T0330211

FROM TOTALITARIAN
TO DEMOCRATIC HUNGARY
Evolution and Transformation
1990-2000

Edited by
Mária Schmidt and László Gy. Tóth

Social Science Monographs, Boulder, Colorado
Atlantic Research and Publications, Inc.

Highland Lakes, New Jersey

Distributed by Columbia University Press, New York

2000

EAST EUROPEAN MONOGRAPHS, NO. DLXXI

Copyright © 2000
Atlantic Research and Publications, Inc.

ISBN 0-88033-472-X
Library of Congress Control Number 00-136293

Printed in the United States of America

ATLANTIC STUDIES ON SOCIETY IN CHANGE

NO. 116

Editor in Chief, Béla K. Király

Associate Editor in Chief, Kenneth Murphy

Editor, László Veszprémy

Table of Contents

Table of Contents...v
Preface to the Series and Acknowledgments.................................vii

Anzelm Bárány
　　There was Once a Freedom of the Press.............................1
Bertalan Diczházi
　　Property Changes in Hungary..75
Tamás Fricz
　　Democratisation, the Party System
　　and the Electorate in Hungary.......................................106
András Gergely
　　József Antall:
　　Prime Minister of the Change of Régime.......................147
Zoltán Illés & Balázs Medgyesi
　　The Role of Green Movements
　　in the Change of Régime..163
Frigyes Kahler
　　Moral and Legal Justice...187
János Martonyi
　　Values and Foreign Policy...220
György Matolcsy
　　Hungary's Debt..232
Tamás Mellár
　　Economic Policy Conceptions
　　and Political Force Fields..267
Attila Károly Molnár
　　The Open Society and the Chaotic Prison......................294
Csaba Őry
　　Workers' Footsteps Resound...323

Mária Schmidt
    The Role of "The Fight against Anti-Semitism"
    during the Years of Transition..........................339
Tamás Sepsey
    A Short History of Compensation....................386
Gyula Tellér
    Four Essays on Communist
    and "Post-Communist" Hungary.....................432
László Gy. Tóth
    The Post-Communist Government Coalition
    in Hungary...462
László Tőkéczki
    Education, Culture and the Loss of Values....................496
Tamás Fricz
    The Orbán Government:
    An Experiment in Regime Stabilization....................520
Biographies of Key Personalities.................................571
Contributors..592
Name Index...597
Place Index...607
Volumes Published in
    "Atlantic Studies on Society in Change"..............609

Preface to the Series and Acknowledgments

The present volume is a component of a series that intends to present a comprehensive survey of the many aspects of East Central European society. It is also part of a sub-series which in-the-making exposes Hungary's history between 1848 and 1998.

The books in this series deal with peoples whose homelands lie between the Germans to the west, the Russians, Ukrainians and Belorussians to the east and north, and the Mediterranean and Adriatic seas to the south. They constitute a particular civilization, one that is at once an integral part of Europe, yet substantially different from the West. The area is characterized by a rich diversity of languages, religions and governments. The study of this complex area demands a multidisciplinary approach, and, accordingly, our contributors to the series represent several academic disciplines. They have been drawn from universities and other scholarly institutions in the United States and Western Europe, as well as East and Central Europe. The authors of the present volume are prominent Hungarian experts of their theme.

The editors are responsible for ensuring the comprehensiveness, cohesion, internal balance, and scholarly quality of the series they have launched. We cheerfully accept this responsibility and intend this work to be neither justification nor condemnation of the policies, attitudes, and activities of any person involved. At the same time, because the contributors represent so many different disciplines, interpretations, and schools of thought, our policy in this, as in the past and future volumes, is to present their contributions without major modifications.

Ms. Andrea T. Kulcsár gave extensive help in arranging, refining, type-setting of the text, and preparing the appendices. I wish to express our gratitude to her.

Budapest, August 20, 2000

Béla K. Király
Editor in Chief

Anzelm Bárány

THERE WAS ONCE A FREEDOM OF THE PRESS

Media and Politics, 1987-1997

If we are to understand the changes in the media, it is unavoidable to briefly outline the context in which these took place: namely, the change of system itself. The debt crisis in the 1980s brought to the surface the economic and social crisis, and the legitimacy of the Kádár regime based on the increase of living-standards started to erode. As a consequence, the intellectual groups which had been isolated until then began to receive a growing—though not overwhelming—support from the population, while the MSZMP (Hungarian Socialist Workers' Party) and its two successor parties only achieved a result of about 15 percent in the 1990 elections. Running into debts, nevertheless, had two other, more lasting consequences. One of them was that the country has carried out a turn of orientation in foreign policy after the dissolution of the Yalta system. Behind the festal slogan "Back to Europe" there was, of course, a much more prosaic reality concealed: the fact that we returned to our usual system of dependence. At the same time, and by no means separately, a significant shift of power took place within the internal relationships of the political elite of the late Kádár era in favour of the financial technocracy, respectively against the party apparatus and the large entrepreneurial sector.

Beginning with 1990 however, the benevolent passivity of the population had started to shift to nostalgic feelings towards the achievements of socialism, to a much greater extent and at a much quicker pace than the deterioration in living-standards. The most surprising thing, though, is that by today not only the losers of the system-changing intelligentsia (mainly those working in the fields of culture, education, and the public sector) have become frustrated, but also the winners. According to statistics, 64 percent of the population feels that they are the losers of the system change, and only 6 percent consider themselves its winners.

Before 1989, alongside the general anti-Communist disposition, there existed a romantic image of future capitalism. Yet, anti-romantic, wild capitalism has dissolved all our illusions. Reality following idyllic images is of course always a disappointment, but in this case it meant more than inevitable disenchantment. After getting acquainted to semi-peripheral capitalism, it has become more and more clear that our choice is not between the Austrian and Finnish ways, but between the Greek and Turkish ones. The media had canalised this growing disappointment into the area of politics; politicians—particularly Government representatives of that time—had become punching bags for the media. By 1997, romantic anti-capitalism had gained ground as a logical consequence of the "no alternative" propaganda of governmental parties. If there is no other capitalism, most people think, the whole thing must be thrown away, both baby and bath water. Furthermore, the best Hungarian disciples of global-crats are already cooking the uncaught hare. Trends of globalisation, to make everything uniform, undoubtedly exist, though the final results are still unborn. It is not yet known what will be the result of the fight between the neo-liberal American model, the so-called Rhenish capitalism of social market economy and the mixed model of traditional and corporate elements of South-Eastern Asia. One of the most important scenes of this battle in Hungary, as in the rest of the world, is exactly in the media—the subject hereby examined.

When the heretofore balance of the change of system is drawn, only the treasury's optimism can paint a positive picture. The living standards of the population have decreased by 30 percent during the past seven years. The redistribution of property has resulted in a Latin American structure of society. The share of property in foreign hands reminds us of the banana republics. The welfare state baptised as a premature infant is being constantly disciplined and punished. (By the way, has anyone heard of prematurely born Western wage-levels mentioned when talking about the managers of state-owned companies or banks?) Instead of a Marshall Plan there is the pumping of resources, a decreasing number of inhabitants, a decreasing average life span, a growing number of mental health problems, while the strategic assets of the state—this would be the national specificity—were put in foreign hands to such an extent as has perhaps happened only in Argentina.

Much smaller crises than this leads to demonstrations, blockades and early elections in Western countries. Why does this system then seem, in spite of that—at least for the time being—stable and viable? Reasons can be looked for in many directions. The hope or the illusion of the political alternation delays the time when the system can be questioned. The other similar social psychological reason is that all defeats have a paralysing effect: after the suppression in 1956, long years of concentration of energies and regeneration had to pass until social resistance could renew. There are people now who think that even the years of 1989/90 represented a defeat, while others think the same about 1994 (the year the former communists were re-elected). The third such reason is that the security valve of the black economy built on the reflexes of the Kádár era still operates quite well in letting off steam. The fourth reason can often be heard from the sympathisers of today's opposition parties [now—post 1998—the governing parties, ed.], and that is the role of the media. According to this concept people are simply not aware of the processes taking place in the country. Due to a lack of information they are not in a position to form an opinion: they merely endure, rather than comprehend the situation, thus not being able to effectively influence it either. The reason for this is not to be found on the demand side, but rather on that of supply. In other words, the problem is not that the people—reconciling themselves to their situation—would prefer to bury their heads in the sand, ignoring these serious problems and only expecting narcotics from the media. The problem is much more on the side of the press, which instead of revealing the facts and articulating interests, in most cases only disinforms and misleads. We also see this as the main reason for the fact that mass dissatisfaction grew to much more considerable proportions in Hungary during the Antall government than under and against the Horn government, although the latter implemented measures with much more serious consequences. Should we accept this explanation, we have to ask two further questions:

1. How can a nation be misled to such a great extent? Isn't it possible that the demand side is not faultless either? Might it be true that all societies have the media they deserve?

2. Why does the media manipulate and how can it do this so effectively and professionally?

Revolution or Revolt?

While the development of civic mentality in the West brought the independence of social subsystems—though there, too, myths exist in connection with their functional differentiation—Stalinism in Hungary crushed media autonomy, making it much more the maidservant of the party than art or science. The slow economic liberalisation of the 1980s left the press basically unchanged. Private individuals were allowed to start economic enterprises much earlier than journals. The 1986 Media Law has kept the rigid system of licensing newspapers introduced in 1938. Journalists had no prestige among the politicians of Kádár's generation, who did not consider the media an independent branch of power but rather a tool of their own. In spite of this, the media of the 1980s was not entirely "gleichschalted". Although sometimes the press administration made concessions concerning the contents ("dripping publicity"), it never offered institutional guarantees. Concessions were always granted informally, as a favour, so that they could always be taken back. The general principle regarding the print media was that the fewer the number of published copies, the higher the level of Glasnost. Dailies of the 1980s could be read in 10 minutes, while reality was hidden in the so-called reports on the general disposition, under headings of confidentiality that restricted their access, done by a separate information department within APO. The press can be practically considered free from the moment these reports on disposition ceased to exist.

Most of the magazines, though, were readable before that, and in spite of the restricted publicity, one could find critical, investigative articles in one or two weekly magazines. Naturally, real reportage was something editors were afraid of, and on television it could only be broadcast if about events in distant countries (see László Benda, or the reports of Alajos Chrudinák).

By the middle of the decade one or two programs destined for certain parts of the population were worth listening to also on the radio, like for instance the *Night Owl* of Miklós Győrffy. The boundaries of the free expression of opinions were made the narrowest on the largest media channel, the television. This, however, did not mean that in a few areas (quiz programs, foreign policy, talk shows) valuable works were not born at all. The limit of taboo topics was marked by the party-state intervention in connection with Sándor Sára's documentary entitled *Pergőtűz* (Drumfire). As Kádár himself did not like television—according to Gyurkó he did not even have his own TV-set at home—the President of the television needed to be on good terms with the Central Committee secretary in charge of the media. Although the Hungarian Television, MTV, complained at that time about the lack of proper conditions, the number of employees was growing constantly, reaching 3600 in 1990.

Then, among all genres the skit possessed a special political significance. Writers of leading articles about capitalist overproduction or socialist deficit-economy could hardly have a resounding success. Humorists, on the contrary, were in an entirely different position. At a time when policemen were not only collecting jokes, but were sometimes, in village pubs, also the joke-tellers, most people did not see the embodiment of the jester's freedom in Géza Hofi or the role of the security valve in György Moldova, but rather the spokesmen of men-in-the-street, who tell the comrades a few home truths about what the average folks think.

The deepening of the economic crisis, the ghost of Solidarity, and the spreading communication technologies in the 1980s made orthodox communists more and more anxious. The spread of copy machines increased the range and effect of the *samizdat* press. A Free Europe satellite television would have certainly been much more effective in the ideological battle than Radio Free Europe (RFE), although we could see that West German TV stations by themselves could also only loosen the East German system, and not overthrow it. Furthermore, communism was not so much defeated after all by the ideology of the "free world", but rather by the dream world of the consumer society.

The press administration of the late Kádár era quite often had to use the tools of direct control—in spite of the strict filter of loyalty in the case of journalists and a self-censorship that had well become a habit. Some of the intellectual revolts could only be put down by means of prohibition or replacement of the editorial staff. At the same time, the younger generation of information employees that had visited the West, with a knowledge of foreign languages, was trying to loosen somehow the pressure of the controlling agit-prop apparatus. In spite of that, we must not forget, though, that the writers' boycott that followed after the closure of *Mozgó Világ* was broken precisely by the members of this new generation. Many of them later filled in leading positions (György Baló, András Domány, Henrik Havas, Ferenc Vicsek). In 1987, as a part of *Fordulat és reform* (Turnabout and Reform), some background material was published entitled "Reforming Proposal of Publicity and Mass Communication", written mostly by correspondents of the *HVG* and the Institute of Mass Communication. The study criticised the 1986 Media Law and contained the theses of a democratic law on mass media.[1]

Nevertheless it would not be correct to overvalue these endeavours of independence. While the Writers' Association revolted both in 1981 and 1986 against the political power, reading the protocol of the MÚOSZ (Hungarian Journalists' Alliance) general assembly in 1985, one can find only very cautious and marginal critical remarks in one or two of the speeches.[2] This explains why it was for many difficult to understand why, in its second decision of January 23, 1989, the Publicity Club took a stand against its earlier owner, the Writers' Association, and supported the editorial staff of *ÉS* (which had played an inglorious role in 1956) in an attempt to establish an alternative Writers' Association. The reference to editorial autonomy did not take into consideration the obvious fact that the rising prices of publications reduced demand, and that a new paper is disadvantaged by one that had already existed. *Magyar Napló* eventually did not succeed in reaching the circulation of ÉS, which from 1990 to 1994 unambiguously represented the general political line of the Democratic Charter.

The Hungarian *samizdat* press, with its one to two thousand copies could not reach the effect of its counterpart in Poland. Reading them today it is evident that the paper was determined by the way of thinking of intellectuals from near the circle of Alliance of Free Democrats (SZDSZ), though the co-operation of the opposition was producing even in May 1987 such common declarations as the one signed by István Csurka, Gyula Hernádi and György Konrád, concerning the Raoul Wallenberg monument.[3] The real allure of *samizdat* was primarily due to the civil courage of its contributors. Its other important merit is the fact that it broke the information monopoly of the MSZMP. A journalist of the *Wall Street*

Journal Europe characterised the leaks in banned news with the metaphor of a dripping tap. There are no reliable surveys about the audience reached by the programs broadcast by RFE. It is generally estimated that 10-20 percent of the population was listening more or less regularly to the station in Munich. The samizdat press remained the reading material of an intellectual subculture; it propagated ideas first of, all and it could not acquire the skills necessary in the economics of the media. Without such skills, after the freedom of press had set in these publications could not adapt to the new circumstances and could not compete with the professionally more qualified editorial staffs. The attempts to break out from the intellectual ghetto and widen the reading public by writing about new topics, adopting a more common and newspaper-like editorial style were not more successful, either. While in Poland the staff of the most widely read daily newspaper, the *Gazeta Wyborcza*, had started mostly within the framework of the underground press, only a few of the collaborators of the Hungarian *samizdat* press (Ferenc Kőszeg, Miklós Haraszti, János Eörsi and the publicist Péter Sneé) remained in the business. The legal *Beszélő* had become a paper of the party opposition from a party journal, which is perhaps why it was reduced to a monthly journal from a weekly. By 1997 *Beszélő* turned out to be of the same quality and size as it had been as a samizdat; only its printing technique was better and the financing source has changed.

In May 1988 in the Jurta Theatre János Kis summarised the responsibility of the intellectuals as follows: "Until 1985-86, the entire public opinion of the Hungarian intelligentsia has had essentially the same perspective regarding fundamental questions. Its change of direction has barely preceded by one year the turn of the general disposition. We have to declare: we must assume responsibility for the fact that the country could be kept for such a long time in state of ignorance concerning the real situation, and that the leadership could practice untroubled its catastrophic policy for such a long time. If the aversion of bankruptcy—supposing that this is still possible—costs that much for society, then the illusions we ourselves had diffused are also to be blamed, and we must not be silent about it. If we do not speak about it, our words will not be trustworthy any more to the people of this country, and we shall not be in a state of equilibrium with ourselves either. Stifled bad conscience gives birth to perfidy, and perfidy to bad actions."[4]

While 1987 was the year of partisan actions, 1988 was that of "the burst of the dike" (János Berecz) and 1989 was undoubtedly the year of the breakthrough. In the autumn of 1987, *Magyar Nemzet* succeeded in publishing the declaration of Lakitelek only within an interview with Imre Pozsgay, though in April 1988 we still could only learn from a police communiqué that the FIDESZ had been established. Beginning with the autumn of 1988, though, the limits of publicity were enlarging day by day.

On the 15th of May the MDF (Hungarian Democratic Forum), after discussions about the minority question and constitutionalism, organised a conference on the subject of publicity in the Jurta Theatre. Here the front line characters of the future media-war: Dénes Csengey and János Kis, Gábor Czakó and István Eörsi were still present together. Professionals were represented by such personalities as Richárd Hirschler and András Szekfű. The debate was dominated by the subject of facing the past, while concerning the future there were much more questions and dilemmas than ready answers and solution proposals. The spirit of the time was imbued with some kind of naïve belief: if the informal censorship will cease to exist, democratic publicity will automatically come into existence.

The announcement was made on the 14th of January 1988 that the Publicity Club was born. Most of those 208 persons who first signed the announcement were the correspondents of *HVG* (12 people), *Magyar Nemzet* (17 persons), *Magyar Hírlap* (24 persons) and *Világgazdaság* (8 persons). Among the institutions the MKKE, the

Center for Cultural Research, the Center for Financial Research (*Pénzügykutató Központ*), the Center for Research in Mass Communication (*Tömegkommunikációs Kutató Központ*) led the way; and there were 11 persons from the Hungarian Radio, respectively five from *Népszabadság* as well, among the signers. Nobody had joined the announcement from *Népszava* and from the strictly controlled Hungarian Television.[5] The signatories were mainly the supporters of the present-day governmental coalition. At the time of the establishment of the association, in November, the number of the members was put at 600-700 persons (MÚOSZ, the official journalists' organisation, had approximately 6000 members at that time), but only 234 ballots were gathered. Among the members of the Association there still are such persons as Mihály Bihari, Attila Mélykuti and László Sólyom. Dénes Csengey greeted its establishment in the *Hitel*. Amongst the plans of the journalists fighting for the possibility to freely establish magazines—and whose struggle at that time was not free from risks at all—was to register all events meant to hinder the freedom of press, the publishing and managing of a so-called Black Book. The power was seen in the Publicity Club of the ghost of the Petőfi Circle and of the alternative Writers' Associations. I myself would rather lay the stress on the differences between generations, on the revolt of the generation of 1968. And that most of this team has by now become part of the establishment, a fact which is signalled by the fact that they are more and more often the targets of the attacks of the next generation, that of 1989.

1989 was the year of the intellectuals. The lettered moved into the limelight, and the borders of glasnost enlarged to such an extent as by the middle of the year we could safely talk about freedom of press. Although in January 1989, Pozsgay qualified as an insurrection the events of 1956 in a radio program ("168 hours"), the leading medium of the era became undoubtedly the television. On March 15, 1989, demonstrators no longer marched to the Bródy Sándor Street, but to Szabadság Square. While the target of the

March Youth in 1848 was the printing offices of Landerer and Heckenast, it was the Radio for the generation of 1956. While Petőfi and his companions in the name of the people had effectively taken over the press and the revolutionaries of 1956 tried to occupy the Radio, demonstrators in 1989 were contented with slogans demanding a Free Hungarian Television; and for Dénes Csengey, with the symbolic occupation of the institution. The television leadership at that time did not deign to tremble by that kind of symbolic policy, and they did not return to the norms of civil service. The author of the still samizdat *Beszélő*, after analysing the provable impersonalisation, the de-politicisation and the distorted information in the evening news program, concluded that: "Although the political openness of Hungarian Television (MTV) has significantly improved compared to its earlier state, giving a large scope this year to non-official festivities, it also had nevertheless tried to do its utmost to minimise the political significance and effects and to 'tame' the radicalism of these events."

All in vain, as more than seven hours of demonstrations, with 80-100 thousand taking part, could not be presented as though nothing were happening at all. The structure of the information in the news program was quite similar to the structure of the official journal of the MSZMP; amongst the national dailies this organ could be considered as the best "spiritual ally" of the MTV.[6]

Outside Budapest the situation remained the same. The *Békés Megyei Népújság* did not publish Attila Herpai's article about the Recsk concentration camp, (*Beszélő* did), in which the young journalist gave an account of how Pál Vastagh [minister of justice in the MSZP-SZDSZ government, ed.] and his comrades from Battonya had been joking about the new parliament spending its four years at Recsk concentration camp. Instead of publishing the article, the editorial board tried to discredit the young journalist.

The winds of democratisation and freedom of the press could not eventually avoid the television either. The reburial of Imre

Nagy and his companions, and the opening of the round-table negotiations were already transmitted live, but it was almost impossible
to gain worthy information about the mid-level talks. "Later on the
press itself had demanded the presence of the journalists at the mid-
level negotiations. This proved to make not too much sense,
though, as the political fight went on in the garment of a professionals' debate, being fairly boring for an outsider and often hard to
follow. After the initial enthusiasm, the commentators were hardly
present, and as a consequence the news published was also full of
mistakes and inaccuracies."[7] The meetings of the workers' committee were private, although representatives of the Opposition
Round Table had insisted on publicity earlier as a means of pressure
against the power; but they eventually retreated as a result of the
MSZMP protest. Something similar had happened as a matter of
fact in Poland, too, where the transition was also characterised by
negotiations. While the citizens of Gdansk could listen live to the
negotiations between Walesa and his companions and the delegation of the government before the Lenin-shipyard in August 1980,
the negotiations that were the basis of the 1989 transmission went
on behind closed doors. Solidarity was granted an hour in the television every evening to give account of the situation. In spite of
this, those events are even now hidden in a kind of mist.

In the case of Central and East Europe, quite a lot of articles
have been written about the revolutions being led by the media. The
most provable role seems to be that of the West German channels'
catalysing demonstrations in East Germany. The Czechoslovakian
media changed sides overnight. The Romanian revolution and its
transmission on television, however, still raises a lot of questions.
Some other questions are also unanswered, like why the Hungarian
Television fell behind with the live transmission of such a significant event in world history as the fall of the Berlin wall, or why it
dealt to a surprisingly insufficient extent with the overturn of the
Czech and Slovak domino. The much-glorified TV transmission of

the Romanian revolution could not enter behind the scenes either, just as CNN could not during the Gulf war.

Only a part of the population, mostly the intellectuals, were the producers and consumers of the new journals and books that had been on the index. Eliminating the blank spots of the near past was a compensatory work, though retrospectively it is quite conspicuous how superficially the questions that determine our future and concern the financial change of the system were mentioned, while the re-evaluation of the past and the events of the political scene were analysed in detail. The priority was completely different for writers, journalists and men of words than for an economist or a manual worker. It would have been indispensable to awake the population to the consciousness of the origin of the financial crisis, in order to successfully neutralise the myth of the 1970s and 1980s and the nostalgia of the Kádár-era. Even *Beszélő* published the first article about the catastrophic proportions of debts, realising the gravity of the situation only in 1988. Meanwhile János Fekete has never been troubled with questions like how he had succeeded to cause a damage of approximately 600 million dollars to the country by speculative manoeuvres. The time bomb of the demographic development was not treated in conformity with its importance either.

This kind of missing could scarcely have become widely known at that time, as this was the period when the media led in the list of popular confidence in institutions with 75 points. It is important because the power of the parties was only sufficient to batter the walls, and without the support of the media they could never have forced the MSZMP, paralysed into a draw game, to retreat so quickly. The transformation did not happen in the streets, but in front of radio sets and televisions. The minority was demonstrating in the public squares, the majority was watching the events at home. This situation had the disadvantage that the organic growth of the opposition parties had become a secondary function for their own leaders, who had considered their primary task to gain positions in the media rather than establishing a broad base in society. Hence their vulnerability, which highly exceeds West European proportions and this is the reason also for their sudden increase—and decrease—in popularity.

Why did the society of journalists revolt against the press administration of the APO? The reasons could be classified into three large groups:

a) **Political dependence**. "Nation-wide known journalists could be—could(?!)—condemned to silence, prohibited, thrown out of leading political TV programs, without the least possible reaction of the MÚOSZ. As far as I know, but it's possible that I'm wrong, at the selection of the leaders of the national dailies, the national radio and television the opinion of the MÚOSZ was never asked."[8]

b) **Income**. "By and by, professionals consider ridiculous the smiles they get as an answer to questions concerning their salaries. If this is how we are valued, the political leadership should not be surprised by the fact that this is all this gathering is capable of and that it can serve politics to such an extent only. I am convinced that the society of Hungarian journalists could much more better and efficiently serve this policy, according to its ideas, only it were allowed to and optimally inspired to."—said Sándor Szathmári (*Népszava*), the president of the department of internal affairs within the MÚOSZ at the extended board session on the of June 16, 1988. While the press generally represents business in the West, most Hungarian journals lived on donations. Journalists started to consider their comfortable cages extremely confining when it came to the light that innovative editors (such as those of *ÖTLET*, for instance) were capable of holding their own, and moreover earned a much better living than they had before.

c) **The professional disorder of the press**. "In our view the biggest mistake of this system is that it does not allow itself to be served intelligently"—István Sándor quotes the outburst of one of his colleagues.[9] And the radio journalists coming back from his study-trip draws the following lesson concerning the efforts to obtain independence of the journal of the Austrian Socialist Party: "... the real support does not mean the unconditional following in every case or the neglect of criticism, but the effective emanation of a system of ideas, with the convincing appearance of independence."[10]

These endeavours were present in the ad-hoc committees of the MÚOSZ, which were dealing with the rethinking of the system of political institutions and of the MÚOSZ's relationships, and respectively were trying to build the partnership between politicians and journalists. Gábor Fodor, lecturer of the College of Political Science, proposed an alliance on new grounds based on Halberstam's book: "they over there suddenly realised again: if politicians raise claim to the press, then the journalists cannot be considered mere devices of transmission summoned only for their services... And for that most politicians—even if grinding their teeth and swearing—were ready to pay a high price, including all those inconveniences that involve the acknowledgement of the relative sovereignty of mass communication which naturally did not go without the personalities of journalism... Today such a gigantic machinery is necessary (for selling policy—the author's remark) in which it is unquestionably true that the journalist is at least as important as the politician is. We haven't got there yet, although the ice has broken."[11]

If you can't beat them, join them! Perhaps this English saying could have led the more foreseeing reform-communists, when they accepted the contractual proposal of the professionals. József Csikós, one of those responsible for the MSZMP-media in 1988, offered his help during the program of Reform Evenings of the KISZ (Communist Youth Association): "I help them as a rear-guard in so far as a detached unit can be helped from behind." Until the autumn of 1989 the intellectuals and technocrats of the late Kádár era had not been considering a change of the system but were only thinking in terms of a change of model, and the society of journalists was not an exception either. The general assembly in January still accepted—with one vote against and six abstaining votes—the proposition of Katalin Bossányi that "our national interest is to realise a democratic socialism without having bloody conflicts or explosions."[12]

After the general assemblies in 1989, some has-beens—like József Pálfy, the leader of the MÚOSZ, Károly Megyeri, the general secretary, László Szabó, Ernő Lakatos or Pál E. Fehér from the police column—retreated for some time or retired on a pension. Several new names appeared at that time, comet-like careers began, but the one-sidedness—as it came to light later—survived. No wonder the workers in the press felt this period as liberation. Those who would have been satisfied with enlightened absolutism at the beginning, then with a partnership with politicians and eventually with a change of the model, began to sense the historically rare possibility that was unfolding in the vacuum of power caused by the erosion of the MSZMP. "The party guidance of the TV has soon ended also *de jure*, and the new owner, the Minister of State, strove to keep himself out of the affairs of the institution. For the first time in its history of 30 years, MTV remained without supervision and guidance. This state of affairs is unknown in the case of national televisions, both in the East and the West"—János Horvát described the situation.[13] After the direct guidance of the press and the phone calls to the editorial offices had ceased, journalists would have liked to escape from the owners of the magazines which did not have "even a paternalistic experience."

The desire of the completely sovereign, existentially independent press soon became stabilised as a natural state, although the journalists did not codify it. This state of affairs can be desirable, but by no means can it be natural. The existence of a completely independent press is illusory even in the West. This would mean that a journal owned by its editors was supported solely by its readers. Since about 70 percent of the journals' total revenue comes from advertising, this almost inevitably means a certain degree of financial dependence, too—although much smaller than in the case of Hungarian journals. Besides that, as much as the media is financed by public money the institutionalisation of social control becomes a natural claim. The journalists, however, keeping pace with the spirit of the time, pushed for privatisation instead of socialisation of the mass media. After the circulation had decreased as a consequence of the drastic rise of the price of paper, the journals' dependence on advertising grew constantly. Bismarck noticed that journalists are all people that have missed their vocation. Media is the scene for social dialogue and the mediation of interests, and journalists are first of all chroniclers and mediators of the process. Their secondary task is to play the role of the watchdogs of democracy. Power should not be supervised primarily by the press, but by another power. The division of power, the principle of "checks and balances" is based on this comprehension.

While the SZDSZ generally challenged the existing structure with self-made organisations (samizdat vs. official press, League vs. MSZOSZ, SZDSZ vs. MSZMP) they did not try to build up an Anti-MÚOSZ organisation from the Publicity Club—although the APO was afraid of that. They felt the power relations to be suitable for a take-over. The famous sentence of Gáspár Miklós Tamás: "Bolshevik chalk cannot be turned into democratic cheese" did not refer to the journalistic establishment. Already in 1988, the leadership of the MÚOSZ was under strong pressure to organise an earlier general assembly. An extraordinary general assembly was disapproved because its participants would have been the delegates of the former general assembly. The first "change of power" however—in accordance with the spirit of the time—occurred in the economic department.

Since the framework conditions and the transition models in
the Hungarian change of system were decisively formed by the
Western powers, the groups with Western experiences and information had an obvious advantage. Besides financiers and diplomats, journalists also belonged to that group. The nomination of
Zoltán Király and his election as a Member of Parliament in 1985
had already indicated how strong a sympathetic TV personality
considered trustworthy could be. Amongst the journalists generally
inclined to policy-making, more found a political career attractive
in 1990 than in 1994. Most of these started in the colours of the
MSZMP: Katalin Bossányi (*Magyar Hírlap*), László Róbert (the
leader of the MÚOSZ), Julianna P. Szűcs (the editor-in-chief of
Mozgó Világ), Antal Réger (the editor-in-chief of the Political
Programs Department of the Hungarian Radio), Zoltán Árpási (the
editor-in-chief of *Békés Megyei Népújság*), Frigyes Marton (the
leader of the editorial staff of the Hungarian Radio), Sándor Fekete
(editor-in-chief of *Új Tükör*). Bossányi was the only one who succeeded in getting into parliament. In addition to her, Csaba Ilkei,
Zoltán Király and Zoltán Speidl representing the MDF, Miklós
Ómolnár (reporter of the Hungarian Radio and the managing editor
of the *Kis Újság*) from the FKGP, György Giczy (*Új Ember*) from
the KDNP have also been elected. Király was the first to leave the
faction, Ilkei belonged to the party opposition. Bossányi also
returned as early as January 1991 to *Népszabadság*, where an
inquest had been started against her in the summer of 1988 because
of her activity in the Publicity Club. On the other hand, all the 1988
black sheep of the MSZMP, excepting the popular socialists, have
returned by now to the bosom of the successor party. In the case of
the SZDSZ, apart from the editors of the samizdat, only Tibor
Fényi, reporter of the Austrian *Die Presse* could be found at the end
of the list.

First Shots in the Media-war

Why wasn't the Media Law born in the negotiation phase of the transition?

The prestige of the media was at its zenith in 1989, and the intellectuals—but not only them—were enjoying with a happy enthusiasm the blessings of the free press. What could then be the reason that feelings vary today from wry disillusionment to bitter disappointment in connection with the press? What are the reasons for the hopes set on the freedom of press coming to nothing so quickly? There is a strong interaction between the crisis of the Hungarian democracy and the miserable conditions of the freedom of press, we can see them as two processes that reinforce each other. Let's see the characteristics of the low-altitude flying of the media.

Two latent directions were present all the time in the cultural policy throughout the 1980s. The first one had been connected to Imre Pozsgay (nowadays an advisor to the MDF), and the other one had been stamped by György Aczél, who—by his own account—voted for the SZDSZ in the 1990 elections. The latent rivalry between the two groups became apparent in the media after the November referendum of the "four yes", on January 9, 1990, when the Leadership of the MTV released the editors-in-chief of the Híradó and the Hét. The dismissed person was Endre Aczél, the present commentator of foreign affairs at *Népszabadság*, one of the main journalists of the governmental coalition. He was replaced by István G. Pálfy, the former party secretary of the news program, considered a popular socialist, and Pozsgay's man. On January 14, István Csurka's commentary was broadcast on Vasárnapi Újság: "Reveille, Hungarians! You are being misled again! The aster revolution is over, this is the period of Béla Kun, even though the new Lenin-boys are scolding Lenin." The next day Miklós Győrffy, the manager of the program resigned in protest, the general editor Béla

Győri was severely rebuked and 50 persons out of the 146 correspondents of the Political Program's editorial staff sign a letter of
protest against the commentary. "Former lies are replaced with new
ones", declared Imre Pozsgay on January17th, and he resigned from
his supervising position of the radio and television. Miklós
Haraszti, the media politician of the SZDSZ, agreed with the decision of the State Minister.

The followers of the present governmental coalition generally
explain the outbreak of the media war with the unsuccessful media
policy of the MDF or with its arrogance in power. The unfriendly
behaviour toward the MDF, the "first smack in the face" however
dates much earlier, from the period preceding the elections. In the
left liberal press from abroad (*New York Times*, *Dagens Nyheter*)—
with whom the *Beszélő* circle had excellent relationships—the
charges of nationalism and anti-Semitism began to spread already
in 1987-89.

The SZDSZ had started its media campaign against the MDF
in the autumn of 1989, in the drive for the referendum. The MDF
was charged at home that they had entered into a secret pact with
the communists and abroad that they were right-wing extremists,
anti-Semites and irredentists. Beginning in the autumn of 1990,
after a tacit alliance with the MSZP, the accusation became the
same at home and abroad. During the electoral campaign a text
entitled "Fathers and Sons" appeared stating that the mentality of
liberal sons is similar to that of their Bolshevik fathers. It is difficult to decide what kind of role the MSZP played in the conflict
between the two strongest opposition forces, but it is a fact that they
gained the most profit from this fight on the long run, as the laughing third party.

The MDF was not acting uniformly in the respect of how to
relate to the media establishment. István Csurka announced a policy of toughness in the early spring of 1989.[14] According to Csurka
the most severely censored institution was the MTV, where "the

staff of the television—with very few exceptions—fulfilled 'voluntarily and merrily' all the expectations of the cultural policy, 'having made a deal', as counter-selection here did not primarily aim the exclusion of the talented—though, of course, that was one of the reasons—but rather the exclusion of accidental resisters. Even today not just the chiefs of the party and of the ministry of the interior keep a firm hand on the institution, but also voluntary lewdness. Hungarian TV has learned how to manipulate and mislead the audience with delight. Masters of sophisticated irrelevant talking, of telling partial truths and of nearly invisible lies have grown up. The programs and announcers diffused the worst spiritual insignificance." Since Csurka saw a conspiracy even in the structural and partly spontaneous processes, after such a diagnosis his conclusion could not be other than that the manipulative leadership of the television stands in the way of the nation. Symbolic politicking though, with fist shaking and without the demonstration of power, turned against Csurka, and later the MDF—even against those individuals with whom it may have been possible to establish correct relationships. Many were startled by the slogan of the "spring-cleaning" but as it was not followed by actions, its only result was that the antipathy and distrust towards the MDF turned into barely concealed and later open hostility from the leading circles of the journalistic community. After the pact between the MDF and SZDSZ, these journalists were less and less afraid; more than that, they started to consider and sell their fight for privilege as a war of independence, and looked up to the SZDSZ as their guarding angel.

The reason for the later escalation of the media war was that the parties that—according to the spirit of the time—had formerly been thinking that the best organising principle in the field of the media was the "invisible hand" of the market, colliding with the unpleasant phenomena of reality, swung to the other extreme and started to deal with the media almost exclusively from the point of view of power. This meant the priority of the informal exertion of

power and of personnel policy, something not unusual in Western
Europe either—only it works more indirectly there and is not the
only tool of media policy. Party programs hardly contained an
abundance of ideas about the connections of media structure and
democracy, just as few people racked their brains publicly to define
a national information policy, or within that, to outline the role of
the media in the development of bourgeois mentality. Neo-liberal-
ism had become the dominating intellectual trend of the era. Under
its aegis, the technocracy of the late Kádár-era, which before 1990
had even been considering a reformed dictatorship, and the *samizdat* opposition, which earlier had placed itself left from the centre
on the political palette as well, found each other. The influence of
the Western political forces and the fact that neo-liberal policy was
very much in the favour of both groups' interests, equally played a
role in the change of direction. The party of grey matter was not
able to do anything else in the media policy either, other than to
copy the Western model in a distorted way, without new ideas.
Everyone was speaking of human rights on the level of slogans, yet
nobody tried to extend these in the area of communication and
media.

For those on the inside, the status quo was fine. But in the declaration submitted by György Szabad as a representative of EKA on
June 21, 1989, a separate paragraph still dealt with the media. "We
consider the elaboration of a new information law indispensable
also for the reason that the electorate can vote not blindly, but to the
possible extent armed against the demagogic efforts of influencing,
for the effective representatives of their recognised interests.
Consequently it is justified that when the fifth draft law regulates
again all the means of the formation of consciousness having in
sight the requirements of democracy, freedom and public morality,
it also took care that all the political organisations that are participating in the elections can carefully and constructively use the possibilities offered by the press, the radio and the television—but

without abuse. (It needs to be mentioned here that the wider protection of personal rights must be expanded to the modern information systems as well.)"

Another key-figure in the discussions recalls: "Furthermore I
took part in the working group on publicity, but it did not work the
way I would have liked. It would have been desirable that the new
media law and the law on the protection of data and the freedom of
information was born as quickly as possible. I made a draft for the
latter one more than one year ago—I had been officially commissioned for that—and it could have been a good opportunity to carry
it through." According to László Sólyom, these laws could not be
carried through at that time because such daily political matters as
the giving back of confiscated *samizdat* or printing equipment had
superseded them from the discussion arena. After Sólyom had been
elected as a constitutional magistrate, there was nobody in the MDF
who could have been capable of working out a draft law that could
have constituted the starting point of the discussions. For Haraszti
and his companions on the other hand—as they were inside the
property—the status quo was quite suitable, so they did not urge the
creation of the media law, or its inclusion among the cardinal laws,
although for their media experts from around the Publicity Club the
creation of a draft law could hardly have represented a problem.
Perhaps it is not uninteresting to mention that in the I/5 political
working committee, in charge of problems of publicity and information, FIDESZ was represented by István Hegedűs (who is
presently close to the SZDSZ in the Owners' Counselling Body)
and András B. Vágvölgyi (the longtime editor of ultra-radical
Magyar Narancs), the League by Endre Hann (a founding member
of SZDSZ earlier, presently the leader of the Medián, a company
for public opinion research); the MDF in the beginning was represented by the literary historian Károly Alexa, later by the literary
historian Szigethy Gábor; the SZDSZ by the writer Miklós
Haraszti; while the MSZMP by a certain József Csikós (earlier

from the Ministry of the Interior, later from the Ministry of the Interior, nowadays the suspect in bombing attempts). Unlike in Hungary, the cause of the media was considered as one of the most important sub-roundtables in Poland, and this was also reflected in the fact that the delegation of the government was led by spokesman Urban, and that of the opposition by the later prime minister Mazowiecki and Michnik, today the editor-in-chief of the most important daily, the *Gazeta Wyborcza*.

The MDF-SZDSZ Pact stated that the planned amendments of the constitution would include that "the law that regulates the supervision of the public radio, television and news agency, the nomination of their leaders, furthermore authorisation for the establishment of commercial radio or television stations, respectively the law that impedes information monopoly, will have to be accepted by a two-thirds majority in parliament." On position 14 of the list of the laws, which need a two thirds majority, there was the media law and the law on information. Appendix IV of the pact stated as a basic principle that the national media cannot become the prey of the skirmish between political parties and kept on the frequency moratorium until the law on information is passed. Participants at the negotiations without exception recall that the pact was not media-motivated. Against this, József Debreczeni, the MDF representative of the cultural committee, saw that the media "has become the main subject of MDF-SZDSZ pact, since the SZDSZ in exchange for giving up some of the two-thirds laws has been promised that the government will not annex the mass media"— just as István Csurka had declared.[15] Knowing how utterly important the media was for the SZDSZ, it is indeed difficult to imagine that this was not the most important issue for them in the pact. The contradiction can perhaps be resolved by the negotiators of the MDF giving up with absolute naivete, without expecting anything in exchange, what the SZDSZ was ready to fight tooth and nail for.

The phrasing of Miklós Haraszti is telling when he states that the media does not belong to anyone, and besides: "I am not announcing know that the media is free but that the journalists are free". The whole strategy of the SZDSZ was built on having behind them a majority of sympathisers in both mediums, thus the slogan of the self-management and freedom of professionals served well the defence of its positions in the media. As a matter of fact the freedom of providing information is usually emphasised by the American liberal model, while the West European, particularly the German, concept about public service lays the accent on the freedom of receiving information. As Felix Frankfurter said, the media is not a purpose in itself, but rather an instrument: the instrument of reaching to a free society. The question of the primacy of media makers or media users leads, though, to particularly high tensions where the political sympathy of the media makers differ sharply from the political relations of power. Left-liberal journalists are a majority in the West as well, but this state of affairs is at least balanced by the fact that among the editors there exists an equal predominance of right-wing, conservative publishers. The recruitment of media workers in Hungary, primarily for historical reasons, has resulted in an almost exclusive left-liberal majority. The results of a survey made in 1992 are quite edifying. According to it the preferences for a political party of the MÚOSZ (journalists' association) members were the following: FIDESZ: 38 percent, MSZP: 13 percent, SZDSZ: 12 percent, MDF: 6 percent. Negative preferences are even more instructing: FKGP: 34 percent; MDF: 20 percent; SZDSZ: 5 percent; KDNP: 3 percent. By 1994 the situation has changed in the sense that earlier FIDESZ sympathisers changed over to the MSZP and SZDSZ.[16] Much more important than the party preferences of field journalists are of course the sympathies of the leading editors of political programs, which unfortunately had not been surveyed. The situation in Hungary is even more aggravated by the fact that—for various reasons—the owners of the papers also support the MSZP and the SZDSZ.

Advance!

The written press became the main field of the end-of-regime's, spontaneous privatisation program. "The publishing of newspapers also fell under foreign control, as the heads of publishing houses and the editorial offices did not wish to wait until the new government was formed following the free elections."[17] The procedural flaw was that precisely the privatisation of the forums of publicity has especially lacked publicity and the possibility of competitive bidding. Papers and periodicals were then followed in 1990–92 by printing houses, after that with the public disposal of the Danubius shares, foreign institutional investors also joined in.

While the MDF's men of letters felt that even the biweekly publication of *Hitel* was a great success, the MSZMP had pieced together an "independent" weekly (*Reform*) and an afternoon tabloid (*Mai Nap*) as early as 1988. The founding staff of *Reform*, published with the support of János Berecz, was provided by the *Vasárnapi Hírek*; the editor-in-chief was Péter Tőke. The journal declared itself independent, but increased the confusion rather than contributing to a clearer viewpoint. The preservation of power went on after the establishment of the MSZP, too. The editorial staff of *Ludas Matyi*, led by József Árkus, which was an independent local MSZP organisation, one bright day simply established a limited company inside the bosom of the *Mai Nap* Kiadó Rt. (publishing company) and started to edit *Új Ludas*. Gyula Fekete, on behalf of the MDF, made mention of this danger as early as the MSZMP–MDF debate forum in January 1989: "As I observe, the salvation of monopolies is going on in our days; such and such monopolies of politics and economy switch from one dimension to another. It settles from one sector to another by means of nominations and salvage of capital, and once its new positions are built, it becomes the loudest follower of both free market and democracy. This change of the costumes of power monopolies is obviously also acting against the reforms."[18]

Opposition parties tried to improve their media positions by establishing new party organs (*Magyar Fórum, Beszélő, Magyar Narancs, Kis Újság*). These papers, however, not only did not reach the size of edition of the already existing weeklies, but what is more, sooner or later became the mouthpieces of their own internal party opposition.

Why did the opposition forces not also ask for a halt to privatisation in the field of the written press, similar to the frequency moratorium? A strong warning that the cases of media privatisation would be re-examined would have probably restrained some of the investors. But since this pre-emptive step was not taken, it encouraged the MSZP. Especially MDF members outside Budapest felt the significance of the press, and—although it was formally initiated by the SZDSZ—the assembly of the sub-committee in charge to investigate the privatisation of the press is partly due to their vehement protest against the transactions.

According to András Fabriczky, leader of the economic office of the MSZP, the county newspapers had received the authorisation to negotiate with foreign owners in February 1990, as only foreign ownership could guarantee them being relieved from all kinds of party influence and provide the necessary investment in infrastructure. After the MDF had won the first series of negotiations, the editors of seven papers set to work and switched to Axel Springer Budapest. The MSZP made an allusion that it had been on a general defensive for months, besides the readers' interest comes first, and did not stand against these moves legally; more than that, it even placed the lists of subscribers and the editorial offices at their disposal. What seemed to be the plundering of the MSZP at that time, retrospectively can rather be considered an orderly retreat, or even a salvage job. Also between the two rounds of the election, on March 28, the MSZP had conveyed the establisher's right of *Esti Hírlap, Vasárnapi Hírek, Figyelő*, and *Magyarország*, all papers founded by itself, to a limited shares company, which practically meant the conveyance of ownership in this case. The hasty action was nevertheless condemned by many at that time. Mátyás Eörsi from the SZDSZ questioned the lawfulness of the action by pointing that ownership can only be acquired from owners, and as a press monopoly could form again, a press moratorium should be instated in a similar pattern to the frequency moratorium. The paper of MÚOSZ started its gleanings with the following: "The journalist society, administered to death until now, ruined by permanent control, never habituated to take decisions, being suddenly abandoned by its APO-gee, proved of course to be unable to realise and defend its own interests—its fate and future was not decided in a deal but in an exigency."[19] Imre Nagy, who represented the MSZP on the negotiations between the journals belonging to Hírlapkiadó Vállalat (Newspaper Publishing Company) and the leaders of the editing company, argued that it was not old papers that were being sold, but rather new ones were being established.[20]

The change of system took place by means of negotiation between élites, and it was concentrated in Budapest. It did not permeate into the whole of the country, and the old structures of power, even if somewhat changed, firstly reorganised themselves here. In the local elections of 1990 continuity had been strongest in the rural areas, and roughly at the same time the citadels of the freedom of press had fallen. Let us make a roll call here, as a payment of respect and memento: *Dátum* (Szekszárd), *Úton* (Debrecen), *Debreceni Krónika*, *Helyzet* (Pécs), *Tér-Kép* (Győr—Szombathely), *Heti Hírnök* (Miskolc), *Prés* (Gyöngyös), *Bácskapocs* (Baja), *Somogyország* (Kaposvár). A few journals declaring themselves as social-liberal, such as the *Világ*, or *Köztársaság/ Respublika* with its ambitions to become the Hungarian Spiegel, have shared the same destiny—although for different reasons. *Somogyország* had had to announce its own demise as early as the spring of 1990, i.e. before the political disgust set in. The *Úton* of Debrecen was reformed into the county journal by its new owner, the Austrian Funk, Verlag und Druckerei GmbH. "Economic leaders were pushed not to advertise in our magazine", declared János Kepenyes, editor-in-chief of *Délkelet* in Békéscsaba before the elections. The editorial staffs that had been supporting the system-changing opposition also felt later that the new parliamentary forces coming into power did not adequately support them. They did not receive exclusive news or interviews from them, or even a rotary press, which could have made them become profitable. Thus their fall sooner or later in the face of the tremendous financial superiority of the county papers was predictable. The Hungarian Post, with its monopoly in distribution, often hindering rather then helping their distribution, had played a key role in their failure. There was a constant complaint in the country that post offices did not accept subscriptions for these papers. The supply of papers had increased explosively while the capacity of kiosks remained the same, so it depended on the sellers which journals were on top and which were under the counter.

Thus in the case of many new papers the unsold number of copies reached even 50 percent. The management of journals was characterised by an enthusiastic and optimistic lack of experience. The readers' demand was over—while the resistance of forces with opposite interests was underestimated. They did not only represent an economic challenge for the county journals in a monopoly situation, but also because their existence slackened the existential defencelessness of journalists.

"There are plenty of good people, but show me an able one"— Antall's words, turned since that into common saying, are often quoted. MDF media politicians complaining about the lack of cadres could have better relied—as happened in Poland and the Czech Republic—on talented and non-compromised youngsters that were testing their wings around these journals. These idealistic poor fellows, who had previously constituted an internal opposition in the county papers, after the economic bankruptcy of their independent journals, were standing jobless as the first losers of the change of system. Few of them could take back their former positions, and what remained was either Budapest or a change of career. Their fate was an object lesson for the correspondents of the county newspapers.

Finally, only those papers remained in operation where at least one of the following three conditions has existed: a market gap, professional know-how, considerable capital. The most successful one became *Kiskegyed*, but *Mai Nap* and perhaps *Blikk* can also be counted here.

Foreign Ownership: Friend or Foe?

The big Western investors appearing in the field of the print press varied from country to country. In the Czech Republic it was the Passauer Neue Presse and Ringer AG, in Poland the Passauer Neue Presse and Jürg Marquard, while in Hungary Springer, Bertelsmann, Murdoch, Hersant, and later the Swiss Ringier AG and Marquard again all descended.

During the years of the press administration, in meetings of the editors-in-chief organised by the APO, it was of no importance whether the owner of the paper was the MSZMP, the Patriotic Popular Front or even the trade union. In the course of privatisation, however, this started to play a certain role. The *éminence grise* of media privatisation was István Horváth, the ambassador in Bonn between 1984 and the autumn of 1991, the representative of a Bavarian bank after his return home, and later the counsellor in matters of foreign policy for Gyula Horn. The Ferenczy media group and the Springer concern appeared in Hungary with his assistance. The Axel Springer Budapest Ltd. started its activity as a common company of the two firms in February 1989.[21] We shall hear about it again as a representative of Bertelsmann's RTL-Klub when the commercial TV stations participate later in a call for tenders.

The newspaper of the MSZMP's Central Committee, *Népszabadság* had already been negotiating with Bertelsmann in 1988, and when Pál Eötvös, who became editor-in-chief with a journalist background, finally brought *Népszabadság* Ltd into being on July 30, 1990, the media concern from Gütersloh obtained 41 percent of its shares, worth of 140 million Forints. The fight for the profile of the paper burst out after the MSZP had been born, and was won by the "bourgeois section" of the MSZP against the popular-plebeian reform circles, which strengthened the line of Nyers and Horn and reacted upon the internal fight for power.[22] The socialist paper had risen to its feet earlier than the socialist party. Though the edition size of the newspaper had fallen from 695 thousand copies in 1987 to 337 thousand in August 1990, it became stable around 300 thousand. Apart from inherited financial superiority, the fact that the intellectuals of the Democratic Charter established in the autumn of 1991 had *started* to publish in *Népszabadság* as early as the summer of 1990, resulting in higher level of debate and making the former party- paper accessible to new readers, has also contributed to this. Robert Maxwell—the English publisher of the works of Honecker, Kádár, Brezhnev, Ceausescu and Zhivkov—bought the paper of the government, *Magyar Hírlap*, in January 1990. The deal had been done with the contribution of the Minister of Commerce, Tamás Beck, who also sat on the board of directors of the stock corporation for a while. The new editorial line of the paper is well described by the fact that after the mysterious death of its owner, Gábor Demszky defended it on March 15, 1992 with the slogan "Hands off *Magyar Hírlap*" to prevent the government buying it back using its right of pre-emption. Pallas had no money and anyway no intention of doing that, thus the newspaper was finally bought by the Swiss Jürg Marquard.

The privatisation of *Népszava* was necessitated by its owner, the trade unions, expenditure of all possessions to cover income shortages before the local elections. The League was afraid that the partners brought by Sándor Nagy would be straw men of the Bertelsmann, but the deal fell out of the frying pan and into the fire when it chose the VICO of János Fenyő as a partner in 1993. The media offensive of the VICO-empire, a former video seller, has occurred with sharp conflicts both in the case of *Nők Lapja* and the *Színes RTV*. The ex-photographer Fenyő, returning from America, paid 100 million Forints in cash of the 340 million purchase price for the bankrupt paper, and a part of the purchase price (87 million Forints) went to legal proceedings.[23] Fenyő and his companions also got the journal's valuable estate on Rákóczi street. The paper had effected a risky complete change of profile, but due to extremely stable consumer habits it only lost a few its low-income, leftist regular readers. Behind a certain EKH Ltd., the present owner of the newspaper established in 1900 by the Social-Democratic Party, stands a company registered in a Caribbean tax haven.

The most important organ of the system-changing intelligentsia, *Magyar Nemzet*, which in 1989 had reached by a dynamic expansion a number of 170 thousand published copies, started its decline in 1990, and by May 1991 its edition size sunk to under 100 thousand again. The conflicts between the system-changing parties were also reflected in the divergence of opinions within the editorial staff, especially on the question of whether the government-supported conservative-liberal Hersant-group or the Swedish left-liberal *Dagens Nyheter*—preferred also by the SZDSZ—should become the new owner. The partial editorial strike of the "Swedish-wing" in October 1991, which emphasised editorial autonomy against ownership rights, has remained unprecedented ever since in the recent Hungarian history of the press.[24] Since then journalists have fallen into an open conflict with owners only in cases when they did not get their wages. The editorial statutes of Western papers have never taken roots in our written press.

The organisation of *Mai Nap* was started in May 1988, the first issue coming out on February 8, 1989. The staff had come over from the socialist tabloid *Esti Hírlap*, the editor-in-chief, István Horváth, had been the domestic politics columnist of *Esti Hírlap*. The print run grew from 45 thousand copies to 110 thousand within one year. The Hungarian Credit Bank provided 90 percent of the HUF 10 million core capital of the journal. Murdoch purchased 50 percent of the shares for 3 million dollars in 1990. The concurrent *Esti Hírlap* also went into foreign hands; it became the property of Maxwell.

The MDF-lead Government was greatly affected by Axel Springer Budapest's acquisition of seven local county papers (all of them in a monopoly position) out of the existing 19, making use of the vacuum in ownership. At the same time, *Szabad Föld* published in 500 thousand copies found a buyer for 100 million Forints. The group highlighted with the name of Mark Palmer (US Ambassador to Hungary) acquired the latter. The American ambassador, who took a very active role in the change of system, was supposedly dismissed with immediate effect in the winter of 1990 exactly due to his economic conflict of interests. Dénes Csengey has pointed out as early as April 1988 that "as long as in the provinces there is no press and a political publicity defended, even over-defended, by laws, nothing has happened in this country that could not be withdrawn."[25] Why did the MSZMP's county papers prefer Western "exploiters" to the democratically-elected local governments in the autumn of 1990? Technical development and guarantees of employment are most often invoked as reasons. However, as long as public opinion did not come to know some angel-faced maidens among the young power technicians of the MSZP, the explanation holds fast that the party did not only receive moral appreciation for letting its papers become independent.

It would have been the task of the first supervisory committee of the newly elected parliament, initiated by the SZDSZ, to investigate the cases of media privatisation. The MDF members in the committee intended to examine all cases of privatisation, while the

SZDSZ would have preferred to limit the investigation to the German concern of Springer. Such a restriction would have unavoidably had the appearance that German capital was undesirable in Hungary. The committee had drafted a report, and after Miklós Haraszti resigned, it finished its activity without a worthwhile result. The Antall Government probably did not want to pick a quarrel with Western media Caesars (Maxwell, Murdoch); it did not want to jeopardise our integration to Western Europe with an incidental press campaign. The West (or at least a part of it) on the other hand considered the area some sort of a fire-trap that needed to be pacified and which deserved a little brainwash after the communist indoctrination anyway, even if the term of 're-education' was not used. Consequently, Western governments resigned themselves to the thought that their publishers acquired dominant positions in the media market here. Thus, everything remained basically the same, laws against monopolies have not been adopted since, and we haven't got a media strategy either—well, perhaps only if we consider the principle of "selling everything" a strategy.

While in the Visegrád countries big Western investors appeared one after the other, in the Balkan states these were almost completely absent for a long time. The reason for this was not primarily the lack of interest of Western investors, but that the political forces there did not give a chance to foreign capital to penetrate their market. The nationally-owned media did not prove up to the task in the Yugoslav war—to put it mildly—but the same goes for the majority of the Western media as well.

It can hardly be doubted that acquiring control over the tools of the formation of consciousness is qualitatively a different kind of activity than selling a brewery or an ice-cream plant. By all means, the creation of a secure financial background, the development of the technological background and of intellectual know-how is a certainty on the short run. *Pest Megyei Hírlap*, the local paper of Pest county, was the only one that did not pass into foreign ownership and that went bankrupt. We must not forget though, that due to the gravity of Budapest, this paper was not in such a privileged situation as the other county papers had been. Journals remaining in Hungarian hands could also be technically modernised provided they had a good management (e.g. *HVG*). The VICO-owned *Nők Lapja* was not far behind the Springer-owned *Kiskegyed* either.

According to Zoltán Farkas, independent journalism was defended in Hungary by foreign capital.[26] In the internal political fights, foreign ownership as such has indeed reduced the possibilities of action of the governments in power, but the situation is far more complicated than that. In the privatised papers, the development of external appearance has only partly been followed by the improvement of the content and of the ethical norms of journalism. Published opinions were and remain extremely ill-proportioned because the one-sidedness of the media workers' view and disposition in our country was not limited or balanced by the opposite one-sidedness of the owners. The majority of the publishers in America are Republican, in England right-wing, in Germany conservative, while journalists, on the contrary, everywhere are mostly left-wing and liberal. Why are old editorial staffs good enough for the new owners, for the Bertelsmann concern, or for the expressively right-wing Springer—as opposed to former East German papers? Western buyers in Hungary have undertaken not to dismiss anyone for a determined period (1-2 years), which seemed to be an attractive offer in the uncertainty of the media market. New owners have easily paid that price in exchange for what was a very reasonable transaction for them. In the case of county papers the monopoly situation has in advance secured profitability, and the economic policy after 1994 has completely served Western businessmen. This Western behaviour was a disenchanting experience for the Hungarian right-centrist forces, although we could read from Heinrich Böll already in the 1970s that the slow-down there had also been realised as a consequence of fraternisation between

Western capitalists and communist functionaries. We will only find out to what extent foreign capital indeed defends independent journalism, when the opinions of newspaper writers will clash in some crucial question with the interests of owners. At any rate, the limited reshuffles done during the privatisation of the electronic media do not back up Farkas' optimism.

Apart from the selling of national assets at a sacrificial price, two other fears had been expressed in the beginning by the humanist intelligentsia (Dénes Csengey, Ferenc Kósa) taking a leading role in the change of the political system in Hungary. One of them concerned the question of cultural integrity, namely that the values of Hungarian culture are dissolved in the impersonal international (or more correctly, Hollywood) mass culture. The other one was the concern that the country that sells its newspapers, also sells the public opinion, a part of its political sovereignty. The SZDSZ's Tamás Fodor, on the other side, had only emphasised business manipulation and the danger of monopolies, and warned about the discouragement of foreign capital.[27] Later radicals were speaking about media invasion and media colonisation, while the moderates suppressed the question as the inevitable price of integration and globalisation. Nevertheless, it cannot at all be ruled out that the foreign owner—should his interests demand so—can block or disturb the recognition and realisation of our strategic interests as a nation. Later, when commercial taxes were given in a concession, such considerations did not even arise in the forums of publicity. Interestingly, one of the exceptions was an economic monthly magazine, which quoted Albert Camus, according to whom the nation that sells its press also sells its right to determine national self-consciousness. It is still a question whether in a similar manner to other branches of the economy, the big foreign fish will eat up the small Hungarian fish also in the written media.

Why did the Centre-right Press not Hold Its Ground?

The opposition paper *Hitel*—the child of the populist writers—was able to publish in the autumn of 1988, after a long struggle; and making use of its positional advantage could in no time reach a print size of 60 thousand copies. Nevertheless, after competition had appeared this number quickly decreased to the regular level of cultural magazines. *Új Magyarország*, launched with HUF 250 million, wanted to become the "shield of trust" against the pessimism continuously generated also by the press. The paper managed mostly by writers—as a daily published weekly magazine—has had a confusion of roles for a long time and its sphere of influence did not reach beyond the core audience of the MDF. The equally loss-making *Pesti Hírlap* stopped publishing one day after the 1994 change of government. *Új Hírek* started by the MDF couldn't break the monopoly of the local papers because there is no tradition of regional papers in Hungary. In the publishing company of the North-Transdanubian paper distributed in five counties, the Post Bank and the Commercial Bank had shares of 49-49 percent each, while 2 percent was owned by the National Foundation. The publisher was liquidated in the beginning of 1994 due to lack of success.

In his analysis, Pál Tamás emphasises the permanently unfavourable marginal conditions aside from mismanagement. What were these conditions? According to Tamás the conservative press "lacks for the moment that kind of intellectual power which could have shown attractive neo-conservative visions." Péter Esterházy goes even further when he considers the saddest mistake of the MDF was that it had created a parody of its own system of values. This is an unjust over-generalisation, but examining the activity of at least some of the party's media people, the statement is correct. The 1989 *Hitel* is light years away from the 1994 *Parabola*.

Between 1990-94, it was still partially true that the conservative side had gotten a lamp but was lacking the oil. By today though, the situation has changed radically.

The most burning worry now is not so much the lack of intellectual ammunition, but rather the lack of means to convey the message. The papers of the old regime have inherited the infrastructure and the know-how, while the disadvantages of starting from scratch could to this day not be overcome by the new papers. They have no money, they are unable to pay even for the service of MTI (the Hungarian news agency), not to speak about maintaining a network of correspondents abroad, so they are permanently one step behind. Their competitors say that their edition sizes are small because these papers are not competitive. The truth is rather the other way round: as they are not competitive regarding their financial background so their edition size is small. There is another serious charge made by a former editor-in-chief: "There is no other country where banks and representatives of business life—against their own financial interests—would boycott with their advertisements a paper which has a continuously growing number of subscribers and where the edition size approaches those of the papers with a much longer history. Unfortunately political neutrality is not prevailing in the case of our paper, and as a consequence we are in a much more difficult position."[28]

The early-afternoon deadline, the view of the editors working with blankets on their knees and the suspension of the missions abroad spoke for themselves. With full knowledge of the incomes at other newspapers and of the wages paid often with one-two months delay at Iván Kelemen's, working at the *Új Magyarország* "had become a matter of honour and glory" since 1994. Here are some data, just to illustrate the proportions between the well-to-do newspapers and the ones in need. In May 1997, advertisers at *Népszabadság* spent 441 million forints, at *Népszava* 45 million forints, at *Magyar Hírlap*, with a not much greater circulation than that of *Új Magyarország*, 250 million forints, in *Magyar Nemzet* 67 million, and even in the *Kurír*, with its 25th position, 37 million. *Új Magyarország*, meanwhile, was not present in the top 25 regarding press advertising incomes, had to get by one a mere 35 million forints in 1996.[29]

The dividend of party-preference of the right-centre powers is in excess of the readers' interests in the conservative-liberal magazines. These magazines are mainly read by the powerful core of the right. Traditional voters of the FKGP and the KDNP are not obsessed magazine readers, just as the young supporters of the FIDESZ do not start their day reading newspapers, either. On the other hand, these parties cannot permanently acquire the great number of wandering voters, as this would exactly require the everyday "maintenance" fulfilled by the media. Loose connections can easily be neutralised by systematic counter propaganda. It is always easier to destroy than to build, and this is why destructive, discrediting campaigns are always more successful than constructive ones. And if the voter becomes apathetic and stays at home, that is half a victory.

Because the present opposition parties lack the serious capital to undertake financing of a daily magazine and making it well-known, nothing is left but to "ask for the friendly help of foreign capital". The short-term interests of Western capital are nevertheless better served by the economic policy of the MSZP-SZDSZ than by that of the bourgeois powers, which would rather support the strengthening of the national middle class—the competition. The Western media investors are consequently not interested in setting up a daily magazine whose spiritual trend would not correspond to the so called "neo-liberal globalisation."

All-out War

Theatrical performance or war? This is title the political scientist István Schlett gave to his book which analyses the events between 1990-94. If this question can refer to the whole, why couldn't it refer to any part of it? Media war, as a generally used expression/*terminus technicus* makes it almost completely unnecessary to seriously analyse the question, since, how could it be a theatrical performance if it is a war? True, it was fought with words and images, but its soldiers have received and inflicted lifelong wounds and at stake in the fight was nothing less significant than political power. But the question should not be put aside with the stigma of conspiracy, as the followers of this view also have a few thought-provoking arguments. History knows about operetta armies and operetta wars, so why could not an operetta change of system also exist? Compared to the importance of the shifts set in the last ten years—in contrast with the foregoing experiences of Hungarian history and with the present experience of the economic micro-sphere—the political transition was unusually smooth. Even in stable Western democracies political crimes occur, but in the last decade in our country such things fortunately did not happen, or at least we do not know about it. Journalism is not a completely secure profession even where the self-defence and solidarity of professionals is better, but the peak of the politically motivated atrocities in Hungary was when the MIÉP (Hungarian Justice and Live Party) demonstrators trod on the foot of a TV reporter. Although the chief warriors of the media war often complain, their standards of living—regardless of whether their favourite party is in the government or not—far exceed those of university professors, although differences can of course be extremely significant among them. While the losers of the élite are relative losers, the losers of society are absolute losers.

It must be made clear that the author doesn't agree with the followers of the conspiracy theory, but as such elements were present in almost all historical transitions, there is no reason now to exclude them even hypothetically. The Hungarian transformation has too many undiscovered areas for that. The "makeshift Europe" theory of Jenő Szűcs has a greater explaining power in the description of the change of system and in that of the drawbacks of the media-transformation. Our institutions are formally Western-like but most of them are deformed to such an extent by informal functioning mechanisms and by imbalanced social and power relations that a new makeshift situation is taking shape. This kind of "neither censorship, nor freedom of press" is characteristic of the period after 1994 for the very reason that the media workers had missed the moment of clemency to stabilise their prestige and create institutional guarantees for their independence between 1989-1994.

Why exactly had the media become the battleground of the system change?

It is worth quoting at greater length from the media policy ideas of the MDF, published by a member of the campaign staff before the elections. According to these, mass communication should be impartial from the political point of view, but morally partial; should seek for the truth without shading it; should be reactive and co-operative; should be characterised by the compliance of the costs and the outstanding role it plays in social renewal; should not be described by an aristocratic detached attitude; should identify itself better with the problems and their solutions; should not produce or increase tensions but work them off; should promote love of work and eagerness for action taking; should increase the effect of perspectives, pointing out regularly and bravely where and why the positive processes of transformation get blocked; should not be against any of the parties; should foster national traditions and support social progress; should transmit European values; and should not be dependent on parties and political organisations. Regarding the institutional set-up, in his view a new media law and such relations are necessary whereby media workers can elect and if necessary replace their leaders themselves. Members of the Superintendent Committee of the national media would be delegated by the government and the parties, while the Independent Professional Council would consist of professionals.[30]

The National Renewal Program pointed out three strategic goals:

1) guarantees must be created for national culture in order for it not to be disadvantaged by international commercial culture;

2) the Government should encourage improvement of possibilities for the reception of Hungarian radio and TV channels in the neighbouring countries;

3) more effective social organisation requires more differentiated orientation and information management.

While media researchers in the West have been warning firstly against the dangers of commercialisation and economic concentration, in our country—surprisingly, to a certain extent—they most often elicited the phantom of political repression as the main danger between 1990-94. One of the few exceptions is—although the current political and purposeful cloven hoof is showing also here—the 17th article of the Democratic Charter: "There will be democracy only when the freedom of press is not restricted, either by state monopoly or by the financial burden of the banks dependent of the state, or by intimidated journalists."

The main explanation of this kind of reduced media policy is that the leaders of the 1989 change of system had come from the cultural sphere. Television for them was first of all a conveyor of culture. For the technocrats that showed up later, or had rather remained in the background earlier, media was business in the first place and culture only much later. The *Kulturkampf* existing in several countries is consequently taking place in two theatres of war: on the one hand between the two camps of humanist intellectuals (this was characteristic of the former cycle), on the other hand between the camps of the humanist intelligentsia and that of businessmen (the latter unequal battle is still rather in latent phase). Values-led humanist intellectuals are more inclined to fundamentalism and to open battle than the technocrats, who are more capable of compromises, covering themselves up with the regularity of the market. This is why while in the former cycle the country was resounding with the noise of cultural battle, now everything is quiet—grumbling can be heard at most—as the victorious part of the humanist intelligentsia has acknowledged that it can only have a subordinated role in the new line of power.

Péter Ákos Bod sees the essence of media war as follows: "The media battle does not help. On the contrary, it slows up and hinders the political emancipation of the population. As prime minister, Antall had to expend a lot of energy in the 'cultural battle' fought above and below the normal multi-party political confrontations. The majority of the directors and operators of the media were far from the value-systems they were representing. It is not only that the media in most modern societies stands to the left of the imaginary political centre, moreover—as a result of its function of social supervisor—it is inclined to criticise the government. It would not be unexpected on these grounds to witness some kind of excess in the criticism of the system of values and functioning of the Antall government. But in the Hungarian conditions the point at issue was something completely different, and this was also marked by the fact that the majority of the media was not standing against the government, the MDF and Antall to a modest extent only but rather to a very considerable degree.

"There is no room here to analyse all the possible reasons and factors. Obviously, the starting fact is that the leaders and the determinant personalities of the media had belonged in the past to the severely supervised inner circle of the party-state—which presumed a particular selection and socialisation—and had played a role in the cultural resistance. This circumstance could explain—at least partially—the distrust of older journalists in leading positions towards the new political power in opposition and within it towards the MDF represented by József Antall. And because the privatisation of the press—that of the written press in the first place—had already started before the 1990 political change of system, at the time of the extant hegemony of the MSZMP, the political powers inherited the developed structure of publicity. This structure prefers the values of the left side and the preservation of the positions of *nomenklatura*, whereas it does not support the forces that propagate the radical transformation of the system and those that endanger the financial, economic and cultural positions of the *nomenklatura*. The reason for that was that the determinant personalities and supporters of the right-centrist movement had not belonged to the former *nomenklatura* before, their appearance and growth—just like every unknown and foreign phenomenon—may have caused fear and distrust, and what is more important it endangered settled positions."[31]

The MDF met the aversion of the media right from the beginning. The television broadcast of the elections was characterised not only by the failure of the computer system, but that of the professional crew led by György Baló, as well. No exit polls were organised, correspondents did not inform viewers about the result of the manual counting of votes, voters were not asked to comment. The viewers basically did not receive definite information until early the next morning, and this did not help to dispel the rumours about electoral manipulation. It also happened of course that MDF politicians—as a consequence of the "besieged castle" effect—at times became hypersensitive and overreacted to unfriendly statements thought to be insulting. Such a classic case was Mihály Vajda's opinion only partially based on facts stating that the more developed parts of the country had voted for the SZDSZ and the backward ones for the MDF.

The main reason for the media war can be found in the desire of those inside the possession to have the autonomy of the BBC, but without its objectivity and professional, moral standards. The MDF government and the mainstream of the media interpreted the goals of the change of system and within it the function of the media in two completely different manners. The BBC sees the media's task of public service as the threefold unity of information, education and entertainment. "The new political parties leading the system changing state were not prepared to appear in the mass media, and in the absence of a coherent national information policy of the government they could not sustain it with information."[32]

Society of course was even more unprepared for the changes than the new political forces. There was no revolutionary situation in Hungary in 1989. To paraphrase Lenin's definition: those in power could not reign in the old way, while the people wanted to go on living as they had done. Or perhaps a little bit better. Regrettably, this was not possible because of the debt crisis, and therefore the legitimacy of the old system, based on the standard of living, had collapsed. The media, however, rarely gave information to society on the transformation of the system. The big questions essentially determining the future relations of ownership (election of councils in plants, compensation, joining in privatisation) were surrounded by silence in the mainstream media , almost a news blackout. In other tactics, instead of providing factual information, commentaries came at once. For the problem is not that the media analyses the government program meticulously, with a critical disposition, and interprets it according to different interests and values; but the problem is that the program cannot even appear in the media without distortion. The situation was a little bit similar to that before 1989, when certain writings had been slanted while the reader was not even granted the chance to read the original writing. Media is naturally not the transmission belt of the government, but—with adequate distance and criticism—it has a service function as well. The idea that in a similar way to Dr. Brain's 1968 successful series entitled "explaining the mechanism" on MTV, now it was the market economy that should have been brought closer to the viewers, was followed by the clamour of liberal journalists in our country.

Insufficient knowledge leads to the malnutrition of the society. The 40-70 percent participation of the media's "evening class graduates" in the elections also marks that something is wrong with this Hungarian democracy. Everybody could find the suitable proposal on the supply side of the multi-party system. Yet, if this does not happen then the media bears heavy responsibility for two reasons. On the one hand, because it de-politicises the voters; and on the other because—to quote Bálint Tóth—it tries to detach the potential voters of the opposition parties using three strategies (distortion, concealing, overstating).

It was interesting to observe how flexibly the journalists' notion of roles declared by the mainstream was adapting to the current political situation. While during the Németh government the slogan was that the real press is independent of everything, during the Antall government a new slogan took its place, according to which the press by its nature is always in opposition. András Kereszty, the former president of the MÚOSZ was assuring the representatives of the governing party during the MDF government that journalists will undoubtedly love them once they go into opposition. Instead of that, the innovative professionals succeeded to invent anti-opposition journalism after the change of government, and in the spirit of independence they now joyfully accept financial support from different ministries, too.

The transmission of values was also refused by the mainstream media, citing its neutrality of ideology. Of course this did not seem very convincing from the mouth of the ideologists of "otherness". Then it came to light that in the category of entertainment, "otherness" means Hollywood for them. Among the movies broadcast by MTV (Hungarian state television) almost only late in the night can non-American productions be found. The refusal to transmit values is also a problem because the biggest obstacle in the birth of a powerful bourgeois middle class is that work, diligence and honesty are not considered and appreciated as values. The winners of the change of system are considered by the public as groups interwoven with speculation, black economy, black market and corruption. Original capital accumulation however did not mean firstly Drake's pirates in the West either, but the dominance of Protestant ethics as recorded by Max Weber. The values of reformation were diligent work, saving and the intact family. As a contrast, the world concept of the show business that dominates television is based on hedonism, egoism and the primacy of consumption.

The other basic goal of the government, besides the transformation, was to create a balance between acting in accordance with its mandate and restoring trust in social truthfulness. The first goal would have been served by the media if it had also shown the inevitable difficulties and limited options instead of creating tensions, while the second one could have been accomplished if the media had performed the role of the watchdog of democracy; if we could have relied on it in the sense that the good eventually gain their merits and the bad their punishment. As in America, several interests had to meet for the Washington Post to make Nixon resign, so to say, likewise in Hungary the press obviously had a certain role in Privatisation Minister Tamás Suchman's downfall, but the decisive factor was constituted by those forces for whom the privatisation minister proved an obstacle. The press was a great power between 1990-94 because it met powerful allies facing a weak enemy. And today it is weak because these powerful allies, acquiring even the main power in the state, though applying new methods, succeeded essentially to restore the former relation of dependence.

Antall endured the antipathy coming from the media's mainstream for a long time with patience, and in the MDF-SZDSZ pact he gave his consent to the nomination of candidates for key media positions based on consensus. This step of his, however, was regarded by many of those who had already packed up not as generosity but as a sign of weakness. It was at the least a sign of insensitivity towards the historical moment when instead of moving the Champion League Final to another channel, the swearing in of the freely elected government was prevented from being broadcast. The next conflict was caused by Hungarian Radio chief Csaba Gombár, who as a member of the MSZMP had been present in 1987 in the tent in Lakitelek, when he personally stopped advertisements for the weekly newsmagazine *Magyar Fórum* ("A paper which is not edited by former communists"). Comparing negative advertising is indeed not accepted, but it is also obvious that in the case of similar ethical errors the president did not take such firm steps. And when before the local elections TV president Elemér Hankiss did not allow the prime minister to appear on TV (imagine this in the case of Gyula Horn!), the psychosis of the war developed in the MDF. The besieged castle syndrome started to shape up in the prime minister's office. Antall enjoyed using the comparison of the 80 hussars or that of the kamikaze-government. It has to be added that the editor-in-chief of the most important news-program, the TV-Híradó was István G. Pálfy at that time. There were some who stoically or rather only nervously saw the press as the weather, with which one has simply to put up: the government is supposed to govern, the press is supposed to criticise.

József Antall did not like the term "system change": one changes one's underwear, he used to say. His constitution as a politician—as well as his research theme—carried the style marks of the 19th century liberal parliamentarianism, based on the suffrage with census. He was not able, and he did not even wish, to adapt himself to the requirements of modern media democracy. This can be seen maybe as an occupational hazard. "He does not use striking commonplaces, 'one-liners', 'sound bites'. This style is archaic, of the last century for the contemporary media.", an ex-minister wrote about him.

And what was his even greater deficiency: not only that he didn't possess an economic politician of Erhard's calibre, but he didn't even have a media politician with similar qualities. His sense of powerlessness eventually showed up in verbal duels with the media: thus he called a sad-faced Mickey Mouse László Lengyel, who had wanted to be his adviser earlier and who himself often used animal-allegories in his essays written about politicians.

A dual power stabilised relatively quickly in the former cycle, where against the fragile Antall government, just weakly embedded in society, the barrage of propaganda was led by the heavyweight Charter. Why did the opposition possess better connections from the point of view of the media? Because mass communication was a confidential profession and therefore required absolute loyalty. Members of the old middle class, resigned to passive resistance, were glad if their children could at least enter the politically neutral technical and medical universities, and the profession of journalism had never been touched by the limited liberalisation of the Kádár era. For this reason, the lack of an organic development resulted in a lack of cadres and that is why the MDF had to accept the service of the hirelings.

Antall endeavoured to reach equilibrium in the media field, too. He agreed in the pact about the nomination by consensus of the radio and television presidents, then realising the imbalance in the media and the danger of the MSZP's strengthening, he proposed to the SZDSZ the dividing-up of the two TV channels akin to the Italian model. Hankiss' idea about the alternative television news program was accepted without special resistance, too. But the SZDSZ preferred to undertake the media war than a media pact like this, which would have undoubtedly been disadvantageous for them in the short run. Thus they could stand as a guardian angel near the journalists, protecting their unlimited freedom; and from this transitional identity of interests they drew many the misleading conclusion that the media was in favour of the SZDSZ. In 1997 the opinion leaders of the media—let's not count now the militant party-soldiers and political sympathizers—saw the success of their interests in the MSZP government and therefore they served up "success propaganda". After the policy of equilibrium had failed, it was replaced by the policy of counterbalance in the electronic media (nomination of vice-presidents). In the unbalanced written media, a counterbalance was attempted by the foundation of new papers. And the functioning of the swing is based on the principle that the more one sits at one extreme, the more the other needs to sit at the other extreme as well. The equilibrium of the extremes is of course not an ideal state, but the logic of things increasingly took on the characters of the events in this direction.

"For thousands of years the North Star has been the most certain point of orientation for seamen. In democracy its function is fulfilled by the free press. The great impediment to our progress is that the main part of the Hungarian media is over-politicised. It interprets and explains instead of informing. It shows up scandals instead of conflicts. It judges but doesn't ask. Many journalists lack general and professional knowledge. The television and radio are mostly responsible for the fact that thousands and millions of people do not have basic information about the process of system change; that tens of thousands of people haven't got the slightest idea of how they could have benefited from the sharing of co-operative property; or how they could get their land back, which are the basic characteristics of market economy and so on... Meanwhile the television is full of stupid quiz programs, video clips, and of talk shows interesting to nobody. A reporter and editor style and practice characterised by the lack of knowledge, aggression, prejudice, grammatical mistakes is becoming dominant nowadays. We can only hope for the time being that the concerned part of our press will grow out of these infantile disorders", wrote Ferenc Grezsa from the MDF front-line in April 1992.[33]

The media war has distracted attention from reality. It covered the "original capital accumulation" in the economy and in the media. Public television has become commercial not only because in a country with low wage-level this national institution could not have been sustained from subscription fees. With appropriate personnel reduction and a more effective collection of operation fees this would not be an unsolvable task. Advertising and sponsorship was permitted by the producer firms in the TV to milk it as a cash cow because they hoped to yield the capital they needed to enter into privatisation. The income of the TV had increased from HUF 3.7 billion in 1996 to HUF 33.8 billion in 1997. If we could tell what exactly happened to this tremendous amount of money, we would surely understand better the history of the media war as well.

Two media policies lived together inside the MDF: Antall's and Csurka's. A Csurka-style hot war was in the beginning lacking in political will and later sufficient power. His conception was built on the approach characteristic of France: he who owns political power also owns the national media. In spite of that, in the first months even Csurka had supported the pact with the SZDSZ—as an inevitable compromise—signed by Antall behind the back of the party, which essentially preserved the status quo in electronic media. Inside the political base of the MDF, the opinion that compares 1945 to 1990 can often be seen. The elections were free in both cases according to this opinion, but pressure from abroad was lying heavily on the coalition agreements. The difference was, that the constraint of the coalition in 1945 became the constraint of the pact in 1990.

The government was walking the path of conciliation and constitutionalism. But in 1992, the parties of the present coalition had no intention of effecting a reconciliation with Antall and his companions but rather of defeating them. "Csaba Gombár is right when he says that the political field of forces has changed, and the SZDSZ-MDF pact is dashed to pieces. But this is no excuse for Csaba Gombár not to succeed in promoting the impartiality of the radio", wrote one of the national liberal cultural politicians.[34] The constitutional method preferred by the government was impracticable, in spite of the decision of the constitutional court. "It was the result of this process of 'Weimarisation' that the President of the Republic was not allowed to sign the decisions concerning the replacements of media presidents, and he has been under a continuous pressure to avoid that, although these were supposed to be signed on grounds of the constitutional law", said Antall in January, 1993.[35]

The president of the constitutional court states more diplomatically: "We have clearly defined what the head of the state can ponder and what he cannot, but did not state with a single word whether he should relieve Elemér Hankiss or not, because that was not within our sphere of authority to decide, but within the president's. Consequently we could neither take a stand on the question of whether the president has applied correctly the rule deriving from the constitution. The only case where we are not at the mercy of further political definitions is if the constitutional court itself declares a law null and void."[36]

Due to this deadlock situation the Antall government was put under ever increasing pressure from its political base. The media law failed to pass in December 1992, and the time of the MDF congress on January 23, when the question about power and leadership ("Antall or Csurka?") would be openly raised, was coming dangerously close. Gombár and Hankiss resigned on January 6, 1993, in this increasingly tense situation and the management of the two institutions was taken over by vice-presidents Gábor Nahlik and László Csúcs. Thus Antall could temper the vigour of the radicals and win a victory of 16:5 for his men in elections to the party's presidium.

The year 1993 was characterised by a two-directional process. While Antall was consolidating the governmental party by pushing Csurka out, the hidden bar brawl, ready to break out any time, had started over again after the taxi drivers' blockade in the electronic media. Activists of the governmental party had given up their philosophy of "Not he who strikes is stronger, but the one who stands his ground" and started an offensive. Some opposition TV and radio programs were halted with the slogan of de-politicisation, investigations were started in connection with the management, and in the end, the tool of firing was also used in Hungarian Radio. This tool had first been used as a matter of fact by Elemér Hankiss himself when he had dismissed István G. Pálfy and Chrudinák, who were later on put back to their positions by the court of labour. When in March of 1994 László Csúcs finally decided to take the same measures, this was a completely counter-productive step two months before an almost certain election defeat. Otherwise, two radio reporters (Eszter Rádai and Ferenc Vicsek) out of 129 dismissed had been among the first 200 signatories of the appeal of the Publicity Club. It is difficult to judge, also subsequently, which the proper conduct in a bar brawl is. If your opponent sets on you it can happen that you can disarm him with the manners of a gentleman, but it can also well happen that he will see in his victim an easy prey and become even more aggressive.

Stabbed in the Back?

When the activity of the two vice-presidents is judged, there are opinions in opposition circles that while in Italy the media empire of Berlusconi gained a victory for the Forza Italia, in Hungary the opposite occurred: the government was overthrown by its own media. Facts do not support either contention. Media—when skilfully used—can indeed be a powerful institution, but not an omnipotent one. The whole party system was crushed by a corruption scandal in Italy, so a party which was similar to the 1990 MDF could easily appear to fill the vacuum. On the other hand, not only the Italian party system had become discredited, but together with it the public channels distributed among the parties as well. Thirdly, the Italian written press is extremely heterogeneous, so the

TV channels of Berlusconi did not have to suffer a massive systematic campaign aimed at discrediting them. Until the winter 1990 blockade of the taxi drivers, the operation of the electronic media had not really been criticised, yet the MDF had still lost the local elections. The nostalgia for the Kádár era was not reborn in 1994 because the population was dissatisfied with the media of the governing party, but because their standards of living had decreased. The directors of the news programs had visibly assessed the situation wrongly, and their programs addressed the regular customers of the governmental parties. Continuously mentioning the danger of the left wing was in this situation rather counter-productive. Recalling at every step the Rákosi-era and the ÁVO did not bring votes, because the majority of the population already during the Kádár system had perceived the break with the Rákosi-system and its Stalinism. And the MSZP was not identified with the 1950s at all. The anti-1956 past of Gyula Horn had left people grown up in the Kádár era indifferent, too, a fact later indirectly proven also by a survey, according to which only 2 percent of the population considered October 23 the most significant date in the calendar. There is truth to the argument that instead of economic and social problems the TV placed the historic recent past in the centre of the campaign, further reinforcing the image of a history-obsessed, socially insensitive, economically amateur government. Votes could have been gained from the history of the recent past perhaps only if the corruption cases of the 1970s and 1980s, particularly those of the local petty monarchs', and the enormous national debts would have been revealed. After the resignation of Hankiss and Gombár, the News Program led by Pálfy came under such heavy fire that its effect was strongly diminished. The success of this campaign of discrediting was also helped by the fact that István G. Pálfy, who was considered to be Pozsgay's man within the MDF, was not enjoying Antall's confidence, and was trying to acquire it with overdone loyalty. This overcompensation however only strengthened the public belief that the News Program was not trustworthy, as it was supporting the government. The critics of the News Program of Pálfy of course forget to mention that the index of confidence of the television continuously remained on the same level ever since the change of government. Judging, on the other hand, by the negative campaign of the previous weeks—which as a matter of fact, in spite of the widespread opinion, is not connected to the name of Pálfy but that of Chrudinák—is extremely difficult. For, in the last week before the 1994 elections an opinion poll was conducted, the results of which, according to the law, could not have been made public. In that the support for the MSZP fell back to 25 percent. It is not possible to tell whether this was compensated by the compassion votes of the Horn accident or by the boomerang effect of the negative campaign.

According to the researcher, though, the issue is far more complicated: "Concerning the relationship between the government and the information of the public, the present situation is mostly characterised by the fact that the favoured social groups do not support the government either, as the informative activity of the government does not offer a suitable handhold for that. The social mirror role of this information is simply not working: thus the whole of the Hungarian society is not aware of the real processes, of the intentions of the government, the irrationality of its own (social) behaviour, and about what helps and what hinders economic development. The lack of effective information, causes—according to experts—a loss on the order of HUF 100 billion by distrust towards the economic programs and the excitation of inflational expectations."[37]

Aside from conciliation or the use of force, the Antall government had a third option as well: trying to open new frontlines instead of continuing the hopeless trench warface. In the field of written press the foundation of new papers were such attempts (*Új Magyarország, Új Hírek*). Radio Free Europe, losing its listeners, carried on negotiations with the government about starting to broadcast on a new VHF-band from within the country, but this plan failed as a consequence of the fierce protest of the SZDSZ. The Németh government, as a result of the opposition's pressure, had imposed a frequency moratorium on the electronic media, which blocked the media privatisation. The MDF government did not want to believe until the last moment that it was going to lose the elections, and—unlike the MSZ(M)P in 1989—had not taken any steps to create infrastructure for the period when it would act in opposition. The plan to privatise the Russian Army channel was raised by György Schamschula a few weeks before the elections, but due to the protest of the MSZP and the SZDSZ he retreated. So finally this was also just fuel to the fire, and proved to be just as counter-productive as the dismissals at the radio. The question of why the MDF did not initiate such a pre-manoeuvre in the fall of 1989 is entirely justified. However, in the atmosphere of hectic changes, an expectation which supposes such considerable political consciousness from a newly-formed party without a solid infra-structure and no governing experience, may seem exaggerated.

Almost the only long-lasting act of the MDF media policy was the establishment of Duna TV. The satellite station starting at Christmas 1992 was condemned as an illegally born alternative governmental television by the opposition of that time, headed by the SZDSZ. This accusation however did not stand. The satellite channel is very popular in Transylvania and at home it has fulfilled the role of a cultural television, filling a gap in this sense, and keep-ing itself at a distance as much as possible from internal political fights.

Cannon Fodder

Do politicians and journalists sit in the same boat in Hungary? The relationship of the two professions alternates between distrust and interdependence even in the West. "Don't trust any quotation unless you yourself have picked it out of its context", advises Johannes Rau, the former SPD nominee for chancellor. The Swiss Hans Gottfried Bernrath emphasises the positive facts of the relationship: "They are better informed than us. They can at least buy some information. If they did not exist, we would know even less."

While journalists had been afraid of politicians during socialism, between 1990-94 the situation took a turn: non-leftist politicians began to be afraid of the policy-making groups of the press. One can often hear the opinion today that a politician who is on good terms with a television reporter can make a better career than the politician with a strong background in a particular region. Correspondents are also fully aware of their power. A good example of that is the statement expressed by the former co-editor of *Magyar Hírlap* about FIDESZ on the 1993 media boat: "We have picked you out of the litter bin, and we are now going to throw you back just there." This situation is not unknown in the West either. Helmut Schmidt considered the confrontation with the Springer papers political suicide, too.

But the influence of the media can here be far greater and above all quicker than in Western Europe because—as Béla Pokol has argued—there are no stable party-preferences in this area, traditional political relationships based on family relations have broken off, and civil society is weak. Some 50-70 percent of the electors are "wandering voters", they can easily be convinced to switch by press campaigns. And what is more, 40 years of de-politicisation has made the people give up communication beyond mass media, the power of mobilisation of public meetings and public debates is small.

In a country where the proportion of electoral participation is small, neither the politicians nor the journalists can be satisfied with their performance in the field of democracy. Ideally the success of politics is typically in the interest of both kinds of professionals. In a country where basic questions are being openly raised for the first time in decades, both kinds of professionals are burdened with negligence for not being able or not wanting to explain to the people with the right to vote, what was at stake in politics.

The question, of course, is whether the functioning of democratic publicity is indeed the priority which makes the characters of media move. The fact that media consumers are not convinced about that either can also be demonstrated by the index of importance of the press being 88 percent in 1991, while its index of confidence 67 percent, the latter falling back in 1996 to 49 percent and remaining essentially the same ever since.

The prestige of the journalists is nowhere in line with their wages and importance. The three most dreaded jobs in England are: 1) second-hand car dealer, 2) journalist, 3) politician. According to this it indeed seems to be suicidal to attack each other, and an agreement would be obvious, as it seems that they indeed share the same boat. Helmut Schmidt said once that journalists and politicians are alike. They both have statesmen and crooks among them. Instead of the recognition of the partial identity of interests, in the campaign against Antall many were driven by a distorted psychological reaction: if I had prostituted myself then the others could not have remained honest either.

Who Goes Home?

The most sensitive field of the media is the question of hirings and firings. Some 7,500 people, representing half of the correspondents of the public DFF, were dismissed in Eastern Germany, beginning with those who had worked with the Stasi. Nobody could remain on the TV screens from the former presenters of political TV programs; key positions were filled by West German "foreign workers" who chose whom they would employ (or take back).

Csurka's radicalism required both change of the system and the change of persons. The media establishment took the view "Change of system, yes, change of persons, no" and regarded Csurka's statement as a declaration of war. Its actions of supposed self-defence were then directed against the whole of the MDF. "The Presidium of the MÚOSZ is worried by the unmistakable declarations of the representatives of different parties concerning 'purges' and dismissals in the press after the elections. These certainly individual opinions evoke the bad spirits of past times, and do not fit at all with the desired tolerance of a society progressing towards democracy", rang the storm-bell of the "freedom-fighters" of MÚOSZ.[38] In the face of Csurka's radicalism Antall tried to reach an agreement. The presidents of the television and the radio were nominated with the agreement of all the political parties represented in parliament. The application for the leading position of the MTI also concerned by the nomination law was announced without previous co-ordination, and according to Sándor Révész it was tailored to the person of Ottó Oltványi.[39] Oltványi, who previously occupied the position of the president of the Owners' Advisory Body of the MTI as the candidate of the MSZP, in 1992 was charged for one more year with the leadership of the national institution. His position was taken over by the editor-in-chief of *Heti Magyarország*, the MDF member Károly Alexa only in the fall of 1993. In the spring of 1990, many journalists in the electronic media were waiting for their dismissal with their things packed. Why did Antall not force the changes in personnel?

1) The prime minister did not have a very high opinion of journalists but he had applied in their case, too, the thoughts of Deák that he had been quoting in his exposition: "We must try to endeavour to make friends in this present transformation out of those who

are not its friends at the moment; we can accomplish goals only by shaking hands, and if we fall out with ourselves then no enemy will be needed."

2) The media really played its part in the shake-up of the old system. "If you mean personal changes by the change of system, then we hardly had one, for today the same people are working in the press as before. There has of course been a change—although I do not know whether I should dare to call it a change of system— in the sense that people started to think independently, which they had been made to give up, or more exactly, they were not trained to do."[40]

3) Some journalists of the former regime discovered that the best form defence is attack: the easiest way to become exempt from prying into their past was to accuse their critics of anti-Semitism. The SZDSZ representative Miklós Szabó wrote about this issue in the *Népszabadság*, on May 26, 1990. "If anti-Semitism was in the beginning a matter of bankers in the Rákosi system, it became a matter of functionaries and today it turned into an issue of television. The proportion of intellectuals with a Jewish origin in the press surpasses indeed that of the Hungarians with a Jewish origin in the population. Let's put capitulative explanations aside and stop trying to prove that this proportion is 'not that conspicuous'... Regarding the present-day situation, the country possesses a journalistic society with excellent standards, sensitive and loyal towards democracy. Some sort of cleansing or changing of the guard in this field can only cause a decline in this level and political damage. It is the vital question of the blossoming democracy to dare to fight and not to make the slightest concession for any kind of anti-Semitic spirit."

4) The mainstream in our country had been suggesting till then that basically everyone in the media had been forced to make a compromise. The only difference is that the better ones, who have nothing to hide in their past, are brave enough to admit it, while

those who changed sides to the MDF government are the ones who lie low, pretending that they were born in 1989 and do not dare to assume their past. To unveil just this, *Beszélő* started a series in 1992 to make the writings of youth of the MDF journalists known to the general public. Former masterpieces of Miklós Vásárhelyi, Tibor Várkonyi and his companions could on the other hand be enjoyed in the *Magyar Fórum* and *Demokrata*. The problem was not that it was said countless times that István G. Pálfy used to be a party secretary, but that the same individuals have never written about the news director of the radio, Iván Bedő for instance, that he had been trying to enlarge the "boundaries of the freedom of press" as a member of the old workers' militia. If anyone would like to get a taste of how the match of the two parties completely lacked any kind of fair play, I would like to bring to their notice the telephone conversation between Tivadar Farkasházy and András Sugár in the spring of 1994.[41] The ex-editor-in-chief of the *HVG* had the following opinion about the metamorphosis of professionals: "I can see two typical attitudes. The total changing of sides, the unconditioned service of the new power, in a similar way to the former. The other one has got exactly the same amnesia as the total about-face: 'It's no concern of anyone what I had written then, and how I had licked the boots of the old system, I am now a fierce opposition person, give me a break with what I had done before.'"[42] By the way, this kind of personal concern could have been the reason for dealing rather with the 1950s and with 1956—almost totally irrelevant from the point of view of present-day politics—instead of the Kádár-regime. The Poles probably had a more correct procedure when they put the so-called Pampers generation, i.e. young, unstained individuals, into key-positions. On the other hand by calling the journalists that were attacking them "hirelings", certain MDF-politicians have partly even strengthened those of the mainstream in their belief that they were the embodiment of real, steadfast journalists, while those in favour of the government were weathercocks; and with their delimitation they showed that they are not willing to make common cause with them. The SZDSZ was not that fastidious about its own compromised hirelings (Tamás Ungvári, Mihály Sükösd) when it accepted their services.

Or, as an editorial in the *Budapest Sun* stated the issue:"Unlike in other former communist countries, communist journalists were not expected to disappear in Hungary. Most national and local papers were instead privatised in the last days of communist government, with the condition that the new owners are not allowed to change the editorial staffs. So instead of sending them away for having misled the public opinion for years, the firms of Bertelsmann and other foreign investors have rewarded them with a rise in salary and a renewed security of employment. Most Hungarian journalists—as no-one forced them to do so—have not changed... Briefly: Hungarian journalism has but slightly changed since communism."[43]

"In 1990 in Hungary there hadn't been a considerable clean-up within the staff of public offices, in spite of the fact that there was not a simple change of government going on but a political change of system. The change of senior public servants was of a smaller degree then, than the one that followed the 1994 social-liberal transformation of the government", writes the political scientist.[44] The same is true for the media. The smoke in the case of the 1990 changes was bigger than the flame. The 1994 "carpet bombing" of the media, in turn, has reduced to silence all the "political dissidents" except for the *Vasárnapi Újság*, left there as an alibi.

On the Parade-ground

What conditions and norms does the media system create for journalism? Let's take a look first at the relationship between performance and compensation. The salaries of those with some status are far better than the average wages of the intellectuals. In other places this is more differentiation. A Dutch employee of German TV, Rudi Carrell, has said that the media talent would be broken if they wanted to become chancellors, for they would only earn half as much. However, while the only public servant in Germany who earns more than the chancellor is the President of the Bundesbank, in our country not only the salaries of the public TV and radio presidents exceed that of the prime minister, but also the incomes of many editors. It is a natural thing, according to Elemér Hankiss, that the jester earns more than the king, but in the view of the author of the present paper neither their performance nor their responsibility give grounds for that (and I am not trying to praise the prime minister when I say that).

What seems to be a casual and interesting job for an outsider, often covers self-destructive working conditions. On the other hand just as journalism seems to be a desirable dream profession for those who are choosing their career, so does its prestige fluctuate in the view of the population. Within the editorial offices then, there is a wide abyss between those with status and the part-time correspondent pariahs. While salaries at Axel Springer are regulated by means of a collective contract, in many other cases they are subject to case-by-case bargains only.[45] Fees paid for a standard page of text vary from 1000 to 3000 forints [5 to 15 dollars].

Are journalists bums?

Experts and politicians, and a part of the readers, too, often complain about the superficiality and unreliability of journalists. The question of what kind of constraints the structures of media institutions press on the journalists is less examined. Economic constraints and/or temptations often deprave papers to the level of open prostitution. The *Budapest Business Journal* related its experience in July 1996, that main daily papers in the capital—with the exception of *Magyar Hírlap*—had been accepting or even asking money (100-300 thousand forints) for publishing articles paid for by advertisers as editorials. Most people see in the fight for a living the reason for the commercialisation of the press. The Hungarian market in their view is not capable of supporting seven national dailies.[46]

Political constraints appear indirectly, in most of the cases, generally through the owners. This is in our country particularly facilitated by the circumstance that—unlike in Germany, for instance—the primary profiles of many owners of papers is not media and they only use the press to enforce other interests (e.g. Kordax, Postabank, VICO). This also partly explains the strange fact why loss-making political papers are so virulent in Hungary. Just like in Italy, certain owners in our country use their daily papers for the indirect validation of political and economic interests, rather than direct profit making.[47]

Organisational constraints derive from the tensions that exist among the three phases of producing a paper (collecting information, selection, processing/boiling down). Often-witnessed lack of journalistic competence, for example, derives from the principle of one party/one journalist, whether the topic of the press-conference is a nuclear power station or the closing of theatres.

Investigative journalism, apart from the fear of press lawsuits, is also hindered by the lack of financial interest. If a high ranking author even by the richest daily is only paid 35 thousand forints for an investigative column after five weeks of collecting information, one cannot really wonder why the majority prefers to choose the more well-paid genre of article writing. As a natural consequence to that, opinions infiltrate dominate news items in the media.

Another important question concerns the expectations regarding the roles of journalists. The ethics of emotions undoubtedly dominates the ethics of responsibility in Hungary. A small sign of that is that rapidity is more often mentioned as a viewpoint in the news competition than reliability, although readers value it exactly the other way round. The consequence of the primacy of rapidity is that the press is teeming with half-baked thoughts that are unsuitable for publication, yet are published. Tongues are sharp as swords, but minds are blunt as blocks—one could quote Madách.

The next question is the identity of Hungarian journalists. János Berecz said once that the most humiliated stratum in Hungary during the system of Kádár was that of the journalists. In spite of that, the depravities witnessed in 1956 ("We were lying during the day, we were lying in the night, we were lying on every wavelength") we have been spared—so far. Coming to terms with the past has not failed to occur only in the press, though. "... I find it miserable that now, seven years after the end of things, we still know nothing more about the Kádár era than during it. The fact that society has rejected this undoubtedly very difficult, very painful process... we don't even know the facts that could be known."[48] There has been only one attempt worthy of appreciation: the volume of interviews entitled *Behívattak* (I have been called in). The failure to deal with the past then gives birth to sentences that obfuscate the different degrees of responsibility, such as those of Ákos Mester, according to which people who were listening together to János Kádár on May 1, 1957, have by now organised in different parties.[49]

Power reflexes originating in the power of press are dominant in certain journalists. Aside from for the famous litter bin of Iván Gádor, we could also read sentences from Péter György that can be considered as threatening, saying that Viktor Orbán should not act foolishly, for journalists are more powerful than him anyway. Péter Zsolt had written in *ÉS* that the media worker of the present considers him/herself rather an intellectual than a journalist, and this mentality is indirectly reinforced by the praises of the political parties. These media workers either play the role of the public prosecutor or that of the defending counsel, according to their party sympathies. The attorney role of the men-in-the-street is, on the other hand, losing ground—it is a role that was even overplayed in the Kádár system. Hankiss has written about how the press—as some sort of a righteous, but distant King Matthias—could occasionally help people in trouble who had sent complaining letters when some local petty monarchs took advantage of them.

Independent information is also damaged by the widespread practice that leading personalities of the public media work as PR consultants for different institutions. Thus József László (still at the radio at that time) was working for György Surányi, the leader of the column on economic policy of the MTI for the ministry of finances, and István Javorniczky from *Magyar Nemzet* for the constitutional court.[50] What kind of a gendarme does a journalist make, who supplements his income by working as a part-time highwayman? The identity crisis of the journalist is his private business, but the conflict of interests between the two roles is already a public affair. For such a request addresses the position of the journalist at least to the same extent as his abilities.

The hotbed of power-centred information is constituted by the widespread practice that certain institutions hand feed easygoing journalists through their press-informers, while the former do not even notice how they become mouthpieces of PR-specialists.

It was an offence to the spirit of public service when the producers of the political satire programme on the radio were campaigning for the MSZP-SZDSZ in the spring of 1994; likewise, the participation of two leading correspondents of the MTV, János Horvát and András Kepes in the election campaign of Gábor Kuncze was not reconcilable with the impartiality of public service.[51] Provided, but without permission, that this was only a reaction to the biased pro-governmental attitude of others, the example of Martin Bell, the star-reporter of the BBC, is still far more to be followed, as he immediately stepped out of service when he started to run as a candidate in the 1997 elections.

Regarding the ability of the journalists, in spite of improvement it is still true that the fact that God has given someone a microphone does not mean that he has also given competence along with it. Training in journalism was for a long time centred on one-year intensive courses, while the most problematic feature of the present-day training situation is its political one-sidedness.

Surfers of the mainstream rush from one employment to another, are basically uninformed, do not read magazines and opposition papers; moreover, the persons thinking in a more differentiated manner on their own sides also hardly get enough space in their programs.

Just as Greek thinkers degenerated into sophistry once they lacked the original ethos, the moral crisis of the mainstream media has also turned out to be the breeding-ground of cynicism. "If the conditions are like that, it's still better if I make my pile than others." The media policy of Gyula Horn was successful because he knew this moral crisis and was aware of the fact that the majority of journalists would change sides from the SZDSZ to the MSZP on grounds of the principle of the stronger dog.

One of the most delicate areas is the one concerning the trustworthiness of journalism. Journalists were eventually left out of the law on agents and informers. That was of course the least of the average reader's cares, but this field became the hotbed of mistrust and suspicion among the circles of politically active citizens. Those who consider themselves the conscience of society should not allow their moral trustfulness to be overshadowed. That is naturally also true about the churches. Although the constitutional court has eventually taken both institutions from the power of the law, they somehow should have voluntarily requested their own screening for former secret service activities. The absence of this gesture, moreover, the anti-campaign the mainstream of the media has conducted against the law did not increase one bit the trust towards journalists. Only once has an aborted attempt happen in this sense. In November 1993, 22 editors of Hungarian Radio asked for their screening when the SZDSZ representative Imre Mécs declared that a great number of the editors of the Hungarian Radio, the

Hungarian Television and the Hungarian News Agency (MTI) had worked in a way or another for Office III/III (political informants). The parliamentary faction of the SZDSZ did not identify itself with the declaration of Imre Mécs, while Gábor Kuncze apologised to those concerned.[52] The strong position the Office III/III held in the press is well demonstrated by the press scheme elaborated for the reburial of Imre Nagy in 1989.[53]

The other very sensitive area is the question of foreign correspondents as agents of intelligence. There is a saying about the English that all their journalists abroad are spies. As data are not accessible, one cannot know how general the practice was in the former regime to use correspondents sent abroad also as agents. Treating this issue confidentially can of course be an interest of national security, but the problem is worsened if these persons have worked for Office III/III in another capacity as well. This is again an area where there is a great deal of gossip, but little is written.

Lying Low

"By forming a consensus they do not only have the chance to determine what they will talk about but also to decide what they are going to keep silent about. From the American press, for instance, one can gather much more accurate information concerning the nature of the military-industrial complex than about the telecommunication monopoly. Those who are making a living by publicity in the real sense of the word do not seem to like publicity when they are personally concerned", said Péter Vajda in the February of 1985 on the theoretical discussion of the Department on Agitation and Propaganda of the Central Committee of the MSZMP.[54] The statement of the editor of the news and information column in *Népszabadság* is still true. Media is still an unknown territory in the media. There has been as much talk about the media war as there has been little else published about the other aspects of the press.

Most papers do not have an audited print run up to the present day. The monitoring service of the ORTT that has existed for almost two years now has not yet made public a single report. In vain could one wait, of course, for a newspaper to expose itself. This would roughly be as meek of a desire as the statement of the MSZMP that there was no need for an organised and legalised opposition, for the party itself fulfilled the role of its own opposition at the same time.

However as the "multi-journal" system is even less developed in Hungary than the multi-party system, in vain we also wait for the controllers to monitor each other mutually. As the power relations between the governmental and the opposition press is truly reflected in the difference between the media-ship (MÚOSZ) and the media-boat (MUK) setting off each September, a question raised by an opposition paper can only be put on the public agenda if one of the factions of the governmental press also endorses it. For in the present situation, instead of being the watchdog of democracy, the governmental fox is watching the hens of the public welfare. Besides, this news blackout originating in the media structure is one of the reasons why the press has more prestige than the parties: spectators do not know the salaries of the media aristocracy, they rarely hear about their scandals. Although the index of confidence has decreased in all categories, that of the television is higher than that of the press in our country. On the one hand readers are less unprotected against the tricks of printing than against those of visual manipulation, on the other the aura of officialdom is still connected to the electronic media. Apart from that, users of the written press belong to the more educated and more critical stratum of the population. A typical characteristic of the fragmentation of self-reflection also resides in the fact that even the handbook on the history of the Hungarian press only covers the issue until 1982. If we look for refreshing exceptions in the public sphere of publicity, then we can mention Ágnes Vándor, Zoltán Kovács, and András Bruck (*ÉS*) from the side of the (smaller) coalition party (SZDSZ), Ferenc

Langmár and László Seres from *Magyar Narancs*, Gabriella Lőcsei and Kinga Hanthy from *Magyar Nemzet*, respectively István Lovas and János Kecskés Székely from the side of the opposition (*Magyar Demokrata*). Classic examples of what kind of tempers criticism can induce—even if it comes from the same camp—are the writings of Gábor Szűcs, editor-in-chief of the *Kurír*[55] and László Juszt in response to critical articles about them in *ÉS*.

Who should then control controllers if we are lacking competition, i.e. there is no self-control within the branch and journalists more or less also defend their fellow-journalists?

A minimal requirement that should be imposed to ensure the transparency of this basic institution of democracy would be if the media sub-committee of the Parliament—in a similar way to the Austrian Parliament—elaborated or had someone elaborate, at least every fourth year, a comprehensive report about the situation of the media.[56]

Whose Victory?

The Cold War was lost by the communists also on the front of the propaganda. The successor parties of the losers have learned their lessons well this time. Recognising the increasing importance of the media, they have made huge and successful efforts to save their media positions. Today—with the exception of Poland and the Czech Republic—they have in their hands the decisive greater part of the written and the electronic media. The MDF was thinking about a longer transition in 1988-89 and was caught unprepared in many areas; it did not have either cadres or a conception for the case of a rapid change of power. The return of the successor parties cannot of course be explained solely by their strong media positions. The post-communist successor party could also return in 1993 in a Poland where its influence on the media was considerably smaller. Relying on the remains of their infrastructure and system of relations they could deliver their message to the voters even where their media positions had been shaken.

Topics of the media were not determined by the big dilemmas of the change of system but by the arguments of the top-fighters of *Kulturkampf*. Though the latest act in the 'populists vs. urbanists' argument was at the same time the clash of two different possibilities for development, its contents and language did not meet the everyday concerns of people. Partly due to the low level of the argument, partly because of lack of interest, the prestige of the media has decreased between 1989 and 1994 from 75 degrees to 50. The communicational defeat of the MDF government was partly caused by the fact that its media élite were not able to introduce the main questions of the change of system into the political discourse. Thanks to the relative balance of power, conditions for a liberal freedom of press were more conducive especially in the period of 1989-1994 than during the whole history of the 20th century. By not being able to make the best of the opportunity, journalists unwillingly helped to create the conditions for a new dependence. Most of them now realise that there was more freedom of press under the Antall government than when the blue-ribbons came into power.[57] Media conditions for a rotational economy do not exist today in Hungary. This deformation however is the story of the "media peace."

Notes

1. *Medvetánc* [Bear's dance]. Supplement of the number 1987/2.
2. "Közgyűlésen és közgyűlés után" [During and after the General Assembly]. *Beszélő*, no. 19.
3. "A SALOM állásfoglalása és három magyar író nyilatkozata" [The statement of SALOM and the declarations of three Hungarian writers]. *Beszélő*, no. 21.
4. Bába, Iván, ed. "Szószék" [Pulpit], *Alternatív krónika*, no. 88 (Budapest, 1989), p. 124.
5. *Mozgó Világ*, no. 7 (1988).
6. Tóth, István János. "Tömegtájékoztatás és párt(atlanság), avagy március 15-e a TV-híradóban és az országos napilapokban" [Mass media and im-party-ality, or March 15 on TV news and in the national dailies]. *Beszélő*, no. 26.
7. "Interview with László Sólyom" in: Richter, Anna. *Ellenzéki kerekasztal (1990)* [Opposition round-table]. (Budapest: Ötlet Ltd.)
8. Gálik, Mihály. "Hol folyik a Rubicon?" [Where does the Rubicon flow?]. *Magyar Sajtó*, no. 10 (1988).
9. *Magyar Sajtó*, no.14 (1988).
10. Domány, András. "Sajtótörvény, sajtószabadság Ausztriában" [Media law and freedom of press in Austria]. *Magyar Sajtó*, no. 10 (1988).
11. Fodor, Gábor. "Irigylem Halberstamot" [I envy Halberstam]. *Magyar Sajtó*, no. 10 (1988).
12. *Magyar Sajtó*, nos. 3-4 (1989).
13. In: "Televízió 90". *Jelkép*, no. 1 (1990).
14. "Lesznek-e halvacsorák a Hungaroringen?" [Will there be fishermen's parties on the Hungaroring?]. *Hitel*, no. 6 (1989).
15. Ferenczi, Krisztina. *Előjáték a sajtószabadsághoz* [Prelude for the freedom of press]. (Budapest: Telehír, 1994).
16. Vásárhelyi, Mária. *Az újságírók helyzete, gondolkodása és szerepvállalása* [The position, way of thinking and acting of journalists]. (Budapest: MÚOSZ, 1992).
17. Diczházi, Bertalan. "Külföldi beruházások Magyarországon" [Foreign Investment in Hungary]. *Valóság*, no. 10 (1996).

18. *A demokrácia alternatívái hazánkban (1989)* [Alternatives of democracy in our country]. (Budapest: Kossuth Könyvkiadó), pp. 114–115.
19. *Magyar Sajtó*, no. 9 (1990).
20. *Népszabadság*. April 2, 1990.
21. Horváth, István. *Európa megkísértése* [The temptation of Europe]. (Budapest: Láng Kiadó, 1994), pp. 126 and 220.
22. "A Blahától a Bécsi útig. Beszélgetés Eötvös Pállal, a *Népszabadság* főszerkesztőjével" [From the Blaha Lujza square to Bécsi street. Conversation with Pál Eötvös, the editor-in-chief of *Népszabadság*]. *Kritika*, nos. 10-11 (1993).
23. Kormos, Valéria. "A nagy puff és etikája" [The great bam and its ethics]. *Magyar Nemzet*. May 14, 1996.
24. Murányi, Gábor. *Volt egyszer egy Magyar Nemzet?* [Was there once a *Magyar Nemzet*?]. (Budapest: Héttorony Könyvkiadó, 1992).
25. *A titok korszaka* [The era of secrets].
26. *Mozgó Világ*, no. 7 (1991).
27. In: *A megyei lapok eladását vizsgáló bizottság megalakításáról szóló országgyűlési határozati javaslat megtárgyalása 1990. május 15-én* [Discussion on May 15, 1990 of the parliamentary decision proposal concerning the establishment of a committee to investigate the selling of county papers]. Hiteles Jegyzőkönyv, colums 160-180.
28. "Interjú Franka Tiborral" [Interview with Tibor Franka]. *Világgazdaság*. March 7, 1996.
29. *Média Figyelő*, no. 14 (1997).
30. *Jelkép*, no. 1 (1990).
31. Bod, Péter Ákos. "Értelmiségi a politikában—Antall József miniszterelnöksége" [An intellectual in politics—Antall József, the prime minister]. *Valóság*, no. 12 (1996).
32. Csorba, József. "A magyar tükör" [The Hungarian mirror]. *Hitel*. May, 1994.
33. In: Grezsa, Ferenc. *Számadás* [Rendering of account]. (Budapest: Haza és haladás alapítvány, 1994).
34. Elek, István. "Gombár Csaba és a kulturális bizottság" [Gombár Csaba and the cultural committee]. *Magyar Hírlap*. May 21, 1992.
35. "Az MDF egységéért" [For the unity of the MDF].In: Antall, József. *Modell és valóság*. (Budapest: Athenaeum, 1993). Vol. II, p. 508.
36. "Interjú Sólyom Lászlóval" [Interview with László Sólyom]. *Magyar Nemzet*. October 22, 1997.

37. Csorba, József. "A magyar tükör" [The Hungarian mirror]. *Hitel.* May, 1994.
38. *Magyar Sajtó,* no. 4 (1990).
39. Révész, Sándor. "Rekontraszelekció" [Buggins' turn]. *Beszélő.* November 25, 1993.
40. Mester, Ákos. In: Kasza, László, ed. *Metamorphosis Hungariae 1989-1994.* (Budapest: Századvég, 1994).
41. "Ne várd a májust..." [Don't expect May...]. In: Farkasházy, Tivadar. *Nem értem* [I don't understand]. (Budapest: Helikon, 1984), p. 190.
42. "Langmár Ferenc is discussing with Vincze Mátyás". *Beszélő.* March 28, 1992.
43. *Budapest Sun.* December 13, 1995.
44. Körösényi, András. "A közigazgatás politikai irányítása és a patronázs" [The political control of public administration and the patronage]. *Valóság.* December, 1997.
45. *Hírlevél.* May, 1996.
46. "Matkó István PR-szakember" [Matkó István, PR-expert]. *Magyar Toll,* issues 7-8, 1996
47. *Magyar Hírlap.* December 17, 1997.
48. In: Kasza László. *Metamorphosis Hungariae.* (Budapest: Századvég Kiadó, 1994), p. 293.
49. Esterházy, Péter. *Egy kék haris.* [Bluestock']. (Budapest: Magvető, 1996).
50. Langmár, Ferenc. "Kiszolgáltatott újságírók és olvasók" [Defenceless journalists and readers]. *Magyar Narancs.* January 16, 1997.
51. Kóczián, Péter and Weyer, Balázs. "Felelősök" [Responsibles]. *Figyelő.* (Budapest, 1997), p. 41.
52. *Az Országgyűlés hiteles jegyzőkönyve* [Official minutes of the Parliament]. November 24, 1993, p. 31812.
53. Kenedi, János. *Kis Állambiztonsági Olvasókönyv* [Small reader of state security]. (Budapest: Magvető, 1996), pp. 280-282.
54. In: Horváth, Jenő, ed. (Budapest: Kossuth Könyvkiadó, 1985).
55. *Kurír.* January 29-31, 1997.
56. *Massenmedien in Österreich.* Medienbericht 4, Buchkultur. (Wien, 1993).
57. Vásárhelyi, Mária. "Hivatása: Újságíró" [Profession: journalist]. *Népszava.* November 3, 1997.

PROPERTY CHANGES IN HUNGARY

One of the most important processes during the change of regime was the creation of an economic structure based on the dominance of private property. The mechanism of privatization in Hungary was influenced by different political interests, including the economic élite, managers, workers, the media, and foreign and domestic investors. A national consensus regarding privatization and property strategies never existed. However, the process of privatization continued, with each regime selling according to the current legal regulations and developing its own strategy. Governments of different political principles respected previously-concluded contracts and agreements, and this brought legal stability. At the same time, capitalist changes necessarily increased the differences in property and income: they favored certain regions and territories and hindered the development of others. The economic élite that played an active part in the privatization process (consultants, managers, mediators) took decisions that affected whole generations.

Conceptual Arguments
Regarding Privatization at the End of the 1980s

The large number of prefixes (such as spontaneous, wild, hidden, pre-, management, leasing, installment payment, stock exchange, company, self-, giant, etc.) that precede the word *privatization* demonstrate the complexity of the privatization process that took place here.

Politically-speaking, opposition organizations were initially involve (in the creation of proposals and concepts concerning the separation of powers, democratic rule and the creation of a state of law. Thus privatization and property changes came into discussion only in 1989. Parties formulated their concepts of property in their programs. The Hungarian Democratic Forum (MDF) and Alliance of Free Democrats (SZDSZ) developed a fairly detailed but quite general concept, listing priorities and expectations.

The discussion also began in professional circles: how is privatization possible if, compared to the HUF 2000-2500 billion in state property, individual savings and demand is small. Who shall become owners? Should they be private individuals, institutions, public foundations, foreigners? How should a state property, the value of which is diminishing day by day, be passed quickly into private hands? In answer to these questions, four main theories were developed:

a) Local government and public foundation theory

László Kotz suggested that, because of the dramatically low demand, local governments and public foundations should receive the shares of the joint-stock companies. With this method the budgetary support of the institutions in question could be redeemed. Local governments and public foundations could manage the received property and could even sell it. The argument supporting this suggestion was that in Western economies many holdings and concerns are owned by foundations. Family wealth—for taxation and personal reasons—is often transferred to a foundation, although family management continues.

b) Privatization credit

István Csillag's proposal linked privatization with the reduction of state debts: investors buying state property would have to take over a certain part of the state debt. The Hungarian National

Bank (MNB) would offer a quasi-credit to the investor, who pays with real money to the MNB by installments from the purchased company. In balance with the amortization the MNB tempers its claims toward the state. Privatization credit was later introduced, combined with MNB fixed interest. Because of the high interest rate this did not work. Later the so-called existential credit was based on this concept.

c) Cash privatization

According to this concept, companies which lack capital and have large debts should not be sold: instead the capital of the share companies was to be increased by cash or technological apportion. By the increase of capital, the debts would become redeemable and companies could be modernized on the cash taken in. The aim of this proposal was not a quick attainment of private status, as the increase of capital could have been performed by other state companies as well. This would have resulted in cross-ownership of state companies but later, with the consolidation of the private sector, the proportion of private shares could have been increased. Company management accepted this idea easily because the profile of the enterprise would have remained the same, they would have conducted the process and meanwhile they could gain some time. This model was represented by the Németh government, which managed to balance the company power that developed by the end of the 1980s. Later this concept changed and cash capital was accepted from foreign partners as well. Thus, if the management reached an agreement with the foreign partner without a penny of state privatization income, the foreign company could obtain a majority stake in a property. As a consequence, under the Németh government whole sectors were taken over by foreigners and no income was brought in. The legal grounds for such moves were the company law, the partnership bill which came into force in 1989 and the reorganization bill in effect at the middle of 1989. This was in fact a hidden privatization strategy, which left the process to the mercy of insiders, without any state or community control.

d) Public shareholder model

In my opinion an equal distribution of free bonds should have been performed: coupons of a value of 300,000 HUF each for every citizen of legal age. They could have been used to purchase state shares or business shares. State companies would have become public share companies and could have used the coupons at public quotations. Besides, investment funds could have been established to gather the coupons and change them into investment bills. As capital organizations, investment funds could have purchased majority ownership within state companies. This would have resulted in quick privatization and fair distribution, and the state property would have remained in Hungarian hands. This concept was followed in the Czech Republic, and partly in Poland, Slovakia, Romania, Russia. The Hungarian method of compensatory certificates is similar to this proposal.

Financial Processes in the Period 1988-1990

With the strengthening of opposition and the weakening of the power of the communist party, the workers councils founded in 1985 became more independent after 1988. Having become independent of the control of the state party committees, and due to the absence of a national strategy and a state property organization, a certain number of enterprises tried to find a way to change by themselves. Without state control over property it was possible to appropriate entire firms without any compensation. It is still unknown how many billion HUF of state property was stolen and by whom. There are only suppositions. Some managers were surely trying to preserve the activity and the working culture, with the goal of saving the property from the creditors and expropriators. Others focused on saving their own positions and transferred the property far under its real value into a mixed company. Still others transferred a small part of a firm to an investment company in which the other owner represented his own personal interest. Some people tried very hard to save assets, sometimes not for themselves but to serve the interest of a partner from abroad lacking a favorable reference and preferring risky investments. A labor contract for five years and the promise of a good Western car proved to be sometimes sufficient motivation. The foreign investors were of course interested in the cheap purchase of a firm promising good short-term market possibility. This meant the preservation of non-viable state companies.

a) Cross-ownership of companies with several units

This model was applied mostly in the case of heavily indebted companies. In this model the different factory units were transformed into separate firms in such a way that the other factory units became shareholders in addition to being the center of the enterprise. The transformation was motivated by the fact that the functioning units had to eliminate their credits, as to be able to start a new economic activity. In the case of the liquidation of the enterprise core, the factory unit may live on. By the payment of dividends and defining the rent of immovable properties and fixed assets, the income could be modified by applying specific internal prices. This model was made use of especially in the machine industry, textile industry and building industry.

b) Subdivision of the enterprise's property into a new economic entity

By apportioning company units and fixed assets, and with the machine and cash apportion of the new partner, the founding of a new enterprise was possible. Entire companies thus became the property of foreign partners, e.g. road construction enterprises in different districts, the cement industry. The most unpleasant process took place in the small retail sector, where company leaders transferred the businesses into mixed companies at a very low price, thus not falling within the law for privatization (Ápisz, Röltex, etc.) A similar process took place in the newspaper publishing business.

c) Capital investment according to the law of transition

According to the transition law coming into force in the middle of 1989, some state companies entered into alliance with foreign partners (e.g. firms in the sugar industry and textile industry).

d) Large-scale privatization

A few convincing examples of major privatization: Tungsram, which found itself in an impossible financial situation during socialism, became the property of General Electric with the mediation of an Austrian bank. GE wished to increase its market share in the lighting sector. The credit bank sold the shares. More disputable is the case of the insurance company Hungária Biztosító: it sold 49 percent of its shares to the German company, Allianz, with a further purchasing option. Because of this move, more than half of the Hungarian insurance market passed into foreign hands.

Overall, the Németh government did not develop a conscious strategy for privatization, so these processes took place without any framework. There has been no plan concerning the purchasing of national property and the privatization of certain branches. The ÁVÜ (State Property Agency) founded in the string of 1990 lacked strong authority; the legislators created a weak organization.

The First Stage of the Antall Government (1990-1992)

The plans for property reform hastily constructed by the Antall-government in 1990 created a complex property transfer strategy. The different organizations, interest groups and even the coalition partners expressed very definite demands and ideas. Some legal order had to be established in the spontaneous privatization process; the anarchic developments in the provincial factories had to be normalized. The new concept of collective property had to be given up. A new election law had to be created in order to calm the demand to replace the old leadership of the enterprise; the effort of the coalition partner to re-privatize had to be slowed down. The property demands supported by the opposition (which at the time consisted of the left-liberal Free Democrats [SZDSZ] and the former communist Socialist Party [MSZP]) had to be restricted and many tasks e.g. land reform, privatization of small businesses—required serious efforts. All these had to be done in spite of an unstable state apparatus and a hostile mass media.

At the same time, the Antall government could not afford to suspend the whole privatization process—even for only a few months—to work out the necessary strategy and create an organizational system. Foreign currency reserves were low. The property reform from 1990 concentrated on the fundamental factors that determined the later privatization process. Any political and legal uncertainty would have ruined the strategy of privatization as a whole.

Concerning agricultural land this concept aimed at the re-establishment of original ownership, but for other types of assets (flats, shops, factories, banks) it suggested a compensatory system of ownership certificates which could be turned into a share of property.

By voting for the pre-privatization law in the autumn of 1990, legislators decided on privatization instead of re-privatization. The constitutional court dismissed a governmental motion concerning agricultural land and therefore a compensatory system and the regulation of public sale had to be created in order to make possible the return of agricultural land (a very complicated process).

A debate took place with local authorities over the ownership of approximately 300 enterprises previously founded by the local workers' councils. The Antall government wanted to establish a self-governmental system in a short time and organize local elections, and therefore it forced the passing of the two-thirds law. Despite warnings from experts, a consensus concerning the law was only possible without the concrete definition of public utility companies. This later caused serious disputes over the title to property between the government and the local authorities. The compensation and disputes over the ownership of the authorities overburdened the political atmosphere and the government.

The reaction of the government against the campaign for the managers' replacement was that it called for re-election of the councils (which also controlled the social security funds). Through a governmental regulation it offered legal and procedural rules concerning the separation and independence of provincial factory units. The law of the ÁVÜ amended in the summer concerning property protection and transition created control over the privatization processes. The amendments served first of all the creating of state initiative, collective control and competition. The undertaking initiative and the possibility of privatization through foreign investments was still present in the privatization methods.

No unit privatization strategies were elaborated in this busy period. The rules appeared within the framework of payment conditions of the privatization. The durable state and national property had not been settled. No concept for the large-scale application of privatization on the stock exchange was created. Privatization was still a spontaneous process: foreign investors and managers had a strong influence over it.

The coalition parties determining the government program urged preservation of the small and medium-sized enterprises mainly in state property and the creating of large-scale property acquisition conditions. The possibility of company purchase by employees as well as the programs concerning small shareholders were created later.

Privatization of Enterprises (1990-1992)

The privatization law started to deliver about 10,000 businesses to domestic private firms. An existence-credit program was set up, simplifying purchases.

More rapid privatization was greatly hindered by the fact that foreign trade functioned from 1991 at world-market prices and in foreign currencies. Many companies of the machine industry, textile industry and food industry producing for the Russian market lost their assets, they went bust. The laws of accountancy, banking and bankruptcy were elaborated in 1990, hoping to halt the debts of many hundred billions of HUF. Passing a severe financial-economic law was the government's goal and it wanted to bring to light where the losses came from. At the beginning of the 1990s, Western economies were fighting a recession and internal demand was also declining. All these processes shocked the system and therefore only a few companies could be sold.

The producers of consumer goods, companies with favorable national market position, as well as a few companies with world positions were the first to become private properties during this period (Chinoin, Lehel, the insurance company Állami Biztosító, companies belonging to the food industry and commercial companies).

The Second Stage of the Antall (Boross) Government

The strategy adopted under the leadership of the privatization minister, Tamás Szabó, based on the property structure in use in European states, defined the domains of durable state ownership in the main branches. Concepts on branch privatization were born with corresponding organizational systems. One of the most important elements of this concept was the introduction of favorable payment structures by which many national companies could join the privatization process. The reduction to seven percent interest on existential credits, the delayed grace periods, the starting of an employee share purchase program, the possibility of leasing privatization, the right to rent or buy made purchasing companies possible for domestic managers, workers and investors. Through self-privatization, almost 400 small and medium-sized firms became private properties. The Agency for Compensation began its activity by distributing compensatory certificates and raising the internal demand for state property. Doubtless the founding of the ÁV Rt. (State Property Co.) and attempts to manage property slowed the privatization of large companies. Difficulties were created especially by the fact that few public capital issues were organized. The organizations for privatization had to face the difficulty caused by the existence of many different payment methods (cash, credit, compensatory certificate). This made judging the applications very difficult. In spite of the domestic demand, foreign investors were still interested in taking part in this process because the yearly budget included cash payment of a defined sum for the privatization organizations.

The greatest achievement of this period was the creation of conditions whereby privatization was possible not only for foreign investors, but domestic investors could also become owners. This represented the interests of national participants and increased the motivation of the managers and employees. They expressed their favorable view of privatization. This made possible the selling of almost 700 firms in this period of time, mostly to domestic interests.

It should be mentioned that foreign investors aimed at finishing their privatization acquisitions before the end of 1993, as in 1994 a suspension of the special tax allowance benefiting foreign interests would take effect. In the first half of 1994 sales to foreign investors greatly decreased.

The bank, interest and credit consolidation of this period aimed at clarifying bank balances. Saving those 13 large companies that are still the engines of Hungarian industry can be considered a success.

After the state had consolidated the dubious bank credit demands, the banks sold their credit demands to private companies without any competition. These were not for sale to the ÁVÜ, but different groups of investors appeared as creditors of many state companies with cheap credit offers. By this they presented the privatization organization a *fait accompli,* and they could also purchase the enterprises at a low price. The exclusive closed business with the credit demands is part of the process of property transfer. This form of privatization has been broadened since 1994.

The "slow shock therapy" from 1991-92 led to the bankruptcy and liquidation of many enterprises. The liquidator appointed by the court of justice could sell the assets. As the majority of creditors were state banks and state servicing enterprises, the credit committees did not show much interest in the liquidation process. The liquidators could privatize former state enterprises, consisting of valuable real estate, offices, machines and tools without any restrictions. The assets of more than 400 companies became private property through the process of liquidation and final settlements. The great liberalism of the liquidation process accelerated the liquidation, as it increased personal interest. Earlier this process lasted for years; in this period, the number of such actions grew. The assets that became private property were doubtless quickly put into use.

Privatization of Enterprises (1992-1994)

The most spectacular transition of this period was the privatization of MATÁV through a significant capital increase. The privatization of banks began with the partial sale of the Hungarian Foreign Trading Bank (MKB). Such important firms as Centrum (a chain of department stores), the Cable Works, the Kőbánya Brewery, MMG, Egis, etc. were sold. A quick privatization was characteristic for the food industry, retail, service enterprises, building industry and the machine industry. The strategic sector (energy, raw material industry, bank, public service) were practically not affected by privatization.

A Year of Transition (June 1994-June 1995)

This is the period when the former privatization strategy was not valid any longer and the new one was not yet born. What is characteristic for this period of time? The laws remained valid. The ÁV Rt. was waiting—for reasons easily accounted for—and many applications were being processed by the ÁVÜ. The financial experts and the new coalition partner SZDSZ (Alliance of Free Democrats) wanted privatization through cash and the sale of the strategic branches to foreign companies. The now-ruling MSZP (Hungarian Socialist Party) was also satisfied with the former privatization strategy because the cooperatives could buy firms in the food industry for compensatory certificates and the managers could purchase the enterprises for credit together with a consortium. Employees were also interested in payment allowances. The practice of the ÁVÜ did not show any changes after the invalidation of some of the applications: privatization based on preferential techniques continued. A larger percentage of cash was requested of the applicants. The government halted the privatization of the HungarHotels, which raised substantial interest abroad. Foreign investors had the impression that the left-wing government did not want to privatize. Being influenced by this, an over-compensating mechanism was born, which turned the new privatization strategy and the new law to the advantage of the SZDSZ and the financial managers. In the period mentioned above, the privatization of the pharmaceutical company Richter began through the stock exchange. Many firms in the food industry and retail had been privatized (cheese production in Répcelak, wine producing factory in Balatonboglár, three regional Tüzéps, etc).

The Privatization Politics of the Horn-Government

The privatization strategy from 1995, in contrast to European practice, included the sale of energy production, gas and public electricity supply as well as bank branches to foreign companies. With the exception of state farms, the government wanted to maintain a lower percentage of durable state ownership in the other sectors as well. To the advantage of foreign investors and national financial groups, cash as modality of payment came to the fore. The smaller firms were privatized through a new method called simplified privatization. Its main point was that smaller firms could be sold for cash at a limited price. The other points of view (employment, development and protection of the environment) were not taken into account any longer. Financial experts explained the sale of the energy sector as vital for economic regeneration.

Many advisers and lawyers appeared to hand over the equivalent of national assets, taking huge handling fees in exchange for this. About HUF 10 billion is thought to have gone to consultants to the detriment of the privatization profits.

The bank consolidation went on based on new techniques (MHB, Mezőbank, Post Bank, etc.). The privatization of the chemical industry was doubtless a success. Considering the potential, privatization through the stock exchange was less successful, as the energy and bank branches could have brought bigger public capital issue. The privatization of middle-sized enterprises was delayed by the fact that the ÁPV concentrated upon cash income.

Foreign Greenfield Investments

The modification of the national economic structure was influenced by the significant number of greenfield investments. Foreign investment with active capital has been possible since 1972 in our country. Some 166 enterprises with foreign interests were registered by the end of 1988, with invested capital estimated at some USD 250 million.

According to the concept of a mixed property economic system, the Németh government passed the laws that made possible foreign investments. The new law (XXIV/1988) on foreign investments meant a change concerning the regulation of the influx of foreign capital, promising many allowances (first of all tax allowances) beyond the fundamental guarantees (as against nationalization and dispossession, the support of the free profit repatriation and of 100 percent share of foreign property).

Greenfield investments proved advantageous to foreign investors because of the search for markets and lower production costs. Great investments were made in the car industry, packaging material production, telecommunication techniques, financial branch and the building of office blocks. The production of electronic and computer fittings and retail has also been of interest to foreign investors. One third of foreign capital investments in our country belong to greenfield investments.

Foreign Industrial Greenfield Investments

According to the evaluation of the Privatization Research Institute, 75 percent of the increase shown in the last years in the Hungarian industrial production is due to greenfield investments. The dynamic increase in production in tax-free areas underlines this fact.

Foreign industrial greenfield investments totaled more than USD 3 billion. More than half of all greenfield investments come from seven foreign investors (General Motors, Audi, Suzuki, IBM, Ford, Philips, Guardian Glass). These companies are believed to bring in 50 percent of the income in their sector, in spite of the fact that only 20 percent of all employees work for the firms mentioned above. Northern Transdanubia enjoys 70 percent of all investments. The machine industry receives two-thirds of all investments. Within the machine industry, car mounting, engine production, the production of mountings and cables and the production and mounting of electronic fittings are the most important. Compared to the value of the investments only 50,000 jobs were created. These multinational companies were supposed to be followed by more and more suppliers. However, the new firms created through greenfield investments continue to function in an isolated manner; they rarely cooperate with domestic enterprises.

The relatively large number and value of the industrial greenfield investments is a successful result of the transition of the Hungarian property and structure. New industrial branches were born in our country; effective labor organizations are functioning, which pose a challenge for the other industrial participants.

Foreign Greenfield Investments in Other Sectors

In the financial sector new mixed-property banks appeared (CIB, Citibank) even before the two-tier system of Hungarian banking was formed. A great number of national banks appeared during the change of regime. The new foreign banks are, first of all, financing the foreign enterprises. The higher-income population has made use of their services from the middle of the 1990s. They had a significant contribution to the loss of influence of the former state banks, in spite of the fact that they had opened only a few branches. The banks with foreign ownership are usually following their country's enterprises. Thus the system of bank-to-enterprise relations and networks has been reorganized in Hungarian investments as well.

The role of greenfield investments gained ground in the retail sector especially in the middle of the 1990s, through the building of shopping centers, supermarkets and discount networks. Today's building boom in the whole country reorganizes retail structures to the detriment of small businesses with Hungarian ownership.

In telecommunications, mostly foreign companies took part in the building of the mobile phone network, as well as of the locally concessioned fixed-wire system. Here, foreign capital contributed a great deal to the elimination of backwardness.

In the building of office blocks, more than 90 percent of the 50 new office buildings in the country were built using foreign capital. The middle of the 1990s brought a boom in the building of greenfield warehouses and logistic centers.

In summary the foreign greenfield investments contributed to:
- the establishment of new industrial branches in our country
- the quick development of the backward services sector
- the spreading of modern technological and technical methods
- the development of professional marketing.

In comparison to privatization investments, greenfield investments created new capacities, new jobs and new services, which constitutes one of the sources of Hungarian economic growth. They played an important role in the process of accumulation of fixed capital in Hungary.

The Organic Development of the Domestic Private Sector (without Privatization)

The wave of liberalization at the end of the 1980s created large-scale possibilities for private individual undertakings and partnerships. A lot of private undertakings appeared in the retail, services, building industry and agriculture. This mainly concerns undertakings with little capital and few employees. In comparison to the 320,000 private undertakings functioning in 1989, at the end of 1996 their number was about 750,000. In the case of private partnerships their numbers grew from 40,000 to 300,000. But this impressive numerical increase did not mean the growth of the enterprises as well (incomes, capital, number of employees). Only a few small undertakings were able to develop to medium size. Some of the top enterprises from the 1980s even disappeared or were sold to foreign firms. From the "Top 200" edition of the year 1996, only the Sepsiker company can be considered to be a quickly growing and expanding private undertaking. The other firms are privatized enterprises or new foreign firms. The well-known firms of the 1980s like Kontrax, Microsystem and Kontroll disappeared. Kordax and Stadler, which appeared suddenly in the 1990s, must have had an uncertain and dubious activity, as the tax and customs authorities took action against these firms. These undertakings were quickly halted, however, due to different pressures.

Of those domestic private undertakings that could not take part in the privatization only a few developed into medium-size or large firms.

The poor record of private enterprises expanding their operations is due to:
- competition from imports
- insufficient internal demand
- high interest rates
- unsatisfactory accounting and financial advice
- quick re-utilization of the income generated.

According to Zoltán Pitti the value of property assets run by medium-sized individual enterprises is about HUF 150-160,000. This means that the individual undertakings are characteristic for fields that do not require much capital.

At the end of 1997 the majority of the enterprises in Hungary were functioning at the level of individual undertakings, micro-undertaking and at most small enterprises with little chance to expand.

Internal Property Conditions at the End of 1997

The year 1997 was marked by primary privatization running on course, change in business ownership for the second or third time, unprecedented speculation on the stock exchange and keen debates over ownership of agricultural land. Our country became capitalist. Some 70-75 percent of the GDP was produced by the private sector.

Despite the important developments in progress, it can be stated that the major property transformation has been concluded—with the exeption of agricultural land. The Hungarian capitalist structure is a specific Hungarian model. It is unlike the South-Korean *chebol*, the Japanese structure *keirechu* and the family model in China, Hong Kong and Taiwan. It is unlike the American model, where a great part of the companies are public companies present on the stock exchange and where the investment funds, retirement funds, institutional investors and small shareholders are the majority owners. It is unlike the German property structure, which is characterized by the cross-ownership of banks and enterprises as well as by family ownership. In our country the proportion of state-owned property is already smaller than in Latin Europe.

The Hungarian property structure is also unlike the structure of the other post-communist states. It is unlike the Slovenian management-employee ownership, the Slovakian management property structure true to government or the confused cross-ownership of the Czech state-bank investment funds.

What is the essence of the Hungarian model? The characteristic of the Hungarian ownership is the dominance of foreign property. Multinational companies, foreign national enterprises, foreign family undertakings, companies present on the foreign stock exchange, as well as foreign organizational investors are the main owners and leaders of the national system, of enterprises and banking.

About two-thirds of industry, more than 90 percent of the telecommunications, almost 60 percent of energy production and distribution, 70 percent of the banking sector and half of the retail is under foreign control. Today state property is dominant only in the agriculture sector.

We can ask ourselves: Why have foreign companies played such an important role in Hungarian privatization? It can be argued in different ways:

- the state is highly indebted, so the foreign currency income was necessary for the external financing of the economy

- with the cash income it received, the state could lower its debts and the privatization incomes could be used for economic development

- the dominant financial-economic conception and the media preferred foreign ownership, as only investors with great capital are considered to be good owners

- the position of the financial-economic elite was saved through their relationship with foreign companies

- the insufficient influence of the potential Hungarian owners on the economy and politics

- weak national identity

- the political elite could not reach an agreement concerning a general national privatization strategy.

Enterprise Types

Due to the privatization of state companies, the settlement of foreign enterprises, and the development of the domestic undertakings, four major types of enterprises were formed. The criteria of classification were as follows: property structure, size of enterprise, the area of product distribution, the export/import participation and the type of activity.

To the first category belong the concerns in Hungary led by international companies headquartered abroad. These enterprises were formed through privatization, mixed enterprises or greenfield investments. The Hungarian concerns of the multinationals are well represented in most economic sectors. They represent 110 of the 200 biggest Hungarian companies. They are dominant in telecommunications, electricity supply, food industry, machine industry and building industry; but their position in the chemical industry, retail and banking sectors is also growing. According to their globalization strategy, these companies are trying to integrate their Hungarian subsidiaries into all aspects of their functioning—including sourcing, IT, marketing and human resources. At the same time, the effectiveness of the activity of the multinational companies depends in many cases on local legislative and regulatory decisions—which is why they take such an interest in the politics of the countries they are in.

Certainly, the existing forms as well as the number of general regulations (taxes, social insurance contribution, customs regime, rate of exchange, labor question) significantly affect the activity and profitability of international firms. This means that despite the majority being private property, state and governmental decisions have a strong influence on the success of enterprises. So the question is raised whether there are possibilities for the multinational companies to exert their interests in our country. It is widely believed that the multinationals have considerable influence on the government. Due to their international economic importance they deal only with the government and have access to the prime minister. The governments and Hungarian embassies of the states they are settled in are intensively engaged in lobbying. Such companies often subject their investment to conditions. Tariff rates are a particular burden. Multinational companies employ the most expensive consultants and contact men to promote their interests. They influence the decisions through personal relationships. The international financial organizations (IMF, World Bank, EBRD) representing the free-market principle and the return on financial investments influence the general economic environment in our country as it relates to the multinational companies.

To the second category belong the firms of domestic leadership with export possibilities. These are enterprises of Hungarian property or firms with their shares sold to financial investors being negotiated on the stock exchange. These are independent Hungarian firms; the decisions of the enterprises are taken here and their leadership defines their strategy. The property structure of this group was actually formed through the privatization of state enterprises on the stock exchange and through their sales to management; but many domestic firms with great capital and/or with export potential belong to this category. These firms stand a good chance of international expansion. The government is expected to protect the domestic market and to support their expansion to foreign markets. Large and medium-size firms belong here, because they already have or in the near future will have an international position (participation in foreign markets, capital investment). What is good for these firms is good for Hungary as well—we can assert in connection with the example of the American car manufacturer, General Motors. They play an outstanding role in economic growth of our country, as they can export a great part of their production, so the limited domestic market does not impede their growth. The above mentioned enterprises are present mainly in the chemical industry, but they are also represented in the machine industry, food industry, building industry and software servicing. These are firms with great capital, quality products and an extensive export distribution network.

Some of these firms could grow into Hungarian basic regional multinational companies. So far, however, the government does not seem aware of the importance of this category. As a result, their capacity to exert their interests is inferior to that of the multinational companies, but the consolidation of these companies, their increasing capital and their growing exports can sooner or later make them a significant economic power. They act according to the mechanism of interest representation that grew up in our country in the previous period, so that personal relationships are deemed vital. Only a few can reach the ministerial level, and not even these can make reference to NATO or EU entry.

The third group is formed by the medium-size enterprises of national ownership producing mostly for the domestic market. Their property structure was formed by certain preferential privatization; they grew from small enterprises into mid-size firms. They employed significant labor, their global role in the economy is also significant, but individually they do not represent power. Their capital is usually weak, it is difficult to obtain credit and maintaining daily liquidity requires serious management. The depression of internal demand in the last two years has been a trial for these firms; many enterprises were purchased by the multinational companies and the large national companies. A great part of the food industry, retail, building industry, machine industry and services belongs in this category. Their concerns are not strong. The fact that the media prefers and aims at foreign capital is unfavorable for them. Their influence is stronger in local society. They are expecting an economic policy from the government that makes possible the increase of internal demand. The tendency of recent years shows an economic decline of mid-sized firms. There is also no reinforcement in the small enterprises. A part of the medium-size firms tend to export or want to become importers for the multinational firms. Such a strategy creates a stronger position. Another part of these firms turn to the black market.

The fourth category is made up of the hundreds of thousands of small undertakings. The small firms with a maximum of 10 employees mostly work for the domestic market and are present in the less capital-intensive sectors. They turn to the black market to avoid taxes and social insurance charges. Many jobs appear and disappear. The majority of these businesses are small-trade, small producer, retail-oriented and family undertakings. Most of them are in the services, retail, public catering, building industry, and light industry. In spite of the many concerns their influence on the government is weak. They play cat and mouse with government financial leaders and their cooperation is distrustful. They, too, try to gain ground in local society (local government, local economic elite etc.). They believe in acting alone, but sometimes organize to solve certain problems.

Several Characteristics of the Hungarian Capitalist Transition

a) The lack of conscious privatization

The whole period of transition was marked by arguments regarding privatization but a consensus was never reached. The strategy and legal background of privatization were constantly changed by the different governments in power. This was not a peculiar Hungarian phenomenon; it occurred in other countries, too. But in the Czech Republic and Slovenia, say, the process of property change was more balanced.

b) Uneven distribution of benefits

Existential credits, compensatory certificates, leasing, installment paying, mrp-allowances, bank consolidation, etc. created the
possibility for the Hungarian citizen to participate successfully in
privatization. The employees of enterprises, banks and cooperative
societies could participate preferentially in privatization, in a normative manner. Pensioners, public functionaries, state employees,
teachers and health service employees did not receive normative
allowances. Very important advantages could be obtained by those
in connection with the banking system. Information, inside knowledge and speculation played an important part in the manipulation
of compensatory certificates. By changing compensatory certificates to shares, buying preference shares and self-government
shares, the persons connected to broker agencies acquired fortunes.

c) Property redistribution instead of accumulation of capital

Foreign greenfield investments were the ones that created new
factories, capacities, real assets and other fixed assets. The redistribution of the already existing corporate property to private persons
was the main characteristic of the process. While the classical capitalist accumulation of capital implied the quick expansion of the
economy and its exponential increase, the Eastern European
changes were characterized by stagnancy. Besides, during the first
five years of the changes, a significant recession hit which was later
followed by slow economic development.

d) Insufficient stock exchange privatization

A wide privatization publicity would have been accomplished
by stock exchange privatization. At the beginning of the 1990s
Hungary lost the market of the Commonwealth of Independent

States. Because of the Western recession, strict financial laws (the public accountancy and banking bill and the bankruptcy and liquidation bill) and slackening domestic demand, many Hungarian companies ceased to exist and the others were not successful. Thus a wider stock exchange privatization was practically impossible. The period following the bank consolidation and economic recovery would have offered proper conditions for stock exchange privatization. Successful transactions were concluded mostly in the chemical industry (MOL, TVK, Richter, Borsodchem, Graboplast and Pannonplast).

e) Weak position of domestic enterprises

Following the Bokros economic program, many domestic investor groups which obtained companies at the beginning of the 1990s gave up their industrial investments. Some of them were probably only fronts: they bought companies from the state for foreign investors only to benefit from the preferential payment opportunities accorded only to domestic customers. In 1996-97, a large number of domestic companies, some of them of long-standing tradition, were passed into foreign hands. This was characteristic especially of the food industry and commercial companies.

f) High number of liquidation proceedings

One-quarter of the 2000 state companies were turned into private property by liquidation or final adjustment proceedings. Property was sold without any audit or real competition and the state did not see any income.

g) Local government shares were sold at half price

According to the law adopted in 1989, local governments received shares of capital in exchange for downtown territories.

The small amount of property allowed little interference for local governments because this shares could be sold at a lower price only, except for the officially quoted stocks. Some 10-15 percent of the total state company shares were transferred to local government property, a significant part of the industry of electric power generation and distribution among others. Selling at a low price could have been avoided by a concerted selling strategy elaborated by the central and local governments.

h) A large part of the privatization income ended up in the pockets of the brokers

Certain drafting errors of the transformation bill (the parts concerning local government shares and the proportion of value) generated legal uncertainty. In order to recover their "claims" from the state, local governments and companies made contracts with different counseling companies, influential joint ventures, lawyers, financial counselors, legal advisers, lobby companies, political mediation companies with limited partnership and other companies specialized in negotiation and mediation. Dubious contracts of success-remuneration were signed which caused losses to the state. A part of the income from privatization ended up in private pockets. The political scientist Gyula Tóth described the privatization process as the expansion of *kleptocracy.*

i) Most privatized companies function well

We do not have final results, but we can already state that most of the privatized companies work well. The new owners reorganized them and reduced expenses, thus creating efficient company structures. The concentrated leadership generated a "shocking company diet." In former state companies, marketing policy and financial policy were the first things to be reorganized.

j) In companies owned by foreign investors, technological envigoration is quick

Technological revitalization has been one of the most characteristic features of companies run by foreigners. Production-transfer was often used in the machine industry. Owing to low expenses, a large number of multinational enterprises placed a good part of their production in Hungary (e.g. GE, Elektrolux, Linamar, ZF, Knorr Bremse, Siemens, etc.).

k) Home-grown plutocrats

Persons forming the domestic plutocrat groups and their former careers aroused everybody's interest. No detailed analysis in this matter has been made so far. We can hear certain vulgar statements and simplifying inquiries but these are not suitable for a real study. We often hear that a capitalist nomenklatura class has been born. Others speak about managerial capitalism. Taking into account the experience of the last six to eight years we can define five different groups. The range is arbitrary, of course, but is based on proper criteria. The influence of certain groups cannot be evaluated. It is a well-known fact that property holders hide. The real background of many fronts is still unknown. So we can consider only known persons in economic life.

Enterprise managers

In the 1980s, managers worked on various levels of enterprise management. When the enterprise councils were reelected they gained ground and occupied higher positions. They could become owners in the process of spontaneous privatization unless they chose the protection of a foreign owner. Serious enterprise purchases could be undertaken beginning in 1992 when the participa-

tion in the MBO-MRP consortium and the managerial buyout started. Stock exchange privatization offered managers of large companies the possibility to acquire reduced rate shares, in accordance
with their achievements. Enterprise managers usually were the
owners of a single firm but several groups started a powerful
expansion. The overlap of managerial and holder functions is quite
peculiar but it seems to work.

It is probable that the majority of owners belong to this group.
Among them we can find persons who were leading personalities
in the 1980s, others became managing directors in 1989-1990 and
many of them occupied their positions at the beginning of the 1990s
or after 1994.

Members of the former nomenklatura

This term concerns people holding important positions in the
former regime. Some high officials of the socialist institutions
(ministries, higher authorities) and political organizations (MSZMP
[Communist Party], KISZ [Communist Youth Alliance], SZOT)
became property holders during the change of regime. They started
on a shoestring and became wealthy by using their connections as
a form of capital. Using state funds, the money of political organizations and their own capital, they created consulting companies
and "privatized" their corporate part. By establishing these companies and using their former relations, they managed to obtain capital. Their economic database was extremely rich. Owing to their
relations with different enterprises and banks, their participation in
the process of privatization was very successful. The former KISZ
network became a joint interest. However, it should be noted that
their real property holder positions are not as big as the public
thinks.

Young financiers

Brokers, financial counselors and young bankers soon after finishing their studies took advantage of the changing market with great affinity. They established investment funds, mutual aid funds for pensioners, leasing firms, purchasing companies, dealt with compensatory certificates and successfully managed their funds and the share capital. Some of them offered their services as fronts for foreign enterprises. They took shameless advantage of the differences between the market price of the compensatory certificates and the price offered by the state. They bought firms on credit, sold them for cash and invested the income again. They traded preference shares and local government papers. They managed to accumulate large amounts of capital and most of them are active financial investors.

The entrepreneurs of the 1980s

Many people took advantage of the possibilities for enterprise created at the beginning of the 1980s (in commerce, computer assembly and service, construction business, services, etc.) At the end of the 1980s and beginning of the 1990s, these entrepreneurs enlarged their field of operation by organizing new markets and buying enterprises. Former GMK owners and small cooperative societies were less successful in the huge redistribution of property.

People returning to Hungary from the West

These returnees brought with them capital, market knowledge and market conduct. They realized quickly that capitalism is developing in Hungary too, so they should acquire enterprises, market and land. They established relations with the adequate political, financial and state forums. Beside their own resources, the sums necessary for purchase were obtained from the money market, foreign banks or multinational companies. Privatization was their main motivation. Many of them succeeded in establishing huge enterprises.

Bibliography

Árva, László. *Külföldi tőkeberuházások Közép-Kelet-Európában.*

Diczházi, Bertalan. "Népi részvényes alternatíva" [Public shareholder alternative]. *Figyelő.* September 1, 1988.

——. "Magyarország a piacgazdaság felé vezető úton 1990-1994" [Hungary on the road to market economy 1990-1994]. *Napi Gazdaság.* February 11, 1994.

——. "Privatizáció és tőzsde" [Privatisation and the stock market]. *Világgazdaság.* August 30, 1996.

——. "Külföldi beruházások Magyarországon 1995 végéig" [Foreign investments in Hungary up to the end of 1995]. *Valóság,* no. 10 (1996).

——. "Kikből áll a tulajdonosi réteg?" [Who is the owners' strata?]. *Magyar Nemzet.* September 10, 1996.

——. "Szaporodó másodlagos privatizációk" [Replicating secondary privatisation]. *Világgazdaság.* March 25, 1997.

——. "Zöldmezőn az iparba—befektetések külföldről" [Foreign investment in Hungarian industry]. *Figyelő.* May 8, 1997.

Harmati, István. "Mi fán terem a korrupció?" [What is corruption?]. *Új Magyarország.* September 13, 1993.

Matolcsy, György and Diczházi, Bertalan. "Filmszakadás a házimoziban (Magyar privatizáció '96)" [The movie stopped in the private cinema—Hungarian privatisation '96]. *Magyarország politikai évkönyve 1997.*

Matolcsy, György. *Eredeti tőkeátcsoportosítás Magyarországon a 90-es években*

——. "Gazdasági és társadalmi sokkterápiák Magyarországon a 90-es években" [Economic and social shock therapies in Hungary in the 90s]. *Társadalmi Szemle,* no. 5 (1996).

——. "Milyen gazdaságpolitikával integrálódunk az Európai Unióba?" [Which economic policy to choose for integration in the European Union?]. *Valóság,* no. 8 (1996).

Pitti, Zoltán. *Egészen eredeti tőkefelhalmozás.*

Tóth Gy., László. "Berendezkedés a kleptokrácia birodalmába" [Establishment in the land of kleptocracy]. *Magyar Nemzet.* August 17, 1996.

Tamás Fricz

DEMOCRATISATION, THE PARTY SYSTEM
AND THE ELECTORATE IN HUNGARY

At the time of their systemic change, the Central and East European (CEE) post-communist countries, including Hungary, regarded Western democracies as models and goals, the standard to which they adjusted every step. They tried to transplant the tested, basic democratic institutions of the West to their respective countries, from charters of human and citizen's rights to the constitutional court. Even when political parties were developed, they kept in mind the existence of traditional party families and the characteristic party labels in Western countries. Therefore Western analysts who claim that the Eastern democratic revolutions and transitions did not bring forth any new, spectacular political ideology or philosophy are right. *Catching up and joining* were much more the characteristic features of the case of the Eastern countries.

Yet the CEE countries, and Hungary in particular, attempted in vain to be faithful "copiers" of Western democracies, as the political and social systems they created were qualitatively different in many respects. The systems that evolved in the region are indeed democracies, but differ considerably from West European models. What is interesting is precisely the fact that while the Eastern post-communist countries carefully avoided the invention of anything new, preferring to tread the path of Western democracy, these newly-created democracies brought to the surface entirely new issues and problems, which may be important even when viewed from the West. There may be no new ideology, no new, world-redeeming principle, but there are new sets of problems and new sets of questions emerging in the new democracies. Some of the crises that have surfaced in the region have already been faced by the Western "model" countries, or may prefigure future problems for them. Thus even for Westerners it is worth paying attention to the Eastern "novices".

How far had the CEE democracies stabilised by the late 1990s? How sure was it that the unfolding crises and conflicts would not sweep away these fresh systems and that they would not revert to the past and to totalitarian dictatorships? In the following I wish to argue that by 1998 Hungary was among those post-communist democracies most solidly linked to democracy. Despite all its "differentness" and some crises, a return to the past was hardly conceivable.

Causes of the Souring of Kádár's "Goulash Communism"

After the Second World War the communist party took power in Hungary in 1948 with the vigorous support of the Soviet Union. Democratic institutions and free elections were abolished or took the form of empty rituals. From 1948 to the systemic change of 1989-1990, a communist dictatorship held sway politically in Hungary, while economically the so-called "socialist planned economy" was introduced.

More than four decades of communist rule can be divided into two periods: a period of *totalitarian dictatorship* from 1948 until the democratic revolution and war of independence of 1956; after the revolution of 1956—despite the fact that it was suppressed by the armed intervention of the Soviet Union—the regime could not continue unchanged. The communist party put forth a new leader in János Kádár after 1956, who, apart from the very last months in 1988-89, remained a decisive figure of the modified and reconstructed post-revolutionary system until its fall. The Kádár regime tamed the former dictatorship and there were some elements of economic and cultural, though not political, liberalisation. This second phase of communist rule may be called *authoritarian dictatorship* in the political sense, as a limited freedom of movement was permitted in various spheres of society, while political pluralism was totally excluded.

Economically the Kádár regime was nothing but a centralised redistributive system under vigorous state control, which only very exceptionally permitted private ownership.[1] The regime was unable to run the state-owned establishment efficiently, and ultimately this led it into an ever-deeper crisis. Unlike the earlier Rákosi regime, the Kádár regime did not base itself on terror, but on the legitimisation of consumption, i.e. the fact that people enjoyed some freedom of movement and could maintain extremely moderate living standards which seemed to be stable for a long time. The Kádár regime's compromise with the society worked relatively well in the 1960s and 1970s when there was hardly any inflation, everybody had a job and the citizens could even travel occasionally, usually to other East and Central European states.

However, a system which is regarded as legitimate only as long as it is able to maintain relative well being is based on extremely precarious foundations. Kádár's system, built exclusively on state ownership, suffered continuously deteriorating efficiency. In the 1970s, the government began to borrow money from abroad in an attempt to sustain the apparent stability and to ensure that legitimisation by consumption should not be hurt. By the time the Kádár system fell, it had accumulated a foreign debt of more than USD 20 billion, causing serious damage to the country and leaving an incredibly difficult economic legacy for subsequent democratic governments to solve.

However, foreign borrowing did not help promote economic productivity in the long run. Inflation increased rapidly from the late 1970s, and in the late 1980s the economic system, built more on appearances than on reality, collapsed like a house of cards. This meant the political legitimacy of the Kádár system was also lost: a system with no political foundations, which has exclusively worked on the assumption of legitimisation by consumption, logically becomes illegitimate when consumption is impaired or reduced beyond an acceptable point.

Nevertheless, the communist system did not fall primarily because of internal fermentation and the loss of legitimisation by consumption. Widespread dissatisfaction with the living standards did not lead to confrontation with the system, or to the creation of broad mass movements, spectacular demonstrations or organised action. Nor did it lead to the reorganisation of "civil society". Rather, the demise of communism resulted from an important politico-cultural characteristic of the citizens, namely their vigorous introversion into private life, the distance they kept from politics, apathy and a large degree of disillusionment and pessimism regarding their possibilities for action. These features were consolidated during the decades of communism in Hungary. A limited amount of embourgeoisement was seen in the 1960s and 1970s in Hungary,[2] but at the most it was able only to create conditions favourable to the market, provided other conditions necessary to it were already present. Thus, although liberalisation was actually manifest in some fields, the system ultimately did not fall as a result of vigorous pressure coming from below, but as a consequence of pressures coming from outside and from above, namely the Soviet-led processed of *glasnost* and *perestroika*.[3]

Nevertheless, some social groups, mostly within the intelligentsia, did emerge during the last decade of the Kádár regime, and their activities did contribute to the disintegration of that system, and to transition towards a new system.[4]

Firstly, there were limited groups of the intelligentsia, working totally or partly underground, with the express goal of reforming, and later increasingly replacing, the political system. Three of these groups which were ready for a possible transfer of power from the second part of the 1980s. The first of these were members of the so-called "democratic opposition". Initially they opposed the system from the left at a highly theoretical level. Later on they shifted to liberal politics, founding the Alliance of Free Democrats (SZDSZ), which was to play an important role in parliament right from the outset.

The second of these groups was the circle of the so-called "populist writers", who criticised the existing power structure mostly from the angle of national survival, national independence and national "self-confidence". This group, which turned against the system only towards the late 1980s, subsequently founded the Hungarian Democratic Forum (MDF), the victorious party in the first free elections.

The last group of intellectuals to be considered here were the young democrats, who appeared in the second part of the 1980s and pressed for radical democratisation right from the outset. They were to found the Federation of Young Democrats (FIDESZ), which became a stable parliamentary party after the first democratic elections.

Another set of actors pushing for change were reformers within the Communist Party, the MSZMP (Hungarian Socialist Workers' Party), who strove in the late 1980s to renew the party and to democratise the political system within limitations. These reformers played an important role in the internal disruption of MSZMP. Significantly it was these reformers who represented the Communist Party at the decisive National Round Table in the summer of 1989.

Finally, opposition came from the young generation of technocrats, who came increasingly to the fore in the 1970s, and particularly in the 1980s, and who tried to promote the renewal of the bureaucratic machinery of state administration and the institutions owned by the state in the broadest sense of the term. Their pragmatism, free of ideology, clearly prepared the reform of the bureaucratic and increasingly inadequate state institutions. A group of reform economists among them used rational criticism to challenge the system as a whole.

However, it should be borne in mind that these groups of intellectuals had little contact with broader sections of society, in contrast, for instance, to the organisations of Polish intellectuals, who were linked to social movements by their contacts with Solidarity.

Thus by 1988-9 Hungary was ready for some systemic change in the sense that it had narrowly based opposition groups who were prepared for democratisation, yet lacking wider social contacts. The mass of citizens meanwhile had become atomised during the four decades of communism and showed no inclination towards being organised or mobilised. Hungarian society was dissatisfied and waiting for "something better", but also passive and helpless, since citizens were not integrated politically. Thus it was the extremely narrowly based critical and opposition groups of intellectuals rather than larger social groups that were able to influence the processes of systemic change and democratisation.

Characteristics of the Development of the Party System

The process of party formation in Hungary was rather different from party formation in Western countries, which have often been regarded as the models of functioning democratic party systems. In contrast to Lipset and Rokkan's model which shows that party systems in Western Europe emerged as part of a "bottom-up" process, in Hungary new party formation was expressly organised from the "top-down". After four decades of communist dictatorship, social groups and citizens had been completely pushed out of politics, they were atomised and lacked any real means of expression. Social cleavages, which played such a considerable role in the development of Western societies and parties, did not become the norm and so did not form bases from which people could organise; hence they did not inspire party formation.

Consequently the establishment of parties, the evolution of party competition and the articulation of interests fell into the hands

of those narrow groups of opposition intellectuals who were ready
to set up parties and political organisations. Thus, a process of elite
party formation occurred in Hungary, with most of the parties
organised from above, on the initiative of opposition intellectual
groups. This top-down process had one inevitable consequence:
namely that the newly-established party system did not represent
society with its various divisions, but rather reflected the conflicts—either ideological and theoretical or cultural—among the
opposition groups within the intelligentsia. Right from the start
these elite-led parties suffered from a lack of social foundation,
reflected *inter alia* in low membership figures. Thus they attempted, rather unsuccessfully, to forge links with assumed or actual
social groups which they claimed to represent.[5] In this respect the
"traditional parties"—the Independent Smallholders' Party (FKGP)
and the Christian Democratic People's Party (KDNP)—had better
chances, as the electorate identified them with their predecessors
which had functioned before 1948, hence they could be linked to
specific social groups. The newly-established parties without
antecedents and traditions, for example the Hungarian Democratic
Forum, the Alliance of Free Democrats and the Federation of
Young Democrats, had a far more difficult job, as social groups
were unable to identify with them unambiguously. As I shall
demonstrate later, the communist successor party, the Hungarian
Socialist Party (MSZP) was in a special position. In addition the
new parties misjudged the situation and made the mistake of pre-
suming the existence and functioning of groups in the market economy which simply did not exist in Hungary at that time.

   Here it is worth making a detour and discussing those radical
legal-constitutional changes which have produced the legal framework to the emergence of a democratic multi-party system in
Hungary. The so-called National Round Table Talks played a fundamental role in the process of transition from dictatorship to
democracy, where the Communist Party (Hungarian Socialist

Workers' Party), exercising authoritarian power, and the emerging opposition parties and political organisations of the day participated, together with other political formations. The talks lasted from June 13, 1989 to September 18, 1989, and were concluded by an Agreement which essentially contained the legal framework of democratisation. An agreement was reached upon six, so-called key issues concerning the amendment of the 1949 Constitution, the setting up of a constitutional court, the functioning and finances of parties, the election of representatives, the modification of the penal code and of penal procedural law. The agreements of the Round Table of historical significance were shaped into law by the then parliament, of which Act XXXI of 1989 is of the greatest significance as it modified the 1949 Constitution. On this basis Hungary obtained a democratic constitution, though formally it is still only a radically modified variant of the 1949 Constitution. (Hence—and of course due to other reasons too—the parties have the intention, it may be said to be based on a consensus, to create an entirely new Constitution.)

Act XXXI of 1989 created the framework for a democratic and liberal state based on the rule of law: Hungary again became a republic, there is parliamentary democracy based on a multi-party system, where human and citizens' rights are respected to the maximum. A constitutional court was set up, the State Audit Office was established and the institution of the ombudsman was introduced along the Scandinavian pattern, to protect the rights of national and ethnic minorities; further, the institution of the commissioner for data protection also started to work. The constitution acknowledges market economy, the freedom of economic competition, the equality of public and private ownership.

The constitution states that parties can be freely established and may freely operate, and they have an important role in the shaping and expression of popular will. (In 1990 there were about 80 parties in Hungary, in 1998 their number is between 150 an 180.)

The law also regulates the conditions of financing the parties by the state.

It is also an essential question in what kind of electoral system the parties can compete for parliamentary mandates. The Hungarian electoral system is a complicated, mixed one of two rounds, which equally has elements striving to achieve proportionality as well as majorities. Of the 386 MPs the citizens elect 176 in individual constituencies, and 152 MPs are elected on territorial party lists. The national list of 58 mandates is distributed on the basis of a complicated method of calculation when the fragmentary votes are counted. However, only those parties can get mandates from the national list which have garnered 5 percent of all the votes cast. (Up to 1993 the parliamentary threshold was 4 percent). The experiences of the first three elections (1990, 1994, 1998) show that *the electoral system shows majoritarian, rather than proportional elements*. This is not only because of the 5 percent parliamentary threshold, but also because it greatly prefers the relatively sure winner. (Examples are the elections of 1990 and 1994: in 1990 the MDF obtained 42 percent of the seats with 24 percent of the votes polled, and it is even more conspicuous that MSZP obtained 33 percent of the votes cast, but that brought 54 percent of the parliamentary mandates! In 1998 this effect could not assert itself because FIDESZ could overtake its great rival, the MSZP, only in a very close competition.) One may say that the majoritarian effect, the so-called "Westminster" method is stronger in the Hungarian electoral system than the proportionate one, but this, in itself, does not shift the Hungarian party system towards a two-party one.

It was within this normative-legal framework that the new stratum of politicians entered the scene in 1989-1990, with the objective of building democracy and a multi-party system in Hungary. Due to the nature of things, after 40 years of communist rule the founders and leaders of the new parties had little or no experience in democratic politics, and earlier did not take up political roles. (With the exception of those who had been active in the political life before 1949.) This stratum was recruited overwhelmingly from the intelligentsia of the humanities; on the one side there were writers, poets, historians, and on the other there were social scientists, such as sociologists, economists, lawyers, political scientists and philosophers. For instance, the writer István Csurka and the poet Sándor Csoóri were among the leaders of MDF, representing the populist-national camp, whereas SZDSZ, representing the urban-liberal trend, had the philosopher János Kis, the sociologists Bálint Magyar, Miklós Haraszti and Gábor Demszky, the economist Tamás Bauer, and the list could be continued. They and their associates were the people who determined the discourse and tone of the new Hungarian democracy in the first years. What has characterised it? There was little political professionalism, and much more of "redeeming" faith, ideas and ideologies—as a result the political and party disputes of the first years there were mostly discussions between different cultural outlooks.

Since that time eight years passed with three parliamentary elections, the founding fathers have been and are being gradually pushed into the background, they relinquish their place to a younger generation of politicians who are more professional and, what is more important, are more pragmatic. But the traces of the initial politics of strong cultural and ideological nature are still very much present.

Now let us see the election results. Six parties were sent to parliament in the first free elections to the National Assembly in 1990. That composition proved quite stable for some, although the FKGP split into two in February 1992. Primarily because the Acts on restitution and re-privatisation related to agriculture were unacceptable to them, the majority of FKGP members, led by József Torgyán, left the coalition, while the Smallholder MPs called "the 33" continued to support the Antall government. Moreover, while effectively the same six parties were returned to parliament in 1994,

some fragmentation did occur. In 1996 a group broke away from
MDF and formed a new parliamentary faction, the Hungarian
Democratic People's Party (MDNP), although this new party was
rather weak.

Table 1 *Results of the parliamentary elections of 1990*

Participation in elections: 1st round   65 per cent
                                2nd round   45 per cent

Order of parties	Trends	No. of mandates	Governing coalition
1. MDF	national conservative	164-42.49 %	+
2. SZDSZ	radical liberal	92-23.83 %	
3. FKGP	radical conservative	44-11.40 %	+
4. MSZP	socialist, social democrat	33-8.55 %	
5. FIDESZ	pragmatic liberal	21-5.70 %	
6. KDNP	Christian democrat	21-5.44 %	+

Table 2 *Results of the parliamentary elections of 1994*

Participation in elections: 1st round   69 per cent
                                2nd round   55 per cent

Order of parties	Trends	No. of mandates	Governing coalition
1. MSZP	socialist, social democrat	209-54.14 %	+
2. SZDSZ	radical liberal	69-17.88 %	+
3. MDF	national conservative	38-9.84 %	
4. FKGP	radical, right wing populist	26-6.74 %	
5. KDNP	Christian democrat	22-5.70 %	
6. FIDESZ	national liberal-conservative	20-5.18 %	

Source: *The annual issues of the series* Magyarország Politikai Évkönyve
(Political Almanac of Hungary) 1991-1995.

Developments in the Party System between 1990 and 1998

Three important political cleavages characterised the Hungarian party system between 1989 and 1998. The main party cleavages were between, firstly, the communists/socialists—until 1989 the Communist Party (MSZMP) and later its successor, the MSZP—and anti-communist/anti-socialist parties and groupings, effectively all the other parties with the exception after 1994 of SZDSZ. There were also conflicts between the so-called populist-national tendency—broadly, the MDF, KDNP and FKGP up to 1992, and from 1994 FIDESZ—and the so-called European-liberal parties and trends, including SZDSZ and MSZP and prior to 1994 FIDESZ. Finally the parties were divided between the radical, right wing populist parties and the moderate parties and trends, dividing the FKGP, partly supported by the KDNP, from all the other parliamentary parties.

These three lines of conflict helped determine party competition in Hungary, although their relative weight and proportions inevitably differed over time. In this respect four periods can be distinguished:

1) 1988-1990. The last years of the communist regime and years of transition were characterised by the communist/anti-communist cleavage between the MSZMP, exercising a monopoly of authority, and the newly-emerging opposition parties. At the National Round Table talks held between June 13, 1989 and September 18, 1989, the opposition parties stood jointly against the communist party, forcing it to accept democratisation and to implement the amendment of the constitution.

2) Autumn 1989 to 1992/93 Shortly after the Round Table Talks, in October 1989, the MSZMP dissolved itself and the MSZP was formed as its successor. Opinion poll data indicated that the MSZP would not be able to play a decisive role in the 1990 spring elections. Conflicts between the opposition parties became pre-

dominant with spectacular speed. The two strongest parties, MDF and SZDSZ, were divided on ideological and cultural lines, with the MDF representing a national and Christian attitude, while SZDSZ stood for the European-liberal trend. This populist-national/European-liberal cleavage can be traced back to the so-called "populist-urban" disputes of the inter-war period. It became politicised during the period of democratisation and is essential for understanding Hungarian party politics in the late 1990s.[6] This division did not mean that the parties such as the liberal-conservative FIDESZ categorised as "national" would be fundamentally opposed to the process of European integration or to Hungarian membership in the European Union; nor would "European" parties such as SZDSZ support European integration to the exclusion of national interest. The terms do, however, reflect the dominant tendencies in the parties.

The dissolution of MSZMP and its successor party's unsuitability for government pushed the communist/anti-communist conflict into the background, so the national/European confrontation dominated the first parliamentary term, increasingly replicating the conservative-liberal divisions frequently seen in Western Europe. This was especially evident when the "national" parties, headed by MDF, formed the government, while SZDSZ and FIDESZ were in opposition.

One should speak separately about József Antall, one of the most characteristic politicians of the first years, who was chairman of MDF and also the prime minister of the MDF-led coalition government up to his death in November 1993.

In the period after the first free elections there was a sharp debate in public whether national conservatism, represented by MDF, the government, and, naturally by József Antall, pointed towards the past, or the future. The socialist and liberal opposition said that the Antall era would lead the country back to the feudal-style, nationalist, anti-liberal world of Miklós Horthy in the inter-war period, as the personality of József Antall itself is the manifestation of that age. However, at the most Antall represented old-fashioned conservatism and an intolerant respect of authority at most in its formal elements; his political activities pointed towards modernisation.

Antall was an exception within the populist-national camp in that compared to his associates, who were writers, poets and historians, he came from a family of politicians; his father was a politician of decisive weight in the Smallholders' Party before 1948-1949. Antall was given a thoroughly conservative education, but his vision was European and an open one. He "exploded" into political life at the National Round Table Talks between June 13 and September 18, 1989, and at once became the decisive politician of MDF. Antall soon became an internationally acknowledged politician and this also played a major role in his rapid emergence. He was particularly welcome in the conservative European circles and had excellent relations with Giscard d'Estaing and especially Helmut Kohl. (He was given positions in the European Democrat Union and in the Union of Christian Democratic Parties as well.) Antall's take-over in the MDF meant that the radical populist-national line, representing the so-called 'third way', was pushed into the background within the party (István Csurka, Sándor Csoóri, Zoltán Bíró and others), and the conservative, right wing politics of the centre, open towards Europe, were becoming increasingly decisive.

As prime minister, József Antall implemented an "enlightened" conservative policy from May 1990 until his death in November 1993, which was not at all oriented towards the creation of a kind of a feudal, nationalist, paternalistic society. The government policy of Antall aimed at the consolidation of a democratic state based on the rule of law, the strict respect of basic liberal rights, and at social justice. The reason why József Antall and his government could be blamed for "lordly pride", and an patrician paternalism, etc., was nothing else but a kind of political style, which, though rarely, was woven into the political content as well. Antall's personality was truly of keeping a certain distance and it was characterised by a kind of aristocratic superiority, therefore the majority of the citizenry respected him at the most, but did not love him. On the other hand, it is also a fact that with his somewhat old-fashioned style, Antall could not, or could only with difficulty, fit into the modern, and modernised world of politics and was unable to transmit his message convincingly to the people through the media.

Summing up, the period of MDF governance between 1990 and 1994, the "Antall-era" pointed toward a modern, European conservative policy in its content as well as in its practical steps; however, it retained such traditionalist traits, characteristics and style in its form which provoked the sharp criticism of the opposition political circles.

3) 1992-1994. MSZP gradually ceased to be perceived as an "unfit" party that was merely tolerated, and from the autumn of 1992 it started to prepare for the 1994 elections as an increasingly strong and popular party. The party's changing fortunes were due partly to the radical and somewhat antidemocratic "populist" trend within the MDF, and to the SZDSZ. The populist trend in the MDF was closely associated with István Csurka, a rather tainted figure and a leading force within the governing coalition, who wanted to divest the media from communist control and tried to push national, specifically Hungarian culture to the fore. SZDSZ, as a fundamental adversary of the MDF, claimed a danger from the extreme right, and from this perspective made contact with the MSZP through the Democratic Charter, which was created by the intellectuals surrounding the SZDSZ. MSZP politicians and intellectuals actively joined the work of the Charter. At the same time, the two liberal parties, SZDSZ and FIDESZ began to distance themselves from each other given their different attitudes to the Democratic Charter, which essentially outlined "antifascist" goals.

SZDSZ regarded MSZP as a partner in opposing the radical national forces and thus brought the MSZP into the group of accepted opposition parties. From being the most militant anti-Communist political force prior to the 1990 election, SZDSZ made a spectacular *volte face* in 1992, compromising with the successor party to the communists as a result of its European credentials, even going so far as to enter into a governing coalition with it in 1994.

The growing strength of the MSZP contributed to a strengthening of the national/European cleavage, but also led to the establishment of a socialist/social democratic pole as the socialist party modernised itself; and from 1992-3 it set electoral victory as its definite goal and became a real electoral alternative. A left-right cleavage had reappeared alongside the national/European one, but it was based on a socialist/anti-socialist rather than a communist/anti-communist cleavage. Thus the party system was characterised by two dominant cleavages: left/right and national-conservative/liberal-European.

4) After 1994, the formation of the MSZP-SZDSZ coalition government following the 1994 elections indicated that SZDSZ perceived the national-European cleavage to be decisive, although that position came only after considerable internal disputes. The coalition was unusual in bringing together parties divided on economic (employee-employer) and ideological (left-right) cleavages. The result was that the decisive national/European and left/right cleavages strengthened each other, increasingly with the radicalism of the political-ideological confrontations. From May-June 1994, the national/European and the socialist/anti-socialist cleavages sharply divided the parliamentary parties into two camps. The two governing parties—MSZP and SZDSZ—were in the European (liberal) and also leftist camp. MDF, FIDESZ, MDNP and, to some extent, the KDNP were in the national (conservative) and right wing camp. These divisions meant extremely sharp confrontations, with minimal possibilities for consensus.

Here it is worth talking about the personality of Gyula Horn, the prime minister of the governing coalition of 1994-1998, who was also chairman of the MSZP. All the more so as he is undoubtedly the second decisive politician of the post-1990 democratic period after József Antall.

Antall and Horn belonged to the same age group, yet a word, a period and a system separated them. While Antall's roots went back to the inter-war period, Gyula Horn already had leading political positions in the 1970s and 1980s, at the time of "goulash communism", associated with the name of János Kádár. One may say that two "pasts" have returned in their personality after 1990, namely, a more conservative one between 1990 and 1994, and the period of state socialism between 1994 and 1998; these only to relinquish their place to a generation of young politicians after the elections in May 1998, to the Federation of Young Democrats (FIDESZ), synchronous with the age, headed by Viktor Orbán, the new prime minister.

Antall, as well as Horn, attempted to modernise, and both more or less succeeded, but there is no doubt that Horn could adjust far better to the world of the media and to constant appearance in public than Antall. Undertaking the image of modern social democracy, Horn could admirably merge two kinds of attitudes: on the one hand he used a technocratic "market" language, divested of ideology (he very much needed it as the MSZP-SZDSZ government had to assert a very tough neo-liberal economic policy), and on the other hand he made efforts to testify his "social sensitivity", recognising that there was a strong nostalgia for the quiet and modest petite bourgeois existential security of Kádár's state socialism in a very broad circle of the society. One of the important secrets of the landslide victory of the MSZP in 1994 was that the party, and mostly its leader, were capable of simultaneously representing and symbolising two kinds of—contradictory—demands (capitalism and social sensitivity) present at the same time.

Another important feature of Gyula Horn, the "Great Integrator", was his excellent tactical ability: he was capable of implementing the principle of "divide and rule" to the utmost. On the one hand it was Horn who guaranteed for four years that the MSZP-SZDSZ coalition did not disintegrate, on the other hand also that the various platforms inside his party should not destroy it. It can be stated about the latter that the MSZP as the biggest catch-all party has been internally the most articulated one. Radical (Marxist) leftists, syndicalists, populist-nationalists, social democrats and social liberals, near to SZDSZ, could also be found inside MSZP, not mentioning the technocrats. Often these trends have been in sharp dispute; however, Gyula Horn, being in the centre, was able to keep the balance of the party and its unity toward the outside world right until May 1998, when the party lost the elections. Horn only fell out of his role at the last minute, between the two rounds of elections (May 10 and May 24, 1998). It was at that time that is became clear: the MSZP may lose the elections as against FIDESZ, and Horn had a rather poor, almost panicky reaction. Surprisingly his state socialist rhetoric returned from the past, he began to speak about dangers of the right wing, and even of the extreme right wing and called the leftist "comrades" to join forces, projecting the socialists as the only and exclusive depositories of the future. All this backfired, the MSZP lost the elections and stood second. It lost the government and Gyula Horn had a major role in this failure, just like in the great success of 1994. In the summer of 1998 every indication suggests that there would be a replacement of the Chairman of the MSZP.

In the period after the 1994 elections the Independent Smallholders' Party, led by József Torgyán, pursued an increasingly marked rightist, radical and populist policy, deviating from its earlier image as a traditional conservative party primarily organised to represent the peasants and farmers. The FKGP had been regarded by many as the only party representing particular interests or strata. However, after its relatively successful performance at the 1994 elections, the FKGP made a spectacular turn, appointing itself as the leading party of the opposition and announcing a policy of "saving the country", which contained all the traditionally significant elements of a right wing, populist policy of national salvation.[7] Following a change in the party presidency in January 1995 the KDNP also joined this populist trend, albeit rather reluctantly.

The populist/moderate cleavage emerged ever more markedly from 1994 to join the main fault lines. The FKGP and to some extent KDNP were on one side (creating a fierce struggle between the moderates and the radicals in the KDNP). Opposed to them were other parties, committed to democracy and refraining from radical propaganda and politics, including the national and European ones, the leftists and the rightist. Although the members of the moderate camp could not reach agreement on many issues, they stood unambiguously and uncompromisingly against the often irresponsible policy represented by the FKGP.

The political cleavages, basically defining and shaping the nature and conflicts of the Hungarian party system, were strongly ideological, even cultural in character, with cleavages based on more pragmatic issues almost totally pushed into the background. However, the parties strongly supported democratic practices, with almost all the parliamentary parties clearly respecting the democratic legal order and the rule of law.

5) Finally, I would only deal with the election results of May 1998 and the short time passed since, because a proper scientific processing is still missing.

First of all, let us see the results.

Table 3 *Outcomes of parliamentary elections*
May 10 - May 24, 1998

Electoral participation: Round I: 56 %
                             Round II: 57 %

Order of parties	Trends	No. of mandates	Governing coalition
1. FIDESZ	national conservative liberal	147-38 %	+
2. MSZP	social democrat	134-34.7 %	
3. FKGP	radical, rightist populist	48-12.4 %	+
4. SZDSZ	left liberal	24-6.2 %	
5. MDF	national conservative	18-4.6 %	+
6. MIÉP (Party of Hungarian Justice and Life)	anti-liberal, radical rightist	14-3.6 %	

As we can see, a kind of breakthrough has taken place: the MSZP, which had a sweeping victory in 1994, obtaining 54 percent of the mandates, was defeated four years later by the Federation of Young Democrats. Though it should be added that the MSZP remains a rather strong party with a very stable social, economic, cultural, local, etc. network of contacts. The failure of MSZP, its loss of governance, however, requires explanation. Political scientists and experts agree on the following reasons in their brief analyses produced in the first weeks after the elections.

a) First of all the electorate had to be disappointed in the nostalgic illusions linked to the MSZP. In the period between 1993 and 1998 the social democrat MSZP, together with the liberal SZDSZ, asserted a vigorously restrictive economic policy, aiming at the improvement of the balance of the state and its finances, which was accompanied by a significant decrease of the living standards of the population. On the one hand there were the excellent indices of the macro economy and the appreciation of the international financial and economic organisations, whereas there was a slump in consumption, a reduction of incomes and a growth of unemployment on the other. And what is very important: the governing coalition proved unable to demonstrate convincingly to the people that there was an interrelationship between the improvement of the macroeconomic indices and the potential long-term improvement of the "micro economy". The electorate was only influenced by short-term effects at the ballot boxes.

b) In 1996 a huge corruption scandal erupted around privatisation (the 'Tocsik-case'), which was followed by other, minor cases of corruption up to 1998. It did a lot of harm to the authority of the government.

c) Public security had dangerously deteriorated in Hungary by 1998, and grew even worse in the run-up to the elections.

d) The government, and Gyula Horn himself, became incredibly conceited; they thought, just on the basis of their broad network of contacts, that the elections could not be won by anybody else but the Socialists. Setting out from this premise they projected the opposition to the public as lacking in seriousness, and the government lacking an alternative, and it backfired.

e) It is also due to the latter item that the MSZP and the SZDSZ conducted a campaign of extremely little success, particularly during the two weeks between the two rounds. The television duel between Gyula Horn and Viktor Orbán just four days before the second round was won decisively by the 35-year-old Chairman of FIDESZ.

But the closeness of these election results have produced a curious situation. The features, discussed earlier, of the rigidity of party structure combined with the lack of flexible centre parties forced FIDESZ to enter into coalition with the radical populist Smallholders' Party in addition to MDF (its ally of little weight) and so partly to give up its own ideas. As for FIDESZ it was a basic issue of principle to push the MSZP, the communist successor party into the background (in other words, the socialist-anti-socialist fault line), so therefore it preferred to made allowances along the populist-moderate fault line. No doubt the governmental co-operation of FIDESZ, of young men of technocratic orientation, speaking a modern political language, and of the Smallholders' Party of older politicians, using an archaic, populist political parlance, is a rather piquant one.

It is a fact however, that the proportion of mandates between FIDESZ and the Smallholders is two thirds to one third, which gives FIDESZ the chance to assert its modern governmental ideas in the face of the professionally less prepared politicians of the Smallholders. However, what will really happen can be seen only in the coming months and years.

Relations between Parties and Voters, 1990-1998

The political cleavages created from above by the parties and party elites were not sufficient to articulate the real divisions in society, hence the parliamentary parties were not successful in integrating the citizens into the political competition and democratic institutions in the 1990s. Apparently the citizens were divided on other, more pragmatic issues closer to their daily lives. Although the political parties did evolve during the 1990s, the changes still did not permit voters to distinguish between the parties on the issues which concerned them most.

The voters were particularly affected by the consequences of systemic change, of transition to the market economy and of the processes of privatisation. Within a few years changes in market competition led to broad social differences in Hungary and polarisation between the narrow stratum who became significantly wealthy and the great majority whose position had deteriorated—

between the "winners" and "losers". Yet this social cleavage saw no corresponding cleavage in party politics. Only the populist FKGP appeared, later on, to stand for the 'losers'. Thus the voters regarded both governing and opposition parties in parliament as elite parties, jointly representing specific elite interests which, if necessary, they would co-operate to preserve. They seemed indifferent towards the real problems preoccupying the citizens.

These problems were reflected in a variety of ways:

1) The generally low level of participation in elections. Turnout in the first free elections was rather low at 65 percent, dropping to only 45 percent in the second round. Nor had a sense of civic duty developed by the second free elections of 1994. On that occasion 69 percent went to vote in the first round, and 55 percent in the second.

In May 1998, on the occasion of the third parliamentary elections, voter participation was further reduced as only 56 percent cast their votes in the first round, and to the great surprise of all, participation went up to 57 percent in the second round. (The reason for the latter was decisively the fact, that, as contrasted to expectations, the first round did not produce the unambiguous superiority of the MSZP—though it could obtain the leading position before FIDESZ—so it evoked tremendous interest among the voters. The second round had become something which had stakes, and big ones at that, as an unexpected but clear chance for the replacement of the government emerged, which "mobilised" voters, dissatisfied with the past four years.)

At the local elections—one may say quite naturally—participation was even lower. In 1990 40 percent of the electorate went to vote in the first round, and 29 percent in the second. In 1994 local elections were conducted in a single-round system, when 43.4 percent of the electorate showed activity. At the so-called by-elections participation often dropped below 20 percent on parliamentary as well as local governmental levels.

Such figures, low in comparison with most Western European elections, suggest that some citizens had no confidence in the basic institution of parliamentary democracy—elections—and did not see any sense in backing it by participating.

2) A marked lack of attachment to parties. The regularly published polls and comprehensive empirical surveys clearly show that the most characteristic behaviour of the voters is electoral uncertainty, with a large number of "floating voters". This has on occasion been true for more than 50 percent of the voters, while only a fifth of the electorate regularly practised partisan voting.[8]

The primary figures of participation of the 1998 elections show that the number of non-voters, protest-voters and floating voters has further increased in the past years. It is partly manifest in decreasing electoral participation and in the fact that a significant part of the 1994 voters of the MSZP either did not vote for anyone, or migrated to FIDESZ.

Various empirical surveys have shown that the classic cleavage between worker and capitalist, and more recently between employee and employer, which has constituted the basis of left-right division in West European countries for decades, was virtually non-existent in the emergent Hungarian party system.[9] This phenomenon has three basic causes. First, society as a whole lost the ability to express interests during the decades of communist dictatorship; the only trade union organisation, the Central Council of Trade Unions, occupied a monopoly position, functioning as part of the ruling elite. In any case, in the absence of a free market, no clear appearance of economic interest was apparent, even if workers had had a vehicle for representation, which the Central Council of Trade Unions clearly was not. Under communism practically everyone, irrespective of position, was both employed by the state and politically subjugated. Economic interests and lobbying groups emerged only latently during the Kádár era, and did not lead to the appearance of autonomous agencies of interest representation.

Rather such groups cozied up to the government in order to obtain additional favours, while claiming to be "lobbying for interests" as László Lengyel put it. Conflicts between industry and agriculture were moderately articulated by the Smallholders' Party until that party shifted to a populist platform from 1994 onwards.

A second reason for the lack of interest articulation was that the newly-appearing opposition parties concentrated on the comprehensive tasks of systemic change, involving the entire country and society rather than on specific interests. Thus, with the exception initially of the FKGP, they wished to appear to be catch-all parties, representing the interests of the nation, standing above specific groups right from the outset. And thirdly it should also be noted that the party which willingly projected itself as leftist and social democratic, the MSZP, also functioned as a catch-all party and not the specific party of employees, just as much as the other parliamentary parties.

3) Fluctuation in electoral behaviour since 1990. It is understandable that Hungarian voters were uncertain about which party to support at the time of the first elections in 1990, as they were inevitably unfamiliar with parties established a few months or at most one or two years earlier. What is less comprehensible was the dramatic shift between the first round, which put MDF and SZDSZ neck and neck as winners, and the second round only two weeks later when the decisive majority turned away from SZDSZ and voted MDF. Support for MDF, with its "Calm Force" slogan, seemed to be motivated by its platform as a moderate political agent, committed to maintaining relative continuity and not threatening everyday basic peace –as against the radical and at that time strongly anti-Communist SZDSZ. Indeed it appears that what was decisive was the emphasis MDF laid on gradual transition rather than its advocacy of a national, populist and partly conservative policy. Similarly, SZDSZ was rejected at the last minute not because it was a liberal party, but because voters had reservations

about its anti-communism which appeared to be excessively radical, some feeling it might endanger everyday peace if SZDSZ came to power.

The second free elections held in 1994 saw a huge and sweeping change in electoral behaviour compared to 1990. The majority of those who had voted MDF in 1990 cast their ballot for the MSZP in the first and second rounds. This shift was indicative of uncertainly rather than mature preference on the part of the voters. The MSZP's landslide victory was not the result of its socialist ideology, but people's reaction to the bitter experiences of the four years following 1990—falling living standards, unemployment, inflation, rising crime and so on. MSZP represented the hope of restoring the old, peaceful world "free of excitement". There was a clear relationship between voting for MDF in 1990 and voting MSZP in 1994: in both cases important pragmatic, practical, "everyday" considerations played a decisive role, explaining how voters could shift support from a conservative party to a socialist party within a period of four years.

Apparently due to the above causes—and of course due to other reasons too, which I referred to earlier—changes of electoral behaviour continued at the third free elections as well, together with the dominance of the floating voters, as a not insignificant proportion of those who in 1994 voted for the MSZP now voted for FIDESZ in May 1998. Thus the trend that in Hungary—as contrasted to most West European countries—there are only a modest number of disciplined, active voting strata, strongly attached to parties, has not changed. The electorate is primarily influenced by the changes of their personal vote, by the changing political mood, thirdly by the actual public disputes of the pre-election weeks and months, and finally, by inscrutable emotional motives.

At the same time attention should be called to a new phenomenon in relation to the elections of 1998. Empirical surveys show that of the two strongest parties (FIDESZ and MSZP) it is primari-

ly the civic, small and medium-size entrepreneurs of the more
developed, Western counties who cast their vote for FIDESZ, advocating a conservative liberal "Hungary of citizens", whereas the
socialist MSZP won the votes of the inhabitants of the less developed Eastern counties, of the unemployed, people of little income
and of a disadvantageous position. What does it suggest?
Perhaps—and one should be cautious for the time being—that the
confrontation of left and right economic policies may have obtained
some meaning for the voter. How lasting that trend may be, would
be more precisely stated in the year 2002.

4) Public dissatisfaction with the institutions of 'big politics'
was significant right from the outset—and grew annually. Regular
public opinion polls show unambiguously that there was great mistrust toward the most important political institutions, including both
parliament and government. They also indicate that citizens' confidence in political parties sank very low. Distrust of big government
has been rising in Western Europe as well, but it seems to differ in
weight and nature from the distrust apparent in Hungary and other
East-Central European states. In the West distrust was more moderate and predicated on a basic trust of the system overall, whereas
in the East this bedrock support for the system was lacking.[10]

This lack of public confidence in the political parties explains
why the party system had to struggle to find legitimacy. The majority of citizens did not desire anti-democratic solutions, but they did
not trust the political parties and personalities shaping politics.

Can the Past Return:
Or, How could the Socialists Win Again in 1994?

How was MSZP, successor to the former communist party,
able to gain a landslide victory of sensational dimensions in 1994?
Was it the return of communism and party dictatorship for four
years? These questions should be answered even if we know that

the elections of 1998 were lost by the party and it fell out of governance. It should not be disregarded by any means that after eight years the MSZP is the first party which has been able to retain its high-ranking political positions from one election to another, and has been able to stabilise itself with its 34.7 percent result. At the next, 2002 elections the MSZP has every chance of regaining its just lost governing position. Therefore the study of the success of the MSZP continues to be a topical issue. Certainly the party's success did not mean that the voters wanted to bring back a communist or socialist system in a political or ideological sense. Rather, they sought their basic expectations from democracy: peace, order, quiet, consolidation, jobs, and a compromise with a modest, but sure standard of life. They blamed the MDF government for the failures of the years after 1990 and for the loss of security in everyday life. Yet voters did not blame government alone, but also the opposition parties. Only the non-elite MSZP, which symbolised Kádár's good old policy of consolidation, seemed to be clean in this regard. Again pragmatism rather than a demand for the return of the old regime led the voters to support MSZP. In fact MSZP always protested whenever it was accused of harbouring intentions of restoring the old regime—a protest supported by its actions during its period in office.

Yet, if citizens were voting for a better and quieter life, in many ways this was a vain hope. Their disappointment with the MDF government of Antall arose from a loss of illusions about democracy, which they associated primarily with high living standards, rather than with freedom, participation in decision-making, or the right to vote.[11] This apparently paradoxical phenomenon can partly be explained by the fact that although in the 1980s everybody knew that the Kádár system only maintained itself by Western loans and was essentially built on appearances, by the run-up to the 1994 elections the memory of the majority of the citizens was working selectively. They suppressed their memories about the lack of pro-

ductivity in those days and remembered only that life had been better and calmer in the Kádár era. In this light it was only natural that
the "old ones" should return. Yet in practice, MSZP became considerably more liberal over time and finally announced an almost
neo-conservative, monetarist economic policy because it faced an
extensive economic crisis. Thus austerity measures, including tax
increases and trimming of social services, became as inevitable for
MSZP as they would have been for a party of a different political
complexion.

A second, political factor was at least as significant in securing the election of MSZP. This was that voting MSZP was a kind
of surrogate activity for citizens in whom the new political agents,
parties and other organisations such as the independent trade
unions, had not evoked any emotional attachment beyond a merely
rational acceptance.

Democracy is basically a relationship based on confidence and
the most important functional deficit of the new political elite was
that it was unable to develop such a relationship with the electorate.
Thus the lack of a confidence-based relationship between the new
political forces and the citizens contributed to a major breakdown
of confidence in the new democratic institutions—parties,
Parliament and so on—when the inevitable and drastic fall of living standards set in after 1990. This was the other fundamental
cause of the success of the MSZP in 1994.

Had the electorate been politically integrated, it would not
have turned back to the MSZP. In the event, the majority of citizens
returned to the socialist party because it symbolised a once-existing
good world in which a large part of the people had been integrated,
albeit in a distorted, schizophrenic manner. They became fed up
with it by the late 1980s, but nevertheless it represented a reassur-
ingly known quantity.

In addition, support for the MSZP did not involve the danger
of a real, systemic return to the past either in the short or the longer

run. By 1998 it was already clear that the party's time in government had strongly tested the confidence of citizens in the party: affection and support had changed either into hatred, or into passivity and indifference.

A Special Feature of Hungarian Democracy and Party Competition

One characteristic of Hungarian democracy worthy of note is the persistence in office of former members of the *nomenklatura*. Although systemic change has unambiguously taken place in Hungary from dictatorship to democracy, from socialist planned economy to market economy, certain leading circles of the former communist regime have succeeded in retaining certain advantageous positions in the democratic system, or, characteristically, in developing new positions of power and influence. On the one hand it is a fact that a number of the politicians who had been attached to the former state party (the MSZMP), continued their career in the MSZP, they could even return to the front line of political life after the party went into a governing position in 1994 by its election victory. MSZP Prime Minister Gyula Horn never made a secret even of his active—militia—participation against the revolutionaries in 1956.

And what is perhaps even more important is that three important groups, linked to the former centre of power, have acquired significant *economic capital* under the new market relations. The three groups are the following:[12]

members of the so-called *nomenklatura* (that is those who possessed significant state jobs),

heads of former large state companies,

a young stratum of technocrats who got into lower and middle managerial posts in the 80s.

If Pierre Bourdieu's categories are used in this respect[13], then one can say in summary that the influential strata, linked to the former system, have retained their political capital to a lesser extent, but have converted their authority and influence to a larger extent and more characteristically into economic capital, a far more realistic one under the new conditions. And in the background there was the capital of contacts (largely among themselves) which allowed for the maintenance of power and influence, though in a changed form.

Systemic change in Hungary was characterised by this paradox: transition from dictatorship to democracy took place without bloodshed, it was peaceful and negotiated. Its zenith was the National Round Table, held between 13 June and 18 September 1989, when the opposition parties, acting in unison, agreed with the delegates of the communist party, the MSZMP upon the scenario of peaceful transition by legal means. That in itself was an indisputable achievement, proof of the wisdom and sobriety of the groups conducting the political negotiations.

Despite all the positive qualities of the negotiated character of transition without bloodshed, it is a sociological fact that it also meant that the Hungarian public did not show any predisposition towards radical personal changes after the systemic change. Nor did they press for the removal, even by administrative measures, of the remaining leaders of communist commitment who were still heading the most divers institutions. The government headed by József Antall, which entered into office as a result of the 1990 elections, made some weak attempts to implement the changes of personnel as required by the logic of systemic change, but these attempts met the strong resistance of the media, and the opposition parties—particularly SZDSZ—vehemently raised their voices against the governmental intention to remove communists. That MSZP, the communist successor party, should have opposed such changes was not surprising; the case of SZDSZ was more complex, since at that time it projected itself as militantly anti-Communist. However, when SZDSZ's chief opponent, the "nationalist" MDF, got into power, SZDSZ felt distancing itself from MDF was even more important than removing personnel with Communist backgrounds: a clear sign that the national-European cleavage, described earlier, had become more important than the communist-anticommunist fault line. Consequently, it can be stated that the Antall government proved unable to implement personal changes related to systemic change, partly because of the peaceful, negotiated nature of transition, and partly because of the resistance of the parliamentary opposition. People who had been involved with the former regime in Hungary were able to preserve their influence, to acquire favourable positions, mostly in the economic sphere, but partly also in politics, and also in the field of the media and of the press. They did not seek to restore the former regime but rather to enjoy all the advantages of the market economy and system of private ownership which they had come to endorse. However, the new situation did endanger the realisation of openness and equality of opportunity seen as an objective in a free society.

Rather a strong concentration of political, economic, cultural capital and capital of contacts did emerge with the MSZP-SZDSZ governing coalition formed in 1994. Right from the start of the regime change, SZDSZ, mostly created by influential intellectuals, enjoyed a favourable position in the media and this capital of publicity, influencing public opinion, supplemented the MSZP's economic and political capital. Thus, despite internal strife, the ruling coalition from 1994 to 1998 wielded significant influence in most spheres of the society, consequently limiting to some extent the mobility of the opposition parties. Nevertheless, the opposition, more exactly FIDESZ, enjoyed some success in organising capital as the results of the 1998 elections demonstrated.

Here it is worth mentioning that the Federation of Young Democrats started almost from scratch in 1994 and has been tenaciously working on the building of an alternative social network in opposition to the governing coalition. The apparently hopeless objective reached fruition by 1997-1998, so much so that by the elections of May 1998 there were important and influential social groups and circles standing behind FIDESZ.

They have succeeded in accomplishing a breakthrough against the "monopolies" of MSZP and SZDSZ:

a) Certain influential circles of people working for the media (journalists, editors), have "changed" and started to show tolerance, and even some appreciation of FIDESZ;

b) As a result of the party's resolute enterprise—and market-friendly policy, part of the stratum of major domestic entrepreneurs and multinational companies started to support FIDESZ by 1996 and 1997, as they were getting fed up by the often unpredictable market- and taxation policy of the governing parties, and mainly of the MSZP;

c) Certain circles of the money and banking world have also turned towards FIDESZ;

d) By the setting up of various civic associations, clubs, organisations, etc., it succeeded in winning the support of authoritative circles of intellectuals and in creating a base of social science in the backyard of the party. The party created an alternative governing policy and it set up its shadow government by the beginning of 1998;

e) The party has acquired influence in a certain spheres of foundations playing a significant political, economic and cultural role in Hungary;

f) Last but not least, FIDESZ made efforts to develop support bases in the local governments and in the settlements, not without success.

It should be immediately added that despite the achievements, FIDESZ did not totally break up the hegemony of MSZP, and partly of SZDSZ, in respect to economic, cultural, social capital and that of contacts. It is beyond doubt however, that having had access to governing power, it has a chance of stabilising its social base and integration, and to further strengthen it.

All this is eminently significant primarily from the angle of the consolidation of party political plurality, party political alternatives, that is of democracy.

It is a significant difference that in the West the emerging democratic institutions offered the framework for the struggles and conflicts of the political actors and the parties gradually grew into them, whereas in the East, in particular in Hungary, the democratic institutions did not offer a framework for the political parties which had to organise themselves within a couple of months. They were, rather, institutions to be consciously created; in other words, they were goals in themselves. Thus democracy in Hungary is not yet the natural field and framework of political competition, but it is a goal. It is what is at stake in political disputes, a part of the set of arguments in the political struggle.

The new, original parties established during the transition did not evolve into democratic institutions, but dropped into them. This was true even for the parties having historical traditions—the FKGP, KDNP—as, re-established decades after they had been shut down, they were faced with entirely new challenges under almost entirely new party leaderships. Nor did MSZP, as the communist successor party, have any democratic experience and practice. Effectively each political party was new, original, and unknown by the others, and if the cultural-ideological cleavage playing a decisive role among the party elites is added, then the result was inevitably a large degree of mutual suspicion. Democracy in Hungary did not appear as part of a process where each political actor was able to prove his or her democratic commitment convincingly. A situation evolved in which every actor thought himself democratic, while doubting the democratic credentials of his political adversaries. This absence of mutual tolerance rendered it difficult to reach that consensus which is absolutely essential to the operation of democracy, or to agree on the basic safeguards of the fairness of political competition. Hence, in the period 1989-1998, political parties in government very often ignored the measures taken by their adversaries, demonstrating reluctance to build on each other's achievements. For instance, after the electoral defeat of the Antall government in 1994, the Horn government felt that everything had to be shifted to new foundations. Thus there was the danger that every change of government would always mean a kind of starting anew, a *tabula rasa*, as a result of which democracy would undergo excessive shocks, and the long term effects of this have still to be seen.

Democracy in Hungary, as elsewhere in East Central Europe, was very much an ideal in the 1990s, yet was never an ideal realised in practice. Thus, although Hungarian citizens were committed to the values of democracy, they became extremely dissatisfied with the practice and mistrustful of the operators of democracy. At the time of writing, it was not clear whether the political parties and other elite groups would be able to renew themselves and to transfer to quite a different, more tolerant politics without any external assistance. Help could come from the outside, from the society, if citizens adopted their own rules of self-organisation, which would lead to the creation of a real civil society with the setting up of authentic organisations of interest which would have a proper weight and autonomy. That civic community could eventually force the political elite to carry on an entirely different politics, both in behaviour and style.

A lot of negative features of Hungarian democracy have been outlined, but there is one positive point to be made: the citizens as well as the political parties take very resolute steps against political or social groups who openly turn against democracy. Therefore even if the parties and citizens are frustrated in many respects with the practice of democracy, they are able to turn against the enemies of democracy.

However Hungary's experience since 1989 is assessed, one thing is definite: the situation in the late 1990s was not the final picture. Stabilisation of the Hungarian party system required greater experience of everyday democracy, with new rounds of elections, with the collation of interests, with citizens' initiatives and most especially the change in government arising from the 1998 elections, which allowed all the responsible political parties to show their credentials in government as well as in opposition.

Notes

1. The first precise description of the socialist economic system was given by Iván Szelényi and György Konrád in their work written in the early 1970s. It was originally a *samizdat*, to be read illegally only. Konrád, György and Szelényi, Iván. *Az értelmiség útja az osztályhatalomhoz* [The Intelligentsia's road to class power]. (Budapest: Gondolat, 1989).

2. Cf. Szelényi, Iván. "Polgárosodás Magyarországon: nemzeti tulajdonos polgárság és polgárosodó értelmiség (Bozóki András interjúja)" [Embourgeoisement in Hungary: a national owner bourgeoisie and an embourgeoising intelligentsia (Interview by András Bozóki)]. *Valóság*, no. 1.

3. Cf. Kiss, József. "Többpártrendszer Magyarországon 1985-1991" [Multi-party system in Hungary 1985-1991]. In: Bihari, Mihály, ed. *A többpártrendszer kialakulása Magyarországon 1985-1991.* Budapest: Kossuth, 1992).

4. The following enumeration is based mostly on Erzsébet Szalai's analyses, and particularly on her work: Szalai, Erzsébet. *Útelágazás. Hatalom és értelmiség az államszocializmus után.* [The Parting of roads. Power and the intelligentsia after state socialism]. (Budapest: Pesti Szalon—Savaria University Press, 1994).

5. The total membership of the six parliamentary parties was around 150,000, little more than two percent of the seven million enfranchised voters. Fricz, Tamás. *A magyarországi pártrendszer 1987-1995* [The Hungarian Party System 1987-1995]. (Budapest: Cserépfalvy, 1996), p. 141.

6. Cf. Fricz, Tamás. "A népi-urbánus ellentét tegnap és ma" [The popular-urban conflict yesterday and today]. *Napvilág.* (Budapest, 1997).

7. For the comparative and Hungarian characteristics of populism see Bozóki, András. "Vázlat három populizmusról: Egyesült Államok, Argentína és Magyarország" [An outline of three populisms: the United States, Argentina and Hungary]. *Politikatudományi Szemle*, no. 3 (1994), pp. 33-68.

8. See the comprehensive survey conducted by Ferenc Gazsó and István Stumpf: Gazsó, Ferenc and Stumpf, István. "Pártok és

szavazóbázisok két választás után" [Parties and voting bases after two elections]. *Társadalmi Szemle*, no. 5 (1995).

9. Cf. Bruszt, László and Simon, János. "A Nagy Átalakulás. Elméleti megközelítések és állampolgári vélemények a demokráciáról és a kapitalizmusról" [The Great Transformation. General approaches and citizens' opinion on democracy and capitalism]. *Politikatudományi Szemle*, no. 1 (1992), pp. 78-98. and Simon, János. "A demokrácia 'másnapja' Magyarországon" [The "aftermath" of democracy in Hungary] in: *Kutatási résztanulmányok*. (Institute of Political Science and Research Institute of Sociology of HS, 1992), pp. 39-74. Angelusz, Róbert and Tardos, Róbert.: "Pártpolitikai mélyrétegek" [Deep layers of party politics]. *Magyarország Politikai Évkönyve* (1991), pp. 647-670. Angelusz, Róbert and Tardos, Róbert. "A választói magatartás egy mögöttes pillére" [A background pillar of electoral behaviour]. *Politikatudományi Szemle*, no. 3 (1995), and Tóka, Gábor. "A kakukk fészke. Pártrendszer és törésvonalak Magyarországon" [The cuckoo's nest. Party system and fault lines in Hungary]. *Politikatudományi Szemle*, no. 2 (1992), pp. 123-159.

10. Cf. Fricz, Tamás. "A bizalom szerepe a posztmodern politikában" [The role of trust in post-modern politics]. In: *Rendszerváltásban Magyarországon*. (Budapest: Villányi úti Konferenciaközpont és Szabadegyetem Alapítvány, 1996).

11. Cf. Bruszt, László and Simon, János. *Op. cit.*, and Simon, János. *Op. cit.*

12. See Szalai, Erzsébet. *Op. cit.*

13. Cf. Bourdieau, P. *Towards a Theory of Practice*. (Cambridge: Cambridge University Press, 1977) and "Cultural Reproduction and Social Reproduction" in: Karabel, I. and Halsey, A.H. (eds). *Power and Ideology in Education*. (Oxford: Oxford University Press, 1977).

144   Tamás Fricz

Bibliography

Ágh, Attila. "A pártok parlamentesedése Magyarországon (1989-1991)" [The emerging parliamentary parties in Hungary]. *Politikatudományi Szemle*, no. 1 (1992), pp. 125-140.

Almond, G. "Comparative Political Systems". *The Journal of Politics*, vol. 18 (August, 1956).

Angelusz, Róbert and Tardos, Róbert. "Választói részvétel Magyarországon 1990-1994" [Voter participation in Hungary 1990-1994]. *Politikatudományi Szemle*, no. 4 (1996).

Beyme, K. v. *Die parlamentarischen Regierungsysteme in Europa.* (München: Piper Verlag, 1970).

—————. *Politische parteien in westlichen Demokratien.* (München-Zürich, 1984).

Bihari, Mihály, ed. *A többpártrendszer kialakulása Magyarországon* [The development of the multi-party system in Hungary]. (Budapest: Kossuth, 1992).

—————. "Az állampárt végórái. Egy pártkonresszus szociológiája" [The final hours of a state party. The sociology of a party congress], in: Bihari, Mihály: *Demokratikus út a szabadsághoz.* (Budapest: Gondolat, 1990), pp. 81-89.

Bozóki, András. "Posztkommunista átmenet: politikai irányzatok Magyarországon" [Post-communist transition: political trends in Hungary], in: *Magyarország Politikai Évkönyve* (1989), pp. 96-111.

—————. "A magyar átmenet összehasonlító nézőpontból" [The Hungarian transition from a comparative perspective]. *Valóság*, no. 8 (1991), pp. 16-33.

—————. "Modernizációs ideológia és materialista politika: szocialisták szocializmus után" [The ideology of modernization and materialist politics: socialists after socialism]. *Századvég*, no. 3 (1996).

Bruszt, László. "Miért támogatnák a kapitalizmust a kelet-európaiak?" [Why should East Europeans support capitalism?]. *Politikatudományi Szemle*, no. 3 (1995).

Czakó, Ágnes and Sík, Endre. "A hálózati tőke a posztkommunista Magyarországon" [Network capital in post-communist Hungary]. *Mozgó Világ*, no. 6 (1994), pp. 17-21.

Czizmadia, Ervin. "Ismétlődő pártlogikák" [Recurrent party logics]. *Valóság*, no.7 (1991).

————. *A demokratikus ellenzék I-II-III.* [The democratic opposition I-II-III]. (Budapest: T-Twins, 1995).

Enyedi, Zsolt. "Az ésszerűen nem racionális párt" [The rationally irrational party]. *Politikatudományi Szemle,* no. 3 (1995).

————. "Tekintélyelvűség és politikai tagolódás" [The principle of authority and political articulation]. *Századvég,* no. 2 (1996).

Fábián, Zoltán. "Szavazói táborok és szavazói hűség" [Voters' camps and voters' loyalty]. *Századvég,* no. 1 (1996).

Fricz, Tamás. "Politikai tagoltság Magyarországon" [Political articulation in Hungary]. *Valóság,* no. 5 (1991).

————. "A pártszervezeti demokratizmus kérdéséhez" [The issue of democracy in party organisation]. *Politikatudományi Szemle,* no. 2 (1994).

Gazsó, Ferenc. "Az elitváltás Magyarországon" [The replacement of the elite in Hungary]. *Társadalmi Szemle,* no. 5 (1993).

Kitschelt, H. "Formation of Party-Cleavages in Post Communist Democracies: Theoretical Propositions". *Party Politics,* vol, 1, no. 4 (1995), pp. 447-472.

Kéri, László. "Illúziók, csalódások, várakozások. Politikai megjegyzések az elmúlt évről" [Illusions, disappointments, expectations. Political remarks about the past year]. *Társadalmi Szemle,* no. 5 (1991).

Körösényi, András. "Újjáéledő politikai tagoltság. Független és ellenzéki politikai áramlatok és szerveződések Magyarországon 1988-ban" [Political articulation renewed. Independent and opposition political trends and organizations in Hungary in 1988], in: *Magyarország Politikai Évkönyve* (1988).

————. *Pártok és pártrendszerek* [Parties and party systems]. (Budapest: Századvég, 1993).

————. "A magyar politikai gondolkodás főárama" [The mainstream of Hungarian political thinking]. *Századvég,* no. 3 (1996).

Klingemann, H. D. "Die Entstehung wettbewebsorientierter Parteiensysteme in Ost Europa", in: Zapf, W. and Dierkes, M., eds. *Instituionsvergleich und Institutionendynamik. W. Z. B.—Jahrbuch.* (Wissenschaftzentrum Berlin für Sozialforschung, 1994).

Lengyel, László. *A rendszerváltó elit tündöklése és bukása* [The rise and fall of the systemic change elite]. (Budapest: Helikon, 1996).

Márkus, György. "Pártok és törésvonalak" [Parties and cleavages]. *Társadalomtudományi Közlemények,* nos. 1-2 (1991).

O'Donnel, G. "Delegative Democracy". *Journal of Democracy,* no. 1 (1994), pp. 56-69.

Plasser, F. and Ulram, P. A. "Demokratikus konszolidáció Kelet-Közép-Európában" [Democratic consolidation in East-Central Europe]. *Politikatudományi Szemle*, no. 1 (1995).

Richter, Anna, ed. *Ellenzéki kerekasztal* [Opposition round table]. (Budapest: Ötlet Kft, 1990).

Róbert, Péter. "Pártok és választók" [Parties and voters]. *Politikatudományi Szemle*, no. 1 (1994).

Rokkan, S. "Die vergleichende Analyse der Staaten- und Nationenbildung: Modelle und Methoden", in: Wolfgang Zapf (hrsg.) *Theorien des Sozialen Wandels*. (Köln, Berlin, 1970), pp. 228-252.

Schlett, István. "A politikai tagoltság determinánsai Magyarországon" [The determinants of political articulation in Hungary], in: *Politikai kultúra és állam Magyarországon és Cseh-Szlovákiában*. (Torino: Giovanni Agnelli Foundation, 1990), pp. 66-79.

Schmitter, P. C. and Terry Lynn, Karl. "From an Iron Curtain to a Paper Curtain: Grounding Transitologists for Students of Post-Communism?" *Slavic Review*, no. 1. pp. 173-185.

Schöpflin, G. "Post-Communism: The Problems of Democratic construciton". *Daedalus* (Summer, 1994), pp. 127-141.

Stumpf, István. "Pártosodás és választások Magyarországon" [Party formation and elections in Hungary]. *Társadalomtudományi Közlemények*, nos. 1-2 (1991).

Szabó, Máté. "A szabadság rendje. Társadalmi mozgalmak, politikai tiltakozások, politikai szervezetek a magyarországi rendszerváltás folyamatában" [The order of freedom. Social movements, political protest, and political organizations in the process of systemic change in Hungary]. *Politikatudományi Szemle*, no. 4 (1995).

Szilágyi, Ákos. "Vox populi, vox dei". *Kritika*, no. 12 (1990).

Tóka, Gábor. "Parties and Electoral Choices in East Central Europe", in: Lewis, P. and Pridham, G., eds.: *Rooting Fragile Democracies*. (London: Routledge, 1996).

András Gergely

JÓZSEF ANTALL:
PRIME MINISTER OF THE CHANGE OF RÉGIME

Beginning in the 1970s, Western correspondents in Vienna had been passing a hint to each other: if they go to Budapest, there is a strange gentleman in the curator's office of the small Museum of the History of Medicine, who is not only studying the history of medicine but the history of the 19-20th century. What is more, he is studying politics, too. His expertise is up-to-date, and he is willing to share his opinion. He keeps a close watch on internal politics but does not identify himself with any of its legal trends. He seems to be out of current social space and time when he puts forth his opinion in the strange milieu of his room with half-closed window-curtains, among spirits, deformed skeletons and old medical instruments similar to torture tools. He himself talks like a fine precision instrument, veiled in discretion, in an old-fashioned manner uncharacteristic of his age, sparing no time. Yet his views are not those of an eccentric. On the contrary, Hungary—especially for a fresh inquirer—can only partially be understood without getting to know him personally and his opinion. In the 1980s diplomats accredited to Budapest also took the courage to visit the birthplace of Semmelweis, the Museum of the History of Medicine, to have a discussion with this gentleman competent in Hungarian and international politics, yet obviously keeping a distance from those, with visibly no desire to take an active role. This gentleman was József Antall.

József Antall came out of his study in the museum in 1988. Until then mostly only the historians and the intellectuals of his age group—and the competent comrades of the ministry of interior—

had noticed his person. The latter had not forgotten that József Antall decided in favor of this peculiar way of "submerging" following his activity in 1956. Though he continued to participate in scientific life, no one who knew him would have thought to ask him to write political articles in a daily paper or to participate in a late-evening TV discussion with intellectuals.

For József Antall—unlike many—did not think that the system could be reformed. Not that he identified the 1970s and 1980s with the 1950s and not because he did not know anyone honestly serving the system yet truly wanting to improve it. Rather because he thought that this was not his cause. Antall had rejected the whole of the system: he did not only want to repair the house but rather to pull down the patched and mended building, so he was just watching when the plastering tools would be put down and when the guards would leave, if that were to happen in his lifetime at all. That is why he could become the leading figure of the change of system: as an accurate observer he knew which cornerstones of the past needed to be preserved, when the work had to be started, and he had a plan for the new construction.

As was already mentioned, he actively rejoined political life in 1988. Following his father's trail, in the beginning he tried to find his place in the re-established Smallholders' Party, but eventually—taking notice that its mostly aged leaders were unsuitable and had a narrow base and political program—leaving that circle he became interested in the Hungarian Democratic Forum (MDF). He had nevertheless reservations also concerning the Forum (which was turning into an association in the fall of 1988), as he noticed the political naïveté of some of the initiators, the "Third Way" feature of their program (between socialism and capitalism), or more precisely, the conception regarding long-term cooperation with the ruling circles. He participated in but did not rise to speak at the 1988 Lakitelek conference, when the Forum was declared an association. Half a year later he appeared with a speech already suggesting a political program on the first national meeting of the Forum, in March, 1989. The speech written and read aloud did not receive a warm welcome; delegates used to striking slogans did not really understand the deeper thoughts of the treatise and they received with aversion his ideas concerning the necessity of becoming a political party. He therefore declined election to the leadership, and in fact in smaller circles he even asserted his reservations regarding the group.

A few days after the first national meeting of the Forum, as a result of the initiative of the Independent Lawyers' Forum, the Opposition Roundtable (ORT) was born. The ORT was a common coordinating organization of opposition parties, party-cells and social unions that was established to prepare the negotiations with the state power. June saw the start of the so-called trilateral talks between the ORT on one side, the MSZMP (Hungarian Socialist Worker's Party) on the other and various social organizations supposedly somewhere in-between. Then Sándor Csoóri and György Szabad, both members of the presidium of the Forum, made a common proposal: the MDF should involve József Antall in the negotiations as one of its leading personalities.

József Antall, first in political circles and later throughout the country, became well known during these negotiations. (He only rarely participated in those of the ORT itself.) His education in constitutional law, his ability in reaching compromises, his expertise in pondering power relations while considering foreign policy, made him a distinguished personality not only for his own political side but also in all the groups participating in the negotiating triangle. He had a significant, occasionally decisive role in the creation and acceptance of many concrete solutions in the field of constitutional law, sometimes also including negotiations behind the scenes.

That is how the "trilateral" agreements could be signed on September 18, 1989. A few weeks later, roughly at the same time when the last communist parliament accepted and enacted the agreement, József Antall was elected president of the MDF at its second national meeting.

As a president Antall turned his attention primarily to reorganization. By that time the majority had accepted (his election as party president also showed it) that the MDF must become a political party. He tried to create a real party out of the loosely structured, politically heterogeneous opposition organization, not hiding the goal that it was meant to be the political background of a government, a governing party. He slowly and gradually made it accepted that the MDF needed to adjust itself to European party structures. In this sphere two of the three theoretically possible directions were already taken: the renewed and still-popular social democracy, represented by the newly reformed MSZP (Hungarian Socialist Party) which arose amid the ruins of the MSZMP, and the SZDSZ (Alliance of Free Democrats) as the liberal alternative. The SZDSZ looked small at first but later became larger due to its militant anti-communist slogans. The MDF therefore could only fulfill the role of a center—right-center party, approximately in the same position in Western Europe of Christian-Democratic parties. The opposing or at least the very different currents of thought within the MDF—the populist tendency, anti-Bolshevism, the traditions of 1956, "Third Way", constitutional liberalism, Christian morality—could only be kept together on that platform. Antall also succeeded later in drawing nearer to each other the three political parties oriented in the same direction, which had been competing earlier and watching each other jealously: the MDF, the FKGP (Independent Smallholders' Party) and the KDNP (Christian Democratic People's Party).

One personality could very rarely intervene in the shaping of party relations in such a decisive manner during the history of Hungarian internal politics—perhaps only the role of István Bethlen after 1920 was similar. In addition, Antall exerted much effort in realizing a "Western-style" reshaping of the Hungarian domestic political scene. He organized and made the working group on foreign affairs of the MDF function (that was the only area personally directed by him), and thereby built a relationship with diplomatic missions in Hungary, foreign parties and press. The results of his activity are well shown by the fact that the party represented by him was the first one to be admitted to a European organization: the EDU (European Democrat Union).

Antall was an adherent of peaceful transformation, of gradual change. From the point of view of internal politics, building a constitutional state was a more secure approach—even if for that sake one had to give up spectacular actions demonstrating the change of the system, such as convoking a constitutional assembly. From the point of view of foreign politics, on the other hand, Antall was in favor of gradual transformation because he thought that the politics of the weakened Soviet Union was highly unpredictable, and so a transformation based on consensus offered less opportunity for external intervention. Besides, the MSZMP was still the most popular party of the country in the summer of 1989. A coup-like election would have meant a victory for the MSZMP at that time. That was the reason Antall also agreed to bring forth a series of laws that required a two-thirds majority with a change of the constitution: the opposition could only be sure to obtain more than one-third and so it was hoped the winning Socialists would have to make a compromise.

That was not the case. Elections in April 1990 brought a parliamentary victory of the former opposition and with that of the MDF.

The candidate for the position of prime minister, József Antall, had now two choices considering these laws that needed a majority of two-thirds to pass. He could either form a so-called "grand coalition" with the SZDSZ, the second strongest party of the election, or try to reach a compromise with this party to restrict the range of the "two-thirds laws" which at that time even included the budget. (The MDF/FKGP/KDNP coalition could obtain a two-thirds majority neither together with the MSZP nor with Fidesz, the sixth party that made it into parliament.)

Antall—even before his formal appointment—had to take his first, perhaps most difficult decision. There were more arguments against a grand coalition than for it. Most of his party was opposed (the presidium of the MDF endorsed the possible admission of FIDESZ into government, but the parliamentary faction of the party rejected even that). Besides, the Smallholders—having more a right-wing orientation in politics than a centrist one—could have hardly co-operated with the liberals for a longer period of time. The latter, at least on the level of ideas, had already begun their orientation towards the MSZP months earlier, in the so-called March Front. Apart from that, in Antall's view the more than 75 percent parliamentary majority of a possible wide coalition was excessive and dangerous for the development of the young Hungarian democracy. In that case only FIDESZ and the MSZP would have remained in opposition, while Antall judged—wrongly, it can now be said with the wisdom of hindsight—that the MSZP would hardly recover even for the next cycle.

In favor of narrowing the range of the "two-thirds" laws and signing a "pact" there was the fact that it seemed unlikely that the Socialists would regain their strength in the short term. With such a modification, normal democracy could take shape in Hungary at once, offering good opportunities in the future for the opposition as well. Thus, the coalition of the parties with a related system of values was enough for governing based on the principle of majority.

In reality though—and this became clear only later—Antall had not been in a position to decide. For the SZDSZ came up in its economic program with a plan that was not only irreconcilable with the views of the winning coalition, but was also highly harmful for the whole country. Therefore they excluded themselves from all coalition negotiations with a plan that could be qualified in the best case as dilettantism and high treason in the worst. Antall only spoke about this plan in his last TV interview: "Simplified, this would have meant that in a Hungary having a debt of more than twenty billion dollars, we turn Hungarian enterprises into stock companies and pay debts back by selling these stocks... It is easy to weigh the incalculable consequences that could have had... it would have meant the devaluation of the country, which would have been catastrophic. I must add that the initial program of the SZDSZ included that." Although the SZDSZ soon gave up this adventurous idea, the whole issue made many people insecure about their competence and political commitment, excluding their suitability for the coalition.

The only possibility consequently remained that of a "pact". Antall decided—and that was his own personal decision—that he would make a compromise with one of the political parties regarding the laws which must still obtain a two-thirds majority. Those partners were the Free Democrats. He also decided, again assuming personal responsibility, to negotiate on his own and relay the results to his party only afterwards. He was afraid that a detailed dispute of the whole negotiation process (on the level of the party committee or the parliamentary faction) would be conducted with little sense of compromise by the winning party of the elections, and in this well-intentioned but rather uninformed medium in the field of constitutional law, the whole thing would only lead to political crisis rather than any results. As a consequence, his popularity decreased for the first time within his own party—and also in the parties that did not participate in the pact—when he announced at the end that they either accept what he had negotiated or he would resign. Antall rightly emphasized that he didn't need to offer much in exchange, for the opposition had created by the deal the conditions for its own ability to govern, for its future government. (The two most important concessions were in fact that he gave the position of the President of the Republic to the SZDSZ and he leave the opposition media positions unchanged.)

For the functioning of the prime minister and the government, the firm 62 percent majority in parliament of the three coalition parties was enough, because there was another important element in the pact, a solution included due to the wise foresight of József Antall: namely, the legal institution of the so-called "constructive no confidence vote" which, unlike in the case of other countries that are transiting from communism to democracy, in Hungary has ever since made lasting governing possible.

What was the political aim of the prime minister? What did he try to obtain during his four years of activity (out of which fate would eventually grant him only three and a half?

His political opponents again and again emphasized that apart from his declared goals, József Antall had secret plans: that though he had been speechifying about creating democracy and rule of law, in reality he was up to reinstate the Horthyite system, meaning land given back to big landowners, factories to the upper middle class, fulfilling the political activities of Christian churches, introducing laws against the Jews, and in concordance with that, handing the country over to the Germans. These were the charges against him, although seldom were they formulated so tersely. True, even though the first serious biographer of Antall, Sándor Révész, though he barely hides his antipathy for him, dismisses it as pure fantasy.

Searching for explanations, let's first simply formulate what others had said: József Antall was a gentleman and a democrat.

We do not state that József Antall personified the one and only shape of a gentleman, but there was something in his nature, in his appearance and way of speaking that inspired the feeling that he was not "from among us". That was obviously also because he was a gentleman in an era when a whole series of generations had not met that kind of creature. It could be known about him that his gentlemanliness was rooted in the past, and in order to denigrate him his detractors identified him with a denigrated past. Antall—

whether this was his virtue or his fault—never aimed to produce the feeling, "I am one of you". His way of speaking went down well only in higher intellectual circles, his long sentences and complex trains of thought often tried the patience of his audiences, recalling unpleasant memories from school. Antall himself felt that his audience followed him with difficulty and to help he sometimes did not finish his longer sentences; he suppressed his further references with "and so on" or "as I have already said". If his audience was not present, as during his TV or radio speeches, then it was even more difficult for him to communicate. He did not therefore seek his presence in the media, but his less talented fellow politicians needed so many corrections and guidance that his appearances were regular until his illness took over. Furthermore, Antall took his role seriously: he did not use satire in his speeches. He had rather hid his humor and avoided patronizing gestures. That is why he was new and modern: he was the first truly democratic politician in decades. He seemed to be an old-fashioned gentleman because of the role he had assumed, and as such he could not be popular and successful. Antall was not willing to make concessions for the pseudo-democratic requirements shaped earlier for media appearance, not even if that meant a loss of popularity. Although we cannot say that he was an expressly unpopular politician, his successor in the following cycle began with higher popularity and became much more unpopular. Antall's popularity curve had also gone down a bit, but it never fell during his years as prime minister. It is interesting that in spite of the fact that he was an excellent conversationalist and demonstrated remarkable skill in political negotiations, as a speaker in front of an audience he did not give a very good performance.

At the same time, when considering the Antall image reflected by the media, we cannot disregard the strange, almost personal enmity the representatives of the Hungarian media have treated Antall with. One cannot decide clearly whether Antall had an aversion to the modern media or was rather disturbed by its virulent ani-

mosity. In any case, partially it was due to the media that the image
on the surface of this man—József Antall—showed a person considered to be the embodiment of the old world, and who wanted to
bring that time back.

Over and above the surface, the accusation had a deeper political reason which was indeed connected to Antall's appreciation of
the situation.

József Antall was aware that this country would be plundered.
He saw and could list the ever-growing number of laws since 1986
that pointed to the expropriating privatization done in favor of the
nomenklatura (the former party-state élite). He knew the corrupted
state apparatus and the moral decline of the country. The first document he studied after becoming prime minister was the list of
informers. Only his closest friends knew how the learned truth had
embittered the prime minister (and restricted him in his personnel
policy), even though he had been suspecting much (and not hoping
too much).

"In a transforming country the danger of corruption is very
high. People suddenly get close to very much money... this is
something that must be thought of when talking about the dangers
of Hungarian politics."—József Antall was trying to find remedies
for that, in order to prevent the general decay of the country.

As the task of privatization was urgent, he could not think of
creating institutional guarantees, of completely reshaping the structure of the state apparatus. He was willing to give in conceptually,
as long as he could hope for some sort of personal guarantees. As a
young man he had lived to see the catastrophe resulting of the 1944
dissolution of the Hungarian state and the coming to power of the
Arrow Cross (Hungarian Nazis). Striving to strike a balance, he
turned for moral support to the times before 1944: he hoped to
obtain some sort of guarantees from the mostly older people that
still preserved the traditions of the former Hungarian middle class
against the period of private property confiscation. (This was the

subject of one of his greatest speeches at the end of 1990, at the fourth national meeting of the MDF, which is unfortunately unpublished and therefore not known by many.) The old middle class—he declared in 1991—"succeeded to survive somehow. Although the communist régime tried to do everything to wear out its nerves and morality. Its spirit of taking initiative, love of work, ethics were kept suppressed but remained."

In his view—compared to former and later processes in the Balkans—the old Hungarian middle class did well before 1944, and the priority of the first plundering of the country in 1944 was to push that class out of power. He considered that age group worthy to turn back to. "We are indeed for continuity, for the continuity of values, and our opinion is that what had been forcefully done against the development of the nation, against organic development, the veins and roots that have been violently cut, must be replanted. For our political culture, our political heritage is indeed connected to the previous political culture", he said in one of his speeches. He was well aware that this middle class had been partially destroyed, partially broken in two; yet he felt that he had no other solution for the historic problem that had arisen. He trusted his own age group, his own circle and those younger people who had a family background that vouched for them. He did not believe in "new, fresh forces" because he had lived to see the moral decay of the Peasant Party, the Social Democratic Party and the Smallholders Party, organized mainly by new forces after 1945.

His undertaking could not be successful. In vain had he hoped that there was tradition and continuity, and that these could have saved the country from Balkanization. The past forty years produced morally intact individuals, but not whole strata of society. And the individuals could not immediately be organized into an élite. His undertaking was heroic and utopian because the moral was more often an appearance than reality, as it had not been tried by modern times and had no skills in politics, no schools to test its ability.

But his experiment was far from futile. He had struggled with dubious elements of his own party, with those veering towards the far right, with the political dilettantes, the daydreamers and the passionate. Nevertheless, in spite of some burdensome elements, this party succeeded in its own sometimes expert sometimes dillentantish way to prevent the plundering of the country for four years. True, this was sometimes achieved at a cost: slowing down privatization, a process that should have been speeded up. Names could be recalled that gave an inadequate political or professional performance; but if such a roll call is made it is easy to realize that not one of them became a millionaire. Yes, a representative of the governing party made absurd accusations and predicted as early as 1993 that the price of the bread would reach 100 Forints; but he did not pocket the food industry. Several of his ministers had made several mistakes but none of them have reared their children in crystal palaces.

The gist of Antall's social-political concept, to be built around the remains of crystallizing spots of the old middle class, was to separate the political and economic élites, i.e. to keep the political élite out of the financially promising process of "original capital accumulation." (This renouncing attitude of sacrifice was later given the name "conscience of calling.")

The prime minister could not accurately measure the social support for his view and the state of the society—he lacked the necessary measuring instruments for that. He relied instead on social continuity, undoubtedly wrongly. He compared in several of his speeches the 62 percent majority of the coalition in the parliament to the results in the 1945 elections of the Smallholders and other small middle class parties, and he believed he had discovered in that same proportion the proof of social continuity. In actual fact, the 1990 coalition did not have the 62 percent support of the people but rather only in parliament (42 percent was what it received from the voters). But even if we leave that correction out of consideration, it is apparent that the agrarian-industrial society of the mid-century had turned into an industrial-service type of society. Its schooling, customs of consumption, habits and most of all its values cannot be measured by those earlier decades. The moral demands of society and the requirements its politicians had to face did not reach a level that would have appreciated Antall's endeavors in that sense, either. A single example is enough to prove it: during the Prime Minister's medical care abroad, people were not preoccupied by what exactly the therapy consisted of, how painful or successful. The public was rather preoccupied by how much it cost, who paid for it, if social security paid it then why do they make an exception, etc. One cannot find a more spectacular example for the change of the way of thinking of society, the spreading of a grossly materialistic, non-humane spirit. And to assume to undertaking of value-based politics in this world—that was József Antall's real "kamikaze" flight.

Undoubtedly the most successful area of József Antall's time as prime minister was that of foreign policy. The departure of Soviet troops, the dissolution of the Warsaw Pact, the admission of the country into the Council of Europe, the recognition of the claim of integration into Euro-Atlantic organizations, the shaping of the regional cooperation of the Visegrád countries, the building of new diplomatic and economic connections abroad, drawing attention to the issue of Hungarian minorities in the neighboring countries, the formation of the six-party mechanism to harmonize views concerning foreign politics, making contacts with political parties abroad regular and support for non-governmental foreign policy were all known areas of this success. Yes, Antall was bothered by the fact that he was less known abroad than Walesa or Havel, but was compensated by having the greatest prestige of all the politicians of the area in circles of international politics.

The prime minister sometimes felt disappointed. We have already referred to the disappointment he felt in connection with the performance of his own circle, the politicians of the coalition. We must admit objectively that his personal choices and decisions had not always been fortunate; moreover, he often delayed their correction. Real disappointments in this respect reached him from the outside, though. One of these was the reluctance of the intelligentsia to assume public duties not directly connected to the party (neither to the old party, nor to the new ones). "Where previously were those pugnacious individuals, those really leading intellectual professionals who appraise so fastidiously some of our measures today, saying that this and that could have been done better?" The answer is undoubtedly that certain circles of the intellectual élite had bade their time, they were afraid of "going back to the bad old days", and later of the unfair attacks of the media in opposition. Lacking their supportive cooperation then, the government performed worse than would have been otherwise possible.

Another disappointment was the strong passivity of the state apparatus in the beginning, when it was still sure that József Antall would eventually have to call the MSZP into the government due to the difficulties he would to face. Although after 1991 the upper state apparatus had started to move at last, after 1993 it sank again into gradual passivity, already squinting at the approaching elections.

The three and a half years when József Antall was prime minister can be divided into three main periods. The first lasted for some six months, until the famous taxi-drivers' strike. This blockade clearly showed the government that the social discontent about which there had been much discussion before, was indeed undoubtedly present. The government was forced to change its politics and communication strategy.

The need for a change and the difficulties involved made József Antall aware of the inner insecurity of the MDF and of his own political background. Former opponents of the MDF becoming a political party wanted now to surround it with a democratic social movement which would follow social wishes as a driving force, eventually creating a governing party that would control the government from its center. Antall favored Western-type models, a party that puts the center of its activity into the parliamentary faction between two elections, and he managed to make the party weightless by his own weightless candidate appointed as a deputy. This step on the other hand meant he narrowed his base, as the activists did not find enough space to operate and began to drift along with the populist current within the party. (The history of the MDF as a party is not our topic at the moment.)

This period became known for the different opinions expressed by the coalition partners (eventually leading to the departure of the Smallholders Party), internal fights over economic policy-concepts, new difficulties caused by the situation of international economy, increasing social discontent generated by decreasing living-standards, the narrowing support of the electorate. These all led to a turn in the economic policy of the government in 1992, and the pace of privatization was slowed down. Seeing these worrying signs, the right thing would have been to accelerate this process so that a possible new, less anxious government should not have anything else to privatize. (The background and the real reasons of that process are little known.)

The third and last period is characterized by limited activity due to the grave illness of the prime minister. It is not possible to determine exactly the time when this final period started, in which the prime minister, not so much because of his disease but rather due to the repeated medical treatments, was hindered in his activity, the governing activity was partially paralyzed and partially—exactly as a result of all this—characterized by the personality of the appointed deputy, Péter Boross. Out of an understandable consideration this was seldom mentioned at that time, but we can state today that it had its role in slowing down the activity of the government and in the decrease of its social acceptance.

It would have been necessary, at the latest by the beginning of 1992, to reorganize the structure of the government in a way that would have introduced a deputy prime minister into the government and the office of the prime minister. But Antall would have interpreted all such initiatives as recognition of his defeat in the battle he was fighting with his disease.

Eventually, as we all know, he was defeated. The disease won. His heroic fight to establish a new Hungary only brought partial success. But the change of the régime was successful and with this József Antall has entered his name forever into the history of our country.

Zoltán Illés & Balázs Medgyesi

THE ROLE OF GREEN MOVEMENTS
IN THE CHANGE OF RÉGIME

Experience has taught us that the phenomenon of environment pollution has occurred in every social system. Expanding and increasing environmental problems infiltrate into the daily life of a society influencing not only the everyday life of people but the working and decision processes of the economy as well.

From the point of view of society, the importance of the environment is interpreted quite simply: the development and existence of a society, despite the technical achievements and the increasing separation from nature, has a strong connection with the environment and nature. On the other hand, this relation—presenting a certain level of dependency—does not occur with proper importance in the activity of society and economy.

One of the reasons for this is the lack of information of individuals and businesspersons. In the complicated system of environmental, social and economic relations even specialists can face difficulties in the evaluation of certain elements and their interaction. The decision-making majority that is inexperienced in the matter of environment protection is seldom familiar with the direct environmental reaction that acts upon the decision-maker himself, not to mention the social effects.

The other, probably even more important reason, is the separation of individual and social benefits and expenses. Despite the existing social rules and regulations the person harming the environment, similar to a "free rider", often volunteers to undertake all social expenses occurred as a consequence of his activity, even when his profit is dwarfed by the expenses caused to society. All this is only for obtaining the maximum profit.

Individuals and social groups that face the consequences of environmental damages feel that their "sore spots," their basic needs are jeopardized.

The history of environmental protection proves that social expectations regarding subsistence, healthy environment, the sustenance of human race and the assurance of similar opportunities to our descendants generate political pressure. The proportion of this is similar to the one represented by the lobbies having certain interest in environmental damage. However, nowadays in those areas where environmental interests are more transparent, a higher proportion of the society is "environmentally aware". Thus the political importance of environmental protection may exceed the power of the lobbies.

Let us not forget: political and social pressure in the area of environment and nature conservation is represented by green movements. The movement is quite different in many countries of the world. The grassroots groups work on basic democratic principles. The other important group in the movement is represented by those organizations which, by developing a larger, often international organization, attempt to balance the "negotiation power" and power position of well-organized sectoral lobbies and the centralized state administration. This is realized by the development of a network of smaller organizations merged by "umbrella organizations". The third and in many respects determinant group is formed by organizations specialized in a certain field conducting research on the boundary of politics and science and becoming more and more institutional. However, there are important overlaps among the above-mentioned categories.

According to the above-mentioned, the movements of the democratic countries manage to cover environmental issues very efficiently, not only in the sectoral but in the social respect as well, this ranging from the creation of political will, large-scale social control and research to public information.

The Socialist Context

Similar to the West, the environment of the former socialist countries was polluted due to incorrectly interpreted and short-term interests. In the 1970s and 1980s environmental problems grew to considerable proportions both in East and West, in many cases threatening the existence of the society.

However, there was an important difference between Western democracies and former socialist systems: the latter were characterized by the lack of the freedom of speech and of institutions of publicity. Up to the 1980s in the countries of the Eastern Bloc it was impossible to discuss environmental problems, not to mention publications or public debates on such issues.

In Western societies, especially in the beginning, the instrument of protest of those concerned toward those harming the environment (despite their possible pressure) was exactly the freedom of speech. They gained publicity in the media, and in the framework guaranteed by the constitution and the laws they were able to organize their groups and organizations which represented their interests. Local and national protests as well as conflicts with those that polluted the environment formed the representatives who defined the aim of their political activity the prevention and cease of pollution and environment destruction.

At the end of the 1970s and beginning of the 1980s, those in power declared firmly that there wasn't any environment pollution or destruction of nature: this phenomenon could occur in capitalist economies only. In consequence, those who spoke about pollution and environmental harm in Hungary were spreading Western enemy propaganda, were spreading alarming rumors and worrying people for no reason at all. A good example in this matter was the campaign started for the publication of the data regarding air pollution that was simply ignored by the authorities on the basis that it was only a false alarm.[1]

Police were often deployed to impede and make impossible the work of the "undesirable environmental organizations". They wanted environmental issues to remain unfamiliar even to such a small audience; they did not want green movements to gain strength and have an inner public support.[2]

Roots and Early Activity of the Hungarian Green Movements

No matter how consistent the information policy concealing environment problems of the old regime was, at the end of the 1970s a process of maturation began which by the beginning of the 1980s created the basis for the Hungarian green movements. In the beginning the preparations of the movement started in several independent directions and were based on the process of evolution. According to Dr. György Lajos, who played a basic role in the establishment and functioning of the movement, the independent Hungarian environment protection had three sources.

The first group (existing since 1945) was the independent religious community known as the Bokor Bázisközösség (Bokor Basic Community). Earlier they were famous especially for their religion-based disobedience: their members refused military service and assumed the grave legal consequences of that time. By the beginning of the 1980s the Bokor-movement became stronger and extended its activity to the area of environment protection and nature conservation.

The other group originates from peace movements. At the beginning of the 1980s they captured public attention with their impressive demonstrations for peace. In this movement the ideologies integrating pacifism, related with it or categorized as traditionally alternative ideas (including green, pacifist, human rights), were easily accepted and environmental protection gained increasing importance in their activity.

The third group included those scientists, researchers and students that during their work or travels abroad became acquainted with environmental problems and learned about those new trends which proposed to solve these problems. On the other hand, this third group was based on the spreading lifestyle-movement as well as on small progressive communities.

In the beginning the third group, influenced especially by Western environmental movements, was characterized not so much by organized group demonstrations but by the isolated actions of individuals. Thus the antecedents of the massive Bős-Nagymaros demonstration (September 12, 1988) can be traced back to the early 1980s, when an article by János Varga concerning the giant Bős-Nagymaros Barrage was published in the periodical *Valóság* in 1981.

The process of evolution that prepared the establishment of green groups had "grown ripe" by the middle of the 1980s, when the important groups of the movement appeared. They could be considered communities rather than organizations, as the regime did not tolerate any legally functioning group except for the ones initiated by party officials.

The first important green group playing a significant role later was the ELTE Természetvédelmi Klub (ELTE Nature Conservation Club) founded in June 1983, which recruited its members from the natural science department of the university. Among the pioneers was the Duna Tájvédelmi Egyesület (Danube Region Conservation Society) as well, founded after a debate in the Rakpart Club. This was the heart of the Duna-mozgalom (Danube-movement) that protested against the river barrage. The groups consisted of university researchers and students, although many outstanding members came from the peace movements.

From the mid-1970s several nature conservation groups were working in Hungary but they avoided political display. One of these was the Magyar Madártani Egyesület (Hungarian Ornithologist Society), which merged several member organizations.

The first wave of green groups appeared in 1985. In the spring of 1985, at the Days of University and High School Youth, representatives of green communities in higher education initiated a special discussion and consented to keep in touch regularly. Groups were formed in universities (Debrecen), agricultural universities (Gödöllő, Debrecen), at the Sopron Forestry University, in teachers' training colleges (Nyíregyháza, Szombathely, Szeged). The Zöld Klub, Zöld Kör (Green Club, Green Circle) started in the college of the Budapest Technical University and played an important role later.

From the very first moment of their establishment the organizations solidly supported the interests of environmental protection and nature conservation, often exceeding the framework created by the socialist state for the spontaneously organized groups.

The pioneers of environmental protection realized quickly the advantages of a network system, and they developed strong collaboration between different domestic groups and established relations with foreign movements.

In 1985 the ELTE Club, which had already joined the campaigning for signatures organized by the "Danubers", founded the Szigetköz work-group. In addition, together with the Czech, Slovak and Polish movements working more or less in the same conditions, they organized an Eastern European environmental protection network which later published the Greenway Newsletter. (Their center was moved to Bratislava later.) A result of the cooperation was that the "forest caravan" organized by Western European movements which was protesting against acid rains crossed the countries of Europe and ended in Hungary in June 1986.

The international reaction started to amplify as well: in October 1985 the Duna Kör (Danube Circle) (at that time they were known by this name) received the Proper Lifestyle Award established by J. Uexküll, the Swedish writer, an award as well-known as the alternative Nobel Prize.

Lectures, debates and individual publications played an essential part in the preparation and early period of the movement. The Interdiszciplináris Tudományos Diákkör (Scientific Interdisciplinary Student Circle) had organized different debates and lectures regarding environmental problems since 1981 and later accepted and integrated the basic principles formulated by the Bokor movement. The movements organized within the universities sympathized the slightly political, scientific, educational and attention-arousing activity, which was dealing with ecological problems. An important result of this activity was the constant increase in the number of professionals, this gaining fundamental importance later in the actions against party propaganda.

This contributed to the development of the social and intellectual support. Within the limits of the system, the solid motivation of ecologist intellectuals implied the increase of political interest and activity as well. No wonder that later, during the change of the political system, both professional politicians and the developing political elite "searched for resources" in green movements.

Except for violent attempts of suppression, the strengthening green groups did not obtain answers from the elite of the communist regime to their requests and presumptions reinforced by debates and regular exchange of opinion. Thus the main, and often the only available scene for the activity of the green groups was the street.

The *Duna-mozgalom* had an essential importance in street protests. Their first campaign for signatures against the construction of the Bős-Nagymaros barrage started in January 1984. This was followed by a number of smaller demonstrations in the next few years, which were not ample enough to familiarize the representatives of the regime with such manifestations of civil initiative. Even years later, on February 6, 1986, the police simply dispersed the walk organized by the Duna Kör in the Batthyány Square.[3]

Another kind of demonstrations were those campaigns which, beside their political aims, intended to amplify the environmental awareness of the public. An example of this was the Savas Eső Hét (Acid Rain Week) in Budapest (April 20-25, 1987), when conferences, lectures, walks, marches and meetings were vastly publicized in press and television. The organizers were the Zöld Kör (Green Circle) of the Budapest Technical University, the ELTE Természetvédelmi Klub (ELTE Nature Conservation Club), green groups from the Horticulture University and the Light Industry College as well as the Biológus Klub (Biologist Club) of the ELTE TTK.

The open attitude of the movement accelerated the influx of those interested in politics and rapidly "politicized" environmental protection. Slowly the movement became a nucleus for politicizing citizens. From the very beginning it disapproved firmly of activities that harmed or destroyed nature or the environment. In the absence of local groups and grassroots, these campaigns involved green groups from the capital and the larger cities. They used their professional skills and growing experience to confront the environmentally damaging activity conducted by giant state companies and the authorities, their activity being governed by directive rules and contrary interests. One of these was the Szársomlyó-affair[4] connected with the name of the ELTE Nature Conservation Club.

The "Expert" Régime

Ecologists exploited with growing efficiency the small possibilities for publicity, their presence and their activity became more obvious and their activity slowly became a matter of common knowledge. This process was enforced by various environmental problems such as air pollution, improperly handled dangerous waste and the growing evidence of nature destruction. This did not cease the hostile actions against ecologists, but the elite of the regime had to find new means to handle the phenomenon and to interpret it for the public opinion. A propaganda apparatus that previously barely focused on environmental issues, now started to function.

The communication strategy of the state party focused on the idea (long ago discredited by the West) according to which the representatives of green movements are not professionals, their statements prove the lack of information and lack of the power of discernment. Professionals could only be those who supported the official point of view, thus those in power positions were defining arbitrarily what "truth" meant and who it was represented by.

The success of this communication strategy proved to be quite ambiguous: environmental problems that occurred one after another made the affected people support those who pleaded for environmental issues. At the same time, it became obvious that the problems raised were not only real, but the existing social system was responsible for their appearance and development.

The "expert campaign" was further discredited because it slowly became obvious that the positions of ecologists were supported by real professionals. This was repeatedly proven, and the standpoint of professionals was supported by accurate documents. Their opinion was nevertheless completely neglected by the communist party hierarchy, which was controlling the science as well.

Attempts at "Inclusion"

The enforcement of environmental awareness occurred not only in limited professional, intellectual or political circles, but among larger masses as well. Due to their number and their nature ecologists posed no serious threat to the power elite, but their activity and the growing awareness of the population turned the strengthening groups into a political factor of increasing importance.

The tension was further increased as, after the revolution of 1956, the first group acting firmly against the regime and progressively increasing its social basis and publicity was founded by greens. In the 1980s being an ecologist in the Hungarian People's Republic was equivalent to belonging to the opposition.

The party elite realized that environment protection—which became an important political factor in the Western block—determines the boundaries of political power balance, receives increasing significance in the international policy of those countries which were important factors of world economy, and through the population, it was going to determine political power in internal affairs too. Therefore they used every effort to separate environment protection from the self-organizing green movements that opposed the regime, and tried to connect them to controlled, neutral organizations founded by the authorities.

The first such attempt—partly as a result of the movements organized within the universities—involved the KISZ (Communist Youth Alliance), a tested "political drill-ground" of the party. In 1984, by collaborating with the power-enforcement machine of the state, it was their mission to prevent the Duna-mozgalom from founding the Duna Tájvédelmi Egyesület (Association for the Protection of the Danube Region). In June 1984 the KISZ KB (Central Committee of the Communist Youth Alliance) held a three day conference on environmental issues in Kecskemét. They had two aims: to link environment protection and official structures in people's minds and to provide an "official framework" for green activity. In this conference the spontaneously formed green groups discussed the future of the independent movement in long evening informal sessions. As a consequence, taking into account the historical antecedents and the "supervision coming from above", they dropped the idea of integration and fusion.

As the national presidium of KISZ wanted to turn the development of the "green cause" to good use but could not subdue the already existing groups, they decided, as a counteraction, to create the Ifjúsági Környezetvédelmi Tanács, IKT (Youth Environment Protection Board). Founded by the Central Committee of KISZ, the "specialized organization" was designed to organize cooperation between environmental protection groups, control them and finance their programs. The IKT established relations with many groups but because of the circumstances and aspects of its creation and its attempts of neutralization the spontaneously formed groups could not accept it as a partner.

The presidium of the KISZ expected some other benefits from the puppet organization as well: through environment protection and nature conservation they hoped to refresh the empty and quite disgusted KISZ groups by offering them a useful activity.

Environmental Samizdat

In the press controlled by the Hungarian Socialist Workers Party independent movements found little space and the journalists which supported green movements were jeopardizing their existence if they wrote on the activity of green groups.

In October 1985 János Varga, representing the Duna-mozgalom received the alternative Nobel Prize. This was an event of national and international importance. However, if the *Sajtószemle* issued by the ELTE Club and the *ITDK-Levlap* (ITDK-Leaflet) had not reported on it, the Hungarian press would not have mentioned the event until 1989.

Since the founding of the ELTE Természetvédelmi Klub in 1983 the *Sajtószemle*, today called *Gaia Sajtószemle* had been reporting on the activity of domestic and international movements, new achievements of environment sciences and different tendencies of green philosophy. Owing to its comprehensive view, its information and news, it became an important forum and the "great generation" of the alternative green movement "grew up" on its issues printed on a stencil duplicator.

Many groups linked to institutions of higher education were publishing leaflets on a regular basis. Beside the above mentioned *ITDK Levlap* and *Természetvédelem* there were others too: the *Kari Papír* (Faculty Paper) issued by the Faculty of Architecture of the Budapest Technical University, the *Kék bolygó* (Blue planet), a publication of the BME Zöld Klub (Green Club of the Technical University), the extras of the Sopron University (later published under the name *A Helyzet,* [The Situation]), the *Túlélés* (Survival) issued in 1988-89 and a number of other publications. A similar source of information was the booklet of the Biokultúra Klub (Bioculture Club).

Similar to the illegal publications of the Bokor movement which were available only for a limited number of people, the *Newsletter* of the Duna Kör and the *Watermark*, papers of the Duna-mozgalom, were also known as samizdats.

The Movement's Political Début

The growing movement, the increasing number of members interested in politics and the immunity of the MSZMP (Hungarian Socialist Labor Party), the only representative of the official policy, compelled the alternative green groups to use political instruments.

As a consequence, certain members of the green movement dared to investigate the possibility of enforcing the "legal achievements of the people's democracy". In the nomination meetings preceding the parliamentary elections of 1985, some of the representatives of the Duna-mozgalom wanted to participate as independent candidates, but this was firmly opposed by the MSZMP and the popular front, which prevented any kind of application. The old regime could not accept the political institutionalization of any green movement. And this was valid not only for parliamentary membership but for green groups working in organized conditions as well. The first wave of green organizations established within institutions of higher education made the party elite realize the political opportunities of the expanding organizations included into a strong network. Thanks to that, in the summer of 1986 the Political Committee of the MSZMP stood up against the founding of green organizations. This could not hinder the communication between different groups that was based on personal relations, their attitude managed only to prevent open national displays.

The strengthening movement could work only in non-institutional circumstances, isolated from publicity. For the same reason the idea of infiltration into various institutions had occurred, the movements wanted to enter the political scene (in a different context) and fight using political means. In the summer of 1987 a report regarding the situation of the environment in Hungary submitted by the OKTH, Országos Környezet- és Természetvédelmi Hivatal (National Office for Environment Protection and Nature Conservation) was discussed by the parliament. The representatives of the movement became indignant as the report submitted by the secretary of state concealed the real situation. They wrote letters to certain MPs that seemed willing to discuss the items of the agenda and asked them not to accept the OKTH report. (They enclosed detailed professional explanation.) Although a number of MPs promised to refuse the report, the result proved again the mode of operation of the communist state mechanism. The report was agreed unanimously, with one abstention only.

The Second Wave

In 1987-88 the ecological activity labeled as oppositionist behavior increased visibly. Similar to the first wave, the second wave was also linked to a process of maturation: the heart of the movement won its way from underground movement to half-illegality, from anonymity to growing recognition. The political opposition became stronger as well. The ideas formulated by the green movement reached more and more people, they "ripened" in the minds of the socially active people and mobilized them.

At the beginning of the wave it was obvious that the number of the followers of the Duna-mozgalom grew continuously and the number of groups protesting against the barrage increased too. The "Blues" (A Kékek) announced their appearance, the Bajcsy-Zsilinszky Társaság (Bajcsy-Zsilinszky Society) founded its Környezetvédelmi Csoport (Environment Protection Group) and many other individual green activists fought against the "Danubesausur" too. In order to correlate their activity, the movements and the new political forces realized the necessity of collaboration, therefore they created the Nagymaros committee, which organized many actions but also became the scene of hard internal discussions and fights. Because of the internal problems even the Duna Kör itself changed several times, many people retired and new members continued their activity. In the summer of 1989 even János Varga himself left the circle. László Sólyom, one of the founders of the movement, characterized briefly the odd reason for the internal problems: "The Duna Kör is neither a legal nor illegal organization." The activity of the circle was neither prohibited nor allowed, although the authorities tried to hinder its creation several times.

The Duna-mozgalom was not the only expanding group and many towns enriched the national green movement with vigorous organizations. Beside the Holocén groups of Miskolc created in 1987-88, many other groups were founded on local and county levels too. Among the first we shall mention the Reflex Környezetvédelmi Egyesület (Reflex Environment Protection Society) from Győr, its successful actions made it famous both in the country and abroad. Active green groups were founded in Nyíregyháza or Mosonmagyaróvár and in many other towns as well.

In Opposition

The second wave of the development of oppositionist green groups coincided with the public appearance of the political opposition. The separation of "political" and "environmental" opposition would be artificial and illusive, both considering the aim or the activity of the individuals from a group. There are several reasons for this.

The green movement managed to gather those people who were politically active. Thus it was almost natural that many important representatives of the opposition came from the alternative movements. The Duna-mozgalom was "represented" by important characters of the moderate organizations which later became rather famous. The "Danubers" can be found both among the advisors of the SZDSZ (originating from the Free Initiative Network) and the founders and former governmental advisors of the MDF. FIDESZ was not only "subsisting upon" the Duna-mozgalom but participated in every important Danubesaurus event as main or co-organizer. Owing to its relations with the colleges and the age of its sympathizers, it was strongly bound with green movements from the universities. Its Környezetvédelmi csoport (Environment Protection Group) founded in 1988 was practically born from a group of the ELTE TK.

The goals of environmental protection and those of the embryonic opposition were quite similar, not only because of the same roots and individual overlaps but also because forty years of experience proved that it is just as hard to imagine democracy without environmental protection as to guarantee environmental protection in the absence of democracy. Ecologists working for oppositionist organizations did not abandon the green movements, they participated in green activity as individuals or representatives of their organizations. It was also natural that oppositionist organizations reserved an important place for environmental protection issues among their goals and, some years later, in their political platforms too.

After the passing of the unification bill the oppositionist organizations gained more self-confidence, clarified their oppositionist status, the style of their activity and practically started to function as parties in a country that formally still had a one-party regime. The traditional framework for party activity (well known in any Western democracy) did not exist in Hungary; these organizations continued to use those civil techniques which were characteristic for green movements and civil grassroots initiatives. The traditions of the green movement were respected both in topic and form. A large amount of the green mass meetings were linked with these organizations, for example, the series of protests against the storage of the radioactive waste from the Paks nuclear power-plant in the neighborhood of Ófalu (the MDF played an important part in this action), the protest of women against the Nagymaros barrage organized by the FIDESZ, the barricade built on the Mártírok útja as a protest against the consistently neglected problem of air pollution.

Endgame

Beginning with the summer of 1988, the greens had been an impressive success and had gained determinant importance in the change of the communist system. Working in full force, the movement became a true accelerator of the change. The accelerator role was not only a result of the political maturation of the movement. Slogans asking for a change of regime occurred first in green demonstrations, and the Nagymaros protests were powerful enough to convince the hesitant and skeptic that the change of regime is possible.

A real chain of demonstrations started against the Danubesaurus. In May 27, 1988 three to five thousand people participated at the demonstration organized by the Duna-mozgalom and the Zöld Csoport (Green Group) of the Bajcsy-Zsilinszky Társaság. By the autumn of 1988 the Duna-mozgalom had become so "accepted" that on the first day of their conference they could use the chambers of the Academy.

From September the Duna protests became weekly events. On September 12, 1988 about 30-50 thousand people were demonstrating against the barrage in front of the Parliament. The women's demonstration on September 17 counted four hundred people; this was followed on October 3 by a living chain on two bridges and both sides of the Danube in Budapest, and October 30 was the day of the famous torchlight procession. The 30,000 participants of the procession were asking not only for a referendum regarding the barrage but for free elections as well. This was followed by another campaign for signatures, and as a result 150 protesting signatures were submitted to parliament in February 1989. On April 13, 1989 several thousand people were protesting in Nagymaros along the fence of the construction area. Finally Miklós Németh, the prime minister of that time, suspended the building process of the Nagymaros barrage. Thus the greens overcame the political power of the party, the teenaged David defeated the shrewd, experienced and well-nourished Goliath. Despite every effort of the discredited regime, what in 1983 was potential threat by 1989 became historical fact. As the Danubesaurus, the megalomaniac socialist investment symbolizing the regime itself, the abolishment of the construction process symbolized its collapse.

In spite of the famous speech made by Károly Grósz in November 1988, the year of 1989 bore the mark of the approaching change of rule. Green movements started to spring up like mushrooms. The activity of the "pioneers" was characterized by three trends: they continued the campaigns that strengthened environmental awareness, the preparations for functioning in a multi-party democratic system and approached the organizations that gradually took the role of a political party. Characteristic to the period, the latter had the strongest influence. This is illustrated by the support given to the green movements by oppositionist political movements and by the realization of the fact that democracy is essential for effective environment protection. By the elections the parties which later were admitted into the Parliament (except perhaps for the Smallholders Party) had already found the support in the green movement on which they could base their green activity later. Besides the connections named above, we must mention the links between the BZSBT ecologists and those of the MDF, as well as the connections between the greens of the Keresztény Értelmiségiek Szövetsége (Society of Christian Intellectuals) and the KDNP. Obviously, the new parties developed more or less strong relations with many other organizations as well.

The MSZMP was very reluctant and did not reduce to ashes its own political realm and, in the terms of possibilities, made long-term attempts to consolidate its economic and social power. The political component of this activity meant not only the establishment of the MSZP (Hungarian Socialist Party) and the democratic social-democrat self-definition: they did not renounce any group, they attempted to "employ the energy" of the green movement. The KISZ KB tried to accomplish two further integration attempts: in 1988 they founded the Ifjúsági Környezetvédelmi Szövetség (Young Ecologist Society) that merged more green groups, later the MME (Hungarian Ornithologist Alliance) started its activity, then they established the MTVSZ (Hungarian Ecologist Society) which joined more regional organizations. Assessments of the role of the latter opinions differ, with certain sources claiming that the reason for its separation was the centralizing tendency of the IKT and others saying that the IKT was no longer "accepted" and therefore needed a new umbrella-organization attractive for the alternative movements. Although the MTVSZ became stronger through the MME and had a significant number of members, the oppositionist green groups continued to remain distant.

Independent from the "generalist" political forces, the green movements continued their activity. In March 1989 several "old warriors" of the Duna-mozgalom started the Kék Lista (Blue List) which, during its brief existence enriched the green movement with many initiatives (Ecoservice, support for the Fidesz-academy, workgroups for settlement policy).

The Independent Green Party

As a consequence of the general character of the parties and the successes of the West German greens, many ecologists considered that an independent green party should be finally created. In the summer of 1989 some members of the Duna Kör and the Magyar Természetvédők Szövetsége (Hungarian Ecologist Society) initiated the discussions aiming at the establishment of the Magyarországi Zöld Párt (Hungarian Green Party). Many of the old members of the movement participated at the first few sessions, and they suggested the creation of a loose elective organization. Those who wanted to found a party gained the upper hand and created the Hungarian Green Party that included only a small part of the green movement. The founding of this party was "experimental", its creators hoped that the common goal of environmental protection would reconcile the divergences between the alternative movements and the KISZ-protected MTVSZ. We will never find out what the results (in optimal conditions) would have been, even if now, from the distance of ten years, it is quite obvious. However, the conditions were far from being optimal. The Hungarian Green Party was at least a year late. By the time of its creation the activity of the Oppositionist Roundtable[5] was practically over, the parties which later got into parliament had already accomplished not only their self-definition but their regional structure and representative system as well. They managed to "set" successfully the ecologists and the social groups linked with these. On the other hand, the

MDF and Fidesz had recognition of over 60 percent in Budapest while eight months later the Green Party entered the elections as a practically unknown formation. The inner tensions, non-elucidated issues and the strained competition made the situation only worse. It is not surprising that in the general elections of 1990 no representative of the Green Party managed to get into parliament. The results of the election, synchronized with the political processes, mirrored the Western trends: environment protection was included in the activity of the traditional political parties.

After the Fall

After these long-desired changes, the Hungarian movements could work in the same formal framework as their Western colleagues. The success and social support of the campaign against the BNV, the "movement cells" which continued to spread quickly even after the change and the journalists sympathizing with green movements predicted a bright future for the movement. However, the new situation meant an important challenge for the movement: it had to find its place and function in the new, developing democracy and, besides the traditional division, it had to face the division lines between the new political parties, the government and the opposition. The movement that originated mostly from the same source suddenly found itself both in the new government and in the opposition. The half-legal green groups were suddenly turned into social instruments.

The movement could finally fulfill those functions which are traditionally linked with an independent social green organization: to arouse the attention, to increase environmental awareness and social control. Owing to the special situation following the change of the system, the movements had one more important role: to keep the initial base and form such a professional background which can be used efficiently in civil social activities and as "political assistance" as well. As the many newborn green organizations were successfully fulfilling the role of the grassroots, the former generalist groups (except for the Duna-mozgalom) had the opportunity to become specialized. A frequent phenomenon was the creation of specialized umbrella-organizations beside the already existing groups; thus the Hulladék Munkaszövetség (Waste Workgroup) functioned beside the Reflex, the ELTE TK members founded the Energia Klub (Energy Club), the Levegő Munkacsoport (Air Workgroup) joined several organizations and concentrated on air pollution problems. An important feature of the latter is that it later managed to gather the ecologists of the parties represented in parliament which were still in connection with green activity. In the case of certain groups specialization occurs not only as a sectoral activity but as regional function too.

Specialization is strongly connected with the process of professionalization. In this period not only the university workshops had to gain modern professional knowledge but every group which was interested in public policy. A significant help in this process was offered by the cooperation between the different scientific workshops, the favor of certain professionals working in different fields of the ecology and the huge and systematic amount of information provided by foreign social organizations.

Social environmental awareness mirrors the activity of the movement. At this time the relation of society and the environment was less influenced by shocking new environmental problems. The protection of the environment and nature became a general expectation which implied not only the most important needs (a healthy life) of people, but democracy too. Great masses of people began to realize the importance of environmental problems and the real or presumed conflicts of interest between environmental protection and economic development were emphasized. However, we must not forget that after the change, civil activity decreased quickly and influenced the mobilizing power of green movements. Green groups became more diversified and environmental problems were treated very seriously, therefore the decrease in social activity and mobilizing power has not been caused by the diminution of environmental awareness.

New Directions

As a consequence of the professionalization of movements, regularly paid personnel began to appear where previously there were only volunteers. This is partly the result of specialization. Time forced many ecologists to decide: they either continue to work and earn their living or choose environmental protection. Many of them combined these two aspects and linked their existence with the newborn nonprofit sector. Still, everything has a price: nowadays being existentially linked to the Hungarian nonprofit sector implies political dependency. "Fundraising" became a keyword in Hungarian environment protection, its importance began to precede environment protection and reverse the role of instrument and goal. The main financial source of the movement is the central funds redistribution system practiced exactly by those social authorities which should be controlled by environmental protection groups. While during the change of system only a few groups had real administration (especially the larger ones which were not in conflict with the regime), after the change many groups had to face the difficulties of providing regular funds for their administration.

Owing to this, the concentration of social organs and the development of their representative system was not only a political but an existential question as well. The efforts regarding the creation of an organization which can gather, coordinate and represent the movement intensified especially among those groups which were specialized in fundraising and employed more people. This idea was brought up repeatedly in the exchange of opinions of the yearly national meetings. According to the opinion of the alternative groups, such concentration was unfamiliar with the spirit of the movement, so for several years they tried to stop at any means the creation of a supervising organization. However, the alternative movements only slowed the process; they could not stop it. Later the representative system was legally formalized by new legal measures. Thus, through the Országos Környezetvédelmi Tanács (National Council of Environment Protection), the representative ecologists could receive official decision-making and distribution licenses.

Thus, while preparing their actions and positions, the representatives of the movement consider not only the character of the environment problems, but certain groups of the movement support the goals of the ministry.

Notes

1. It happened again at the middle of the eighties when the green move-
    ments from Budapest asked the data on air pollution measurements
    to be published and to place indicators in different places of the city
    which could inform citizens on the quantity of pollution, in compar-
    ison with the allowed limits. Authorities refused such requests on the
    reason that people should not be worried.
2. The representatives of power were trying to hush up the struggle
    against the destruction of the natural reservation (*természetvédelmi
    terület*) of the Szársomlyó Mountain. Thus could happen that in
    November 1984 because of the repeated pesters by police and other
    authorities the ELTE Nature Conservation Club could not organize
    the Szársomlyó-meeting in Pécs.
3. As in August 1985 the government agreed again upon the construc-
    tion of the barrage, in January 1986 twenty-two German, Austrian
    and Hungarian ecologists signed the Budapesti Nyilatkozat
    (Budapest Declaration) in the Zöld Fa (Green Tree) restaurant and
    announced a walk on the bank of the Danube on February 8. In the
    Batthyány square, the starting point of the meeting the police mal-
    treated and dispersed the participants roughly. After this incident
    police officers often confiscated Duna-badges from students or
    young people.
4. In autumn 1984 the ELTE Nature Conservation Club began its strug-
    gle against the destruction of the Szársomlyó Mountain threatened
    by the extension of mining in the area. Only in January 1988 took
    place the press conference in which the leader of the Országos
    Természetvédelmi Hivatal (National Office for Conservation of
    Nature) and the representatives of the ELTE Club declared that the
    mine shall not be extended to the reservation.
5. Under political opposition we understand the organizations that par-
    ticipated in the activity of the EKA and later became parties. Not all
    such organizations declared themselves oppositionist or alternative
    and we disregard the actual organizations and those being trans-
    formed.

Frigyes Kahler

MORAL AND LEGAL JUSTICE

Why do Justice?

After decades of communist dictatorship, Hungarian society began the reconstruction of its democratic institutions. The then embryonic state had to face up to the politically-motivated moral, legal and material damage to Hungary's citizens inflicted by the previous regime. The situation was exacerbated by dictatorships prior to the communist take-over: especially the German invasion (19 March, 1944), which cancelled out Hungary's sovereignty. The ensuing ultra right-wing regime of the Arrow Cross-forces, backed by the German invaders, also inflicted considerable damage on the lives, freedom and material goods of the citizens.

Prior to the transition, the last parliament of the *ancien regime* began an unfinished and rather complex process that was designed to provide some degree of moral, legal and—to an extent—material justice to those who had been affected. The first freely-elected parliament of the Third Hungarian Republic vowed to undertake the task (judged impossible by many) of passing laws to serve as a basis for historical justice and reconciliation.

If a survey had been carried out on the vocabulary of the period between 1991 and 1994, the phrase "doing justice" is likely to rank very high. Historians, lawyers and politicians used this phrase, as did the millions of victims and the smaller, yet more vocal, group of perpetrators. The latter group, of course, looked on it as a "witch hunt."

Surveys revealed that the majority of society advocated some kind of justice be done; however, it was not so simple to decide what that justice should entail. The debate even split experts. The focus of justice at one point meant the *liability* of the people who caused the damage. The passionate debates between advocates and opponents restricted the scope of the solution to cover only a part of the issue, though: that of liability in court.

By "justice" it should be meant, I believe, a process whereby the new legal state will, on the one hand, seek to remedy the injustices of the dictatorships of the past half century; and on the other hand, will also demolish the structure of an oppressive dictatorship and its discriminative system. From this, it follows that, first and foremost, justice will mean the compensation of victims legally, morally and, to a degree, materially; secondly, it means the liability of the living perpetrators of the crimes; and thirdly, it will also mean the unearthing of the history of the Bolshevik-style dictatorship, its theoretical critique and the destruction of its institutions. Finally, justice should mean the re-establishment of democratic institutions. Throughout this process the partial remedy of the damages done by the consequences of the Bolshevik dictatorship will be of utmost importance. Due to the specific historical conditions it was also inevitable, however, to tackle the question of compensation for the crimes committed during the ultra right-wing dictatorship that preceded the Bolshevik era. This meant it was necessary to revisit the injustices caused by the Jewish laws and regulations passed before the Second World War[1] since the post-war compensation efforts were hindered by the Stalinist dictatorship.

Without citing the compensation laws[2] here we, nonetheless, must refer to the most important compensation principle, that of *ex gratia,* which the Constitutional Court recognises as the very foundation of the compensation process. It guarantees that, in addition to the victims of the injustices done during the Bolshevik era, compensation will also be granted for the violation of property rights, loss of property, and right to freedom or life for political reasons. The 1992/XXXII statute clearly guarantees that the legal state interprets the discriminations of the different dictatorships as no different and equally unlawful.

The ink on the discriminatory legal documents of the short-lived Nazi dictatorship had hardly dried when a new camouflage of social progress marked the beginning of the process meant to "behead," then annihilate Hungarian civic society. Throughout this period, the framework of ownership was radically changed (through nationalisation), the annihilation of the rural food producer class took place (forced cooperative-ization), and the Hungarian legal system and administration were re-structured. The Hungarian intellectual class was muted: from the primary schools all the way to the Hungarian Academy of Sciences, the exchange of ideas was standardised. In sum, the foundations of a "Soviet World" were being laid down. The big powers at Yalta passed Hungary into the hands of the Soviet Union. The establishment of the Temporary National Assembly and the Temporary National Government and the attempt to start a civic life were all part of reconciliation. In the first, military phase of this process, the new rulers began the annihilation[3] of the potential enemies of the future communist state by way of holding war criminals accountable in court. From the very first moment of its invasion of Hungary the Soviet government monitored and instrumentally controlled the silencing of the intellectual and non-communist political leaders of the civic society. They oversaw the destruction of civic society and the annihilation of all real or imagined opposition within the Hungarian power elite. The Ministry of Justice, responsible for the fabricated show trials, was headed by Stalinist "consultants" N. Ritshkov and J. Kolianov. With similar Soviet help, the political police was set up. Within the political police, the State Defence Department (ÁVÓ) began operation on December 10, 1946 (to be re-named the Interior Ministry's State Defence Authority on 6 September 1948). This, then, became the independent State Defence Authority (ÁVH) in 1949 headed by deputy general F. Belkin and operating with 2,500 inspectors, 7,000 officers and 40,000 informants. (The informants were still employed under the supervision of the Interior Ministry's III/III

Office until the collapse of the dictatorship.) After the establishment of ÁVH, the Hungarian Communist Party (MKP) and Mátyás
Rákosi had a special military arm.[4] The new ruling class passed a
whole series of amoral laws that laid the foundations for the creation of a most shameless dictatorship which deprived Hungarians
of basic human rights.[5]

The onslaught against the church[6] and the offensive to dissolve all civic organizations[7] requires an independent inquiry. This
was orchestrated to go hand in hand with a great deal of violence,
Soviet-style fabricated show trials and mass trials affecting hundreds of thousands of people.[8] The government, in fact, waged war
against the population. Thus, the monolithic power not only
crushed the fine structure of Hungarian society and halted its organic development while keeping the country in war psychosis, it did
more: Hungarian history itself was criminalized.[9]

By 1949, also known as "the year of the turn," Hungarian society, according to Zhdanov's classification, was divided into two
segments: the leaders of the party state and their disciples—the new
class—and "the non-communists." In Hungarian Communist
leader Révai's words, the latter were "reactionaries," which meant
an enemy to be annihilated.

In criminal as in civil law, the common root of the damage is
due to this Bolshevik class discrimination.

After the first chapter of the Communist dictatorship, which
led to the 1956 Revolution, another series of moral and legal violations ensued in the form of reprisals, either outside the legal framework or with the help of the law. The post-revolution retaliation[10]
resulted in the execution of approximately 400 people, the imprisonment of about 21,000 people and others interned,[11] the victims of
the December retaliatory shootings[12] as well as the murder victims
of the ÁVH officers.[13] Without investigating the activities of the
military police set up after the 1956 Revolution, those of the
Interior Ministry's Political Department (and their subdivisions in

every county), the no-trial judgements, the operations of the people's judiciary committees and the other retaliatory machinery established by the Hungarian Socialist Workers' Party (MSZMP), my conclusion is that, although the authorities resorted less and less to fabricated false trials than before the revolution, there was just as much class discrimination, inequalities and violation of basic human rights as before. With regards to the treatment of politically motivated damage and its compensation, the time period up to the passing of the 1993/4 statute is a separate area of law.

The focal point of the violations committed between 1945 and 1957 is the murders (mass murder) and aggression committed by the authorities. The bloody secrets of our recent past had been kept untold until the transition, and at the beginning of the 1990s, still only few of these secrets were revealed. To compensate the victims morally as much as materially the following classification was devised:

I. From 1944 to the 1956 Revolution: murder of individuals (e.g. the series of murders in Gyömrő, the Lakos murder, murder of priests); ÁVH operations where guns were used against unarmed groups of people (e.g. the unarmed people of Beszterce when they tried to protect their priest in 1949).

II. Between 1956 and 1967: shootings, which are further classified into three subcategories:

First, mostly ÁVH incidents (including the border guards also known as "green ÁVÓ") before November 4, 1956 when unauthorised random shootings were official violations. These shootings took many lives in Debrecen, Mosonmagyaróvár, in different parts of Budapest (the best known incident took place in Parliament Square), Győr, Miskolc, Esztergom, Beszterce, Tiszakécske, Kecskemét, Ózd.

Second, during the Soviet intervention from November 4 to December 6, 1956 shootings by the Soviet squads (again, the crowd they shot at was unarmed) in Szombathely, Sárbogárd and in different locations of Budapest.

Third, the shootings by the re-organised officers (the so-called "pufajkások") in Budapest (Nyugati Railway Station), Tatabánya, Salgótarján, Eger.

The murders committed by the officers constitute a separate category e.g. the murder of the Salgótarján revolutionaries, whose bodies were fished out of the river Ipoly, or the murder of peasants beaten to death after they quit the co-operative in Hajdú-Bihar County.

III. Between 1963 and 1989, when the number of people tried for political reasons decreased considerably.[14] After 1963, the dictatorship became "softer," consequently the *methods* of asserting power changed, too. Legal punishment was less often used. Class discrimination, which was still the foundation of the system, did not change. In the meantime, the Kádár regime ratified documents of universal human rights like the International Agreement on Civic and Political Rights.[15] In practice, however, the soft dictatorship continued violating the domestically ratified, but actually unrecognised rights of those who were in conflict with government interests.

Violations of private law (property rights) spanned from 1945 all the way to 1987 (!) and occurred in all areas of the economy.[16] These violations were also addressed as part of the compensation scheme.

In the areas of labour law and social security law, a great number of steps was taken especially with regards to public service to compensate for loss of pension and time spent in forced labor.[17]

One of the essential characteristics of the war waged against civic society was that it monopolised the intellectual and cultural life of the country. The nationalisation of the schools (1948/XXXVI statute), the strict supervision of university education, the destruction of university autonomy, research and lecturers' freedom all transpired under the aegis of class discrimination.

Compared to these violations, others appear almost marginal, and they are very difficult to handle within the framework of the law. The other violations include harassment of religious people, restriction of travel, freedom of speech, freedom of press, right to gather and organise, etc.

Justice for the Victims

Is it possible to compensate for irreparable injustices that go back to more than half a century and affect two or three generations? What could be the philosophy of justice? What will be the common denominator that society will accept and through which it will be able to understand the historical mistake it was forced to endure? And what is the purpose of justice at the beginning of the 1990s?

This last question will determine the answers to the rest of the questions. Justice must serve one purpose: reconciliation. It must serve reconciliation and not vengeance. Reconciliation will turn suffering into the strength of the soul to eventually manifest itself as the energy of the future. Only a part of the violations and suffering could be accounted for through compensation. In the case of the rest of the violations and suffering, politics, morals and the law intertwine. The legal consequences of fabricated show trials had been over long before the nullity laws were passed. The victims were cleared of the disadvantageous consequences of their criminal record; nonetheless, morals and the conscience of society demanded that this should be guaranteed by the law. The legal procedures against them were never lawful.

There are aspects of justice that will never be realised as legal formula, not even partly. These are purely a matter of morals. In this respect, although a considerable part of society is affected, we are lagging compared to other similar-sized countries like Austria. This is the consequence of losing our way in history.

Let's return to the part of justice that is a matter of the law. Fair play and the betterment of the lives of the victims demand that these people should be able to live their life the way they did before the violations. This is the principle of, in the terminology of Roman law, *in integrum restitutio*. The question arises if this is possible. In Roman law, *in integrum restitution* i.e. the restitution of the conditions prior to the violation, is only possible if "the restitution of the original conditions prior to the violation does not pose a greater disadvantage than during the violation." This formula, unfortunately, is not applicable, however attractive and just an option it appears. On the one hand, the violation is not an act; on the other hand, the violator does not benefit from or take advantage of the act. We inherited the task of restitution for state-orchestrated violations of a half century. In this time-frame, criminal sentences affected a number of lives throughout generations which cannot be rectified by way of the law alone. These sentences affected the lives of children, spouses and relatives. The loss of material deeds is a similar issue. The principle of *in integrum restitutio* cannot be but the repetition of life without the violations. This is impossible! The only solution, therefore, is the declaration of moral-political and legal restitution as well as the correction of the relevant labour and social security conditions; and furthermore, compensation based on the principle of *ex gratia*.[18] This was realised through the statutes of 1991/XXV and 1992/XXXII.

The first group of restitution laws were nullity laws, which defined moral, political and legal compensation.

On 1 November 1989, Parliament passed a decree[19] whereby they obliged the Ministers' Council to put forward a bill that defines the guidelines of compensation for the victims of unlawful criminal sentences made between 1945 and 1962, as well as compensation packages for the internees and deportees. The reformers of the self-dissolving party-state realised that this broad social demand needed to be met. The first 1989/XXXVI nullity law was passed by the last parliament of the *ancien regime*. The first nullity law and its measures set out a number of restrictions.

To understand these laws, it is vital to investigate the legal nature of nullity. The first nullity law is based on the *ex lege* nullity, which means that the law declares court sentences null. Consequently, the sentences of previous court procedures, be it imprisonment or even death, need to be regarded as if they had not taken place. The nullity principle had been used before in the history of Hungarian law. The 9590/1945 ME decree made it possible to regard sentences as if they had not happened.[20] These were passed on the basis of socialist, anti-fascist or democratic convictions, attitudes or activities.[21]

The question arises: why have the institution of nullity when the justice system made it possible to submit extraordinary legal remedies? During the time period in discussion, there were two types of remedy: re-trial and appeal on legal grounds.[22] These legal options, however, did not adequately treat hundreds of thousands of convicts whose sentences were based on existing legal norms at the time, but where the very foundation of their sentences was amoral in legal norms. It was also impossible to handle the tens of thousands of sentences which were based on "flawless" legal norms but the sentences were executed unlawfully. To re-try these cases would be extremely difficult as there was no evidence in existence (huge amounts of relevant documents were missing due to wide-scale shredding in the 1960s). Furthermore, the courts were overburdened with re-trials and there was no capacity to undertake more.

There were objections to the *ex lege* nullity due to the fact that Parliament's judiciary committee essentially trespassed into the territory of the courts and revoked court sentences. Without an in-depth legal philosophical inquiry into these concerns, let it suffice to say here that there are not even theoretical bases to these worries. These court sentences invalidated by nullity were not sentences of independent courts in a constitutional sense but the sentences of a monolithic power, which cancelled out the independence of the courts in the first place.

The first, 1989/XXXVI statute in the series of nullity laws was passed by parliament on October 20, 1989. The title was "Restitution of the sentences related to the 1956 people's uprising." The much-criticised preamble of the law did not yet have the courage to define the events of 1956 as more than an uprising. It was essentially a revolution, a battle for freedom fought for the independence and democracy of the Hungarian people. Nevertheless, we would deny historical justice if we refused to recognise the significance of this ambivalent effort: it was the very first preamble in Hungarian law to accept that the freedom fighters of 1956 "acted in the name of the country's political evolution and independence." This phrasing was already a breakthrough in comparison to the most "permissive" point of view during the years of the Kádár restoration. The Kádár regime granted pardon to the 1956 victims in the 1988/20 decree on October 6, 1988. At this time the convicted victims who were "sentenced to imprisonment or life in prison on charges of treason of the state or crime related to counter-revolutionary activities between October 23, 1956 and May 1, 1957 were exonerated from the legal consequences of their criminal record."

The 1989/XXXVI statute (in line with the practice of the previous retaliation) revoked the sentences of "political crimes related to the people's uprising" as well as the sentences of "murder, robbery, threat to the public and assault" committed between October 23, 1956 and April 4, 1963.[23] The *ex lege* nullity was declared by the first-degree court or its successor in a revocation document.[24] Besides the *ex lege* nullity, the law introduces nullity declared by the court's constitutive decision.[25] However, this is the jurisdiction of the Supreme Court alone.

The second nullity law, 1990/XXVI was passed on March 14, 1990 by the last session of parliament. It was announced on March 31, 1990. The concept of the second nullity law is more far-reaching in its implications than the first one. It actually demands seeking pardon from the nation. "Parliament will not forget the times after the Second World War when the Stalinist state was created in Hungary, which deprived the country of independence, shaming humanity, justice and the law. It deprived hundreds of thousands of innocent people of their freedom. Some lost their lives. The one-time deportees and internees lived as refugees in their homeland. The pardoning gestures were hardly satisfactory for the unlawfully persecuted masses[26] because *crimes that were not committed are not pardonable*" (italics mine). It was now possible to say what the first nullity law did not specify, namely, that the persecuted are innocent and that crimes that were not committed are not pardonable, and that the Stalinist and post-Stalinist eras (i.e. the counter-revolution laws as well) are essentially the same.

The law *ex lege* revokes criminal acts against the internal and external safety of the state, crimes of pricing and distribution, crimes of not reporting criminal activities detrimental to public property[27] as well as other less serious criminal acts within the same categories with the exception of "war crimes and crimes against the people."

The courts issue a declarative verification of the nullity. The reason of nullity is defined according to the rules of special procedures.[28] The second nullity law does not recognise nullity declared by the court's constitutive decision, not even as correction. Appeals[29] on charges of refusal of nullity verification can only be considered if the reason of nullity was not reported by mistake.

The law was widely criticised even by the members of the drafting committee. On the one hand, the group of revocable acts was defined too narrowly; on the other hand, the judges did not have the power to adjudicate less obvious cases, thus rejecting the possibility of correction. These criticisms were well founded. Furthermore, the time-frame leading up to April 4, 1963 was criticised as too limiting. However, the sentences of the second half of the Stalinist era, the "soft dictatorship," were the jurisdiction of the first freely elected parliament—in the form of law.

The third nullity law, 1992/XI revokes sentences of criminal acts against the state and public order committed between 1963 and 1989. The minister's justification of the third nullity law and the above-mentioned committee both point out that after the passing of the 1963/4 law "guidelines defining and sentencing the criminal acts against the state and public order were still in effect which resulted in a judiciary practice that was completely against the fundamental principles of the existing constitution, the generally recognised principles and rules governing human rights as well as the value system of society." The third nullity law denounces the *ex lege* principle, and entitles the courts to declare the individual sentences revoked. The court investigates whether or not the criminal act was carried out in line with the basic rights of the International Agreement of Civic and Political Rights accepted on December 16, 1996 by the XXIV Convention of the United Nations.

If the court finds that the answer is yes then it declares, essentially, that the sentence for the criminal act is revoked.

The nullity laws include the *ex lege* nullity of sentences based on racial discrimination, namely the third Jewish law, 1941/XV § 9, 10, 14, and 15.[31] The 200/1945 ME decree (the nullity of the so-called Jewish laws) sets out guidelines to invalidate these sentences. It does not declare, *expresses verbis,* nullity. Therefore, it was justified to include nullity as a far-reaching political and moral gesture in addition to a legal one.

The Other Side of Justice:
The Enforcers and Beneficiaries of the Dictatorship

Looking at the other side of the story, we have to investigate the privileges that the executives of the dictatorship enjoyed from special pensions and "reward" property to the university admission of the children[32] of the privileged class.

More serious than this is the practice by which top positions (even the ones requiring expert knowledge) were filled with people on the basis of political background alone. This has its effect on the change of the *nomenklatura* to this day.

The most difficult task, however, is the judgement of criminal attitudes (murderous at times), especially criminal attitudes and acts condoned and required by the state. Here, I will be discussing only scholarly opinions, bills that passed the judicial system and the points of view of the constitutional court. The debates fuelled by passion, manipulation and provocation are of no concern to this investigation.

The first scholarly debate broke out with regards to the bill known as the Zétényi-Takács bill. It is common knowledge that the principal idea of the law[33] passed by parliament was the retrospective change of the statute of limitation rules.[34]

These rules are related to the suspension of the statute of limitations, and more specifically, their suspension for political reasons. This is not unprecedented in the history of Hungarian law. The statute 1945/VII § 9. was similar.[35] The law facilitated the persecution of crimes where the duration of the sentence had expired. With reference to this amendment, serious sentences were passed by the people's courts. Even in 1957, a death sentence was carried out which would not have been possible without this law.[36]

The debate concerning the suspension of statute of limitations in criminal law, or in other words the retrospective persecution of crimes condoned by the state, was greatly affected by a similar debate in Germany. Though the predicament was very similar, §78/b subsection (1) of the German Penal Code could be cited, which applied the suspension of statute of limitations to cases where the state, despite the law, failed to prosecute crimes.

For lack of a similar positive norm in Hungarian criminal law, we faced a difficult challenge. The constitutional and judicial committee of parliament commissioned chief prosecutor Kálmán

Györgyi to investigate the issue.[37] In the first chapter of his analysis, Kálmán Györgyi reviewed the relationship between the conditions and obligations of international agreements and Hungarian law, especially with regards to § 57 subsection (4) of the Constitution.[38] He continued to elaborate on whether or not it is possible to initiate persecution for lapsed crimes. According to Kálmán Györgyi, the statute of limitations is a matter of material legal institution and as such, legislation with retrospective effect is not viable. The analysis appropriately pointed out the constitutional shortcomings of the Zétényi-Takács bill.

The other principal theatre of the professional debate was the ministry of justice.[39] Debating the issue, Károly Bárd reformulated and stepped beyond the limitations of the "statute of limitations debate", which was later published in a study.[40] His study was on whether or not criminal law is able to do justice retrospectively. Arguing pro and contra he arrived at the conclusion that "to summarise, the discrepancy between traditional criminal activity and system-friendly crime condoned and sponsored by the state *is not to the extent that the application of criminal law should be excluded*" (italics in original). He goes on to argue that "The Bolshevik regime did not hesitate to suspend the prohibition of any legislation with retrospective effect and this is exactly how the National Socialists began their reform of the law in 1935. In the history of Hungarian criminal law it is stated in 1950[41] that it is possible to apply the Penal Code to crimes that were committed before the effect of that particular Penal Code if it especially states that its effect is applicable to crimes committed before it has taken effect. To save face, the legislators of the dictatorship never intended to create a legal state. However, if we reject the past in the name of the legal state and we still overstep the boundaries of the law, we question the legitimacy of our own intentions." He also brought up the legislation of the non-extinction of principal crimes[42] and the need to establish a parliamentary committee.

Another important document of the statute of limitations debate is "On the principles and legal conditions of liability, activities and advantages at the expense of social justice, committed between 1949 and 1990" by Imre Békés, Mihály Bihari, Tibor Király, István Schlett, Csaba Varga and Lajos Vékás.[43] The main argument of the paper echoes many of the constitutional concerns raised by Kálmán Györgyi. "It is not yet foreseeable how the constitutional court will interpret the clauses of the legal state."

László Szűk[44] interpreted the institution of extinction as a dogmatic question, concluding that statute of limitations is fundamentally a matter of procedural law; therefore, he found no objections to the Zétényi-Takács bill.

I have argued,[45] and the constitutional court agreed with me,[46] that the suspension of the statute of limitations does exist in Hungarian criminal law regardless of the fact that, as in German law, a positive rule does not state that. For, if the state does not fulfil its obligation based on the principle of legality[47] as stated in the law, time lapse with legal effect (statute of limitations) cannot transpire—only a natural time lapse. The notional condition of statute of limitations, i. e., time lapse with legal effect, is that the state must attempt to fulfil its obligation to persecute crime. By contrast, the state, motivated politically, did not persecute serious criminal activities on the one hand; and on the other hand, the MSZMP violated the principle of legality by way of secret instructions.[48] These secret instructions also violated the citizens' legal equality in an institutionalised way.[49]

The suspension of the statute of limitations was ignored by the law. Based on this, the authorities suspended persecution of the most serious, inhumane mass murders, such as the killings in Mosonmagyaróvár. They never considered the possibility of suspension of the statutes.

The bill as passed by parliament, but incidentally not signed by the president, was ruled unconstitutional in its entirety by the constitutional court.[50] The ruling of the constitutional court was based on the interpretation of legal state citing the following:

1) the principle of legal safety ("The principle of legal safety is violated by the imprecision of the wording of the law");

2) the requirements of constitutional criminal law ("The law violates the requirements of constitutional criminal law in that the extinction of crimes, including the pause of limitations as well as the suspension of the statutes of limitations, must be based on the current penal code in effect unless, during the duration of extinction, new laws take effect that are more favourable to the plaintiff").

After the announcement of the decision of the constitutional court, there was a conference on the issue in Budapest on May 16 and 17, 1992. The event was organised by the Konrad Adenauer Stiftung and was titled "Legal state and justice."[51] A number of respected European lawyers[52] all agreed that the crimes of the Bolshevik and National Socialist dictatorships must be accounted for legally: however, the exact procedures must be devised in the judicial system of the individual countries themselves.

After the 11/1991 (5 February 1991) constitutional court decree, parliament attempted to interpret the suspension of the statutes of limitation.[53] The constitutional court ruled the interpretation unconstitutional.[54] As opposed to "the interpretation of the issue by the parliament (1987/XI. § 54.) it is a constitutional requirement that it is only binding for parliament and its committees."

After the unfavorable ruling on the Zétényi-Takács bill, Zsolt Zétényi submitted another draft, a procedural one this time. According to the new version, the decision whether or not the statutes of limitation can be applied in case of the most serious murder crimes should be in the jurisdiction of the court. When passing the bill, parliament heavily relied on the arguments of the constitutional court. "Limitation is a matter of legal fact; therefore, the law must change the natural lapse of time into a fact with legal effect.

The legal facts of the beginning and duration of limitation must be valid during the time of limitation, and they are valid or they are not valid."[55] This was stated in order to make it possible for the courts to adjudicate between the statutes of limitation and the natural lapse of time, and, to prevent the investigating authorities from throwing out the case citing expiration of the statutes of limitation or to prevent the courts from closing the case on the basis of natural lapse of time,[56] the Penal Code had to be amended. Therefore, Zétényi's draft proposed that the modification of the law should entitle the courts to investigate whether any lapse of time creates legal effect.

The Zétényi bill was passed on February 16, 1993. The review of the constitutional court beforehand ruled the bill unconstitutional again (42/1993, June 30, 1993). According to the majority decision[57] the bill violated 1) the normative concept of legal state as interpreted in the Constitution, 2) the requirement of legal safety, 3) § 8 subsections (1) and (2)."

The decisions of the constitutional court made it clear that the intention to do justice, meant to extend a gesture to the victims as well as hold liable the perpetrators of the most serious crimes, was not well-received.

The government continued looking for new constitutional ways to persecute the perpetrators of the principal crimes, especially mass murders. In the meantime, Germany passed its law regulating the liability of the perpetrators of crimes committed during the communist era but not persecuted for political reasons. In the Czech Republic, a law declared the communist system illegal, while holding accountable the Czechoslovak Communist Party and its members for the systematic destruction of traditional values of European civilisation and the purposeful violation of human rights.

During the debates, the idea surfaced amongst scholars and government and opposition politicians that the events of the 1956 Revolution could be defined as war. The 1961/V § S 114 ministerial argument also reflected this: "The punitive decrees of the proposed rule are applicable to situations of war as interpreted in international law but also to hazardous situations that pose threat to internal order. By hazard to the safety of the state is meant the mobilization of an internal counter-revolutionary force as well."

Similarly, the experts of the Christian Democratic People's Party (KDNP), János Bruhács and Gábor Jobbágyi, wished to buttress their draft using the norms of international law. This was an unprecedented initiative. They wanted to incorporate the generally recognised principles and norms of international law into Hungarian criminal law.[58] The KDNP draft did not make it to the parliamentary debate after the 1993/XC bill was passed.

Having limited the grouping of criminal activities, the Hungarian legal state then attempted to persecute the perpetrators of the mass killings of unarmed citizens during the days of the 1956 Revolution. The criminal procedures did not apply the duality of the suspension of statutes of limitation. Therefore, the prosecutors decided to press charges on the completely new basis that international agreements recognised by Hungarian law were violated. This was reflected in the 1993/XC law.[59] The bill was passed under the title *Az 1956. októberi forradalom és szabadságharc során elkövetett egyes bűncselekményekkel kapcsolatos eljárásról* ("On the procedure related to some crimes committed during the 1956 revolution and war of independence"). As far as its content is concerned, it is the type of law which interprets one law using another law. It states that the norms of Hungarian criminal law must be applied in accordance with the Geneva Accords accepted on August 12, 1949 to protect the victims of war and to persecute heinous crime. The objective of the law was that the crimes committed against the population during the revolution must be prosecuted as crimes against peace and humanity, not subject to the statute of limitations.

What is the difference between ordinary crimes and the crimes in question? The fundamental effect of the Geneva Accords is that it changes the legal object of the crimes. It interprets the legal object of crimes against the life of the individual person as the legal object of the protection of humanity. The 1961 Penal Code reflects a similar approach.[60]

The 1993/XC law reflects the intention that the most heinous war crimes against humanity must be persecuted at all times regardless of whom committed them, the Bolsheviks or the National Socialists.

The president sent the bill to the constitutional court before it was passed. Their decision[61] nullified the law's reference to the statute 1945/VII § 1 arguing that the "crime is not a war crime in international law."[62] It also stated that "...the non-extinction of criminal prosecution is only applicable to crimes which can be prosecuted in accordance with the current Penal Code which was in effect at the time when the crime was committed with the exception if international law defines the crime as a war crime or crime against humanity, and it also rules that the crime is non-extinct or it allows for that option, and Hungary is in a binding international agreement to suspend the statute of limitations."

This law "unblocked" the way to begin investigation into the most serious mass murder cases of 1956. The "blockage" was an oversight: the investigating authorities had not applied the relevant international norms, which were also the basis of future rulings. In any case, investigations of extinct or closed cases started.

The first such case was heard by the Fővárosi Bíróság (municipal court).[63] Some of the gunmen who actually fired into the crowd in Salgótarján were found guilty on charges of crimes against humanity. The ruling pointed out that the legal basis of the verdict was Article 1.b of the New York Agreement.

During the appeal proceedings of the case, the president of the supreme court and the chief prosecutor submitted a request to the constitutional court to nullify the 1993/XC law. According to their argument, "the law refers different aspects of the Geneva Accords to one another and creates an originally non-existent correspondence between them, changing the content of the Geneva Accords, violating the harmony of international law and internal law and hindering the application of generally recognised rules of international law."[64]

The constitutional court found the plea relevant and nullified the 1993/XC law. The arguments of the decision pointed out, however, that "... the majority of war crimes and crimes against humanity were against the law according to the Hungarian Penal Code in effect at the time. The constitutional court would like to point out, however, that international law regulates the definitions of crime and persecution, and all the conditions of criminal prosecution in and of itself. All these circumstances and conditions must be applicable so that a crime in Hungarian law can be judged as a crime in international law."[65]

After the decision the supreme court passed a sentence in the case of the Salgótarján shootings.[66] The legal basis of the verdict was the 1968 New York Agreement.

In the seventh year of the transition, in the legal field, the closure of the past began with this verdict.

Whether or not the means of traditional law are able to adjudicate crime condoned by the state is still an ongoing debate between political scientists and prosecutors. The issues arose after the Second World War when war criminals were being tried.[67] It is widely accepted that, motivated by their own self-defensive reflexes, the civilised nations ignored principles such as *nullum crimen* and *nullas poena* in cases of war crimes and crimes against humanity. Persecuting these crimes means today that we have to judge a crime based on principles that may not have been in effect when the crime was committed; furthermore, there was no objection against expiration of the statute of limitations either. It does not change the fact, however, that "criminal law can be applied mostly to the 'middle sphere' of individual events, and as long as it is put to effect in this area, it will keep its logical consistence and resist contradictions-in-terms."[68] It appears this contradiction cannot be solved in our century: the Hungarian judicial system would not be without contradictions even if the efforts were more assured.

The contradictions are enhanced by the more and more obvious "culture war", through which different groups of the 1956 revolution, even the oppressors, are making attempts to appropriate the memory and international recognition of the revolution.

Criminal law alone cannot be the *exclusive* means of justice, though it is not negligible either. It was similarly needed at the time when we faced our National Socialist past.

As criminal law alone is not satisfactory, many proposed the establishment of a parliamentary committee.[69]

With regards to the establishment of the parliamentary committee, there was, in principle, agreement between scholars and politicians. Still, such a committee was not set up. There is no tradition of institutions like this, let alone the legal framework.

The scholarly investigation and publication of facts began with the Németh government's appointment of the lawyer-historian committee[70] headed by József Földvári and Tibor Zinner. The work was carried on with the Antall government's appointment of the Kahler Committee.[71] The Committee involved researchers from a number of disciplines and during the time of its appointment,[72] it published two reports[73] which mainly focused on the 1956 shootings, retaliation after the revolution and the outpour of immigrants. After the termination of its appointment, the Committee published its third report[74] and completed its analysis.[75] This, too, is part of justice.

Demolish and Rebuild

Doing justice, as I have pointed out above, means, by and large, the historical process, which results in the creation of legal state once the dictatorship of the party state is brought down. This also results in the separation of power and the realisation of fundamental human rights.

The ideal of liberty-equality-fraternity written over the French flag by the victorious revolution to the future betterment of many of Europe's states was only an unattainable dream for other states in Europe for a long time. As the obvious bankruptcy and inevitable collapse of the Bolshevik dictatorship was becoming a reality, the joy of freedom mingled with fear. The question arose whether the space left by the ancien regime would be filled immediately or whether there would be a political vacuum, the power of which would drag the country into chaos. The fear was well-founded as the Balkan war shows. Nonetheless, despite the fact that the Bolshevik dictatorship demolished civic society, the spirit of the 1848 laws and Ferenc Deák and the memory of a liberal legal state equal to nineteenth century Europe was still very much alive. This is all part of what is known as the silent revolution of Hungarians. It is a revolution because it carries the *sine qua non* of revolutions: it replaced the failed system with a new one through general and secret elections, which immediately filled the vacuum following the demise of the monolithic dictatorship. It is silent because it gained power without arms or at the price of citizens' blood, but with the support of the masses. The representation of the new power became an "independent democratic legal state" as announced on October 23, 1989. Many felt, however, that the shift of power was based on too many compromises as if the transition had not been real. The constitutional court's approach reflected a curious historical predicament, "legal transition" in their definition, in which the law had to be harmonised with the constitution of the legal state. Furthermore, at the same time, the transition required the legal state to adhere to the self-governing rules of the law.

A comparison between the revolution of the legal state and a bloody revolution fought with arms should be the subject matter of another study. It will be an important task as well, when time allows for the appropriate historical scope. Such a synthesis would be too early at this point, as is this evaluation of justice necessarily partial. It is important to note here that while a revolution wipes out the legal system and institutions of a regime with force and oppresses the regime's social base, the revolution of the legal state, as a result of a lengthy process, acknowledges the validity of the old legal system, regardless of its legitimacy, on the basis that "every law in effect has to be harmonised with the new constitution of the legal state." Under the aegis of legality the bloodless revolution of the legal state restructures the legal relations of the party state so that the state can still continue operating in safety. This is less of a shock for the population than an armed revolution—although it does deprive the citizen of the catharsis of revolutions, which, in the end, creates a feeling that nothing has changed. The feeling was further enhanced by the fact that numerous well-known personalities of the *ancien regime*—political and economic—re-surfaced in public life in a variety of new positions.

Justice also includes the demolishing of the party state and the building of democratic institutions. The political build-up to the revolution of the legal state nurtured the situation that allowed for the public legal reforms that led to the announcement of the Republic of Hungary on October 23, 1989 and the first free multi-party elections on March 25 and April 3, 1990. The escalating events of the new international situation following the change of power relations in the West resulted in a wide array of judicial efforts to dissolve the monolithic party state and build a civic democracy. The Hungarian democratic opposition was not fully prepared to meet these challenges, and consequently some of these efforts had their shortcomings. However, the most remarkable consequence of these judicial efforts was that in incorporating international norms,[76] basic human rights were guaranteed on the basis of legal equality of the citizens. The laws[77] and decrees[78] passed in 1989 abolished some of the pillars of the party state (workers' guard, State Clerical Office and others). At the same time, institutional guarantees of the constitutional legal state were established (constitutional court and others) and laws guaranteeing the practice of basic human rights were passed.

The parliament passed 104 laws in 1990.[79] Furthermore, the revision of the previous judicial system began ("deregulation").

To promote the idea of the democratic state, parliament passed a law known as the "agent law,"[80] which aimed at facing the past and justice. The law was later amended and its effect restricted.[81] It is still incomplete.

The reform of criminal law was another important aspect of the legal transition. Previously, criminal law used to be the most effective weapon of class discrimination. Criminal law was, therefore, considerably unjust. The first efforts of the reform reviewed the inherent injustices[82] and then revised and devised them[83] to best serve the requirements of the legal state of the future. The process is still under way.

This study could end here. For the personal impressions and emotions of the author can hardly be incorporated here unless they are objectively well-founded. The subject, however, tempts me to share some of them with the reader. Posterity, heavily dependent on written sources, will never quite understand why the Hungarian nation is not optimistic after this half century's paralysing communist dictatorship. It is comparable to the pain of the generation which survived the Second World War and mourned its victims in the debris of their homes. We have homes now. Still, the "apathy quotient" is comparable to the one after the war. I know that the majority of this society is tired and poor. It was no different after the war and still people had hope; what is more, enthusiasm. It is often claimed that the country is torn apart by conflicts of interest along party lines. There are conflicts of interest and party battles in every society—this is hardly a sufficient argument.

However, the diseased suspicion and hate that poisons the public and private spheres has grown out of hand. It is a crisis of values, argue the experts, hastily adding that this is a world phenomenon. There is a grain of truth in this. I firmly believe, though, that the fallout of oppression and the crimes of a half century's dictatorship have done more damage than the oppression itself. Think of the Holocaust, corrupting "goulash communism," racism and communist class discrimination. Sometimes we catch ourselves reacting the same way as the dictatorship had taught us despite our best intentions to oppose and fight the regime. Or, we do not dare act. The question arises: what are the consequences of the regime's zero tolerance for justice? Let's face the truth: it deformed public and private thinking. Public thinking was oppressed by the regime's guardians of culture and censorship, which later turned into self-censorship. As far as private thinking is concerned, the appreciation of national intellectual values was undermined, as intended by the dictatorship, and morals sank to the level of everyday survival. It resulted in a general demoralisation. Although we now live in a sovereign and democratic state, the majority of the nation does not regard liberty as a cornerstone value. Many believe that democracy is nothing more than a synonym for wealth and consumerism. People would not make sacrifices for freedom. This is similar to what the Bible says: "The sons of Israel were in protest against the whole congregation of Moses and Aaron. And Israel's sons tell them: I would rather have died by the hands of God, eating meat and bread; because you have brought us out here in the wilderness to kill this multitude in starvation."[84] Also: "Why is the Lord taking us to that land? to die by weapons? to let our wives and children fall prey? Would it not be better to return to Egypt? And they tell each other: let us find guides and return to Egypt."[85]

This is where we are now as a result of our incompletely processed past. The oppression that attacked the immunity of our soul marred our conscience and led us to believe that crimes are not crimes but necessities of interest. Gyula Illyés's "One sentence on the nature of despotism" is not poetic justice. If Illyés was alive, he might write a "second thought" on the painful recuperation from the dictatorship's poisoning, which we cannot circumvent either. Without knowledge of our own past and its analysis, more chaos will prevail. It is still important though to call crimes by their names and name the victims as well as the perpetrators of the crimes. This, and only this, can achieve reconciliation—through the peaceful, not vengeful, soul—the objective and meaning of justice.

The process of doing justice yielded less than expected results in the first years of the transition. The organism of society was "detoxified" partially. It is now the task of sociologists and political scientists to uncover further conflicts of interest. The lawyer still hopes, though, that the nation has enough healthy "cells" to defeat the parasites of hate, reach reconciliation and turn the past into a lesson well learned.

Notes

1. Especially 1939/IV statute, 3350/1940 decree; 1942/XV statute, 3600/1943 decree; 550000/1942 decree; 4070/1943 decree; 1942/XC statute; 1600/1944 decree; 1830/1944 decree; 26500/1944 decree; 50550/1944.
2. Cf. Sepsey, Tamás. *A kárpótlás története*, in this book.
3. Cf. József Révai's article in *Szabad Nép* published on July 22, 1946. He argues that "reactionary forces" must be fought. But who is reactionary? Everybody who is "anticommunist!"
4. Cf. *Törvénytelen szocializmus*, edited by Vera Révai. (Budapest, 1991). (Tibor Zinner, Sándor Szakács, Miklós Habuda, László Svéd, Imre Szomszéd, György Markó, Margit Balogh).
5. Cf. the following statutes and decrees: 1950/IV on the suspension of judges' independence; 1950/I on the introduction of the local councils; 8800/1945 on the legal protection of economic order; 1950/26 on military staff's border crossing; 2560/1949 on provocation against cooperatives.
6. ÁVÓ had a separate department specializing in clerical matters. The "Clerical Subdepartment" was set up in 1946 and headed by János Tihanyi. After the Mindszenty trial, from May 15, 1951 the State Clerical Office took over the task of the sub-department. Its aim was to make the existence of the church impossible. Cf. Szántó, Konrád. *A meggyilkolt katolikus papok kálváriája.* (Budapest, 1991). Havasi, Gyula. *A magyar katolikus egyház szenvedései 1944-1989.* (Budapest, 1990). Hetényi Varga, Károly. *Papi sorsok a horogkereszt és a vörös csillag árnyékában.* (Abaliget, 1992-1996). Bindés, Ferenc and K. Németh, László. *"Ha engem üldöznek".* (Budapest, 1991). Lénárt, Ödön. *Erő az erőtlenségben. Eszmélődés, élmények és dokumentumok fölött—a magyar katolicizmus helytállása a kommunista diktatúra alatt.* Manuscript in the Kahler Committee's report. See also Gergely, Jenő. *A katolikus egyház Magyarországon, 1944-1971.* (Budapest, 1978).
7. On orders of Interior Minister László Rajk, 901 organizations were dissolved in 1946. Only 24 were fascist organizations. The decision was urged from Moscow.
8. Kahler, Frigyes. *Joghalál Magyarországon 1945-1989.* (Budapest, 1993.). Gosztonyi, Péter. *Magyar Golgota.* (Budapest, 1993).

9. Szakács, Sándor and Zinner, Tibor. *A háború megváltozott természetéről 1944-1948.* (Budapest, 1997).

10. Kahler, Frigyes. *Joghalál....*Kahler, Frigyes. "Megtorlás a forradalom résztvevői ellen a jogtörténet tükrében" in *Sortüzek—1956.* Report II, edited by Kahler, Frigyes. (Lakitelek, 1994), pp. 23-32. Zinner, Tibor. "Az igazságszolgáltatás irányítása és az 1956-1963 közötti büntető igazságszolgáltatás" in *Sortüzek—1956.* Report III, edited by Kahler, Frigyes and Almási, János, pp. 63-111.

11. Cf. 1956/31 decree on arrest for public safety.

12. *Sortüzek—1956.* Report I, edited by Kahler, Frigyes. (Lakitelek, 1993). Cf. Kahler, Frigyes and M. Kiss, Sándor. "Az erőszakszervezet és a forradalom" in *Kortárs*, no. 7 (1996), pp. 73-92; no. 8 (1996), pp. 80-95.

13. Kahler, Frigyes. "Pufajkás ítélet" in *Rebellitas '56.* Vol. II, nos. 9-10, pp. 82-92.

14. The sentences of the period in discussion were individually analyzed by the members of the committee appointed by the president of the Supreme Court and the Minister of Justice. The members of the committee were Frigyes Kahler, Tibor Zinner, Barna Mezey, Sándor Steffler, János Zanathy. According to the material reviewed by the committee, 6,620 persons were sentenced while 696 were acquitted, including those forced to undergo psychiatric therapy.

15. 1976/8.

16. Cf. the following statutes and decrees especially 1945/VI; 600/1945 ME; 12330/1945 ME; 2400/1945 ME; 5500/1945 FM; 1946/IX; 1946/XIII; 1946/XX; 1947/V; 1947/XIX; 1947/XXX; 12200/1947; 1948/XXV; 1948/XXVI; 1948/XXXIII; 1948/LX; 10010/1948; 12770/1948; 22140/1948 FM; 22900/1948. (January 5, 1948); 1949/I; 1949/VII; 450/1949. (January 15, 1949); 690/1949 (January 22, 1949); 1310/1949. (January 12, 1949); 2050/1949. (March 5, 1949). 1949/XXIV; 1949/3; 1949/20; 4091/1949 (June 16, 1949); 4049/1949. (June 18, 1949); 4153/1949. (July 29, 1949); 4162/1949. (July 26, 1949). 4314/1949 (November 13, 1949) MT; 1950/25; 284/1950. (December 10, 1950) MT; 16100/1950. (August 23, 1950); 94/1951. (April 17, 1951) MT; 101/1951. (April 29, 1951) MT; 145/1951. (July 14, 1951) MT; 1952/4; 1956/15; 1957/V; 1957/32; 1957/52; 1958/13; 1959/24; 1960/22; 1965/20; 1965/21; 1967/IV; 31/1971. (October 5, 1971); 31/1971. (November 5, 1971); 32/1971. (November 5, 1971); 1978/I. S 30-32 subsection (4).

17. 5000/1945 ME (and amendments)
18. Cf. 9/1990 (April 25, 1990). AB decree: *ex patria* compensation to provide benefits in kind and not to meet legal demands. The limitations of differentiation are the effect of positive discrimination: equal treatment before the law, unconditionally, with respect to the fundamental rights of the Constitution.
19. Parliament decree.
20. 9590/1945 ME decree. S 3 subsection (1).
21. 9590/1945 ME decree. S 1.
22. In place of the appeal on legal grounds the statute of 1992/LXIX introduced the request for revision.
23. 1989/XXXVI. S 1.
24. Same S 6.
25. Same S 2.
26. The text of the preambulum was passed based on a draft written by Frigyes Kahler, who was a member of the lawyer-historian committee appointed by Prime Minister Miklós Németh in the 3063/1989 decree on 14 April 1989 to investigate the false fabricated trials and to draft the bill.
27. 1990/XXVI. S 1.
28. Modified statute 1973/I. S 356.
29. 1990/XXVI. S 4 subsection (1).
31. 1992/XXXIII. S 18 amends 1990/XXVI. S 3 and 4.
32. University admission of the children was automatic if the parent held the so-called "For the workers' and peasants' power" badge.
33. The bill *"On the persecution of serious crimes committed between December 21, 1944 and May 2, 1990, which were not persecuted for political reasons"* was passed on November 4, 1991.
34. According to the text: "On May 2, 1990 the extinction of crimes committed between December 21, 1944 and May 2, 1990 takes effect. These crimes are defined as treason by the 1978/IV. S 144 subsection (2) paragraph, voluntary manslaughter by S 166 subsections (1) and (2), assault causing death by S 170 subsection (5) if the state has not started legal procedures against these acts for political reasons." Subsection (2) claims: "The sentence that was passed based on subsection (1) can be reduced unconditionally. This law takes effect on the day of its announcement."
35. "In case of the political murders committed in 1919 or thereafter, the persecution of which was *hindered by the ruling regime at the time,*

extinction only takes effect on December 21, 1944." (81/1945 ME) According to the text amended with the 1440/1945 ME: "In case of the political crimes that resulted in the loss of human life committed in 1919 and thereafter, as well as crimes committed by the press *as defined by this present bill*, the persecution of which was hindered by the ruling regime at the time, extinction only takes effect on December 21, 1944." (italics mine)

36. In the case of Mihály Franczia Kiss (Budapest Court, B. XI. 1798/1957; the execution took place on August 13, 1957).

37. May 22, 1991.

38. No one can be ruled guilty and sentenced accordingly on counts of crime that was not a crime at the time of the carrying out the act. (1989/XXXI S 34 effective October 23, 1989.)

39. Of all the debates the one at the Prosecutors' Club on September 27, 1991 was especially beneficial.

40. Bárd, Károly. "Visszamenő igazságszolgáltatás, alkotmányosság, emberi jogok". *Társadalmi Szemle*, no. 3 (1992), pp. 29-38.

41. In tile general section of the Penal Code

42. S 33 of the Penal Code was changed by 1993/XVII: crimes cited in subsection (2)/a-c were ruled non-extinct. Cf. 2/1994 (January 14, 1994.) AB decree.

43. The paper was commissioned by Prime Minister József Antall in *Magyar Jog*, no. 11 (1991), pp. 641-645.

44. László Szűk. *Szakvélemény az "elévülési törvényről."* Manuscript. Presented at the Conference of The Ministry of Justice on September 27, 1991. After his death, the manuscript was not published.

45. Cf. Kahler, Frigyes. "Igazságtétel és társadalmi megbékélés". *Rebellitas '56.* II/3, (1993), pp. 1-41.

46. Cf. 11/1992 (March, 5, 1992.) AB decree argument.

47. I. e., crime must be persecuted by the state.

48. Cf. Kahler, Frigyes. *Joghalál...*, pp. 67-68.

49. Károly Bárd argues: "The fact is, the citizens' legal inequality was violated in an institutionalized manner out of political considerations. The Political Committee of the Hungarian Socialist Workers' Party (MSZMP) passed decrees in 1984 that state that the top functionaries of the party can only be held liable in court after permission for persecution has been obtained from the appropriate party committees. According to the decree, the ensuing procedure is devised based on the instructions of the prosecuting parties. See for example

no. 001/1985 instruction of the chief prosecutor regarding the tasks related to the persecution of persons within certain party ranks." *Társadalmi Szemle*, no. 3 (1992).

50. The papers of the conference were published in *A múlt feldolgozása a jogállam eszközeivel*, ed. by Bank, Erhard von der.

51. Wolfgang Brandsetter, von Bülow, B. Sharon Bydr, Joachim Hermann, Joachim Hruschka, Martin Kriele, Karl-Heinz Schnarr, Jacques Verhaegen, Imre Békés, András Szabó, János Zlinszky gave papers at the conference. Historian Sándor M. Kiss also gave a lecture, amongst others.

52. Wolfgang Brandsetter, von Bülow, B. Sharon Bydr, Joachim Hermann, Joachim Hruschka, Martin Kriele, Karl-Heinz Schnarr, Jacques Verhaegen, Imre Békés, András Szabó, János Zlinszky gave papers at the conference. Historian Sándor M. Kiss also gave a lecture, amongst others.

53. 1/1993 (February 27, 1993).

54. 41/1993 (April 30, 1993) AB decree.

55. 11/ 1991 (March 5, 1991) AB decree arguments.

56. Bc. S 213 a); S 250 I/a).

57. According to constitution judge János Zlinszky, "the bill in question is sketchy and it does raise doubts about some aspects of the procedures but it does not violate constitutional criminal law."

58. The draft was based on the draft of the International Penal Code of the A/46/405 UN decree (September 1, 1991). It wanted to introduce the concept of amended private charge.

59. The bill was passed on February 16, 1993.

60. Ministerial argument regarding S 139.

61. 53/1993 (September 13, 1993) AB decree.

62. War crimes and crimes against humanity of the 1945/VII law were nullified by the Constitutional Court's 2/1994 (January 14, 1994) decree on the basis that they were not in accordance with the definitions of war crimes and crimes against humanity as interpreted by international law.

63. Fővárosi Bíróság, 16. B. 768/1994/88.

64. Cf. 36/1996 (November 4, 1996) AB decree.

65. See above.

66. January 16, 1997. Bf. IV. 1847/1996/10.

67. London Accord, August 8, 1945; UN Convention, December 11, 1946. 95/T decree; Rome Accord, November 7, 1950, Article 7.2;

UN XXI. Convention, December 16, 1966; International Accord Documents, Article XV.2; New York Accord on the suspension of extinction of war crimes and crimes against humanity, November 26, 1968.

68. Bárd. *Társadalmi Szemle*, no. 3.

69. Among the advocates of the proposition are Prime Minister József Antall, President Árpád Göncz, Hungarian Democratic Fórum (MDF) representatives József Speidl and László Székelyhidi (February 11, 1991), Independent Smallholders' Party (FKGP) representatives István Böröcz and Sándor Oláh (February 22, 1991), and Young Democrats' Alliance (Fidész) representative Gábor Fodor (February 3, 1991).

70. The work of the committee was seen as completed by the Antall government. The members of the committee were notified on June 4, 1990 by the Ministry of Justice. (40014/1990. IM. IV/1.)

71. The committee was set up with the government decree 3035/1993 on January 21, 1993. It was led by lawyer-historian Frigyes Kahler, the members were: historian-archives librarian Vilma Alföldi, historian-archives librarian András Borosy, historian Károly Kapronczai, historian Sándor M. Kiss, historian-archives librarian Béla Pálmány, and lawyer György Sándorfi.

72. The committee was dissolved on January 1, 1995 by the Horn government.

73 *Sortüzek—1956*, vols. I, II. (Lakitelek, 1993, 1994).

74. The third report was published in 1996 with support from POFOSZ 1956 Foundation, Veszprém County Government and Werbőczi István Foundation. (Lakitelek: Antológia Kiadó).

75. Kahler, Frigyes and M. Kiss, Sándor. "Az erőszakszervezetek és a forradalom." *Kortárs*, nos. 4 (1994)-1 (1997).

76. Universal Declaration of Human Rights (1948); International Accords of Civic and Political Rights (1966).

77. In chronological order (without amendments): 1989/II on organization rights; 1989/III on gathering rights; 1989/VII on the right to strike; 1989/VIII on constitutional amendment on the vote of confidence; 1989/XVII (amended 1989/XXXIV) on referendums; 1989/XXI on the termination of the workers' guard; 1989/XXVIII on passports; 1989/XXIX on immigration and relocation; 1989/XXXII on the Constitutional Court; 1989/XXXIII on the operation of the parties; 1989/XXXIV on representatives' elections.

78. 1989/14 on the termination of the State Clerical Office; 1989/17 on the operation of clerical orders; 1989/15 on refugee status.
79. The most relevant ones here are: 1990/IV on the freedom of religion and churches; 1990/XVII (amended 1990/XXXII) on the suspension of denaturalization; 1990/XIV on the legal status of representatives; 1990/LXI on local governments.
80. 1994/XXIII on the surveillance of some important politicians.
81. 1996/LXVII AB decree (effective from July 31, 1996; cf. 60/1994).
82. Cf. 1989/XVI abolishes the death penalty for crimes against the state; 1989/XXV revises crimes against the state and abolishes provocation; 1989/XXVI modifies conditions of arrest and entitles courts to put suspects under arrest; also restricts the entitlements of military persecution; 1989/LIV abolishes enforced imprisonment; 1990/X entitles the Minister of Justice to authorize the use of intelligence equipment.
83. 1993/XVI, Penal Code. Cf. 1992/XIII, 1993/XVII, 1993/XLV, 1993/LXXI, 1993/CXII.
84. Moses. II. 16. 3.
85. Moses. IV. 14. 3-4.

Martonyi János

VALUES AND FOREIGN POLICY

The adage that "Politics is the art of the possible" is attributed to Talleyrand (among others), and the master tactician of the 19th century could indeed say that. In the 20th century, though, there might be many more adherents to this idea, making it senseless even to start listing them. Not that the proposition is astonishingly original: the basic question of politics is precisely the assessment and the definition of possibilities, and the setting of goals that arise from them. For, if we understand "possibilities" as a given set of circumstances that holds regardless, politics cannot be anything else but continuous adaptation to them ("intelligent adaptation", as the American competition law says—though in a completely different context).

However, if we accept into this world of possibilities that the existing system can to a certain degree be improved or reasonably changed, we immediately face the question of where the boundaries of such reasonable improvement are: namely, what is possible and what is not? Now pragmatic adaptation is no longer the order of the day, but rather a search for slogans that can provide answers to the most fundamental questions of politics and of foreign policy, too. What are the basic values, principles and norms of political action? To what extent must and can we act on grounds of these values, upholding these principles and norms? What is the relationship between morality and politics (and as a subset of that, foreign policy)? How, in specific cases, can the correct balance between principledness and practicability, between values and pragmatism be struck?

There has been a lot of talk lately about the relationship between politics and morality, and those expressing their view seem generally agreed on the most important issues. We believe together with István Bibó, that political constructions built on lies always collapse,[1] and we are also aware that neither the economy nor the legal system can work without moral values. Nor can society as a whole, so that politics would necessarily fail, too. That is why so many say, and we say it ourselves, that without mental and spiritual, but most of all, without moral renewal there will be no successful modernization in Hungary, no development of the middle class, and no long-lasting national recovery. Political, social, economic and legal order—as the founders of the social market economy emphasized so many times—are inseparable, and this integrated system is based on the order of values, on moral order.

The intellectually and ethically banal view about the confrontation of politics and morality so widespread today is just as artificial as the contradistinction between morality and law, also often spoken about. Politics indeed often comes into conflict with moral values but it also offers opportunities for the highest levels of morality imaginable. As József Debreczeni writes: "There are few areas of human action where one can witness more self-sacrifice, more standing up for principles, ideals, more persistence than in the case of politics. Politics has given numerous heroes to mankind, people who had undertaken the fate of martyrdom, sentences to prison and death, the gallows, burning on stakes for their principles."[2] If we reflect on the fate of the martyrs he lists, well known to all of us, too, it becomes clear that their defeat did not mean failure in a historic sense, but victory: their ideals and goals have mostly been realized. Here, of course, that most mysterious of dimensions, the one that is the hardest to handle, emerges: time. This makes the question of assessing and judging political possibilities and success still more complex.

It is even more difficult to harmonize demands deriving from principles with effective possibilities, to solve the everyday conflict of values and interests in the field of foreign policy, particularly in that of international politics. There is no such foreign policy, nor could there ever be one, that would take allegiance to moral values, ideals and principles as the only correct basis of action. One needs to adapt oneself to the determining trends of the world, which supposes the careful assessment, understanding and the acceptance to a necessary degree of these processes. But foreign policy with the *sole* aim of everyday adaptation, of affirming and reaffirming utilitarianism, cannot be successful in the long-term either. Policymaking along these lines, choosing always the course of least resistance, results in drifting and is quickly disoriented by the slightest unforeseen occurrence. The successful enforcement of interests, therefore, cannot lack well-defined values, ideals and principles—not to mention the aims that derive from these.

International politics supplies a number of examples of commitment to values and policy built on this commitment leading to success. The best known and the simplest is the winning of the Cold War by the Western World. The foreign policy the United States has been pursuing since the end of the forties can of course be criticized: it is up to the judgment of each individual to appreciate the moral contents of certain actions and their success or failure. But what is beyond dispute is that this policy was morally-grounded and attempted to enforce basic values. For a long time, it seemed that this moral dimension of American foreign policy was not an advantage; sometimes it even seemed to get in the way. In the end, however, a number of astute political scientists and Kremlinologists were proved wrong, while a then unknown Hungarian political scientist (now considered to be a brilliant European mind) István Bibó proved to be right when he said—as we have seen—that political constructions built on lies always collapse. The Western world needed only to stand firm.

Foreign policy, like politics, is not primarily about how to adapt and fit ourselves to the world but about how the world can be reasonably improved and corrected under given conditions.

Therefore one must think in the future, about the future and for the sake of future—which in our case means the future of Hungary, the future of the Hungarian state but also the future of the Hungarian nation. This future is addressing both a Hungary that fits into a uniting Europe, integrating into its economic, institutional and legal framework (while also contributing in the meantime to the formation of this framework), and also a Hungarian nation that is integrating with an emerging European nation with all of its material and spiritual power, while at the same time preserving and strengthening its own identity, language, and culture. The creation of a unified Europe, and the fact that both the Hungarian state and the Hungarian nation are participating in this process and benefiting from the results is perhaps even more important from the point of view of the nation than from that of the state. For the nation hopes from the European unity, from this process full of contradictions, tensions, burdened by doubts, yet astonishingly successful, called the building of Europe, alleviation of or even a solution for the problem of its state that was torn apart. That is why we have to believe that a united Europe will be created in the 21st century, and that is why we have to set as a goal in front of us to help the creation of a united Europe and to take an active part in that process. That is why we have to trust that the 21st century will give us the chance of better times for Hungary, for the Hungarian nation, for the whole of Europe, perhaps the whole world.

The basic question is whether it is enough to contemplate, to adapt, and to drift according to the pragmatic demands of each day in order to reach this goal. Will it be enough to go on unchanged, carrying on the thoughts of the 20th century? Will the ideas, models of thinking, paradigms, techniques rooted in the positivism of the 19th century and which came of age in the 20th be enough? In a century when mankind has tamed nature, put it at his service, almost turned back rivers, tens of millions were killed on account of murderous ideologies, and the dictatorships that were born have made one third of the world economically insupportable. According to everyday wisdom all this is behind us now, but there is no clear assessment about to what extent this past, its culture, ways of thinking and techniques are being continued, to what extent does continuity work and to what extent can we as individuals and as a community break out and overcome it. The past must not be completely forgotten, but overcome, understood and remembered so that future can be understood and shaped.

The coming century bears tremendous uncertainties. The possibilities are huge, but the dangers are terrible, too, not only for Hungary but also for Europe and the entire world. We might be approaching a more righteous and secure world, in which citizens and nations have real equality of opportunity. Alternatively, we might be descending into greater and greater inequalities, a time of ecological catastrophes and organized crime becoming the world's leading industry.

The choice is up to us and it is our responsibility. First of all we need to trust in ourselves, in our community and nation. Without a sense of national self-identity, the community which is the most important for our self-definition cannot be sustained. The nation needs confident citizens that are aware of and can enforce their rights, while citizens need a confident nation that is proud of its history and performance, that lives its self-identity and trusts in its success. These are the nations that are able to create that politically and economically united Europe, which can have a great influence on whether the 21st century is going to live up to the possibilities for the world and for Europe which lie ahead of us—or else give rise to new dangers, false, fundamentalist answers and catastrophes.

All this is not possible without an unquestionable national and in the meantime European commitment. Without a national commitment there is no commitment to Europe: without the ability to live the experience of belonging to a nation, European self-identity and successful integration cannot exist. This commitment to Europe offers us the chance not to nurture any kind of inferiority complexes toward the European Union, but to represent our interests determinedly, forcefully, professionally and rationally, building them on our values. European integration itself is built on values and ideals in the first place. The original concept of unity was born in the world of ideas, and at times when progress towards this goal has run into the sands fresh impetus to it has again been given by ideals.

"Une certaine idée de l'Europe" led, for instance, to the declaration by the European Court on the direct application of basic treaties. But the ideals connected to the European social and economic system—such as parliamentary democracy, market economy, the rule of law—were the ones that determined the nature and the character of this whole process, too. We must therefore accept these ideals in order to truly participate in the process. In the meantime, democracy, market economy and a constitutional state also mean that integration does not function under the direction on one omniscient center, and that no political movements or parties are in a position to insist on their view of the transformation of world and society. European integration is built on the determined and honest representation of different, opposing interests, just as operating market economies and democratic constitutional states themselves are. The gist of this system is that everybody is representing their own interests and nobody is expecting anyone else to represent his/her interests. This sharp and determined representation of interests is made possible exactly by the fact that all the participants— apart from possessing the necessary professional and moral standards—are committed to its basic aims and values, and nobody calls them into question.

The question of an appropriate negotiating strategy has been raised several times lately in connection with Hungary's bid for membership, and in this context the issue of to what extent

Hungary should press for derogations from the acquis communautaire. It is well known that the European Union has its own plans in
this sense. No doubt it will try to restrict the free flow of labour, for
example, and in the case of new members it clearly has no wish to
extend the entirety of its agricultural policy and the subsidies that
go with it. References have also been made to the possibility that
new members will not receive the level of financial support from
which current members benefit, and to which they would be entitled under existing regulations. Certainly these would constitute
significant departures from the acquis communautaire, since the
assertion of the four freedoms and the economic and legal unity of
these—which has been created precisely by the rulings of the
European Court—will be infringed, if equal conditions for competition deriving from a common, even single market do not prevail
in the field of agriculture, while in the sphere of financial support
communitarian solidarity and the principle of equal treatment
would not prevail entirely either.

These are very serious questions, which obviously need thorough preparation. The accurate and professional elaboration of the
claims we would like to submit during our membership negotiations, in connection with such transitional periods, is only one element of these preparations. The main question is not whether there
are many or few such claims (their weight is not determined by
their number, anyway). A strategy which tries to limit these claims
in the hope of speeding up the negotiation process is not mistaken
as such, either. But it would be a serious mistake if we gave up
entirely certain demands without exact knowledge of the derogation claims put forward by the Union. It would be an even more
serious failing if we did not recognize precisely the nature of these
claims and the interests these try to represent. As for those that say
that by submitting too many claims, we in fact supply arguments
for and proof of our immaturity and lack of readiness to join, this
type of approach views the accession process as some kind of

entrance examination at which we must demonstrate our fitness on all possible fronts without giving consideration to our actual interests. Especially since the maturity of the other side is a given, enabling it to defend its interests through seeking derogations which are in fact far more significant and extensive than those requested by the supposedly "immature" parties. Indeed, there is a danger that we misunderstand the relationship between the proposed derogations and the level of development of the candidate country. This was clear during earlier enlargement negotiations, as the demand—for example—for the special treatment of chewing tobacco so important for the Swedes is hardly connected with how developed or undeveloped Sweden is. In the case of the current negotiations, it is precisely the more developed existing member-states of the Union which are pushing hardest for the protection of their markets and products.

In our case, it is undoubtedly true that in the field of environmental protection, for instance, we need a transitional period in order to implement the stricter levels of regulation already in force in Western Europe. On the other hand, we will also need a derogation in the area of animal and plant health, where it seems our regulations are actually stricter. Our other demands could be connected to the specific traditions and the names of some of our products (e.g. wine). In the area of agriculture, one has to pay special attention to the fact that support coming from the common budget of the European Union is maximized in the case of each economy. This means that large agricultural enterprises are disadvantaged, since the same maximum of support is as valid in their case as in that of family farms. The question, of course is what is considered more developed: farming built on big agricultural enterprises or the fundamental role of family farming. If we believe that agriculture dominated by big businesses is in fact more developed (and one can often read views to this effect), then the supposed derogation claim that needs to be submitted is again not connected to our development but precisely to our underdevelopment. Several other examples might be given but the main point is to see our interests and the claims that derive from them, and then to represent these professionally, reasonably and firmly. Joining soon is indeed our primary interest but that will depend on the way the Union's expectations of us are handled and on the developments inside the Union, rather than on the nature and number of Hungarian expectations. We obviously cannot make any concessions as long as the credits we receive in return—in terms either of the acceleration of negotiations or moderation of the Union's claims—are not clearly visible.

The main conditions of a successful integration policy, however, are not connected to our negotiation strategy and to how this is implemented. The full and successful incorporation of the country and the nation into the process which will eventually lead in the 21st century to the creation of a unified, more effective and democratic Europe that is much stronger than today, depends crucially on whether we shall succeed in creating a well-working, efficient market economy, an operational, democratic, constitutional state (as judged also by European standards), a more decent public life and greater public security, as well as a more democratic and more just society. It is necessary to embark on a path of lasting economic growth, one that is faster than that we experience today, since the difference in the level of development between the European Union and Hungary needs to decrease. It is also important to obtain further results in the domain of legal harmonization, as this means not only bringing our legal system closer to the European one, but in fact approximating to such standards our entire social and economic system. However, even if we do move closer in these fields but not in terms of social structure, then all these results will become empty and meaningless. For, the real danger is that the actual operation of our political system gradually undermines our economic results, too, and the political distortions, alongside with and as a consequence of the strengthening cultural, moral and mental characteristics of the former system, will act in the direction of a social and political system that is gradually moving away from Europe. Such systems operate in numerous countries of the world, and one hasn't got to travel to the Far East or Latin America to encounter them.[3]

Thus, all the phenomena and manifestations that are today in contradiction with the values and the system of requirements of the democratic constitutional state, are working against Europe. Not understanding constitutionalism, improvisations that are not thought over and the statements that deny political alternatives not only jeopardize the performance of a democratic constitutional state but also seriously damage our Europe policy as well.

What type of society, and within that what kind of political system is created, depends above all on the values that are taken as a basis and on the moral order that originates in them. Therefore the teachings of the intellectual forefathers of the social market economy regarding the connections of different—economic, social, legal—orders is valid. To put it another way: the interpretation of orders is not built on anything else but on the moral order behind them. That is why that politics which is aimed at creating a successful society, successful economy and successful law and order is built on values, and that is why success will eventually depend on how we manage to hold on these values in spite of the necessity of reasonably fulfilling the requirements of everyday adaptation, too.

The requirements of the centrality of value, authenticity and commitment naturally have to make themselves felt not only in our Europe policy but also in that towards own nation and our neighbours. Concerning regional politics, for example, one must trust in a Central European identity and that the historical and cultural reality of Central Europe can be turned into political and economic reality, too. Commitment toward a qualitatively higher level of cooperation built on Central European self-identity will make it possible to step over slogans and revive the true spirit of Visegrád.

Central European cooperation must therefore be filled with content and given dimensions that exceed the economical one. This is in harmony with our Europe policy, too, as filling Central European cooperation with new dimensions also helps the negotiations concerning our membership; more than that, it strengthens our position as a member inside the Union as well. This is even more true insofar as the goals of our national policy are concerned. For the different dates at which different parts of the nation will become part of the European Union make it inevitable to move ahead in creating a system of Central European cooperation, as this system, irrespective of the time of entering, will become more valid in case of Hungarian membership. This is how a successful Europe policy can become compatible on the one hand with a successful "good neighbourly" policy, and on the other with the basic moral and constitutional demands that derive from the obligations of a national policy.

Notes

1. Quotes Viktor Orbán, in his presentation entitled "The Political Message of Bibó István" in Polgár, *Bibó István üzenete* [The message of István Bibó]. Special edition. (February, 1998).
2. Polgár. *Erkölcs és társadalom* [Morality and society] Special edition. (May, 1997).
3. Zakaria, Fareed. "The Rise of Illliberal Democracy". *Foreign Affairs*, (November/December 1977).

György Matolcsy

HUNGARY'S DEBT

This study is a historical essay, somewhere between economic history and economic analysis, examining Hungary's indebtedness and the process over the 25-year period between 1973-1998 by which Hungary became indebted. Wherever possible, I will try to avoid presenting detailed statistics, as I believe the history of the indebtedness can best be understood through intentions, not figures. It is only seemingly important that Hungary's external debt totalled USD 10 billion or USD 30 billion at a given point. What really matters is who wants to use this debt and for what purposes, in a given historical situation. The picture is more subtle as regards internal indebtedness. Figures cut more to the quick here, as the interest service paid after the domestic government debt became the largest expenditure item in the central budget in the 1990s. However, I will also avoid going into deeper financial analyses here; instead, I will try to show what concealed economic and political interests benefited from the accumulation of domestic government debt. Furthermore, I will explore what impacts it is expected to have now and in the foreseeable future. Similarly, I will not go into details presenting the repayment and quiet rescheduling of the debts and the debt service techniques, as I believe it is the sums that matter, not the techniques.

Historical Preliminaries

Hungary's indebtedness in this century is not a new phenomenon. The dramatically rapid and successful economic development that began after the Compromise of 1867 cannot be separated from the foreign loans financing it through the bank system. The establishment of the railways and modern industry as well as the birth of a modern European city, Budapest, largely started with foreign loans; the dynamics of economic development provided domestic resources for further investment only later. Hungary grew out of this indebtedness: the Hungarian economy worked off the earlier capital injections by the turn of the century, creating the necessary internal resources for further development.

Of course, World War I destroyed everything: modernisation, economic advances and the monarchy, including Hungary. However, the economic stabilisation of 1925 was again financed by foreign loans. There was another huge period of indebtedness between 1925-1931, because foreign loans were indispensable to successful financial stabilisation. This was also essential to the political stabilisation of the country after the peace treaty signed at Trianon. While the country's foreign indebtedness after 1867 took place mainly commercially, through the banking system and without political motives, the loans taken out by the government to finance the stabilisation of 1925 were largely made possible through political intentions. Hungary was the weakest link in the cordon sanitaire created in between the great powers winning World War I and the recently established Soviet Union, which the Western powers wanted to reinforce sooner or later. A politically and economically stabilising Hungary was not considered a threat for the new countries of the "protective ring" of the Little Entente, with Germany, which was moving from one crisis to another right until 1933. This country was struggling for survival, with economic progress as such no longer on the agenda. This period is perhaps best characterised by the dilemma of "market and money": Hungary needed both money and the market at the same time for survival, however the former could be expected from the winners (England and France) and the latter from the loser (Germany). Therefore, indebtedness between 1925-31 could only solve half of Hungary's historical dilemma. It provided money, in the form of loans, to stabilise Hungary economically and politically, but did not provide markets.

In 1931, Hungary halted interest and principal repayment of the loans taken out earlier and the National Bank of Hungary closed shop. This was a natural reaction to the waves of the 1929-33 world economic crisis reaching Hungary with some delay. Closing shop was linked with an ingenious innovation: the National Bank of Hungary was willing to repay the debts and interests in pengos (its currency at the time). There was an abundant supply of the national currency, but the reason it was an ingenious solution is because it meant that only creditors who spent the money in Hungary got their money back. Creditors could get their money back if they spent it on Hungarian investments, purchases and travels in Hungary. This solution struck a special bargain with the limits of the national economy, as it closed with the borders of Trianon in the first half of the 20th century: they only paid to those who were willing to reinvest the money into the Hungarian economy.

The international financial system received some shocking blows in 1929-33, and as a result, fewer and fewer financial institutions granted loans to assist Hungary's economic stabilisation. As a result, the debt problem was taken off the agenda after 1933, as one-third of the loans taken out earlier were repaid in pengos, one-third was cancelled and the remaining one-third disappeared due to bank failures. From 1933 until the early 1940s, an interesting dual process can be observed: Germany started providing a solution to the market problem, while money and credit sources from England and France gradually narrowed. The "market and money" dilemma was now solved the other way round; but again, only half of the problem was solved: with external markets expanding and external credit sources narrowing. However, while the Hungarian economy had a more and more urgent need for markets, it was increasingly able to cover financial needs from internal sources. And between 1940 and 1944, a reversed indebtedness process took place as well:

Germany was less and less willing to pay for Hungarian deliveries to the opening German markets. However, the Hungarian state financed these exports, so money followed the market.

Both the indebtedness related to the stabilisation of 1925 and the opening of German markets after 1933 were decisions motivated by political interests. When the new German chancellor came to power in 1933, a political decision was taken to open Germany's agricultural market to Hungary, in order to bind the country striving for territorial revision closer to itself. While the foreign resources of the financial stabilisation of 1925 basically served to preserve the status quo created after Trianon, the opening of German markets after 1933 was aimed at revision, that is breaking up the new status quo of the winners. Both were political objectives, contrary to the indebtedness following 1867. The opening of the German market after 1933 brought a new political indebtedness to Hungary: Germany kept demanding and receiving political, and later economic, concessions. The history of Hungary's indebtedness between the two world wars shows that a country which is unable to solve the dilemma of "money and market", in a very unfavourable historical situation, had to keep alternating the ways of indebtedness measurable in terms of money and power. The country was forced to choose now this one, now the other.

Between 1945-47, there was another successful financial stabilisation in Hungary. Economic history has so far acknowledged its speed and immediate success. We must, however, also note the fact that the successful forint (post WWII currency) stabilisation was carried out without the involvement of foreign resources; in fact, with the burden of compensation payments. In Hungary, there were no major foreign loans, there was no Marshall Plan and almost all institutional-organisational conditions were lacking. However, what was available proved to be the most important assets: good experts and skilled workers, including many young ones, and the will to be reborn of the plundered and the defeated.

From then until 1973, the history of Hungary's indebtedness is rather varied. Indeed, indebtedness as such only became a central political phenomenon around 1965-65 again. In these two years, Hungary accumulated a considerable trade deficit to the Soviet Union as the price for the successful stabilisation after 1956, leading to Hungary's indebtedness to the centre of the Soviet Empire. Of course, this indebtedness was politically motivated: it took place in line with the decision of the Soviet politburo and not business criteria. Its consequences were also primarily political ones, when the Hungarian political leadership decided on the economic reform in 1966. This took place through the economic reform committees, which operated between 1966 and 1968. The indebtedness resulting from political interests was followed by politically-inspired reforms: this was the economic mechanism reform of 1968. It was aimed at preventing further indebtedness to the East, meaning an uncomfortably close dependence for the Hungarian political leadership on a Soviet leadership which considered the loans granted to Hungary as an unfavourable sacrifice.

Playing with Oil Prices

There was a political ceasefire in terms of indebtedness between 1968-1973. In 1973, the explosion of oil prices was followed by the considerable increase of world energy and raw materials prices. Despite reassuring political phrases this affected Hungary as well, and the problem of the rising Soviet energy bill had to be managed somehow. Theoretically, there were three options. First, the performance of the Hungarian economy could have been improved. There were only two little problems with this: the leading figures linked to the economic reforms were dismissed and some of the reforms withdrawn one year earlier; and improving the economy would clearly have required political and economic solutions that did not fit into the minds—and the political

framework—of the time. Second, if it is impossible to improve performances, living standards should be reduced. However, the memory of 1956 was still too close, and the march into Czechoslovakia
in 1968 clearly showed the political leadership that an internal
rebellion would be crushed by external "help", and the presiding
Hungarian leadership would disappear without a trace. As the successful stabilisation of the early Kádár era would have been jeopardised by a major fall of living standards, this option was rejected.
The third option was to accumulate debts to the West.

As became clear later on, this was an important step toward the
revision of the second major European peace treaty of the 20th century, established in Yalta. The indebtedness to the West was perceived as a necessary evil, a temporary move and a financial transaction with a very limited impact by political analyses. If the
Hungarian political leadership of the time and the Soviets had fore-
seen the consequences of the indebtedness of Central and Eastern
European countries in the 1970s, they would undoubtedly have
given up this solution. The indebtedness of these countries to
Western governments and banks was part of a large-scale historical
game, in which the political interest of the West was to break and
later to eliminate the European status quo established after Yalta.
We cannot ignore the connection, which cannot be more than a logical assumption until archives are fully opened, that the US and
Western Europe intended to use the indebtedness of Central and
Eastern European countries to the West to break up the Soviet
Empire. Their argumentation could have been the following: "If the
Soviet satellites take out loans from us and invest them unwisely,
they will not be able to repay them and they will be in big trouble,
and then anything can happen." And they might have gone on like
this: "If these countries happen to invest the loans wisely, they will
generate huge differences in terms of economic success and living
standards on the one hand, and dictatorship and dependence on the
Soviet Empire on the other, and the tension could break up their

dependence on the Soviet Union." This is the ideal type of game: it is good if the loans are used badly by the Central and Eastern European countries and it is also good if they are used well. There are many signs suggesting that the Western strategic analysts and political elites only considered the first possibility seriously. I think they were perfectly right as, with some education and historical sense, nobody could seriously expect these countries to convert loans into profitable investments creating efficient economies without market economies open towards the developed countries, and with dictatorships instead of democratic systems.

With the exception of Albania, Czechoslovakia and East Germany, all Central and Eastern European countries became indebted after the oil price explosion. Albania stayed out of the big historical game called indebtedness due to its relations with China, Czechoslovakia as a result of the invasion of 1968, and East Germany due to its special historical status. The indebtedness basically opened a historical avenue of escape for Central and Eastern European countries, by which they could move closer to the West, step by step through increasing economic reforms, and edging away from the Eastern Empire. After a certain point, economic reforms make social and political reforms unavoidable. The indebtedness following the oil price explosion thus began with a politically-motivated economic decision, which, until a certain point, brought about a number of various economic reforms until the political decision closed the circle with a political reform. This political reform could only be a change-over to a democratic political system and the replacement of the Eastern club with the Western alliance. There are a number of signs suggesting that the oil price explosion of 1973 could not have happened by mere chance. The two major competitors of the USA at the time were Japan and Europe. Both were very successful in the 1950's and 1960's, and started to threaten the economic positions of the country winning World War II. An economic faltering could sooner or later turn into political or military weakening, so it is advisable to take any changes of economic proportions or power relations seriously. This is what US strategic analysts and political decision-makers did when they tried to set their two competitors slightly back in the race through the oil price explosion. Both competitors were highly dependent on energy, while the US was strategically in a far better position as regards energy from domestic sources and also through purchases from neighbours. Another objective was to restructure power relations within the US economy. The renewal of the American economy required an expansion of modern and innovative sectors at the expense of old ones. This internal restructuring of capital was achieved by increasing energy and raw material prices as a result of the oil price explosion. Businesses operating in industry requiring less energy and raw materials, but using more information and intellectual capital benefited from the oil price explosion, while companies unable to advance toward activities with higher added-value and higher information content moved into a difficult position. And the state tapped the profit of the energy companies.

The third objective of the oil price explosion was to break up and stir up the Soviet Empire. Under the above-mentioned logic, both consequences of the game had their advantages and and moved the countries on the fringes of the empire away from the core, while moving them closer to the West. In 1973, it was not yet clear that it was worthwhile to add another strategy to this one, in order to increase tension at the core of the empire. This was the military race accelerated in the 1980's, which increased the tensions and functional disorders originating from the closed-ness of the Soviet Union, the lack of market economy and its centralised power system. The breaking up of the fringes of the empire through indebtedness and the internal breaking up of the core of the empire through the accelerated arms race yielded dramatic results in the second half of the decade. Historical logic overpowered the passing status quo order of history. Change prevailed, the balance was shaken.

If we look at the three objectives of the historical and world economic realignments started with the oil price explosion of 1973 from the perspective of their realisation, we can see that the first objective has not been accomplished. Japan and Western Europe reacted successfully to the first and second energy price explosions, and the economies of both regions moved forward toward advanced technologies, innovation and higher added value. However, this strategy was highly successful in the urgently needed realignment of capital and power relations within the US economy. Industries using less energy and raw materials and more advanced innovation were successful, the internal economic renewal started from the inside and forced by external impacts proved very successful. Of course, as we have experienced, the third objective of the strategy has also been accomplished: the second status quo of 20th century world history has been broken up. Yalta started crumbling, with bigger and bigger pieces breaking off and, finally, the Yalta system died.

Hungary's External Indebtedness

The history of Hungary's indebtedness has a number of exciting twists and turns. Of course, the most interesting of these was the starting-point, when the Hungarian political leadership set off on the path of external leadership in 1973-74 with permission from the Soviet leadership. The motives of this decision were rather clear and reflected the entire logic of the Kádár regime very clearly. After the shock of 1956, the Hungarian leadership had to constantly reconcile two conflicting objectives: operating smoothly within the framework of the Soviet empire and making this acceptable to Hungarian society. The elite of the Kádár regime achieved this by gradually and constantly making political concessions to

Hungarian society, defending these concessions against the Soviet leadership by arguing that they are necessary to suppress dissatisfaction. The system was continuously retreating, but remained basically the same until 1990, even though political power was slowly decentralised, with market economy values, players and processes gradually coming to existence. External indebtedness served to exercise constant external and internal pressure on this political system based on concessions. In 1973, the management of the National Bank of Hungary persuaded the political leadership of the harmlessness of external indebtedness by presenting the necessary loans as small and temporary. The original foreign loans totalled USD 4 billion: this amount was used in the 1970s, mainly to maintain the level of internal consumption, and partly for investments. This means that, of the USD 21 billion debts accumulated by 1990, four-fifths came from secondary loans, taken out to repay the interests and principal debts of earlier loans. Of course, in addition to debt service (interest payment and principal repayment), foreign debts also included the foreign trade deficit (imports exceeding exports) of the given year. The main reason for increasing debts, however, was the fact that the debts were rolled over and over. This is how the little snowball of 1974 turned into an avalanche by 1981, and into an even larger avalanche by 1990.

The political leadership became aware of the situation in 1977, seeing the foreign debts suddenly accumulated between 1974-77. They realised that the indebtedness was neither small nor temporary. Therefore, in 1977, they tried to relaunch the reforms slowed down and effectively stopped in 1972. However, 1978 proved the "black year" of foreign debts, when foreign debts suddenly increased considerably. This stimulated the political leadership to speed up reforms, and they gave permission to draw up and introduce the price reform of 1980.

Developments accelerated, and the Polish people's army marched in into its own country. The finances of the Eastern block were thoroughly shaken by the Polish military coup in 1981. It was suddenly impossible to take out new loans, because the wind of Cold War swept over world politics. It was also impossible to get further loans because it became clear to Western creditors that, as they had suspected, the Soviets do not guarantee the debts of the other countries of the block. These two realisations together pushed Hungary onto the brink of a financial crisis. Kádár received loans from Hungary's Finnish cousins, deputy prime minister Marjai checked foreign trade representatives travelling to the West at the airport to see if their travel abroad was really necessary. There was a crisis, and the only way out was to move forward. The Soviets would not provide funds, but the West would not provide money either. That is, unless Hungary (re)joined the International Monetary Fund and the World Bank. This, however, was a very delicate issue questioning the cohesion of the Empire. Thus it happened for the first time since 1956 that the Central Committee of the party accepted the proposal of the Hungarian political leadership despite strong Soviet pressure: Hungary again became member of the International Monetary Fund, and then the World Bank. The decision shows a very interesting phenomenon: Kádár did not have a majority in the Central Committee until the mid-1980's, he did not have a majority in 1981, and still, in a decisive political issue, economic-business considerations prevailed. This clearly shows how the Western strategy worked out for making the Eastern block indebted made headway with an incredibly powerful logic through the twists and turns of history. Although the majority was loyal to the Soviets in the Hungarian Central Committee, if they did not provide any money the only way out was to move forward toward the West. Of course, there could have been another way out as well: the path taken by Romania. However, the option of actually repaying the debts, which would have resulted in dramatically declining living standards, was not feasible for the Hungarian leadership, mainly because of the Hungarian revolution of 1956. This is another historical warning: if a people lifts up its head and tries to take its destiny into its own hands against any heavy odds, even if it fails, it will be rewarded by history later. If it had not been for 1956, the Romanian path—repayment of debts by means of declining living-standards—could have been taken.

Another interesting turn took place in 1985-86: the internal anti-reform political forces joined forces with the managers of large companies and wanted to break out of the debt trap by accelerating full steam ahead. In 1985, the political leadership decided on an economic policy which broke with the process started in 1966, accelerated in 1968, got stuck in 1971-72 and started again in 1978, with concessions and withdrawals. "Forward, comrades, we've had enough of constant concessions and withdrawals," the command went. Large companies, one of the pillars of state socialism, suddenly realised in the mid-1980s that the continuous withdrawal of the Kádár regime from the central distribution method called socialism was taking place at their expense, while the winners were those suspicious private businesses—which are not even mentioned in the official political slogans of May 1. However, the acceleration went wrong, as the foreign trade deficit dramatically increased in 1985-86 and external loans also rose considerably, increasing the country's foreign debts.

These were already the last days of the regime. History is showing a playful parallel here: the Hungarian political leadership took its decision on acceleration and a cautious withdrawal of market reforms simultaneously with a decisive change in the Soviet leadership. This personnel change reflected the new realisations and new strategy of the Soviet political elite, which the Hungarian political elite obviously was not aware of. The big game was approaching its outcome: the wedges driven in from the outside through the external indebtedness moved the external shell (the Communist allies of the Soviet Union) of the empire away from its core. The new development—and decisive turn—of the game was the split taking place at the core, which accelerated developments. Hungary's external indebtedness continued sending alarm signals to the decision-making points of the shell and the core, warning that even "the happiest barracks" would not be able to resist the whirlwind, will not stand the burden of the external debts.

Developments accelerated even faster in 1987-88, as the party-state's counter-attack lost its momentum, Kádár resigned and the change of the political system began. Meanwhile, foreign loans flew easily to Hungary as a universal signal to everyone that there must have been an agreement here, struck between East and West, on a new current of history. The political changes of 1989-90 affected the external, then the internal shell of the empire, and finally its core as well. The game seemed to end, with the framework of Yalta breaking up and a politically-militarily unipolar world coming to existence. The debt weapon worked well; the West achieved its goal through it by breaking up the Eastern Empire. In the euphoria of the revolution, those concerned in Central and Eastern European countries (particularly Poland and Hungary) believed that the external debts could be forgiven, as they achieved their aim. "The Moor has done his duty, the Moor can go"—this was the general opinion in Hungary and elsewhere in 1989-90.

The West Refuses to Cancel Hungary's Debts

Why did so many believe that the West would forgive our foreign debts? First of all, because they would have regarded such a move as doing historical justice to these countries. We have been the bastions of the West, one argument went, the West let us down in 1956, said others. We have always been a European (that is Western and Christian) country, a third set of opinions held. Such views were also backed by the arguments of economists. If the foreign debts were taken out with political motives on both sides, and these political interests have fundamentally changed because Yalta died, economic logic should prevail over political logic.

This means that only the loans taken out with economic-business motives and used on the basis of commercial business criteria should be repaid. And as the state socialist system in Hungary (just like Romania, Poland, Bulgaria and the Soviet Union) was not suitable for efficiently investing the foreign loans into businesses, the loans could therefore not be used in ways generating sufficient profit to cover the repayment and the interests of the loans. This could not happen in any other way, as the indebtedness came about exactly with the aim of creating bankruptcy. Thus, the loans granted with political motives achieved their goal, the political loans were returned in a political (and historical) dimension. It is not very nice to expect economic return in a situation like this, many thought, since the loans were granted exactly with the aim of political, and not economic, return.

Romania was driven out of the international club exactly because, instead of taking part in the game by moving forward from the grip of the debt trap by continuous reforms, Romania quit the game by repaying her debts and cancelling the historical tacit agreement. Romania was not regarded as a model child at all by the West; in fact, she was an enfant terrible because she quit the game. Romania did this exactly in order to avoid having to gradually move closer to the West through reforms, and to avoid having to prepare an internal change of system by making concessions to society. Thus, it was not only the logic of the historical game that made Hungary (and other countries) think with reason that the debt weapon could be placed back into its case, the reversed example of Romania also seemed to reinforce this logic.

However, just as Romania received no reward for its unsuccessful and redundant sacrifice, Hungary was not rewarded either for her conduct as a model student. It was all for nothing to manage the external debt in an admirable way, to take part whole-heartedly in the big historical game: there was no reward. Between 1989-91, the new political elite made an exploratory attempt at having the external debts cancelled by the West, but we did not manage to achieve what Poland did. Perhaps the most interesting attempt was that of George Soros, who offered what later became the leading governing party to make half of Hungary's debts disappear by an ingenious but risky method. This would have been the following: after coming to power, the new government cancels all foreign debts, refusing to undertake the liabilities of the past system; the "market value" of Hungary's debts falls to half or even less; debts worth USD 10.6 billion owed to governments and banks are transferred at the market price mentioned earlier to a financial group led by Mr Soros, which "buys off" the debt at the Hungarian state as an investor group, receiving state-owned assets in exchange for debts. The plan was ingenious, but very risky; therefore, the prime minister of the day did not accept it.

Another reason why the proposal was rejected was that the bulk of the debt was owed to Japanese and German creditors, while the idea and the solution would have been American. It was also rejected because another possibility seemed to present itself, and it was one without major risks. A fast privatisation following the political change of system theoretically offered the opportunity for the Hungarian government to quickly collect a large amount of foreign currency in exchange for selling state-owned property, which could be used to reduce foreign debt. This solution is basically identical to the one proposed by Mr Soros, the difference is that the debts have to be repaid at nominal value.

In addition to this rational, safe game, the new government's strategy as regards foreign debts was also motivated by constraint. In the first months of 1990, foreign banks withdrew deposits from Hungary at such a pace that forex reserves fell to an alarmingly low level, below USD 1 billion. This was partly due to the fact that the Soros-plan leaked out: who wanted to see his forex deposits frozen and who wanted to lose 50-60 percent of the nominal value of his receivables? Nobody did, this is why banks withdrew deposits;

thus, the new Hungarian government found itself in a case of necessity even after rejecting the Soros plan. Our Western friends also advised the new Hungarian government against using a desperate and aggressive method to reduce the foreign debt, in favour of applying a quiet, continuous rescheduling and using privatisation revenues for reducing the debts.

This quiet rescheduling took place indeed between 1990-1993. The National Bank of Hungary and the government carried out the conversion of Hungary's short-term debts into medium-term and long-term ones expertly and with Western assistance. The quiet rescheduling and the simultaneous agreements with the IMF jointly ensured that Hungary's foreign debts ceased to be a number one political and economic burden between 1990 and early 1995.

The Moor has not Left ...

Then something interesting happened. Although we received help for quiet rescheduling and started selling state-owned property mainly to foreign investors, we did not emerge from the debt trap. This was perceivable on two levels right until the beginning of 1996. One of these was the accumulation of further debts: the gross foreign debt increased from USD 20 billion in 1990 to USD 32 billion by the end of 1994. The snowball set off in 1973 grew into an avalanche by 1990, and the avalanche did not bury the country, but rather it grew further. And this avalanche was not only growing, it was threatening Hungary as well, as it could come crashing down at any time.

The other level was the area of threat. Between 1990-92, the way of thinking and values of the International Monetary Fund became a major influence shaping Hungary's economic policy. During this period, leading Hungarian government officials exclusively chose solutions in fundamental issues of the economic policy which complied with the values, logic and way of thinking of the

IMF. The way these solutions came into existence was that, in some of the most important workshops of Hungarian economic policy (National Bank of Hungary, Finance Ministry), there was a strong inclination to the IMF way of thinking, to applying purely monetary and neo-liberal recipes. These inclinations were reinforced into economic policy decisions by the IMF delegations, in the form of a concealed threat with the foreign debts. There were requests made and advice put forward at the negotiations between the Hungarian government and the IMF delegations. However, the advice presented in a quiet and objective way had a hidden message: the threatened avalanche of Hungary's external debts which were very high by international standards and kept on increasing. "If the IMF does not sign an agreement with Hungary or cancels the existing agreement, then, although there will be no financial bankruptcy, the time of inconveniences can return,"—this is how leading Hungarian government circles read the encoded message.

As in the second half of the 1970s and throughout the following decade, the role of foreign debts was again to force out economic reforms. This happened despite the fact that the debt weapon proved a political weapon. Apart from a short detour, it again worked as a political weapon in the first half of the 1990s. The attachment of the bulk of the Hungarian political and economic elite to monetary and neo-liberal recipes is a story with many aspects, which I do not want to discuss here. However, the outcome is clear: Hungary's economic policy switched over to a path inspired purely by monetary and neo-liberal principles between 1990-92, in the first—and therefore most important—two years of the establishment of the new system. This, to a considerable extent, was due to the foreign debts, accumulated earlier, but still increasing further.

Why did the West not Cancel Hungary's Debts?

Hungary's foreign debts totalled USD 21 billion in 1990. This seems a lot, but it only amounted to a fraction of the total debts of the "developing world". It also accounted for an insignificant share of the receivables of the Japanese and German financial systems. Although Hungary's external debt was outstandingly high in the first half of the 1990s compared with the performance of the economy, as a result of the admirable debt management and the country's assessment, this carried no threat to creditors. Furthermore, everybody knew that the official economic performance (official GDP) and the real economic performance had nothing in common with each other. At the end of 1997, Hungary's economic performance was registered at an official USD 40 billion as against a GDP of USD 80 billion. Thus, the indebtedness was considerably lower compared with the real economic performance, and this was and has been clear to all decent experts in the West and Hungary alike.

Furthermore, between 1990-92 there was still a general upward trend in world economy, thus there was no reason to assume an intensification of the debt problem. Although Hungary's official GDP fell 20 percent between 1990-93, it did not decline by such an extent in reality, as privatisation was under way and the debts had been successfully rescheduled. Despite all difficulties, the country operated successfully, there was no reason to fear for the receivables. Finally, despite all Hungary's economic difficulties, there was general agreement in the West between 1990-92 that, as Hungary had been the showcase of economic reforms earlier, she would accomplish economic restructuring and Western integration the fastest and easiest of all. This was also where the strength of monetary solutions came from: the representatives of the neo-liberal ideas, which already had some momentum, knew exactly where and how the reforms begun earlier had to be continued and completed through monetary moves.

Well, these arguments hardly recommended the forgiveness of Hungary's external debts. On the contrary, they confirmed the assumption that, with some external help, the country would successfully overcome its difficulties by itself. Why should we make a gift to a country strong enough to get on without it? Poland did not seem as strong, and its condition gave cause for concern to the West. Poland therefore received debt forgiveness. There is no question of historical merits here: there seemed no need for special help to Hungary from the business point of view. The West could not see any urgent need for a new Marshall plan, or a European Baker plan, or a Schmidt plan for Hungary—they considered it enough to partly open the European markets to Hungarian products, to quietly reschedule the debts and to make foreign capital investments.

We cannot disregard the historical fact that Poland was more important to the West than Hungary. Poland, which has a population of 40 million, lies between the West and the East, and, through its historical traditions, cannot be considered either pro-Russian or pro-German. However, there are 6 million American citizens with Polish roots. Furthermore, as a result of the internal military takeover of 1981, Poland experienced a deficit of reforms in the 1980s and therefore deserved assistance more than Hungary. Also, Germany strongly hoped for historical reconciliation with Poland, her old-new direct neighbour. Thus, the strategic decision of the West as regards debt forgiveness favoured Poland and not Hungary.

Finally, we cannot disregard either the fact that Hungary's foreign debts provided a constant pressure toward opening markets and privatisation. Hungary opened its markets to foreigners the fastest and to the furthest extent in the region. The Hungarian governments of the 1990s applied no market protection measures, which, in addition to the neo-liberal way of thinking, was also due to the constant pressure of the foreign debt. This privatisation had a double effect: dollar revenues were very much needed just as was the other result of privatisation, a more efficient private economy, which—theoretically—would be stronger in carrying the burden of the external debts. There was a third area where the pressure of the foreign debts was perceivable: the way foreign capital investments were received. Hungary has basically sold her domestic markets to foreign suppliers, mainly as a result of privatisation and other foreign capital investments. Instead of selling off the markets cheaply, it would have been historically much more favourable to open markets more cautiously while supporting greenfield foreign investments.

The Debt Trap in Early 1995

The external debt problem, which intensified for a short time with the change of the political system in 1990, did not play a major economic and political role until early 1995. As we have seen, however, it played a key role in shaping economic policy in a concealed way. However, in early 1995, the threat of financial bankruptcy emerged almost out of nowhere. The consequence and solution of this situation was the new government's new economic policy: the Bokros austerity package and the sale of Hungarian monopolies to foreign investors. Thus, in 1995, the foreign debts again became a key factor, shaping the Hungarian government's economic policy in a decisive way, just as in 1977-78, 1981 and after the acceleration in 1985.

How could a dull minor character become a leading figure again? First, because 1994 was election year, when privatisation came into the centre of political struggles; and although it was not suspended, it still seemed to be the case in foreign observers' eyes. Many expected the new leftist-liberal government to slow down privatisation. And indeed, when the new government came to power it did not take steps to speed up privatisation, but waged fruitless battles on the new privatisation act behind the scenes. The quasi-halt of privatisation was more than just an ideological issue to Western observers: it meant that no privatisation revenues were collected, and, as a result, the foreign capital inflow could not curb the large foreign trade deficit, reducing it to a lower current account deficit. The Hungarian economy's proportions established by the mid-1990s meant that the deficit increase from imports considerably exceeding exports could be reduced by tourism revenues (the positive balance) and the forex revenues from foreign capital inflow (FDI), even though it could not be fully counterbalanced by these revenues. For lack of this reducing effect, there was a record current account deficit of USD 3.9 billion in 1994. This suddenly reinforced foreign concerns regarding the Hungarian economic policy (who knows what the new government will do) and the debt service. They found that if privatisation did not yield sufficient revenues and other revenues from FDI did not reduce the foreign trade deficit, Hungary would gradually slide into financial bankruptcy.

However, developments accelerated in late 1994, and the perspective of a few years shrank to a few months. In Japan, an estimated USD 1200 billion worth of bad corporate debts held by Japanese banks threatened to blow up the financial system of global economy. Share prices plummeted on the Tokyo stock exchange. As a result, the value of Japanese shares held by Japanese banks dropped, which meant that there was lower coverage for these bad debts held by the banks. Due to Japan's economic weight and particularly its special role in the financial world, this internal problem jeopardised world economic stability. Then, the USA and Japan concluded a large-scale, historical agreement, successfully reducing the risk of a collapse of the financial system.

During these nervous, anxious times, the Hungarian economy kept sending alarm signals to the control centres of the world economy. These alarm signals came from Hungary's financial sector, and they were directly put on the danger zone maps of international financial institutions. Moreover, this happened simultaneously with Mexico's financial collapse, and the obviousness of the very negative Hungarian financial figures was only separated by months from the Mexican financial crisis and its successful solution. Mentioning Hungary and Mexico together equalled slander, though such whispering had already started in international financial networks.

This was reinforced by some irresponsible and careless statements by the finance minister of the new government, expressing his concern that Hungary was facing a near financial bankruptcy. This slip of the tongue, unprecedented in the financial world, stemmed from the finance minister's intention to persuade the new government's leading party and the prime minister by the spectre of bankruptcy to introduce a financial austerity policy. He did not succeed. However, on the waves of international and domestic anxiety, the new finance minister announced one of the toughest—and let us add least successful—austerity programmes of Hungarian economic history. All the good news coming from the Hungarian economy in 1997-98 concerning industrial production, economic growth and investments does not result from the austerity programme of 1995, but rather in spite of it.

In 1995, the Hungarian energy and telecommunications sectors were sold off to foreign investors, and the government used the USD 3 billion revenue collected from this to reduce the foreign debt. There could have been better options: they could have spent it on urgently needed infrastructure developments, financing a second tax reform, or investing into education, which all would have been more useful in the long term than reducing external debt. Thus, the foreign debts fell below USD 30 billion by 1996, and the external debt problem returned to the comfortable and slightly dull role of a historical minor character.

Hungary Can Emerge from the Debt Trap
through the Right Policies

The external debt problem, as a minor character, will certainly play a role in Hungarian governing and economic policy for a further 5-10 years. By now, debt forgiveness has ceased to be a topical issue, and it has become historically possible to grow out of external debts. The reasons for this surprising change are divergent. Hungarian exports have been steadily and dynamically increasing in the second half of the 1990s, and this trend is expected to continue into the next decade. Annual export growth is projected at USD 1-1.5 billion, and imports are expected to expand even faster. As a result, the foreign trade deficit will increase in the coming 5-10 years. This in itself would result in intensifying the external debt problem, as the increasing foreign trade deficit of the coming 5-10 years would have to be financed from further loans, which would further increase the interest burden and the repayment obligations.

Fortunately, this will not be the case. The foreign trade deficit will be continuously curbed by the positive balance of tourism and foreign capital inflow. As for tourism, the picture is clear: tourism has produced a USD 1.5-2 billion surplus in the second half of the 1990s, and this could steadily increase in the coming 5-10 years. The maturation and profitability of tourism will be the most important factor reducing the foreign trade deficit in the Hungarian economy. On the model of Austria, Italy and France, Hungary's tourism industry will become one of the driving forces of economic development. The inflow of foreign capital will have an ambiguous effect on the increasing foreign trade deficit. Foreign capital investment in Hungary could amount to a minimum USD 1.5-2 billion a year in the coming 5-10 years. This will have a double effect: the inflowing foreign capital will improve the current account, reducing the need for borrowing; however, on the other hand, investors will repatriate profits, which will deteriorate the current account, increasing the need for borrowing. Currently, the profit of the FDI totalling USD 16 billion so far can be estimated at USD 3-4 billion, and only a fragment of this appears in official statistics.

Thus, the financial indices of the Hungarian economy are considerably better than the official statistical figures, and this is why I believe Hungary could grow out of the external debt problem. Of course, there are less optimistic scenarios as well. In case of a political crisis, external debts could bury the Hungarian economy. As a result of the extensive foreign capital investment, Hungary has become so vulnerable as regards the current account and the foreign trade deficit, that the loss of the annual net foreign capital investments or even a temporary decline of tourism could result in an almost unsolvable financial situation. In such a situation, the external debt problem could again play a key role, not by itself, but through other, more important factors. Another, also negative possibility could be if the upward trend of the Hungarian economy stopped, its capabilities attracting and absorbing foreign capital were exhausted and the dynamic growth projected for the coming 5-10 years failed to come about. Contrary to the previous scenario, this would not mean immediate financial bankruptcy; however, it would bring laborious struggle of decades for the Hungarian economy. For my part, I do not believe in either of these negative scenarios, and consider it definitely possible to emerge from the external debt trap if the economic policy is able to sustain dynamic growth.

Evaluating Indebtedness

Evaluating the historical role of Hungary's recent 20th century external indebtedness, we can see that it shows a high degree of similarity with the earlier. This is no surprise, as they were all attempts at solving the dilemma of "money and market". After 1867, the Hungarian economy managed to break free from the double grip of "money and market" by the early 1910s, because it simultaneously used the extensive markets of the monarchy and the financial sources of the monarchy and other creditor countries. Dynamic economic growth relied on both sources and resolved one with the other. It used money to create market and ability to obtain market, and used market and steadily strengthening market operators to attract and create more money. It managed money and market together.

The indebtedness waves of the 1920s and 1930s were unable to manage these two together: focusing now on money, now on markets. Therefore, if one was successfully secured—as Hungary managed to take out international loans for financial stabilisation, the other problem was left unsolved, as happened between 1929-33.

There was a similar double dilemma and ambiguity between 1948-90, although in a different dimension of "money and market". In the Hungarian economy, closed to the West and open to the East, neither money nor market forces worked. This was the historical situation of "neither market, nor money", which the continuous economic reform tried to resolve here and there, but could not break free from. External indebtedness became an instrument for resolving this problem with the strategy that letting external money (external loans) into the Hungarian economy would strengthen internal money, thereby gradually reinforcing the role played by market. Without market economy, multi-party system and opening the economy to the world, however, it was impossible to shift from the state of "neither money, nor market" to the state of "money and market".

After 1990, Hungary was again given a historical chance to resolve the dilemma of "money and market" at the same time. In the meantime, money and market have become international, in fact, global, and therefore Hungary's Eastern dependence has been replaced by a global dependence.

Hungary's external indebtedness conceals major historical paradoxes. The Hungarian political elite and Western strategic decision-makers equally expected the indebtedness to break the Eastern Empire, and they proved right. However, the disintegration of the empire also happened to countries (such as Czechoslovakia) which—through no fault of their own—could not become indebted. They obtained freedom without having to pay for it with external indebtedness. The first historical paradox is that Hungary undertook the largest share of the realisation of the Western strategy, while she received the least in exchange, and had to pay the highest price for the historical liberation. There is another paradox, however, as the first one suggests that Hungary could have obtained freedom without having become indebted. Yes, we could have obtained freedom, but the chances for economic progress and social mobility in the first decades of the next century may be higher as a result of the slow internal fermentation of the 1970s and 1980s than they would have been without the external indebtedness. Through its retreats and concessions, the system forced to constant internal reforms by the debts resulted in a rise into middle-class status of large numbers of people, in a way unique in Hungarian history. The real historical paradox is that we would not have had to pay the high price of foreign indebtedness for freedom; however, in order to seize our historical opportunities, we needed the internal fermentation of several decades, which, without this big adventure, would certainly have been omitted from Hungarian history.

Hungary's Internal Indebtedness

By the time of the change of political system, Hungary had considerable external and insignificant internal debts. On the other hand, by the end of the 1990s, the country will have net external debts of USD 10 billion and a significant internal government debt of USD 15 billion. The insignificant internal government debt inherited from earlier decades has grown into a considerable amount of internal debt over a decade, equalling the net foreign indebtedness by order of magnitude. What is striking here is the further slow increase of the external debt and the rapid growth of the internal debt.

The sudden swelling of the internal debt in the 1990s is one of the strangest phenomena in Hungary's economic history. This happened at a time when the external debt perceptibly narrowed the Hungarian government's scope of action, and it did not take special imagination to foresee that the internal indebtedness of the government would have similar consequences. It was also easy to foresee that the convertibility of the forint will make the difference between forint and forex debts disappear: debts earlier held in forints will turn into forex debts, with all the burdens of forex debts. However, it was indeed difficult to foresee that this would take place with the bulk of the government's domestic forint debts being transferred to banks, which, in turn, would be mostly acquired by foreign investors, and, thus, forint debts would become foreign receivables.

From the point of view of economic history, it is difficult to get away from the idea that what happened to the state externally over a quarter of a century between 1973 and 1997 happened to it internally over 5-6 years: it became considerably indebted. It is difficult to get away from this idea even though the state did not accumulate all its internal debts over 5-6 years: it also inherited some, and it also pretended as if it did not matter how much it actually inherited. The inherited domestic government debt included an item (the government debt of HUF 2,000 billion with zero interest) which was only pseudo-inheritance: it existed or did not exist as they wished. In 1996, the government decided that this zero-interest government debt is its existing domestic inheritance. Now, even if we postpone the debate concerning the inheritance, the domestic indebtedness of the Hungarian state happened surprisingly fast between 1991-97. No less surprising is the pace and the order of magnitude by which the process is expected to continue in the coming 5-10 years. Although history is speeding up and it can become particularly fast for a company drifted out from a closed harbour to the stormy sea of global economy. However, even considering this, the internal indebtedness of the Hungarian state happened surprisingly fast and reached a surprising level.

Thus, we have to ask the question: what caused this internal indebtedness? In addition to the inheritance, it had two main sources. The first source was the legislation package of the "monetary coup" adopted in 1991. In the new central bank act, the state gave up the possibility of financing at cheap interest rates the costs of the transition to market economy, globalisation, modernisation and Western micro-integration. This was carried out by a stroke of the pen, while it made it possible to finance the annual central budget deficit only up to 3 percent of annual central budget revenues by money issue (this was the encoded meaning of the zero-interest central bank lending). The remaining—and overwhelming—part of the annual central budget deficit was financed from loans taken out on the financial market, in line with the provisions of the central bank act. Representatives of the state may have believed that the economic transition of the 1990's and the other powerful historical processes would not incur extra costs on the side of government expenditures and the central budget deficit would be low; thus, the government would not accumulate major domestic debts. Perhaps they thought that the historical changes would involve major financial burdens but the costs would be concentrated in time, so Hungary would overtake the difficulties of modernisation and restructuring within a few years and the government would not accumulate major domestic debts. They may also have thought that the changes would incur major costs over a long period of time, however the interest rates of the loans taken out on the domestic financial market would be low, and therefore it would not result in major domestic indebtedness. Finally, representatives of the

Hungarian state might also have come to the conclusion that the transition would be both costly and lengthy, however a major domestic indebtedness of the state would not a bad thing at all.

For my part, I believe that the government officials of the first half of the 1990s, and particularly those aware of all the prospective economic consequences, followed this latter train of thought. These consequences can be summarised as follows: "The state will also become considerably indebted domestically, which may be inconvenient, but at least it will prevent governments from overspending." Of course this is true, as, in 1997 for example, the over HUF 700 billion interest paid after the domestic government debt was one of the largest expenditure items in Hungary's central budget, so the government certainly had to restrain itself from all kinds of wage increase, welfare and investment adventures. Those who believed they had enough of "the state's adventures" in investments and welfare services thought the easiest way to prevent this was to undo the money-bag of the state at the bottom and let the money trickle out so that the state would not find any money in its purse when it wanted to take some out at the top to finance some outdated investment or welfare adventure.

The easiest way to undo the money-bag at the bottom was to increase interest burdens, just as family households also have to pay for food and electricity first and therefore further expenditures are only possible if there is money left for other purposes. If the interest burden paid after domestic government debt increases to such an extent that no money will be left to finance the investment and welfare functions of the state, the Hungarian state will be prevented from such doubtful adventures. The representatives of this view believed that, historically, it is still better to prevent the state from financial adventures and make it indebted domestically than to let it get involved in financial adventures and increase its foreign indebtedness.

Another important source of the accumulation of domestic government debt was the bank consolidation. The Hungarian state spent approximately HUF 450 billion on consolidating the economy between 1992 and 1996, mainly on providing assistance to financial operators. Since then, it has become clear that this financial consolidation strategy was wrong in every respect, as it did not accomplish its objectives. Instead, it considerably increased the domestic government debt. Furthermore, the government bonds transferred to banks at 20 year maturity and at market interest rates have spoiled the Hungarian banking system to such an extent that it still—after a major capital injection, after privatisation and in possession of a major capital surplus—does not work as a complex of real banks. In fact, we have to evaluate this financial consolidation operation of the state as an unsuccessful adventure. The state undertook considerable financial commitments for 20 years unnecessarily, and the country did not receive a well-functioning bank system in exchange.

The swelling of the domestic government debt ties the hands of the state, because it accumulates a huge item on the expenditure side of the central budget, in the form of interest payments. This is considered to be good by representatives of the monetary and neoliberal economic theories– for my part, I consider it bad. The ship of the Hungarian economy has sailed onto the stormy sea of global competition, where rules and control have changed and, in addition, the ship must navigate with its sails and steering-wheel tied down. Under the laws of sailing, this will result in rolling and pitching, not navigation. The ingeniously tiny and almost invisible 3 percent solution of the new central bank act introduced in 1991 is the rope and the peg condemning the ship of governing to writhing instead of navigation.

There was another purpose that the accumulation of domestic government debt could be used for: an original redistribution of capital carried out as against an original accumulation of capital.

This is another very simple and ingenious solution, just as the 3 percent rule. Let us just imagine that we have some money to invest, and we have to choose between investing it into the economy (industry, agriculture, real estate) or into some financial investment instrument (government bonds, treasury bills). If we are in our right mind, we will choose the investment form with the lowest risk and the highest yield. If financial investments yield more than any other economic investments and, in addition, they are guaranteed by the state, we will not hesitate in purchasing government securities. It seems we will come off well and so will the state, as it receives money to repay its debts and interests; however, both will come off badly. The state will see its debts increase, and although we will continuously collect interest after our government bonds or treasury bills, the country we live in will not be able to use its development opportunities, which means we will also lose in the long term even if we win in the short term. If motorways, universities, new homes and plants, and the networks of the modern information economy are built more slowly or not at all, we will also lose as individuals even if we win temporarily, simply because our lifetime is limited. There is a difference between living in a good country and a struggling one.

Historically, the domestic government debt also worked as a tool redistributing capital and profit on a very deep and extensive scale, in addition to small individual profits. If I as an individual have won by purchasing government securities instead of investing into my own business, and this is done on a large scale by large numbers of people, it will move capital and profit from the real economy into the financial sector. Similarly, a considerable amount of capital and profit is transferred by the swelling of the domestic government debt through interest payment from domestic operators to foreign operators, because the operators of the financial sector—the winners—were largely foreign-owned financial institutions, investors and brokerage firms in this decade. In a rather strange way, the domestic government debt also carried out another major redistribution of capital within the real economy, not only between the economy and the financial sector. For the greater part of this decade, the average real rate of return on investments in the economy (the average profit above inflation of non-financial investments) was considerably lower than the average real rate of return of investments in the financial sector (the average profit of government securities and treasury bills). In this situation, the economy will narrow and the financial sector will expand, which also means that it will be increasingly difficult to generate income in the economy and a growing number of businesses will have to pay wages and other costs from savings and assets accumulated earlier. Thus, the real economy has been losing assets in this decade and the assets lost there largely appeared in the financial sector, with only a small part of it being redistributed to outstandingly successful operators of the real economy.

There was a further ingenious and concealed redistribution of capital between generations, partly as a result of the accumulation of domestic government debt and interest payment obligations. Let us imagine a 50-year-old worker employed by a mining company and a 25-year-old expert with two diplomas, one from a Budapest university and one from Oxford, employed by a brokerage firm. Let us imagine how ephemeral the job, the income and prestige of the former is compared with the position of the latter. What has happened in the case of two individuals has also taken place in the relations of large social groups, resulting in a redistribution of capital between generations at the expense of the older generation. This is mainly related to differences of qualifications and labour capabilities between older and younger generations. Well-qualified younger generations, increasing in numbers, are flowing in a natural way to professions and jobs benefiting from the redistribution of capital within the real economy and between the real economy and the financial sector. The level and the amount of interest paid after the domestic government debt has worked as a latent steering-oar in redistributing the properties, positions and prestige accumulated in Hungary in the earlier decades. If the level and the amount of the interest is high or considerable compared with the amount of profit available in the real economy, there will be a fast and large-scale redistribution of capital from the real economy into the financial sector, from domestic businesses to foreign investors, from the unqualified to the well-qualified, from the older generations to the younger ones. Of course, this also has a geographical dimension: Hungary's western part and the northern part of Transdanubia in particular as well as Budapest have benefited from the gains of this large-scale redistribution of capital, while the country's northern, eastern and southern regions have suffered its losses.

The domestic government debt is increasing due to the order of magnitude of the annual interest, while the foreign debt is growing at a slower pace. As it is now advisable to manage the two together, the overall indebtedness of the Hungarian state can be slowed down if the further increase of the domestic government debt can be slowed down. This can be halted, or in fact reversed, if the economic principle applied in this decade, the monetary/neo-liberal line is changed. That would create the possibility of covering at least the interest paid in forints by zero-interest central bank lending (money issue). As long as the world without Euro makes it possible, this could be implemented. The other option could be the taming of inflation, as the interest payment obligation at market rates is not as oppressive below 6-7 percent inflation as with double-digit inflation and double-digit interest rates. However, inflation is largely the result of the monetary and neo-liberal economic policy redistributing property and investment resources into the financial sector instead of the real economy, infrastructure and intellectual capital investments. The Hungarian economy is still in an artificially cooled state, just as it has been for the larger part of the decade. It is not utilising its human and physical resources to a desirable extent, keeping inflation at a higher level than it should be. This means that the original redistribution of capital through the domestic government debt and its interests is continued. The circle has closed, the grip of the debt trap is still tight due to the further increase of the domestic government debt and historically it will take longer than possible in releasing the country.

Epilogue

Being a small country, Hungary has seldom had the opportunity to determine the decisive turns of its fate in the past five hundred years of its history. This has also been the case in this century concerning the country's indebtedness. It was particularly true of the external indebtedness after 1973, which took place as part of a strategic game of great power politics. Its real aim was to create tension on the edge of the Eastern Empire in order to break up the empire itself and put Yalta under revision. The strategy proved successful and beneficial for our history, as we are again part of the West, where we have always belonged and where we longed to belong over the past decades. Similarly, the history of the internal indebtedness resulted from an external, and not internal strategy. The West has embraced us, but never disregarded its own rules of the game and its own interests. I am convinced that it did not realise its real interests when it forced the recipes of neo-liberal economic philosophy onto us in the 1990s.

The external indebtedness served to open up the closed Empire and, historically, we benefited from it. The internal indebtedness serves a close and strong dependence on Western integration, and, historically, we are losing by it. Central Europe and Hungary will emerge from its shackles as well as from the grip of the debt trap in the coming decades. This will happen because our historical situation found a country ready for catching-up, leading to a handshake of opportunities and capabilities. Hungary's rise and economic progress will be successful in the coming decades not because it chose the right strategy or, rather, the right strategy was forced onto it, but in spite of that. The source of the success will be the country's readiness for this historic leap.

Tamás Mellár

ECONOMIC POLICY CONCEPTIONS
AND POLITICAL FORCE FIELDS

Analytical Perspectives

The eight years which have passed since the change of system may be regarded from a certain point view (i.e. from the point of view of the economic policy analysis) as long enough to thoroughly evaluate events. From another point of view, however (i.e. from the point of view of the history of economy), this period is too short for a serious and sound evaluation. Nevertheless, this does not mean that only short-term and current policy-centred analysis could and should be attempted. Short-term may often mean short-sighted and it can easily mislead the analysis, because the road that appears ideal in the near-term may not lead the country towards the right final goal.

Therefore, this study intends to apply a system of in-depth perspectives over three different time-scales. This three-layered system may be thought of as based on the three tasks Hungary faces following the change of system: namely, economic consolidation, market-economy transformation and modernisation. Obviously, these three goals are interdependent: the achievement of one may be often promoted by progress in another of the fields. Still, it should be emphasised that the results obtained in one of them cannot counterbalance the under-achievements in the other, and the completion of one of these goal should not be carried out by sacrificing the other two.

In more concrete terms, the political and practical temptation is to sacrifice long-term modernisation goals for the sake of the

267

short-term consolidation goals. The results of the latter entail much better political returns for the period between two elections compared to the ones produced in the other area. Nevertheless, if all governments fall into this trap, we may easily end up like the person falling from the top of a skyscraper, telling himself to relax since during his descent no damage was done. Thus, all three perspectives and systems of goals will be regarded from here on as of the same rank and equally important elements of our analysis.

The judgement of the economic situation, beyond a strictly professional evaluation, may also become quite broad-based. The opinion of different walks of life is very important, and political judgement is essential as well. This latter basically depends on whether the opinion-maker is on the government's side or on the opposition's side, whereas the first is relative to the person's position within society and to the changes this position has undergone during the recent years—particularly how committed the person is to certain principles and to what extent this person may become the subject of manipulation. Professional evaluation needs to surmount these contingencies and subjective influences; nevertheless it would be very naive to assume that this can definitely be done. Obviously, the expert cannot free himself either from the influencing factors determined by his principles or even particular position. Moreover, facts are sometimes ambiguous, the data never accurate and every coin has its reverse, etc. These factors all weaken the exactness of a study in general and of this study in particular, too. All that the reader has to do is to be aware of these limitations and to take them into account and eventually form his or her opinion accordingly.

This study deals only with the issues raised by the Hungarian transition and no comparative analysis with the other former socialist countries will be carried out. Nor is this meant to be an economic analysis based on quantitative indices extracted from statistical data, but rather an economic policy evaluation focusing on qualitative aspects. Our study is not based on statistical data partly because they are not reliable enough, and partly these seem to conceal the essential message, the crucial moments and their change over time. This, of course, leads to an increase in the level of subjectivity and of the possibility of errors. Nevertheless it may render the study more interesting and the personal aspects of the conclusions are also explained.

Difficulties of Economic Consolidation

Subsequent to the political system change, economic consolidation appeared clearly the most important task, as the country inherited a deep economic crisis from the old regime (it was exactly the economical troubles that overthrew the regime). The transition to a market economy even worsened the situation in the short-term, as the feeble and unprepared socialist economies were shocked by the dramatic changes. Moreover, the world economy conjuncture occurred to be unfriendly in the early 1990s. The need for consolidation appeared in five main areas: 1) production and employment, 2) surplus of demand and inflation, 3) budget deficit and public finances, 4) lack of balance of foreign trade, 5) accumulation of foreign debts. Let us review these areas in more detail.

1. Economic growth and unemployment

Following the change of system, Hungary's stagnating economy slid into recession quite rapidly, leading in just two or three years time to a fall in GDP of some 20 percent.

The reasons for this significant regression are well-known: disintegration of outdated production cultures and structures, loss of the Eastern markets, drying-up of state subventions, insecurity due to the change of system, appearance of new competitors, etc. Simultaneous with the decrease of production, unemployment appeared and rapidly increased to over 10 percent. Moreover, the decrease of the economic activity rate from the former 50 percent below 40 percent meant an even more serious problem: over one million people were excluded from the category of active citizens and the already great number of those dependant started growing.

The economy, just recovering from the shock caused by the change of system, managed to produce a 2.9 percent growth in 1994; nevertheless, because of equilibrium tensions and the change of government another recession followed. Bringing the story up to the present, though economic growth will reach a level of 3-4 percent in 1998, due to the 1995-96 stabilisation measures this improvement will only return us to 1994 levels. Indeed, in spite of the relatively high rate of growth expected for the forthcoming year, GDP will hardly reach by the end of 1998 the level it had attained prior to the change of system. All this would not mean any serious problems provided that the regression and reconstruction were based on a fundamental structural, institutional and technical renewal of the economy, since in this case the entire process would become cost-effective. Unfortunately, only a partial and in many cases just a formal transformation and renewal is to be observed while the tensions and problems of the past live on unchanged.

Perhaps an even greater problem is the fact that despite economic growth, unemployment has remained practically at the same level. At first sight this could be regarded as positive, proving that productivity has considerably increased. However, this is in contradiction with the other fact that lately employment has gone up primarily in the services' sector where the growth of productivity is well below average. This is more about the growth of economy fostered by temporary (external) sources. Data from the last eight years tends to prove that the natural unemployment rate in Hungary is set around 10 percent. This may not seem very high and is in line with West European standards. However, it is certainly high for Hungary, especially if we take into account that this is a country where there was no unemployment before the change of system and that the activity rate has significantly decreased.

The third serious shortcoming of the production-based consolidation is the fact that the growth in production and prosperity failed to spread to the entire economy, benefiting only those more frequented areas of the country: Budapest and the western half of the country, while the south and east were almost completely omitted. In point of fact, prosperity applied only to joint ventures and the multinationals: these companies stand behind economic growth and they are the ones to take advantage of it as well. The small domestic undertakings did not feel any of the beneficial result of the economic recovery. So prosperity is very limited from the structural point of view, since exports have grown basically on wage-labour based activities involving goods imported from the West, consequently having no impact on the domestic suppliers' circle. Therefore, it is not surprising that neither the usage of the domestic forces of production and domestic wage policies nor consumption could live up to the trends corresponding to the boom.

2. Surplus of demand and inflation

The socialist economies, due to the lack of an active market and to the principle of centralisation, were economies of limited supply and therefore of forced savings and un-spendable incomes leading to the accumulation of a considerable surplus of demand. This was expressly the reason why it was expected that subsequent to the change of system the liberalisation of prices and commerce would conclude in a high inflation rate and the gradual loss of value of the domestic currency. The high inflation and the unstable national currency would result in a chaotic economic system rendering impossible the transition to a market economy. Therefore, especially the foreign financial experts recommended a radical currency consolidation policy and a dramatic restriction of demand—

in more common terms the application of "shock-therapy" was suggested.

As opposed to other former socialist countries, in Hungary the surplus of demand meant no real jeopardy (at least certainly not on the consumer goods market) due to the partial liberalisation of prices and markets carried out during the economic reforms implemented in the socialist era. Consequently, it would not have made too much sense to undertake a "shock-therapy" kind of consolidation. The first government after the change of system did not give in to the pressures of the professionals calling for this and decided for a moderately-paced, step-by-step consolidation. Nevertheless, the Antall cabinet could not avoid "shock-therapy" and shock effects, because the measures taken during the change of system had cumulated and concentrated so that their effects entailed serious, shock-like consequences.

The "shock-therapy" sort of consolidation had not been cancelled for good either. The liberal economists who came into power after the second parliamentary elections eventually managed to wangle the introduction of "shock therapy". The restrictive programme known as the "Bokros-package" was implemented following eight-months of conscious manipulating and influencing public opinion to create a sense of crisis so that the programme was regarded as a redemption. Its officially declared objective was to create equilibrium in the foreign trade economy, to avoid insolvency and the debts crisis. These aims could have otherwise easily been reached, provided that the controlled currency devaluation and extra customs tariffs had been introduced thus rendering unnecessary the radical restrictive measures applied in different areas of the state budget and public finances. Why were these necessary and why were they introduced? First, the Socialist Party cabinet of prime minister Gyula Horn wanted to restrict the old-style redistributive role of the state (obviously because Horn wanted to make place for a new-style role); second, the government wanted to reduce the incomes of the middle strata (and to render some balance in the incomes of the lower layers); third, the government wanted to strengthen the financial and banking sphere by providing them with extra revenue under the auspices of overall monetary and fiscal restrictions.

Concerning inflation the same remarks can be made as in the case of the GDP: subsequent to the 1991 nadir (35 percent) marking the shock of the change of system, the inflation rate started steadily improving (in 1994 it was only 18.8 percent); however, it then began to worsen for two more years after the coming to power of Horn. Later the inflation rate started to fall in 1997 and the decreasing tendency remained constant and hopefully will continue for the year 1998 as well. It has to be stressed, however, that the rate cannot be maintained steadily under 15 percent since there are no such reform conditions in the real economy or in the public finances (therefore, the decrease of the inflation rate is a mere election promise for the government); moreover inflation can only temporarily be reduced with the risk—even in the short term—of worsening the trade balance.

The present spectacular inflation rate decrease is due to the artificial increase carried out in 1995. The government used inflation for restrictive purposes and succeeded in reducing the level of real incomes by more than ten percent, which is quite unusual for economies in peace time. The preparations for the 1998 elections require no reduction of incomes, so inflation may be decreased. This means at the same time that in Hungary—contrary to the basic thesis of classical economics—there is no correlation between the inflation rate and an increase in GDP (and decrease of unemployment). Generally speaking, inflation goes up when the GDP decreases and falls when production grows. It seems that this is a particular feature of the four-year recurrent Hungarian business policy cycle. Another aspect means that inflation in Hungary is not determined by the volume of demand (the surplus of demand) but by the volume of supply, i.e. costs. Consequently, this means that inflation can be significantly and constantly reduced if the aggregated supply increases steadily and the cost of production as well as the central subsidy decreases.

3. Budget deficit and public finances

The budget (and public finances) deficit managed to get on the top-list of the most serious economic problems Hungary had to face following the change of system. This was a direct consequence of the decrease in production, because on the one hand this reduction has decreased (tax) revenues and on the other hand it has increased public expenditure needs (social-welfare support and consolidation costs). The change of system further aggravated the situation, because privatisation decreased the number of taxpayers and the volume of taxes paid, while the creation of new institutions and the establishment of the new financial and banking system meant further burdens for the state budget.

Consequently, the budget deficit was not caused by the classical over-expenditure, but rather by one-time expenses related to the burdens inherited from the previous regime and to the costs of the change of system. The main factors of the accumulation of the deficit were the payment of interest rates on our foreign debt, losses due to the devaluation pertinent to same and the outstanding expenses related to debtors'- and bank-consolidation. The superseding effect well-known from textbooks seems to have not worked amidst the particular relations of the Hungarian transition; on the contrary, an inverse reaction appears to be valid. According to the classical superseding principle, the prime public expenses of the state (i.e. welfare and investment-development costs) cause the deficit, and due to the need for financing the deficit interest-rates increase leading to the decrease of private investments.

In our case the shift in the market-profile as well as the market-conform financing of the deficit and the handling of the debts led to an increase in the volume of debts and liabilities related to payment of interests, so resulting in a considerable growth of the budget deficit. Budget control could have only been sustained if prime public expenses were reduced, besides maintaining a certain method of financing. Therefore, interest related payments superseded public expenditure pertinent to welfare and state investment expenses. The 4-5 percent (of the GDP) total budget deficit was reached by producing a 3-4 percent surplus on the prime expenses' level counterbalancing the 8-9 percent liabilities related to payment of interests. Obviously, this also means that in spite of the deficit the budget made no contribution whatsoever to the over-expenditure, to the creation of surplus in demands or to the picking up of the economy. Moreover, from the production and the important distribution systems' point of view the budget must be considered as a genuinely restrictive one. The budget may be considered permissive only from the financial sphere point of view, since it has redirected the tax-forints saved at the expense of the social distribution system to the banking system and to the important financial investors.

No significant changes or improvement in the balance of the budget and public finances occurred during the past few years. This does not mean, however, that no considerable restructuring was carried out in the state budget on the expenditure and the revenue side as well. On the expenditure side the social and welfare expenses, the local government subsidies as well as the development costs have been significantly reduced, while the interest expenses increased considerably. On the revenue side the ratio of the general (VAT-like), indirect taxes has grown. The levied taxes did not decrease; nevertheless, the taxation system became more complicated.

According to official statistics the redistributive role of the budget has considerably reduced over recent years. This change may be welcome in itself provided that we did not know the background of the decrease of the expenses, which is a cut-off of the expenses carried out by the "lawnmower method" instead of a reduction of actual money-waste based on a well-defined conception. It is also known that the public finance reform is still delayed, therefore further changes and burdens are to follow (the reform of the pensions' system has already signalled what the social-liberal reform means: a higher individual burden and less guaranteed safety in change); the redistributive role of the state is still important outside of the budgetary items (as in the case of the use of the privatisation revenues and the role of the State Privatisation and Assets Agency in this respect). Consequently, these sorts of statistics and declarations should not be taken seriously at all.

Concerning public finances, the replacement of the change of system and modernisation objectives with consolidation can easily be identified. The decrease of the budget expenses and the severe austerity according to their promoters serves three objectives: firstly, it decreases the importance and role of the state; secondly, it rules out inefficient organisations; and thirdly, it allows for the change of the structure. This means that the new organisations emerging in the place of the old ones may be implanted right from the beginning in different structural frameworks. Experience and facts, however, have been shown to contradict these positive expectations. The lawnmower-method of cost-reducing has ruled out not only the redundant or the inefficient institutions, but also the efficient and necessary ones. Meanwhile, the steadily decreasing role of the state cannot render the ruins into the shape of a new structure. On the contrary, in order to carry out a structural reform a more significant state action and support is required.

4. Foreign trade imbalances

Due to the market transformation and to the liberalisation of the foreign trade it was expected that imbalances in foreign trade and insolvency problems would appear. This was even more obvious because one of the basic problems in the economy of the former (reformed) socialist system was the very same issue. Interestingly, though, in the first two years of the change of system the problem of a foreign trade deficit did not occur. The explanation for this phenomenon is very simple: because production fell back significantly due to the change of system and was reduced accordingly, the volume of imports and exports could have been kept at the same level since warehouse stocks were still available. The situation dramatically changed following the commencement of economic activities after the shock of the change of system. One of the most serious economic problems during 1993-94 was the extreme growth of the foreign trade deficit.

The overly rapid foreign trade liberalisation, which left unprotected the newly born Hungarian market economy as well as the particular type of import-based development of joint ventures created with foreign capital and that of the multinational companies, played an important part in unbalancing foreign trade. Nevertheless, the main reason for the lack of foreign trade balance was the low competitiveness of the Hungarian economy, its weak capacity for adaptation and the inappropriateness of its technical standards. The foreign trade consolidation policy of the Horn cabinet did not take into account these facts, and instead built its concept on the foreign trade imbalance being generated by the overexpenditure of the government and by the budget deficit. Therefore, the government aimed mainly at reducing the budget deficit in order to create foreign trade equilibrium. Since after 1994 the budget presented no more deficit on the primary level the restrictions targeted at this level were unnecessary and proved to be insufficient regarding the managing of the problem mentioned. Statistical data have rather clearly shown that the main part of the foreign trade deficit (from 1993 on, the constantly growing part of it) was being produced by the sector of state undertakings.

No matter how efficient the treatment of the lack of balance in the foreign trade may be by the means of financial instruments, in the long-term this can only be considered a symptomatic treatment since the basic reasons should be looked for in the real-economy sphere. The controlled currency devaluation rate mechanism and the extra customs tariffs introduced in 1995 alleviated the problem but did not solve it. Extra customs tariffs may be used as a temporary measure but they cannot be considered a reliable long-term solution. The continuous monthly controlled devaluation may only be effective if a strong restriction of demand is applied as well (as happened in 1995-96). Otherwise a devaluation/cost increase/inflation/devaluation spiral-like process commences. On the other hand, incomes cannot be permanently held back, especially when elections are to take place. Therefore, the 1997-98 picking up of the economy might easily annihilate the improvements obtained with such severe constraints during the recent two years.

The renewal of the problems related to foreign trade imbalance can already be identified; still the government rejoices cheerfully because of the successful foreign trade consolidation. It is undoubtedly true, however, that the public debts deficit seriously decreased during 1996-97; nevertheless, the improvement is far less spectacular regarding the foreign trade deficit. In addition, the latter is expected to worsen in the very near future. In order to evaluate the actual state of equilibrium the evolution of the foreign trade balance is more important (since it reflects the actual evolution of the real economy processes) than the budget deficit, which may improve due to certain positive changes in one-time financial factors. Still, none of these deficit indicators improved to such an extent that they would bring about a new situation from the quality aspect, solving for good the problem of foreign trade imbalances. The new situation would not occur even if the public debts deficit is counterbalanced for the moment by the active capital presently invested in the country. The active capital presently invested in Hungary represents a short-term financing criterion and has very little to do with the real balance of economy.

5. Accumulation of foreign debts

Perhaps the easiest to deal with and the simplest to compute of the serious problems inherited from the socialist regime was the accumulation of foreign debt. The interest liabilities exceeded 5 percent of GDP already at the end of the 1980s and therefore the spectre of foreign debt trap bearing down on the Hungarian economy became more and more threatening. Due to the seriousness of the issue many opinions were developed after the change of system concerning the management of the debt problem. One of the extreme poles was the "let's pay back nothing and ask for rescheduling or remission of the debts" while the other said "let's pay back everything along with the interest even if we have to sell our family jewellery". In practice we had a solution closer to this latter option. Through the state revenue obtained from privatisation (which primarily meant the selling to foreign investors of the energy sector), an opportunity was created to significantly reduce the foreign debt. On the other hand, due to the flow-in of foreign active capital the foreign debt could have been converted into internal debt (through state treasury bonds).

The possibility of having a debt crisis has considerably decreased since the state debt has fallen from the former 85 percent of the GDP to below 70 percent of GDP. The net foreign debt has more significantly decreased than the gross debt, whereas the volume of domestic debt has not decreased to such an extent as the foreign debt volume has. In spite of the reduction of foreign debt and the alleviation of the inflation rate resulting in lower interest rates, a significant decrease in interest liabilities could still not be achieved. This means that the shift of the external debts to domestic debts was not efficient enough and the conversion of central bank financing to treasury bonds financing entails a considerable growth of interest rates. This process was most obvious when transforming the so-called "zero volume", since the conversion declared as a mere technicality cost the government over HUF 120 billion (net) in extra expenditure.

Of course the total cost of reducing the volume of foreign debt includes some items which are very difficult to compute, such as forced privatisation, technical monopolies and the selling to foreign investors of the markets and production lines. These costs already exist and will exist both in the near and further future as well. Moreover, it needs to be stressed that the long-term consolidation is ensured not by the debts/GDP ratio reduced under 60 percent but rather by steady and significant economic growth. There are several dynamically growing and developed economies that have borne a debt/GDP ratio over 100 percent for decades; still, due to the positive evolution of their real economy indicators they have no reason to worry because of the relatively large amount of foreign debt.

6. The permanence of consolidation

Concerning consolidation, let us review briefly in conclusion whether the positive changes of the recent years in macroeconomic figures reflect a successful consolidation and system change as well as the shift toward long-term sustainable growth, or whether they simply mean a temporary improvement as witnessed in 1994. A temporary turn would mean keeping the country on the waiting list for achievement of true quality improvement. The answer is that, unfortunately, transition has not been concluded yet and the Hungarian economy has still to undergo a very serious and basic transformation in order to display a solid competitive market able to produce high-rate growth without the external or internal balance being disturbed. This opinion is based on the fact that underneath the present positive changes there are some reasons which may be explained not by the inherent operation of the domestic market but rather by external circumstances.

The 3-4 percent economic growth of 1997 was produced by the artificial state-driven upturn of the economy and not by spontaneous functioning of the private sector. Despite the fact that state property has been reduced to less than 30 percent of the production capital and the direct state subsidy of the economy is decreasing, the influence of the state is still too significant. The state exerts itself partly through indirect economy policy instruments such as monetary and budgetary policy measures (e.g. tax-, interest- and loan policy, etc.) and partly through extra-budgetary expenditure, which pumps extra resources into the economy. It is obvious that while preparing for elections the government strives to boost the economy at all costs. The former government did the same (and thus started the political business cycle, which took over the place of the socialist-type of planning cycles) and this is mainly what the governments of more developed economies do, too.

Another aspect regarding the weakness of consolidation is that improvement was not based on internal factors continually present in the economy but rather on one-time external factors such as increase of privatisation revenues, levy of import customs taxes, continuous devaluation of the national currency, in-flow of high volume of foreign active capital, etc. All these factors contribute to the accidental character of positive changes, as there is no insurance respective to the steady effect of these factors or to the future existence of them when further consolidation efforts will be required.

The criterion for shifting to a new positive evolution of economy is not that the economy produce in one or two favourable years higher growth figures than the previous growth trend. There is more to this, namely that a real economic basis for growth is established and sustains itself: the volume of capital undergoes a quantitative and qualitative improvement process, the professional standards of labour increase and the overall technical and technological standards improve. However, following the change of system no crucial positive changes could have been registered in these areas, especially not after 1994. Due to the consolidation measures implemented with the so-called Bokros-package investments decreased by over 10 percent, while the block grants intended to support education and research have fallen considerably as well. Nevertheless, these are exactly the fields in which the state has to assume a special role, as due to its nature no one can expect that these activities will be actively maintained by the private economy and supported by the rules of the market economy.

The Results of the Change of the Economic System

Subsequent to investigating consolidation, let us briefly review some important issues relating to the establishment of a market economy and the change of economic system.

1. Choosing a model

The main guidelines of the change of economic system were essentially influenced by the intention of initiating political changes and democratic transformation as well as creating civil society. Under these circumstances any kind of rigid or centrally controlled model of economy was ruled out from the very beginning. Concerning planned or market economy options, with almost no debate everybody voted for the latter alternative. Nevertheless, there has been a small group of professionals devoted to the idea of undertaking a so-called "third option," intermediate solution, which was intended more to impose state or socially (Workers' Council, small communities, etc.) controlled limitations of market economy rather than to preserve a socialist-type planned economy. The only competitive option, however, remained the market economy, as it has already historically proven its viability whereas the non-market-based economic systems lead almost as a rule to a state of impossible operation or to a centrally controlled model.

Subsequent to accepting the system of market economy the issue of what to choose needed to be addressed, as there were several operational market models available both in time and space. There were three types seriously considered in Hungary: the Anglo-Saxon liberal model, the Scandinavian welfare model and the German social market economy model. Evidently, the different political parties embraced the options more appropriate to their political beliefs: the social-democrats chose the Scandinavian model, the liberals considered the Anglo-Saxon alternative while the conservatives reviewed the social market economy model. The conservative government that came into power after the change of system won the elections by using the slogan of a social market economy without being able in the given situation to create it. Nevertheless, this does not mean that the majority of the society really wanted a social market economy.

The vast majority of the electorate misunderstood the social market economy model and thought of it as some kind of particular combination of Kádár-style socialism and the Western-type of market economies. They imagined that this special mixture would obviously bear only the positive elements of both ingredients. When people realised that this could not be brought off, that socialist relations would still apply for the production process but the consumption part would be more Western, they rejected the conservatives and began supporting the socialists, who had earlier realised at least one part of their dreams. However, the social market economy did not really fail in Hungary as it was not introduced in the first place. The Antall cabinet strongly committed itself both politically and rhetorically to it but due to the particular circumstances the government could not take any firm steps toward the introduction of this model. The introduction lacked on the one hand a solid governmental decision and the adequate professional and specialist background, and, more importantly, on the other hand it did not have the support of the external and internal economic factors.

The creation of the social market economy was not in the interest of the foreign investor nor of the (new) domestic group of entrepreneurs (private investors), as the broadening of competition, the creation of equal opportunities and the establishment of background institutions for the market would have all enhanced the competition, infringed the rights earned and eventually would have lead to the loss of monopoly positions gained through political machinations. Therefore, the idea of the social market economy gradually was taken off the agenda due to the false reason of the still weak Hungarian economy being unable to socially support the losers of the market economy. The real reason for this is that there was no intention of involving wider groups of society in the selling out of monopoly positions, state owned markets and production capacities which was and is still going on instead of market economy transformation and market creation. The model presently being implemented in Hungary does not correspond to either of the aforementioned options but rather shows resemblance to South American economies or Western economies of the XIXth century and may be described properly by comparing it to state-monopoly capitalism.

2. The transformation of the ownership system

It was widely agreed that the main task of the change of economic system was the transformation of the ownership structure by rendering private ownership dominant within the system. It was also commonly supported that the transformation should be carried out by restructuring state property, i.e. by privatisation. The real disagreements occurred when deciding how to undertake privatisation. Concerning privatisation, the classical triangle of questions may be asked: *what?, how?, for whom?* The latter two questions were regarded as most relevant at the start of privatisation. It has become obvious for the time being however, that the first question was at least equally important as the other two.

Passionate debates emerged regarding the *'privatisation for whom?'* issue. Basically four 'privileged' groups were brought into discussion: former owners, citizens, workers and whoever would like to buy property. Connected to this, the question of *how* gave birth to answers ranging from returning property free of charge to former owners through below-price selling to sale at full market value. In practice the business-type privatisation won and became the decisive method. Nevertheless, in certain domains discount-based privatisation techniques as well as mixed methods were applied with no significant influence on the privatisation process as a whole (except for agriculture, where compensation and the return of the property share pertinent to the member of the collective farm created a special situation). The business-type privatisation was supported most significantly by the fact that due to the management of debts the Hungarian economy needed extra resources and it is more likely for efficient management to be performed by those who purchase the instruments than those who just obtain them free of charge or at a discounted price. The requirement of obtaining revenues compelled Hungarian privatisation to a forced evolution: the principle of "sell fast and sell all" prevailed and, therefore, the new owners' obligations concerning production, employment, technical development and investment has not been emphasised properly.

The 'what to privatise' issue raised less debate. All the same, important disagreements appeared here as well and could have been identified as the ever changing list of undertakings envisaged to be preserved as state owned property in the long term. In spite of the debate and changes, the concrete results are depressing: some of the sectors sold out would have been better from the future objectives' point of view to remain for a certain period of time under state ownership (e.g. the fiscal areas, sugar and tobacco industry, food industry because of the development of the agricultural production). On the other hand comprehensive market (monopoly-oligopoly) positions and full sales chains were sold out as well (e.g. the privatisation of the commercial sector). Finally, the technical monopolies and the strategic industrial branches were privatised without proper guarantees. The selling out of the energy sector as well as the bank privatisation are eloquent examples of how not to privatise.

From a quantitative point of view the transformation of the ownership structure has been carried out, as more than 70 percent of GDP is produced today by the private sector. Considering the qualitative aspect, though, a major problem is the lack of a healthy organisational culture—there is no middle within the pyramid of undertakings, in other words there are no middle layer entrepreneurs. The base of the pyramid displays many small undertakings (rather micro-undertakings) and a part of these are not genuine but compelled undertakings created just to avoid strict tax regulations. The other part of these undertakings are in a very unstable situation; they are virtually levitating between being and not being and being legal or illegal, respectively. The weak situation of small and medium-size undertakings occurred due to the fact that during the change of the ownership structure the official economic policy focused almost exclusively on privatisation and omitted the appearance of the sphere of new entrepreneurs. In spite of repeated promises, there are no effective development and initiative support programs for undertakings even in these days. The position of the large concerns is maybe more stable and stronger than it should be, as is very difficult for others to enter the competition and get hold of market share in the respective domains. Simply stated, during privatisation the former state monopoly positions were converted into private monopolies.

3. Creation of the institutional and legal background

According to the original conceptions "shock-therapy" referred not only to the consolidation but also to the change of system and the privatisation that should have been carried out under its auspices as fast as possible in order to allow the almighty market to exert its beneficial effects. Related to the creation of the institutional and legal background it has become clear that this conception is wrong because the profoundness and the professionalism of the changes as well as the sustainability of the operation and the creation of an appropriate market function are far more important than speed and radicalism. Subsequent to the first years' experience with the change of system even the Western advocates of the radical solutions (including the experts of the World Bank) had to revise their ideas regarding fast transition.

The institutional and legal background for the functioning of a market economy has been realised to a great extent in the past eight years. During the creation of the legal background, the servile copying of the legal solutions of the more developed Western states appeared almost as a recurring error leaving out the national particularities and the special features of the transition period. Therefore, the need to reformulate adopted positions regularly recurred after the enacting the laws, often rendering them too complicated and controversial. The lack of a solid legal background negatively influenced the efficient functioning of the market: the laws on taxes for instance were modified on average every second week in the last five years.

The slow and unprofessional functioning is characteristic both for the newly created and for the old but transformed institutions. The old norms and bad traditions tend to live on. There are no professional personnel, the good specialists moved away and the entire structure depends too much on politics. One of the great failures of the transformation of the institutional structure is the continuous postponement of the reform of the important distribution systems. There has been a plan for reform of the pension system and new practices were implemented. However, several aspects of this reform may be subject of criticism and it seems doomed to failure right from the beginning. Moreover, nothing has been done in the other areas, rather the good old principle of "restrictions instead of reform" was applied. Nevertheless, it would be crucially important to transform the national health, education, culture and welfare systems since while these provide low-standard services and dispose of a poor management they are becoming more and more impossible to finance on the macroeconomic level. Reform requires sound concepts, wide-ranging social debate and consensus. The goal is evident: a smaller but more efficient provision system needs to be created which does not concern a welfare-type of revenue redistribution but improves equality of opportunity.

In the present state of development of the market mechanism, it is easy to see that neither the system of laws nor that of the institutions serves the goal of creating and sustaining a properly functioning broad market economy but rather the preservation of the particular interests of certain groups. This is attested to by the defectiveness of the tender regulations, the ever growing corruption and the tenacious expansion of the black economy. The defectiveness of the tender regulations is obvious if the lack of competition in the economy is considered, as well as the conservation or creation in several industries of monopoly or oligopoly positions due to the deployment of multinational corporations taking advantage of their virtually limitless power. Participation in the market is hindered by several obstacles in many areas as the small and medium-size undertakings are unable to face the market siege of the powerful mammoth corporations.

Corruption also belongs to the heritage of the socialist regime and is well embedded in the conscious of the political-economical elite and the state bureaucracy, as well as in their behavioural patterns. The change of the political system and the publicity could not make much difference in this respect. The overall morality, the ignorance and the almighty web of nepotism and relations maintain corruption at a steady level. Moreover, the return of the socialists to power expressly increased corruption since all they needed to was to brush up their old relations and start using their good old practices.

The black economy is not a new phenomenon, either: its longevity and expansion are not a consequence of the shift to a market economy. The black economy survived primarily because of the inadequate regulations of the market and the inappropriate role of the state in market creation. In order to curtail the black economy, changes in three areas need to be considered. First, the taxes and duties levied on businesses should be decreased as well as other financial liabilities pertinent to their operation. In addition, accountability and administration should be simplified in this respect. Second, the integration into the officially registered forms of economy should be supported by incentives and preferred formally. Financial support and tax reductions should be linked to fully legal operations. Thirdly, non registered and illegal operations should be addressed by strict punitive measures.

The Issue of Economic Modernisation

The third aspect to be analysed is the level of long-term development and the modernisation of the Hungarian economy. Let us review the evolution of the events of the years subsequent to the change of system and the important tasks that remained unaccomplished.

1. Modernisation strategies and conceptions

The relatively underdeveloped nature of the Hungarian economy bears a long historical past; maybe King Matthias' medieval Hungary belonged for the last time to the group of the most-developed countries. The Kádár-led socialist regime, famed for its "goulash communism", did not intend to be the "saviour of the working class", but instead wanted to modernise Hungary and eliminate its centuries-long underdevelopment. In spite of some initial successes, the experiment failed and in the 1980s the distance between the developed countries and Hungary began increasing instead of decreasing. Therefore, the socialist system proved to be a failure as a modernisation model, too. Subsequent to the political change not only a system but a modernisation strategy should have (also) been chosen.

The professionals' debate brought seriously into discussion three options out of all the possible modernisation strategies: the classical model, the underdeveloped—recovering model and the Far-East model. According to classical modernisation theory, successful modernisation requires an adequate behaviour on behalf of the society. The key to success is a strict work ethic, a considerable willingness to save and an outstanding standard of professionalism. However, a society needs a considerable amount of time to acquire these "Protestant" virtues even under fortunate circumstances. The underdeveloped/recovering model presumes that recovery may be ensured only by the active role assumed by the state, creating rapidly the institutions which could be developed only slowly if pursuing the natural course of organic evolution. The more underdeveloped a country is, the greater state involvement is required. The Far East model implies a powerful state as well that should not take responsibility solely in the creation of the institutions but also in the enforcement of strictness and discipline. This is how hard work, high rate of savings and considerable surplus of exports is achieved.

There were no extensive and passionate debates on these modernisation strategies. The liberal parties could not even interpret the problem and stated that the market would solve the issue of modernisation (as all other issues as well). The conservative parties embraced rather the Far East model; however, they sensed that the Hungarian state may not be able to apply such tough centrally-directed measures. The socialist parties adhered more to the recovery concept, but in their dreams in fact they were pampering the reformed socialist-type of modernisation. It was this the reason that right after their coming to power they elaborated a modernisation concept reflecting the work of several well-known experts and spending significant resources. The central elements of the modernisation strategy concept of the government was quite questionable (and as a matter of fact the experts questioned them), while the issues of realisation and the methods of financing were not clarified altogether.

Therefore, it is not surprising at all that the implementation of the modernisation programme proposed by them has never been seriously taken into consideration. The Horn administration is genuinely concerned only with short-term problems and does not take into account the long-term effects of its decisions. The government seemed to have found the panacea to the long-term problems of Hungary in Hungary's joining the European Union. This attitude suggests that if Hungary seriously considers integration, it should do whatever it is told and all the problems should be solved with the methods proposed within the framework provided by the EU. In reality the success of integration entirely depends on how well the country is prepared, while its position and role in the community depends on whether Hungary disposes of a constructive vision and of a feasible national strategy.

A modernisation strategy should be developed which deals with a 25 year period and formulates a comprehensive programme for the various subsystems of society providing them with concrete objectives and tasks. Obviously, the financial conditions of such a programme should also be ensured by delimiting a certain percentage of the GDP each year for the purposes of this plan.

2. Special areas of modernisation

Maybe the most important area to be developed is the infrastructure. Hungary is well behind in this respect, which hinders the overall development of the country. The differences in development levels and incomes existing within the country may be reduced to the infrastructure background. Eastern Hungary, for instance, where there are no motorways and an adequate network of roads is missing, produces one fifth of the incomes per capita as compared to the central or western regions of the country. The motorway concessions should be revised and a national motorway-construction programme should be initiated. The pubic utility development programme is also very urgent in the eastern part of the country as well as in the smaller localities.

Another important area is the technical and technological development. The newer economics theories have clearly established that technical development is not a "free" exogenous factor or a positive external contribution that is automatically produced by the market economy, but it is an endogenous factor which depends on the amount of labour and capital invested in it; moreover, due to the non-rival and non-exclusive features of the technological development the private economy has neither the will nor the power to create it. In this respect nor the small undertakings nor the multinational corporations or joint ventures can be taken into consideration. These corporations usually deploy their out-dated technology to Hungary leaving behind in their homeland their development departments. Therefore, both basic and applied research need strong state subvention. The dissemination of developed techniques and technologies should be supported directly by block grants and indirectly by tax reductions as well.

Equally important is the third item on the list, which is the development of human capital and modernisation of education. According to the most recent growth theories nearly one-third of the GDP is known to be produced by human capital contribution and therefore, each modernisation theory should put special emphasis on this issue. Concerning education the relative advantage Hungary previously had is slowly disappearing provided that nothing is done in this respect or if the restrictive policy started by the Bokros package is continued. An overall reform is required, which eliminates wasted resources and poor standard education and results in a more efficiently working flexible and focused education system.

In conclusion: the regional and area development issue needs to be stressed. Hungary has fallen into three parts from the development point of view and the most developed regions are six to ten times ahead of the least developed ones. The previously existing gaps have grown even wider after the change of system. The traditionally backward regions were unable to integrate themselves into the market economy system solely based on their own resources. Unless there are effective state programmes these huge gaps would destroy the frames of operation of the economy. Market creation, revenue redistribution, tax reductions are required in the backward regions.

Attila Károly Molnár

THE OPEN SOCIETY[1] AND THE CHAOTIC PRISON

> *"All that I say is just a story,
> not meant to be advice."*
>
> *Montaigne*

1.

When our liberals were in opposition, the ideal of the open society became the measure of everything.

Although this ideal has been dropped from their discourse now that they are in government[2], sooner or later again they will end up in opposition again, where they will rediscover this ideal and use it to its critical potential. In the following I will try to present the concept of open society and a critical image of the modern society, an image which also characterises Hungary after the change of regime. This image of society is what I call the "Chaotic Prison". Due to its nature, my description does not mean to be precise, but rather *enlightening*. When one describes a lion, it is not important whether the lion is precisely described or not, but that one can convey the picture of the lion.

The utopia of the open society[3] does not suggest a static situation, it does not look like the static utopias of Thomas More and others, in which we get the detailed description of institutions and human relationships. In Karl Popper's and his followers' writings the open society is first of all a negation, the negation of the closed society. From Popper we find out more about the closed society than about the open one; and, which is even more important, he identifies the closed society with his contemporary totalitarian

294

states and first of all with fascism. Advocates of the open society have ever since been talking about societies and public actors in a dichotomy characteristic of Manichaean heresy. The Manichaean language looks upon the political world as the constant fight between good and evil, truth and wickedness. In this way advocates of tolerance are systematically intolerant towards their debating-partners and, based on this Manichaean approach, condemn them. Thus people who do not support their view can only be situated on the other side in this scenario, that is on the side of the closed society, which is identified with fascism. For European intellectuals, the fact that it is identifiable with fascism is quite enough as an argument against anything and anyone.

The ideas and arguments of the open society are supported by the literature of religious freedom: among others, the most popular are Milton's *Aeropagitica*, Locke's *Letter on Religious Patience* and J.S. Mill's *On Liberty*. These writers, in advocating individual freedom, brought up the arguments of truth, peace and progress, which also occur in Popper's writings. But neither these writers nor Popper mentioned political structure, institutional organisation or the traditional issues of power: who and how exercise it and how it can be gained. The Hungarian liberals' critical thinking and the ideal of the open society, which they have so much impressed on the public, does not mention the most important matters of state and politics, power, coercion, compliance, their control and limits, etc. Of course one cannot expect one particular piece of writing to thoroughly discuss everything, but this shortcoming is more than conspicuous, since fascism, which is mentioned as the negative counterpoint, was a political system, a totalitarian *state*. Furthermore, Popper quotes from the writings on state theory of Plato and Hegel, two "disliked" authors, enemies of the open society. Thus, the ideal of open society is opposed to the *reality* of totalitarian states and political *theories*. (This peculiarity of the principles and arguments of the open society is even more conspicuous if we consider that

Plato, whom Popper so thoroughly criticised, did not like democracy and the type of democratic man. Plato mostly disliked democracy, because its theory and the Greek practice unavoidably[4] lead to tyranny. The ideals of political community offered by Plato and Hegel, which according to Popper are radically opposed to the open society, were indeed different from democratic ideals but also from the ideals of dictatorship, because their principal importance was the defence against tyranny.) Despite this, we do not know anything at all about the function and role of power in the open society. Due to this contrast, it seems that the open society is tacitly also opposed to power and coercion: in a community of free, rational beings there is no need for coercion, power, and therefore they do not exist. This is why I call the open society a *rationalist utopia*.

In the open society there is no common culture, which contains not only common meanings recognised by everyone, but also the coercion, the rules connected to them. In the totality of common meanings, which make social life possible, the elements of the nomos are cognitive (we all know what "red light" means) and normative at the same time (we all know has to be done when the light is red). The cognitive element cannot be separated from the normative. The plan to do away with the nomos (law) does not only view the norms, but it also views the cognitive elements. Without these, is it possible to live and act rationally?

The tendency to erase social group differences ("we" and "you") is increasingly moving toward the dissolution of all former moral limits. The dissolution of barriers between social groups promises peace: since the source of conflicts is the separation of mankind and thinking in categories, then the demolition of the separating walls is done in the name of peace. For the sake of peace, groups of people have to melt into universal humankind. This takes us back to the platform of the French Enlightenment: the domination of universal human reason, that is the abolition of particular arbitrary prejudices, makes way for the rational consensus of humankind. Besides the ancient argument of peace, the other important argument for the dissolution of social, cultural and moral limits (what is right and what is wrong) is the fact that limits are arbitrary and difficult to define. Simmel's[5] argument against this, is that though we find it hard to precisely determine the time, the limits of dawn and dusk, we still clearly know the difference between day and night. However unable people are to precisely express this difference in words, they still know that there is day and there is night. It is the same with cultural and moral limits. However unclear the dividing line between right and wrong is in practice, rational men know exactly that there is good and evil, right and wrong.

The deficiency of the closed society, Popper says, is that besides the intellectual oppression and darkness, it divides humankind and therefore it is a source of unrest. The victory of individual intelligence, of the critical reason that questions everything, coincides with the advent of world society and of eternal peace. This double hope and promise was not new in Popper's time, either. Earlier, this charge of division was only used against the Pope, then against the Catholic Church and now against the closed societies. The world of identity, of common meanings and duties, has always separated those who know the meanings and rules from those who do not know them—or do not recognise them. The basic idea of Durkheim's sociology was that integration is always accompanied by segregation, that the common knowledge and rules that allow the functioning of a society divide a certain society from others. Further, the difference may produce conflicts. The hope of the open society and, generally, of rationalist utopias, is that segregation, the "we" and "you", can be eliminated in such a way that inner integration will not be affected, and the outer peace will be maintained. The elimination of conflicts between societies and groups requires that the integration of groups be sacrificed for the sake of a hopefully new integration. It requires the sacrifice of our common knowledge, meanings, rules that make co-operation possible; everything that connects us has to be sacrificed, because this everything also separates us from others. A price has to be paid for the elimination of conflicts between groups and societies—disintegration or anomie, which is accompanied by increased conflicts among individuals, loss of reason and the sense of chaos. According to Popper, only an open society is absolutely homogeneous, that is, it excludes the possibility of group conflicts. Only such differences can survive that do not lead to conflicts and in this way they do not give rise to the need to solve conflicts. The reason for homogeneity is peace, and in this case decisions and coercion can be eliminated. For instance, if some people want fried potatoes, others mashed potato, and still others baked potatoes for lunch, then the chef will have to decide—and the legitimacy of his decision is another problem. But if everyone has fried potatoes, and the only difference is how much salt and pepper they will have on them, then the chef does not need to make any decision. And the provision of salt and pepper is only a matter of economy. The condition is that everyone becomes a "potato-eater" (i.e. an "open-liberal-democrat").

The open society is a negatively worded utopia: its advocates never or hardly ever write about what it actually is. They prefer to write about what it is not. That is why when one describes the open society, one has to put the picture together from fragments. It is clear that: 1) the openness of the open society is first of all cultural and moral, and that 2) in an open society the state has serious social and cultural (educational) duties. The open society differs from the closed one in that in the former the individual enjoys absolute liberty in matters of culture and morals: "the society in which the individuals are faced with personal decisions is an open society".[6] Closed societies are characterised by a "magical attitude", which "exists in the magical circle of unchanged taboos, laws and customs, which they find as natural as sunrise or the cycle of seasons or other similar obvious regularities in nature."[7] In comparison with this, the open society is that where people find norms and rules artificial, and they believe that "our duty is to improve these as much as we can".[8] In the open society people are critical, there are no taboos, individuals make decisions based on their own intelligence only. The essence of the open society is absolute moral and cultural autonomy. This, however, as Popper says, does not happen automatically, but it needs scientific policy and social engineering. So the creation of open societies requires scientific policy, despite the fact that Popper considers that the open society will necessarily come into being.[9] Though history will necessarily bring it about, it is better if we do not trust history and do something for it, participate in the creation of the society that will inevitably come. This historicism is odd: Popper himself trenchantly criticised histories[10] that claimed to describe trends in history, and thus pretended to foresee the future. In the case of the open society, like all other utopians, he writes about tendencies in history and situations that will necessarily come forth.

The promise and hope for the individual that creates his own self, destiny, thinking and duties does not belong to Popper, but it is much older. The open society is only a new name of this hope: "man is master of his own destiny, and in accordance with his goals he is able to influence or change human history, in the same way he does with scenery. He does not believe that these goals are forced upon us by our historic past or by historic trends, he rather believes that we ourselves have created them freely, just as we create new thoughts, masterpieces or buildings and new machines."[11] Every cultural or moral element, institution, every human relationship depends on individual decisions: "Transformation occurs when social institutions are first recognised as conscious human creations, and when their conscious transformation is discussed in terms of how appropriate they are for the realisation of human goals and plans. The closed society will dissolve when fear of the supernatural, with which they regarded social order, makes way for the active involvement and for the conscious pursuit of individual and group interest."[12] Every society in which the individual cannot arbitrarily change his institutions, duties, identity, because these or part of them are accepted as undoubted, is closed. This world of unquestioned, common meanings, duties and rules, called biological world by phenomenology, is the opposite of the open society.

In the closed, tribal society (in the biological world) there are few problems; the individual never doubts his way of action. The right way is always determined. It is determined by taboos, magical tribal institutions, which are never analysed critically.[13] In the open society everyone has the right and responsibility to make their own life and do their own thinking, as long as they do not bother others. Individual openness concerns one's private life rather than public life, since the latter is the job of social engineers. (Naturally, what counts as disturbance cannot be established rationally, but only arbitrarily, from one case to another.) Freedom is first of all not political, but a moral, everyday matter: everyone can live as they like.[14] As regards private life, the open society is conceptually opposed to any kind of human group that contains common meanings, duties or rules. The question is whether there can be any kind of human cohabitation or society in the absence of common meanings. In the open society there is no valid map or compass for the individual; everyone can wander and has to wander. This confusion and inability to orient oneself can be that which gives the feeling of liberation, but also of defencelessness. The frontier—like in the heroic period of the wild west or in the big cities at night—is the world of the bare fist.

The open society promises two attractive things: liberty and harmony. Liberty first of all means the liberation from moral constraints, and this is to be achieved in such a way that whatever moral life someone leads should not have any disadvantageous consequences, which means that should not be a responsibility. But what kind of liberty is this, since the open society emphasises the liberty of the individual choice. But it is a real choice if it does not involve responsibility, if it does not have consequences? This myth of liberty is opposed to the myth of the tragic hero, who is tormented by antagonistic expectations and predictable responsibilities, and he chooses—he makes a decision. The decision and the pertaining responsibility belong to him, and he is free because he can do this. But the liberty ideal of the open society is the choice that has no consequences which, therefore, is not a decision. There is no role conflict, no tragedy whatsoever; every decision can be undone. Liberty is enhanced by doing away with choices and decisions. For every step can be undone, and the goal is that one will not have to give up B if one chooses C, and D will not have to be tolerated as the unwanted consequence of C. This liberty consists in the lack of unwanted consequences, and not in the choice between good and evil. There is no good and no evil. Anything can be done, there is no need to hesitate, because hesitation comes with weighing the foreseeable consequences and with the search for the not so obvious results. The dilemma of the "Who am I?" supersedes that of the "What shall I do?" The ideal open man, when he thinks rationally, has the same dilemma as others do under the influence of drugs. In order to have a viewpoint, a standpoint, we need a point, an identity to be able to look upon the world. The loss of this point is the loss of our viewpoint as well, but despite this, or exactly because of this, we can still be onlookers and can have a stand. Openness is psychic fluidity, and this is the very opposite of identity.

With the disappearance of law (nomos) neither the state, nor the individual can be judged, except in comparison with itself. There is no standard for either. The individual and the state bureaucracy have become sovereigns. Thus in the open society individualism and bureaucracy have become partners. The languages of the former's "rights" and that of the latter's "utility" are meant to cover these forms of human arbitrariness. Both languages have been established to face arbitrariness.

Piecemeal social engineering is connected to the illusion that since every generation can think freely, it can rescue itself and can do whatever it finds "rationally right". Scientific policy promises to do away with arbitrariness in the name of rational thinking, weighing and of the lack of prejudices. The initially positive thinking of the open society is in a specific and intimate relationship with rationalism. It concomitantly needs and supposes the social role of critical rationalism in the formulation of possibilities and in the choice made between them, and also the efficient domination of rationalism, which leads to the most useful solution under any circumstances. The rationalism connected to the open society only values and approves of those actions which are conscious, and are not based on prestige or coercion. It links the unconscious certainty to the repulsive closed society. It only accepts as valuable and free the action based on individual choice. The value of the action is not given by its course, content or result, but the fact that it has been preceded by conscious choice. (And it has also produced the correct result.) In the open society every action is a choice, and every action-choice has to be linked to reason. This removes arbitrariness from the surface. It is expected that every action is the result of conscious reason. This further means that every belief and knowledge is measured on a more basic, more universal and more important scale, on "reason".

2.

The Chaotic Prison is the very specific consequence of the disappearance of barriers, that is of moral rules and laws. Now every individual and group has been entrusted with the making and interpreting of its rules and thus, in practice, the earlier clear meanings of rules and the barriers have been lost as a result of the diverse individual and group interpretations. It seems that, after the political revolutions and, later, after the industrial revolution, such an image of the society emerged which at once admits tyranny and chaos and disorder in the society. Neither the above nor the below are restrained by rules and laws. There is too much and too little control in the society at the same time. Those thinkers and movements that only perceived one aspect of this paradox, and only sensed the tyranny or the disorder, wanted either only liberation or only order.

The same writings of the same authors describe and judge modern life from two standpoints, often at the same time. On the one hand the life form, the world image is becoming plural, and there are infinite opportunities. So the common image of the world is falling apart. On the other hand, the life form, the image of the world is becoming homogeneous—the consequences of the system, of administration are becoming uniform at the structural level. If we accept the simultaneous validity of the two images then there is disintegration and interdependence at the same time (because of the systemic integration we depend on each other more and more).[15]

Anarchy (feet without a head) can exist in the absence of freedom and defencelessness; slavery can exist in the absence of legality, of respect for and acceptance of superiors.

Tyranny and anarchy are equally abnormal or anomalous, because they only recognise the will of the strongest as the rightful, most important measure. The good that exists independent of the individual or of the tyrant(s) is the barrier to be destroyed by the most important tyrants. The characteristic of tyranny is not the wrong law, but the absence of Law. Let us think it over: do we feel oppressed by the interdiction of paedophiles out of moral principles? No, because we are not like that. But most crimes and aggressions are committed against unimportant people, since the rich live in well-guarded palaces. The law is first of all to the benefit of the lower social layers. By now maybe several people have learnt that the law protects the lower classes against the powerful and against each other's violence. The law first of all protects the weak from the tyranny of the powerful—either collectively or as individuals. Chaos, disorder and lawlessness favour speculators, who can lure people to join them by stating that the laws and rules oppress them. But if law, rule and barrier disappear, then there will be anarchy and/or tyranny, and the only ordering principle in both is violence (see the case of Albania). In both cases those who suffer are the lower classes. The defining characteristic of the modern world is that chaos and tyranny are not present as alternatives, but that they co-exist.

Two concepts off man are linked to the image of the Chaotic Prison. According to one, man can be shaped from outside with the aid of social sciences. In this, man has no intrinsic importance but rather receives it from the society and the relations that exist in it. So the social engineer can shape men with these relationships. In the society only the social engineer is active, all the other men are dummies, raw material. In this concept, man is the creature of the cause/effect relation. He is not a personality, but a consequence. In contrast to this, the autonomous person does not have causes, but reasons. The autonomous person is innovative. He himself chooses what kind of person he will be. Free action is opposed to action that can be explained with causality. In the case of free action he does what he wants.

But where do we get our willpower? The rational actor is at the same time free and the appropriate object of science. As a result of his actions he is at the same time the follower of rational goals and the subject of rules.

Secularisation, the elimination of laws, matches coercion with anomie, with sins. For Saint Augustine sin is equal to the absence of laws, with anomie. Sin is non-existence, since all that exists comes from God, and God cannot be the creator of sin. So Saint Augustine concludes that sin is the absence of the laws of God, sin is anomie. Sin, anomie is not another society, the world of other laws, but the absence of society and of laws. This even if there are several intellectual rationalisations of sin, of anomie. These are only subsequent explanations and partly creators of anomie, of the spread of the initial sin. The paradox of abstract idealism is that the strict moral expectations are supported by the least respectable feelings. However, the appearance of the least respectable feelings are celebrated by the humanist intellectuals as the realisation of the strict moral expectations. The disappearance of the living world (the world of common meanings) results in the world of chaos and uncertainty. Together with the common meanings, the common norms and the expected behaviour also disappear. From this anomie comes our sense of chaos. The absence of laws brings about "wilderness". When everyone exercises their natural freedom, then nobody is free.[16] This is because there is no need for freedom in chaos.

And although no one wants to admit anyone around them, yet everyone is at the mercy of the finance minister's sympathy, of agreements and of invisible specialists, and as a result of these the income of any big social group can be reduced, independent of their hard work or of their earlier investments. Neither the Turks nor the Tartars nor natural disasters took away (or gave as much) as people who are to us effectively anonymous. Invisible hands give or take away opportunities, and the individual tries to compensate himself by continually breaking every expectation. Instead of the lost essential decisions the individuals win some freedom in insignificant political matters—they can warm up, can buy or sell children, can have abortions, can cross the street on the red light.

The absence of laws—chaos—only brings short-term liberation. In chaos it only matters who is more powerful. Today's specialists call these people "those who have better opportunities to enforce their interests". The disorder of lawlessness favours speculators: anyone who speculates about the change. They convince people to join them by telling them that the law is the oppressor. But if law is lost, then the two situations of lawlessness or their mixture occur: tyranny and disorder. In both, violence is the only ordering principle. The best measure for how closed a society is to this situation is the popularity of lotteries, the belief that "anything can happen", the "why can't I be lucky?" These people are easy to fool because they can be attracted to relations they easily accept, but whose rules they do not know, which are known only by the speculators, who, however, can change the rules of the games as they wish and when they wish. The belief that "anything can happen" shows the absence of rules. Everything is possible because there are no rules. Why does the society-shaping intellectual speculator support the risk-taking capitalist speculator, if not that both of them hope to make a profit from the change, from the stabilisation of "provisionality"? Speculative profit can only be made from the "anything is possible" state. Speculation and anomie precondition each other. The more chaotic the world, the more believable the chance and the luck. (That is why the world of Renaissance was dominated by the theme of "luck", and this theme disappeared after the Tridentinum and after the Puritan orderliness.)

Why did bankers and capitalists support left-extremist radicals (see the history of Hungarian and German working class movement) in past centuries, and why does one of the most popular financial speculators do this with the open society? Uncertainty breeds irresponsibility: we cannot be responsible for the unpredictable consequences, but only for the consequences that can be predicted based on experience and using the everyday rational mind. Responsibility implies that our world, our environment, is rational and can be known—even though this knowledge remains unreflected and it is not worded into theorems and rules. And even if this knowledge is never absolute or certain, we can still live as if it were. The society that can be known is not the same as the rational-mechanic society (see Montesquieu's story of the blind man who can find his way in Paris better than those who can see.[17]) Inherent in responsibility is competence—the knowledge of my world to some degree. In the case of a stirred up society everything becomes fluid, mobile and uncertain. This feeling of uncertainty comes with responsibility, and both are accompanied by speculation. Intellectuals and financial people are prone to speculation. Speculation means change, because only change and its results can be speculated about. As a result of the change the rates of exchange can rise, new groups can come to power. Revolutions show the risk of changes: no one can know the final result for sure. The continual change can make a habit of games of chance, it can spread speculation. At the same time chance means disorder and injustice. Everyone is more and more forced to play chance games, but their rules are only known to the few, and these can change them to their advantage even during the game.

The elite must preserve its prestige rooted in the past, its culture, its connections and its income. The speculator has to achieve all these by using his outstanding knowledge. This outstanding knowledge appears to the others to be the sin of self-confidence and ambition. Burke was the one who first pointed out the danger of rising groups of prestige-thirsty people. He said they did not only want to rise, but also to disrupt society for this purpose.

In an earlier writing about the open society, I already mentioned the problem of how defenceless an amorphous, unstructured mass—which can only be called a society out of laziness or laxity—is in front of the ambitions of a well-organised group acting as a "closed society". The unstructured mass is easy prey to the "closed" interest group—whether that is a cultural minority or a career group, a club or anything that acts as a community. What happens if a "tribe" penetrates the always fluid open society? Is this state of the open society not ideal for the "tribes" of career groups? They can move forward without encountering any obstacles, gaining more and more influence. The open society has no structure, no moral or cultural expectations, no coherent feelings; the feeling of solidarity is absent. Thus, the open society can be easy prey for every purposeful "tribal" community, because this latter stays closed as compared to the majority: it preserves its identity, its self-knowledge, its inner solidarity, its moral and cultural expectations. To such a "tribe" the rest will be the "you", that is the strangers.[18]

Utopias and society-building plans always refer to the ruling group that "leads" the rest and dominates them—even if they do not interpret their activity as domination. But we are getting farther and farther from the promised and hoped-for, happy, free and harmonious world's actual variety, and it more and more seems that the relationships and institutions of the society are changed in order for the "leaders" to dominate the rest. Social science, social engineering is the basis of society-shaping, and it changes and improves people by changing social relationships. "Someone will want to become a sociologist not only because he wants to understand society, but also because he wants to change it."[19] Piecemeal engineering works based on technical knowledge. Popper does not want to understand how society and politics work, but he chooses the more enjoyable way; he tells people what to be like, how to shape their life and society.[20]

3.

The concept of an open society does not allow for violence and coercion, and that is why it is so attractive.[21] The sources of conflict are economic and cultural differences, so if they are eliminated, then conflicts can be eliminated by making human thinking homogeneous. In this way there will be no need for coercion, violence and all that accompanies them: laws, obedience, law enforcement and judicial institutions. But an important precondition for this to happen is to eliminate the sources of conflict—differences in thinking and in material possessions. And this has to be done, say the old liberals, by the state. In order to open up the society and to keep it open, the assisting, and not the compelling state has very important duties to see to, both in redistribution and in cultural liberation (retraining). The ideal of the liberal open society is not the minimal state, but minimal coercion. (Unfortunately, coercion is still needed against the fascists, that is against people who have joined the not-yet-open, not-yet-universally rational and generally well-meaning homogeneous mass.) The coercive activity of the state is reduced and governing is superseded by bureaucratic influence. Coercion can be minimised and the problem of obedience with it because influence is growing and spreading. People can be made open and kept open with the omnipresent influence of the state. In this way the (material and cultural) differences that cause conflicts will cease to exist, so conflict will disappear and there will be no need for coercion. All we have to accept is that the only sources of conflict are these differences. In the open society one cannot hear about the minimal limited state, only about the minimal violence. The limiting of power is not a problem, the only problem is whether the adequate group, (good) will and (real and useful) knowledge get the power. In this case it is pointless to talk about limiting the (good) will and the (good) knowledge, because the occasional problems and conflicts can be solved with knowledge and goodwill. This power should be unlimited, because being so it can secure progress, liberty and happiness. The liberalism of the last century sought limited government, whereas Popper and today's liberalism want a lot of influence—first of all, in economy and culture, because they are the principal means of exerting influence. The cause of the still existing problems is either economic or prejudices inherited from the past. So they will be solved in the course of development, which is the same as getting rich and getting rid of trouble-causing prejudices.

In the open society it is not the sources of power, their operating mechanisms, their limits, the sources of submissiveness and the cases of confrontation that are being debated, but the very existence of power. The most serious lese-majesté is not to say that the power has violated some limits and has turned into a tyrant, but that "X group has power". To someone with any historical knowledge, this phenomenon sounds odd and definitely unique. Throughout history, the powerful have been proud of their power, they have claimed and legitimised it under different pretexts. But this type of power wishes to legitimise itself by stating that it does not even exist: this is really a new experience in legitimisation, and it goes well with today's dominant anti-power culture. Today's experiment in legitimacy is based on the fact that no one has power. If anyone mentions having power, he must be from the extreme right. The experiment in legitimacy is not only based on "we do not have power", but also on "we are not a group"—if anyone states the opposite, they are "plotting". The sheer fact that one group or another is called by a name—without mentioning their power—is extremism in a society that claims to be homogeneous.

Since the Exodus, the first step in the revolt meant to achieve collective freedom is the naming of the responsible people in power who use their power badly or to a wicked end. Let us imagine that Moses wants to stir his people to revolt by simply promising Canaan, and he fails to name the power of the Pharaoh as the source of their troubles. Let us imagine how efficient his mobilising power would have been if he had said that they did not have to fight the Pharaoh, but the low water of the Nile. In this case the Hebrews would probably still be in Egypt. And because ever since Moses the first step in a confrontation has been to name the source of troubles, the evil power, it is understandable why the public figures become so touchy if they are called by name. And it is especially the case of those who think that people do not do this or that because the power forces them to do so, but because they themselves have decided to do so. To admit that "We, group X, have the power" would bring along unpleasant consequences.

Firstly, the idea of naturalness of the world created by them would disappear. One of the biggest problems of today's intellectuals is that they are the slaves of their prejudices about the past, and they want to replace their past inheritance with these. It is typical that they should blame the old times, when debate on the power was open and those in power were proud of it, because this period, that world, that society was unquestioned. People living then perceived their relationships as a natural, not an artificial creation. This only changed at the parents of today's intellectuals, when they stated the artificial man-made nature of the existing society. The social structures before the political revolutions were also man-made, but they were the result of unconscious creation. On the contrary, today's society is characterised by the fact that it is the consequence of conscious human creative intention—though this consequence does not always coincide with the creative intention. Despite this, leading intellectuals do not feel it necessary to prove the artificiality of present relationships. The old period was natural and unquestioned for those who lived in it, although the debate on power was open—who can have power and why, to what purpose it can be used, etc. Today the leading intellectuals do not talk about, and especially do not debate, power, nor the man-made nature of their relationships—they try to make people not see any alternatives. Despite this attempt to naturalise, this period is not natural and neither without problems. However, Popper states that closed societies are characterised by naturalness and lack of problems; advocates of the open society, one can notice that they are trying hard—though with little success—to make their power natural. In the case of adequate power exercisers, they do not talk about power as the actor with an outstanding role and responsibility in shaping these relations. Social science, which criticises the naturalness and non-reflectiveness of earlier periods, tries to naturalise today's obviously and visibly man-made world. It does this by accusing hatred, it tries to make it impossible for topics that question this world to exist in public thinking. What does today's pluralism and openness mean when one cannot even talk about the existence of power? And what does the closeness of old societies mean, if it means anything at all, when the power and its responsibilities and limits were obvious?

Secondly, the unpleasant consequence of admitting to power is that one has to take responsibility for the consequences. Power means action, and action has consequences. However, responsibility is the least known word in the open society. Naming things and taking responsibility are in a very intimate relationship with each other, because this time it is not simply the responsibility of the elected politicians. Though the leading intellectuals do not mention the power of government or of the parliament, it is even more remarkable that they do not mention people in power, who have never been elected, and therefore they cannot be replaced every four years. The politically adequate people's anger can be aroused especially by naming groups in power that cannot be held responsible by any institutional means. Those whose activity can be controlled least of all or not at all are counter to the democratic ideal that dominates the public. Naming certain people and admitting to the power brings along the unpleasant consequence of responsibility in the case of those whose allegiance to a group and whose power are not obvious.

Popper and the liberal tradition oppose power to truth, which, of course, was only known to them and represented by them. What happens if those who know the truth win? Will they take power? Do they have power? Do they need to limit truth? Are we allowed to think of limiting the truthful?

Of course, the answer to all these questions is "no". Power itself and every type of coercion will cease, and people, just like the wolf and the child, will embrace. When the truthful and the truth are in power, there will be eternal peace. In the open society "no one has power", and this matches the people's taste for anti-power. The repulsive power and coercion will have disappeared from the political community, which will become an economic association and a huge re-training camp. Side-slips can be prevented by means of better unemployment rates and educational work. Only these solutions require more knowledge. It is not accidental that the intellectuals feel so much attracted by this type of politics, which reserves such an outstanding role to knowledge and the knowledgeable. And their activity will not be regarded as exercising power, but as service, assistance, well-meaning counselling. In the case of specialists, obedience will not be a problem any longer, since they do not make decisions, but rather point out and make use of natural coercion; or, they lead us up to the right decision, which we will eventually make ourselves. In this latter case, the specialist only helps us to reach the right decision. He avoids the problem of disobedience in both cases.

In the open society the individual—freed from the limiting and also protecting ties of the community—will increasingly need the assistance of specialist bureaucracy. And thus, he will have to accept the iron cage of bureaucracy's utilitarian rationality. This is the price of individuality: a dependent person, unable to provide for himself. The dissolution of closer family ties will need a more and more developed social network: pensions, child allowances, old people's homes, council flats. The importance of specialists in this mode of thinking is that they promise the possibility of solutions that will please everybody, that is they will not have to decide against anyone. Specialists will be neutral, they do not take sides with groups or individuals. There is no decision-making, so there is no coercion. Because they take into account and meet every interest and position—except for that of those who are sworn enemies of progress—they do not have to decide. Politicians are not decision-makers. Progressive politics has popularised not only the possible advent of the kind of society where there is no conflict and no one feels frustrated, but also the image of political action which does not involve decision-making. This is not to mean that every progressive politician is unable to make decisions, though some of them certainly are. Rather, it means the way in which they regard themselves and their activity, and the image of all these.

The "this is not a political, but a professional matter" means that there is no debatable alternative—because politicians are the debaters. The "professional matter" means that there is only one solution, which results from the nature of the matter and the representatives of the "profession" know it. But what is even more important is that in "professional matters" it is not some kind of—*horibile dictu*—individual or group authority that makes the decision, but the solution results obligatorily from the thing itself. Those who are in a position to make decisions—with the very promise of the elimination of politics, with the promise of "professionalism"—do their best to call more and more matters a "professional matter", because in this case not only are they, as the representatives of the profession, the only people entitled to decide, but they do not even have to account for other possibilities, or for the inevitably harmed interests of some people. For the "professional decision" in "professional matters" means that every step was necessary, that there were no alternatives. Therefore, the "professional decision" is not actually a decision, but only the recognition of a necessity.

The illusion of "professionalism' and "professional politics" is (was) based on the idea that arbitrariness can be excluded from political decisions and political problems, and conflicts can be interpreted and solved as if they were some rational clear matters of social engineering. This would mean the end of politics, the end of arbitrary decisions, which is the height of naiveté. The popularity of the concept is based on the tacit presumption, which today is not defended by too many people openly, according to which the rational decision is at the same time the decision that favours the majority. The ancient enemy, the source of every moral and economic problem, is authority. The non-authoritarian, but "professional" decision is exactly the opposite: remedy for our moral and economic troubles. But if in debates the better arguments or some rational standard were to decide, then why should we need a majority and a government responsible to the majority? Moreover, why should we bother to debate on "professional matters"? The majority parliamentarianism tacitly accepts that there are several kinds of rationality, there are several equally good arguments, and what decides among them is which argument serves the interest of the majority. If it were not so, then the wisest people could have one single representative in a meeting who would then convince everyone with his arguments.

The necessity that derives from the nature of things is coercion, which is why leaders choose one or another solution on the way. But there is no mentioning of arbitrariness, not even of decision. There is nothing about the politician's personal attraction to a certain decision. Professional actions are either obviously to everyone's benefit, or if this sounded exaggerated, then some kind of serious necessity—maybe the discovery of America—compels the politician. The nature of this necessity that forces the poor specialist is that it does not even leave him alternatives. The leader could only do what he did.

Scientific politics claims that its arguments are rational, its assessments are impartial and unprejudiced. Professionalism is more attractive than politics, because it presumes that it does not have to decide among compelling ambitions, but instead, by making use of the adequate knowledge, it can find a solution (not a decision[!] since that is always *against someone*) that will be acceptable to everyone. In the open society, the domination of "professional matters" and of the professionalism of social engineers leads to the end of competition among alternative solutions. This is because in the case of the "professional matters" the technical rationality only admits for one efficient solution, just as 2x2=4 cannot possibly have another solution. The professional solution to professional matters promises this technical solution, which means the exclusion of any kind of group or individual influence. For the professional, knowledge is devoid of such sentimentality. Due to their lack of sentimentality, specialists stay above politicians morally because the latter are bound to some particularity—group, ideology—by their own choice, whereas professional politics only has in view the matter, without any sentimentality. Those who get into a leading position in the open society do their best to eliminate politics, and to specialise in their activity. The more matters can be labelled professional, the fewer those in which one has to bother with alternatives and problems of legitimacy in decision-making. Professional solutions need not be legitimised, just like gravitation—it is there, unavoidably, it is pointless for mortals to debate it. The professional solution does not only bear the halo of correctness and efficiency, but also that of necessity. Where is the openness in the open society if there is no place for alternatives in the most serious matters of public life? Popper and his direct predecessor in positivist liberalism, John Stuart Mill, or more recently John Rawls, perceive openness as life-form freedom, that is the possibility of moral and cultural alternatives, and not the presence of political domination and economic alternatives.

The open society is a rationalist utopia, whose model and pattern is the scientific community: according to the positivist rationalist ideal, science continually progresses through purely rational, unbiased and unprejudiced debates; and scientists are only driven by the knowledge of the truth. (This assumption, i.e. the exclusive thirst for truth, characterises Milton's and J.S. Mill's arguments.) It is important to point out that the ideal of the open society is to transform society after the imagined pattern of the scientific community. One of the problems that arises here is whether any kind of transformation is possible; and if yes, then whether it is possible to transform and maintain a society after the pattern of the imagined scientific community, and finally whether this is desirable. First of all, however, we have to note that basing the ideal of the open society on the scientific community is rather questionable. Based on the experience of the years spent in a scientific community or on

Kuhn's theory of paradigms, we can boldly state that the scientists' community is not characterised by openness to alternatives. As Kuhn described it, and our own experience proves it, debates within a scientific community are always strictly limited. They are equally limited by political-cultural preconditions and scientific-paradigmatic preconditions, by which questions are legitimate scientific matters, which data are really data, which answers and arguments are valid, and which experiences—that upset the preconditions by being their opposite—are not accepted by a certain paradigmatic scientific community; furthermore, which questions, points of view, arguments and answers are illegitimate, that is "non-scientific". The scientific community is probably much more closed than the positivist-rationalists generally assume; moreover, it is probably more closed than the "closed" or "tribal" societies. Science cannot work without the common standards and tacit preconditions established by practice.

Openness is not a final state, but a continuous journey. The open society, judging by its ideal, means openness to the future, that is the preservation of several—as many as possible—alternatives of action and thinking, which result in the unpredictability of the future. The future does not develop after a previously imagined scenario, but rather accidentally. History does not come to an end. The utopia of the open society in this respect means the continual journey of the society, its transformation and change contrary to a formerly planned form on the basis of which relationships, people and institutions should be modelled. However, if the advocates of the open society only think of this ideal and nothing else, why all this bother? Until the advent of rationalists, history developed like this, and it is the rationalist themselves who find it possible, and even feasible, to transform society after ready-made theoretical constructions. This interpretation of openness—which then tries to preserve as many alternatives as possible in the name of historical openness—is hard to connect to the upheaval of open/closed society. The old, closed societies may well have had all kind of common meanings, morality and limits, but they also contained numerous alternatives. The proof for this is history itself. And, surprisingly, the coming history has to be protected first of all from these rationalist intellectuals who advocate the ideal of the open society. This is the group that finds it imaginable and desirable to plan and transform society in the present in such a way that it would also determine its future, that is it would eliminate history by doing away with alternatives. (History is unavoidably always the history of the ruling groups. The wish to end history—that is to decide once and forever on the future—is at the same time the wish to preserve the present leading group and its descendants in their position. The decision on the future in the present means that as many alternatives as possible will be eliminated and, together with them, the possibility of future changes. The more alternative leading groups are eliminated by the ruler, the better his chance to preserve his position.[22] This is why Herod had to kill an entire generation.)

Chaos exists and may exist without liberty. In this chaotic situation fewer and fewer people enjoy liberty and the majority's often only liberty is to choose between homosexuality and drug-addiction. The concept of liberty has successfully been switched to private libertinism. It is worth reminding readers that the issue of liberty for our forefathers in the course of European history came up in connection with taxes, levying taxes and using taxes. Now by liberty is meant "the freedom of lifestyle". Professional liberty advocates fail to remember and prevent others from remembering that up to them liberty concerned public matters: taxes, tax-collection and tax-utilisation. The oppressed mass of people are forever being told that they have never been so free. They have never had such well-meaning rulers. They have never been so close to the happiest of worlds. The open society clams up: this is the only possible (rational, useful and moral) political institutional system— "this government and this politics have no alternative". Those who will not see this are either stupid or mad. The open society is polit-ically closed. Yet, the openness, according to Karl Popper, means that alternatives are possible, everything can be questioned and debated and then changed. In practice, members of the open soci-ety can only change their sex freely. Public matters are subject to the strict, but well-meaning order of professionalism.

The open society is a Chaotic Prison because the nomos (the order of the common, cognitive and normative meanings) has van-ished from it. The opinion and culture of the rulers (governors and intellectuals) and of the mob have rarely been as close to each other in history as at present: no norms and volunteerism. But this coin-cidence still does not mean legitimacy, and in no way does it mean abiding by law. If both the electorate and the governors and the leading intellectuals have the *mentality of the mob*, that does not mean legitimacy and that will not secure minimum obedience. Because for the mob—whether situated at the bottom of society or at the top—no one is legitimate, they do not obey anyone. But this disobedience goes hand in hand with inability to co-operate in pri-vate life. The "everyone is his own judge, he decides and interprets his own rights and enforces them, if he can" is unbearable in pri-vate life as well.

Popper and the liberal reason homogenise the society and thinking for the sake of peace, they would eliminate the differences that are held responsible for conflicts, and in the name of individ-ual freedom destroy the biological world; at the same time, in the name of technical efficiency, they do not tolerate contradiction, alternatives, but only the one, so-called rational solution. The hero of the open society is a creative individual and technical scientist in his private life, and he also draws the "boundaries" of private life. The emphasis on the individual gives the libertarian aspect of the thought of the open society and the emphasis on professional social engineer gives it the "reconstructional" aspect. Opposed to the vol-unteerism of the individual and of the specialist there is the law of

God, the thought of the existence of normative order. This is because a godly law—or any kind of non man-made law, for that matter—would limit the individuals' and the specialists' will. That is why the masterless man—"We are free to live as we like"[23]—is a natural ally of the specialist in shaping the anomic, amoral society. This is the enemy of the arbitrary individual and of the arbitrary social engineer, and therefore, the "norms were made by people"[24] is the main feature of both groups. The anomic society makes anarchy possible at the level of everyday life, and despotism in public life at the same time. The despot is not immoral, but amoral. He does not have bad laws, but is lawless. Though the professional social engineer promise the creation of a new normative order—according to Popper in the open society there can be no new common *belief* without humanitarianism[25]—what will come true out of this promise is coercion, not the norms. Because the existence of norms, their acceptance and prestige are independent of their "scientific" justification; and the absence of godly/moral law is a sin. Sin is not another reality, not another nomos, as opposed to the godly one, but the absence of the godly.

Though in the above I have much debated Karl Popper's views, I still agree with his initial platform: we have to understand totalitarianism so as to be able to fight it. But, and this is the essence of the above-written, Popper missed his target.

Notes

1. Though I am related to the Poppers, I am not dealing with the issue of the open society again out of private reasons, but because the editor of this volume asked me to do so, for which I thank him again.
2. I am not going to analyze in detail the language, problems and standpoints of the liberalism turned from opposition into government. I did this in the *Magyar Szemle*, nos. 10-11 (1996).
3. Many elements of what I have stated about the open society are summed up in an earlier work. *Hitel*, no. 2 (1994), and re-published in *Konzervatív Szemmel*, '94 (1995).
4. Plato: *Állam* [Republic], Összes művei II. [Complete works II]. (Budapest, 1984), 555b-579c.
5. Simmel, G. *The Philosophy of Money*. (Routledge, 1990).
6. Popper, K. *The Open Society and its Enemies*. (1944), Vol. I, p. 152.
7. *Ibid.*, p. 49.
8. *Ibid.*, p. 50.
9. *Ibid.*, p. 1.
10. Popper, K. *A hisztoricizmus nyomorúsága* [The Misery of historicism]. (Budapest, 1979).
11. Popper, K. *The Open*.... Vol. I. p. 17.
12. *Ibid.*, p. 246.
13. *Ibid.*, pp. 151-152.
14. *Ibid.*, p. 163.
15. The idealized description of this can be found in Durkheim's utopia on organic division of labour. There is no collective conscience here, only the respect of individual freedom. At the level of culture and moral freedom this is unlimited. The issue of social control, of coercion can be solved by the division of labour. Due to their interdependence resulting from the division of labour, people adjust to each other *spontaneously, without the feeling of coercion*. A similar image occurs at Elias.
16. Diggs, G. Dudley. *The unlawfulness of subjects taking up armes against their sovereigne*. (Oxford, 1643).
17. Montesquieu: *Perzsa levelek* [Persian letters]. (Budapest, 1981). XXXII. levél [Letter XXXII].
18. Molnár, Attila. "A felnyitott társadalom és barátai" [The opened society and its friends]. *Hitel*, no. 2 (1994), p. 81.

19. Macrae, D. G. *Ideology and Society*. (1961), p. 178.
20. Hayek, F. A. *The Counter-Revolution of Science*. (Liberty Press, 1979).
21. This is a rather funny argument, according to which power is not a problem because the institutions of democracy are working. The establishment of democratic institutions rather intensified thinking about power. It is enough to mention French aristocrat de Tocqueville's writing about American democracy. Popular sovereignty, if it exists in practice, only increases sensibility around matters concerning power.
22. In the trials against the Regnum Marianum in the '60s the accusation was that this Catholic organization was preparing for the overthrow of the system, and that is why it was trying to train an opposition elite. That is why the organization was dissolved, its members were imprisoned in the supposedly idyllic Kádár regime, because they were trying to rid themselves from a possible competition. But they could not stop history; several of the members of the non-communist government in 1990 belonged to the Regnum.
23. Vol. I, p. 163.
24. *Ibid.*, p. 50.
25. *Ibid.*, p.161. The direct descendent of humanitarianism is positivism, A. Comte's and J. S. Mill's *Humankind religion*, which had a major influence on Popper's scientific theory. Our suspicion about the collectivist tendency of the open society is only enforced by the fact that Popper considered 1789 the fight for an open society. And up to that time in history there had been no such ideological state and such power and violence concentration as in the state of the French Revolution. And then all this joined with an endless anarchy and speculation in the appearance of the Chaotic Church.

Csaba Őry

WORKERS' FOOTSTEPS RESOUND...

Many have said so often enough: the 1989 change of regime seemed to be the problem of only a few thousand intellectuals. Intellectuals have spoken in their own language, in the organisations set up by themselves, about democracy, the institutional safeguard of freedom, the multi-party system, the long-awaited economic reforms.

They are chatting, they can afford it—I often used to hear—and, indeed, what proved this was that most people did not really trust in success. This was even more so in the case of the working class.

Trade unions were not popular, but neither were they disagreeable. They belonged to the category that caused bearable discomfort. The reservations people had against them were counterbalanced by a kind of everyday utilitarianism: people could get assistance and preferential package holiday arrangements through trade unions, in exchange for small services, such as a couple of communist Saturdays a year and the usual beer-and-sausage marches on May first.

However, all this was not too exciting.

It was not mere coincidence that in the autumn of 1987, when a group of the researchers from the Academy were threatened with firing, historians remembered that the trade union was the organisation where they could discuss their problems and decide on further steps. Of course, historians live in the past in a certain respect, but the existing trade union soon proved that the suggestion had nothing to do with historians' idiomatic expressions. The answer to the initiatives was a twisted refusal. The trade union activists supported it verbally, but avoided seeing to the problems in practice,

323

trying to calm down the noisy intellectuals with bureaucratic techniques. Under the usual circumstances the noise should have
stopped. This had happened a few years earlier when in the Institute
for Philosophy some suggested setting up a research department;
and this had happened earlier, when it had proved enough for the
system to take it out on some enthusiastic sociologists who had
organised a kind of workforce agency without previously obtaining
permission and approval. The group of researchers did not give in
this time. Why they did not is answerable in many ways. First of
all, in the circle of sociologists it was no secret that the system had
used up its resources and that some change was due to happen soon.
Trade unions—also called activist-cemeteries at the time—were
headed by clerks and former activists who had been left out of the
important political scene. These clerks and activists felt abandoned
by the power and in their own defence, sacrificed them in order to
calm down spirits.

There was some truth in this.

To the political planners, the activities that trade unions
engaged in were a sort of lab experiment, in which they could
observe the realisation of different scenarios. They could follow the
movements and development of the actors. They could include different initiatives in the "experiment", and they could analyse the
way they were received, shaped and carried out. To make it clear, I
do not mean to say that events developed according to some devil-
ish manipulation scenarios written beforehand, but I do think that
the establishment of the new trade unions was a useful experience
in planning the later political strategies for both parts: the rulers,
unsure of their position, and the opposition getting ready to take
over.

The Coordinating Committee that was formed in the Rakpart
Club (i.e. Wharf Club) on February 19, 1988 was really mixed.
Among its members one could encounter trade union agents, intel-
lectuals fired for political reasons who lived on temporary employ-

ment, members of the party who kept in touch with the power and people from the so-called "democratic opposition", populist and urbane, people with humanistic interests, and disciplined people with technical knowledge. The initiators have long since split up and are supporting different political trends. Back in 1988, when trade unions were being set up, ideological differences were of a minor importance and were deliberately pushed back. The Coordinating Committee, which was preparing the ground for the later TDDSZ, first met in a private house on February 26. On this first occasion the participants agreed upon some basic principles. First they decided that their activity should be regarded as legal organising with the purpose of renewing trade union movement, and therefore they would only meet at their workplace, and that they would do their best to use the infrastructure of the local trade union to finance their activities. No one was trying to hide political sympathies. Members of the MSZMP (Hungarian Socialist Workers Party) often mentioned that if the committee made certain decisions, they might have to leave the Coordinating Committee. Being legally organised therefore also meant that the power was present at the meetings not only through its secret agents, but through its legal representatives as well.

The openness of the preparatory stage (anyone could join in and participate in the meetings, where decisions were taken based on the principle of consensus) made it possible for the political strategists to experiment and gain experience. Members of the MSZMP who were on the Coordinating Committee often brought "messages" from the party headquarters, making it known to the opposition that after the party congress planned for May they were going to ease the strictness of the system. It is true that such messages had hardly any impact on the participants. Other leaders of the system made sure about this even unintentionally. The official trade union structure made use of its still-existing influence to isolate the organisers. From one side, from high positions, came the

encouragement to moderation in exchange for recognition of legitimacy; from the other side there were the practices of power
demonstration carried out by the party-state. Damning statements
were being made, recorded radio interviews were being banned,
threats with unclear contents were being sent through acquaintances and "friends." The events are characterised quite relevantly
by the case when the then vice-president of the SZOT (i.e. Trade
Unions' National Council) (now the person is still vice-president,
but this time of the bigger governing party) invited the organisers
to discussions over tea. This person stated without reserve that
they—that is the heads of the trade union—followed the initiatives
to renew trade union with much interest and sympathy, and cate-
gorically denied that the allegations published in the press calling
the activities "ill-willed political turbulence" referred to the guests;
moreover, the person added, they did not even busy themselves
with the well-meaning initiatives of the researchers in the extraordinary meeting they had held in order to state their position. The
lady, who was at the time a simple clerk in the trade union, probably was not aware that the minutes of the meeting she had mentioned had reached the Coordinating Committee by that time, and
her guests knew precisely that she was not telling them the truth. As
for the who and why of the statement "ill-meaning political agita-
tors", the numbered, top-secret labelled minutes will probably
never be found out.

What happened in and around the Coordinating Committee
shows clearly enough that the mellowing political changes did not
take the power as much by surprise as the participants in the events
had suspected. It is now part of history that the first legal organisations of the change of regime were the FIDESZ (the Federation of
Young Democrats), the TDDSZ and the Network of Free Initiative.
These organisations were publicly announced in the spring (April,
May) of 1988. A week after the TDDSZ was founded Kádár was
dismissed. The period between May and December was the time

when the new organisations became stable. Meanwhile, other independent organisations were formed, and in December 1988 the Democratic League of Independent Trade Unions (FSZDL) was born. Many of the better-known activists of the independent trade unions became involved in the newly-established parties. It was in 1989 that the LIGA (at the time still FSZDL) got to the point that it could show itself publicly. In this period the "spontaneous privatisation" had already begun. The Németh government decided to support the new owners' readiness to invest, and in this respect to force the strike bill through parliament. The SZOT agreed tacitly, but the LIGA started a protest campaign against the initiative. They organised a committee of action against the strike bill with the participation of the new opposition parties. The trade union activists had the opportunity to make their stand known in party programmes, and the parties themselves protested against the proposed legislation. The action was successful, and instead of a limiting strike law, parliament passed a permissive one. The relationship between the LIGA and the opposition parties became stronger. When in May 1989, as a result of the initiative of the Independent Lawyers' Forum, the Opposition Round Table (EKA) was established, the LIGA was naturally present. The leaders of the independent trade unions did not doubt that their place was beside the changes, therefore beside the opposition. At the same time this was the moment when the content of the relationship between trade unions and political parties had to be clarified. Members of the trade unions were also members of some organisation belonging to EKA; moreover, some leading party politicians were at the same time on the board of some trade union of the LIGA. It was at that time that LIGA decided on party neutrality, and after some debate managed to secure its status of observer in the meetings of the Opposition Round Table. The accepted formula—drawn up by Dr György Szabad, if I remember well—recognised LIGA as an equal, but outwardly mentioned it as an observer. Party neutrality became part of the identity of LIGA, as it helped the organisation to become stable and at the same time prepared the ground for later conflicts. The decision forced by politics met the expectations of the lower levels in the trade union. Leaders of the trade union and representatives of the member organisations were convinced that party debates had to be shut out of the trade union forums. Their ideology was also created: if political debates were allowed to penetrate the trade unions, they could easily upset the order of the still-fragile organisation.

In the course of discussions at the National Round Table the LIGA had to clearly define three objectives:

- to keep the party organisations away from the workplace;
- to secure employee participation and statement of opinion in privatisation;
- to realise the distribution of trade union funds in order to ensure working conditions.

As regards this last objective, it was not discussed at all in the course of the meetings. There was no agreement on the issue of workers rights in the process of privatisation, either (though they were mentioned in one or another board meeting). Finally, the removal of party organisations from the workplace was done, though it did not go smoothly. It is a fact that in that particular ceremony when the FIDESZ, the SZDSZ and the MSZDP did not sign the agreement with the MSZMP, the LIGA also refused to do so, claiming that the omission of this matter was their main objection. Later the four "yes" votes decided on the matter. The participation of the LIGA in the EKA was successful in the respect that it made a useful contribution to solving inner disputes. As regards the free trade union objectives, the LIGA did not achieve what they had proposed.

The refusal to sign had many decisive consequences. In the circle of national conservative Christian parties it strengthened the conviction that the LIGA, which had a strong intellectual character, was in fact a liberal, left-wing organisation which they later regarded as an SZDSZ-concern. Leaders of the trade union denied this repeatedly, though we should admit that the trade union leaders who participated in the EKA meetings, except for Imre Kerényi, who was at the time a member of the MDF committee, were politicians close to FIDESZ and SZDSZ. Later, when the relationship between the MDF and the SZDSZ became impossible, the prejudices that had solidified in the EKA gained significance, as they made it difficult to communicate with governing parties. The Antall government—at least this is what it looked like from the trade unions' position—did not like trade unions. It was suspicious about them, and it repeatedly stated that trade unions were conservative organisations that impeded the change of regime. The relationship between LIGA and the SZDSZ was strengthened by the fact that politicians of the liberal party emphasised the necessity to change trade unions. They co-operated with trade union lobbyists and accepted several of their initiatives, and even represented them in parliament. The initiative about the obligatory reduction of tuition fees is connected to Ferenc Kőszeg, a member of the SZDSZ (at the time—after 1994). The XXVIIIth Law,[1] passed in 1991, which settled the principle of trade union funds, was drawn up with the consensus of the parties that supported the change of regime. The situation, however, was more complex and contradictory. This is especially true now that we know the four-year performance of the Horn government. During the Antall government the framework of the so-called social dialogue was set up. The Interest Reconciliation Council and the Budgeting Institutions' Interest-Mediating Council were formed. Through compromises, but basically with the consensus of the participants in the interest-mediation, they drew up the employment law, the labour code, the social law. And though the trade unions did not directly participate in privatisation afterwards, there were some agreements worth paying attention to on this topic as well. The government undertook it and included it in the law that part of the revenue from privatisation would be spent on solving the problems of people who would become unemployed as a result of the change of ownership. In order to cover these expenses a certain percentage of the revenue was allocated to the Employment Fund. It was also made possible for the trade unions to delegate a permanent member to the supervising board of the ÁVÜ (the State Property Agency). It is a sign of their mistrust in trade unions and of the illusions they had about their future role that they included such a provision in the labour code that places the detailed regulations concerning work relationships under the decision of the sides, that is the employer and the local trade union. The legislator presumed that the spreading and powerful trade unions would be able to fight out the details, taking into account the concrete situation at the workplace. It has since been proven that the trade unions have not gained in force but have weakened, and under these circumstances the general rules only help the employers to move more freely.

The distrust of the Antall and Boross governments in trade unions is also shown by the unsuccessful activity to support the Workers' Councils, which had been set up in the meantime. The MDF secured a deputy's seat in the parliament for the chairman of the Workers' Council, it ran a work-group concerned with employment in its parliamentary fraction, and it concretely co-operated in organising workers' councils to such extent that at one time the Bem square party branch paid certain activists of the Workers' Council. The Government, in close co-operation with the Workers' Councils, created the MRP law, and in the course of preparations for the XXVIIIth Law it made it clear to the representatives of the LIGA that the condition for the law to be passed was that the Workers' Councils should be recognised both internationally and nationally as an equal partner. The XXVIIIth law itself helped divide the trade unions. The LIGA and the Workers' Councils found it unsatisfactory, whereas the trade unions that were born from the late SZOT turned it down, and have called it the anti-trade union law ever since. In connection with the National Round Table Meetings I have briefly mentioned that the newly-formed trade unions demanded that the change of regime be extended to trade unions as well, that their legality be made clear and that their running conditions be seen to. For this last demand there should be provided some explanation. The dispute originating from their operating conditions was named by the press of the time as quarrels over the wealth, and in this respect the press pointed out the contrast between the poor safeguarding of workers' interests at the workplace and the bickering trade union leaders. This presentation of the problem was unfair, and it was based on superficial knowledge of the matter. Back in the Kádár regime the practice was that one percent of wages was trade union membership fee. In the old regime most of the membership fee went to the central offices, but it is equally true that the local trade unions actively participated in the division of social allocations and assistance that originally must have come from the state budget. After 1990 the situation changed radically. The state ceased financing social allocations at the workplace, and the private companies did not find that this to be their duty. Therefore, the trade unions spent most of their funds from membership fees on compensating for these social allocations and assistance, thus causing a financial crisis in the running of the organisation. The one percent of the relatively small wages could not possibly cover the increased spending of the significantly changed post-1988 business federation structure.

In Hungary there is trade union pluralism nowadays, a fundamentally Latin pluralism. This statement is meant to say that the trade unions are not being organised in a so-called unit-trade union, but they belong to parallel, competing trade union centres. As compared to the model of the so-called unit-trade unions this means that in our country at each level of trade union movements there are several competing trade unions. Though the practice of "one company—one trade union" is not forbidden, it is not obligatory either. In today's Hungary one might even find several trade unions at the same workplace, and it is not impossible that they represent the same employees groups. Their co-existence is not limited by any professional or position-based definition. The presence of trade unions is based on the constitution, on the provisions of the right of public meeting—that is, such organisations can be established as long as 10 persons agree to it—and on international agreements that have been included (ratified and publicised) in the Hungarian legislation. Trade unions can therefore be set up based on the principle of freedom of association.

What is true at the level of workplaces is also true at higher levels, that is several trade unions represent the same profession, and of course there are several different trade union confederations at the same time. By confederation I mean the federation of federations. The more or less legal definition can be found in the law of local administrations, in which the conditions established for a confederation are the following: five professional federations representing at least five economic sectors and at least five regional federations at the same time, and also the existence of at least one hundred basic organisations throughout the country. It is possible, therefore, that at a given company there are simultaneously several trade unions belonging to different confederations; moreover, it is not impossible (there are such examples) that in the same company there are rival trade unions belonging to the same confederation. Belonging to a confederation is possible, but not obligatory. There are, consequently, trade unions operating in a certain company which meet every legal requirement and can even sign collective work agreements. But the opposite case is also true: it is not impossible, in principle, that trade unions operating outside the companies are present at the workplace through their representatives. The definition of the concept of presence, since the alterations introduced last May, has been transferred by the labour code to each trade union's statute.

In their composition, trade unions show great variety. Their smallest units can be the basic organisations or groups, but there are examples of organisations that consist of 10 persons in all. So, there are organisations that are nation-wide, divided into basic organisations and local groups, or they may be organised in so-called regional secondary organisations within the larger organisation, or they may set up professional, inter-professional or special layers of organisation. Other trade unions are organised from the bottom, and form associations with independent organisations (regional and/or professional associations), and further organise themselves in special layers or inter-professional organisations under an umbrella organisation. The trade unions then are grouped in professional and regional federations, which in their turn make up confederations. A mixture of models, traditions and historical coincidences contributed to the formation of this intricate, hard-to-understand structure. The traditions of pre-war professional organisations are mixed with elements of the German-Austrian, Scandinavian and Mediterranean-Latin models. The real situation is even more complicated than the presentation above. There are trade unions whose local branches are independent organisations constituted as legal body, in other cases the fact that they are a legal body and independent can only be applied to larger units, whereas the smaller units are guided by the regulations included in their statute. The MSZOSZ for instance is the federation of 47 professional organisations, the LIGA includes at the same time professional and regional trade unions as their basic organisations; but the trade unions set up at workplaces also form professional and regional organisations, which are also part of the confederation. In some regional organisations of the LIGA the members can be individuals, workplace organisations or can be the local, so-called secondary groups of a national professional organisation. The ideology of autonomous, bottom-to-top self-organising is part of the identity of the LIGA. Any kind of doubt about the inner pluralism of organising can lead to inner problems, such as the dispute over the alteration of the above-mentioned structure at the beginning of 1994, which caused a minor disruption in the LIGA. As compared to the fundamentally regional way of organising in the Workers' Councils, the professional organisations are secondary formations. In the case of the SZEF almost the only criterion to become a member is to be a civil servant. The case of trade unions (or professional associations, professional unions or national confederations) in which all the above-mentioned types co-exist is not rare. In all, one can note the co-existence of old, dissolving, traditional structures and of the new, developing structures in this present transitory period.

The trade union centres are forced to reduce their bureaucracy, to demolish their training institutions and to let their specialists go. On the other hand, the LIGA and the Workers' Councils are coming up with good-quality professionals and an expanding good-quality training, but the leaders of both organisations knew that these all depended on the temporary support from abroad, and it could not be maintained for long without financial support. The old trade unions saw the condition and guarantee of their survival in their wealth, while the new ones regarded wealth as the condition and guarantee of their gaining force and becoming stable. Among other things, this is the explanation for the clamorous disputes around the division of wealth, and this is the essence of the long-lasting controversy between trade unions.

The situation of business federations was aggravated by the changes in the economic structure. Ownership and size of the companies have changed, some sectors disappeared, others have been upgraded. Almost 800,000 small companies employ fewer than 11 workers, who most of the time are family members and relatives. In such places there cannot possibly exist trade unions. It is generally true that membership in business federations is falling, the number of collective contracts is decreasing, and despite bureaucratic efforts, the role of professional, collective meetings is becoming more and more an illusion. Consequently, the Antall government established the framework for social dialogue in accordance with international standards, but it was indifferent to the hardships accompanying the changes in business federations. If not in other matters, at least on this all rival trade unions agree. The dramatic fall in organising trade unions supports their standpoint.

The number of members is an important point of view in judging trade unions, but it is not overwhelming. At present in Hungary the trade union that has most members is the SZEF, but its capacity to promote its own interest is relatively small, mostly because it consists of loyal employees, civil servants and clerks. At the other end, there are the professional associations that have few members, but have a great capacity to promote their own interests. The examples are well-known: pilots, airport mechanics, railway workers, lorry drivers, energy producers and distributors. The prestige of trade unions, besides their capacity to promote their interests, is also influenced by their activity. The trade union can be large or small, but if it communicates well with its members, if it keeps them informed and prepares activists, it will enjoy greater credibility and its organising ability will increase; and due to the fact that many employees listen to it, they will take its advice no matter whether they are actually members or not. The trade unions therefore have a variety of forms, and the number of their members, as well as their influence, is hard to assess. It would require another analysis to detail the problem of what can be considered a result of the change of regime, and what is the emulation of international trends. Many analysts regard trade unions as the product of the industrial era, and in the present post-industrial period, in parallel with the spread of globalisation, they do not trust the future of trade unions.

Since the formation of the Horn government, many people—including the interest groups under discussion—have been waiting for the generalisation of discussion-agreement politics, the coming of a calm, calculated interest mediation instead of the earlier clamorous disputes, and the growth of stable trade unions. There was no shortage of public statements and theatrical gestures meant for the public. Let us remember the long-gone Social Economic Agreement. While the institutional structure of interest mediation was getting more and more complicated and divided, the real participation in the preparation of political decisions was null. According to the logic of administrative formalities the issues to be debated were more and more, committees grew like mushrooms, public institutions of interest mediation were downgraded, whereas the informal meetings and employer-customer relationships were upgraded. Both the Antall and the Boross-governments, and the Horn government stated that there should be stronger trade unions. The arguments supporting their declared goals were roughly the same. They mentioned sharing the burden of transition, the need for social dialogue and the importance of credible, open-dialogue business federations. Their arguments underlined the need for strong business federations saying that in their presence even the agreements that were disadvantageous for the employees would be kept—that is, the federations should be strong enough to withhold their members if needed, not only to make demands on their behalf. This is basically all right. But the last seven years' experience has shown that every government has paid little attention to the problems raised by federations, and has been more concerned with neutralising them. During the Antall government this meant that based on the principle of "divide et impera", the government often stated its ideas about how to organise business federations. The government made promises and threats, and postponed decisions. However, the continual threats and vigilance did good to trade unions: the feeling of danger somehow strengthened their organisations. The Horn government, on the other hand, corrupted trade union leaders. In exchange for certain advantages they offered to trade union bureaucrats they expected passive enforcement of their interests. Eventually this did happen. "The dog barked, but it did not bite," that is despite the loud threats the government finally extended its field of action through the noisy assistance given to business federations.[2] In the long run, however, this proved a costly enterprise. The dissolution of business federations, and among them of trade unions, was accelerated. Its signs were obvious. The number of professional and branch collective contracts fell rapidly[3]—employees' wages were seriously reduced without making a clear, at least long-term promise of compensation. The Horn government, in this respect, has a cynically professional policy. It is not worried in the least about the problems of society, more precisely of the employees. It treats employees, bureaucrats and workers as if they were the same. It negotiates with the bureaucratic elite respecting their interests. If needed, it makes sacrifices in exchange for their goodwill, as it did recently for the sake of organising the new electoral federation. What I previously called the corruption of business federation leaders is the essential element of the Horn policy in treating business federations. It builds a centralised corporation system by means of employer-customer techniques. It invites the representatives of employees—even if sometimes tardily, after the actual decisions have been taken, mainly for the sake of appearances—to discussions regarding national decisions, and in exchange it makes sure that people who are loyal and indebted to the government get to positions of "regular collaborators". This is a thorough and well-calculated arrangement, which weaves an invisible web with the participation of people of similar backgrounds, and which grants a flexible and easy passage among trade unions, parties and governmental organisations. If all goes on like this, then the Kádár regime will get back into the world of business federations, through its system based on old friendships, business and party connections and common interests.

Notes

1. XXVIIIth Law from 1991 about safeguarding the wealth of trade unions, equality of opportunities for all employees to organise and run their organisations.

2. The very refined version of this concurrence was visible in January 1998. In 1997 the government made a smooth agreement with trade unions on wages for that year, before passing the budget. As compared to this, trade unions began protest actions at professional levels in January this year (i.e.1998); they have been threatening with strikes repeatedly, but so far no trade union has actually stopped work (except for a few, which are really unimportant in this context, such as the workers from the Tatabánya brick factory desperately protesting against the fact that they had not been paid for some months). The complaints coming after the agreement, out of the political season, during the January holidays, suggest that that might have been a carefully planned action.

3. At present we know about 415 local collective contracts. The number of branch collective contracts is only 19.

Mária Schmidt

THE ROLE OF
"THE FIGHT AGAINST ANTI-SEMITISM"
DURING THE YEARS OF TRANSITION

Those not with us are against us (the Rákosi period)
Those not against us are with us (the consolidated Kádár period)
Those not with us are anti-Semites (the decade of the transition)

A Phantom Menace

As the party system was living through its last days, all of a sudden, as if by magic, courtesy of a provocative article carefully placed in the government's paper, the opposition intelligentsia— which had unanimously stood their ground against the party state until then—started to polarize along the lines of the "Jewish question." It was in the thirties that "the Jewish question" last divided the Hungarian intelligentsia when, in the middle of a more and more brown-shirted Europe, the public was caught up in the so-called rural vs. urban debate.[1] The strengthening of Nazism and militant anti-Semitism endangered the lives of Hungarians who were even just thought to be Jewish.

But after the inhuman terror of the Holocaust, during the more than four-decade long communist dictatorship, no dialogue could develop. Apart from a short two- or three-year long period, Hungarian Jews were not able to discuss the traumas of humiliation and persecution. Any discussion of the sufferings of Hungarian Jews was only allowed to take shape as general crimes at the expense of the oppressed. During the Kádár period, every issue concerning Jews was turned into a taboo to the degree that even the term "Jew" was excised from public discourse. Furthermore, one of the sad side effects of decades of brutal political manipulation was that many took an "it's-not-even-true-anyway" attitude. Consequently, accounts of the Holocaust were simply seen as lies.[2]

Only during the decade prior to the transition did it become gradually possible to debate in public the humiliation and persecution of Hungarian Jews. I do not claim that facing the past took place in a satisfactory way. The fact is, however, that a wide array of books, films, studies, memoirs, adaptations, essays, commemorations tackled the dreadful horror and terrible twists of fate that Hungarian Jews endured in the years between 1938 and 1945. The majority of Hungarian society reacted positively to the uncovered facts unknown to them until then. These were reactions of genuine catharsis, compassion and empathy.

On the other hand, we cannot ignore the fact that the Holocaust, the tragedy of European Jews during the Second World War, was only discussed in the United States of America and afterwards in Western Europe at the end of the sixties and the beginning of the seventies. The media only tackled it on a regular basis as of the end of the seventies.[3] Before this, the suffering of the Jews in the Second World War was not a prioritized subject among so many other horrors. Most European countries, having tried the criminals who committed the greatest and most war atrocities against humanity, seemed to forget about these crimes for decades. The states situated west of the iron curtain created their own myths of resistance and at the same time, denied their role and responsibility in the rise of Hitler's power. They made it seem as if their countries had been united in a large-scale anti-Nazi resistance movement. The reevaluation of their past served as a tool to achieve national harmonization and boost the national confidence of their disillusioned population.[4] Under the democratic conditions that had been forced on them externally, and under which every citizen was a voting citizen, the major players in the political arena of France, West Germany,

The Netherlands, Italy, Austria, etc., did not want to lose the millions of votes of those who had sympathized or collaborated with the Nazis and the fascists. Moreover, they especially wanted to ignore the responsibility and possible liability of those who participated passively or deliberately in the deportation and slaughter of Jews. Even the victims themselves preferred silence. Firstly, silence suits the endurance of terrible losses better than talk. Secondly, all that the deported, the humiliated and the persecuted masses had endured and lived through took on a whole new meaning in the context of the free world. Most of them were unable to, and did not wish to speak. To this day, it is their sons and grandsons, and not they, who speak. The second and third generations. They speak to the descendants of the perpetrators and the ignorant. Personal liability is an option only in the case of few old people still alive. Those who made the decisions and their executives are no longer with us. That is why we had to wait 35-40 years to bring to public attention the fate of European Jews during the Second World War.

After the demise of fashionable progressive concepts "socialism with a human face" or Third Worldism, the thematization of Nazism and the Holocaust came in handy for the left-wing intellectual circles of the United States and Western Europe as they were thus able to circumvent the confrontation with the practice of socialism and the collapse of the socialist utopia. They meant to prop up their ruined identity by way of relentlessly rejecting Nazism, fascism and anti-Semitism. These ideologies, however, had long lost their power.[5] This is the reason that they did not turn their attention to uncovering the cold harsh realities of communism. Instead, they have all this time more and more intensively emphasized the cruelties of the inhumanities of the Nazi system and the horror of the Holocaust.[6]

It is also important to note that ever since its creation, Israel has been heroically fighting for its safety and the interests of the Western world against the Arab world, which has never resigned itself to Israel's existence. As such, for Israel, the Holocaust has become one of the most important legitimizing bases. The Holocaust acquired really widespread public influence when it became the subject of American mass culture. Then it was "Americanized,"[7] that is "Hollywood-ified." Since then, anybody who is associated with anti-Semitism is politically dead in the most influential circles of the USA.[8] It is very similar in the countries of the European Union. Consequently, all of the above will have to be taken into consideration when we discuss the characteristics of the Hungarian "Jewish question."

In Hungary and the other countries east of the iron curtain, the era of collective persecution was not yet over. After the transition, when all the persecuted and humiliated social groups sought ways to publicize their suffering, it turned out that not all such initiatives met the approval of our opinion-forming media intellectuals, who previously seemed inclined to take an active interest in these efforts. The fate of kulaks, internal deportees, executed anti-communists, the imprisoned, the forced laborers, the Soviet deportees was not of interest. Their sufferings did not become a cathartic, moving and disturbing experience due to the fact that the majority of intellectuals who have all this time influenced and controlled the greater part of public opinion, was not interested in unearthing the inhuman practices of the communist dictatorship. They were not interested because they did not want to face their own responsibility and resolve the question of how they had been able to serve the system and cover up its horrors. Therefore, the people who were persecuted during the communist dictatorship in the fifties or after 1956 and who were unwilling to compromise themselves, became portrayed in the media as pitiable, unsuccessful frightening and, most of all, ridiculous wrecks. The opinion-forming elite was an ever-ready and faithful assistant to support the Rákosi and Kádár system. Their influential positions in the strictly patrolled mass media, television, radio, publications, universities and colleges were due to their loyalty and resignation to the party system.

Naturally, so far as they were concerned, the system should only have changed as long as their positions stayed unscathed. The seriously compromised opinion-forming intellectuals inside the party state structure were clearly motivated to cover up the harsh realities of the communist dictatorship and keep the truth from the information-deprived public. They were not interested in prosecuting or adjudicating the most serious criminals legally or morally. Furthermore, it was certainly against their interest to fundamentally re-evaluate Hungary's twentieth century history in the light of Hungarian national interests after decades of foreign, first Nazi, then Soviet, rule between 1944 and 1990. Instead, for tactical reasons, they concentrated on the "Jewish question."

"He is not one of us"—wrote a dedicated socialist-liberal publicist about the world-famous Hungarian architect Imre Makovecz in an article published in the largest Hungarian national daily.[9] On the pages of the former government's central daily, "not one of us" meant that those who were not loyal to the party state and its successor party were not "*nash*" (the term used in Russia). If someone was "*nash*," they were "one of us": they were ours, they belonged to us. Not the others. The world was that simple. It was divided between progressive forces and reactionaries, anti-fascist and fascist. "Ours" and "not ours." For the "*nash*," the collapse of communism did not change anything. On one side there are the reactionary, fascist anti-Semites, and on the other "us": we who take pains to fight for the "progressive cause" against the "fascist forces."

Taking the "Jewish question" public had a number of advantages. Firstly, those who were or could have been held accountable for their role in the Kádár regime, and happened to be of Jewish origin, shielded themselves with their Jewishness. What is more, any legitimate or unfounded critique concerning "Jews" or "non-Jews" was made to become anti-Semitic, as were the critics themselves stigmatized anti-Semitic, fascists and ultra right-wing. This is how they avoided accountability and facing the conclusions of their own true judgments. Stigmatizing as anti-Semites the post-transition intellectuals, who chose to actively or passively resist the Kádár regime, resulted in another indirect advantage: in front of the political public and those Western European and North American, mostly left-wing or liberal intellectuals, unfamiliar with the internal political situation yet interested in Hungary, the relatively unknown non-nomenclature intellectuals could be easily discredited. Being an anti-Semite, as I pointed out above, is rather passé in the more developed parts of the world. At the same time, coming clean of anti-Semitic or fascist charges is practically impossible.

The anti-communist ideology of the self -proclaimed liberal ex-democratic opposition group, the Alliance of Free Democrats (SZDSZ), used the most critical anti-communist rhetoric during the time of the transition. They were also the most radical opponent of the previous party elite and their intellectual wing. Their anti-communist politics was only upheld until the 1990 elections. The minute the election-winning Hungarian Democratic Forum (MDF) formed a government without the Free Democrats, the smooth political transition was less important than the discrediting of their former ally. Labeling them "provincial", "common" and "rude" was more a priority than demolishing the party state structure, which had organically integrated itself into the fabric of economic and social change. This structure was now propped up by former connections, advantageous positioning and foreign capital. Misjudging the situation, did they, perhaps, wrongly entertain the supposition that these communist *apparatchiks* in the guise of social liberals, to whom they had always condescended, were powerless by now and would therefore subject themselves and their political and economic influence, like some beaten army, to the genuine, more educated, more Western-oriented and more trained liberals, and accept their leadership? We do not know the answer. The fact is, however, that they decided on the overexposure of the

"Jewish question" and the discrediting of the Forum's government while legitimizing the survival of the ex-communist nomenclature. Naturally, the ex-communists, now in political and social quarantine, took full advantage of this opportunity.[10]

The escalation of the "Jewish question" and its interpretation as a dividing line in political and public spheres made it impossible to consider any other option. The policy was that, through continual pseudo-scandals and provocative stunts, unfounded accusations and false statements, the national-liberal-conservative forces, as well as the non-communist, non-left-wing governing forces were put on the defensive. Their discrediting efforts resulted in the derogation of concepts like "national" and "Hungarian."

"Péter Esterházy said in the Society of the Cultural Association of Hungarian Jews that it is not possible to interpret what a writer or a politician means when they say 'Hungarian'. When they say that, they mean something else."[11]

In order to achieve their objective, they combined the experiences and methods of the twenties i.e. the fight against "social fascism"; those of the thirties, i.e. the "people's front"; and those of the forties, i.e. Rákosi-style "salami tactics." The essence of this Bolshevik technique is that, given their media control, they (those fighting against anti-Semitism in this case) decide who can play the enemy's role. They inflict pressure on the enemy until the enemy is completely isolated from the rest of the population. This is exactly how Rákosi gradually took power despite the electoral majority won by the Smallholders' Party in the 1945 parliamentary elections.

And, this is exactly how the post-communist socialists and left-wing liberals have operated to weaken their opponents. It is important to note that they also financially support the establishment of new parties and movement in the opposition. The left-wing post-communists and "liberals" united all their forces and, in the style of people's front politics, have taken control of the political

playing-field against a completely disunited right wing. The cooperation of the communists' successor party and their once sworn
liberal enemies is only shocking at first sight. Thus argues Bill
Lomax, an outstanding English researcher of the 1956 revolution:
these liberals rejected Marxism-Leninism only formally, and they
are in fact Leninists in the guise of liberals.[12] This cooperation
could only be legitimized by way of reviving the spirit of "anti-fas-
cism" through the well-known terminology of the period between
the two world wars.[13] When worst comes to worst, when the worst
enemy has to be fought, the communists, the ex-communists (just
like in the thirties) become the lesser evil. We know from Koestler,
who knew this mechanism inside out, how this works:

"We learned to prove that anyone who disagrees with us is a
fascist agent,... and acts as an agent of fascism."[14]

Against this background, when one has to fight shoulder-to-
shoulder against an artificially created and continually updated
"fascist threat," then it is best not to, what is more, it is forbidden,
to talk about what happened in the past 45 years. Most of all, it is
forbidden to ask who committed what, who is responsible for what.
The "fascist vs. anti-fascist" confrontation has the advantage that
the former opposition is able to unabashedly justify, both at home
and abroad, why they abandoned their plan to change the system
and the nomenclature, why they formed an alliance with their former enemies, and why they legitimize them retrospectively both
morally and politically. The "fascist threat" was never real as it
turns out from their statements.[15] As far as the "Jewish question" is
concerned, it never has been a real concern to most of them; as a
matter of fact, it served merely as a careful calculation.[16]

I do not doubt that they made some of the formerly persecuted believe that their lives were in danger, but it is beyond doubt that
some of those in public and those in the background knew exactly
what the point of the "anti-fascist" fight was. This people's front
style of politics divided not the old nomenclature and the pro-tran-

sition forces. The dividing line, rather, was an artificially fabricated one between a virtual extreme right-wing danger and the pro-democracy post-communist-liberal forces under the banner of the Democratic Charter.[17]

This is why ever since the post-communists and the party of the one-time democratic opposition, the SZDSZ,[18] have governed the country, the "Jewish question" is all of a sudden not so central any longer and the fascist threat has vanished overnight.[19]

Ever since Michael Wolffson's *Deutschland Akte* ("Germany Files") was published, we know from his authoritative research in the Stasi archives that between 25 December 1959 and January 1960 in West Germany, the anti-Semitic, neo-fascist campaign (graffiti, desecration, etc) consisting of 470 incidents was organized and orchestrated by the Stasi. During the Eichmann trial in 1961, the West German extreme right movement collected money publicly to support Eichmann's defense, which again was orchestrated by the Stasi's XX/4 department. The archives also revealed that the Stasi was behind the extreme right's organizations: they were financed, organized and directed by the Stasi. They printed the money collection forms, for example. Under the aegis of the "J-plan," this same department was in charge of sending out hate mail as well as readers' response letters to the editors of West German publications. Wolffson also claims that those who blamed the Stasi for these provocations were made to look ridiculous by the "mainstream infallible," who to this day have not apologized to them.[20]

"Anti-Semitism Today is a TV Question[21]

György Domokos's reader's letter titled "The minority and oppression" was published on 29 April 1990 in *Népszabadság*. The letter was published along with Iván Völgyes' response. Domokos's letter was written in a naiv, good-natured vein. His writing proves how little impact anti-Semitic phraseology had on the generations born in or after the fifties, and how little resistance they have against such rhetoric. These generations are not aware what these thoughts once meant—or mean today, for that matter. Domokos had no clue that he had penned a letter abundant in anti-Semitic cliches, despite the fact that his intentions were innocent:

> "I wouldn't allow the drawing of conclusions or seeking explanations concerning why so many Hungarian and foreign communist leaders were Jewish. Much more than the proportion of their numbers in the population. I would report anti-Semitism because this is the only way to avoid the general recognition that we really hold together for our survival and we really strive for power. I want publicity, namely the acquisition of the tools of publicity. But at the same time, I do not allow people to know how many of us work for the largest media, television, and the radio, the press, what pull we have and the numbers that we represent. Or in the economy, finance, banking. Culture, health care... That's exactly why Jews themselves ought to work toward understanding and curb their drive to attain exclusivity and more power. That's why Jews ought to be considerate not to put only Jewish reporters on a 24-hour TV programme reporting on the first free elections that will determine the future of the whole Hungarian nation. And if they invite experts, they ought to make sure that those are not all Jewish..."

Domokos's opinion on the intertwining of communism and Jewry is a real anti-Semitic stereotype. It is true that many communist leaders are of Jewish origin, but their proportion in the whole of the race is negligible. Jewry is, in fact, strongly conservative and traditional, typically in favor of private property and private enterprise. Hungarian Jews were mainly pro-government and conservative politically all the way through their political emancipation leading up to the tragedy of the Holocaust. In absolute numbers, there might have been approximately ten thousand secularized Jews during the above-mentioned seven decades who were associated with some left-wing movement (the social democrats, mainly), while there were about two thousand Jews who joined some marginal communist organization during the same period. Even if this number grew to tens of thousands in the time after the Second World War, the claim that Hungarian Jews sympathized with or supported the communist regime's dictatorship more than non-Jews is unsustainable. Thus argues Sándor Révész:

"As much as Jews do not have to feel ashamed about Rákosi, Gerő, Farkas, etc., they do not have to be proud of Menuhin, Oistrakh, Stern, Perlman, etc either. They have as little to do with the crimes of the former as little they have to do with the artistry of the latter. All of the above could be substituted with Hungarians—Szálasi, Szentgyörgyi, Csutár, Rácz... etc."[22]

By contrast, Miklós Szabó, one of the founding members and ideologues of SZDSZ, seems to embrace Domokos's argument. Szabó claims:

"Masses of small Jews joined the camp of the 1919 republic because already then they saw that full social emancipation could only take place in a future socialist state... The communist party was primarily made up of Jews between the two world wars. Those who survived 1944 and stayed in Hungary saw the communist party as the sole governing power...they saw the party's rule as a guarantee that 1944 would not happen again. Jews expected from the communist party's state a fresh opportunity to assimilate. Although Jews were Hungarian-speaking Hungarian citizens, although they Hungarianized their names and converted to Christianity, they did not become Hungarian... The paths of Hungarian Jews and socialist, later communist movements, met when this association meant the clearest disassociation from anti-democratic systems.[23]

The representative, who tends to pose as a philosemite, claims no less than that Jews picked socialism in the middle of the 1910s on a racial basis a la Hitler. And that they have fostered a good relationship with it ever since, while together with the socialist and communist movements, they all disassociated from anti-democratic systems. Perhaps it never occurred to them that the relationship between communism and democracy left much to be desired at times. In addition, his claims concerning the Jews' inability to assimilate is beyond the wildest stretch of imagination.

The above was written by a qualified historian and active politician. By contrast, Domokos was stigmatized and ostracized. Miklós Szabó's reputation is still immaculate.[24]

Domokos believes that in order to counterbalance the attempts at exclusivity, descent and representational proportions should be taken into consideration. Why descent though? Would descent classification help to bring to an end the communication monopoly that the left wing has so carefully built up for over forty years? Why is it not more important to pay more attention to the fair and proportionate representation of the different viewpoints rather than the proportionate representation of experts of the different descents, religions and/or cultures in TV programmes?

There are countless arguments. However, three days after the formation of the Antall government, the Domokos-incited debate prompted the above-quoted Miklós Szabó, the most aggressive member of the SZDSZ to coin the following slogan: "Anti-Semitism today is a TV question!" He argues:

"If anti-Semitism was once a question of bankers and, in the Rákosi regime, a question of function, then today it is a TV question. There are more intellectuals of Jewish descent in journalism than the proportion of Jews in the Hungarian population. [He must have counted them. M. S.] Let's not start explaining that this proportion is not that 'outstanding'... As far as the present is concerned: the country has an excellent group of journalists, who are democracy-oriented and loyal. Any cleansing or changing of the guards in this field would lead to a loss of quality and political damage. The future of our budding democracy lies in its courage to fight against the most minor manifestation of anti-Semitism."

This is how all the efforts of the new, democratically elected government to demolish the mass media's post-communist dominance became ab ovo anti-Semitism. That the former nomenclature's media intellectuals did not wish to give up their positions without a fight even after the transition is more or less natural. That the intellectuals who did not get to fill these positions for one reason or another during the pre-transition years, but now aspired to take over, is self-evident. But there are two things that made this situation very peculiar. On the one hand, the "victorious soldiers of a defeated system," as László Gy. Tóth called them, turned this question into a "Jewish question." On the other hand, they managed to win over the support of the former democratic opposition and their intellectual support base. The influence of media, especially electronic media, on our lives is a commonplace today. What the mass media is able to do to us and what responsibilities the players of the media have is aptly described by the following quote from Mihály Babits in his study *Az írástudók árulása* ("The treason of the literate"):

"The soul of the era must be sought in the literate. They make the century move and their power is quickly growing in this era of the newspaper. Modem journalism absolves the masses of thinking, delivering ready-made ideas to them... for all this the literate are responsible."[25]

The ownership of the fourth estate (the media) is very important, if not *the* most important issue in modem mass democracies.
The rather monolithic power elite that filled the key positions of the
media in the last few years before the transition did a lot for the
transition. Many thought they were making politics—a role they
very much liked and were unwilling to give up. Their connections,
inclinations and political reflexes all pulled them to the post-communist-liberal camp. It was almost natural that the two groups met
in the search for the control of the media positions. To describe the
media intellectuals and the media situation, I will quote Béla
Pokol's pithy analysis:

"Despite the multi-party political system, the constitutional
court, and millions of citizens' voting rights to influence government, the opinion-forming processes are still controlled for us by a
couple of hundred editors, reporters, journalists and politically
affiliated intellectuals concentrated around the Budapest-based
media."[26]

The media war, which produced hundreds of TV and radio
reports, articles, and public statements, demonstrations and
protests, signatures, demonstrative bans, etc., only preserved the
disadvantages of the new aspiring transition elite that had fallen
behind all this time anyway. The symbiosis between the opinion
formers and the media intellectuals won the support of those who
were led to believe that at stake is not the survival or demise of the
old party state structures, but the emergence of "anti-Semitic
nobodies."[27] They won over to their side those who were financially dependent on them. And those who were misled and taken in.
And those who saw through them but did not have the courage to
fight the "sign of the times" for fear of getting the cold shoulder.
For those who dared to reject the legitimacy of the Jews vs. anti-
Semites confrontation or even pointed out the falsity of the division, or even attempted a fair perspective were ignored or misrep-
resented (if the person happened to say he or she is Jewish), or sim-

ply were grouped with the anti-Semites (if the person happened to say he or she was not Jewish). At the time of the media war, from about 1990 to 1994 we, the "Belgians," did not know where to stand.

Today, in the eighth year of the transition, it is clear that the media war was won by the post-communist elite. The self-proclaimed liberal transition intellectuals who fought the most charging battles of the media war were also defeated (András Bánó, Ákos Mester, István Bölcs, Iván Gádor, etc.). The result is that the media today can be described as uninteresting, servile and desperately partisan.[28]

Lyre or Orb

Hitel, the national literary periodical published their editor-in-chief, Sándor Csoóri's, diaries. In 1990, an article titled *Nappali hold (2.)* ("Day-time Moon") appeared:

The nation together as one? What kind of outdated wish is that? There were many who expressed their disgust at that: we had to idolize socialism so far, now we'll have to idolize the nation? The nation, that for us is no more than a sack full of Horthy memorabilia?... Many live, why not, in this country who are bored with the usual Hungarian whining: Mohács, Nagymajtény, Világos, Trianon and other vicissitudes. You might be bored with all these but that won't make them disappear from the unsolvable problems. It is funny that as long as one can adapt to Hungarians in a natural way, through assimilation or even intellectual association, these hereditary problems didn't bother, or irritate, the Germans, or the Jews who integrated here after the Compromise. Ady was surrounded by Ignáczi, Hatvany, and Jászi, who shared his problems as much as they could. I reckon that Ady's time is the last period when the nation's problems and the problems of Hungarianness were still existential and historical problems for the Jews. The Jews learned the language and the pain that the language delivered. With the Republic, the Horthy era, and especially the Blood era, the chance to be one in spiritual togetherness vanished. Of course, there have been, and will be, people like Antal Szerb, Miklós Radnóti, György Sárközi, István Vas, György Harag, Ottó Orbán, György Konrád, György Faludy and Tamás Zala but there are signs of reverse assimilation in the country: now the free thinking Jews wish to assimilate Hungarians both in style and thinking. To achieve this they have built a parliamentary platform that they had not been able to build before. If we had a new Endre Ady, Béla Bartók, László Németh, István Bibó, Gyula Illyés, this would even be a challenge: let excellent forces battle to remedy these century-long diseases... But we have no Ady, Bibó or Németh. On top of all that, we have no intellectual life either, which would serve as a backdrop or context to the competition. There is only the political arena, here insult prompts insult, and slap follows slap. Anti-Semitism and nationalism? These are rather the main characters of a badly written political play and not of souls or a real situation. Instead of an army, squads equipped with bellows march about and blow everything out of proportion to help cover up the issues to be solved...

Sándor Csoóri is a poet and a good one, too. He is master of images, symbols, implications and intuitions. All the above was written with poetic license (even if his words are imbued with the overvaluation of "Jewry" and the undervaluation of "Hungarianness"[29]). It is only too bad that he was toying with politics. I never understood those who opposed him and I never understood those who opposed György Spiró for his poem *Jönnek* ("They are coming"). Spiró too overreacted, exaggerated and levelled accusations. But still, he sensed something that only the truly great are able to. He was motivated by the same feeling as Csoóri: "I am angry for you, not against you."

> *The deep-bosomed Hungarians are coming again*
> *Doggerels, dog fans, they're coming from the shit...*

The difference between Csoóri's diaries and Domokos's article is that, while the latter was published in the largest daily and the debate it sparked took place there as well, Csoóri's diaries were published in a literary magazine, but the nearly two hundred readers' letters it prompted, some of which called him anti-Semitic, came out in national dailies and weeklies.[30] Reading the hysterical lines of leading intellectuals, I recall Juliett Greco's radio interview when she said giggling: "It is perhaps better to be wrong on Sartre than be right on Raymond Aron."[31] It appears that a great number of Hungarian intellectuals went to war to prove that they are in fact "*nash*".

Hundreds of thousands of readers, who read only arbitrarily quoted excerpts from Csoóri's work, did not have the chance to understand its underlying context, the rich layers of meaning and its moods. This method became widely used. Writings that were judged anti-Semitic appeared in marginal, small-circulation alternative publications. However, between 1990 and 1994, national dailies and weeklies reaching hundreds of thousands of readers, not to mention the publicity the TV stations and radio stations provided, tackled the "Jewish question" in depth. The pretext was that the extreme right (read fascist) forces, are preparing a coup d'etat. Publications such as *Hunnia*, *Szent Korona*, that came out in a couple of thousand copies, came in handy (the question arises: who financed these publications?).

And of course, there was Albert Szabó. Szabó materialized out of thin air, all of a sudden—having spent years abroad, he returned to Hungary, and armed a neo-Nazi group of a few members. Szabó and his conspicuously attired group turned up at every non-social-ist-liberal demonstration and received prompt media attention. Ever since 1994, Szabó and his posse have not been on TV. (Another question: were they perhaps given a new assignment?)[32]

The real star of the transition was István Csurka, however. He was a founding member of the MDF, an MP, a successful and tal-ented playwright, an excellent author, bohemian, great talker and drinker. He is a folk hero par excellence. He outraged the public that was ever-so-ready to be outraged. He outraged everyone, be it because he spoke his mind (or they thought he had), or because he had kept it a secret, or because he was irritated or because he him-self irritated everybody. According to the archives of Press Monitor of The Parliament Library, between 1990 and 1994 there were 1,603 articles, studies, essays, interviews, etc., in the title of which terms like "csurkaist", "csurkism", "the Csurka lot", "Csurka" sur-faced.[33]

It is for posterity to decide who was a politician doing writing, and who was a writer doing politics. All we know for sure is that the oeuvre of a writer is judged on a different basis from the work of the deputy of a parliamentary party, let alone that of a governing party. Csurka's writing, therefore, can and ought to only be investi-gated from this point of view here. For it is expected from the MP of a governing party to measure every sentence he writes in terms of the effect it will or might have. It is unforgivable if he did not do that. The ruling MDF was not able to associate with his political activities, which led to the breakup of the party. The MDF has not been able to recover from that blow. Csurka's "literary activity" buttressed the socialist-liberal camp, which in turn weakened the transition. His August 20 study was a provocation. He knew what to expect and still he published it. The scandal reached New York.

He received from József Antall the envelope that proved that he was an agent. Then we read in *Magyar Fórum* that, although he had been recruited, he had never reported on anybody. The MDF split. His party, the Hungarian Justice and Life Party (MIÉP) got 85,000 votes on the 1994 elections.

Magyar Fórum published his *Néhány gondolat a rendszerváltozás két esztendeje és az MDF program kapcsán* ("Some thoughts apropos of the two years of the transition and the MDF program") on 20 August, 1992: an essay in his usual voluble style, tackling generalities about history, politics, the present and the future. His analyses are brilliant at times, sometimes witty too, and sometimes dull or simply ludicrous. Incredibly naive observations mingle with precise insights. He is at his best when diagnosing. He is like a quack when it comes to prescribing treatment.

Csurka was right when he argued that the collapse of the Soviet world empire had taken most of the world by surprise—including the Hungarian pro-transition forces. It is also true that Hungary is in a dependent situation due to its geographical location and economic performance. It can only act on its own with limited success. His arguments regarding the definitive control of the IMF, the World Bank and foreign capital point to givens that a heavily indebted and geopolitically closed country like Hungary has to accept. He was right when he predicted the following:

"The future lies with the 'experts'. The public was led to believe that the expert, party leader, institutional and economic decisionmaker, nomenclature of the last years of the Kádár era, were not hillbillies, like the nomenclature of the previous communist elite. Quite the contrary, they were 'European', endowed with Western connections."

(Did the MSZP lift its 1994 campaign slogan, the "Let the experts govern" from Csurka's writing?) Csurka's prophecy regarding the coalition between the SZDSZ and MSZP also came true:

"It was impossible to feed the public that the most famous anti-communist party was, in fact, part of the nomenclature. They guaranteed the smooth transition."

He was probably right in saying that "Dunagate" was just a "Hollywood tale." But throughout his writing, he shows inferiority and resentment. At the same time, he flings insults at his opponents ("Mickey Mouse", "Aczélists", "nomenclature", etc.). So why is he disturbed when he receives criticisms such as "peasant", "foot stench", "poor boy"? He made it in politics. He is active in his party and a representative in the parliament. What about Csoóri? And what about the rest of the elite of the MDF, who were also writers (with the exception of Boross, who was only a politician). Why?

Csurka seems to believe that Hungary is the center of the universe, while writers are the center of Hungary. There is a world conspiracy including capital, the international media, the vice-president of the USA, international Jewish organizations, the influential Jewish World Congress, George Soros and György Aczél, and the Aczél "parachutists." They get together sometimes on Rózsadomb, or Tel-Aviv or New York to discuss what to do with the world.

> "One day when times are quieter, someone might reveal how the parachutists function in the body of Hungarian society. They sometimes act as the Galilei Circle, sometimes the periodical of civic liberal thinkers, then they come out as terrorist assassins of Béla Kun and Tibor Szamuely, then they morph into the Muscovite immigrants headquartered in Vienna and Berlin, then they side with Attila József until he dies. This squad takes numerous shapes, they are everywhere, they reject whatever they did previously but they take part in every major social transition."

What Csurka means by "parachutists" is interpreted as the following by Péter Kende, a "Leninist liberal":

From free masons to feminists and the fight for the lay intellectual schools, everything associated with the more Western notion of egalitarian, civic and emancipatory initiatives is stigmatized in Hungary as Jewish initiatives, conspicuous Jewish presence and mass Jewish participation. The forerunners of social development do not want to integrate into the national society but rather, they are working to replace today's conservative Hungary with a Western-style Hungary open to the modern world, which they can integrate into from inside.[34]

Csurka's claims in his ill-famed study are true. Csurka and the MDF had to battle the accusations of anti-Semitism from the very first day of the transition. The charge besmirched the MDF, the right wing and József Antall himself. It was unfounded in their case. Csurka, however, although he does not call himself anti-Semitic, made a good number of anti-Semitic statements in his writings.[35] For example, he writes that the USA did not try to intervene in the 1956 Uprising because Eisenhower was told that Jews were being murdered in Budapest.

"There are two players wrestling here: the national center, which has a Christian wing as well as a nationalist and peasant base with socialist inclinations, and the left block, which has been the loudest anti-communist group but which has sustained power ever since 1945. This, of course, includes the sustaining of Jewish influence, most importantly the preservation of financial means and the succession of power."

What kind of Jewish influence does he mean? What kind of Jewish influence has been exercised here since 1945? Rákosi, Gerő et al represented Soviet rule in Hungary as kings of a Bolshevik totalitarian state. But then, what kind of influence did they grant the Jews as a community? Or Kádár? Csurka must know that the politics of the Soviet Union was marked by sharp anti-Semitism all along, even if, at one point, they termed it "anti-Zionist." How much more influence might the National Representation of Hungarian Israelites have had than, say, the Unitarian Church? Would it not have been better to restrict himself to discuss what mistakes the MDF made during the first two years of their government? Why did Csurka recommend Elemér Hankiss and Csaba Gombár to head Hungarian Television and Hungarian Radio? Why did Árpád Göncz become President? Why did Csurka and the MDF itself not communicate better with the journalists, editors, intellectuals? Or society as a whole, for that matter?

One-time opposition star-writer György Konrád was the emblematic leader of the Democratic Charter at this time. The SZDSZ-affiliated politician-writer[36] intended to nominate the SZDSZ's top representative prime minister when the election-winning Hungarian Socialist Party (MSZP) went into government with the SZDSZ in 1994. This anti-democratic attitude, ignoring the majority's will, went unnoticed in socialist-liberal circles in Hungary or abroad. They also turned a blind eye on the fact that Konrád collaborated with the secret police on one occassion.[37]

Konrád is a writer. He has taken a great deal of interest in writing about the "Jewish question" lately. Different things every time. But, then, he is only another writer doing politics, or politician doing writing. Before the transition, he said, in the usual left-wing liberal style: "I have stepped out of Jewry somehow." And: "If Jews collectively take credit for the heroism of suffering they endured, then they should also take responsibility for the suffering they caused." However, when in 1997 he published his collection of selected writings, these statements were cut. It appears he re-evaluated his relationship with Jews in the meantime.[38] The following might well have been inspired by Domokos and Csurka:

"It is justified that Jews should not be overrepresented in political departments. Their performance should be personal. Jews should exercise reserved self-restraint and accept that the majority sees them as a minority."[40]

Why justified? And what else would their performance be but personal in the political department? What Jews? Those who got there without their personal performance? How much reserved self-restraint should be exercised in politics? Would it be enough, for example, if they did not insist on appointing the prime minister?

Péter Polonyi argues that Konrád's *Láthatatlan hang* ("The Invisible Voice") is a cultural and biological race theory. It is sadly typical of Hungarian public life that he hastens to clarify in the beginning that he himself is of Jewish origin. (Who cares?) This is how he justifies his argument:

> "Jews... took a major role in the establishment of communication links, mass media, commerce, intellectual dialogue, the development of the Earth and its inhabitants into a living world... This is the single one world nation and hence their mission... The people that elected itself to carry out clerical functions have stood aside and held up the notion of one God and one humankind. Jews are not going to become streetsweepers because the intellectual capital that has accumulated throughout centuries will be passed on. We blend sensitivity, disposition and intelligence in our gene cocktail, which will be our children. This is a portable heritage and it will work everywhere."[41]

To summarize: "Jews" are the cherry on God's cake on the one hand, on the other, "Jews" have been a pool of intelligence for centuries. Probably because of the gene cocktail. My goodness! If only Csurka, Csoóri and Konrád had discussed all the above with one another at their own peace talks.

Pseudo-Scandals

On 18 October, 1990 MTV2 and the tabloid paper *Kurír* reported that while Péter Tölgyessy was making a speech in the first democratically elected parliament someone shouted "Give the Jew a barrel." The investigation of the Supreme Court of Hungary did not find any evidence that this had happened. Its report said:

"It has been confirmed that the comment that was shouted to Péter Tölgyessy during his speech in the Parliament was: 'Give the speaker a barrel.' Our experts analyzed the sentence in question perceptionally and technically as well as phonetically. We can safely confirm that the word 'Jew' was not said."[42]

Historian Péter Hanák published an article titled "Tradition and Future" attacking Csoóri in *Népszabadság* on 29 September, 1991. Afterwards, it was reported, his wife received threatening phone calls, then she was physically abused with a leather belt (!?). On 18 October, after the investigating officer had left the house, she was stabbed by an attacker, who had climbed in through the window. "This is the first pogrom since the world war"—wrote *Magyar Narancs*. This statement was not withdrawn later.[43] Contrary to the active imagination of the sociologist Mrs. Hanák, further investigations proved that it is impossible to stab somebody through the window or the front door. *Beszélő*, the then Free Democrats' Alliance (SZDSZ)-affiliated periodical, claimed that "there are some who want Jews and liberals to live in fear, all who do not belong to the National Majority."[44]

Csurka noted the following in his radio commentary:

"There are filthy little press battles going on in Hungary. Last fall, when every single day there was news and coverage whether or not there is anti-Semitism in Hungary, and if there is, who generates it, a woman, a historian's wife appeared in public and claimed that she had been lashed in the face with a whip just because her husband had written against the spread of anti-Semitism. Then she went on to claim that she had been stabbed through her window for the same reason. Her claims made a huge impact, there was signatures to support her, and intellectuals started protesting against the revival of anti-Semitic brutality. They conjured up a phantom for the public: the picture of the Hungarian nationalist, a terrorist, who stabs defenseless women just because the populist literate prompt them to do so. The case was picked up by the Publicity Club, which was originally established to monitor the fairness of mass communication. Now it turns out that the whole case is a tissue of outright ties. The woman is ill and there are no whip-equipped Hungarian fascists. The window through which she was stabbed is five meters high. In the meantime however, the historian has been talking about the spread of Hungarian nationalism, the peril it brings, and now there is this guilt trip. The historian did not harbor any guilt, despite the fact that he is a historian and that he does not know his own wife. Ever since, however, the Publicity Club, with its minuscule membership, has been thought of as the bastion of press ethics."[45]

The much younger Attila Novák pointed out the following:

"The Hanák and barrel cases reflect the 1944 experience and fear of persecution. The same was prevalent in other 'scandals' that were related to political and religious minorities. When judging minority-related issues, they *envisioned* a possible Auschwitz, the horror of which promptly canceled out any dialogue and grouped other non-extreme right wing opinions with the brownshirts. This is appalling since generations that were not direct victims of the Holocaust are still affected by it nonetheless. Thus, harping on the 1944 experience be came the single one acceptable form of communication as well as the single Jewish problem. Relentlessly comparing the present with 1944 became a schlock topos. This hurt mostly the Holocaust and the survivors, as their experience and suffering was now made politically available. It is intolerable and unfair that in the nineties, any perspective regarding group differences is associated with the criminals of the Holocaust."[46]

Speaking at a Hungarian Democratic Forum event (MDF) Jenő Fónay, president of POFOSZ, made the following statement on September 8, 1992:

"Whoever tries to reject fascism in 1992 is a shameful servant of Bolshevism."

"The statement stirred up quite a bit of scandal"— reflected the editor in *Egyenleg*, a political TV program. Jenő Fónay had been elected one of the deputies of the Hungarians' World Association three weeks prior to his statement, about the time when Csurka's study appeared. His Óbuda speech clearly cast a darker shadow on the recently re-formed association. His interview in *Egyenleg* was widely quoted in TV news, radio news as well as dailies the following morning. Prime Minister József Antall took a stand and said morals dictate the rejection of Nazism, fascism, communism and Bolshevism altogether... *Egyenleg* replayed Fónay's words and took the opinion that given the tension and passions of the Hungarian public arena, politicians ought to pay more attention to the responsibility of their words in public. Fónay eventually published a letter of apology."

Egyenleg created a pseudo-scandal.[47]

Fónay was on death row after the 1956 Uprising. On the day of his execution, he was led to the pillar, where he was informed that he had been granted a pardon. He was a 56-er hero not "*nash*". Through him, the other "bigs" could easily be targeted: Csoóri and Csurka, the MDF itself. Furthermore, it was easier to prove that the 56-ers who did not belong to the communists, or reform communists, or post-communists, or even the SZDSZ were fascists. For Fónay had the courage to say that in 1992, after the collapse of more than forty years of communism, two years after the transition, the fight against this virtual fascism exclusively served the purposes of post-communists, who still held power. That is why he fell prey to the media commando. The scandal around Csurka's "Nazi" study had been going on for three weeks then. The statement that "Fónay had been elected one of the deputies of the Hungarians' World Association at the time the Csurka study was published" served one purpose: to montage Fónay and Csurka together and lead the casual reader to believe that Fónay's statement had more to do with Csurka's study. The presentation of the issue prevented the public from analyzing it and arriving at a judgment for themselves. They were served a judgment ready-made.

On 23 October, 1992 Árpád Göncz, the SZDSZ-affiliated President of Hungary was not able to deliver his speech at the Kossuth square commemoration as the audience, mainly made up of 56-er veterans, received him with 67-second-long booing and whistling. The president did not even attempt to talk to the crowd. He was looking around befuddled then marched off with resentment on his face. To save his unprecedented cowardice from public shame, the public was fed the "fascist demonstration" tale. (There were about two or three boys wearing neo-Nazi caps and waving Árpád flags.) The commentators argued that the president was shocked by the neo-Nazi caps (he must have had excellent eyesight!) and decided against delivering his speech due to the "fascist provocation." Later on, Sony investigated and analyzed the footage

shot on the square and it turned out that the coverage broadcast on
Egyenleg had been edited. By the time the president took the podi-
um to give his speech, the neo-Nazi attired youths had left the
premises escorted by the police.[48] From this point on, however, this
demonstration was not about the president's flight or why most of
his co-56-ers turned against him.

The 56-ers held grudge against the president on a number of
counts. Primarily, abusing his constitutional power in office, he
stopped the transition government from removing the presidents of
television and radio, who had vested interests in sabotaging the new
government. Secondly, Göncz also turned against those who sought
justice for the victims of communism, and punishment for its executives.[49] As interpreted by the former democratic opposition, these
modest efforts to punish the most serious criminals on charges such
as treason, murder and mass murder became a "showdown" and
"vengeance."[50] The media did not allow room for those who
demanded justice. Those who advocated investigation were pillo-
ried. To add insult to injury, the president arrogantly prevented the
representative of the 56-ers' organizations from delivering his
speech at the commemoration event on Kossuth square.

The socialist-liberal politicians, opinion-forming intellectuals
and their allies in the media accused the Antall government, and
interior minister Péter Boross, personally of organizing the "fascist" demonstration. Their synchronized media offensive defamed
the border guards. They spoke about organized provocations that
endangered the existence of the republic to make the public forget
that the country's president is so incompetent that he runs from a
protest of this scale. These dedicated anti-fascist socialist-liberals
repeatedly promised to investigate who was responsible for the
Kossuth square incident on 23 October, 1992. Ever since they have
not fulfilled this promise.

"I will never forget that 23rd of October when we abandoned
our revered president of Hungary, Árpád Göncz, one of the most

respected and popular politicians of Hungary. Only because we did not want to be associated with 'that lot'... ."[51]

The state of the public and passionate overreactions are best reflected in chief rabbi György Landeszmann's interview in February 1993:

"If we identified all the contribution of Jews to Hungarian culture, and then took it out of the culture, we would be left with nothing but peasant's pants and schnaps."[52]

On Patriotism and "Lymph"

In Hungary between 1990 and 1991, it was not just forty-odd years of socialism that collapsed. It was the end of half-a-century-long foreign invasion too. It was only logical that nearing the millenium, upon the demise of a bipolar world order, we needed to re-evaluate the most salient issues of Hungarian, European and world history. We wanted to face the most important challenges of our own national history. It was unavoidable, as generations had grown up in the tight grip of an exclusive and oppressive ideology, which propagated that once we take the right road, we will march toward a just and happy future. The right road happens to lead through socialism into communism as Leninism imagined. Every player and event in history was measured against the unfilled promises of this future. The transition politicians wished to investigate the heritage of the past through realities, not an abstract idea, of the real happenings, driving forces, traps, lies, real or imagined options of our own national history, the history of the continent and the world. This attempt was against the interests and raison d'ętre of the media elite and the opinion-forming intelligentsia. On the one hand, as chancellor Kohl put it, "Who ever owns the youth's vision of history, lays hands on the future as well." On the other hand, these people had been explaining to the public that their system, the socialist system, is normal and just, and it works. These same people wanted to limit the public's perspective on the past, their communist past as well as the eras before.[53] It is in their best interest to keep the public in the belief that the outdated notions such as "the fascist Horthy era", "modernizing left wing" and "retrograde, obsolete conservative right wing" still exist and hold water. In effect, we are told history as if we were still living the lies of the darkest days of the fifties.

Much quoted above, chief liberal Miklós Szabó's vision of history aptly reflects these characteristics, almost to the degree of self-parody at times. A lecturer in history at the "flying universities" organized by the former democratic opposition, this SZDSZ MP said the following at a Holocaust memorial organized by the HIT community:[54]

The MDF government intellectually reinstated the Horthy system and revived anti-Semitism. It could not restore the historical landholding system though. It rehabilitated the pre-Second World War territorial revisionism, the German alliance and the anti-Soviet fight, Arrow Cross style. The MDF propaganda had close links with the extreme right wing Hunnia Kör. The MDF-affiliated *Új Magyarország* organized an event with Hunnia Kör. This Horthy-ism was basically anti-Semitic. Its anti-communism rejected communism on account that it rid the aristocracy of their power and they thought that power was an exclusive entitlement. Power was handed over to the proletariat and Jews, which they interpreted as the desecration of Hungarianness. This mindset surfaces in MDF's politics. The Antall government has often chosen to follow the swastika course in the past few years. You do not have to go far: think of Horthy's reburial and the rehabilitation of numerous war crimes. The conservative forces in search of tradition are falling back on the revival of the worst heritage of the Horthy era rather than facing up to the charging tasks of modernization.[55]

The SZDSZ-affiliated politician-historian used the imagery of the Horthy era and the post-transition democratic changes for two reasons. Utilizing the worst hackneyed, vulgar-marxist traditions, he re-activated the buzzwords that were in use between the two world wars and during the Second World War up to the end of the sixties. (This jargon lost its appeal afterwards in better circles.) He did so in order to montage the jargon with the transition government's politics. Terms like anti-Semitism, restoration, large land-holding, Arrow Cross, anti-Soviet, ultra right course, aristocrats vs. proles, as far as Szabó and his disciples were concerned, described best the Antall-Boross era. It is easy to sense, though, that there is a degree of lymphatic alienation and suspicion in him just as in Sándor Révész:

"The truth is that although Antall's vision of the ideal society is closer to me than that of Aczél, I still find Aczél's personality and its context more comprehensible and familiar than Antall's. I was brought up in a communist family of Jewish descent, this is what I have an internal image of. I have no such image of the middle class that raised Antall."[56]

The metaphor of lymph first surfaced when parliament decided on the use of the one-thousand-year-old crowned coat of arms. The debate was seemingly about the crown: however, its real stake was whether or not the Republic of Hungary was willing to accept our one-thousand-year-long history or, like the People's Republic of Hungary, it will pick and choose from the course of history to best suit the so-called revolutionary and progressive ideas.[57] This would have been similar to what the late Péter Hanák asserted in his provocative writing:

"I believe in the national liberalism of the Reform Era and the socially reformed national and political programs of the turn of the century. These are good traditions. I reject the kind of national conservatism which is nationalist and conservative. This has rushed the country into tragedy twice already on a scale that outdid Mohács. It also played a large role in forcing us into the acceptance of Trianon, the Soviet's 1945 invasion and the harsh realities of the 1947 peace accord."[58]

Former writer of the Rákosist *Szabad Nép* Péter Kende proffers a similar account:

> "That Hungary collapsed by itself in 1944. Hungary's Soviet invasion would not have happened the way it did if the old Hungary had not brought upon itself the misery of 1944... The old Hungary was responsible for Hungary's problems, which made continuity impossible... However, Antall still tried ... and the urban intellectuals thought for a minute that the white or green scare is back again, and it is time to organize one more time ... The games the Antall government played with the past, the traditional tassels, the national costumes, the noble feathers, to put it metaphorically, immunized the country against bringing back the past. That done, now it is time to take a modernist course."[59]

Is it perhaps that Kende and Hanák do not know history? Is it perhaps that they are unaware that the war was still raging in 1944? Is it perhaps that they never heard of Yalta and the clash for world dominion among the great powers? Or that the Soviet invasion hit passive, collaborating Czechoslovakia as hard as victimized, resilient Poland? Why write at all? For the cause of modernization?

The famously "objective" SZDSZ-affiliated president Árpád Göncz evidently shares the above views on Hungary's history over the past half decade:

> "Although the Stalin-orchestrated genocide murdered people on a similar scale, the Holocaust is different in that the Stalinists pretended that they served some moral values... The Horthy era that was brought back in the past four years

did not accept that society had changed. It did not accept that during forty years of socialism a very strong secularized and civic society had evolved, which was looking forward to liberation, coming out into the light ... The system did not notice that there is no administration but local governments. Or that there is no military police and that we had lost the war... The 1994 elections responded to anti-Semitism and class issues. The countryside said a unanimous no. Only a few gentry circles said yes."[60]

It is good to know that according to our president, the Stalinist genocide is only different from the Holocaust in that the former "served some moral values." The fact is, however, that the Hungarian civic society was born from socialism. Unfortunately, the president does not recall the fact that local governments were revived during the Antall government. He confuses them with the socialist council system. He also should be informed that administration has been and will be in existence as, without it, no state can function. As far as anti-Semitism, class issues and gentry circles are concerned, those comments must be from a different writing. He may have written those for *Szabad Nép*[61] in 1952.

The above texts illustrate how the left wing presents itself as a progressive Westernizing and modernizing force as opposed to the right wing forces, whose sole objective is to reinstate days long gone. This polarization has, since the thirties, been typical of another divide: the rural vs. the urban polarization.

"The two sides in this debate are not equal partners in that one represents progress, the future, while the other embodies the past, a retrograde pull. Therefore, it is beyond doubt that the rural side need not be involved in dialogue but rather, they have to arrive at a compromise, they have to be subdued and excluded from the political circles of the country... The rural side are persona non grata in this sense... ."[62]

"Hungary has very little conservable national heritage"[63] or "Its history is nothing other than a series of failures ever since Mohács"[64]—argue those who look at our past and traditions with some degree of suspicion and alienation as if it is to be measured up to some elusive set of ideals. They want to prevent the nation from building up justifiable self-confidence and fashioning a national identity after more than half a century of invasion. The very existence of Hungarianness is at stake at this time of new globalization unless we, the nation, grow strong. Despite the tragic consequences of the twentieth century, some of the Marxist-school intellectuals stuck in their beliefs still fail to understand that the notion of nation is a far stronger call than class. It also signifies a stronger tie than economy. National cohesion can form a commonly shared identity that reaches beyond educational and occupational divisions, or even differences of age, gender, race or ethnicity. Nation, therefore, is a positive notion, a kind of political and legal contract that free and equal citizens make on the basis of their rights and duties. The nation is made one by common rituals, enterprises, schooling, conscription, national celebrations, the anthem, symbols, wars and revolutions as well as victories and defeats, glorious moments, failure or mourning. Hungary is all its history. Some might be interested to cover up the less victorious chapters of their own personal past; still, they will not be able to wash away the shame of their betrayals and actions. Hungary must have its heroes back. We must learn about the real and truthful history of the time between the two world wars, the time during the Second World War as much as the reality of the decades following 1945.[65]

One of the members of the Academy of Sciences, Péter Kende, argues along similar lines:

"Communism, with its successes and failures, apotheoses and shame, is still a shared adventure involving and striking the whole of society together. It is a common enterprise. If we refuse to accept this, we will be bound to misinterpret the national history of the past half century."[66]

It is sad that Péter Kende, who used to publish internal articles for the longest years during the bloodiest times of the Rákosi era, is still able to receive publicity at all in democratic Hungary.[67]

"Every nerve in our body detests American imperialism, which intends to plunge the whole world in a sea of fire just a few years after the Second World War... Appreciating our national heritage means that we follow the wise Stalinist peace politics of the Soviet Union... From the Kremlin a voice, a firm, kind and wise voice, says to the peoples of the world: peace will prevail if the nations undertake the cause of keeping world peace." "Stalin's words provide hope, encouragement and guidance to the simple people of the world." "Mindszenty can but try to validate his clerical eminence in vain. More and more people understand that the catholic church is just a repository of reactionary forces. Mindszenty's religious associations are party organizations of reactionary politics and Mindszenty's in-house apostles are Hungarian agents of American imperialism." "The government of the people's democracy will not tolerate that irresponsible swindlers use the church for reactionary purposes in any shape or form."[68]

They all worked on this "shared adventure" for a "secularized and civic society." Some used to persecute enemies on the pages of *Szabad Nép*, others were B-listed. Between 1945 and 1950, approximately 300,000 people were persecuted in fabricated pseudo-trials on false charges. Hundreds were executed. Attics were swept clean of crops. The country was cleansed of kulaks. Not to mention the atrocities after 1956. Will we have a chance to talk about it? It seems unlikely, since today, executioner and victim lay wreaths at memorials together. That is why their restless activists write that, these days, calling people names like "executioner" and "yid" is one and the same.[69] Or, to put it in another way:

"[today's anti-Semitism] packs discrimination in the guise of calling people communists."[70]

Seven years after the transition, calling people names like communist, traitor, spy, executioner is regarded anti-Semitic. In his television interview, Hungarian Socialist Party (MSZP) representative Péter Lusztig said that he was "stigmatized with a yellow star" when the transparency investigations revealed that he once worked as an agent.[71]

The circle has closed here.

**"The Historical Change was Painless.
As if it had not Ever Happened"[72]**

The former democratic opposition, their political party, the SZDSZ, the sympathizing opinion-forming intellectuals and the media elite betrayed the transition. One of them, Ferenc Kőszeg writes:

> "In the summer of 1990, the SZDSZ demanded that the names of the secret agents responsible for keeping secret the real amount of the government's debt should be identified. But when the right wing demanded, in their somewhat aggressive language, that justice should be done, the liberal party turned it down flat. They prevented the ÁVH torturers and executioners from being tried. At issue is not that a dozen old ÁVH officers were let off without a trial, but that crimes against humanity committed in the name of communism were now reduced to little anecdotes as opposed to Nazi war crimes, which, and rightly too, still outrage the world."[73]

The point is, however, that with the formation of the MSZP-SZDSZ coalition government, the right wing threat disappeared at once. The country took the modernizing course. The Charter was dispersed. Similar organizations such as the Publicity Club, Act Against Hatred, etc. limited the scope of their own activities or folded.[74] The socialist-liberals won the media war by a longshot. Calling people Jews became an everyday habit in mainstream publications on the part of mainstream journalists and politicians.[75] But since the anti-fascist war is over, the media commando ceased their operations too. It is clear from the above, Jews and anti-Semitic statements mattered the least in all this. It is who said what that mattered. This is how we reached the point where the president of the SZDSZ, minister of interior Gábor Kuncze, granted pardon to a murderer: the ÁVH officer, Tibor Vajda. The same officer was represented by the legal office owned by SZDSZ deputy foreign minister Mátyás Eörsi.[76]

Most of the former transition politicians turned out to have no qualms about the system at all. They were only disturbed by the fact that they did not get to govern it. Between 1991 and 1994 they fought a cruel war against the then government. From their media bastions they shouted accusations and lies to the world without ever buttressing their points. The horror story that the Antall government wanted to reinstate the Horthy era was only ever based on the fact that parliament accepted the crowned coat of arms and that the design of the parliament guards' new uniform was based on the historical Bocskai-style attire. They also resented the fact that some government ministers attended Horthy's reburial when his ashes were returned to Hungary.[77] Other than this, nothing else pointed to the revival of the Horthy era. Then, it was widely rumored that the MDF government wanted a dictatorship and would not hold elections in 1994. There were accusations that the government was militant, exclusive, anti-Semitic and anti-democratic. None of these accusations were supported with facts.

There were unfounded accusations, statements and slander. According to some strange logic, simply disliking the several presidents of the SZDSZ—namely Kis, Pető, Kuncze—is anti-

Semitism. This is how the president of FIDESZ, Viktor Orbán became a "climber of a little nobody, who calls people Jew as dictated by the lowest of the low ultra right."[78] He probably deserved this after he refused to join the MSZP-SZDSZ coalition in 1994 despite MSZP efforts to recruit him in their reign. How many anti-Semites were created like this in the nineties in Hungary? Everyone who is not a post-communist and/or a left wing liberal.[79]

We know from the experience of history that any transition only removes the elite[80] completely if that change happens through revolutionary terror or the force of a foreign victor or invader. Peaceful transitions usually do not remove the political, economic and cultural nomenclature. Nonetheless, there was a dire need to at least symbolically hold the criminals accountable in public and to remove the most serious ones. The whole of Hungarian society has paid a huge price for this. A lack of adherence to the law, the devaluation of moral values, the relativization of personal responsibility undermine the development of democracy. Lawlessness prevails, argues the Central European expert Anne Applebaum, when thieves elude liability and living a life of luxury they laugh in the face the public. To many, uncovered past crimes mean that it is not worth being decent and fair. Or, the wise men were all collaborators. Corruption pays better.[81]

As the perpetrators of the Holocaust were held accountable a generation after the crimes were committed, so will the communist criminals. Those, too, will be held liable who hampered the transition, sustained the entire post-communist elite in power and sabotaged any effort to come clean. And they will be asked to justify why they used the anti-Semitic/anti-fascist rhetoric in favor of the post-communist power elite. They knew that anti-Semitism has born a new meaning since Auschwitz. What about playing with it?

Notes

1. The latest notable book on the rural-urban debate was published by Fricz, Tamás. "A népi-urbánus vita tegnap és ma". *Politikatörténeti füzetek* VII. (Napvilág Kiadó, 1997).

2. See Pelle, János. "A zsidó reneszánsz esélyei a rendszerváltás után." In *Holocaust emlékkönyv.* In commemoration of the fiftieth anniversary of the deportation of rural Jews. (Budapest: TEDISZ, 1994), pp. 384-385.

3. The so-called Auschwitz trial took place in Frankfurt in 1964-65. Willy Brandt kneeled in front of the Warsaw ghetto statue in 1970. The Fibinger case resulted in the resignation of the CDU prime minister due to his past Nazi involvement. The extension of the validity of Nazi war crimes coincided with the screening of the American television series titled "Holocaust". (January 1979, November 1982, etc.)

4. More on this Tony, Judit. "A múlt más világ". *2000,* 5/9 (September 5, 1993), pp. 11-21.

5. See more on the Western European intelligentsia, especially the French intellectuals collaborating with Moscow, and their relationship to the past Besancon, Alain. "Forgotten communism". *Commentary.* (January 1998).

6. In the above-quoted study Besancon mentions that according to the records of one of France's leading dailies the term "Nazism" occurs 480 times, while the term "Stalinism" only 7 times, "Auschwitz" 105 times, "Kolima" 2 times in the time period between 1990 and 1997. The "Ukrainian artificial famine," which is guestimated to have taken the lives of six million people in 1933 alone does not factor at all.

7. Rosenfeld, Alvin H. "The americanization of the holocaust". *Commentary.* (June 1995). 99/6, pp. 35-41.

8. Ball, Georges W. and Ball, Douglas B. *The passionate attachment. America's involvement with Israel.* (New York, London: W. W. Norton, 1992), p. 217. The AIPAC (American Israel Public Affairs Committee) lobby organization regularly prepares an "enemy-list", which includes the politicians who are not Israel-friendly or have not gotten carried away to make anti-Arab statements.

9.   Szűcs, P. Julianna. *Népszabadság*, November 20, 1995. The
     Communist Party appointed Julianna P. Szűcs editor-in-chief of the
     magazine *Mozgó Világ* in 1983. The party did not approve of the
     political openness of the magazine's previous editors. Szűcs and her
     magazine were treated with a widespread boycott.
10. "I belong to those liberal intellectuals whose writings and actions
     considerably helped the Hungarian Socialist Party (MSZP) to break
     out of its isolation. As far as that is concerned, I have absolutely no
     regrets." György, Péter (SZDSZ). "More than a sin—a mistake".
     Népszabadság. (December 15, 1997).
11. *Mazsike Newsletter*, no. 7 (1996).
12. Lomax, Bill. "The strange death of 'civil society' in post-communist
     Hungary". *Journal of Communist Studies and Transition Politics*.
     Vol. 13, no. 1 (March, 1997).
13. This anti-fascist rhetoric was silenced at the time of the German-
     Soviet friendship (1939-1941).
14. Koestler, Arthur. "Fallen god". *2000*, II/7-8, p. 36.
15. Miklós Tamás Gáspár, one of the main ideologues of the SZDSZ,
     MP between 1990 and 1994 said in the radio programme called *168
     Hours* on May 7, 1996: "I never claimed that these movements were
     so dangerous that the extremist torgyánists, csurkaists, szabóists
     would be able to bring down the republic." He said in *Magyar
     Nemzet* on June 23, 1994: "In the fall of 1992 those who did not think
     that democracy is in danger had lost their mind." In Tóth, Gy. László.
     The inheritors of Kádárism and a civil Hungary. (Budapest: Kairosz,
     1997), p. 276.
16. According to the results of a Gallup survey of all the parties the
     membership of the post-communist successor party, the Hungarian
     Socialist Party (MSZP) turned out the most number of anti-Semitic
     responses. It is also common knowledge that during the 1990 elec-
     tions the party's youth organization, the Left-Wing Youth
     Association (BIT) painted over the posters of the Young Democrats'
     Association (FIDESZ) to say ZSIDESZ (Hungarian acronym for
     Jewish Youth Association). This also surfaced in graffiti.
     Furthermore, the bastardized version of the poster was also pub-
     lished in the New Year's Eve edition of *Népszabadság*. László
     Kövér, FIDESZ Hungarian Civic Party deputy's statement. *Magyar
     Demokrata*, no. 6 (1998), p. 310. The then leader of BIT is today the
     labor minister of the MSZP-SZDSZ government.

17. The Democratic Charter was issued on September 26, 1991 signed by 162 people. Among those: György Konrád (SZDSZ), Iván Vitányi (MSZP), Zoltán Szabó (MSZP), Gyula Hegyi (MSZP), László Donáth (MSZP), András Gerő (SZDSZ), Iván Pető (SZDSZ), Miklós Jancsó (SZDSZ), Gábor Fodor (FIDESZ, later SZDSZ), György Surányi (President of the Hungarian National Bank), Lajos Bokros (MSZP), Rezső Nyers (MSZP), etc. The Charter was also signed by the extreme left-wing Münnich Ferenc Society. When Prime Minister József Antall removed György Surányi, president of the National Bank on account of signing the anti-government Charter, advertisements were placed in the press saying "You could be next!"

18. "Today's SZDSZ used to be left-wing opposition. This is the term they used to use in the seventies. Later on Miklós Haraszti coined the term 'democratic opposition'... they were criticizing the Kádár regime from an ideal socialist platform. Abandoning this platform they switched to a third-way point of view after István Bibó. After the Polish Solidarity they propagated workers' self-justification. Finally, they ended up promoting capitalism. They keep saying that they and only they are right. They would never admit that they have made a mistake... SZDSZ is a Bolshevik-style party. In fact, when I say Bolshevik, I do not mean an ideology. The structure of the organization is Bolshevik. That a selected few decide on everything... Their mindset is aristocratic. They think they are all superior." György Krassó's interview. *Dátum*. (April 5, 1990).

19. "In 1994 as the socialist-liberal government took office the official anti-Semitism temporarily stopped." Tamás Gáspár, Miklós. "A magyar kérdés másodjára". *Magyar Narancs*. (September 9, 1997).

20. Schmidt, Mária. "Az antifasiszta NDK". *Magyar Nemzet*. (August 16, 1996).

21. Szabó, Miklós. "A kárhozottak összeesküvése". *Népszabadság*. (May 26, 1990).

22. Révész, Sándor. "Zsigány a ködben". *Mozgó Világ*. (January, 1998), pp. 27-30. It is incomprehensible and shocking at the same time that the three-part series called, *Ávósok* in the Hungarian Television's series titled *Magyar félmúlt* caused so much outrage: "Israeli groups and a number of other Jewish groups protested against the broadcast. These organizations and rabbi József Schweitzer were appalled at the fact that the Jewish origin of some of the guards was so over-empha-

sized. This is very insensitive especially at the fiftieth anniversary of the Holocaust." Excerpt from the letter written by Hungarian Television's programme director dated March 25, 1994. The photocopy of the letter was published in Kubinyi, Ferenc. *Fekete lexikon. 1945-56.* Vol. I. (Thousand Oaks, California: Malomfalvi Kiadó), p. 198.

23. Szabó, Miklós. "A magyar zsidóság és a kommunista mozgalom". *Szombat.* (May 1995).

24. Typically, my writing critiquing Miklós Szabó's article was rejected by *Népszabadság*, which otherwise shows major interest in the subject. My piece was eventually published in *Új Magyarország* titled "Az antiszemitizmus szerepe a baloldal érvrendszerében". (June 14, 1995).

25. Babits, Mihály. "Az írástudók árulása". In: *Élet és Irodalom.* (Budapest: Atheneum), p. 140.

26. Pokol, Béla. *Médiahatalom. Selected writings.* (Budapest: Windsor publishing, 1995), p. 29.

27. The History of Politics Institute of the Hungarian Socialist Party (MSZP) held a session on apropos that "there is clear and present danger that the post-transition conservative government intends to monopolize on the media, and the appearance of extreme right wing politics in the parliament. The main question was whether or not there was a possibility for a new right wing government to take over," in Székely, Gábor. "Fasizmus, diktátorok, Németország—Adolf Hitler". In: *Akik nyomot hagytak a 20. századon. Diktátorok—diktatúrák.* (Napvilág Kiadó, 1997), pp. 48-49.

28. During the Antall years when the media was supposedly smothered by the government the "liberal" president of the television did not allow an interview with the Prime Minister József Antall to go on air. Today, in the year of "media peace" Prime Minister Gyula Horn is on TV more often in the space of a month than Antall used to be in the space of a year. And that's not counting his appearances on the commercial TV stations.

29. Imre Kertész' sentence rich in meaning cannot be reduced to mean that Szálasi and Teleki stood for the same: "What exactly separates me from the Hungarian Christian middle class (which is not a real middle class only a middle class of intellectuals)? That for them it is important to be different: does Count Teleki call people Jews, or does Szálasi, for that matter? It is the same as far as I am concerned, the

final outcome is still Auschwitz." Kertész, Imre. *Valaki más.* (Magvető, 1997).

30. "For one of the *Nappali hold* [Daytime Moon] pieces, let's not beat round the bush, they stoned me publicly. They attacked me in over 180 writings. For the longest time I did not know if I was going to be able to take the blows. I was. What's more, among my feverish nightmares I discovered some frightening truths as well. That's how I realized that if you want to remain truthful, you cannot back away from becoming temporarily truthless. For sometimes the breakdown will show your opponents the dramatic and tragic entirety of reality." In Csoóri, Sándor. *Nappali hold (2.).* (Budapest: Püski, 1991), p. 6.

31. Quote in Nyéki, Lajos. "Reflexiók Párizsból a magyar értelmiség hivatásáról". In: *A (magyar) értelmiség hivatása. Studies, essays, letters, confessions.* Edited by Fasang Árpád Mundus Jr. (Magyar Egyetemi Kiadó, 1997), p. 320. Besides the much-glorified left-wing guru Aron Sartre (1905-83) was the most influential non-marxist French philosopher of the time.

32. While all the left-wing parties as well as the media were frightened that the extreme right might take over, no one bothered to investigate how these groups were financed, where they got their guns, their uniforms, etc. Interestingly, they never took part in demonstrations organized by the Democratic Charter or at Horthy's re-burial. Horthy was not exactly the Nazis' favorite either.

33. The data come from the chief "csurkaologist," László Karsai, who worked his way into the "right" circles by way of his publication *Kirekesztők.* Karsai, László. "Búcsú Csurka Istvántól és a Magyar Fórumtól". In: *Holocaust emlékkönyv*, p. 383.

34. Kende, Péter. *Az én Magyarországom.* (Budapest: Osiris, 1997), p. 108.

35. Csurka is rumored to have called the Jews names and Aczél blacklisted him for that reason.

36. Konrád was member of the National Council of the SZDSZ and also of the policy-making think tank of the party.

37. Did the German writers know this when they appointed Konrád to head their academy? Or reporting to the "Hungarian Stasi" is altogether different?

38. Komoróczky, Géza. "Egy magyar író aki történetesen zsidó". *Élet és Irodalom.* (December 19, 1997). Komoróczky reviews Konrád's *Láthatatlan hang* [Invisible voice]. (Budapest: Palatinus, 1997).

Komoróczky never missed an opportunity to prove his "*nash*"-ness in the time period under discussion. In one memorable statement he says: "We are all responsible for the Holocaust. Even those who did not live at that time, even those who—horribile dictu—did against it." "The middle of and the end of the thirties, sometimes all the way to 1944 seems to come alive again in the radio, on TV and in the press"—he wrote in the fourth year after the transition. *Beszélő*. (1994/IV/14). (The article was also published by *Magyar Hírlap*). (My article that I wrote in response was rejected by *Beszélő* even as a letter to the editor. Instead it appeared in *Pesti Hírlap* on May 25, 1994.)

40. Konrád, György. "Tartós várakozók". *Szombat*, no. 3 (1995), p. 5.
41. Polonyi, Péter. *A zsidó identitásról*. Konrád, György. "Láthatatlan hang". *Mozgó Világ*. (January, 1998), pp. 121-123. The Konrád quotes are on p. 227, and *Magyar Zsidó Almanach*. (1996-97). p. 39.
42. *Magyar Nemzet*. (September 13, 1990), p. 2.
43. Quote in Alexa, Károly. "The Landeszmann files". *Heti Magyarország könyve*, vol. 10 (1993), p. 10.
44. *Beszélő*. Vol. 39.
45 Csurka, István. *Vasárnapi jegyzetek*. (Püski - Magyar Fórum, 1991), pp. 77-78.
46. Novák, Attila. "Zsákutcák". *Szombat*, no. 10 (1996), p. 4.
47. *Egyenleg. Képtelen történetek.* CET Könyvek. (Belvárosi Könyvkiadó, 1993), pp. 67-73.
48. In Varga Domokos, György. *A váratlan tanú. 23 October, 1992. Véletlen vagy összeesküvés?* (ESÁ Média Bt, 1995), pp. 30 and 112 quotes János Lázár police deputy and György Suha, police spokesperson's accounts of the event.
49. Between March and July 1992 the president refused to countersign the documents that would have removed from office the presidents of Hungarian Television and Hungarian Radio. According to the Constitutional Court's ruling the president has power to do so only under conditions extremely hazardous to democracy.
50. "I blocked transparency efforts [to investigate past activities] and liability"—said a very proud Domokos Kosáry, president of the Hungarian Academy of Sciences. *Magyar Nemzet*. (May 14, 1997).
51. Kartal, Zoltán. "Kinek a zászlaja?" *Magyar Hírlap*. (March 12, 1992).

52. *Heti Magyarország.* (February 26, 1993). The reactions to the Landeszmann interview were collected and published by *Heti Magyarország.*

53. "A kommunizmus mítoszának hideg valósága. Interview with historian Judit Tony in four parts". *Pesti Hírlap.* (May, 1994).

54. In *Népszabadság* on March 7, 1997 speaking about the alliance of the HIT community and SZDSZ Sándor Németh, HIT's chief pastor said the following: "At the foundation meeting of SZDSZ, there were approximately 800 people present. At least 450 of them were HIT members. That is more than half of those present. ...Even the name, the Alliance of Free Democrats, comes from us." According to the late Péter Uzoni, HIT's former president "the time will come when God judges nations on the basis of their relationship to Israel and the Israeli Jews." *Magyar Nemzet.* (January 12, 1996).

55. Szabó, Miklós. "Horthy rehabilitáció és antiszemitizmus". *Holocaust emlékkönyv,* pp. 358-359.

56. Révész, Sándor. *Népszabadság.* (January 25, 1997).

57. Miklós Szabó (SZDSZ): "If we are going to have a crowned coat of arms..., we will express a longing, a nostalgia for the pre-1945 aristocratic Hungary." Parliament, second day of sessions. (June 18, 1990). "Furthermore, this coat of arms, which was the coat of arms of historical Hungary and the revisionist Horthy government, will understandably antagonize the neighboring nations and their people." Bauer, Tamás. "Megint a címer". *Beszélő.* (June 30, 1990).

58. Hanák, Péter. "Hagyomány és jövőkép". *Népszabadság.* (August 29, 1990). Hanák divided his own life into right and wrong, acceptable and unacceptable periods. He rejected the time period when he worked on vulgar-marxist historiography and reported on his civic colleagues. Instead, he embraced the time he spent "in resistance". See: János Kőbányai's interview novel: Heller, Ágnes. "Biciklizö majom". *Kortárs.* (November, December, January 1997).

59. Kende, Péter. *Op. cit.,* pp. 230-231.

60. "A magyarországi holocaust a magyarok ellen irányult. János Kende interviews Árpád Göncz. *Múlt és Jövő,* no. 4 (1994), pp. 4-14.

61. Árpád Göncz has not publicized the findings of the transparency judges. There are nationwide rumors concerning his past involvement.

62. Fricz, Tamás. *Op. cit.,* pp. 108-109.

63. Szabó, Miklós. "A jobboldali alternatíva". *Népszava*. (December 18, 1996).

64. *Magyar Narancs*. (June 20, 1996).

65. It is revealing that between 1990 and 1994 the name Miklós Horthy surfaced 407 times in titles of articles and studies while the name Mátyás Rákosi only 109 times. (The most number of occurrences was in 1993, 273 times while in the same year Rákosi surfaced 18 times.) Data from the *Press Monitor of the Parliament Library*.

66. Kende, Péter.*Op. cit*. p. 118.

67. The following is a selection of Péter Kende's "best' writings published in *Szabad Nép*.

68. See L. Lovas, István. "Péter Kende: Kérlelhetetlen harcot—semmi liberalizmust". *Demokrata*. 24 July, 1997.

69. Eörsi, István. "Az emberi jogok és a politika". *Magyar Narancs*. (November 20, 1997).

70. Ungvári, Tamás. "A parvenü és a pária". *Világosság*, no. 8 (1991), p. 800.

71. September 1997.

72. Radovanovic, Milivojc. *Magyar Napló*. (April, 1997), p. 30.

73. Kőszeg, Ferenc. *Op.cit*.

74. Even the organization called People Living Under Subsistence Level (LÁET) folded. Interestingly, they were very active between 1990 and 1994. After 1994, it seems no one lived below subsistence.

75. Q: "Did Iván Pető lose his chance to be the Free Democrats's Prime Minister candidate because he is Jewish?" A (Imre Szekeres, Socialist Party fraction leader): "I know from the papers that that was the reason... in such cases the individual cannot make the decision but rather, political considerations have to be heeded. One needs to decide between a favorable candidacy or losing voters." in *Szombat*, no. 1 (1995), p. 8. Pál Bodor in *Népszabadság*, Miklós Tamás Gáspár in *Magyar Narancs*, András Bruck in *Élet és Irodalom* pointed out that the chief editors and many of the journalists at *Népszabadság* are Jewish.

76. There are a number of employees working for Eörsi's office who used to work as senior ÁVH officers. The son of one of them, Tamás Bauer, is an SZDSZ representative in parliament. His father's past is of no interest. But then, if a former ÁVH officer can take advantage of his family connections that is a public matter and an embarrassing one too.

77. When Horthy's ashes were returned to the family's crypt as request-
    ed in his final will, the very tolerant Leninist Charter boys created
    havoc in the form of counter-happenings to anti-fascist media fren-
    zy. In 1997, president Árpád Göncz, Prime Minister Gyula Horn,
    interior minister Gábor Kuncze attended the wedding of György
    Habsburg in Bazilika (broadcast on TV). There were no articles
    about the restoration of Habsburg power.
78. Kornis, Mihály. "Naplórészlet". *Élet és Irodalom*. (September 24,
    1996). See on this: Elek, István. "Nyugtalan szélsőségek" in: *Polgár
    és kora*. (Osiris, 1997), pp. 220-221.
79. "The majority of the six parliamentary parties (read, opposition or
    right wing) are not reliable anti-fascists" said János Hajdú (MSZP)
    speaking at the Progressive Forces' Forum (!). *Új Magyarország*.
    (December 13, 1995). On this Ferenc Kőszeg (SZDSZ): "Every
    opposition party has radical right wing tendencies." *Magyar Nemzet*.
    (May 13, 1997).
80. By elite I mean a very limited group of government, economic, polit-
    ical and cultural leaders.
81. *Schmidt, Mária. "Elmaradt igazságtétel amerikai szemmel.
    Megválaszolatlan kérdések, mérgezett közélet." Magyar Nemzet.*
    (November 22, 1997). The article analyzes Applebaum's articles
    published in *Prospect* in April 1996.

Tamás Sepsey

A SHORT HISTORY OF COMPENSATION

Writing the true and authentic history of compensation will be most certainly a task to be accomplished by posterity. Many years will have to pass until it will become possible to sum up objectively and without taking into account current political criteria that vast sequence of legislation we used to call compensation. Only then will it be possible to evaluate those long chains of desired social events that became reality as well as those that—despite the intentions of the legislators—did not become reality or became reality just partially.

The purpose of the present paper is to give a brief overview of the events leading to the promulgation of laws regarding this legislation, the aims of the legislators and to sketch out the stages of implementation. Naturally, one must also summarise the experiences gained throughout the process. In this respect, the author wishes to apologise in advance for the inherent subjectivity of the analysis which is due to his direct involvement in the process.

One can approach the history of compensation in several manners. The legal approach seems to be the natural alternative because of two reasons. First, compensation means post facto reparation for wrongs done by legal means by the state. Second, the framework of reparation is also defined through legal norms. The legislation when attempting to regulate these legal relationships tried to apply the criteria of constitutionality to a relatively unexplored domain. The principles of regulation that can be distilled from the numerous rulings of the constitutional court also suggest that an approach setting out from statute law is the most appropriate.

However, the observance of economic priorities is as important as the legal aspects. Through compensation, the legislator made an attempt to couple reparation for wrongs done by previous political regimes with the establishment of a social market economy. For, compensation has been a device that besides putting the principles of rule of law in practice, accomplished legal reparation through transferring state property into private ownership as well.[1]

The impact of compensation on the stratification of Hungarian society, the social processes ensuing from this legal measure, the sociological aspects of its implementation are all areas of research that have hardly been explored yet. Therefore an analysis of compensation that lays emphasis on these points of view is necessary.

Finally, one cannot omit the administrative aspects of compensation. Having to give rulings on petitions for compensation, the administrative apparatus of the Hungarian state faced an unprecedented professional challenge that was both intellectual and technical. What method can be applied to give well-founded rulings in millions of cases, in a relatively short time considering that it is time-consuming and incredibly difficult—sometimes even impossible—to establish the facts, since evidence is incomplete or has been destroyed during the years?[2]

However, solving the technical problems alone is not equivalent to efficient implementation of legislation. At the end of the day, outcomes depend on acting human individuals, and legislation has to prove itself effective within a social environment that itself influences implementation. Therefore, one should not omit those people who took part in the implementation of these pieces of legislation. I do not mean now only my closest collaborators, the employees of the reparation offices. It is true that without their commitment, sense of calling and love for their fellow humans there could not have been achieved any result at all. I refer especially to the employees of the land repartition offices, who took out from the back of the archives the old files and put themselves at the permanent disposal of the clients, and to the personnel who prepared the auctions; to those persons who undertook a thankless task for the benefit of the public, who took part in the activity of land inventorying and land-distribution committees, of interest-mediation fora; to archivists who giving the fullest measure of their professional honesty faced the unceasing attacks mounted by the entitled persons; to notaries and employees of agricultural co-operatives who helped provide information to the public; to the volunteers who operated the free-of-charge consulting service organised by the MDF (Hungarian Democratic Forum) who contributed significantly to publicising the regulations concerning material compensation. In sum, when analysing compensation it is necessary to take into account the human factor, too.

Why was It Obligatory to Offer Compensation?

Compensation represents the partial reparation of property-related and other kinds of injuries committed by the state during the last five decades.[3]

Redressing such kinds of grievances is not, unfortunately, an act without precedence in Hungarian history. After the Second World War many regulations were adopted—laws, decrees issued by the prime minister and other authorities—in order to annul the so-called Jewish Laws and the decrees pertaining to them, the objective being the mitigation of injuries done to the Jewry in Hungary. In some respects, this compensation was ill-conceived for a number of reasons. First, the reestablishment of property rights did not apply to "large estates", i.e., estates exceeding 1000 *hold*s [Translator's note: the Hungarian unit of measure *katasztrális hold* (or briefly *hold*) is equal to cca. 0.575 hectares or cca. 1.42 English acres.] According to Decree No. 600/1945 of the prime minister these were to become state property. Second, the fate of the so-called Jewish deposits has not been settled and, finally, the possessions of the persons who deceased during persecutions or deportation and left no heirs have not been handed over to the National Reparation Fund for the Jewry.

Decree No. 9590/1945 of the prime minister concerning the annulment of discrimination against persons who manifested socialist, anti-Fascist or democratic attitudes was also a repertory measure. This act prescribed that discrimination suffered by persons for their socialist, communist, social-democratic/anti-Fascist or democratic political convictions, attitudes or activities—including activities supporting the 1918-19 revolutions—should stop. Sentences given for the above reasons were to be considered as nullified, together with any negative legal consequence following from such a sentence. The persons who suffered injuries, or their surviving relatives could apply for compensation.

One must also mention the rehabilitation proceedings that took place at the beginning of the 1950s. These proceedings entailed compensatory payments made to certain communist victims of the so-called cult of personality and their relatives. Under the economic circumstances that prevailed during that time, these payments represented large amounts of money.

This short listing of cases illustrates: trying to redress the legal injures committed during a historical period and to compensate for their negative material consequences after the period ended and the social conditions have also changed is far from being unprecedented in the Hungarian legal tradition.

After the first free elections the new parliament had to face the incredibly difficult task of re-establishing the rule of law and of dealing with the question of reparation after a long period of time (1939-1989) when the rights of millions of persons had been infringed upon. Persons who had been persecuted for political reasons, former property owners, those who had suffered of property-related or other kinds of injuries were all expecting some legal reparation for the wrongs they suffered.

Compensation was, hence, both a legal and a moral obligation of the legislative body that had to be fulfilled under any circumstances.[4]

The majority of the laws sanctioning the withdrawal of property[5] deprived owners of their assets promising indemnification. However, a law on compensation for nationalised properties was never adopted. Consequently, the proprietors who suffered injuries never had the legal opportunity to enforce their claims for compensation. The authorities or courts they appealed to systematically dismissed their petitions pretending that they could not give a genuine solution because the relevant piece of legislation is missing.[6]

The most eloquent evidence that eliminating violations of the constitution committed by failing to fulfil legislative obligations is a matter connected to compensation and represents a legislative duty forming an organic part of compensation is Ruling No. 27/1991 (dated the 20th of June) of the constitutional court. Articles 1 and 2 of this ruling declared several laws sanctioning the withdrawal of property unconstitutional and annulled them. However, according to Article 3 the court suspended its proceedings in all the cases where the plaintiffs complained that the law-making bodies did not adopt the piece of legislation—thus, making themselves guilty of violating the constitution through omission—that had to regulate the manner and amount of compensation and has been promised by the laws that were annulled.[7]

The constitutional court established the violation of the constitution through omission as a fact, since the laws that were promised in order to regulate the manner and amount of compensation have never been made by the competent bodies. Bearing in mind that the government brought in a bill on this matter[8], the court suspended its proceedings on all the petitions that requested the constitutional court to summon the lawmaker to put an end to this unconstitutional state of affairs. After the adoption of laws on property-related compensation the court closed all these proceedings arguing that by passing such laws the parliament ended the state of unconstitutionality caused by omission.[9]

Similarly, legislative obligation had to be fulfilled in the case of those persons who have been illegally deprived of their liberty or lives for political reasons. The constitution stipulates unambiguously: "Persons subjected to illegal arrest or detention are entitled to compensation."[10]

It follows from the constitutional stipulation cited in the previous endnote that if it has been proven about somebody that he/she suffered an illegal arrest or has been detained illegally that persons is entitled to compensation.

The obligation to compensate has not been prescribed only by the constitution. Decisions made by the parliament of the party-state regime created legislative obligations for the parliament elected in 1990 and the coalition government formed by the MDF (Hungarian Democratic Forum), the KDNP (Christian-Democratic People's Party) and FKGP (Independent Smallholders', Farmers' and Civic Party), too.

The previous government issued Decree No. 72/1989 of the Council of Ministers (dated the 4th of July) already during the summer of 1989. This decree settled matters regarding employment and social security for persons who had been detained and kept under surveillance of police authorities (using a term of common parlance: internees). In a few months, it turned out that the decree should also apply, for similar reasons, to persons interned before the first of January 1949, to persons forcibly relocated by the police, to persons convicted by Soviet courts, to civilians deported to the Soviet Union for forced labour as well as to those who after returning from the Soviet Union where they were deported for forced labour had to work in labour camps in Hungary.[11]

Observing the continuously increasing force of the political disagreement—and sensing the disillusionment of the population—parliament adopted Law No. 36/1989 (from this point onwards: 1st Law of Nullification) concerning reparation to persons convicted in connection with the popular revolt from 1956 after the government made a proposal in this respect.[12]

The last parliament of the socialist period was quite active in what concerns the prescription of compensatory tasks. Its Resolution No. 19/1989 (dated the 1st of November) instructed the Council of Ministers to bring in a bill regarding compensation for people who had been illegally convicted, interned or forcibly relocated by the police between 1945 and 1962.

Another resolution was adopted on the very same day (parliament's Resolution No. 20/1989 dated the 1st of November), in which the legislative body presented an official apology to former internees and people who suffered from forced relocation by the police.

The 2nd Law of Nullification was promulgated on the 13th of March 1990. Article 6, paragraph 2 of this law (No. 26/1990) providing for the nullification of the sentences given between 1945 and 1963 stipulates that a separate regulation will deal with the compensation of persons who suffered injuries.

The 4th of March 1990 is a significant date concerning the compensatory process that involved people who were subjected to political persecution. Four resolutions that defined in detail the legislative obligations connected to the compensation for injuries suffered by persons who has been politically persecuted were adopted on this day.

Parliament's Resolution No. 34/1990 (dated the 28th of March) called for the reparation of injuries done to persons who had been deported or wronged in any other way between 1938 and 1945 because of their racial or ethnic origin, or because their attitude towards Nazism. Parliament instructed the Council of Ministers to bring in a bill providing for the compensation of persons who suffered discrimination during the mentioned period of time.

Parliament's Resolution No. 35/1990 (dated the 28th of March) mended a quite old omission pointing out that: "the deportation of Germans from Hungary and their subsequent relocation were unjust procedures, representing also severe infringements upon human rights. Innocent persons were made to suffer because of their ethnic origin." Therefore, parliament presented its condolences to the relatives of the deceased and expressed its sympathy to the survivors. Consequently, the Council of Ministers had to bring in a compensation bill stipulating equal treatment for Germans as compared to other Hungarian citizens who suffered similar injuries during the given period and were not ethnic Germans.

Parliament's Resolution No. 36/1990 (dated the 28th of March) provided for the compensation of Hungarian citizens who had been deported to the Soviet Union to labour as indemnity for war damages, or had been convicted by Soviet courts but were later rehabilitated because they had committed no crimes. The Hungarian parliament condemned those means of violating human rights that meant that tens of thousands of people deprived of their freedom and kept in detention far from their homeland under such inhumane conditions that most of them did not survive. Parliament presented an official apology to the victims and undertook the obligation to provide guarantees that in the future no foreign state will deport or convict Hungarian citizens in a similar fashion. Furthermore, it instructed the government to prepare a law on the compensation of the victims.

The last resolution that was adopted on that day—parliament's Resolution No. 37/1990 (dated the 28th of March) prescribed the compensation of people who had been wrongfully limited in their personal freedom between 1945 and 1963. In accordance with Article 55 of the constitution the resolution stipulated that all persons who were persecuted within the context of the Second World War or afterwards during the Stalinist dictatorship should be compensated. The deputies, bearing in mind the proximity of the forthcoming elections, called the attention of the next parliament to the necessity of a law on compensation and recommended as the guiding principle for passing such a piece of legislation the following: injuries against the life and personal liberty of human individuals should be redressed according to the possibilities, taking into account the sense of justice prevailing in society.[13]

The new parliament fulfilled its legislative obligation.[14]

While adopting compensatory legislation one could not disregard the fact that Hungarian citizens suffered property-related or other kinds of injuries not only in a manner that has proven unconstitutional or illegal, but the dictatorial exercise of power itself caused damages to a huge number of citizens.

Therefore it had to be assessed which societal groups suffered damages during the last decades and how serious were these damages. Furthermore, establishing the amount of compensation that was to be awarded required taking into consideration the country's capacity to carry economic burdens. There is not much need to argue that compensation lacking the necessary economic basis would have yielded no other benefit than the one of political slogans.

Using as a criterion the damages that have been caused, one can distinguish between three broad areas of compensatory legislation.

The first kind of losses were incurred by citizens because the state acted in a wrongful manner and damaged their properties. The partial reparation for these damages is called property-related compensation. Second, the compensation awarded to persons who have been subjected to political persecution means the satisfaction of claims that arose because of the politically motivated infringement upon their personal freedom—including even taking their lives. Third, alleviating the health damage suffered by persons because of well-defined reasons (such as, wrongful detention on the basis of political reasons, arbitrary decisions made by authorities, injuries of military origin) was also a task to be accomplished by compensatory legislation.[15]

One could realise already at the very beginning that the law-maker undertook an incredibly complicated, complex and, in the end, thankless task when he tried to partially compensate some well-defined societal groups that were marked off in a manner that not even a constitutional objection could have been raised against it. A legal reparation of this extent and covering such broad areas was unprecedented in Hungarian legislation. Thus, the legal institution that was given later the name "compensation" had no precedents either in legal literature, or in legislative practice.

The parliament and the government ended up in "no man's land", where finding one's way about was a very difficult, sometimes even an almost impossible, job. One had to lay down the legal/theoretical fundaments of compensation during the elaboration of pieces of legislation that succeeded each other, the experiences gained from implementation were put to use during the process of drafting the laws and, meanwhile, the constitutional court performing its extremely important and massive task enriched and refined the theory of compensation.[16]

During the preparation of compensatory laws some aspects had to be given priority: compensation was a non-recurrent act that took place under special circumstances; redressing property-related and other kinds of injuries could be construed as part in a process of transition targeting the system of properties; compensation represented a salient part and a manifestation of a process that aimed to do justice to people.

Redressing Property-related Injuries

It was impossible to deduce from the constitution a requirement that the state should give back the properties that had been withdrawn by previous regimes in a manner that can be considered unconstitutional if one applied the standards of the newly-established rule of law. Neither the constitution nor other laws included stipulations that the state had to indemnify or compensate such losses entirely. Furthermore, the state was not constitutionally obliged to retroactively alter general regulations in the civil code or in the procedural codes in order to make possible the compensation of former owners or the return of their original properties.

It follows from these facts that nobody had a constitutional right either to regain his/her initial property in kind or to receive full compensation. Therefore, establishing the unconstitutional or illegal character of the laws on nationalisation or of single acts of the authorities did not entail that the property right of the state over the assets in question ceased to exist.

Transferring state property into private hands, and as part of such an action returning it to former owners, was at the present owner's (the state's) discretion. Of course, during the process of preparing the relevant pieces of legislation, the possibility of giving former owners their initial properties back was thoroughly examined. However, this method of compensation seemed neither legally nor economically feasible.

Property-related compensation intended to provide subsequent and partial reparation to those citizens who have suffered well-defined and mostly provable property-related injuries during the last five decades as a result of the state's law-making and implementing activities.

However, it was not a matter of controversy that, even if in the same period, hundreds of thousands of people have suffered losses that had a material consequence (regarding employment, membership, study and carrier opportunities, the quality of life etc.), there were no financial possibilities to make a full inventory of these and award compensations.

Therefore, the law-maker saw no constitutional reason for treating former proprietors and persons who suffered legal injuries or material losses during the previous regime in a preferential manner entailing the total satisfaction of their claims by the legislature as *opposed* to a society that bore the burdens of transition.

In order to fulfil the criteria of constitutionality, the legislator—considering what was the country's capacity to carry burdens—had to divide the costs of transition among all societal groups. In this way, it laid a proportional burden on those who were otherwise the beneficiaries—in this case the persons who were to receive compensations. The partial character of the compensation, its incompleteness, can be perceived as the cost of transition. The same constitutional principle was applied when acknowledging that it was constitutionally acceptable to use parts of the property of co-operatives as a resource for compensation and when it was made possible—or at least facilitated—to purchase flats that were to become property of local governments using compensation vouchers.

During the drafting process of the law redressing property-related injuries, the lawmaker approached the establishment of the facts that provided a basis for compensation from the point of view of the outcomes. The reparations law intended to award compensation not on the basis of the amount of property that has been taken away; the law-maker conceived the problem not in terms of claims made by single subjects. Instead it took into account that previously the state endeavoured to systematically and purposefully eliminate private property applying various legal means. For the proprietor in question it was of lesser importance what means did the state make use of in order to deprive him/her of his/her property, or of the possibility to dispose of or use it. On the contrary, the occurrence of the outcome was the general criterion that allowed for the subsequent settlement regarding their claims.

For these reasons, it became irrelevant whether somebody had been deprived of his/her property rightfully or wrongfully considering as basis of judgement the legislation in force at that moment of time, or whether the nationalisation law promised compensation or not.

Thus, the process of making compensation laws under the special and non-recurrent circumstances of transition disregarded the original legal nature of the separate property-related injuries. Compensation was awarded not according to the original claims, but in the context of the tasks and possibilities characterising the new situation and taking into account also the necessity to divide the costs of transition. Compensatory legislation made the process of reparation completely independent of the original entitlements, because instead of a case by case treatment of claims, it settled the compensation of former proprietors and persons subjected to political persecution applying the principle of distributive justice to the whole process of transition. Furthermore, when satisfying their claims, it took into consideration parallel constitutional tasks as well.

After all, recognising the necessary and unavoidable character of compensation would have required that the rest of society somehow realised that here and now, there is no possibility to award everybody rightful and total compensation for wrongs suffered during the last decades. Instead, one should look for a social consensus to define those grievances that will be acknowledged as amenable to reparation; nevertheless, bearing in mind that other persons have suffered damages that do not create an entitlement for material compensation, the first category of individuals will receive only partial compensation for the incurred damages.

This social consensus, unfortunately, did emerge because the parties represented in parliament, primarily those who were in opposition then, were very keen on pursuing their political goals instead of seeking agreement. Hence, they were not interested in uncovering injuries done in the past and in compensating for these according to the possibilities. They were rather interested in escalating social tensions to a degree that under the pretext of compensation would have resulted in overthrowing the government. Furthermore, the MSZP (Hungarian Socialist Party) was obviously interested in exposing to the population of the country the atrocities committed in the last forty years to the smallest degree possible.[17]

After the regime change the political forces that wanted the return of the former regime did everything in their power to turn the persons who suffered damages against the government that intended to compensate them. Thus, they told the population that they were entitled to receive more and, in the meantime they tried by all possible means to diminish the amount of partial compensation. On the other hand, referring to the country's capacity to bear burdens, they partially blamed the worsening living conditions on compensation. Their goal was to prevent the masses who had not received compensation for property-related injuries, or because they had been subjected to political persecution, from realising that the worsening of their material conditions is the result of the irresponsible and erroneous economic policy pursued in the last decades.

Even if there were no constitutional stipulations to give back the properties that had been taken away, *in integrum restitutio*, the restoration of the initial situation seemed the handiest solution for those who suffered property-related losses. This, however, was neither legally nor economically feasible.

Compensatory legislation intended to provide reparation only for a part of the injustices committed during half a century; namely for the ones that are more ore less provable and acceptable as basis for the calculation of damages. There also have been other injustices, but in those cases it was impossible to compute the extent of the damages caused and therefore one could not establish a precise amount of compensation to be awarded. Moreover, establishing the type and the numbers of such injustices was also impossible. For all these reasons it was justified to acknowledge that the whole of society suffered losses and—after admitting that there are no possibilities to compensate for all the damage that was wrongfully caused by the state during the last fifty years—grant partial compensation to those groups that had been identified according to constitutional criteria.[18]

Certain inescapable facts also ruled out the possibility of returning properties to their original owners. For instance, since the Second World War the country's agricultural land decreased by an area equivalent to Szolnok County; industrial plants were transformed; substantial investments were made by the state that changed the character of the plants; there was a massive sale of flats transferred into state property; the so-called deposited movable properties were long since unavailable. Moreover, one could endlessly enumerate those difficulties that would have rendered the possibility of restoring the original situation even under favourable economic circumstances.

The lawmaker, being aware of the special bond between most members of Hungarian society and agricultural land, tried to find a way of satisfying within the given constitutional framework the rightful desire to regain their assets felt by former proprietors of agricultural land.

For this purpose, Prime Minister József Antall turned to the constitutional court requesting interpretation of the constitution regarding two issues. The first question asked by the government was whether it represented discriminatory treatment—according to the stipulations of Article 70/A, paragraph 1—if the former properties of certain persons, depending on what was in their possession, would be re-privatised; whereas the former properties of others, on the basis of different privatisation and compensation principles, would not be returned to them. The second question was whether the law could allow for taking away property from co-operatives, but without resorting to the procedures of expropriation and indemnification.

The ruling given by the constitutional court in this matter[19] stated that it represents unconstitutional discrimination if the former properties of certain persons were re-privatised depending on what these assets were, while other persons' properties not, unless there were constitutional motivations justifying such a measure.[20]

The statements of principal importance that were made in the motivation attached to the ruling—and the presentation of which cannot be made in this paper—have significantly contributed to elaborating the legal/theoretical fundamentals of compensation, and became crucial for the subsequent process of drafting compensatory legislation.

After receiving the answers from the constitutional court, the government finalised its bill on property-related compensation and presented parliament in December 1990 its Bill no. 1020 on the settlement of property relationships and concerning the partial reparation of unjustly caused damages by the state to the property of citizens after the 8th of June 1949.[21]

Nothing proves the vehemence of the dispute that took place in parliament more eloquently than the fact that 415 amendments were handed in and fifty-two deputies appealed to the constitutional court requesting the preliminary judicial review of certain stipulations contained in the bill.

The constitutional court dismissed[22] all these motions without even inquiring into their substance because all of them requested preliminary judicial review of a draft that was not the final one. However, the court made some remarkable principal observations in Part Three of the ruling.

Among other things, the constitutional court considered it acceptable that the state renewed its compensatory obligation postulated in previous pieces of legislation, and in a manner that was similar to the *novatio* restated the same debt while creating new entitlements, giving it a new extent and formulating new conditions. Thus, fairness became the unitary legal basis of compensation, because the renewal of the obligation excluded the possibility to refer to previous entitlements.[23]

The measure of encumbering plots of land owned by co-operatives with rights to purchase them also passed the test of judicial review. The constitutional court did not consider *per se* unconstitutional two connected facts. First, that the state permitted citizens to purchase agricultural land that had not been state property using as means of payment compensation vouchers. Second, that the state regulated the distribution of a limited means of coverage having a special legal status differently from other properties allotted for compensation. The state used as coverage for compensation vouchers land owned by agricultural co-operatives that was withdrawn from citizens in a manner that fell within the competence of the compensation law. According to the ruling of the constitutional court, because during the process of eliminating societal property the laws shaping the system of properties divided both the costs that spring from the former creation of societal property and the obligations that ensued from the establishment of the rule of law among those who were to freely acquire societal property, the future subjects of the new form of property have no constitutional rights to claim either the unencumbered transformation of what has been previously societal property into private property, or its unencumbered transferral to a new owner. The burdens that had to be divided do not represent only legal obligations. Compensation promised by nationalisation laws, burdens ensuing from pieces of legislation that increased the property of co-operatives, and the costs of societal transition are all burdens that have to be divided among those who will freely acquire societal property.

Considering these reasons, there were no obstacles in constitutional law that would have prevented the usage of agricultural land owned by co-operatives as coverage for compensation.

The passions incited by the compensatory laws, however, remained as intense as they were at the beginning. The president did not sign the bill that had been voted in by parliament and requested the preliminary judicial review of the stipulations that raised doubts.

Thus, the constitutional court had to take a stand again in a very short time on the controversies about compensation. These were cloaked as legal disputes, though in fact they were of political nature.

The court[24] objected neither to dividing the compensation process into several phases nor to leaving the situation of persons who in spite of not having suffered property-related damages, were harmed in a manner that affected their estate or material condition, unsettled. Nevertheless, in order to insure constitutionality, it ruled that the law should specify those pieces of legislation the implementation of which caused property-related damages requiring compensation. It also required the law to specify the deadline for adopting the next compensatory act.

The judges forming the constitutional court stressed again: purchasing rights based on the compensation law and encumbering co-operatives are not *per se* unconstitutional.

However, they objected to a particular discrimination present in the bill. The stipulation they criticised might have lead, because of the different manners of computing the amount of compensation to be awarded, to full compensation in kind for land that had been taken away. Meanwhile, any other usage of compensation vouchers would have meant a partial indemnification of former owners equivalent to only a small fraction of the current market value of the lost asset.

The court declared it unconstitutional to oblige local governments to accept as means of payment compensation vouchers if the beneficiaries intended to buy flats that were already owned by local governments on the date when the law became operational.

In order to put an end to the unconstitutional character of the stipulations, the lawmaker had to fundamentally alter the method of compensating for previously owned agricultural land. It had to legally solve the difficult problem of maintaining the limited amount of agricultural land as coverage for compensation while securing the equality of opportunity and avoiding the jeopardising of agricultural life.

Consequently, the lawmaker eliminated the separate methods of computation prescribed for the cases of compensation awarded for loss of agricultural land, and other withdrawn properties, respectively. By creating the institution of the land auction, it accomplished the observance of the constitutional criterion that required equal treatment of all beneficiaries. In keeping with the constitutional framework, it managed to identify the persons who were allowed to participate in these auctions in a manner that granted a subjective right to former proprietors to bid for plots of land owned by co-operatives that were using their previous proprieties. Allowing members of the co-operative in question and inhabitants of the locality where the co-operative was located made it theoretically possible for the price of purchase—the highest bid—to reflect the relationship between supply and demand.[25]

Parliament adopted the law in its final form during the session held on the 6th of May 1991. The Hungarian Bulletin published Law No. 25/1991 on the settlement of property relationships and concerning the partial reparation of unjustly caused damages by the state to the property of citizens. The law comprised the detailed rules of compensation: however, it granted partial compensation only for losses incurred as a result of laws made after the 8th of June 1949. These laws were listed in Appendix 2. The parliament also undertook a legal obligation to pass a law compensating for losses caused by the implementation of legislation made before the mentioned date. (The set of laws pertaining to this category were listed in Appendix 1.) The legislature set the deadline of adopting the second compensatory law for the 30th of November 1991.

Parliament failed to meet this deadline. The government brought forth the relevant bill (Bill no. 3623) in November 1991, yet as a result of the lengthy debate that took place in parliament, the law was voted on only on the 7th of April 1992 and entered into force on the 8th of June 1992. This so-called Second Law on Compensation (from this point onwards: LC2)—Law No.

24/1992—was by far shorter than its predecessor, The First Law on Compensation (from this point onwards: LC1). Nevertheless, it managed more than just regulating compensation for damages caused by implementing legislation passed between the 1st of May 1939 and the 8th of June 1948. Capitalising on the experiences gained through the implementation of the previous law, it added some new items to the list of laws that caused losses amenable to compensation. Bearing in mind the specific character of properties (jewellery, paintings etc.) that have been taken away, it also prescribed several methods of computing indemnities.

Some 817,855 petitions were handed in on the basis of LC1 and 78,801 petitions on the basis of LC2. During the spring of 1994, the reparation offices registered 532,787 so-called supplementary claims. All in all, there were approximately 1,000,000 claims for compensation that had to be processed and settled.

The Government established, on the basis of the authorisation given by means of LC1, an independent administrative organ with national jurisdiction—the National Reparation and Compensation Office (from this point onwards: NRCO)—and its county-level subsidiaries: county reparation offices (and the Budapest reparation office).[26] The NRCO, besides implementing the provisions of the laws on property-related compensation, also handled matters concerning the indemnification of material losses incurred by persons who had been subjected to wrongful measures that limited their personal liberty. (In this respect the NRCO acted as the legal successor of the Reparation Office.) On the other hand, it co-operated in the process of preparing and elaborating legislation connected with compensation.

To put together the administrative organisation that had to deal with reparation, to secure the necessary conditions in terms of personnel and logistics and to begin the implementation of the laws required an enormous amount of work.[27]

The county reparation offices managed to complete inventories of the claims made for compensation in agricultural land before the deadline prescribed by the law. They also sent so-called totalled notifications to the co-operatives owning plots of land that have been claimed.[28] In December 1991, approximately one hundred rulings on the first degree in matters regarding property-related compensation were handed down. One had to begin to give rulings this early because the system of computerised processing needed to be tested and the issuing of compensation vouchers had to be checked in practice. Effective activity began in the spring of 1992, after these experiences had been processed. It soon became obvious for the government as well that the county reparation offices were severely understaffed. With the personnel employed at that moment, it would have taken ten years to implement LC1. After the budget of these offices had been supplemented at the beginning of the summer, more personnel were hired and trained. However, the beneficial effect of increasing the number of employees could be felt only during the following year.

Auctions began in August 1992. In order to make the rules regulating the auctions known among the staff of the offices, the NRCO ordered a demonstrative video and held several simulations of auctions. After the aversion felt at the beginning towards auctions decreased and people learned how to behave during auctions, the number of participants began to grow constantly.

Because of the delayed processing of applications, many people felt that when they finally received their compensation vouchers there would not be enough farmland to bid for. In order to eliminate this problem, parliament adopted on the of June 23, 1992 Law No. 49/1992 on certain aspects of the usage of compensation vouchers for acquiring agricultural land. This piece of legislation allowed people who wanted to buy farmland and pay with compensation vouchers to announce to the county compensation office this intention within a given period of time. If a person proceeded in this manner his/her claim had to be settled within 60 days. In order to prevent abuses, persons who were entitled to receive compensation in kind were not given compensation vouchers. They were given so-called certificates of deposit that could have been used only for participation in auctions. It can be concluded that this legal procedure made the plans of the lawmaker come true. Tens of thousands of people obtained their compensation rulings because of the employment of this summary procedure and were able to participate in auctions.

The compensation offices organised approximately 26,000 auctions up through the summer of 1997. In this manner a total area of farmland equivalent to 36 million golden crowns (unit of measure used when assessing the expected net benefit yielded by a plot of farmland) has been transferred into private ownership.

These figures speak for themselves. However, one must also mention that there have also been scandals around these auctions, alleged or real abuses have been committed and there have been persons for whom these auctions meant a disappointment. In certain regions of the country—especially in areas that were considered to be valuable because of the possibility of putting the land together, allegedly creating more efficient use in the future—aggregates of estates came into being that are inappropriate for farming.[29]

However, one must point out that during the auctions the participants themselves made deals with each other though being fully aware that some deals were contrary to common sense; that the manner in which they drew the borderlines ruled out the possibility of independent farming on the plots in question.

The hypothesis of the lawmaker that rationality would prevail proved to be false. Nor did it prove a powerful deterrent against speculators, even though a double obstacle was built into the law. Introducing the heavy income tax that had to be paid if the acquired land was abandoned within the first three years was inefficient because the people who bought land for compensation vouchers were unaware of this stipulation, or they could hardly believe that the state would claim the tax in question. On the other hand, the stipulation that no farmland was allowed to be withdrawn from cultivation within the first five years and if sold the new owner was also obliged to use the land for agricultural purposes, went ignored. These regulations were broken in many cases because there was no deterrent to stop offenders: neither did the state police this aspect of the law nor were the sanctions prescribed in the law applied against transgressors. The amount of abuse was insignificant both as compared to the total area of land that had been sold via auctions and to the number of people who acquired properties. However, within the given microenvironment or exactly as a result of the magnifying effect media accounts had on the popular perception of these events, they were appropriate for influencing the general mood.

All in all, it can be concluded that the institution of the auction passed the test of judicial review. Nevertheless, its economic and social-psychological impact can be assessed after the passing of a longer period of time.[30]

Almost all stipulations of the law on property-related compensation were challenged before the constitutional court. The length of the present paper permits the presentation of only two rulings of the court.

Ruling No. 15/1993 (dated the 12th of March) of the constitutional court dismissed all but one of the constitutional pleas handed in as a challenge to the dispositions of LC1. The sole disposition that was found unconstitutional was contained in paragraph 24 and referred to the institution of the agricultural entrepreneur's warrant.[31]

Ruling No. 16/1993 (dated the 12th of March) of the constitutional court referred to petitions concerning deposits made in gold and jewellery before 1945. The ruling stressed that the unitary legal basis of compensation laws was fairness and that the renewal of previous obligations that fell on the state was constitutionally permissible. This *novatio* was declared acceptable with regard to every claim generated by the withdrawal of an object of property as a result of the implementation of legislation made by the state. The court specified furthermore that in this respect it mattered neither whether the withdrawal of property generated a real legal claim or a claim pertaining to contract law, nor whether this claim required compensation or reparation.

The constitutional court declared in this ruling that an infringement of the constitution had been committed, namely through omission. That is, Hungary failed to satisfy the requirements of Article 27, paragraph 2 of the Paris Peace Treaty. On the basis of the disposition referred to by the constitutional court, Hungary restated the obligations it undertook when adopting Article 26 from 1946. This piece of legislation required that the assets, rights and interests of persons, organisations and communities against whom—as individual or as members of communities—harassing laws of a fascist kind have been adopted because of racial, religious or any other reasons, be transferred into the propriety of organisations representing such persons, organisations and communities in Hungary, unless within six month of the treaty's entry into force an heir presented himself/herself or a claim has been formulated by somebody for these assets, rights or interests. According to the stipulations of the Peace Treaty these organisations were given the assets in question if they pursued certain acceptable goals, that is, they used them for supporting the victims who survived and their organisations.

However, neither the above stipulations of the peace treaty, nor the almost identical dispositions of the 2nd paragraph of Article 26 from 1946 were implemented. Therefore, the constitutional court concluded that the Hungarian state did not fulfil its obligations towards the legal entities specified in paragraph 2, Article 27 of the peace treaty. Moreover, under the new, completely different historical circumstances it cannot fulfil these obligations in their original form. In what concerns natural persons, the constitutional court considered the adoption of LC2 a satisfactory fulfilment of legislative obligations. For this reason, it set a deadline for parliament to settle the matter with regard to legal entities.[32]

The government and the organisations in question initiated talks in 1993, and these continued after the 1994 elections. Finally, the government put an end to this omission that lasted half a century by setting up a public foundation.

Nevertheless, the parliament has to adopt another compensatory law.

Article 29, paragraph 1 of the peace treaty reads as follows: "Any of the Allied or the Associated Powers has a right to arrest, withhold, detain or to order any other measures concerning all assets, rights and interests that are on its territory on the date of this Treaty's entry into force and are the property of Hungary or of Hungarian citizens." According to paragraph 3 of the same article, the Hungarian government undertook the obligation to indemnify all Hungarian citizens whose properties had been irrevocably taken away on the basis of paragraph 1. Furthermore, in addition to the Paris Treaty, Hungary signed international treaties regarding property rights with certain countries (e.g. Czechoslovakia and Yugoslavia) through which Hungary explicitly renounced the Hungarian properties located on the other party's territory. These assets were considered part of the indemnities claimed from Hungary. Thus, an obligation to indemnify the citizens who lost their properties fell on the Hungarian state.

Naturally, no legal norm regulating the process of indemnification was adopted during the decades of socialism. The preparations for adopting such a law began in 1993 and the government also managed to discuss the first draft of the bill. However, there was neither time nor enough political courage to pass the bill before the elections.[33]

The new government that came to power after the 1994 elections showed no disposition whatsoever to bring forth a bill on the compensation of property-related losses suffered as a result of international treaties. For this reason, the author of this paper was forced to appeal to the constitutional court. The court found his application well-founded. Ruling No. 37/1996 (dated the 4th of September) of the constitutional court concluded that an unconstitutional situation occurred because Hungary failed to comply to the dispositions of the 3rd paragraph of Article 39 of the Paris Peace Treaty, dispositions restated by Article 18 from 1947. The necessary measure had to be taken by parliament by the 30th of June 1997. The deadline was missed, no results were accomplished because the government, though it has been included in its legislative agenda, did not bring up a bill concerning this matter.

Hence, the process of property-related compensation has not come to an end. The parliament passed Law No. 33/1997 on problems concerning the closure of the processes of property-related compensation on the 6th of May 1997.[34] The subtitle of the law is misleading—obviously for political reasons—since it suggests to uninformed citizens that property-related compensation is over.

The above-mentioned ruling of the constitutional court created unambiguously an obligation for the parliament to adopt a measure. Thus, compensation did not come to an end, not even on the level of lawmaking. On the other hand, as long as a considerable amount of compensation vouchers have not been exchanged for other assets and unless the state offers properties of satisfactory quality in a sufficient quantity for persons owning compensation vouchers and intending to invest them, there is no sense in speaking of the closure of compensation.

Compensation of Persons
Previously Subjected to Political Persecution

From all that has been said thus far it might seem that the Antall cabinet forgot to award reparations to persons who were subjected to political persecution. It appears that the legislature considered compensation for property-related injuries a priority. Hence, all the people who had been active participants in the struggle against communist dictatorship and suffered losses because of their attitude, under the new political circumstances, became the victims of the new regime as well.

Such an interpretation is at odds with the facts. After the 1990 elections the government faced a shocking fact forgotten by many people, either intentionally or because of carelessness. The country was facing imminent economic collapse. Therefore, adopting compensatory legislation was not on option in the short run. First, the economic basis of the planned compensation had to be created in order to elaborate rules regarding compensation in accordance with the economic fundamentals that were to be laid down. The logical consequence was that the first step to be taken was to settle property relationships. A position had to be taken on the issue of privatisation versus re-privatisation as well. After solving this question, in accordance with reparations carried out by means of compensation vouchers, the creation of the law on compensating persons who were subjected to political persecution began.

The Antall cabinet did, however, take several steps to partially eliminate the legal disadvantages experienced by persons who had been persecuted, and tried to mitigate their severe material hardships, too.

The government issued a decree in November 1990 on the settlement of matters regarding employment and social security for various categories of individuals.[35] The target groups were persons who suffered wrongful convictions between 1945 and 1963, persons convicted because of involvement in the revolution from 1956 as well as other persons who were subjected to measures restraining their personal liberty. Furthermore, the previous reduction of pensions applicable to the second category was annulled.

The settlement of matters regarding employment and social security for persons who were deported, detained in labour camps or limited in any other way in their personal liberty between 1938 and 1945 because of their racial or ethnic origin, respectively because of their attitude towards Nazism, was completed during the summer of 1991.[36] The government also alleviated the disadvantages regarding the pension-related rights of former public servants during the very same year.[37]

One year after the communists seized power in the aftermath of the Second World War, the provision awarded to the relatives of heroes who have been killed in action and to the *honvéd*s (soldiers in the Hungarian army) who became invalids was terminated for most of them because of political reasons. The government, on the one hand, resumed by a decree[38] the payment of the—otherwise rightfully awarded—allowances that were denied because of political reasons to invalids and widows of war; on the other hand it made possible to apply once again for such allowances.

Because of a ruling given by the constitutional court a regulation had to be adopted regarding the changing of the so-called dollar warrants, too.[39]

The last piece of legislation was the one completed in December 1992 concerning the settlement of matters regarding employment and social security for persons who executed forced labour within the bonds of the army and subsequently were discriminated against in the period between 1951 and 1956.[40]

Capitalising also on the experience gained during the implementation process of the mentioned decrees, the government brought in Bill no. 3413 on the compensation of persons who had been wrongfully deprived of their liberty and life because of polit-

ical reasons. A fiery debate came about during which personal
attacks were launched at each other by deputies. Finally, parliament
adopted Law No. 32/1992 on May 12, 1992. The implementation
of the law was the responsibility of the NRCO. Some 368,395
applications were submitted by the original deadline and a further
532,787 applications by the supplementary deadline. Persons entitled to receive compensation could choose between two methods of
payment: a lump-sum indemnity payable not in money but in compensation vouchers; or a monthly allowance.

Neither could this law elude judicial review. Almost every
aspect of the law was carefully examined by the judges. It took
almost three years of detailed study until they came up with a decision. The ruling they made declared several stipulations in the law
unconstitutional.[41]

It is impossible to give a detailed account of the ruling.
Nevertheless, it must be pointed out—as the constitutional court
itself did—that this compensatory law is fundamentally different
from all the previous ones in that it does not award compensation
for property-related or material injuries, but on the contrary, for
other kinds of injuries having a personal character. Furthermore, no
obligation regarding reparation for these wrongful personal damages fell on the state – not even a partial one – since the state did
not directly undertake such an obligation before a new constitution
was written after the establishment of the rule of law.[42] This law is
part of a series of measures taken by the state in order to accomplish political reparation. More precisely, it is part of those measures that besides granting political reparation tried to offer some
material compensation as well. The unitary legal basis for such a
retroactive compensation is fairness, the compensation itself having
an *ex gratia* character. The standard used by judges during the
process of constitutional scrutiny has been the criterion of treating
everybody as people of equal dignity. The liberty of the lawmaker
manifested itself when it was allowed to differentiate among per-

sons according to certain details, since the differentiation did not apply to people possessing an *a priori* entitlement. Under these circumstances the barrier to differentiation is the principal limit of positive discrimination: the unconditional observance of the principle to treat everybody as people with equal dignity as well as of the fundamental rights postulated in the constitution. For these reasons the unequal treatment was justified by a sound motivation, otherwise differentiation would have been arbitrary.

These categories are according to our opinion rather insecure, moreover insufficiently concrete and articulate. Therefore, on this basis one can hardly decide already at the very beginning whether certain legal differentiation introduced during the process of elaborating a law are unconstitutional or not.

In order to eliminate unconstitutional parts, the Horn cabinet brought in Bill no. 1268. However, before taking the final vote the competent parliamentary committee requested a review of the bill because a stipulation might have been unconstitutional. The ruling of the constitutional court given in answer to this motion confirmed that some sections were unconstitutional.[43] Bearing in mind this ruling, parliament adopted Law No. 29/1997 that broadened considerably the pool of people holding an entitlement for compensation because the loss of their lives.

Other Compensatory Laws

The first freely-elected parliament adopted two more compensatory laws. These were Law No. 52/1992 on national care and Law No. 45/1994 on the provision of military care. The first law awarded a monthly allowance to parents and widows of persons who lost their lives because of arbitrary decisions made by authorities (including deportation and forced labour in the Soviet Union as well), or to persons who for similar reasons or because of politically motivated deprivation of liberty became invalids. The latter stipulation regulated military care in a unitary manner and provided a lump-sum indemnity for those persons who were previously denied care for political reasons.

Compensation as a Means of Privatisation

Compensation has been a crucial component of the overall transition since it played a pivotal role in eliminating societal property.[44] The government estimated that the value of compensation vouchers that had to be issued on the basis of LC1 would be HUF 100 billion. In the case of LC2 the estimate was HUF 20 billion, and finally the value of vouchers to be issued on the basis of the law on the compensation of persons who had been subjected to political persecution was estimated at 53 HUF billion. The total nominal value of the compensation vouchers issued by the summer of 1997 is HUF 135,3 billion. There have been also warrants issued the total value of which amounts to HUF 3,7 billion.

As compared to the total value measurable in several thousands of billions of HUF of the property that is going to be privatised, this sum of money does not seem large, even if one takes into account the increase in value attributable to the interest calculated after the value of the vouchers.

All in all, compensation did not represent a possibility that could be underestimated by persons who received indemnities, because by making use of their vouchers—due to the various ways these could have been employed—they could not only stabilise their living conditions under the circumstances of a social standard of living that was declining at a fast rate, but they also were enabled to acquire estates that could have represented a solid base for their future and that of their families.

Naturally, the majority of the persons who were entitled to compensation—taking into consideration their large number, too—could exploit these possibilities only if there did not remain only legal stipulations but were transformed into practical opportunities.

In our view, Hungarian governments that held political power in the past, hold it now and will hold it in the future were, are and will always be responsible for two things. First, to offer—taking into consideration the investment intentions as well—properties of satisfactory quality in a sufficient quantity to allow people to make use of their compensation vouchers and to create possibilities for investments in this context. Second, to inform people owning vouchers about the possibilities available for their usage.

All in all, it can be said that neither the previous nor the present government acquitted itself of this duty. However, the former government has the mitigating circumstance that it was the pioneer of this whole process and, therefore, it had to attend to several matters simultaneously. Almost all negative aspects of transition hit Hungarian society between 1990 and 1994. The legislative difficulties that followed from the reshaping of the legal system, the privatisation lacking practical preliminaries and the obstacles raised by the previous ruling élite—together with the malicious criticism of the so-called democratic opposition—prevented the comprehensive processes of societal change that have been initiated from developing according to their full potential. Naturally, one cannot avoid mentioning the responsibility of previous governments and their members in what concerns the occurrence of this negative outcome.[45]

However, the reason for Hungarian society only partially accepting the process of compensation is to be found neither in objecting to re-privatisation nor in the modest sums that partial compensation represented. It is beyond doubt that compensation involved millions of people. Nevertheless, the majority of the population did not benefit from it. Awarding material compensation to certain groups, to the "chosen ones" under the circumstances of a society that experiences poverty, pauperisation, everyday problems of existence and feels bitterness because of facing gloomy perspectives for the future gives birth to adverse feelings, especially if some politically-motivated groups breed disappointment. Thinking about certain persons' entitlement to compensation and understanding it, comprehending the relationship between its value and the extent of damages that have been suffered depends more or less on the subjective judgement made by the individual. Younger generations who did not experience the decades of most severe oppression, but possibly only benefited from the advantages offered by socialism, naturally opposed all forms of compensation because it diminished their proportion of the scarce material goods that had to be redistributed among societal groups. The beneficiaries of the former regime, and those persons who actively contributed to depriving hundreds of thousand of people of the fruits of their hard labour, of their liberty and lives were not interested in compensation and its success either. They rather made all possible efforts to reduce the number of people who were supposed to receive compensation and to prevent the process from being a success. Similarly, economic groups that themselves wanted take part in privatisation and to acquire—as it turned out later, rather successfully—the state properties that promised to be solid investments were not interested in the successful implementation of compensation. They perceived people who were entitled to compensation as their competition who might be able to grab the merchandise they wanted to take possession of.

The focal point of the political battles that took place in the years that followed the regime change has been compensation. This explained to a large extent why this part of reparation ended up being at best only partly successful.

All of us know that compensation has not been unanimously hailed even among those who were entitled to receive indemnities. We are not alluding to those people who held that the only acceptable method of compensation would have been the in kind return of the proprieties taken away. It must also be mentioned that most of the people who eventually received indemnification did not even consider the possibility of receiving compensation decades after losing their proprieties or their liberty. In fact, compensation came rather late for many of them: their age or health conditions made compensation an act having only symbolic value. This was because it was impossible to compensate either for the decades that elapsed or for the hopes and plans that never came through. Similarly, it was impossible to retrieve the youth that had gone, or to give back one's lost health; not to mention that it was totally impossible to compensate for lost lives.

Since compensation did not make use of cash but of a special securities, the compensation voucher (annuities need not be taken into account because of their modest value), the actual accomplishment of reparation, required that beneficiaries actively co-operated. They had to choose among the opportunities and to accept the consequences of their choices.

Regarding this topic one can again only scratch its surface. We can only allude to the fact that during the years of socialism a "caring" state, capable of "solving everything" surrounded the citizens making them give up the habit of deciding independently. To thoroughly ponder the consequences of investing, of taking material risks was in many cases an almost impossible task for beneficiaries of a rather old age and medium level of education. Most of the notions connected to the usage of compensation vouchers had a semantic content that was unknown to them; moreover, they were forced to realise that the semantic content of the notions they have been using in their everyday lives has also changed.[46] Another factor that had an inhibiting effect on some people who experienced persecution and suffering was fear.

The beneficiaries of compensation were forced to accept that the idea of re-privatisation had been dropped; nevertheless most of them hoped that indemnification would help them acquire an estate that would represent a secure source of income.

Making use of compensation vouchers by buying a flat owned by the local government was a real opportunity for the smallest number of people. Nevertheless, this proved to be the most fortunate investment.

A very small number of people requested the exchange of vouchers for an annuity. The are several reasons explaining this. The payment was due only up until the beneficiary's death and as a consequence persons having families hardly ever chose this option. On the other hand, the modest sum represented by the annuity was also a disincentive.[47]

For most beneficiaries of compensation, the least convenient way of using the vouchers was to take part in privatisation. They lacked both theoretical and practical knowledge of the mechanisms of market economy, of the changed economic and legal environment that provided the system of circumstances under which they had to make their decision on how to put their compensation vouchers to use.

Administrative organs tried almost in vain to help in this respect with information and advice. On the one hand, these initiatives came rather late, and on the other hand, the forms they chose were inappropriate. Hence, it can be concluded that the government is largely responsible for failing to prepare society—primarily, the would-be beneficiaries of compensation—in a proper manner for the difficulties of transition. Transition in its entirety, involving economic, social and political issues, swooped down on the unprepared Hungarian society with tremendous speed. Consequently, society paid and still pays the multiple of the price that is a necessary and unavoidable consequence of transition.

Finally, there was another investment possibility that despite being the least secure source of income was hardly alien to most beneficiaries. This was farmland.

We consider that this is another explanation for so many people participating in auctions and buying land. However, our conviction is that if a satisfactory privatisation offer existed and beneficiaries were informed properly, their investment intentions might have been influenced. This would have had not only favourable economic effects, but the beneficiaries would also have felt that compensation was successful. Because providing the necessary privatisation offer was a task to be accomplished by state administration, unsatisfactory implementation raises the question of governmental responsibility.

For the masses who were present at land auctions, the exchange of compensation vouchers far below their nominal value are all consequences of the fact that beneficiaries needed to make decisions lacking information and reasonable investment opportunities.

The government dealt several times with the problem of coverage for compensation vouchers. Among other things it established an inter-ministerial committee for co-ordinating this task and at the end of 1993 passed a resolution regarding the amount of properties to be offered in exchange for compensation vouchers. The relevant aspects of this resolution have not been implemented, yet nobody has been held accountable.

Before the 1994 elections, there had been compensation vouchers totalling thousands of millions of HUF in the possession of original beneficiaries and investors. Several scandals broke out regarding public trading of vouchers for company stocks. We do not necessarily allude only to speculators, but also to abuses that could have been prevented by persons in positions of high responsibility. Yet, these persons failed to do what was their duty.

The Outcomes of Compensation

The implementation of compensatory legislation partially made the initial goals of the lawmaker come true. The state fulfilled its legislative duties in a legal sense, and by undertaking obligations through renewing the corresponding titles, solved problems caused by legislative omissions that lasted for decades. Moreover, it did partial justice to hundreds of thousands of people who had suffered a great deal.

Transferring farmlands into private property, privatisation by using compensation vouchers and the structure of private properties that came into being as a result of these processes meant the fundamentals of market economy, the fundamentals that allowed Hungary to sever its ties with the past and proceed on the path towards social market economy.

From all that has been said it follows that it is not possible to make a final balance-sheet of compensation, because the process ended neither from a legal nor from a social and economic point of view. Therefore, it would be premature to give an answer to the question as to what are the outcomes of compensation.

According to the opinion of the author, the following tasks are to be accomplished by the Hungarian government of 1998-2002. All the areas of the process of compensation have to be analysed exhaustively and thoroughly. Afterwards, decisions and pieces of legislation have to be adopted in order to terminate compensation in a legal sense, and the economic environment required for the meaningful employment of compensation vouchers by their possessor has to be created. Naturally, one cannot avoid the question of compensatory land auctions and the settlement of problems regarding the landed properties that were shaped by the distribution of proportional shares of land.

These tasks are not smaller than the ones aimed at by the previous adoption and implementation of legislation. Banking on the experiences that were accumulated, one can risk declaring that if the parties in power before 1994 regained the confidence of the electorate, they would meet this challenge, too, since they are now possessing the know-how that is indispensable for successful implementation.

Notes

1. In this respect, apart from looking thoroughly at those persons who obtained plots of land, it is a very challenging topic of research to analyse the privatisation process that made use of compensation vouchers, i.e., to examine the effect of vouchers—a special kind of security—on the development of the stock exchange as well as to scientifically explore in what ways did the compensation contribute to the emergence and further development of a way of thinking that is characteristic for private proprietors, of the entrepreneurial consciousness.

2. Among other things a solution had to be found to make computer-assisted rulings, to provide bank logistics necessary for issuing compensation vouchers as well as to store and protect a gigantic database. One also had to face the human and technical difficulties of organising auctions, not to mention those tasks that in spite of appearing as insignificant details to laymen made the implementation of compensation laws an extremely arduous job.

3. Paragraph 1 of the 4th Article from 1929 stipulates—as a consequence of the Trianon Treaty—the establishment of a legal entity called "Assets of Local Governments Destined for Compensation." This seems to be the very first instance when the term "compensation" has been used in Hungarian legislation.

4. The laws concerning the so-called nationalisation of properties that obviously violated constitutional stipulations were still partially in force in 1990. In consequence, the legislature had to solve this contradiction. On the other hand, the lawmaker (parliament or government) had to bear in mind the legal principle according to which it would have been in guilt of constitutional omission if it did not pass the law that represented the precondition for citizens to exercise their rights.

5. Some examples: the 6th Article from 1945 awarding the status of law to Decree No. 600/1945 of the prime minister that outlawed the system of "large estates" and sanctioned the distribution of land to the peasantry; Law No. 24/1949 regarding expropriation for public purposes and housing; Law No. 25/1950 concerning the nationalisation of pharmacies providing drugs for the large public; Law No. 4/1952 concerning the nationalisation of certain residential buildings.

6.   The constitutional court dealt with this special case of violation of
     the constitution through omission, namely by failing to fulfil legisla-
     tive obligations quite early. Ruling No. 22/1990 (dated the 10th of
     October) of the constitutional court stressed the legal principle
     according to which the law-making body is obliged to fulfil its duty
     of passing legislation even if no concrete stipulation in any previous
     piece of legislation prescribes such an obligation, provided that two
     further conditions hold. First, the law-making body observes a prob-
     lem within its jurisdiction that requires a legislative solution.
     Second, the need for this legislative solution arose because the state
     interfered by legislative means with certain conditions of life and, as
     a consequence, it deprived a group of citizens of the practical possi-
     bility to enforce a constitutional right of theirs.

7.   The motivation given in support of this ruling stated that most of that
     part of the country's real estate that consisted of buildings extant
     after the Second World War on its territory—i.e., pharmacies, facto-
     ries, plants, shops etc. owned by private proprietors together with the
     equipment and machinery, property-related rights and securities per-
     taining to these—has been nationalised almost entirely without any
     compensation awarded to their previous owners albeit every
     annulled law stipulated that indemnities were to be paid and made
     the manner and amount of compensation the object of a subsequent
     piece of legislation. The motivation concluded that no such legisla-
     tion has been passed afterwards.

8.   Bill no. 1020 on the settlement of property relationships and con-
     cerning the partial reparation of unjustly caused damages by the state
     to the property of citizens after the 8th of June 1949. Rapporteur: dr.
     István Balsai, Minister of Justice.

9.   The constitutional court closed other proceedings in the matter of
     petitions complaining about the failure to pass compensatory laws as
     a reparation for other pieces of legislation sanctioning nationalisa-
     tion of properties on similar grounds. [Article 2 of Ruling no.
     66/1992 (dated the 17th of December).] We have to point out a fact
     known only by some people: this ruling annulled because of their
     unconstitutional character—paragraphs 4-7, 11 and 17 of Decree No.
     600/1945 of the prime minister outlawing the system of "large
     estates" and sanctioning the distribution of land to the peasantry, a
     decree that has been awarded the status of law by the 6th Article
     from 1945.

10. Law 20/1949 on the Constitution of the Hungarian Republic; Article 55, paragraph 3.

11. Decree No. 104/1989 of the Council of Ministers (dated the 4th of October).

12. The law instructed the Council of Ministers to solve the problems regarding employment and social security for people whose conviction had to be considered null and for people who have been kept under police surveillance. It is worthwhile to recall the motivation given for this specific article of the law. It declared that though the nullification meant the legal, moral and political rehabilitation of the convict, apart from alleviating disadvantages in the field of social security "no further property-related compensation is possible because of the country's [limited] capacity to carry burdens. Paying compensation for the victims of these legal injuries is impossible because this would impose an unjust burden on the present generation."

13. The resolution listed all groups the parliament considered to be entitled to compensation. These were: persons convicted illegally; internees—including also the people who were detained in the Recsk labour camp—forcibly relocated persons; prisoners of war; civilians of whom the majority spoke German as their native language or had Germanic family names, and who have been deported to the Soviet Union for labour or have been convicted by Soviet courts.

14. The parliament adopted the Law No. 32/1992 on the compensation of persons who have been illegally deprived of their life and freedom, the Law No. 52/1992 on national care, the Law No. 45/1994 on the provision of military care as well as the 3rd Law of Nullification, that is, Law No. 11/1992 regarding the nullification of convictions for certain crimes committed against the state and the public order between 1963 and 1989.

15. There is, of course, a considerable overlap between some of these areas. Hence, other classifications may be imagined as well.

16. However, being aware of the content of numberless rulings of the constitutional court it can be concluded that the principles of compensation passed the test of judicial review. Furthermore, most of the stipulations stood the test of time and proved to be executable, legally speaking.

17. While processing compensation claims two things that could be substantiated with factual evidence became obvious to everybody. First,

the so-called liberation and the popular democracy that followed it meant, in fact, a serious infringement upon the liberty of hundreds of thousands of people. Furthermore, communism gained ground in Hungary using the bloody means of terror. Second, the economic system that fell in a serious crisis in the mid 1980s has been created through massive and unscrupulous elimination of private property.

18. Otherwise, unconditional and total compensation of certain persons—either by returning the properties that have been taken away, or by paying them the current market value of the withdrawn assets—would have meant discrimination against other persons whose claims were to be denied. Deciding about the owners' entitlements to have their original properties returned would have already raised constitutional doubts. This state of affairs is due to the fact that the state acquired the property rights over an asset through wrongful application of a certain law several times, and hence—most notably in the case of agricultural land—because of an asset's transferral into state property several persons could have rightfully applied for in kind compensation. One could reasonably argue: the first owner should be the beneficiary of in kind compensation; nevertheless, all the others could claim compensatory payments. The consequence of such a settlement would have been the restoration of the property relationships extant in Hungary before 1945 and the immediate payment of a single, total indemnity equivalent to the current market value of the property to all former owners except for the first one. This solution was neither economically, nor politically practicable. It would have not been workable even if one did not consider the owner from 1945 as the one who was entitled to in kind compensation, because the national economy lacked the financial coverage needed to compensate owners by paying them the current market value of the assets. Most probably not even a delayed payment deadline would have sold this problem.

19. Ruling No. 21/1990 of the constitutional court (dated the 4th of October) on the interpretation of Article 70/A of the constitution.

20. The constitutional court did not find satisfactory constitutional motivations for discriminating between former proprietors, because the motion did not present arguments that could provide a basis for allowing the limitation of fundamental constitutional rights. The answer given by the ruling to the second question emphasised the constitutional rule that the withdrawal of property could be carried

out only without awarding immediate, unconditional and total compensation. Any withdrawal of property that did not satisfy these criteria was unconstitutional.

21. There is no possibility to give an account of the most important details of the parliamentary debate. Nonetheless, it must be pointed out that the MSZP wanted to exempt the co-operatives from bearing the burdens of compensation; moreover, it wished to grant them compensation as well. Furthermore, the MSZP wanted to award a compensation amounting to a total sum of HUF 80 billion not only to the former proprietors, but also to the employees in the form of compensation vouchers having the total value of another HUF 80 billion. SZDSZ (Alliance of Free Democrats) considered that people were awarded only a small compensation and wanted to grant every Hungarian citizen a sum of 20,000 HUF. For the SZDSZ reparation meant return of property or indemnification exceeding this amount of money in value. FIDESZ tried to call attention to the insecure future of younger generations and, consequently, opposed all kinds of compensation. Naturally, there have been recipients of partial reprivatisation even among members of the parties that formed the governing coalition.

22. Ruling No. 16/1991 of the constitutional court (dated the 20th of April).

23. Our opinion is that the constitutional court contradicted itself slightly in this matter. This happened when declaring in this very same ruling that within the framework of compensation the state satisfies claims that are not of a legal nature and discriminates between persons who do not hold *a priori* entitlements, but awards goods to beneficiaries on the basis of fairness. Our point of view is the following: in what concerns a part of the persons who had a right to be compensated, the law-maker renewed his previous, undisputed obligations the basis of which were of various natures. Consequently, one cannot say about these persons that they previously could make no valid legal claims towards the state. Nevertheless, it is beyond doubt that by widening the scope of compensation the same entitlement—namely, fairness—becomes the basis of all claims made by persons who incurred losses, no matter whether previous laws promised them compensation or not.

24. Ruling No. 28/1991 of the constitutional court (dated the 3rd of June).

25. It is not the task of the present paper to give a detailed explanation of the problems related to the legal institution of auctions. It can be established as a fact: the idea of auctions passed the test of judicial review. In this respect, it eliminated in a satisfactory manner the unconstitutional aspect found in the original draft. Moreover, in spite of all the rumours that preceded its application and the fierce attacks mounted against the idea by a wide range of societal groups, its practical implementation proved that it represented a workable solution.

26. Governmental Decree No. 101/1991 (dated the 27th of July).

27. There is no possibility to speak here and now about this process. It is, however, worth mentioning that the narrow-minded approach that took into account only budgetary constraints (this being either a manifestation of carelessness or of bad faith) created huge difficulties that had to be overcome in order to implement the laws adopted by the Parliament. NRCO's budget for 1992 could have easily meant the failure of implementation. A total fiasco has been prevented by the supplementary allotment received during the year. Still, it was impossible to totally eliminate the delay suffered by the process of implementation, albeit all the personnel worked as hard as they could. The six months deadline prescribed by the law for processing the claims was impossible to meet from the very beginning. The lengthy processing of petitions that sometimes lasted for years elicited righteous indignation. This happened mostly with persons who were unaware of the state of affairs. Requiring from the office personnel to perform beyond the limits of their strength, was a natural cause for making erroneous decisions.

28. Making these inventories listing the total amount of land that has been claimed represented an almost unsolvable problem for administrative organs because an incredible amount of data was missing from the applications, the inventories kept by land repartition offices were disorderly and the two month deadline was rather short. The employees of the compensation and land repartition offices worked almost round the clock to fill in the missing and correct the mistaken data. In this manner, it became possible the meet the deadline that was the most critical one from the point of view of the law's implementation. On the basis of these notifications, one could identify the amount of available land and mark off the areas destined for compensatory auctions. Only after valid decisions on identifying the amount of available land have been issued, could one make prepara-

tions for auctions. The workload of the land repartition offices increased. Besides accomplishing their everyday tasks, their personnel had to find and provide the evidence that had to be attached to the applications handed in by the persons who were entitled to compensation or to receive proportional shares of the available land. They also took part in the process of checking the legality of the decisions regarding the identification of available land and of measuring the plots destined for auctions.

29. This paper does not intend to investigate this problem. Above all, defending compensation at any price is not its purpose. The effects of compensation on Hungarian agriculture are extremely complex and complicated; therefore, only a group of specialists having special expertise could satisfactorily deal with it. Formulating a well-balanced, carefully thought out opinion on compensation that is shielded from current political interests requires the carrying out of previous research covering all broad areas connected to compensation and a thorough in-depth investigation.

30. When evaluating the effects of auctions, one must bear in mind that the assets the state offered as an alternative to farmland for being purchased using as means of payment compensation vouchers totalled a far smaller value than that of agricultural lands. This was a strong incentive to participate in auctions even for people who had no intention whatsoever of buying farmland.

31. The constitutional court summoned parliament to eliminate the unconstitutional disposition and set a deadline. Parliament eliminated the disposition in question though it failed to meet the prescribed deadline. In consequence, the legality of the ownership rights over farmland acquired by means of these warrants cannot be questioned any more. The intention of the law-maker when it introduced the institution of these warrants was to secure advantageous starting conditions for entrepreneurs who intended to start an agricultural business requiring a considerable area of farmland.

32. The motivational part of the ruling gave helpful hints concerning the solutions that could have been taken into account.

33. At that moment, already the general trend in public opinion was to object to compensation. Those who were keen on turning public opinion against compensation were unable to realise that a country where the rule of law has been established cannot afford itself to fail to award reparation for legal injuries, even if reparation were partial.

Otherwise, social morals would be shaken from their fundaments and the results would be a severe identity crisis and ethical chaos. And these characterise the state of affairs we experience and suffer from at present.

34. Published in issue no. 43/1997 of the Hungarian Bulletin.

35. Governmental Decree No. 93/1990 (dated the 21st of November).

36. Governmental Decree No. 74/1991 (dated the 10th of June).

37. Governmental Decree No. 112/1991 (dated the 2nd of September).

38. Governmental Decree No. 6/1992 (dated the 8th of January).

39. Governmental Decree No. 51/1992 (dated the 18th of March) dealt with the pecuniary claims and complementary pensions to which former persons who felt as prisoners of war in the hands of Western powers earned entitlements.

40. Governmental Decree No. 174/1992 (dated the 29th of December).

41. See: Ruling No. 1/1995 of the constitutional court (dated the 2nd of February).

42. Our opinion on this matter is fundamentally different. Illegal executions and detentions create an obligation for the state to offer some compensation.

43. See: Ruling No. 22/1996 of the constitutional court (dated the 25th of June). This ruling attests that in this area of regulation it is extremely difficult to elaborate a piece of legislation that would be satisfactory according to all criteria of constitutionality.

44. The coverage of the value of compensation vouchers has been, after all, ensured by the state property that had to be privatised. The explanation is that the compensation vouchers collected during the auctions held for purchasing farmland that was owned by co-operatives, and the ones accepted by local governments as payment for flats could be used by these two in the process of privatisation. Apart form the land auctions, purchasing of flats owned by local governments, exchange for annuity and subsistence credits the privatisation of state property represented another possibility to put compensation vouchers to use. In the conception of the law-maker, this last possibility would have allowed everybody to invest his/her compensation voucher according to his/her own plans and possibilities, intentions and educational background.

45. Paragraph 1 of Resolution No. 3275/1993 of the Government instructed the ÁV Rt. (State Property Fund) and the ÁVÜ (State Property Agency) to offer for privatisation properties totalling 5-6

billion HUF in exchange for compensation vouchers. The deadline to accomplish this task has been set to the 15th of August 1993. Paragraph 2 of the same resolution instructed the organisations controlling state property to elaborate by the mentioned deadline a concerted plan and a schedule regarding the privatisation in exchange for compensation vouchers of properties totalling HUF 220 billion. The ministry of privatisation held the responsibility for carrying out these tasks. The deadline has not been met, no results have been achieved. Still, nobody from the organisations controlling state property, nor the minister has been held accountable.

46. The nominal value of compensation vouchers increased with the interest rate published monthly by the NRCO. There was no need to issue a new compensation voucher having the value of the interest, because the law contained stipulations in this sense. However, thousands of people complained that they had not received the interest and felt that the NRCO harmed them when neglecting to pay the interest. This reaction is very natural: if one deposited capital in the bank, the interest was credited yearly to his/her account and that sum of money could have been withdrawn in cash.

47. The decision made by the government regarding the modest amount of the annuity was made after fiery disputes. The reasons for adopting such a position were fear of inflation and desire to avoid overburdening the budget. The opinion we are able to formulate in retrospect is that these fears proved to be unmotivated.

Gyula Tellér

FOUR ESSAYS ON COMMUNIST
AND "POST-COMMUNIST" HUNGARY

1. The Fall of Man

The working-class struggle under Rákosi

The socialism introduced into Hungary after 1947, in the spirit of Marxism-Leninism, turned the entire economy into "one production plant", in which the place of the proprietor was taken by the newly-established ruling political class (to supervise the planning mechanism), and in which the role of the manager was played by medium-caliber activists chosen by the above-mentioned political class, and in which all the rest became the former categories' employees: industrial workers. The working-class, which primarily resulted from the elimination of the bourgeoisie made up of formerly independent individuals, emerged from rather heterogeneous groups of people: from the politically conscious workers of the industrial regions that developed before 1945; from elements of the lumpenproletariat; from peasants that either could not find employment in or were banished from agricultural cooperatives; from merchants, tradesmen, other independent individuals; or from people who had not been employed earlier (such as housewives). This heterogeneous population was held together by the all-spanning, pyramid-like workers' organization (which included everyone from the Central Committee to porters and cleaning women); by working-class laws that stipulated the duty to work and severely punished any kind of opposition; by trade unions that had become the tools, the "messengers" of the ruling class; by singling out those who did not fit into the socialist hierarchy; by political and physical terror; and by the party itself—the informal but essential component of every organization—that observed, operated and carried out all these functions.

Among the more cohesive forces in such a society, an important role was undoubtedly played by the manpower so necessary for such extensive industrial development (and by the increasing material security and employment rate ensured by it); by the introduction of compulsory 8-year school education; by access to cheap popular culture and inexpensive reading materials; by the perspective of intellectual careers for the working-class and the inclusion of some of its members in different leading and managerial positions. All these were based on the kind of division of goods that brought success to the top one-third of the society, and to the formerly middle-class bourgeoisie—which had previously amounted to two-thirds of society—only ruin.

The ruling ideology meanwhile cheered the workers' life, it raised the welder or miner to the symbolic status of hero, it did away with achievement-based appreciation of workers' performance and it added colour to workers' lives by noisy and spectacular rituals: propagandistic march-songs, demonstrations, beer-and-sausage filled festivals of the people, heroics, high-sounding speeches.

However, behind this spectacular facade, workers tried from the very beginning to gain advantages through open or secret demands for pay rises, while negligence, poor-quality work, obscured production figures, ignorance of new working techniques and losses through pilfering were all familiar phenomena. Members of the ruling class, on the other hand, strove to recover production costs even at a loss, to bring the ratio of output and wages nearer to the planned one.

In 1956, the so often threatened, oppressed and cheated working-class grabbed weapons and rushed to chase away their oppressors and re-establish their pre-socialist way of living. Needless to say, the repression which followed the crushing of the revolution first of all targeted the same groups.

Kádár's compromise

The prudence of the Kádár-regime can be seen in the way that, having put down the 1956 uprising, it then tried hard to turn the confrontations with the workers (whose members still had memories of their middle-class upbringing into the '60s), into a compromise-agreement to cooperate. This compromise became known as the New Economic Mechanism. Its imagined essence was the linkage of income as assessed in a simulated market to the results achieved in factories—and within those to individual performances. This bargain was supposed to be guaranteed by the local representative of the ruling political class, that is the factory manager, the person meant to guard the common wealth (who was well-paid for his job and who later was even included among the political elite).

However, the means of resistance acquired by the workers back in the '50s proved stronger than the managers, who continued thinking in terms of extensive development and demanding more and more labour. In the poorly-organized industrial plants the week-long bad-quality work went on, as did the hasty work at the end of each month. Meanwhile, another compromise was taking shape around the capacity-resources that lay in the workers' hands, which meant frequent change of jobs from one factory to another used as a tactic of both pressing for better-paid jobs and of lowering productivity. In face of the pressure concealed in these means, the circle of factory managers who could not forget '56 and who feared political conflict chose the easier way out. The output achieved by each one's factory was increased not primarily through individual workers' improved performance (which would have meant sharpening the conflict between workers and management), but through acquiring a higher percentage of the centralized income, which involved maintaining the compromise in the political sphere and—as a result of this—making new investments and employing more manpower. This is to say that the distributive struggle between the political elite and society was not successfully decentralized. Moreover, the economy, which was extensively developed and so much concerned with income redistribution at various levels, swallowed disorderly and badly-qualified labour as well. This situation strengthened the basic bargaining-power of workers.

Thus, the compromises of the '60s and '70s only partly led to an increase in productivity and modernization of the economy, and mostly rested on forcefully placing the outflow of income under the tax-ceiling and on the discovery of fresh labour resources. It also relied on the technologically unimpressive state investments; on placing big industrial companies in the provinces; on setting up and developing ancillary plants within agricultural cooperatives; and above all, on allowing the means of production (land, buildings, machines, tools, loans) to be owned and administered privately as sources of private income.

Still, the market-type operation, the more modern means and techniques employed in production, replaced the attitude of the plan-executing company chief with that of the resource-administering manager. After some time, the manager, together with his team of specialists (engineers, technicians, lawyers, financial advisors and economists) took over more and more of the decisions formerly made by planning authorities and party committees, and started administering company property as though it were his own. Thus did the company and institution-leading elite themselves became part of the compromise-agreement between politicians and the society.

After 1956 the ruling political class only once more engaged the old fighting technique of the Rákosi-regime: during the 1974-75 campaign led by Béla Biszku, which ended in failure. The Hungarian working-class—and, to a lesser extent, the managers' class—may have had (and actually did have) the common sense and ultimately the conscience to contribute to the real compromise between the political elite and society.

City on the back of a whale

The socialist economy and society that before 1956 functioned as "one labour camp" had radically changed by the '70s and '80s through the development of the processes begun in the '60s. The system of secondary employment encompassed the vast majority of the economy (household farming, making things on the side, outsourcing to private artisans, intellectual work, private hotel businesses, etc.) and this was the case of the workers with a solid peasant upbringing as well. Put more simply: the workers (and the peasants) usually engaged the smaller part of their manpower in operating the valuable socialist industrial and agricultural equipment, whereas with their manpower's other—usually bigger—part they operated their own private property equipment to produce for the market. From this complementary secondary employment, supporting each other especially in the country, an entire, independent economic sector—the so-called "secondary economy"—emerged. The socialist economy, so badly lacking in output, could not do without the bulk of goods and services provided by this—which is why the political leadership encouraged the practice of secondary employment.

As a result, the individual worker earned himself material security (not too high wages, social security, pension) by working 5 to 6 hours in the socialist workplace, while, by using the remainder of his working capacity, he acquired almost unlimited surplus income, which he used to buy a house, tools, machinery, what have you. The material growth resulting from secondary employment, as well as the necessary specialized and market economy knowledge, caused workers and agricultural cooperative members to differentiate, to turn into a kind of "socialist" workers' bourgeoisie.

All this focussed the workers' resistance around output-planning and income-distribution. The lack of organization in socialist companies, the oscillating capacity-demand, the factories' need for labour resources, made it possible for the negotiations regarding the workers' struggle to be embedded in the working process itself. And in these negotiations the workers, who benefited from unlimited employment opportunities, financial security (thanks to the income from their secondary employment), and who possessed the necessary stamina, were still in a stronger position than their employers. In the low output industrial branches, whose survival could only be secured by massive central redistribution, the trade union and party elite themselves, together with the managers, did their best to maintain workplace stability and, implicitly, the workers' strong position in this bargain. All these encompassed the only safe form of workers' struggle: the unorganized, secluded, profit and individual survival-oriented, but massively one-directional output-, wages- and resource-negotiating struggle, manifested in job mobility and extra income from second jobs.

Under these circumstances, after having trodden on the bourgeoisie in 1947-49, and later in 1956, the ruling political class sinned for the third time: instead of pressing for higher achievements in accordance with their own ideology, or instead of adjusting consumption to production even at the expense of social conflicts, they hid the lack of output sensed in the negative balance of foreign trade and the continual worsening of the exchange rate, and resorted to foreign sources to cover it up. The gradually developing socialist workers' bourgeoisie and, generally speaking, the success and stability of individual workers' lives, thus became similar to the town in the fairy-tale built on the back of a whale: it could go down at any time.

Going down

Starting in the second half of the '80s and during the following ten years, this downfall actually came to pass. The foreign debts could not be sustained any longer, and in the absence of funds, the artificially maintained building industries, steelworks and heavy industrial giants collapsed. As a result of the collapse of foreign markets, the low-technology light industrial plants established in the second wave of socialist industrialization and the third-wave provincial industrial regions, as well as the ancillary branches of agricultural cooperatives, all met the same fate. Alongside the constant, chronic shortage of labour, mass unemployment came into existence. Commuters from the country withdrew in the countryside, where agriculture was also "producing" unemployment. The low-qualified or unqualified workers hoping to find a job dwindled. Decreasing consumption then caused the secondary-employment market to disappear or shrink. Thus, the second support of the workers' way-of-life was shaken. *The double (half-worker, half-bourgeois) life of the greater part of the bourgeois-oriented society was reduced to the status of the proletariat.* Next inflation started to eat up people's savings. Industries that were re-organized or newly-established in the privatization process squeezed workers' right out of the working process, and even of the factory or plant, as factory committees and trade unions themselves began to disappear.

The strength and fighting spirit of the working-class, so well-established in the position of negotiators during the Kádár regime, vanished almost completely within just a few years. The members of the ruling class that had formerly held a weak position as collective owners and of the managing bourgeoisie rapidly gained in strength by becoming private owners. Thanks to their earlier-acquired position of quasi-proprietors, their knowledge and organization, they laid their hands on the once common property, banishing the workers turned into half-bourgeois from using it. They were generally successful in tightening work-organization and increasing manpower efficiency. Making use of the manipulative techniques so well learnt while still members of the political elite, they easily defeated their rivals and enemies who appeared at the moment of change. Trade unions that were supposed to represent workers' interests proved mostly inefficient in organizing and leading the fight at the level of the factory. But the workers themselves were also mostly inefficient in this respect, though their only strength would have been organized group action. As we have seen, they were made inefficient for this both by the kind of action they were used to in the Kádár regime, an action based on individual compromise, individual strategies for survival, which served as a socializing model, and by their spirituality attuned to the half-bourgeois individual presence on the market. In this way the new workplaces (first of all, plant committees) established as a result of the change in the system, were not supported by organized force. And we can add: besides the new proprietors, the new political elite that was undoing the intricate socialist redistribution system was also interested in the destruction of the traditional trade union bureaucracy and in the weakening of a working-class with conservative interests.

Abandoned

At this point of our overview, one can hardly resist the temptation to further elaborate on the political absurdity of the change of system. For instance, we could discuss the steps in which the representatives of the party that traditionally got on well with the traditional trade unions (but also included among its members most of the new manager-owners), did their best to trim the factory committees' mandates so as to meet the expectations of the friendly trade unions, so that in a later step they could strangle these very trade unions that depended on them, by making them sign deals that were unacceptable and by making informal offers to their skilled and earlier brave leaders so that the latter would resign and their followers give up their membership. One thing seems certain: so far, the factory committees have not really made things happen in the companies privatized by this very party's political and managerial elite, and the traditional trade unions of the working class also represented in Parliament proved "disciplined"—just like in the good old times—during and after their great setback. It is hard to resist the thought that, riding the tide of social discontent in 1993, the very people who got into Parliament were those who had done most to give rise to this discontent.

It is also hard not to wonder at how easy it was for the earlier political elite to renounce socialism in favour of privatization, and how quickly they started taking over ownership of the formerly common goods, and how when these ran out they moved nimbly into pyramid-games, vodka-production, counterfeit petrol, imports of non-existing cars, and thousands of other things, all in order to further rob the population and above all the workers. It is clearly visible that the recovery by the population of that part of the national income that had formerly been redistributed has long been dictated not by the needs of macroeconomic equilibrium, but exclusively by the superior power of these owners, whose amazing income accumulation does not result from economic input (and has so far led to hardly any economic output). Finally, we can hardly resist analyzing the surprising fact that the Hungarian working-class deeply trusts these very political forces. Somehow, the "worker-bourgeois" mostly hampered in becoming fully bourgeois trusts the "politician-bourgeois" and "manager-bourgeois" who are doing them out of their inheritance—not to mention their future.

However, instead of recalling political memories, let us stick to present facts. Out of five and a half million employees in 1986, today there are roughly three and a half million. The vast majority of those who have lost their jobs can be called former workers. The working-class, following the pattern they got used to in the Kádár regime and their individual survival strategies, responded not by uniting their forces or by actively striving to establish the social and working conditions of the new system together, but—where it was possible—by complying with the new conditions, and—where that was impossible—by bearing their isolation from economic integration and by arranging their lives so as merely to survive. On the one hand, they responded by unnecessarily giving up the factory council, the trade union, the collective contract, the retraining and professional re-orientation scheme, and on the other by resorting to the black market, small-scale trading, renouncing essential needs, by loosening the forces that had held society together, by criminality, or even passivity, by hopelessness, depression, neurosis.

2. Changes in Land Ownership During the Transition

Marx and Bernstein

Socialism, as a means of solving 19th century economic and social problems, was founded by Marx and his many followers, in essence by taking into account the mid-19th century image of society. It was assumed then that there were no limits to ownership and so to social polarization. As regards industrial means of production and financial capital, this was certainly the case. (As regards land, the situation is different). Taking this process to its extreme endpoint, we find on one side of the fence a handful of tycoons, and on the other the robbed, discontented and revolution-inclined masses of society that have sunk to the status of the proletariat. In other words, society becomes *bipolarized*.

In these circumstances, it is enough for a small group of determined revolutionaries to drive out the handful of owners, take over their property and possessions, and as absolute owners, manage the now concentrated means of production in conformity with a plan and distribute the income among various groups and members of society as they see fit. In this so-established new society, the major means of exercising power is property, and each property is managed by a handful of revolutionaries, by the political elite; all the rest are employees, work is compulsory and the hierarchical and disciplined work organization encompasses the entire society.

Thanks to Bernstein, we all know that—contrary to Marx—from the second half of the 19th century, besides or despite this polarization, the levelling out of income and property made an increasing impression, such that more and more independent small- and mid-scale owners emerged. This happened not only in industry, commerce, state administration, cultural life, etc., but in agriculture as well. In fact, instead of having a bipolar society, a *tri-polar* society emerged. The members of this third pole entirely or partly based their living on the income or utilization of their property. This layer of small- and middle-scale proprietors did not fit in with the above-mentioned socialist image either because of their living standard (which did not depend on large-scale, top-down work organizations) or because of their independent thinking and behaviour (tending to organize things for themselves), or because of their property—which could not be directly included in the planned economy.

The bourgeoisie and socialism

In mid-century Hungary, society—which was both economically and socially fairly well-developed—also showed features of this tri-polar structure. After the 1944-47 land distribution, the small- and middle-proprietors and other middle-class people made up between half and two-thirds of the total population. The largest group among these was that of agricultural small- and middle-scale proprietors. This tri-polar structure was also reflected in Hungarian society's relationship to communism. The number of those who voted for the Communist Party in the two democratic elections before the communist takeover did not reach twenty percent. The Hungarian bourgeoisie did not go in for communism.

Obviously, the main objective—besides other, not insignificant secondary objectives—of the two important campaigns of socialist cooperative organization of 1949-53 and 1958-60 was to eradicate this small- and middle-scale bourgeoisie, who did not fit in with socialism, to expropriate them and to turn them into workers, proles, subjects. The strongly hierarchical cooperatives fitted tightly into the new centrally-run economy, as the Soviet-supported political elite became the exclusive and absolute owner of all means of production.

Still, the result of agricultural expropriation—like that of other kinds of nationalization—was strongly ambiguous. Indeed ownership of land and equipment was denied to these former proprietors. But it is also true that the nationalized property, as well as the property organized in cooperatives, was never really better managed by its new owners than its previous ones.

The emergence of future owners

The consequences, the historical facts are well known. In 1956, the expropriated and humiliated bourgeoisie spoke up. The socialist ownership-class (which in fact meant no owners), operated with high transaction costs, inefficiently and chaotically. The result was poverty, discontent and unrest. Yes, the communist ruling elite—again with Soviet assistance—went on ruling after the revolution as well. And also, the second wave of collectives came only after the revolution. But it is also a fact that the ruling group admitted that they could not rule in opposition to *the whole of society*; therefore, they made compromise-agreements with several different groups. Of these, we are primarily interested in two.

The ruling elite made one such compromise with the average members of society—among these, members of agricultural cooperatives—allowing them to produce in their old, pre-communist way, by using their small assets and manpower, and to acquire extra wealth which would release resources that had formerly been unusable. This was the so-called secondary economy.

The ruling elite made its second compromise with lower-level, party executives and economic leaders. They were trusted with most of the decisions concerning companies and cooperatives. They were thus included in ruling local society and received huge salaries for their services, which were closely related to political loyalty and less closely related to economic output.

The first group consisted of repressed, frightened members of the destroyed bourgeoisie, who were unable to organize themselves politically, who were happy to be allowed to occasionally own and operate at least other people's property—if not what had been their own. The second group dominated the first using all authoritarian manipulative skills: as local authorities, they were aware of their mission, they had their own ethos, they held all the resources of the local community, they felt absolutely necessary, thanks to their experience in ruling, and beginning with the '70s they gradually came to look upon the property (companies, cooperatives) that they operated as their own. They were looking forward to changing their unofficial, occasional ownership into official, real, final ownership. Moreover, they felt they had the necessary power for this, and so they did. Later on, this secret relationship between the self-appointed owner and his future property became the principal driving force, the defining feature of current social and political processes.

The issue of privatization was therefore the outcome of the first, aggressive period of socialism; the group aspiring to privatization that of the second, compromise-prone period; and the final form of property to be privatized the outcome of the third, declining period.

Some features of the process of cooperative property acquisition

It was in the third period of socialism at the beginning of the '80s that the time came for real property acquisition, for the switch from socialist "group ownership" to individual ownership, when, as a result of repeated economic difficulties (e.g. increasing foreign debt, deteriorating standard of living) the power and prestige of the central ruling group, who maintained socialism but who had become old (to use a contemporary expression, "had mummified"), were shaken and socialism itself began to fall. Ever since, the central ruling elite has no longer been able to stop the process of leader-based property acquisition, and the repressed and isolated local community has not been able to, either.

Since the early '80s, under the ideological guise of increased efficiency and democratization, the local political elite and the leading groups in cooperatives have been constantly struggling to demolish the socialist properties that hindered the privatization of cooperative property. This struggle has been marked by some important moments at the level of cooperative movements: the preparation of new laws regarding the cooperatives to serve the interest of those who carry out privatization; the redistribution of the common, indivisible wealth among cooperatives; the removal of party bureaucrats from leading positions and the appointment of new cooperative chairpersons; the subordination of cooperative associations to certain cooperatives (not to the members but to the chairperson); the limitation of the state's legal means of interference; the proclamation of the absolute divisibility of property; the termination of compulsory activity and, hence, the possibility to squeeze out redundant members; the permission for legal bodies to become members; the re-shaping of cooperatives so as to look more like share companies, divided by "inner businesses". This line of struggle includes the two laws concerning cooperatives from 1992. Still more recent developments (e.g. the move to renounce the "one member—one vote" principle; the unlimited presence of legal bodies; and the dispute whether to allow cooperatives to own land or not, etc.) point in the same direction.

The principles and details of the processes of privatization and compensation in the Hungarian agricultural cooperatives, which have been going on since 1989, are quite well-known. The outcome of these processes seems to be the ultradivision of both agricultural land ownership, and estate- and equipment-ownership. In fact, ever since the very beginning of this process of division, and independently of this, there has been a considerable reconcentration as well. Its beneficiaries are the former local managerial and political elite, and to a smaller extent some professional people and other groups.

In 1989, when the cooperatives were allowed to sell land, but nobody was interested in buying it, the chairpersons and managers invested their extraordinary bonuses, voted by themselves for themselves, in considerable stretches of land bought from their own cooperatives. In other words, with the approval of the management, and with the mediation of some outside financial assistance, they transferred land to themselves. The strongly undervalued cooperative wealth (livestock, chemicals, you name it) was simply transferred to their own companies. Later, they cheaply bought up the often intentionally bankrupt cooperative property; stopped the competing new companies from getting loans (thanks to their old connections); caused them to go bankrupt, then bought them up, paying with their own money or money borrowed from banks (again thanks to their old connections); bought up cheap land and undervalued shares—possibly paying for these with cooperative money; set up their own companies based on the most profitable activity of the cooperative, etc. The array of means to acquire such wealth is indeed large.

The probable outcome

The change of ownership has not come to an end. Moreover, we do not have access to reliable information about its most important moments. This is why we can only offer an approximate image of its outcome. According to statistics, one-third of the agricultural cooperatives that were functional in 1988 have gone down and disappeared. Their decent-quality assets were bought mostly by wealthy local leaders. Most—some say one-third, others half—of the wealth and equipment of the former cooperatives that still exist as share companies or cooperatives is in the hands of a closed group of such figures. One-third of the agricultural land that was so much divided in the compensation process is also in the hands of five to ten families in each village. And this is only the beginning.

But why should this be a problem, we might ask. It is really desirable that the ownership of equipment and land should be to some extent concentrated. It is also an advantage that this concentration should be done by those with agricultural knowledge. In the modern world, most developed agricultural sectors operate based on large concentrations of land that is managed and owned by the same concern.

Well, yes, but in these countries, beside the concentration of property, there were also laid the existential foundations of the middle layers of society. In Hungary, however, the new, post-socialist wealth and property concentration led to the serious pauperization of the rural community. In contrast to the Kádár regime's hazy promises of welfare, rural unemployment is around 20%, and in some underdeveloped areas, around 30% (the national average being 11-12%).

All this points to the fact that socialism robbed a lot of people of their wealth, but as a result of the changes this wealth has become the property of the powerful few, while 60-80% of the society is without a means to make an independent living. To go back to the picture drawn in the introduction: as a result of the present changes in ownership, Hungarian society has become similar not so much to its 1947 tri-polar shape, but to the bipolar structural state of the 19th-century Europe or of 20th-century Latin America. Moreover, the political parties now in government, the Socialists and the Free Democrats, as successors of the old Communist Party which maintained the bipolar system of socialist society for over forty years, and as the political representatives of the class of big-time owners, are themselves interested in maintaining this new social structure.

3. The Liberal Approach to Property

The essence of liberalism, in its "pure" form, as it appeared in the 18th and 19th centuries, was the idea of individualism and of liberty. Both ideas were directed against the class relationships and absolute power of late feudalism in all its spiritual, moral and economic dimensions. However, the demand for the individual's respect and freedom developed around two perceptions. One perception viewed the individual himself, without any qualification, and advocated the idea that everyone has equal rights to cultivate their personality, to lead an active and happy life and to possess the means necessary for this life. Therefore, if the injustice of biological or social accidents deprives the individual from developing his personality, or from the means of acquiring these necessary skills or conditions (basic livelihood, education and training, etc.), these means will have to be secured for him by rational—though limited—redistribution. The other perception of liberalism regards the individual as the owner of goods, tools and capital, and urges his absolute freedom in this respect, so that by the freedom of contract, the elimination of class privilege, the avoidance or minimization of state redistribution, he can do whatever he pleases with his property and the fruit of his property, including dominate others. The first perception of liberalism could be called "individual-liberalism", whereas the second could perhaps be termed "property-liberalism".

It is obvious that in the last two centuries individual-liberalism has given rise to social democracy (and its extreme variant, Marxism-Leninism), and property-liberalism has led to "free market liberalism", which now and then gets to govern and fails, and whose major representatives today are the disciples of Hayek and Friedman. Individual-liberalism and property-liberalism have been fighting each other from the beginning, as their interests are related to the same part of a person's income, which should either be redistributed or stopped from being redistributed.

Early 19th century capitalism, which basically relied on the concept of property-liberalism, demonstrated that the owner of capital, now freed from feudal restrictions and advocating unlimited liberty, possessed such power as to be able to dissolve the living fabric of the society, squeezing more and more people out of their social position and forcing them to lead a sub-human life. The resulting phenomena of mass unemployment, urban misery, moral degradation and hopelessness are all well-known. In order to slow down this "raging" destructive capital ownership, in the 19th and 20th centuries several social forces took measures—above all those animated by the principle of Christian charity or humanistic intellectuals. Then, with ever increasing intensity, the state started to intervene to stop society falling apart. Later, the victims themselves began reacting, the working-class organizing its power in trade unions and parliamentary parties. Finally, acting as a kind of bridge across the chasm of polarization, small- and medium-sized property-owners started to emerge, and used their increasing material and spiritual force both to defend their own interests and to limit the destructive power of large capital owners.

As a result of all this, the last-mentioned changed from being one side of a bipolar society, to being one force in a tripolar (owners—middle-layers—workers) world. In the process, the fight for income redistribution was confined to a relatively narrow part of the national income, because on the one hand there was a limit imposed by the falling economic output caused by exaggerated income-subtraction, and on the other there was another limit set by mass discontent and social unrest caused by unfair redistribution. Property-liberalism and its related ethos (property is the driving force of social development, the guarantee of the common weal, etc) and slogans ("everything is allowed as long as it does not limit the like freedom of others") stopped being the defining social ideology and came and went again over the course of the 20th century depending on circumstance. Today we can say that it is one of the central ideologies for Western European societies, albeit always pressed and tested by other social forces and ideologies (socialism, conservatism, Christian morality, etc.) according to the given situation.

In Hungary, property-liberalism was revived under radically different circumstances from those obtaining in today's Western Europe. In the still socialist '80s, Hungarian society was basically bipolar and consisted of the layer of the political elite and institution managers at one pole, and the majority made up of workers and employees more generally at the other. Between them was a broad layer made up of people with a kind of double-status: half-workers, half-small bourgeoisie. But the bourgeois half of their livelihood was not based on genuine ownership and the resultant social relations, but rather on informal political conventions—which fell to pieces in the reforms. The two marginal social groups were not in a dynamic equilibrium with each other. The system was characterized by the fact that it placed too much power (control over property, the position of employer, connections, monopoly of knowledge and information, etc.) in the hands of the managers and directors of institutions, as well as by its helplessness about society's unpredictable movements. In matters of distribution and other issues raised between various elite groups, as well as between the elite and the society, it was the selfish decisions of the increasingly weaker and thinner political elite that established an equilibrium. This was, however, the only role of the late socialist political class. Society as a whole was incapable of organizing itself in front of the power of this elite: it could only exert an amorphous mass power. It was made incapable of organized action both by its moral and its spiritual condition.

The socialist form of ownership and operation of property in which the entire class of political proprietors was linked to the entire stock of property in the country, was only capable of operating the means of production at increasingly low levels of efficiency. Already there were significant changes beginning with the '60s and '70s. The managers, together with more and more members of the local leadership, started treating the property temporarily entrusted to them as if it were their own—indeed, they thought of it as that, and tried hard to achieve the connection between certain means of production (factory, plants, cooperatives, branches, department, tools, land, etc.) and certain people or groups of leaders. This is to say: they connected themselves to the property handled by them.

Under these circumstances, the spreading ideology of property-liberalism had a particular role. Its advocates argued for the necessity of recreating private ownership—in contrast to the views of the political elite, which remained interested in the unchanged maintenance of socialist power relations. In the view of the former, the reason for the low economic efficiency of socialism was that the owner had disappeared and with him all responsibility towards the use of property. So they set up the idealized image of the "real owner", the cliché of "Of course, in a *real* market economy". They tried to justify to other members of the society, in the spirit of this ideology, why they were meant to treat property as if it were their own. Contrary to the ethos of the Rákosi regime, in the Kádár regime—from the introduction of the New Economic Mechanism onwards—the ethos of the manager, who laid the basis of the more-or-less competitive factories, appeared and spread. This was the ethos of the professionalism demonstrated by economic leaders' group. The manager who did not tolerate laziness, who insisted on discipline and order, who could sack the employees at any time, came to be idealized. During business meeting abroad, it became obvious that the Hungarian socialist manager gets along better with the capitalist manager than the Hungarian socialist worker!

To date, the history of reform and privatization, the uninhibited property-acquisition, the criminal attitude of the proprietors, and the deficient utilization of property still in Hungarian ownership, all demonstrate that only the concept of property-liberalism has performed an ideological purpose. So, everything is allowed as long as it does not impede the like liberty of others, but the dividing-line between the two kinds of liberty is drawn by the stronger side, depending on their own interests and power. Liberal morals—just like their socialist predecessor—are those of power and of the powerful.

Advocates of property-liberalism—first of all, "leading economists" and "social philosophers" rather than the property-acquirer—either because of ignorance, or because of ill-intent, have only laid stress on one operating condition of the market economy: private ownership. They have failed to mention such checks and balances found elsewhere as the market framework, democratic institutions, public opinion, private morals and any number of social counter-forces. The fact that the other elements of the system are missing has made it possible for this newly-acquired private property to be used not to increase economic productivity, but to enhance the power that dominates society. Though the property-ideology that emerged in the reform relies on the example of the

20th century western economies, and makes its statements using the terminology of the mid- to late-20th century neo-liberal and monetarist economics, its essence and function likens it to the early-19th century ideology of the "not-yet-tamed" power-grasping proprietors.

Another comparison that may help in clarifying the reasons why the ideology of the property-liberalism gained popularity so easily is one that takes into account the precedents of 20th century socialism, not those of the 19th century capitalism. It is more practical to lay out the contents of the two concepts of property and their adjunct ideologies in a table (see next page).

A surprising conclusion can be drawn from the table without any further analysis: except for the principle of changing group-private ownership to individual-private ownership, the ideology of liberal property is identical with the ideology of socialist property. This means that except for the issue of the actual change to private ownership, the position of owners before and after the reform is in essence the same, and the owners' ideological position from the standpoint of the reform is invariable. This might also account for the ease with which many devoted supporters of the Marxist ideology on property (of Marxism-Leninism) turned into devoted supporters of the (reforming variety of) liberal ideology on property. It is especially interesting to have a look at the list of "leading economists" and "social philosophers". At the same time, the facts and interests mirrored in this ideology have brought along radical changes in the situation of other members of society. On the one hand, the counterbalancing role of the political class has been proved unnecessary; on the other, secondary "proprietors" (small producers, side-workers, etc.) have been separated from their property. From the standpoint of the owners and leaders that have remained, one could reiterate the old political saying: "Everything had to change so that everything would stay the same."

The basic principles of the socialist ideology of property	The basic principles of the liberal ideology of property in the transition
- socialist ownership and property-operation is justified by the universal mission of the proletariat and the superiority of the planned economy	- capitalist private ownership is the product of universal forces that determine economic progress, and the owners are the representatives of these forces
- proletarian internationalism	- capital and market globalization
- operators of property are the elite, the spearhead of the proletariat	- the elite of managers and owners cannot be changed: there is only one such elite
- the ideology of productivity: the planned economy does away with the contradictions and losses of market economy and makes more efficient use of property than capitalism does	- the ideology of productivity: the market economy does away with the contradictions and losses of planned economy, and makes more efficient use of property than socialism does
- the regime of the planned economy is a value in itself, a sacred value: in its development the society is its subject, a variable	- the regime of the market economy is a value in itself, a sacred value: in it, society "lets the tree lie as it fell"
- morals are set by the powerful: everything is allowed to happen if it is a historic necessity; whatever happens is dictated by the ruling minority; "the essence of revolutionary legitimacy is that we are not even compelled by our own laws" (Rákosi)	- morals are set by the powerful: everything is allowed as long as it does not interfere with the liberty of others; the dividing-line is drawn by the powerful
- property is one of the tools of control over the scattered, unorganized, morally fractious society (by means of taking over offices, public institutions, etc.)	- property is one of the tools of control over the scattered, unorganized, morally fractious society (by means of taking over offices, public institutions, etc.)
- the aggregated coordination of capital ownership and group of owners	- the separate coordination of certain property and certain owners

Today's Hungarian capital ownership and the ideology of liberal ownership will be comparable with present-day capital ownership and ideology of liberal ownership in Western economies and societies, if the social, institutional and ideological structure and forces that accompany capital ownership are built up in our country as well. Until then, the Hungarian market belongs to those who make good money from VAT on petrol, produce vodka, fake audio and video cassettes, and invest the dishonestly made money in gilts that pay well.

4. All is Not Yet Lost

The struggle of certain political forces to achieve power is primarily meant to bring them the means of control. The most important such means are the take-over of the legislature, of decision-making positions and executive offices. In order to do this in democratic political systems, in which there are elections at regular intervals, one needs to gain and keep the adequate support of the masses. This is mostly possible if a certain political power has successfully handled the means of decision-making and execution of decisions before, or if it can make the masses believe that it will do so in the future. Certain political powers, however, do not simply strive to occasionally gain the support of masses or access to power, but want to keep that position forever. The question is: What is necessary for this? And do they stand a chance?

The answer to the first question is quite obvious. What is necessary is what we can see around us today. In the short term, possession of the means that facilitate knowledge communication and that influence the masses: newspapers, publishing houses, radio and television, schools, universities, theatres. Also, the means to define concepts and values, which support the communicated facts and the means of their assessment. What are the figures for inflation in newspapers? Do newspapers agree with what the government says they are? Do newspapers approve of the demands and unrest of certain social groups? Do they criticize and threaten someone or, on the contrary, praise them? Do they think that changes in taxation are absurd or unavoidable? Do they admit that the community (the nation) is an independent value and a standard of values? Who do they put in a good or bad light and how often? Do they accept morals and what is the content of the morals they accept? What do they set as the goal of human life? These questions are all important from the standpoint of power and of how that power can be preserved. Equally important are the subjects taught at school, the university curricula, the images and messages we come across in literature or at the theatre. (By all these, we do not mean to deny the importance of first-hand, individual experience, but we hint at its relativity.) It is also obvious that in order to operate the means of short-term and long-term mass persuasion, we need professional people, institutions, organizations, parties and so on. Either these institutions are owned and financed by power groups, or these kinds of state institutions are influenced by activists of the above-mentioned power groups.

At this point of our analysis, it is easy to see how much money is needed for all these activities. First of all, as we have noted, it is the big proprietors that can successfully fight for the power obtainable with the aid of mass persuasion and popular support. Property has more in common with power than we have mentioned above. Standards of living, the chance to get a good education, the spread and power of the system based on personal influence and connections are continually increasing as income increases. Also, this power is enhanced by castes, the cohesion among those who possess similar sources of power: common social circles, clubs, associations, balls at the opera, means of obtaining information and opinions other than official public sources, support granted for someone or other's promotion, etc. All these are advantageous not only in acquiring the means of mass persuasion, but in the operation of democratic institutions as well. The mechanism of power-reproduction is simple: money can exert influence, influence can determine the opinion of voters and the outcome of elections, and the outcome of elections leads to the reproduction of power.

Notwithstanding, we should not conclude that big property, the media operated by it and the influence thereby gained automatically lead to the perpetuation of power. This is because there are rival groups that appear and operate their own means. Using their own money, their own institutions, their own press, they spread their own ideas and opinions, and influence or rather want to influence masses so as to meet their own interests. The voting citizen compares their newspaper articles, their assessments, and he decides who to vote for in the next elections. Consequently, we can say that a certain group striving for power and for preservation of power will want to monopolize the means that help them do this. Therefore they would like to eliminate their rivals and extend the political battle to this terrain. Their actions focused on this purpose vary widely. Let us discuss some such actions.

The easiest way is to limit the rival's means of spreading information or to shut them out completely, for instance, by persuading prospective supporters of the rival paper to give up, by blackmailing advertising firms through business partners or crediting banks, by winning over journalists or by threatening them, by offering better terms to newspaper distributors. A similar approach is the financial weakening of rival educational or research institutions, or the control of state institutions and their "conversion" to a certain point of view. They can also use their power in political offices to destroy the quality of state education, or to support their own high-quality institutions. They can monopolize studying in higher education by declaring that education is "a rich man's passion" and by making it more expensive. They can ignore the moral and human content of state education, which together with the other types of action will turn the present difference in income into a difference in knowledge and human quality, and through this they will forever ensure their chance to acquire power. Here we are dealing with the old feudal privileges that reappear in connection with money, dressed up in the disguise of a free market democracy. For anyone could—apparently—have money. An important means of causing a situation of monopoly is to disqualify rival political objectives by calling them extremist, populist, to dissolve some values that matter in organizing society without putting forward an alternative. These dissolved values, such as the nation, the interest of the community, history, mother tongue and individual autonomy cause separate groups to think and to organize themselves in a specific way. Where they are lacking, society is disoriented and atomized. But also here we can also mention the capacity to dissolve rival organizations by building in groups or individuals that make the organization dissolve, and who isolate themselves, condemn and compromise the organization at decisive moments.

The means of power acquisition and its preservation through property are also provided for by the power already secured. With this, for example, one can change not only taxation brackets and institutional structures, but also the rules of winning and staying in power. The modification of election procedures, an increase in the share of the popular vote needed for winning parliamentary admission, changes to the rules of the house, reframing of the president's powers, all so as to bind the hands of the next set of power incumbents and even to amend criminal law offer thousands of ways to grant and win power. It is actually quite easy to weaken the state by reducing the government's decision-making competencies or by transferring decision-making to independent institutions. By the time the next government comes in, if that happens to be the present opposition, there will be nothing left to decide upon. And if the old government stays, the means of decision-making will still be in the hands of the groups that support it. Such a means can also be an economic policy that deprives certain social groups from the material means necessary in politics and that changes the social structure. It can also direct the flow of income to certain groups, through different economic means; for example, well-paying gilts will direct the budget income towards big capital owners.

The fact that these means together are capable of placing power in the hands of a closed group and of reproducing it in this way was already proved under socialism. Until the lack of economic output made it collapse, power relations in socialism relied on the monopolistic disposal over property and income distribution, on the monopoly of access to political offices, on the elimination of rival groups, on the fact that the ruling caste was irreplaceable, on the control of publicity, on the possession of decision-making positions in offices and institutions, on the monopoly of deciding on society's aims, on the control of information circulation and on the connection of educational privileges and political careers to the caste in power (the advantages that certain socialists' children had at university entrance examinations, the fact that party leaders' children could study abroad, even in western countries beginning with the '70s), on the purposeful transformation of democratic institutions (one-party parliament, elections without any competition, etc.). From this standpoint, in spite of the numerous differences, the power exercised by the ruling elite of the Horthy-regime, the Rákosi-regime and the Kádár-regime depended on similar principles of control techniques.

In the course of power reproduction the socialist political elite came up against one serious problem of control strategy. At a certain level of economic complexity, the power to operate property had to be shared with adequately professional people, that is with groups of managers. So that this shared power would not lead to rivalry, the two groups were always mixed: comrades from the party committees were "delegated" to positions of economic leadership, then they were moved or "called back" to the leading apparatus of the party. In a lifetime, one would have to change positions six, eight or ten times. Today's power-preserving elite is in a more difficult situation. They helped the big proprietors to acquire their property during the reform, but in vain. The groups that officially became owners are not loyal to them and are not connected to them by their interests. There are several elite groups competing to become the political exponents of the quite united owners' group, and the consolidators of their power. Among others, this position encourages the elite in power to dispose of their own sources besides the above-mentioned means, in order to reproduce their power. The necessary technique is not a Hungarian invention: public funds are changed into private funds, then into party funds. Making use of the method that became world-famous when the Panama canal was being built (and which is probably as old as public funds and the state), the ruling political elite takes away the money necessary for the reproduction of power from the tax-payers whom they will afterwards rule over, with the help of that money. The essence of the method is to gain political power, a position that enables them to decide on public funds, to insert their own people into the office that pays public funds, and then to direct (preferably most of) the money towards private channels by means of—sometimes even legal—economic tricks, and finally to change it into party funds. The power bought for this money will become a source of income in itself. It is a mere technical detail whether this means the small money paid for property belonging to local authorities or the big money paid for twenty-page, well-hidden professional assessments, bonuses or tax-breaks. The emphasis is on the last stage, when public funds are used to finance the instruments of certain power techniques, their own newspapers, parties, movements, institutions, schools, ideologies, enabling them to reproduce power.

What should we answer to the second question? The sociologist observes the situation with concern. Several elements of the political elite's automatic power reproduction and preservation—the disintegrating, bipolar society against the organized elite, the property-monopoly, the concentration of publicity and of informational and ideology-creating institutions, the group inequality of the chances of spiritual reproduction, the closed group control of political and administrative institutions, the physical and moral disintegration of alternative elite groups, and the use of public funds in order to keep all these working—are already present. Only these elements have not coagulated into a unified, automatic system yet. The only hope is that the process is still open. Democracy is still fighting for its rights. We can still decide. For the time being, there are some choices left.

László Gy. Tóth

THE POST-COMMUNIST
GOVERNMENT COALITION IN HUNGARY

"The political left has always been ready to do away with its past mistakes to achieve a status of perfection in the present. This is how they got—without much of a hitch—from clearing peasants' cellars of all they had, to the market economy. Now they are excellent in this."

(Attila Kristóf)

SZDSZ[1] as the Smaller Successor Party of MSZMP[2]

In 1998—eight years after the system change and some weeks before the third free elections—a government coalition of the post-communist (socialist) MSZP[3] and the left-of-centre SZDSZ are holding power. The fact that MSZP is the successor of MSZMP is a historical fact, while the question of where SZDSZ belongs has just been clarified after quite some time.

The Alliance of Free Democrats was established on November 13, 1988 by the members of the so-called democratic opposition, along with a zealous group of Budapest intellectuals in opposition—who turned out to have been quite naive in this move. The religious sect called "Hit Gyülekezete" also played an active role in the foundation of the party, but the uninformed founding members learned about it only years later.[4] The popularity of the SZDSZ at the time was based on its intent to radically change the system, its loud anti-communism and the myth of the "grey matter". Although the real level of opposition presented by the party was questioned by many already at the time of its foundation, the moment of truth arrived only after the first free elections in 1990. At that time, the party implemented a substantial change of political direction, and increasing confusion resulted also from the multitude of unclarified conceptual-ideological questions. At the same time, the influence of the neo-leftist and left-liberal intellectual supporters of the party also grew rapidly, and the similar socio-cultural background of the leaders of the party also proved to be dominant. The confession of Sándor Révész was probably not entirely alien to the dominant politicians of the SZDSZ: "The truth is that, while Antall's ideal of the society is closer to me than that of György Aczél, I understand much better the personality of Aczél and its medium and I can live with it much better than that of Antall. One of the reasons must obviously be that I grew up in a communist family with Jewish roots, this is what I have an internal picture of, and I have none such of the middle classes that raised Antall."[5] This may have contributed to the arguments of János Kis, the then president of SZDSZ and its chief ideologist, that it was no longer worth attacking the members of the former communist *nomenklatura*, therefore, SZDSZ—if they want to further the system change—has to oppose the MDF[6] government.[7]

The internal fight within the SZDSZ was decided by the end of 1992: the centre of power around the leading figures of Pető, Magyar, Bauer and Hack, relatively quickly neutralised, and then marginalised, the individuals and groups of anti-communist sentiments demanding a radical system change as a political factor.

In 1992-1993, the members of the formerly anti-communist, so-called democratic opposition did not yet dare to openly express the possibility of collaboration with the former communists; however, they did not leave much room for doubt about it materialising sooner or later. Before the elections, Iván Pető already made the following statement: "for instance, it has been said that in the next elections, instead of today's coalition the MSZP will be the real adversary of the SZDSZ. I do not see this as successful wording. I see the MSZP as a serious rival in the next elections, but at the moment there is no point in the SZDSZ creating an enemy image for itself."[8] After Pető was elected president of the party in November 1992, SZDSZ—then faced with the problem of its identity crisis—was gradually getting closer and closer to MSZP, which then naturally lead to the coalition after the 1994 elections.

As was discovered later, the neo-leftist and neo-liberal militant opinion-leader intellectuals, led by their sense of having to accomplish a mission, had done a great deal of harm to their party in the long run, by introducing a veritable intellectual dictatorship in public life in Hungary. Between 1990 and 1994 they promptly termed as "fascist" anyone who tried to argue against the planned MSZP-SZDSZ coalition. This was one of the causes of the schism that divided intellectual life in Hungary. The "important" individuals were all liberal or leftist. The absurdity of the situation is characterised by a statement made by an ex-communist political scientist—who, along with his companions, used to be experts of scientific socialism—in 1991: "Everyone used to call himself a Marxist, now everyone is a liberal."[9] According to the analysis of Attila Molnár: "'Scientific socialism' has been replaced by 'scientific liberalism', a mixture of neo-leftist and social-liberal views."[10] So "Sci-soc" has been replaced by "Sci-lib".[11]

However, following the institutionalisation of a large part of the liberal principles and values—the establishment of the market economy, the liberal and democratic state governed by the rule of law—liberalism soon turned out to be incapable of evolving into a force to organise society on its own. The real liberal parties are always extremely vulnerable and exposed to attacks: the left usually argues that liberals are socially insensitive while the right calls on them to more efficiently protect national values. A liberal economic policy is usually accompanied by less attention being paid to the principle of social justice and equality, which may result in social tensions. The realisation of this prompted SZDSZ to change its self-definition: this is why the party turned from a "liberal" party into a "social liberal" one, which, in their case, is a version of doctrinaire liberalism mixed with some social values. The SZDSZ represents the American, leftist version of modern liberalism, together with its libertinism. It is the type of liberalism about which Hayek had the following to say: "It is a carefully planned deceit on the part of the American socialists that they expropriated the term 'liberalism'." This was not without any preliminaries: according to Hayek, L. T. Lobhouse published a book in 1911 whose title was *Liberalism*, whereas, the appropriate title would have been *Socialism*.[12]

By the way, the leadership and ideologists of SZDSZ made the right decision—from their own perspective—when, following forty years of communist dictatorship, despite the leftist origins, values and associations of the party, they defined SZDSZ as a liberal party: for in 1988-1989, any declared association with the left would have amounted to political suicide. Nevertheless, one of the most influential personalities of SZDSZ, Miklós Vásárhelyi, stated that the revolution of October 1917 was an event of historic significance even in 1989, and he confessed that "I see no alternative to democratic socialism."[13] It was probably this two-faced nature, the mobilising energy of political schizophrenia, that fired the neophyte determination and vehemence with which some representatives of SZDSZ fought, at the time of the system change, for the exclusive promotion of the liberal tenets they considered the only true ideology. One example of this is the overheated and inexorable anti-state attitude—the fallacy of which they have come since to realise—the consequences of which include the decline of public security, the inefficient operation of the system of administration of justice, the inequalities of opportunity which results in the helplessness and exposure groups, etc. They eventually had to face all of this as part of the coalition. The theory of a state with as limited a scope of power as possible has also turned out to have been wrong from the aspect of the economy: social and economic policy should not have been neglected—indeed even almost phased out—for this lead to the impoverishment of the middle classes. For, where there is a shortage of domestic capital in the economy, the state (may) help local, national businesses and interests in the accumulation of capital.

But the fact that liberal principles and values were highly fashionable in those days resulted in a temporary increase in the wealth and influence of SZDSZ, irrespective of the outcome of the first democratic elections. From this aspect, a statement made by Tamás Bauer of SZDSZ in 1997 is highly noteworthy: "SZDSZ, then in opposition, did play a dominant role in the formulation of politics in Hungary in the years 1990 and 1991 (amendment of the constitution, the blockades raised by cab-drivers(!), the local government act, etc.) and I am not sure whether we have been as capable of influencing the flow of events over the past one-one and a half years, as (we were) during the one year period following the elections in 1990."[14]

Its history, so far, indicates that SZDSZ is truly efficient only when in opposition. The likely reason for this is that the Free Democrat politicians and their supporters have a great need for an enemy and a sense of being under threat because this has proven to be the most efficient force of cohesion, and, for various political reasons and tactical considerations, they have been defining themselves always in comparison with someone else. According to Gábor Demszky (SZDSZ), Mayor of Budapest, executive party official, if MSZP over-wins in the next election, then SZDSZ will appear as an alternative party "on the other side" and in the 2002 elections, it may enter into a coalition with another liberal party.[15] The irrationality of the concept is also proven by the opinion expressed by another MP of the SZDSZ, Miklós Szabó, on the whole of the political opposition: "The factor that results in the formation of parties is not related to ideology, for ideology is essentially uniform from MIÉP[16] to Fidesz[17]. (…) ... including national-ist maximalism, further to the voicing of the so-called Christian values, the privileged ideological exclusivity. The partition of this political right, is, therefore, not along the lines of different ideas, concepts of the world, society or economy, the differences are more evident in political behaviour and conduct."[18] In another article, Miklós Szabó went even as far as to state that "the parties of the right are infused with tendencies that impose the hazard of dicta-torship" and, in essence, all of them are anti-Semitic. In fact, these are the factors that constitute the foundation of the coalition.[19]

It is also generally typical of the left that it does not talk much about national identity, the economy or the determination of the social structures; to the contrary, leftist politicians pay much more attention to the real or assumed exclusion and stigmatisation of var-ious social groups. The phobias originating from a bad assessment of the situation and the missing of the right proportions—along with intentional misunderstandings for political/tactical purposes—have made our political/intellectual public life intolerable and hys-terical. For example, Mihály Kornis, well known for his attraction to the SZDSZ, wrote the following in 1993: "They hate us. Honestly. And we liberals are not capable of saying what I think we really feel, i.e. that we hate you even more than you hate us."[20]

The opinion-leader intellectuals attracted to SZDSZ were not free from the attitude "let us wipe out the past forever" either: "…SZDSZ has become an unavoidable symbol in the Hungarian political life. The essence of this, in simple terms, is that this party is opposed to the social set-up of both the thousand year period pre-ceding 1945 and that of the 45 years following it…"[21] These must have been the considerations which prompted Gábor Fodor, then minister of education, to abolish the obligatory secondary school exit examination in history. This somewhat unusual attitude is also reflected, for instance, by the current church policy of SZDSZ, which is aimed, in essence, at attracting the atheists and those opposed to the historical churches.

Gyula Tellér pointed out first that SZDSZ "is, in essence, a successor party to the old MSZMP itself, and it supports the system change only to an extent where it does not undermine the interests and positions of the former socialist elite groups that are also represented by SZDSZ." For "…SZDSZ, as the interest-representing organisation of certain groups of the elite that was in power during the Rákosi era, made attempts to give access to ownership primarily to its own clients, within the limits defined by economics." According to the author, in the 1990-1995 period, the development of a civic society was "hindered by the personalities with a great sense of having to accomplish a mission, belonging to the same political sub-culture" which participated in the liquidation of the civic society, the middle and upper classes, after 1949. On the basis of his evaluation of the situation, the fact that SZDSZ is a successor party became quite evident by 1991.[22] An important piece of evidence proving the above arguments was that SZDSZ essentially supported the so-called spontaneous privatisation process which enabled the party *nomenklatura* and the technocratic elite of the Kádár era to convert their political power into economic power. Interestingly, the Socialist politician Iván Vitányi made the following statement in 1994: "…these two political movements are, in fact, one. Of course with a large difference, but still, there is a community."[23] At the same time, the previously cited Gyula Tellér recalled that the "communist or former communist party intellectual group that carried strong sub-cultural features" before and after 1956 "remained in the course of the system change in MSZP or joined SZDSZ." Therefore, "re-union is a natural endeavour of this group, which, after the Democratic Charter, materialised most naturally in the MSZP-SZDSZ coalition."[24] At the same time, with this coalition, established without any historical necessity, the Free Democrats broke with the system-changing forces for good; moreover, they unveiled the whole of their earlier behaviour as well, proving, in retrospect, the suspicions of those who saw them as the fifth column of Kádárism all along. Despite its liberal rhetoric and phraseology, SZDSZ had always pursued its policies to promote the interests of the existing left in essence.

Preparation of the Coalition:
Establishment of a Leftist, Anti-Fascist People's Front

The so-called Democratic Charter (hereinafter: DC) entered the scene on September 26, 1991. An organisation reviving old communist traditions, it was, in essence, none other than an effort made to establish an anti-fascist people's front against the Christian-conservative government which came into office after democratic elections. In contrast to the historical precedent, the situation was somewhat unusual in that there was no substantial fascist—extreme right—movement in Hungary to necessitate the establishment of an anti-fascist people's front, so the DC was increasingly turning against the legitimate government. When established, the DC was supported, in addition to groups of leftist and left-liberal intellectuals belonging to the sphere of interests of MSZP and SZDSZ, by the majority of opinion-leader intellectuals as well as the Hit Gyülekezete. The founding document of the DC was prepared by Tamás Bauer and János Kis. Each of the 17 points of the text begins with the words: "There will be democracy, if ... " Without a real fascist threat the task of making unsuspecting citizens believe that there was such a fascist threat was to be performed by the opinion leaders considered staunch supporters of the Charter, drawing on the assistance of the media. Despite the fact that there was not even a sign of an extreme right organisation in the Hungarian society and that anti-Semitism is not even as strong in Hungary as in Europe on average, taking advantage and heavily over-valuing the significance of the few atrocities committed by extreme rightists—which were to be condemned but which did not add up to a substantial threat—with the help of the media, they created an atmosphere where joining forces with former communists of the former ÁVH[25], and their sons and daughters as well, seemed to be a moral obligation of all democrats. It was no mere coincidence that ex-communists were regular participants of the events of the DC. The MSZP owes a lot to the fact that György Konrád, Gyula Hegyi, Gábor Fodor, Iván Vitányi, Zoltán Szabó, László Donáth, Miklós Jancsó and others were so resolute in fighting against the undoubtedly confused views of István Csurka, Izabella B. Király and the former SZDSZ-member Uncle Potyka. The leftist Charter-activists were probably quite familiar with the observation of Theo Waigel, that the extreme-right phenomena always promotes the left. Under the co-operation against the non-existent fascism, this organisation enabled communists to be rehabilitated, the release of the successor party MSZP from political quarantine and the commencement of co-operation between MSZP and SZDSZ, which constituted the highly successful trial-wedding of the former (reform)communists and the leftist liberals. The coalition struck up in 1994 could hardly have been possible without the zealous and active support by the leftist liberal media intellectuals.[26] An interesting aside is that the speakers of the DC enjoyed the support even of the former SZDSZ member Árpád Göncz, President of the Republic.[27] The efficiency and influence of the DC was also proven by the fact that, following the 1994 elections, which were won by the successor parties, György Konrád called on the leaders of MSZP and SZDSZ, on behalf of the DC, to start coalition negotiations as soon as possible.

Through their immense influence, assisted by the media and their capabilities of manipulation, the speakers of the DC made a large contribution to the preservation of the extremely negative and unjust picture of the Antall and Boross governments, the advantages of which are still being enjoyed by the leftist parties. This group of intellectuals with their dual bond (MSZP-SZDSZ) in the 1991-1994 period was successful in temporarily hiding the communist/anti-communist political schism until after 1994. At that time, following the formation of the government, the survival of the structures of the depth of the Kádár era and the reflexes that had evolved in the late Kádár period became perceptible again for an increasing number of social groups.

The Democratic Charter played a dominant role in striking up the current government coalition, for it provided a good opportunity for the compromise between the party *nomenklatura* bourgeoisie, the technocrats of the late Kádár period and the leftist or left-liberal intellectual groups, including the former democratic opposition as well.[28] The DC terminated its operation after the 1994 elections, the previously militant speakers turned into silent spectators of the increasing dominance of "kleptocracy", the breaches of law by the leftist government coalition, the curbing of social rights, the aggravation of the inequality of opportunities and the hasty reform and partial dismantling of the health care and the education system.

Consequently, the former aggressive left-liberal protectors of democracy and human rights were quickly unveiled, for it became evident that their leftist commitment—and power—was far more important to them than the protection of democratic values. The overwhelming majority of "independent intellectuals" turned out to be, in fact, the intellectual mercenaries of either the MSZP or the SZDSZ. In April, 1996 they made a last weak attempt at resurrecting the movement, but by that time, they had lost all of their moral foundations and so the attempt ended up in a quick and spectacular failure.

In the course of its operation, the DC—even if unintentionally—repeated part of the conflicts characterising the left in all times. It is a typical leftist tradition that while it is the representation of a group of intellectuals with a uniform socio-cultural background, they nevertheless pursue their activities in the name of the whole of society. The representatives of the DC created an atmosphere where those calling themselves "anti-fascist democrats" declared practically everyone who was not willing to accept the exclusive values of the left and liberalism and the representation thereof, unfit for any good society. The Nyilvánosság Klub (Publicity Club), for instance, which was dominated by SZDSZ, was among the zealous supporters of the DC, as well as the Tégy a Gyűlölet Ellen (Act Against Hatred), a one-man movement, the organiser of which did not make it a secret that he would like the political right to simply disappear. The aforementioned myth of the independent intellectual was accompanied by a constant reference to "progressive leftist" traditions as well as the operation of the basic democratic attitude in contrast to representative democracy. The intellectuals belonging to the Charter unveiled their own aspirations—which at the same time resulted in their moral collapse—when, in 1994, it essentially gave up its sovereignty as against the new government; it gave up its attitude of criticism, which, in retrospect, destroyed the credibility of its attitude of open animosity against the preceding government, characterised by constantly calling the government to give accounts for its actions. Point 5 of the DC, for instance reads: "There will be democracy here if the state provides elementary social/welfare services to every single one of its residents." However, for instance, in the statement issued by the Hungarian Medical Chamber on March 2, 1998, one finds the following sentence: "The activities of the government has resulted in a further decline of the already sad health status of the population and in the utter deterioration of the position of those working in the health service system." During its four year period, the MSZP-SZDSZ coalition that came into power with the assistance of the DC, did nothing to implement their goals formulated in 1991. This revealed that the former fanatical supporters of the DC, the members of the media commando—and those they succeeded in deceiving—were necessary only until the taking of political power. The Hungarian society may thank the first, leftist, anti-fascist "people's front" of our most recent history for the partial survival of the Kádárless version of Kádárism. The essence of the compromise between the MSZP and SZDSZ was that the former communists won the sympathy of their former opposition, the intellectuals who had been disappointed in the Kádár regime, and, therefore, had come to form an opposition but who were still leftist—Maoist, Marxist etc.—in their attitudes. Leftist people's front movements seem really to have fun carrying out "actions" or exercising power—or this may be their underlying objective.

Historical Justice—Never Done

"The whole of Hungarian society has been paying a heavy price for the failure to do justice. The lack of legal compliance, the devaluation of moral values, the relativisation of personal responsibility and liability has been undermining the foundations of the civic democratic system. Our opinion-leader intellectuals bear much of the responsibility for this process." According to the historian Mária Schmidt, "the loss of the moral ground of SZDSZ became evident for the first time in the debate about doing justice. This is where their marching together with the Socialists, the Charter, the joint governance and the joint misappropriation of assets turned into a fact." With the "halo" of intellectuals of SZDSZ turning against doing historical justice, the formerly more or less united Hungarian intellectual opposition definitively broke into two groups. The conclusion Mária Schmidt drew was: "... the majority of intellectuals no longer have a moral ground to oppose the ubiquitous phenomenon of corruption, moral decline which undermine everything. Where capital sins go scot-free, where a murderer cannot be distinguished from the victim, there will be no consequence to somebody's treason, if someone encourages killing by word of mouth or in writing, theft is not much of a crime. Let alone lying."[29] This may be the reason for so many finding the definition by the political scientist Tamás Fricz an apt one, when he defined our country a country without consequences.

The consequences of the failure of doing justice, the moral and ethical questions and doubts relating to the failure of doing justice was raised in one of her studies by Anne Applebaum as well.[30] (This paper was presented in Hungarian by Mária Schmidt in the November 22 , 1997 edition of the daily *Magyar Nemzet*.) She mentioned it as an interesting aside that in Poland and Hungary the staunchest opponents of the political screening process were not the former communists, but surprisingly, the members of the former opposition, who must have been afraid of the procedures digging up a number of undesired facts about their past. At present the next generation has no chance at all to get to know the past. And this proves to so many embittered people that it is not worth being honest, since honesty does not pay but corruption and opportunism do. Those who work hard will not be successful, but murderers and embezzlers will,"—says Applebaum. The middle classes owe their existence to the civic values—hard work, integrity and the assumption of personal responsibility. But if the business sector is entirely corrupt and is intertwined with politics, then it is not possible to talk about civic conditions in the Western interpretation of the term. Various forms of Mafia will dominate the region and the politicians will act as promoters of the interests of such groups. Applebaum argues that this process has already started.

Quite understandably, the interest of the post-communist left was in the falsification of the past—instead of its exploration. Typically, Béla Biszku was not even questioned in Hungary. He is well known to have said at the December 10, 1957 congress of the Political Committee of the MSZMP that "...there are a lot of light verdicts on political crimes and there is a relatively small number of physical annihilations..."[31]

The turning-point in the life of the SZDSZ, comprised of the members of the former opposition—each of them with leftist motives—must have been the perception of the atmosphere that developed as a result and in connection with the submission and debate of the bill aimed to do historical justice. The complete exploration of the past would have been seen as members of the opposition—who had earlier been communists themselves—who reported people to the police to promote their own interests or prompted by their political convictions or who collaborated with the communist organisations of oppression. The possibility of involvement triggered aversion at first, and later hatred, of any endeavour aimed at revealing or fully exploring the past. That was when the anti-communist attitude was replaced by an immeasurable hatred of the political right: practically all versions of the civic-national-conservative-Christian ideologies turned into their prime enemy and, at the same time, the urge of joining forces against the non-existent fascism became the focal point of political life.

MSZP as a Social-Democratic Party

The basis of reference and legitimacy most often cited by the members of the post-communist left exercising power has so far been the "expertise", pragmatism and social sensitivity, inherited from the reform-communists. These have replaced the Marxist-Leninist slogans. Further, often used political catchwords include: "progressive", "liberal", "social", "socialist" or "social-democratic", "left" and any combination thereof. In the heat of the linguistic-political skirmishes, practically everyone who does not find the above standards satisfactory is considered unfit for good society. The members of the MSZP continue laying down the "foundations of capitalism" with the enthusiasm with which they used—not so long ago—to strive for socialism, which used to be considered as the "lounge" of communism. Their sense of being missionaries had not been without precedent. The former reform—and career—communists who turned into social-democrats in 1989 confessed to have been faced with the biggest challenge of their life: whether they should count on the former members of KISZ[32] or those who were considered to be mediocre from a political and human perspective.[33] The sense of superiority, a characteristic feature of liberals, probably stems from the former communists' sense of belonging to the "elect". (Although the arguments of Magda Kovács Kósáné and Sándor Csintalan are not without a streak of a sense of superiority either.)

The fact that the MSZP is a successor party is also indicated by its excellent standards of organisation, the late Kádárian style, individuals comprised in the party and its supporter background, along with the skilfully and resolutely salvaged immense wealth. The Socialists were enabled by their experience to come to the conclusion that they knew more about the economy and politics than did the new democratic elite which came into power in 1990. It did not even occur to them that the knowledge that had been valid and usable under the circumstances of a state-socialist system may lose some of its value—might even turn useless—under the circumstances of a market economy. Their activities may perhaps most aptly be characterised by the paradox formulated by László Tőkéczki in that "the system of the 'really existing socialism' constantly focused on the resolution of problems, the majority of which, would not have emerged without it."[34] The very same group alleged of themselves that they overthrew their own system, carefully hiding the historical fact that the collapse of the Soviet empire was a result of the arms race forced on the communists by the West. Following the propagation of the tenets of Marxism-Leninism, the new handy fashion was freedom of ideologies: former communists are pragmatic people, preoccupied primarily with questions of the economy. Since their existence is usually dependent on some executive or other senior position, the maintenance of social mobility is not in their interest; therefore, the ideologies created to support their position are aimed at promoting their existential security.

They are the depositories of the humanist left and everyone else is either an anti-democrat or a fascist.

The exclusion of the spirit of competition and of the society of competition substantially contributed to the unparalleled speed of moral decline and degeneration in our society following the conclusion of the MSZP-SZDSZ coalition in 1994. The conditions were aggravated by the arguments of the left-liberal opinion-leaders that these alarming changes were to be considered as inevitable; indeed for the average man in the street the "transparency of the world was completely lost." The events of the past four years and the experience accumulated during the 1990-1994 period definitely show that only a MDF-SZDSZ-FIDESZ-KDNP-Smallholders' Party coalition, a joint effort of the parties bent on transforming the system, could have resulted in a complete system change to satisfy the requirements of the overwhelming majority of the Hungarian population. Only such collaboration could have provided for the general predominance in politics and public life which could have enabled the breaking of the political/economic power of MSZP, the communist successor party so deeply rooted in the society, and the elimination of its formal and informal relationships. The reformers of MSZMP, however, also recognised this danger and using means of the secret service, they spared no effort to divide the opposition, in which they did not fail. Nobody attacked as vehemently the democratic, right-centre system-changing government formed following the first free elections as did the Alliance of Free Democrats.

The History of the MSZP-SZDSZ Coalition

Since the media, consisting predominantly of ex-communists, proved to be a ready partner of the SZDSZ, which comprised the former democratic opposition, in the unceasing attacks against the democratically elected centre-right government of 1990-1994, the returning of the favour had not been delayed long. "If anti-

Semitism had initially been a question of bankers, in the Rákosi system, a question of functions; it has now become a question of television! The participation of intellectuals in the journalist profession is really in excess of the share of Hungarians of Jewish origin in the population. Let us set aside the capitulating explanations, let us not try to argue that this proportion is not that extraordinary. (...) As for the current situation: Hungary has a society of journalists of excellent standards, sensitive and loyal to society. Any cleansing or take-over in this area could only lead to a decline of standards and political damage. It is vital question of the evolving democracy that it should dare to fight and make no allowance to any anti-Semitic atmosphere."[35] This was the "letter of safe conduct" issued by SZDSZ to the media intelligentsia that had served the Kádár regime. From this point on, it was a warning to anyone who tried to dismiss a communist media star who had changed sides in good time, for his or her past.

Looking at the inter-relationships of the process of the system change, one of the biggest mistakes seems to be that the winds of historical change bypassed the media, as a result of which the composition of the opinion-leader intelligentsia hardly changed at all in comparison with that of the late Kádár era. This, then, led to a predominance of the left and the left-liberal side, which is unusual and undesirable in a bourgeois democracy. Taking into account the historic precedent, without replacing some of the dominant individuals of the media, the survival of the intellectual one party system seems to have been inevitable. To prove this poin, let us refer to the relevant section of one of the revoked amendment proposals of Imre Mécs, SZDSZ MP (an individual who would be difficult to charge with being biased): "A large number of the editors of the Hungarian Radio, the Hungarian Television and the MTI, the Hungarian News Agency had, in some form, worked for Department No. III. The republic would lose the work of a very large number of experienced and qualified editors if this point were kept in the text of the law."[36] The television issue, therefore, was not a question of anti-Semitism—as had been alleged by Miklós Szabó—but a question of ethics: what should the future of the ex-communist media stars be who had compromised themselves, who had served the former system without respecting any principles? Would this arrangement not provide an advantage to the communist successor organisations that may be impossible to catch up with? The real intent of SZDSZ was clearly revealed when Gábor Kuncze, then leader of the SZDSZ caucus, prime minister nominee, distanced himself, on behalf of the caucus, in a pre-agenda address, from the statements of Imre Mécs, who, later, even asked the pardon of those concerned... Of those about whom Péter Esterházy wrote the following: "It is the essence, the *sine qua non* of socialist journalism that it is a lie. It is not the people working there with all of their properties, not all of the articles, but the whole of it." Several years later György Baló stated the following: "...the whole of the Hungarian media is rather 'inbred', people in highly similar positions in life and with highly similar motives got in there, very easily, without competition."[37]

An analysis of the events following the system change reveals that the MSZP and SZDSZ proved to be the quickest to realise the immense role of the media under the circumstances of a multi-party society in the information age. Therefore, from their own perspective, it is only natural that they spared no effort in trying to conquer and/or occupy the media. And a large number of those belonging to the media intelligentsia seem not to care much about whether they are serving the lumpen-proletariat or the lumpen-bourgeoisie.

But the SZDSZ was not satisfied with attacking the democratically elected and democratically operating government—at the same time it also completed the moral rehabilitation of the ex-communist politicians and public figures, preparing, thereby, the victory of MSZP in the 1994 elections and its own access to government. The members of the former "Democratic Opposition" substantially devalued and/or invalidated their actions before 1989 against the oppressive system, since, in 1994 they formed an alliance with politicians whom they had previously deeply reproved and detested for their previous actions and political views. They have never succeeded since then in resolving the resulting conflict.

At the beginning of the operation of the coalition, there were severe tensions between the two parties, resulting, aside from the different socialisation and the personal conflicts, primarily from the fact that the SZDSZ found it difficult to accept the rather thankless role of playing second fiddle; and, relying on the so-called liberals within the MSZP, they entered into a protracted rear-guard action before they finally gave in. By 1997, the positions of Gyula Horn solidified and the MSZP's politicians of dual (MSZP-SZDSZ) ties no longer formed any power of any use, so SZDSZ was left to its own resources and has become increasingly defenceless. Prime Minister Gyula Horn, who has a widely known history, still returns to the communist jargon from time to time. In a broadcast of the Hungarian Radio's programme *Világóra* he said recently that 1997 was the year of turn-around. (In the parlance of the communists, 1948 was the year of the turn-around; that was the year of the introduction of open dictatorship.) If we look at the history of the coalition, the meaning and the message, in reality, of this statement of Gyula Horn must be that that must have been the year when the MSZP switched to a one-party government—while maintaining the coalition. Although the MSZP-SZDSZ coalition—taking advantage of its oppressive predominance in parliament—put its own supporters into practically all of the important positions, this process was more favourable for the MSZP, which managed to increase its already existing, substantial influence. This was explained by the fact that the MSZP was extremely deeply embedded in society; they had and have supporters in all walks of life whom they can mobilise when necessary, enabling them even to switch off the controlling functions of civic democracy or at least to render it into something of a formality.

By today it has become possible to consider SZDSZ a satellite party of MSZP. The resulting confusion, the complete abandonment of pursuing policies on the basis of principles, must have been the reason for the statement made by Gábor Demszky, that the time of anti-communism has passed. (Demszky should be aware of the fact that it is not enough to be an anti-fascist to be a democrat—one has to be an anti-Communist as well.) Taking advantage of the defenceless position of the SZDSZ, prime minister Gyula Horn not only shifted to a system of one-party governance but at the same time he started to make up even for the grievances and humiliations the MSZP and himself had personally suffered at the hands of the SZDSZ. The MSZP no longer needed SZDSZ that much, since it had earned a sufficient measure of acceptance abroad, it had fortified its positions in the media, having expelled the SZDSZ from many of those positions. It cannot be a mere coincidence that Mihály T. Révész, the then president of ORTT[38], was a former confidante of Gyula Horn. Another fact that cannot be regarded a coincidence is that, despite the protests of SZDSZ, the Central Criminal Investigation Directorate was removed by the end of 1997 from the scope of competency of the ministry of the interior, which was then governed by SZDSZ, creating thereby a Socialist Party police. But the protests of SZDSZ had also been ignored earlier, at the time of the signature of the agreement with the Holy See, at the time of the settlement of the problems of the social security self-governments and at the time of the arrangement of a number of other important issues. In respect to the Roma issue, Gyula Horn tried to avoid governmental responsibility when, as yet another proof of his dislike of SZDSZ, owing to the protest by the Socialist caucus, the proposal submitted by SZDSZ to disapprove of the discrimination against the Roma minority was not permitted to be submitted to parliament. Nevertheless, the theoreticians of the two parties consider it as one of their big achievements that "official anti-Semitism" was terminated in 1994—suggesting the unfounded and unjust charge that something like that had existed under the preceding government.

The MSZP-SZDSZ coalition, in fact, is such a new state-party in the making, where SZDSZ cuts out the role of the internal opposition whose prime endeavour is to serve its own clientele and potential voter base by all means and at all costs. The Socialists and SZDSZ are still interested in enabling the members of the late Kádárian elite to transform their quasi ownership positions into real ownership positions. There is only so much to add to their often mentioned social sensitivity that while the notorious vodka factory of Zsurk received HUF 80 million in aid, the victims of a natural disaster, the whirlwind in Kunszentmárton, had to make do with a mere HUF 10 million.

In order to remain in power they are trying to make it seem as though the de-politicised intellectual public life were something particularly valuable. But the creation of myths of professionalism, the promotion of "independent" intellectuals as "stars" and the offering of the silence of libraries hides, in effect, the intent of expropriating public life, since the often militant left-liberal intellectual groups do not at all want to give up their incessant involvement in politics or their socialistic and liberal endeavours aimed to transform society and common awareness.

The process of the system change itself may be divided into two stages: in the first, the formal power was still held by the state socialist elite; therefore, in the chaotic period, called democratic transition, they had exclusive access to information and their decision-making positions had not yet faltered. In fact, this enabled them to achieve the system change without replacement of the elite, as a result of which there is no substantial social group in power in the period of consolidation following the system change which could be the basis for the creation and consolidation of the ethos of social democracy. From the aspect of ideology the two parties cannot be seen as equal; for one thing, because, according to its self-definition, MSZP is a social democratic party and a member of the Socialist International while SZDSZ, as a liberal party, is a member of the Liberal International. Obviously, SZDSZ is the more ideological one of the two parties. It is well known, for instance, that the SZDSZ is the major domestic promoter of the theory of the so-called open or opened society. It was Attila Molnár who wrote in more detail on the conflicts—paradoxically, on the closed nature—of the open society introduced by Karl Popper in one of his earlier studies.[39] But Ralf Dahrandorf also voiced his scepticism, who said that György Soros was wrong when he considered capitalism the major enemy of the open society, "since the point of the open society is the very fact that it accommodates a number of ways, including a variety of forms of capitalism. The Asian, the Anglo-Saxon and the Rhine capitalism have already been mentioned, but, in fact, there are a lot of other varieties." (…) "Versatility persists even in the globalised world of economy and capitalism. It is worth, therefore, working on the squaring of the circle, using all of the means that the various countries can provide for their citizens on the basis of their traditions and experience."[40] However, these observations did not change the attitude of rejection displayed by the left-liberal Hungarian intelligentsia against all novel market conforming arrangements.

It may be considered as only natural, however, that for the new elite recruited, for the most part, from among former communists, being leftist was not primarily a matter of principle, but much more a possibility for ensuring a privileged position in life. When the Socialists talk about the necessity and advantages of the creation of a capitalist class with leftist sentiments, all they are doing is trying to provide an ideology for the existence of the MSZP's clientele. This is how they are trying to provide legitimacy for the advance of the interest groups which see the MSZP as their natural political ally. Therefore, instead of common political ideals, it is time we started to talk about profit.

The post-communist socialist MSZP owes its stable political position and base of voters to the fact that it is the only possible party for voters with a leftist orientation. MSZP is just making efforts to get rid of one of its potential leftist rival, i.e. SZDSZ, with which it forms a governing coalition. The heirs of the state party seem to have undermined the existence of SZDSZ during the period of joint governance, slowly and using democratic means, whose founders they used to keep under police control. From the perspective of MSZP, the destruction of SZDSZ is no more or less than succeeding in eliminating one more competitor group of fundamentally leftist motives, one of the groups that contributed to the changing of the system, from among the potential rivals. But this situation is also heavily conflict-ridden for SZDSZ as well, for the Free Democrats have been flirting with the ideology of social democracy ever since the foundation of the party in 1988. Now it looks like it is time they really revealed their cards. Following the joint governance with MSZP, which defines itself as a social democratic party, it seems to be more appropriate for the SZDSZ to revert to liberalism. Of course, it does not alter the fact that MSZP and SZDSZ are fatally interdependent since these two parties are equally interested in reducing the system change to a partial achievement and in the conservation of the position of the left-liberal elite. Moreover, there is no other major party that would be willing to co-operate with either of them. At the same time, prior to the elections, it is vital that they present different, autonomous features. SZDSZ is trying to show itself as the party of "competitive, self-sufficient existence". According to SZDSZ caucus leader István Szent-Iványi, his party "has been demonised by the parties in opposition. This may result from a certain intellectual heritage as well as from bad conscience."[41] Another one of his debatable arguments relating to the MSZP is even more interesting: "These are two different parties, two different worlds as regards values."[42] With elections round the corner, the various interest groups busying themselves in the background, are trying to maximise their profits in the short run, while politicians are trying to emphasise their assumed or actual merits. For instance, SZDSZ is trying to claim credit for the alleged economic achievements of the government, despite the fact that they are not heading any one of the ministries that have to do with the economy.

The point of the history of the MSZP-SZDSZ coalition lies in the fact that MSZP—taking advantage of its extremely deep roots in the society—made efforts to provide all key positions for its own cadres so the members of the late Kádárian elite, while promoting their interests, successfully repressed—besides the representatives of the political right—the leftist intellectuals with a stronger inclination to express their criticism. Meanwhile, the capability of politics to influence the economy substantially declined. The economic elite increasingly detached itself from the political power. The uninhibited exploitation of the political power and the increase of social tensions increased the antipathy of those left behind or excluded, for the coalition. The smallest proportion of those former party members, who had already been entrepreneurs in the communist era, is found within the economic elite. In the wake of the uninhibited, profit seeking pragmatism and unfettered thirst for a career of the former career communists, and those of the KISZ-Demisz[43]-BIT[44] generation, at the time of sharing out the "goodies", the MSZMP's second line and secondary officials also made it into the forefront. This is the basis for the survival of the late Kádárian, small-scale, fully corrupt world. Hungarian society, observing the increasing dominance of corruption, the deterioration of public security, the fragmentation and the increasing uncertainty of existence, quickly returned to the creation and implementation of the covert individual survival strategies, so well known from the late Kádárian era. The appropriateness of their decision seemed to be demonstrated by the fact that moral behaviour did not prove to be profitable even after the system change. The multitude of corruption cases—including the most notorious Szokai-Tocsik-Boldvai-Budai case—and the frequency of other anomalies in public life resulted in the loss of the creditworthiness of politics; therefore, it has become increasingly difficult to make the losers of the transformation accept their dire situation. Furthermore, these, for the most part, honest people have found that the successful not often disparage but also look down on them. This situation almost naturally radicalises part of those left behind in the process. Similar reaction has been elicited from a number of people by the left-liberal opinion that if this coalition does not win this year's election, then chaos will engulf everything, all of the achievements of the system change will be lost. For the time being, the pro-government media will not recognise that the faith in the expertise and social sensitivity of the MSZP-SZDSZ coalition has fundamentally weakened, but it also goes for the integrity of the governing parties. Under such circumstances it grew into a question of for both governing parties that they do not get involved into yet another corruption scandal. This was the purpose of the declaration of Gyula Horn, that—contrary to their election promise—the privatisation of state assets would not be completed in 1997. It must be more than mere coincidence that the reform of the privatisation organisations and the new property management act was removed from the agenda.[45] In a situation where an estimated 60 percent of the national wealth is held by some 1,500 families, the increased caution on the part of government is quite justified.[46] In the system that had evolved by that time, personal relationships had become more important than anything; this is how some personalities of the state-party era could temporarily come to the fore, as for instance János Berecz or Ernő Lakatos.[47] The gravity of the situation is indicated by Sándor Nagy, Socialist MP, who would be hard to blame for bias against the ruling party, when he says that "corruption has increased to a level where it causes unbelievable moral and economic damage."[48]

Viktor Orbán, FIDESZ President, gave a similar description of the situation: "the government—whether intentionally or otherwise—has achieved an atmosphere where not only minor misdemeanours, but even the gravest crimes, have come to be part of everyday life."[49] The close co-operation between the unions and the post-communist successor party has become an important part of our public life. The intertwining of MSZP and MSZOSZ, the legal successor of the former trade unions, has indubitably contributed to the consolidation of social stability, since the unions have practically given up their role of interest representation.

One of the major sins of the new democratic system has been that it has not sufficiently supported the new, democratic trade unions. In order to retain their forsaken membership, the traditional unions conclude spectacular agreements with their partners, under theatrical circumstances, from time to time. The pro-government politicians and the union leaders reconcile what are essentially their own interests; for instance when they are haggling about the number of the parliamentary seats to be offered to union leaders. They learned the techniques and the language of the bargaining mechanism back in the good old times of MSZMP. The most important and gravest socio-political consequence of the co-operation between the two organisations is that the social security system has come to be dominated by MSZP and MSZOSZ. The operation of the self-governments of the social security and the health insurance system is characterised by a multitude of corruption cases and the threat of bankruptcy. Despite numerous warnings by the State Audit Office almost nothing has changed. The case of the CM Clinic was followed by OVER case, then came the headquarters building case, then the case of the settlement with the ambulance operators, personal quarrels, etc. Those involved in the system are, of course, aware of the fact that it is well worth securing positions in the social security distribution system, for the power over the almost unlimited volumes of orders provides immense influence in a variety of areas.

Although a large proportion of society rejects the corruption, the "values", the immorality—of the "pragmatism" of the MSZP-SZDSZ pact, the well-organised minority forming the coalition, can still quite easily manipulate and control a very large proportion of the unorganised and extremely passive majority. The left is very skilled in taking advantage of the opportunities provided by the fact that there is no single possible and good answer to the majority of social/economic questions, there is no absolute objective and scientific explanation; therefore, personalities, promises, sympathies and antipathies, etc., play a very substantial role. This rational acceptance of spontaneity, however, does not disturb the left in its having been awaiting some cathartic rearrangement or the beginning of a new era for about two hundred years now.

Pragmatic Left. No Wind Favours an Aimless Seafarer

Both dominant parties of the post-communist left are interesting social formations. SZDSZ, the real chameleon party of Hungarian politics, seems to have made very bad calculations. It has already been mentioned that the party has lost its room to manoeuvre, its capability of forming some kind of a pole has practically disappeared; therefore, its future as a party on its own is becoming increasing uncertain, unless it will be satisfied with being the satellite party of MSZP. Elitism is still present in the politics of SZDSZ, along with the "neo-leftist" attitudes originating from 1968 and a doctrinaire liberalism on the basis of human rights, but even this party has come to be dominated by politicians who, by referring to pragmatism, pursue only one real goal and that is to keep their position in power, to ensure the fullest possible promotion of their own interest, including the representation of the interests of the cultural and economic groups behind them.

Bill Lomax, English sociologist, and expert of this region, has drawn a very disillusioning picture of the situation that has evolved so far—and of the intellectuals belonging to SZDSZ in particular. There are no signs of equal opportunities, he writes, and "in the area of acquiring wealth and ownership, a group of 'new rich' has evolved, including the managers of former state-owned companies, technocrats, party bureaucrats, as well as gangsters, criminals and Mafiosi." According to Lomax, the majority of the Hungarian intellectuals are not democrats but liberals, yet they continue to have a sense of superiority. Which is none other than the "revival of Leninism in a liberal costume."[50]

Still, the question that determines the future of both parties is whether the new, capitalist elite—comprising the *nomenclatura* bourgeoisie, the group of the successful technocrats of the late Kádárian era, the winners of the spontaneous and the legitimate privatisation, the elite of the financial and banking sector and, from among those accumulating wealth of hazy origin, the ones who have legalised their position by now—will or will not separate themselves from the MSZP. The majority of the members of the new elite owe their enrichment—besides their dexterity—to their privileged positions they had already enjoyed in the party-state, to the operation of the capital of relationships. Two years after the emergence of the leftist coalition, a left-of-centre Italian newspaper wrote things like: "Hungary is governed by communist chameleons. All power is held by figures of the past."[51]

Along with the peaceful transition, a substantial percentage of the capitalist elite is strongly tied to the leftist socialist-social democratic successor parties, and, since the MSZP has successfully retained its extreme influence, the capitalist elite is interested, instead of detaching themselves, in purchasing the socialist-social democratic parties and making them serve its own interests. This would probably lead to the development of a uni-polar political structure where the MSZP will be capable of controlling a substantial portion of the economic-social processes even under the circumstances of a multi-party parliamentary democracy, re-creating thereby the monopoly of access to information, taking advantage of the opportunities offered by the existence of the informal relation systems inherited from the Kádár regime. With these in their hands, the post-communist left may retain its governing position for decades. The sustained existence of the economic and cultural monopolies renders the operation of the institutions of bourgeois democracy a mere formality.

The lesson to be drawn from the past four years is that bourgeois democracy, social market economy and a humane, yet competitive, society can be best achieved by people other than those who had spent decades fighting against the achievement of these goals. There may be no civic Hungary without civic parties and a set of civic values. The parties of the leftist coalition have learned how to manipulate people without ideology and politics. No wonder that both governing parties are expressly "pragmatist". This is to cover up the complete lack of a coherent ideology and set of values and that of a concept of society, a vision of future, that could be professed and represented. The two parties are capable only of observing the day-to-day matters that await solutions. The legitimacy of the exercising and retaining of power is provided by "expertise". In fact, this professionalism stripped of ideology is the actual ideology of the two parties. They also have the monopoly of deciding who belong to the "elect"—the experts. The group of experts has ensured that legislation keeps favouring the same group of society and that no competing groups can be formed as far as possible.

It is a historical sin of the Free Democrats that in 1994 they betrayed the cause of the formation of a civic society, even formally. The MSZP is a party of the past and the present, it is preserving its anti-democratic reflexes. According to the evaluation of the situation by Socialist MP Iván Vitányi, there has been no time for the resolution of important questions of the society, while the centralisation of decision making has demolished democracy within the party.[52] As a result of their governance without ideology, principles and values, Hungary has drifted into a difficult position. Corruption has become an integral element of the system, which is also proven by the fact that, besides the appalling dimensions of crime, signs of the criminalisation and corruption of the police have also emerged. The impoverishment of a large portion of society, the un-planned and uncontrollable form of privatisation, the reduction of education and health into crisis sectors and the dramatic diminishing of the population all go to show that the parties of the post-communist left cannot be the depositories of the future. Also, they cannot be the depositories of the future because they are against the middle class-es. A few loud, new slogans cannot really hide their deeply rooted antagonism towards the middle classes which they inherited from the communist movement, antagonism which pushes large groups—which could otherwise produce culture and values—to the standards of the proletariat. MSZP is known to be representing employers and employees, the winners and the losers of the system change, the exploited wage earners, the unemployed, the deceived pensioners etc. To win the sympathy of this latter group Prime Minister Gyula Horn is capable of delivering any kind of rhetoric. According to its self-definition, SZDSZ is the party of independent existence, but in fact they only represent the interests of plutocracy, the elite of the late Kádár era and some minorities. Neither of the two leftist parties is interested in promoting the development of a civic society, of strong middle classes, in the promotion of small and medium-sized enterprises, in the creation of an economy and society based on competition—operating under correct regulation. No wonder the parties of the government coalition have not been capable of developing and presenting their coherent political prin-ciples and values. They have been satisfied with the "pragmatic" management of day-to-day issues. But the parties in opposition are not in an easy position either, for—while the MSZP-SZDSZ gov-ernment is pursuing an irresponsible policy of promises and demagogy—they cannot bypass the question raised by Tamás Mellár: "Is it possible to win elections with a programme promising a radical restriction, even elimination, of the acquired rights and monopolistic positions of the current economic and political elite, equality of opportunity, possibilities of joining the economy for lower social groups, and stabilisation of the position of and prosperity for the middle classes?"[53]

With the above taken into account, it may be concluded that the long term interests of Hungary would be best served by the development of the conditions for alternation of powers in parliament. Instead of the currently threatening uni-polar political structure a bi-polar system—based on the dominance of the forces left-of-centre and the right-of-centre—could possibly ensure such a regime. If the 1998 elections result in the continuation of the power of the post-communist left, it would entail the risk that social mobility may disappear for decades and the current—undesirable—structure of society may solidify.

Notes

1. SZDSZ = Free Democrats' Alliance.
2. MSZMP = Hungarian Workers' Socialist Party.
3. MSZP = Hungarian Socialis Party.
4. "Beszélgetés Németh Sándorral" [A conversation with Sándor Németh]. *Népszabadság.* (March 7, 1997).
5. "Egy diktatúra főhőse. Interjú Révész Sándorral" [The hero of a dictatorship. Interview with Sándor Révész]. *Népszabadság.* (January 25, 1997).
6. MDF = Hungarian Democratic Forum.
7. Kis, János. "Az elit megmaradásának elvéről" [On the principle of the survival of the elite]. *Beszélő.* (February 9, 1991).
8. "Interjú Pető Ivánnal" [Interview with Iván Pető]. *168 óra.* (November 17, 1992).
9. Ágh, Attila. *168 óra.* (February 26, 1991).
10. Molnár, Attila. "Közösség és piac" [Community and market]. *Valóság.* (June, 1994).
11. Molnár, Attila. "Bevezetés a tudlib tanulmányozásába" [Introduction to the study of "Sci-lib"]. *Magyar Szemle.* (September, 1994).
12. Hayek, F. A. *Végzetes önhittség* [Fatal conceit]. (Budapest: Tankönyvkiadó, 1992), p. 119.
13. Vásárhelyi, Miklós. "'Ellenzékben' című kötetéről" [On his book "In opposition"]. *Népszabadság.* (January 20, 1990).
14. Bauer, Tamás. "Más helyzetben más lehet a teendő" [The tasks are different in a different situation]. *4x4 oldalas.* (September 18, 1997).
15. "Lejár az antikommunizmus ideje [The era of anti-communism expires]. Interview with Gábor Demszky. *Népszabadság.* (January 19, 1998).
16. MIÉP = Hungarian Justice and Life Party.
17. FIDESZ = Young Democrats' Alliance.
18. "Szabó Miklós egyik előadásának ismertetése" [Description of one of Miklós Szabó's presentations]. *4x4 oldalas.* (September 18, 1997).
19. Szabó, Miklós. "Kereszténydemokrácia és keresztényszocializmus" [Christian democracy and Christian socialism]. *Népszava.* (February 2, 1996).

20. Kornis, Mihály. "Vannak-e a szeretetnek határai?" [Is there a limit to love?]. *Beszélő*. (December 2, 1993).
21. Kozák, Márton. *Magyar Hírlap*. (April 26, 1996).
22. Tellér, Gyula. "Harc a hatalomért" [Fight for power]. *Magyar Nemzet*. (August 29, 1995).
23. Vitányi, Iván. *Beszélő*. (May 12, 1994).
24. "Beszélgetés Tellér Gyulával" [Conversation with Gyula Tellér]. *Beszélő*. (June 23, 1994).
25. ÁVH = State Security Authorities.
26. Tóth Gy., László. *A kádárizmus örökösei és a polgári Magyarország* [The heirs of Kádárism and civic Hungary]. (Budapest: Kairosz Publishers, 1997), pp. 182-191.
27. Bozóki, András. "A demokratikus karta története" [The history of the Democratic Charter]. *Beszélő*. (April, 1996).
28. Tóth Gy., László. *A kádárizmus örökösei és a polgári Magyarország* [The heirs of Kádárism and civic Hungary]. (Budapest: Kairosz Publishers, 1997), pp. 25-26.
29. Schmidt, Mária. "Elmaradt igazságtétel" [Justice never done]. *Magyar Nemzet*. (August 23, 1997).
30. Applebaum, Anne. "Az igazságtételről" [On doing justice]. *Prospect*. (April, 1997).
31. "Interjú dr. Solt Pállal" [Interview with dr. Pál Solt]. *Magyar Nemzet*. (October 15, 1992).
32. KISZ = Communist Youth Alliance.
33. Csintalan, Sándor and Kósáné Kovács, Magda. "Szociáldemokrácia—válaszúton" [Social Democracy at the crossroad]. *Magyar Hírlap*. (January 16, 1992).
34. Tőkéczki, László. "A szocialista modernizáció zsákutcája" [The cul-de-sac of socialist modernisation]. *Magyar Nemzet*. (April 9, 1994).
35. Szabó, Miklós. "Kárhozottak összeesküvése" [The conspiracy of the condemned]. *Népszabadság*. (May 26, 1990).
36. "Mit javasolt Mécs Imre?" [What does Imre Mécs propose?]. *Magyar Nemzet*. (November 25, 1993).
37. "Interjú Baló Györggyel" [Interview with György Baló]. *Beszélő*. (August-September, 1997).
38. ORTT = National Radio and Television Board.
39. Molnár, Attila. "The opened society and its friends". *Hitel*. (February, 1994).

40. Dahrendorf, Ralf. "Egy autoritárius század küszöbén" [On the threshold of an authoritarian century]. *Kritika.* (January, 1998).
41. "Interjú Szent-Iványi Istvánnal" [Interview with István Szent-Iványi]. *Magyar Hírlap.* (June 7, 1997).
42. *Ibid.*
43. DEMISZ = Democratic Youth Alliance.
44. BIT = Leftist Youth Society.
45. Mink, Mária. "Ki fut el vele?" [Who will run away with it?]. *HVG.* (September 13, 1997).
46. The Parliamentary address of Ervin Demeter.
47. The persons listed are former members of the supervisory board of Port Rt., a company in a difficult situation.
48. "Interjú Nagy Sándorral" [Interview with Sándor Nagy]. *Népszabadság.* (September 1, 1997).
49. "Beszélgetés Orbán Viktorral" [Conversation with Viktor Orbán]. *Népszabadság.* (February 20, 1998).
50. Lomax, Bill. "The strange death of the civic society in the post-communist Hungary". *Journal of Communist Studies and Transition Politics*, vol. 13, no. 1 (1997). Translated by István Lovas.
51. Sandro, Viola. *La Reppublica.* (February 9, 1996).
52. "Reformkörösök: válságban van-e a magyar társadalom?" [Reformists: is the Hungarian society in a crisis?]. *Népszabadság.* (August 24, 1997).
53. Mellár, Tamás. "A populizmus mindennapi gyakorlata" [The daily practice of populism]. *Népszabadság.* (February 18, 1998).

László Tőkéczki

EDUCATION, CULTURE
AND THE LOSS OF VALUES

The Consequences of the Kádár Era

After the Communists had eliminated the material and spiritual foundations of independent life (private property, non-nationalised institutions and culture), the majority of Hungarian society settled down to surviving. The worst consequence of the repression of the 1956 Uprising was the petrification of this situation: the loss of individual and collective perspectives independent of the state (i.e. outside "real socialism"). In time, even the reprisals themselves would be surpassed in impact by the systematic corruption of Hungarian society.

The main point of "socialism with a human face" was that, in exchange for voluntarily accepting the way of living thematised by the state, Hungarian citizens were granted a kind of "private space" for existing without direct ideological and political constraints in those sectors not touching upon the freely-interpreted interests of the state. The acceptance of this condition was a proof of civil loyalty in itself (as was said at the time: "Those who are not against us are with us"), and this "socialist democracy" could thus provide opportunities for individuals to assert themselves. This forced situation eliminated the possibility of asserting autonomous morals, and forced even honest and self-confident citizens into constant adaptation. Nevertheless, many happily collaborated, using the unchangeability of the situation as an excuse—if the issue of conscience came up at all.

496

What was known as "double education" was often talked about in the Kádár era, while nobody ever mentioned "double existence". What did this mean in reality? Much more than the simultaneity of communist and religious education for a minority of children, it meant that—although weaker and weaker as older generations were dying out—Hungarian society still knew the requirements of ethical action: at the same time, however, people increasingly adapted themselves to those forms of pragmatic thinking—aimed at survival or prosperity—based on the political situation. This meant that they got on in life, not caring about the wider ethical and collective consequences. The vast majority of Hungarian society became rapidly secularised, their materialism/atheism turned against idealism, with a narrow consumer-type selfishness (known also as "self-realisation") being asserted en masse instead of enthusiasm and humanistic generosity.

Those in power were satisfied with this, viewing such social transformation as the best guarantee that the "counter-revolutionary" national-social unity of the 1956 Uprising would never recur. While a vast paid apparatus and propaganda were officially and loudly encouraging people to follow the model of selfless "socialist morals", in reality, even those who lived off this propaganda were laughing to themselves. In addition, the centuries-old tradition of Hungarian society's following Western models tragically reinforced this materialistic trend. Most Hungarians increasingly and uncritically regarded Western consumer and welfare societies as their ideals, especially after the official ideology of the Kádár era ceased making the "enemy" seem so alarming and instead simply took over from the West its own progressive critique of capitalism. Lacking perspectives, people simply wanted to enjoy and possess as much as possible of the material goods available in their own life. Thus, the modernity of Western societies also became the model of Hungarian society without a moral or even work ethic-disciplinary dimension. The circle closed and society effectively disintegrated.

All the more so, as official cultural policy operated with the aim of neutralising (or in fact eliminating) two fundamental value-systems: Christianity and national feeling. These ideas and beliefs had an essential integrating role and power, which communist officials throughout the Eastern Bloc—with the exception of Hungary and East Germany—tried to take advantage of. Only in these two states were no attempts made on the part of the government to live in peace with one—and sometimes even both (e.g. Poland)—of these value-systems.

The simultaneous bleaching of religious morals and patriotism from the awareness of the Hungarian population had two very serious direct consequences. On the one hand, having already experienced major population losses as a result of World War II, exacerbated by the deportations and resettlements of 1945-48, and then compounded by the mass emigration that ensued after 1956, the country underwent a kind of demographical collapse. On the other, this led to leaving to themselves the ethnic Hungarian minorities separated from Hungary by the diktat of Trianon.

But paradoxically, by becoming indifferent to their collective future, the majority of the country's population, with their increasingly consumerist mentality, started undermining the prosperity of the individual as well. Despite sinking into a continuous crisis, as early as the eighties, the country's communist leadership continued to feed this irresponsible attitude. For, while they increasingly had to talk about the worsening conditions of collective existence (indebtedness, deteriorating balance of trade, etc.), official propaganda continued to suggest that, despite all this, improvement in the individual's standard of living was still possible. Everyone should simply look after number one.

Indeed, a successful minority was starting to rise above the rest even before 1989. Of course, this rise was not based on performance or intellectual excellence (although there were always some exceptions), but on political reliability and personal connections.

What kept the Kádár-era elite together was a kind of business executive's solidarity combined with a dose of much-modified (non-communist) left-wing ideology. These were the technocrats of power who delighted in borrowing their language from the West and calling each other left-wing humanists.

The Late Kádár Era
and the Intellectual Emptiness of Hungary's Public Life

After 1948, the Communists either drove out or silenced everyone whom they termed "reactionary". Although the old ideological, moral, and political principles continued to stagger on for a while, this purge made public life empty and infantile. All that was Soviet and "progressive" started flowing into these liberated spaces. Hungary's intellectual world was flooded by principles foreign to reality, mannered ideological-intellectual products—though always, of course, "scientifically-based". The education of the younger generation drew not on established moral principles but on the views imposed by the newly-installed dictatorship.

Nonetheless, even the bloody restoration that followed the 1956 Uprising could not make people forget that it was no longer possible to create a system of communist true-believers in Hungary. Even the party-faithful pursued their mere individual interests while continuously repeating the same slogans over and over and accustoming themselves to self-censorship. The more intelligent representatives of the Kádár era (i.e. György Aczél) could feel the danger, on the one hand, and the opportunity, on the other, in this emptiness, and slowly put classical Marxist-inspired communism onto the path of a Western-style, non-anti-Soviet leftism—while never forgetting to praise those fellow-travellers in the West who perfected this doctrine. The elite thereby affiliated itself to an old trend, liquidated in the East by Lenin but never seriously threatened in the West: namely, a trend of left-wing political forces that considered communism more tolerable than the Christian and/or national right-wing. Originally, they viewed communism as a major progressive experiment. Later, it became clear that this was actually a dead-end in the glorious self-liberation of mankind, but repudiating these experiments would have been even worse, opening themselves to the charges of being "reactionary" or "counter-revolutionary". The way communism is currently treated by the West has caused very considerable damage to Hungarian society. In today's global world, it is hardly possible to "prove" the moral unfitness of people who have committed crimes by any constitutional norms and democratic moral standards without a clear Western judgement. And how can the "average citizen" be expected to respect the law when it is possible to break moral norms and turn one's coat successfully, even gaining in power, wealth and influence?

The issue here is one of withdrawal: political self-denial on the part of those governors once directed from the East. For, from the moral point of view, it is not relevant how skillfully some groups managed their own self-advancement, and whether they were later democratically legitimised by a combination of the vast economic difficulties of the transition and the old propaganda machinery which had been left untouched. At the time of Hungary's bourgeois-democratic transformation in the nineteenth century, the nobility was able to retain power because—in addition to their ancestors' social merits—they also made enormous material sacrifices. Today, those in power are "taking it all", while the lives of millions have become hopeless amid the ruins of the system they created and maintained.

"The time is out of joint" in Hungary and the majority of society is incapable of self-defence, self-organisation and moral or political self-expression, because of their subverted sense of self-awareness. So most people resort to the old methods of "real socialism", simply trying to survive, and their indifference and suppressed frustration support the old-new groups in power. Without the old moral-ideological framework, the old maxim of the average man of the Habsburg monarchy, "live and let live", is turning our country (and the region) into a haven for unscrupulousness. In today's atomized modern world, there is nowhere to withdraw to. The majority of families and small communities are in crisis, and even when they have not totally disintegrated, they are in thrall to the "information society" through TV, radio, video, computer, newspapers, etc. The individual's brain is inundated with millions of messages that cannot be made sense of except against a background of organizing beliefs and ideas.

This is ideal operating terrain for the "experts" that—thanks to the networks of former communists—continue to hold key positions in the mass media. Amid such helplessness and ignorance, indifference and selfishness, they exert a major influence over the bulk of Hungarian society. All the more so, as their formal "Westernisation" took place during the Kádár era, and they are currently "Americanising" the masses as unscrupulously as their predecessors once "Sovietized" them. Contrary to what they often say about themselves, their background lies not in waging a war for freedom, but in the distortion and manipulation of information. Between 1990 and 1994, they used their professional abilities in this sense to organise and foment dissatisfaction against the government of that time, politicising and blaming everything on those then in power. After 1994, they began depoliticising and neutralising everything, backing the new government both directly and indirectly, perhaps even more fully than before 1989, when the media took its part in the power-games of that period by voicing criticism and strengthening the image of an "anti-communist" alternative. Sometimes they even expressed their views openly, as when they said the Alliance of Free Democrats (SZDSZ) should be the political party alternating in government with the Hungarian Socialist Party (MSZP), thereby preserving a monopoly of political power on the left while excluding those they stigmatized as clearly unfit to exercise power. Such a perfect balance-of-power could only have been upset by the populist wing of the MSZP: but they, in turn, were counter-balanced by the advanced Americanisation of society, particularly its younger generations.

Education Policy in the Late Kádár Era

In the late Kádár era, the system's ideology—being mostly about preserving power, come what may—was no longer all-determining, but consisted more modestly of a framework of restrictions setting the boundaries of the tolerated and the banned. The corrupting principle "Those who are not against us are with us" re-emerged. However, those who stayed within these boundaries had a relatively free scope of action, particularly in areas where formally declared "loyalty" and "scientific" ideological principles and concrete intellectual activities could be largely separated. School is an area where—with some oversimplification—one might say that pedagogical activity can be divided into emotional-moral and intellectual education. Under communism, the former took the form of ceremonial verbalism and official "preambles", while the latter amounted to everyday practice, which could still be enacted at a high standard. And the excellent teachers of Hungary's school system have always achieved these standards, establishing a number of outstanding schools.

Where is the loss of values then?—one might ask. Well, by tacitly rejecting the indoctrinating education principles of real socialism, moral socialisation was very seriously weakened in these excellent schools. Unfortunately, the drive-them-hard working methods of honest teachers, designed for entrance examination success, left students to themselves at a time when a growing number of families was also incapable, for a number of reasons, of educating their children. Thus, despite a respectably high standard of education, an increasing moral deficit was created at schools, which had major social consequences. Those driven by selfishness, individual success and competitiveness are not able to think in terms of issues and structures above the individual, not even in ones that are essential for them as individuals. It is well known from practical experience that self-interest does not create public good: the anarchy of a mass of individuals not willing to cover collective operating costs (i.e. not willing to pay tax) leads to social breakdown.

Thus, the school system of the late Kádár era consisted of technocratic institutions concealing a moral emptiness, where individuals were prepared for their self-centred lives regardless of the common cost. Few more libertarian systems have existed in the history of the world—and this thanks to high-quality teachers who actually rejected the lies around them. An anational, atheist, amoral freedom was achieved, which succeeded in further disorienting young people already buffeted by the storms of youth-inspired radicalism.

The school system of the late Kádár era "liberated" the younger generation to an extent only comparable to the East German model, largely observing one single value: instilling discipline focused on individual self-interest. It is no wonder that this has become the only area where we have remained internationally competitive. We are still able to supply excellent experts en masse to the West. But the collective deficit is increasingly obvious in all other areas: disintegrating families, shattered small communities, diminishing respect for norms and the law, loss of identity, steadily-increasing crime and drug abuse, etc. Hungary has risen rapidly up these international league-tables.

In this respect, our schools have actually followed the libertarian principle of "free choice", only slowing down this process by holding back the young from exercising their "sovereign right" through tough performance requirements (which meant that students did not have sufficient time to take those choices). By the time of the deepening economic and intellectual crisis of the late

Kádár era, Hungarian schools were producing morally volatile generations lacking all solidarity. Without the capital of morals and character, naturally competitive individuals are not capable of lessening the crisis of an entire community. The ordinary mass of people, who wanted to pursue their individual consumer interests and regarded this as the only worthy "humanist" path, were enormously disappointed: political freedom did not automatically provide real opportunities for consumption. For a while, they were still motivated, in the main, by consumer dreams: today, however, there are not even jobs anymore, and the state-financed education of future generations has also become increasingly uncertain. For the vast majority, the "freedom" and "free choice" heralded in this area offer nothing but an unceasing struggle on the labour market.

Thus, the necessary liberal erosion of the rigid, highly uniform structures of the school system of the late Kádár era also led to major losses: by undermining a system which at least provided students with equal chances for individual success (including those starting in a disadvantageous position). Now that the number of schools with minimalised requirements and often offering barely relevant knowledge has increased, the need for a school education system that would integrate students—teaching moral solidarity and supplying a stable identity—is even stronger. As it is, the defencelessness of Hungarian citizens has been increased by the fact that their learning and knowledge now largely depend on their limited financial position.

Value Systems and Mentality of the Late Kádár Era

The bulk of the "real socialist" elites hardly had any value systems at all. There was only the myth of technocratic professionalism—and, for some, its reality. But technocrats solve problems only within the parameters of the given circumstances or regime. The experts of the late Kádár era could not, and presumably did not want to, change the essence of the system (they had to be reliable after all), so they could only partly improve social efficiency. To put it more clearly: there must have been excellent experts working on the Eocene programme; however, this did not make it any more meaningful or useful. Eventually, the nomenclature did not and could not permit professionalism to dominate: it could be allowed to play an ancillary role at the most.

It was exactly this element that—combined with the continuous lack of individual and institutional existence—which generated an increasingly deepening gap between private and public matters and private and public morals. The Kádár regime, like all Bolshevik-inspired formations in the world, was a society of organised irresponsibility. There were occasional scapegoats (mainly at the bottom of the pile) but as decisions of substance were taken by "our men", there could be no calling to account. After the suicidal terrors of Stalinism, the nomenclature only acknowledged an anonymous collective responsibility, ritually declared at party congresses. Weaknesses were now only admitted afterwards, once they had been "corrected", as it were ("there are still some problems, comrades"), and they were usually transformed into "objective difficulties". In this context, they were indispensable as well, as they constituted the basis for the action programme of the following plan period and there would be something to fight against.

Hungary could be "the most cheerful barracks" of the Communist block because, due to the 1956 Uprising, it was here that the brutal Leninist-Stalinist system was dismantled to the highest extent. However, this resulted in the least organised "organised irresponsibility". Everybody could start to live for themselves, following their own interests only. Both the fate of public property and the responsibility for future generations also became private matters, while the focus of the individual's life was entirely transferred to individual leisure time, with the job being important merely as a source of income and because of compulsory employment (which, formally-speaking, continued to exist until the end of the regime). The profitability, competitiveness and organisation of jobs remained a matter of statistics and administration, despite the high number of competent departments and officials, and it only mattered to the local management when they were forced to defend themselves as part of some occasional political campaign (staff cuts, profile change, "clean hands", etc.). So Hungary became an interesting shopwindow of socialist private life, with a confusing jungle of state, party and private activities intertwined with flexible boundaries, while the Hungarian state as a collective organisation became dramatically indebted. And the fact that the late Kádár regime could be attractive and admired was because it was able to present some features of the Western consumer private world without changing its own essence. As a "human-faced" left-wing Socialist society, it enjoyed the sympathy of Western fellow-travellers and its own "liberated" individuals. However, this Socialist/humanist shopwindow experience was extremely costly, because Hungary did not have a rich capitalist big brother as East Germany did. The disastrous consequences of living from day to day started to become obvious, but nobody could believe in collective bankruptcy in the Soviet big brother's camp—and grip. The long-term responsibility of filling holes in with loans granted by our "enemies" increasingly started to express the view of life of many Hungarian citizens: we'll manage somehow or other.

While fewer and fewer people felt any collective solidarity, except for their immediate acquaintances and associates with common interests, the growing volume of Western loans placed harder and harder collective liabilities on Hungarian society. This created enormous burdens, divided in an incredibly uneven way, but, of course, nobody cared at the time. The majority continued to follow the path of individual prosperity, at any price. In this increasingly free competition, moral rules or laws became completely redundant. Honest people came to be considered as dupes in Hungary.

The opportunities of the period following the change of system brought back the conditions of 100 years earlier, the unscrupulousness of the original accumulation of capital. The conscious and instinctive destruction of those aspects of statehood discredited by Communism destroyed the institutional and legal basis needed for social balance.

The irresponsible policy of the late Kádár era bred the amoral human types of the new accumulation of capital, letting Hungarian society become a victim of a murderous private struggle. Its long rule saw the return of forms of unequality unseen here for decades, or even centuries—the increasingly unfolding system of fist-law. The roots of Hungary's current "criminal structures" clearly go back to this time, of course.

The Devaluation of Knowledge
and Culture in Hungarian Society

Let us begin at the beginning: after the Communist takeover, the equalising policy directed against the middle-class and intellectual class, did not create the income conditions required for the way of life of intellectuals when creating the new "people's intelligentsia". It can be established in general that, after the en masse retraining campaign of the initial period, learning was not and did not become attractive to the masses. After the economic changes of 1968, it became clear that learning, which, even at the time, required some financial sacrifices, did not secure an advantageous position: indeed, so-called "intellectuals" often found themselves at a disadvantage. Thus, a self-reproducing intellectual class came into being again, living under much worse conditions than in the Horthy era.

The almost complete feminization of important intellectual professions reflected the fact that the given area was underpaid (teachers, health care workers, etc.), as did the appearance of large numbers of unqualified staff. We lagged behind other countries in Europe in terms of the number of students in higher education, while the number of those not completing eight grades steadily increased. An enormous degree of lumpenisation started in villages after the collectivisation and in cities with the creation of mass housing estates with a low level of cultural and collective infrastructure. The discredited official ideology and its increasingly obvious dominance without any intellectual meaning devalued the humanities—social sciences in particular. In higher education, Marxism was still compulsory for all university students, but was considered valueless gobbledegook. We can also say that general knowledge became the professional knowledge of small groups. Forced into dialectic materialism, it was distant from humans, unintelligible, and unfit for debate or further thinking because of the controlling medium. Apart from one or two areas, the development of Hungarian social sciences got stuck, everything was increasingly centred around left-wing theories and views imported from the West. This meant that, if these could possibly have any "harmful" consequences, they had to be "domesticated". And representatives of the real sciences (or theoretical natural sciences) had to orientate towards the foreign opportunities gradually opening up.

The cultural mobility of the average member of Hungarian society did not rise as a result of the Socialist "cultural revolution": feudal features reappeared, and everyday life coarsened—as everywhere in Communist countries, with self-evident behaviour elements of civilian propriety disappearing almost compulsorily. As the civilisational standard rose very little in general, modernisation often brought Western products of disintegration, a general loss of traditions and self-awareness. Of course, this can also be observed in Western societies. However, there at least, production discipline and organisation, and the motivating force of private profit, largely restricted this to private life and leisure time. This survival-type real-Socialistic world is characterised by the highly manipulated inorganic contents of consciousness of existentially defenceless people. This situation was little changed by the above-mentioned quality teaching of many Hungarian schools. However, a society's cultural standard depends on the everyday intellectual average of the masses. Even if we do not idealise the old Hungarian world of the time before 1938 and between 1945-47, we must clearly see that the social capital of morals and solidarity of that society was greater.

Today, the forms of "honest poverty" typical of our region—peasant, petty bourgeois—have been replaced by lumpenisation and increasingly aggressive criminalisation (mainly subsistence crime). Using the slogan of "freedom", modern libertarian propaganda has had increasingly disastrous effects. Increasing inequality of opportunity and also performances, which were already characteristic of the late Kádár era, have become entrenched—particularly since 1994, when the Hungarian government started proletarising masses of people by curbing basic welfare expenditures. After 1945, the foundations for dictatorship were laid down by fully nationalising material assets; today they are establishing a pseudo-democracy by selectively withdrawing intellectual assets (learning, health, security, identity, public order, etc.). A pseudo-democracy dominated by a monopolistic power, where the majority will not be able to assert its will and interests despite possessing general voting rights. This is an old plutocratic model, only this time the counterweights that exist at other times and in other places (strong small and medium-sized property, independent institutions, churches and interest groups, etc.) have been eliminated by Communism.

Our public life operates in the shallows, only serving the interests of a limited minority. As the habits of responsible and independent decision-taking were forced onto the individual and family for decades, the masses of our people were reprimitivised. Just like reading for people who do not or cannot read regularly, democracy and politics are tiresome for people with non-democratic lives.

The majority of Hungarian society is characterised by incredible volatility and impressionability. And the fact that our new situation after 1989 was not attained by ourselves or by our youth, always easily moved to enthusiasm, also has its consequences.

As so many times before in our history, culture and education offered us a way out of this situation. Hungary's current cultural and education policy, however, is not based on the needs of its own society, but is confined to imitating foreign models and strengthening its own power-base.

Why is Hungary's Cultural Policy the Way It is?

The intellectual groups that played a leading political role in the change of system agreed for a long time on the need for eliminating the state (one-party) system which earlier dominated cultural life, and for ensuring as much freedom as possible in culture. There was, however, a major misconception here: these groups believed that everyone shared the same priorities as themselves, and that all members of society are equally independent. This is a perpetual temptation of progressive intellectuals, who also believe that—simply given a free choice in the matter—the masses will opt for the same humanist goals they claim to be theirs.

Let us disregard the fact for now that there are widely differing views concerning values, as well as the fact that it takes a sound financial basis to realise choices (such as going to a freely selected school or even the theatre, for that matter), particularly at a time of austerity measures curbing central budget expenditures. Let us think it over: how does a parent know what his/her child needs, and, particularly, how could he/she know that the modern liberal school—as opposed to the more traditional, "demanding" variety—can only give his/her child, who has a number of disadvantages in a world of intellectual-type public institutions anyway, more inequality of opportunity? Which brings us to the main point:

Hungary's current "liberal" cultural policy is aimed at drowning the majority of society, inevitably poorly-informed as regards education, in freedom. An ignorant, uneducated society is unable to change either politically or culturally-economically: this entrenches the existing monopoly of power and makes the application of still further "austerity" measures even easier.

Global financial capital and the "mass culture" serving it are creating mercilessly anti-democratic and hierarchic structures, with barely any constraints. Lacking the tools of money, knowledge and organisation, an increasing majority is drifting helplessly—becoming, in fact, redundant in the process of efficiency and profit maximization. Although they could play a role as consumer masses, due to their low purchasing power (or even the total lack of it), they are increasingly becoming a welfare burden and a risk factor. This global trend is a much more difficult problem in post-Communist countries than in the West, and particularly in North America, which is far more organised from the point of view of production and social institutions and also has a lot of global economic advantages. Regions that are poor or have become unconditionally dependent through privatisation will either become self-aware and educated, thereby becoming able to assert their interests through natural compromise-based bargaining processes, or turn into colonial-type peripheral regions, where only a handful of individuals might manage to clamber onto the bottom rung of the decision-making ladder. "Mankind" and "universal" humanity cannot be democratically transformed into a "global society". Even nation states are based on organisations operating according to principles of formal representation and occasionally tolerating vast inequalities—despite being supported by strong emotional, identity-communicational and historical communities of interests. Today's financial globalism knows no such compromise as it will not tolerate any restriction of profit.

What does this have to do with public education? In highly atomised societies, only a fragment of the population is able to answer the challenges of globalisation, through financial advantages originating from their social position. And these are not only information challenges, but rather challenges of accumulating a complex social-moral-cultural capital, both individually and collectively. Global economic and power centres—never elected by anybody and largely uncontrollable—can only be counterbalanced by well-informed, cultural-national politicized communities with deep layers of solidarity and culture. Only such an autonomous system of solidarity and values is able to protect its collective interests in a complex way and to protect its individuals from complete defencelessness.

And this is only one side of the coin, the issue of material existence. No less important is the feeling and awareness of national-political affiliation and familiarity, because—for the foreseeable future—the vast majority of humanity will not and cannot be unrestrictedly "mobile", for both financial and cultural (language) reasons. The number of the current group of international managers and bureaucrats is insignificant compared to the number of those, whose destiny is "here you must live and die." This cannot be changed either by the Internet or the fictitious world of television: in fact, in some ways, these even reinforce our state of being bound to the soil, to our home. However, man is a non-economic being, this is what his divine character consists of, thus, he will always be "closer" to those he has directly known as family members or neighbours, whom he grew up together with and can share his emotions and dreams with, to those he is linked with in an often very "irrational" way. We have no reason to assume a rapid and radical change in the fundamental characteristics of humanity. Despite the indisputably increased efficiency of technical civilization, there has been no "progress": mankind has remained the same. The human soul cannot be re-engineered so easily.

This is where the third, extremely important role of schools and education comes in: culturally-mentally (spiritually) and personally counterbalancing civilization and the utilitarianism intertwined with it. Without this, mankind will destroy the life-ensuring natural order and the wonderful balances of the created world, as well as itself, through its narcissistic material "progress". Schools have, and will have, a very tough educational-training duty in this respect, as this is a matter of life and death. Only people educated for self-restraint and self-discipline from early childhood will not want to jump onto trends which could have an unpredictable price and consequences for mankind as a whole. If the concept of humanity has any important contents as regards practical life and survival, that could be used in "environmental education". This is where even the most stupid and selfish can understand that "we are all in the same boat" and the irresponsibilities of individuals and communities unknown to us can also destroy us—and vice versa.

In these circumstances, Hungary's current "liberal" school policy, based on so-called free choice (which can be minimised depending on the local financial situation), is a major mistake. It is an error because a society is not only made up of well-off, educated and rational individuals, who are therefore—theoretically—able to take that choice and to "realistically" assess their situation. Not to mention the fact that, without moral-ethical restrictions, solidarity and mental-spiritual culture, these characteristics often result in intellectual adventurism.

School is an institution with a collective mission, operating considering the values and opportunities of individuality, but which cannot support the disintegration of basic and essential forms, as then the lack of common principles, values, traditions, cultural material, behavioral norms and so on would simply make communication impossible. The world, and, accordingly, schools cannot set the unrestricted self-realisation of the individual as an objective, as neither the natural-material (financial) nor the human-spiritual conditions for that goal exist. It is very important to emphasise this in a world with unusually great inequalities, resulting in boundless opportunities on the one hand, and a depressing and frustrating sense and reality of deprivation on the other hand in human relations. This increases the inability to communicate and everyday unpredictability in interpersonal relations.

True, today, we cannot see any traces of the old poverty of the traditional world. The poor and the young are constantly teased by the effects of television, presenting a world beyond their reach as natural in advertisements. It is no wonder that crime increases among the young and the middle-aged to the injury of property, on the one hand, and in drug abuse, offering a way to escape from reality, on the other, which, in turn, will further increase crime. These trends cannot be controlled by "liberal" punishment and "prevention" methods, based on human rights and emphasising the responsibility of the otherwise neglected community. Education neglected in childhood (training for self-discipline, order and propriety, socialisation for solidarity, determination and integrity, etc.) cannot be substituted by sheer rationality: the "adulthood of reason". Autonomous individuals must be able to adapt to the laws of the community, as those not willing to take mutual responsibility can be excluded easily and with justification.

Schools, yes, we have to admit, are institutions of collective constraint, as they are based on compulsory education: social institutions offering some degree of protection, where the various kinds of hierarchies and inequalities of the "adult world" can be learnt in an artificial form. However, without such preliminary training, after an "alternative" school, representing some artificial childish nowhereland, students can only expect disappointment and tough rebukes later on in life (at work, for example). Today's cult of the individual's self-realisation leads to the inevitable straining of conflicts in human relations, while education should reinforce the willingness to cooperate. This is not directed against also crucial principles of competition and performance, but is aimed rather at integrating these with morals and respect for law, so that the individual will be able to reconcile his/her own objectives with the community's interests.

And this will not be achieved through the miscellaneous information dumping of the Internet. That could serve as a good tool later on, with adequate preparation, nothing more. (Being, by the way, a great business for some groups!) Humans cannot become mere consumers of information. Knowledge (information) remains a tool, by which one will strive for good, the other for evil. The Hungarian school of the future should provide students, the individual with everything that is knowledge and information, but—as much as possible—should bind the same personality to values, faith, principles, order and service as well.

Why do Moral Issues Become Vital at School?

For very simple and understandable reasons: today's Western-type consumer society has failed. This is clearly shown by the increasing masses of "redundant" unemployed, and the austerity programmes of governments, carried out with the increasing profit of the major transnational capitalist companies and banks. The time preceding the great world economic crisis is repeating itself: major efficiency measures in production and yet a lack of purchasing-power on the side of the underpaid masses. The imbalances of over-exploited nature have been giving signals that the chain-reaction leading to the collapse of the entire system could happen any time. And the existential failure, accompanied by social crises reflecting a lack of respect for norms (drug abuse, crime, delinquency, disintegrating families, etc.) cannot be treated with the liberal ideal of rationalist optimism, which has failed so many times before. When increasing profit can only be secured at the price of others' decreasing income, "the hour of truth" is sure to arrive soon.

We must admit that the omnipotence of technology and science, which seemed to substitute for God, is over, as it has hit the barriers of created nature. And we also must admit that another seemingly undisputable pillar of social efficiency, the cult of individuality, has also reached the point where it turns into its own opposite, becoming the source of collective destruction (crime, drug, alcohol and other delinquencies) and deficits. It has become clear that the extremely complex "human phenomenon" cannot be "redeemed" with the simple mechanistic methods of reason. Mankind, and human existence itself, has enormous "idle (neutral) energy needs" (the sources of these are the need for love, individual "defects", emotions, soul, passions), which can only temporarily be ignored in the profiteering of the "desanthropomorphised" modem world.

However, it has also become clear now that the institutionalised welfare policy of the welfare states is unable to cope with increasingly large-scale social problems reflecting a lack of respect for norms. Aid and assistance only provide crisis management (intervention), instead of a long-term solution. It is impossible to put a large number of adults continuously under the care of others, as this, on the other hand, would conflict with the sacred principles of freedom. This is the revival of the proletarian syndrome of ancient Rome, which can still be tolerable for certain groups up to a certain level of expenditure, but its increasingly evident spreading is already shaking the foundations of a system believed to be monopolistic, just as it did before. In modern mass societies, self-protection is almost impossible in public security and public health (for example, as chest X-rays are no longer compulsory, tuberculosis can again infect anyone indiscriminately!). It is also worth considering that, today, anyone with basic (technical) skills can become a terrorist or a criminal, once he/she can create the supply conditions. Will we be able to protect ourselves against professionals lacking all "outdated", "petty bourgeois" public morals in the long-term with anti-terrorist squads and electronic alarms? And is it possible to constantly stimulate the masses for consumption and possession through advertisements and propaganda on the one hand, when there is no real purchasing-power on the other? Is it possible to endlessly talk with pathos about human opportunities and freedom, while all the majority can afford is day-dreaming? These questions could go on and on.

The so-called "modernisation strategy" of Hungary's current cultural czars only reveals a doctrinaire lack of ideas, on the one hand, and a hardly concealed interest of the elite on the other: the old collective structures have to be eliminated and replaced by the disfunctioning of continuous technical modernisation. As a result, the majority of society will have a constant deficit, while the minority, being able to circumvent and substitute for the entire structure of services, will happily do without quality collective institutions. Western forms of freedom are worth very little to society without adequate education, organisation, tradition and material goods. This is why the future Hungarian school has a key position. It is not enough to talk about the requirements of labour market constraints, we should provide opportunities to meet these requirements, in fact—out of individual and collective interest—we should lovingly force people to meet these requirements, in order to avoid the need for costly measures to reduce poverty and crime as much as possible. This is how we can, in fact, we must, follow an economical policy. Unfortunately, our government is rather thinking in terms of supporting the needy, giving them compensation and pay-offs.

Until a greater part of Hungarian society becomes "middle-class" or at least much more balanced than it currently is, it will remain necessary to place a strong emphasis within budget spending on culture and education and on nurturing talents—which is just on the one hand, and the healthiest form of social mobility on the other. We should acknowledge at last that, due to the destructions of real Socialism, culture and education, or becoming a society of

"Bildungsbürger"'s is again Hungarian society's only chance for progress, as accumulation of capital in this sector has and will have no restrictions, and investment in this sector also has much better chances for return compared to the material sector.

Furthermore, in the current situation, when family socialisation has largely disintegrated, the dominant vulgarly materialistic view leading to destruction and mental-spiritual emptiness can only be counterbalanced by efficient community education. A society, which can be efficient in preserving the essential natural and community balances, will acquire enormous advantages. To this end, the first step should be to limit the unrestricted individual and market profiteering. It should be made clear that manmade infinities (in profit, business, power, consumption, possession) are impossible on this earth. A different road, and different roads, will lead us to achieve human dignity on a human scale; thus, even rationality can only play a major role as an instrument. Today, mankind is constantly receiving signals as regards the viability of human life both in society and in nature.

Summary

Hungary's future cultural policy will have to follow Hungarian traditions and seek new roads at the same time, as we are also facing the deadly challenges facing universal humanity (unemployment, drugs, crime, self-destruction). Of course, it will not have to solve these problems alone, but as part of a well-coordinated political programme. However, it will have to play a leading role in this activity, turning back the representatives of the dead-end of paneconomics. We have to act responsibly with a "universal horizon", but in our own historical and moral community, that is in our national, universal Hungarian community, because that is what has been entrusted to us. We cannot follow the path of either mechanistically imitating other models or of self-satisfied isolationism, but have to reject the "modernising" representatives of financial globalisation serving the interests of small groups, who are offering helplessness to the majority while only benefiting themselves.

We must emphasise that this means the application of classical principles and methods proved so many times in historical practice and complying with state-of-the-art instruments of technical civilisation. All we want to do is reject the dominance of these instruments. As we must reject the absolutization of any new initiatives, knowing that there is no self-redemption, and the "total truths" created by human mind and hands have always turned into mass destruction regimes (Communism, Nazism, unrestricted free market liberalism, people's socialism, religious fanaticisms).

The future Hungarian school policy must be based on the experience and spiritual culture and education of both the nation and of humanity as a whole, serving the cause of the Hungarian nation's quality survival. Cultural and education policy is a vital issue, which—paradoxically—should be shaped by representatives of the "old generations" to suit the needs of the new.

Tamás Fricz

THE ORBÁN GOVERNMENT:
AN EXPERIMENT IN REGIME STABILIZATION

The First Two Years (1998-2000)

Allow me to start with apologies. It is a difficult task to present a clear historical picture of a government that came into office two years ago and is still governing. Yet it is my duty to undertake this task since it is clear that the Orbán government is of utmost significance to the history of the new Hungarian democracy and I will do my best to describe what comprises its significance in my essay.

Since this government's activity and influence is being formed at the present time, this is not a "classic" historical description of the period between 1998 and 2000. Instead, I will discuss the Orbán government's political and social significance and its pronounced affects on the process of democratization. My approach and analysis are fundamentally those of a political scientist's.

My thesis will be presented in five chapters. The first chapter deals with the antecedents to the Orbán government: the "heritage" of the Horn government, the causes of the 1998 electoral success of the FIDESZ (Alliance of Young Democrats), and the character of the coalition government established after that election. The second section seeks to grasp the historical significance of the Orbán government—based on their two years of operation—in the Modern Age at the end of the millennium. The third section aims to outline the characteristics of the Orbán government: its place in the divided power structure of the country, its own internal structure, its operation, and its basic governing values as compared to previous governments. The fourth section analyzes the Orbán cabinet's view of democracy and how it puts it into practice. And, finally, the fifth section daringly evaluates possible alternatives for the future.

My entire discussion argues that the Orbán cabinet's third governmental cycle fills an especially important historic role in the stabilization of the new Hungarian democracy.

Antecedents: Circumstances of the FIDESZ Coming to Power and the Creation of the Governing Coalition

Let us begin with the fact that the May 10 and 24, 1998 elections brought along quite an unexpected—unbelievable for many—change in the post-1990 history of Hungarian politics. The Alliance of Young Democrats (FIDESZ), holding a nationalist, socially conservative, yet economically liberal orientation, won the election against the Hungarian Socialist Party (MSZP), the successor to the old Hungarian communist party (MSZMP). The FIDESZ barely made it into parliament four years before with only 5.18% of the vote. It was a redemptive experience, taking the FIDESZ from near total loss to total victory within four years.

The basic question about the results of the 1998 election was how did the FIDESZ, with a party leadership averaging only 35 years old, achieve an election victory that looked like a miracle? A few topics need to be analyzed in order to answer this question. First, "what happened" to the FIDESZ between 1994 and 1998? Second, what general causes played a part in the election results? And third, how much did the election campaign influence the results?

To answer the first question, let us start with the fact that, early in 1993, the Young Democrats entered into a formal alliance with the Alliance of Free Democrats (SZDSZ) in order to win the election. Their goal was to present to the electorate a liberal center alternative to a conservative government coalition comprised of the

Hungarian Democratic Forum (MDF), the Christian Democratic People's Party (KDNP), one branch of the Smallholders' Party, and the Hungarian Socialist Party (MSZP) which was turning into social democratic party. However, starting in the fall of 1993 when Gábor Fodor's league of urban-and-SZDSZ-sympathizers left the alliance, it increasingly lost its rationale for existing, although formally it did not disintegrate until the elections. The FIDESZ did not draw the proper conclusion from the deteriorating relationship between the two liberal parties and did not "turn over a new leaf" while the SZDSZ more and more openly spoke about the possibility of cooperating with the MSZP.

In addition, the Young Democrats committed two more decisive political blunders. On the one hand, they did not separate themselves from the activities of the MDF-led government coalition, even though by then there was a definitely anti-government atmosphere in the country and the FIDESZ itself was dissatisfied with the government. Instead, they spoke about a "half-turn" away from the government, something which did not translate well into vigorous opposition behavior for a dissatisfied citizenry. On the other hand, the Young Democrats had been waging a forceful anti-communist propaganda for some time against the MSZP, the strongest opposition party prior to the 1994 election while a decisive majority of the people in Hungary were turning towards the MSZP as the successor to the communist party with a certain type of nostalgia. These two political mistakes—and several other factors not mentioned here—can amply explain the significant election loss. With 5.18% of the votes, the FIDESZ barely crossed the minimum threshold needed to get into parliament. It had 20 deputies and was sixth among the six parties.

And so the leaders of FIDESZ were posed with the question of how to go on? What could and should they do so that this utter failure would not be repeated after four years and so that the FIDESZ would run with a good chance in the following election? Into what kind of party would they have to transform and what kind of political profile would they have to assume? Further, what alliance should they envision for the coming four years? Anyway, there were mighty few in July of 1994 who believed that a miracle would happen and that the great loser would become a winner in 1998.

There were two factors which helped to form and stabilize the political image of the FIDESZ after 1994. One factor was the political attraction and dedication of the party leaders, while the other factor was opportunities to modify the party's policy positions. Remarkably, the two factors exerted their effects in the same direction. Beginning in 1992-1993 the Orbán-Kövér-Áder-Szájer-Németh team increasingly moved toward a nationalistic version of liberalism while supporting those conservative values acceptable from a modern perspective. On the other hand, between November 1993 and May 1994 the left-liberal party alliance with the SZDSZ broke up and the relationship between the two liberal parties became significantly impaired. It would have been against the FIDESZ's basic principles to shift to the left in order to approach the MSZP. Therefore, the only thing left was to move towards right wing parties with moderate "center right" views which would also tolerate the basic values of liberalism. Finally, the party leadership decided to aim for an acceptable, moderate center-right political alternative for the 1994-1998 period.

FIDESZ also wished to have its own unique political image, different from all the other parliamentary parties on the center right-side of the political spectrum. It was also obvious to the FIDESZ leaders that a unique political profile notwithstanding, they would still not be able to defeat their strongest political rival, the MSZP, by themselves in 1998 and they would have to think in terms of another alliance. However, it was their clear goal to become a leading and decisive force in the center-right alliance.

The social and political vision formed by the FIDESZ and revealed to the public played an important role in realizing their plans. The view of a "bourgeois Hungary"—a bourgeois society and a bourgeois future—proved to be effective in persuading the public and a significant part of the electorate. Further, the idea of a bourgeois Hungary alluded to the progressive heritage of the Reform Era and the past 150 years with the recurring theme of a bourgeois transformation. On the other hand, it also was associated with the petty-bourgeois (lower middle-class) transformation that began under Kádár's state socialism, although it was quite obvious that the FIDESZ emphasized the former association. The image of a bourgeois Hungary also worked well to cement the center-right political alliance since it offered a connection between moderate and right-wing parties without extending that reach to the radical right-wing or integrating their vehemently national and religious demands.

The Civil Alliance with the MDF and KDNP initiated and orchestrated by the FIDESZ was established during the fall of 1994. However, beginning in early 1995 the KDNP gradually moved away from the Alliance, a move closely connected to György Giczy's election as a party president in January 1995 and the radicalization of the Christian Democratic People's Party. The result was to limit the cooperation to the FIDESZ and the MDF. Then the Christian Democratic Alliance separated from the KDNP and joined the Young Democrats in May and June of 1997. In spite of all the controversial problems of the Civil Alliance, the fact is that during these four years the FIDESZ succeeded in forming a unique and strong political image. Therefore, by 1998 the political and ideological message of the Party was obvious and calculable.

As a result, by 1997-1998 the FIDESZ had significantly weakened the extensive existing image in the public that they were "turncoats" who turned wherever political success could be expected and who lacked a real image. Yet it seemed unfathomable at the time that a right or center-right approach would succeed just four years after the 1994 MSZP victory. The FIDESZ profile-reconstruction paid off during the 1998 election partly because the party did not change during the campaign but instead continued with the image the voters got to know during the previous years. This must have created an immediate bond of trust with the citizens.

The question of the party's political language was also essential to the party's strategy. On the one hand, the FIDESZ spoke to the public about a clear political value system, yet its language was not ideological but pragmatic and tried to assume positions on certain topics which were professionally well-founded but dogma-free. Infrequently, however, unsuccessful political and ideological positions were assumed by party leaders which did not enhance the FIDESZ's political image. Rhetoric about the liberal value system, patriotism, compassion towards Hungarians living in neighboring countries, religious tolerance, respect towards progressive traditions, and encouraging the creation of a middle-class did not overshadow discussions about other issues but rather offered a political background to the ongoing political discussions. The party's political language did not change during the campaign either and was not replaced by a radical, ideological, intolerant, or aggressive tone as was typical in 1990 and 1994.

The FIDESZ's ambition to create a wide-spectrum electoral base bore excellent results in 1998. As a result of political agreements and resignations and because many voters turned away from their former parties, the FIDESZ became the party of choice for the moderate right wing. Whether the party would be able to retain its role during the coming legislative period, as well as the elections of 2002, was a different issue.

It seems that the political profile and image of a future bourgeois Hungary reached voters who favored such a value system, while their socio-structural situation inclined them in that way. In way of proof, during the May 1998 elections, counties where the economy was booming—mostly Transdanubian counties—voted for the FIDESZ while counties of the *Alföld* and the Trans-Tisza area gave it less support. The MSZMP was very successful in the latter areas.

All this is especially interesting because, during the past four years, the FIDESZ often criticized the government's social policy, the so-called Bokros package and especially its hasty and unnecessarily irritating elements. Thus, as a "center right" party, the FIDESZ undertook the task of "left wing" opposition. Yet it was not the economically backward counties which preferred the FIDESZ, in spite of all its "social compassion." So why did it happen this way?

In my view, the explanation lies in the fact that the occasional "left wing" rhetoric of the FIDESZ—usually arising from some concrete political challenge—did not have a real impact on the citizens of the "runaway" regions. These people might have believed that, despite appearances, the MSZP was the party that, in line with its political profile, emphasized state support of the unemployed, the socially at risk, state subsidy for low income people, and social care. As opposed to this, inhabitants of economically improving counties, especially the middle class, owners, proprietors, and entrepreneurs, discovered in the FIDESZ a political program and political character whose value system and future vision was most acceptable to them.

Election results, so it seems, proved that the FIDESZ succeeded in drawing together a party identity and a party identification that Hungarian parties had rarely managed to achieve in the past eight years. The FIDESZ identified itself, in the public's eyes, as a moderately liberal and bourgeois central party that responds sensitively to conservative values and this is how the citizens came to identify the party. This fact is one of the most important explanations of the FIDESZ's success in the election.

However, this is only one side of the coin since political and party races are never one-man battles. The FIDESZ's success also depended on the political opposition, on the activities of the Horn government as well as several other factors. Several very important socio-political factors had to occur so that the invincible-appearing "successor party," the MSZP, would lose the elections. Although their 1998 loss was an inimitable moment in recent Hungarian history, it does not necessarily mean a repeat defeat in 2002. However, it does mean that in the 1997-98 period, May of 1998 was the most favorable moment for the FIDESZ. In other words, until about February or March of 1998 there did not seem to be much chance to defeat the MSZP and it may well have been the case that just a few months later and the FIDESZ could not have been repeated its victory. Sometimes there are favorable moments in politics; a good politician grasps them while a bad politician misses them.

Let us not forget that the MSZP, the socialist successor party, had been a forceful agent on the Hungarian political scene, and obviously remained so after the 1998 elections. In 1998 almost the same percentage of people voted for the socialists as during their 1994 victory and their economic, cultural, and social networks continue to remain intact and functional. This is why it is unlikely that the MSZP will significantly weaken between 1998 and 2002. In other words, however mature as center right "catch-all" party the FIDESZ might have become by 2002, it would still not have had the chance to form a government by defeating the MSZP. If we also assume that the Hungarian economy settles on a dynamically progressive course in the coming four years, it is possible that if the MSZP had retained power in 1998, then it would also be re-elected in 2002.

What factors had to come into play for the Young Democrats to win, in addition to their fortunate political preparations? I would emphasize four circumstances.

1) In their rhetoric, the MSZP-SZDSZ government coalition had been unable to show a clear and acceptable connection between the results of macro-economic, financial, and national budgetary policies and these micro-economic and everyday conditions directly affecting the people.

The "Bokros package," named after the Minister of Finance, was introduced on March 12, 1995 and contained stringent financial measures. It led directly to the stabilization of the national budget. However, this "severance" program was loaded with senseless, irrational, and irritating elements some of which were considered unconstitutional by the Constitutional Court. Not to mention the fact that Minister of Finances Lajos Bokros' phlegmatic insensitivity to social conditions was oil on fire.

The economizing program slowly improved the basic indices of the national budget but the Horn government was unable to convince most of the population that improving macro-economic indices incomprehensible to them would sooner or later stop the large-scale deterioration of their living standard. Also, the MSZP and SZDSZ set their "watching eyes" on the EU, the IMF, and other influential international organizations and were mostly concerned about Hungary's foreign reputation. The obvious fact that foreign countries had never won an election for any party was ignored. The Horn cabinet did not have anything to say to the millions whose living standards were stagnating and this attitude necessarily led to failure.

2) The privatization scandal that exploded during the fall of 1996, the so-called "Tocsik case" which tainted both government parties, was a major breakthrough in Hungarian public life. From then onward, corruption cases became a part of political life, and in most cases the government coalition was involved in all sorts of problems. What is more, it also irritated the public that news about corruption involving politicians, ministers and state officials, hardly ever led to negative consequences.[1]

3) The fact that the MSZP-SZDSZ wedding was followed by a dysfunctional "marriage" was less of a problem than its obvious manifestation to the public. There was extremely poor communication between the two coalition parties, conflicts were not resolved behind closed doors, and the coalition conciliation committee

repeatedly failed. What is more, during the last months before the 1998 elections both parties made elementary mistakes in the course of sending messages between them. Prime Minister Horn took the lead in these major blunders when he, as a "simple" citizen, kept complaining about the lack of public safety and kept criticizing the three SZDSZ portfolio ministries. All this finally culminated in the serious defeat experienced by SZDSZ, but also in the decreased numbers of MSZP voters.

4) It is difficult to prove but during the four years of the MSZP-SZDSZ government coalition, the crisis over national values and the pessimism of the Hungarian society did not improve.[2] The government's "results" in macro-economic policy were not "owned" by the society and citizens at large, while their defenselessness and helplessness increased. People also gradually became aware of the different tone that the FIDESZ was attempting to set since the Young Democrats had emphasized early on that, as a governing party, they would achieve towards the nation's goals together with the citizens and that they would count on the entrepreneurial spirit of the citizens to which they would extend governmental help.

Beyond these four factors, a number of events during the last months of the electoral campaign are also worth mentioning. A number of irritating and negative social phenomena increased during the worst possible period for the MSZP-SZDSZ governing coalition. The main issue was not merely corruption but the dramatic deterioration in public security. Bomb explosions, bank and post office robberies, and shootings became everyday events. Needless to say, people are very sensitive about public safety and blame state institutions and the government for its deterioration. In addition to that, nervous and confused statements issued by the Prime Minister, the Minister of the Interior, and other politicians aggravated the situation. It is clear from this that the deterioration in public safety was a major blow to the election chances of the MSZP-SZDSZ coalition.

Finally, while the FIDESZ was successful in the art of democratic electioneeing, the MSZP-SZDSZ coalition was fundamentally unsuccessful. MSZP-SZDSZ leaders could not comprehend that
in democracies, especially in a new one, elections are about new
hopes, promises, and chances for improvement. During the campaign both government parties emphasized that their recent governing performance and political program were outstanding and
even irreplaceable. Therefore, there was nothing to change about it
but rather "to keep the direction" (SZDSZ). This complacent attitude, however, was annoying and irritating for citizens dissatisfied
with their living situation.[3]

Last but not least, President of the Party Orbán's campaigning
skills and participation were also of considerable weight. Actually,
Orbán had matured by the time of the campaign and demonstrated
behavior and attitude that increasingly diminished pre-existing
prejudices about him. What kind of prejudices are we talking
about? Orbán is "too young," "too aggressive," "of dictatorial inclination," etc. These prejudices had the potential of immense negative consequences because as long as this is the way the majority of
the population think about the chief of a party, that party will not
get into power. However, Orbán's campaign was affective and successful in rebutting these accusations. He was calm and determined,
but did not enter into political fistfights nor did he criticize others.
Instead, he spoke about the program of his own party, and was
polite, even gallant, towards his political opponents. These features
were well demonstrated during the memorable televised Horn-
Orbán debate which was decisive to the outcome of the second
round of voting.

Orbán's real character emerged during the campaign and he
appeared to be a real political personality. In spite of his young age,
35, and with ten years of democratic political experience behind
him, he might become the Prime Minister, and a successful one, of
the country. Throughout the campaign, Orbán managed to break

through the psychological hindrances that could have hurt his party. By the time of the second round of voting, the electorate no longer saw a young politician who needed to be trained. Instead, they saw a mature, considerate, forceful young politician with the charisma, ability, and strength to become the prime minister of Hungary.

The significance of the personal factor might be described in the following way: the FIDESZ's every effort would have been in vain had the party not been headed by someone who the public could envision as occupying the prime minister's velvet chair.

However, one should keep in mind that the FIDESZ's victory of 38% of the vote was not enough to form a government. Let us see how cooperation within the coalition evolved.

It is an established fact that in spite its outstanding political performance, the FIDESZ could not have won the elections had the nominees of all the opposition parties not resigned in favor of FIDESZ nominees after the first round. This, however, does not mean that the success of Young Democrats can be fully contributed to the collaboration of the opposition. One has to bear in mind that only a party with good chances for its individual nominees in second round is worth stepping down to another party. In other words, the FIDESZ did not receive these nominations "for free." Rather, the results of the first round empowered them since it became obvious that the FIDESZ was now the only viable political alternative to the MSZP.

It is also worth stressing that the alliance policy of the Young Democrats was the result of clear political vision from months before the election. The FIDESZ's cooperation with the MDF and the Christian Democratic Alliance was not unexpected and the cooperation continued throughout the campaign and election period.

However, it is also true that the relationship with the Independent Smallholders' Party had remained an uncertain issue until the last weeks of the election campaign. The FIDESZ "floated" the question of a probable election or government coalition with the Smallholders. But it was a question difficult to settle. Neither a close association nor a government coalition with the FKGP was very desirable to the FIDESZ. But it was also obvious that without the support of the second largest opposition party, the FIDESZ was not likely to implement a change of government. This was a dilemma that the FIDESZ had not been open and clear enough about until the first election round when it had to deal with this undesirable but indispensable situation. The fact is that after the results of the first round were published, the FIDESZ immediately chose to clarify its obscure relationship with the Smallholders. The one-sided withdrawal of FIDESZ nominees in favor of Smallholder nominees with a greater chance of being elected clarified the issue. At that point the FIDESZ made it clear that supporting the Smallholders was indispensable in order to replace the left center government coalition.

It cannot be questioned that governing with the FKGP and its leader was some FIDESZ wild dream, still after the first round of voting the FIDESZ strove to form and maintain a proper relationship both with the Smallholders and their own "natural" allies.

After the second election round, there was no surprise. As a result of coalition talks with the FKGP and MDF, an Orbán-led FIDESZ-FKGP-MDF government coalition entered into office on July 6, 1998.[4]

The following is a short summary of the political content of the coalition. There is a strong ideological closeness between the FIDESZ and the MDF going back to the Civic Alliance that began in 1994. The two parties feel that their differences can be worked out. That is not to say that the ideological differences between the FIDESZ and MDF, and especially between the FIDESZ and FKGP, are not without controversy. Why is that? In Hungary there are two major political dimensions: 1) the question of socialism versus anti-socialism including one's view of the communist successor party (the MSZP), and 2) the question of cosmopolitanism versus nationalism, which has historically meant the populist versus urban debate.[5] On both of the dimensions, the three parties of the coalition are on the same side—they are anti-socialist and nationalist. Nonetheless, there is a not so significant but still defining difference among the parties as well: the issue of radical right-wing populism and antagonism it produces among the moderate parties. The Smallholders' Party—and especially its leader—is a typical representative of Hungarian radical right-wing populism, and this separates the FKGP from the other two coalition partners. Populism is unacceptable to the Young Democrats because, ever since the party's founding, it has striven for a pragmatic and task-oriented attitude even if it is sometimes thwarted by a forceful ideological undertone.

Beyond an agrarian-oriented populist rhetoric, there is a significant generational difference between the leadership of the FIDESZ and the Smallholders' Party and between their respective electoral bases. The generation gap further increases differences in political styles, which is already considerable, between the two parties, obviously making coalition cooperation more difficult.

Therefore, intra-coalition differences should not be underestimated, nor overestimated for that matter. It can be said that the FIDESZ-FKGP marriage was clearly not made in heaven, but it was not an arranged marriage either. This is a conflict-ridden union that can only be held together by the benevolence and self-restraint of the parties involved.

The experience of the first two years shows that it is a functional marriage because the parties aim at solving the problems between them and not at deepening them and they are tied together by the need to keep their political opponents at bay.

2. The Historical Significance of the Orbán Government

Before venturing out to analyze the first two years of the Orbán government, it is worth examining the significance of the FIDESZ victory, the establishment of the Orbán cabinet, and the FIDESZ-led center-right-right coalition.

I would stress two points. First of all, defeating the MSZP, the successor party of the MSZMP, the former communist party, during the third free election after the fall of communism indicated that the political tasks of changing the political regime and completing the democratization of the country were now completed.

Why is it that the first post-communist election, in 1990, had not brought a real breakthrough from dictatorship to democracy since the successor party to communism had suffered an obvious defeat? The reason is that the important 1990 breakthrough was clearly motivated by a general negative social disposition towards the socialist dictatorship, a denial of the old and helpless regime and an obscure desire for something new. However, the first social outburst and the repudiation of a collapsing regime cannot be considered a conscious and carefully thought-out relationship to a new democratic regime. During the first post-dictatorship election the general public has not yet internalized the values of the new regime but instead wants to restore the lost achievements and social situation of the pre-dictatorship regime in the new democracy. In general, they opt for new parties and democracy because they hope that the "good old times" before the dictatorship can be brought back.

Therefore, a wide-scale social disappointment in new post-communist democracies has been inevitable. The Antall government, as well as all the other new governments of the region, had to face the economic crisis left by socialism and communism, a situation of social disintegration, a multitude of social problems, and high unemployment besides issues concerning national identity and ethnic and nationality controversies. The first democratic governments, obviously, could not have coped with these piles of problems; the Antall government was no exception. As a result, people turned away from it in disappointment because their hopes had not been fulfilled. However, their hopes had still been connected with the pre-dictatorship old regime and it is small wonder that during the second election the successor parties to the communists came back to power. That is how it happened in Hungary in 1994 and the same happened in several countries of the region, from Poland through Slovakia to Lithuania.

At that point, however, a new confrontation occurs. The successor parties again come into power and, for the second time, the public had to face the fact that the successor party—which so far was dispensing illusions and feeding on nostalgia—was unable to redeem the world, not even able to reduce unemployment. This was the political moment when the public realized that the successor party was neither better nor worse than other parties and, from then on, it occupied its own "normal" place in the line of democratic parties. At that point an equal political race among parties was possible and the successor party did not continue to have a special privileged status.

In their study on the Spanish transition to democracy, political scientists S. H. Barnes, P. McDonough, P. A. Lipset, and P. Lopéz made some important statements about this phenomenon.[6] Based on empirical studies they claimed that democratization began following Franco's death in 1975 and that the political change of regime truly stabilized at that point when the change of government was no longer handled as a change of regime. That is, analysis of the activities of individual governments could be separated from analysis of the regime itself. This took place after the 1982 takeover of power by the Spanish Socialist Party led by Felipe Gonzalez and the establishment of a new government. After the experience of a right-wing dictatorship, governmental rule by the Spanish Socialist Party was the first thing that made people believe that a right-left government change did not mean a change of regime.

The same thing happened during the change of regime in Hungary. It becomes clear that during the period when the center-right Antall government and the successor-party Horn cabinet, the government and the regime was not truly separate. Substantive criticism of the MDF-led government also questioned the "credibility" of the new regime and, as such, democracy. Since its achievements were not impressive, confidence in democracy was lowered and a turn towards the MSZP, with its reminiscences of socialism, was the natural reaction needed to come. However, after the performance of the four years between 1994 and 1998 there was no more third chance. For the second time, the nostalgia called socialism failed.

The FIDESZ came to power in 1998 as a second-tier center-right political power in opposition to the successor party. The public had already witnessed that neither the Antall nor the Horn government had destroyed democracy and so a natural democratic "shift system" began to occur in politics. The new center-right FIDESZ government fits this line of analysis and there has finally been a psychological breakthrough among the public: to evaluate the regime and individual governments separately. Gradually, a minimal trust in democracy has been forming. This trust is based on the assumption that democracy is a value and institutional order worth preserving even if a given democratic government does not happen to offer anything perfect or totally acceptable to the people.

Both the FIDESZ and the Orbán cabinet have to be given credit for helping to form this process. On one hand, by defeating the MSZP they obviously pointed out that the power of the successor party could be broken and that there was a new center-right alternative that could be chosen at any time. They also showed that this shift in the basis of the legitimacy of the democratic system had begun and could be counted on. On the other hand, it is the Orbán government's task to create a government that is credible and successful, making the choice for democracy meaningful and stable.

Therefore, it was the Orbán government that implemented the second change of regime and the second defeat of socialism. It also achieved a second, and this time positive and conscious, choice for democracy, one not based on negation.

At the same time the theoretical possibility of choice that appeared with the FIDESZ, and not with the MSZP, does not exclude the possibility that the MSZP could have permanently remained one of the dominant parties of the Hungarian party scene, not as a socialist reminiscence party but as a democratic left-wing or social democratic alternative. Why would this possibility remain, beyond the fact that the MSZP's base is quite stable and hardly decreased between 1994 and 1998? To answer is related to the point that the mere presence of several parties is not enough to consolidate democracy. In order to create a political alternative at least two political parties or centers of power are needed which represent real social, economic, or cultural bases. Even if a party has an appealing political program, if it does not possess political, economic, or cultural (symbolic) capital in Pierre Bourdieu's interpretation,[7] its electorate will not consider it credible enough to implement its program. In the new Hungarian democracy, it is only the MSZP that has had and still has a surviving stock of such capital as a result of the survival of a wide social network. The Antall government could not and did not want to break this social-political force and did not recognize the significance of the challenge. The Antall government also proved to be incapable of establishing an alternative counter-force during its four years in government. And after four years the MSZP returned to power accompanied by the SZDSZ—strong in the field of cultural capital—and reinforced its social capital and social force.

Prime Minister Orbán proved to be an excellent analyst when, shortly after entering into office in the summer of 1998, he outlined the political significance of a FIDESZ-led government. "It is more than a change of government and less than a change of regime," he said. The message of this frequently quoted saying is clear. The "pursuit" of the change of regime has not been over simply because an election had been won. It was also necessary to create a strong alternative to the MSZP's forceful concentration of social power. If we summarize the events of the past two years, it is obvious that while in power the FIDESZ has consciously striven to create an alternative social power center imbedded in the economic, cultural, local, and civic lives of the country beyond the realm of ordinary politics.

It is important to note that the FIDESZ's recognition of this goes back to their severe electoral defeat in 1994. Let us go back in time and let us have a look at how and in what areas the FIDESZ's "construction work" began since this is a story with a morale about the establishment of modern political power.

After the 1994 electoral defeat the FIDESZ faced the upcoming legislative period again in opposition and isolated in many respects, with a narrow electoral base, and a modest infrastructure, and without media or economic connections. Beyond the FIDESZ leaders, member, and a narrow group of supporters, hardly anybody thought that within four years they would end another election period this time in triumph. From a defeated position, the leadership had had four years to devise a way to jump back on their feet and to build a strong and able party capable of replacing the center-left government.

What conclusions had they drawn? They concluded that, by itself, no party could achieve permanent success without a theoretically sound and convincing political and ideological program. In addition, if a party does not have a wide institutional and social network in important spheres of society—political, economic, cultural, and local—and is not socially imbedded through various institutions, it could successfully appeal to a significant segment of the public but the majority will not vote for it. They will not because that party lacks the social, political, and economic power and the supportive base which would ultimately make it possible, upon coming to power, for the party to establish its program both in political and non-political life.

Recognizing this, after the 1994 defeat the FIDESZ engaged itself in persistent and detailed everyday work to construct its missing social network. This construction work involved four important areas:

a) First of all, the interest of intellectuals who help to form public opinion had to be drawn to the party since around 1993/1994 this section of society had almost completely turned away from the FIDESZ. This shift was closely connected to the bitter relationship between the FIDESZ and the SZDSZ which also played a significant role in the FIDESZ's 1994 defeat.

From the fall of 1994 onwards the FIDESZ devised all sorts of ways to approach "benchmark" intellectuals, especially not committed to the left or the SZDSZ or MSZP but who also did not belong to the radical right-wing either. The party tried to find all sorts of institutional forms of rapprochement—forming clubs, societies, associations, and political salons—and these attempts to build confidence gradually led to results. It worked so much so that intellectuals who were disappointed in the SZDSZ but who for theoretical reasons could not identify with the MSZP and missed a European centricity, modernity, and liberalism from the "hard" right-wing sided with the FIDESZ by 1997/1998 and supported the party in publications, interviews, public appearances, cultural and public debates, etc. A narrower group of intellectuals undertook to directly support the party leadership in advisory or other looser roles. One should not underestimate the significance of these activities.

The role of the media and press intellectuals ought to be emphasized because of their importance. Around 1993/1994 the party's media and press coverage hit bottom and this situation needed to be radically changed. In modern politics a party that does not enjoy the attention of the media and the press is unable to perform successfully, and unable to send its messages to the electors. The image the media forms about a party will prevail since electors do not possess suitable tools to check the validity of the image instilled by the media and the press.

The FIDESZ undoubtedly did a very successful job during the past four years. One daily newspaper became a party sympathizer, if not a party organ, while a part of the people working in the media and some of the publishers established a decent relationship with the FIDESZ elite. The media especially began to respect the FIDESZ after the eruption of the Tocsik scandal in the fall of 1996 and its ongoing intensification until the 1998 elections. The appearance of new commercial channels on TV also played a significant role in strengthening the party's press and media positions. On TV young editors and reporters quite openly turned towards the FIDESZ and broke with middle generation of journalists who were still sympathetic to the SZDSZ and the MSZP.

b) The economic sphere was another important area. The party's influence on groups with significant economic power—entrepreneurs, directors, managers, and the banking sphere—was very weak. To change this situation was extremely important because a party that envisions a bourgeois future for the country cannot achieve success without the support of the middle class and upper class nor without the support of the leaders of multi-national companies.

The task was before them and by the end of the four-year period the FIDESZ achieved significant results. Once again, I need to allude to the Tocsik scandal which, along with other corruption scandals which had surfaced, shattered the confidence of certain entrepreneurs and managers in the government. Capital is always drawn towards power. However, it is most awkward for capital if political power becomes extremely corrupted or if the relationship is not defined by an ideological bond or if that bond is a weak one.

As a result of all the above, during the fall of 1996 and in the first half of 1997 a decisive part of the economic elite "changed gear" and began to sympathize with the economic-political views of the FIDESZ. Making contacts with certain circles within the banking sphere was also successfully accomplished.

All this happened—aside from the corruption scandals of the government—because the FIDESZ's opposition policy convinced a certain part of the economic elite that the party was capable of doing well at the elections and able to take power. Therefore, it was worthwhile to invest in the party, literally and figuratively.

c) A party that envisioned the establishment of a bourgeois society and country could hardly achieve its goal without having strong and direct connections with the citizens. This was an especially great challenge for a party with a relatively low membership—it was probably the smallest among the parliamentary parties—and without existing and surviving integral connections in society such as that the MSZP had. In order to overcome its lack of social embededness, the FIDESZ inspired, supported, and initiated the establishment of circles, associations, and clubs that showed any kind of interest in a bourgeois world view, attitude or value system. One cannot say that during these four years the party had fully achieved its goal, but it was able to demonstrate partial results. The social embededness of the FIDESZ is still imperfect. However, the government's position in the coming legislative cycle offers significant opportunities to accelerate this process.

d) The party, as an election majority party, recognized that it faced the same problems at the local level as at the national level. It lacked connections with the leading circles of the local economic, cultural, and public life and without their support political success is very hard to achieve. Therefore, the same thorough attention was given to everyday matters at the local level as at the national level. The results, however, were not always the same due to the nature of the situation. At several places they managed to change the political atmosphere of the local elite, to increase sympathy towards the party, but again, in several other instances, none of these results took place. The party is also only halfway into this process as well as the process of establishing social networks since it is an interconnecting process.

All the above helps prove that the FIDESZ paid attention to minute details and did a very thorough job in order to appear at the 1998 elections as a political actor with an independent and essential part of society behind it. However, besides establishing a strong image and offering a clear political alternative, the FIDESZ was concerned that it provide not just a political alternative but also a governing alternative. In order to do this, the party had to demonstrate a political message and a political team that was convincing both professionally and politically and that could be taken seriously by the voters. A party might be appealing by itself and might say things that appealed to the voters and still not get their votes if the party is viewed as unlikely to do professional and successful work at steering the country.

Therefore, one-one and a half years before the elections the FIDESZ began to build up its "shadow cabinet." The End of the Century Political School (Századvég Politikai Iskola) and its research team, important background institution of the party, had outstanding roles in conceptualizing the hoped-for government's activities, its structure, and its working mechanism. Quite a few months before the elections the FIDESZ set up its shadow cabinet and let known to the public the individuals and their portfolios and tasks who would be part of the government.[8]

This conscious and organized work must have had a positive affect on the voters since it made known who they would be electing to the government should they vote for the FIDESZ. In sum, it can be stated that this 1-1½ years of work played a major role in allowing the voters to see not only an opposing political alternative, but also a real governing alternative in the FIDESZ. The latter must have played a decisive role in the May 1998 success of the party. By then, concerns about the "youthfulness" of the party had diminished.

In addition, the FIDESZ, when later in possession of governing power, continued to construct an alternative power center. This has been manifested in a number of activities: the replacement of certain personnel; the acquisition of certain economic, social, and cultural positions including a part of the banking sphere; the acquisition of certain positions which control the media; control of privatization process; regulation of the client building function of state businesses and investments; and the politically motivated selective work of supporting self-governments. The degree of institutional, personal, structural and legal change has been enormous, so much that it has triggered antipathy in part of the public—something that the opposition parties have taken advantage of. This segment of the public and the opposition describe the FIDESZ government as overbearing, aggressive, and intolerant, while extreme opponents describe the Orbán cabinet as anti-democratic. It is hardly surprising that the MSZP, the successor party, plays a major role in condemning the FIDESZ-led cabinet and in formulating extreme and irrational charges.

Activities that the FIDESZ government has pursued during the past two years in order to establish an alternative center of power sometimes has understandably raised intense emotions in the opposition. However, the intent to systematically implement a change of regime has been behind every government and party endeavor. Contrary to all appearances, simple arrogance and desire to make money has not directed their activities but rather a well-weighed political strategy based on definite principles and convictions. In my view, the interesting part of the situation is that a certain part of the voters and intellectuals would like to make the FIDESZ exhibit governmental self-restraint, typical of long-standing democracies. This would perpetuate the existence and survival of "inherited" power centers in Hungary.

Therefore, the slogan, "more than a change of government and less than a change of regime" reflects the essential nature of the significance of the historic challenge facing the Orbán government.

3. Characteristics of the Orbán Government

After examining the precursors and causes of the 1998 FIDESZ election victory and the significance of the establishment of the Orbán government, it is time to discuss the structural-functional characteristics of the Cabinet in power for two years. What are the most important constitutional, institutional, structural, and functional characteristics of the new government?[9]

There are three major characteristics of the new government.

a) As opposed to the Antall and Horn cabinets, the FIDESZ cabinet has striven and continues to strive to establish a stronger and more concentrated government organization. In this respect, the words strong and concentrated ought to be stressed.

Hungarian democracy is parliamentary, not a presidential system. It closely resembles the German chancellor system with a weak president, a strong head of government—the chancellor—and a strong parliament. In Hungary this structure was essentially founded by the MDF-SZDSZ Pact announced on May 2, 1990—the so-called Antall-Tölgyessy Pact named after Prime Minister József Antall and fraction leader of the SZDSZ, Péter Tölgyessy, played dominant roles in setting it up. Along the German pattern it introduced the motion of a constructive no confidence vote. As a result, the prime minister can only be removed if the parliament also votes for a new prime minister and his/her program. It also decreased the number of two-third majority laws down to twenty, which gives the government dominated by the prime minister a very wide field of action, and it also indicated the person of the president, a traditionally very weak position.

By taking over the model of chancellorship, this constitutional construction allowed for a strong government in Hungary after 1990. For all their intentions, however, neither the Antall nor the Horn governments managed to implement a strong government. In case of the Antall government, this can be explained by administrative inexperience and by what has already been mentioned above. And although the MDF-led coalition held power, it did not possess adequate social power based on economic, cultural, media, or civil social capital. Therefore, it was unable to realize its ideas. It was wriggling in the meat-grinder created by opposition, mostly that created by the SZDSZ and the MSZP, and by public opinion supporting the opposition. Such a forceful and systematic critical voice surrounded the conservative government so that, finally, it became almost completely incapable of action. It could not implement its ideas concerning the replacement of personnel, was unable to gain the sympathy of a significant segment of the media, and was unable to line up substantial economic capital.

The Horn cabinet, in spite of a substantial parliamentary majority, did not manage to create a strong executive power. Because of this, the boomerang effect prevailed: lobby groups, especially the trade unions, inherited from the previous regime and supporting the MSZP, tried to assert themselves vis-á-vis the government and the cabinet was unable to effectively resist. The Bokros package momentarily introduced a more austere government policy. However, the old interest groups soon found their way back once again. On top of that, the Horn government's strength was thoroughly weakened by continuous arguments with its smaller coalition partner, the SZDSZ, since the SZDSZ frequently opposed certain goals of the MSZP and often blocked them.

The FIDESZ-led cabinet is the first one that consciously uses possibilities that the new constitution created by the 1990 MDF-SZDSZ pact allows, including ones created by the chancellery type government, and has been very forceful in the implementation of its goals. The principle of "more than a government change and less than a regime change" makes it act this way. However, it would have been unable to act upon it—just as the MDF was unable between 1990 and 1994—if, during the past few years, it had not consciously striven to develop a social power base. What is more, starting in July 1998 after gaining power, the FIDESZ has continued to expand and widen its social base. It organized the supervision of privatization and of state banks, gained increasing influence in the media, and established wide ranging connections with multinational companies.

Only with this power base in the background could and can the Orbán cabinet pour content into the chancellery model since it did not have to face hostile public opinion.

Its strong governing style manifests in the fact that in order to implement its program, the cabinet, generally speaking, does not negotiate with the opposition. Instead, it asserts its political will by using and utilizing every legal opportunity. It limits negotiating with opposition parties to questions in need of consensus, such as foreign policy or two thirds majority laws. Although in these questions the FIDESZ strives for dominance as well, in other questions beyond these issues still in execution and the force of management are determining factors. All these are supplemented by an assertive and self-assured style that sometimes shows the signs of arrogance that a certain part of the opposition and the public call the arrogance of power or, in extreme cases, dictatorial inclination.

One could raise the question of whether it is justified for the FIDESZ to apply a relentless and systematic style of governing that hardly ever looks for consensus even though it does remain within the framework of a democracy in spite of the criticism from the opposition. We have to admit that the answer is "yes," if we take into account the political goals undertaken by the FIDESZ. If a party wants to establish a base of power against its greatest political adversary—such as the successor party MSZP—how efficient would a government style and practice be that constantly tries to reach agreement with the adversary in opposition or to take important government measures on the basis of a multi-party consensus. It is evident that it would contradict this basic goal since it would help the opposition to get additional opportunities to retain its social power. The FIDESZ would like to avoid this and there is hardly any other governmental strategy or style at hand than what it demonstrated during its first two years. We can also add that the FIDESZ had found partners in the Smallholders and in the, slightly reluctant, MDF to work toward this ambition.

We might also want to note that the possibility of strong government founded the government structure that created by the May 1990 Pact, but not experienced in the first two post-1990 governmental cycles. The Prime Minister's Office, headed by a minister and not an under-secretary of state for the first time since 1990, became a key institution in this structure.

At forming the government structure the FIDESZ considered solutions to two questions of vital importance: on one hand, suitable institutional order would prop up the "chancellery" weight of the prime minister and, on the other hand, diverging sectoral and portfolio interests would still not make the implementation of a unified government program impossible. They found a solution in substantially restructuring the Prime Minister's Office along the pattern of the German Chancellery Office.[10]

What did this restructuring entail? First of all, a minister occupied the head of the Office, made possible by a law passed but not implemented under the Horn government in 1997. Secondly, an increased number of tasks and functions was assigned to the Office in order to prepare the decisions of the Prime Minister so as to strengthen the power of the chancellery type government. Thirdly, following through with the "topics" of the ministries, a kind of mirror-reference system was established to reconcile and coordinate any clashes among the portfolios and, thus, was instrumental in all of the government's strategy. Working out a governmental strategy became the official work of the Office based on the presumption that simply adding up sectoral and portfolio interests is not a real government program but merely eclecticism. Strategic analysis and planning also came to be tasks of the Office, an essential change. Therefore, we are justified in stating that the Prime Minister's Office and, through that the Prime Minister himself, occupy key positions at working out and coordinating government policies and at coordinating and "selecting" the interests of the ministries.

It is important to establish that such a chancellery type concentrated governmental structure is a totally new development in the short history of Hungarian democracy. The Antall government would have liked to have had it, but could not change the previous model of sectoral enforcement of interests. Further, the Antall government was divided among different needs. Gyula Horn and government had already seriously considered the appointment of a chancellery minister—the law was passed—but it was hindered by clashing personalities and clashing group interests within the party and between the two coalition parties. The Orbán government is the first to apply this lesson drawn from the legal framework of the constitution and still intends to continue the change over to a prime ministerial government.

At the same time, it is obvious that the government structure also carries some danger since it is possible that the Office may evolve into a tool to over-concentrate political power or to limit the ministers' independence.[11] However, two years' experience indicates that the István Stumpf-led Office has not become a dictator's office but has, more or less, met expectations. What really limits a successful implementation of the model is the periodic "resistance" of the coalition partners, especially the Smallholders' Party. The Smallholders' Party, led by József Torgyán, are reluctant to subordinate the interests of agricultural and developmental portfolios to all other governmental interests. In key situations this tension eventually dissolves and ends up in a compromise, but working out a perfectly syncronized governmental policy is often hindered by the resistance of the FIDESZ's coalition partner. It causes problems for Orbán and the FIDESZ time and again, but during the first two years they were able to handle most political problems in this manner.

b) The Orbán government is committed to recognize values.

The Orbán government wanted and still wants to encourage the development of national, liberal, and conservative values in society. This was articulated in its election program and in its 40 point program. How new is this compared with its predecessors? The answer is that it is partially new. Although the Antall cabinet placed conservative values in the foreground, it could hardly encourage them due to its weakness and helplessness. Compared to that, the Horn government, also affected by its coalition partner, started out from a kind of value pluralism, or even value indifference, envisioning its primary tasks as the handling of macro-political issues. It was of the view that choosing values was an individual matter with which government should not interfere. However, SZDSZ politicians held the Ministry of Culture and the culture policy they enacted moved somewhat away from actual indifference towards respect for "difference," especially towards a wide variety of minority cultures and value systems. Even if there was not a truly official "value policy," still the SZDSZ articulated an unofficial one by its praises and appreciation of minorities while having little to say about the majority.

The Orbán government radically broke with its predecessor's premises. On one hand, it set itself against the Horn government's embrace of the SZDSZ view of cultural issues by shifting emphasis from minorities to concern with the majority and the average Hungarian citizen. In the Orbán government's view families must play a priority role in establishing a bourgeois middle class and, as such, a bourgeois Hungary. Therefore families and the middle class ought to be supported in every way in order to strengthen the nation. At the same time, support of the poor is also essential in order for them to stand on their own feet so that, sooner or later, they would also become part of the bourgeois middle class.

Furthermore, the government, by token of its own generational characteristics, attributes a prominent role to the young and young families whose support is one of its most important goals. In addition, the Orbán cabinet totally broke with the attempt to "macro manage" society, typical of the Horn era, and always speaks in terms of individuals and families. It tries to speak directly to the citizen and to explain to him/her the consequences of certain measures in terms of his/her individual life. For example, Orbán's New Year's Day 2000 speech concerned the role of ordinary citizens and praised their achievements. It seems to be the goal of the Orbán government that "big politics" be made to be part of everyday life and, that way, gain back the trust of the people for politics.

In the period between 1998 and 2000, the FIDESZ took governmental and legislative measures to encourage its value preferences and its election promises in the area. Let us have a look at a few examples of the steps taken during the first two years of the Orbán government. The following laws and decrees can be mentioned: abolition of university and college tuition, re-establishment of the government's child-care allowance as an individual right, the re-introduction of the child-care benefit beginning January 1, 2000, passage of the law regulating smoking, passage of the law on family doctors' practices, and the introduction of housing loans especially preferential for the young. As a result, the FIDESZ has already implemented quite a few important laws from among its 40 points.

c) Among the values advocated by the Orbán government, its commitment towards national values is especially important to emphasize. It has developed a flexible position and strategy protecting Hungary's national interests in the international arena.

All these are in sharp contrast with the strategy of the MSZP-SZDSZ coalition to conform with the demands of major international institutions, political, economic, and financial, during its four years in power. The Horn government's source of pride was the praise it received from "western" organizations and its source of shame was any reprimand received from these organizations.

The Orbán government broke away from this paradigm and, while it assumed that the country had met the expectations of international organizations since it still strove to join them, it also believed that this should not be an unconditional process. If international expectations came into conflict with Hungarian national interests and traditions, it is Hungary's first requirement to protect its interests since integration does not mean self-sacrifice (or if it does, it is a serious problem.) All these became viable issues in connection both with joining NATO (in March of 1999 Hungary along with Poland and the Czech Republic became full fledged members of the NATO) and in connection with its integration into the European Union. Admission negotiations to the European Union are long and complicated and the interests of the European Union and Hungary have clashed at several points. It is not irrelevant what strategy Hungary's government pursues during these negotiations. As opposed to the essentially accommodating strategy of the Horn government, the Orbán government strove to achieve an equal negotiating position while outlining more autonomous and independent claims. Beyond all that, a nationality-oriented policy was especially emphasized by the Orbán government with its involvement in the lives of Hungarians across the border and in actively supporting their interests.

This ambition manifested itself in protecting the interests of the Voivodina Hungarians during the Kosovo War in spring of 1999, in keeping up official contact with Hungarians and their official governments in Slovakia and Romania, and in the preparation of the "status law" of 2000 which to grant preferential opportunities to foreign citizens of Hungarian origin.

Obviously, the question might be raised whether these value commitments and policies mean a break with certain liberal principles, such as pluralism, and whether such values as solidarity and respect for difference which are not emphasized are thus systematically pushed into the background. Well, after two years of experience one can acknowledge that the conscious state support of certain values and accompanying institutions—such as nation, Hungarians living across the border, family, the development of the middle class, religion, and different churches—did take place but it rarely was accompanied by an administrative limitation of other groups and institutions embodying different values. Therefore, the value policy of the Orbán government is preferential, but not discriminatory.

Yet everything considered, the government's cultural, ideological, and social policies have intensified ideological debates and hardened the line dividing the government parties from the opposition parties, more with the MSZP and SZDSZ and less so with the MIÉP. The breaking points of Hungarian politics had been determined by ideological and cultural conflicts of the politicizing intellectual elite since 1987/88 and even during the decades of communism and socialism. As a result, the society was atomized, de-politicized, and divided into two intensively opposing ideological and cultural sides. The basis of opposition continued to be the same division. On one side are those who are pro-nationality, anti-socialist, and anti-successor party—FIDESZ, MDF, FKGP with the MIÉP having ties here, although its theoretical and radical right wing attitude and frequent extreme views separate them from the coalition parties. On the other side are cosmopolitans, non anti-socialists, and non anti-successor party supporters—the MSZP and the SZDSZ. The Orbán government consciously emphasized values and ideological differences and did not want to launder them for any kind of political compromise. However, neither did the MSZP nor the SZDSZ when they emphasized strong disagreements and even opposition acted to intensify ideological and attitudinal divergences.

In those two years both in political and public life, two widely opposing sides were formed and the front line between them became rigid. There is hardly any cross-over between nationalists and cosmopolitans and few mediating groups, organizations or public figures which aggravates the creation of political consensus, for example on foreign political issues. Moreover the relationship between the members of the leading elite of the two camps is laden with negative feelings and anger—see the FIDESZ-SZDSZ relationship as an example. It should also be noted that an unvoiced mutual prejudice overshadows the relationship between the two sides: anti-Semitism on one side and philo-Semitism on the other. Fortunately, this ethnically driven approach is manifested only in the most extreme members of the two sides—such as the provocation of the Jewish-Hungarian opposition—but it does not improve the political atmosphere by any means.

The value- and attitude-based radical opposition manifests itself in the parliamentary work as well: use of an uncivilized tone of voice, violent and hostile exchanges, and the inability to compromise and reach consensus. All these happened even during debates about primarily non-ideological and pragmatic bills, let alone during discussions of bills embodying contradictory values when opposition was especially intense. The question of establishing media advisory boards, the debate about the minimal number of people allowed in a parliamentary faction (regarding the MIÉP), the issue of monitoring people, or oppositions to the three-week-long parliamentary session all belonged to the second category. In addition, there were foreign policy issues, especially during the Kosovo War and possible strategies to protect Hungarians in the Voivodina. During the spring of 1999 this topic destroyed the foreign policy consensus more or less established during the previous years. As a result, foreign policy consensus in Hungary has been limited to narrow areas. It ought to be mentioned at this point that on certain issues like the media case, the MSZP and SZDSZ constantly accuses the government of conspiring with the "extreme right," that is the MIÉP, not distancing itself from the extreme right. This unfounded accusation, expressly denied by the government, was part of a political strategy aiming to prove that the government itself is part of the extreme right and dictatorial and, thus, to discredit them abroad.

The political debates about values have become especially heated in connection with the Holy Crown Bill (later Act) whose aim was to recognize the one-thousand year existence of Hungary as a nation in a dignified manner. The opposition, and especially the SZDSZ, considered the Act superfluous, both the text of the Act and the aim itself of permanently moving St. Stephen's Crown and coronation regalia to the Parliament Building. The debate forced the government parties to substantially modify the text, yet the opposition boycotted the January 1, 2000 festive parliamentary session. This was symbolic since it indicates that the basic questions of Hungarian history are evaluated differently by the government parties and by the left-wing opposition.

The question is whether the Orbán government, with its strong commitment to specific values, was right to further intensify the ideological-cultural divide between the two political camps. It seems that the FIDESZ's starting point was the belief that in a new democracy pre-existing and sometimes hidden disagreement are to be brought to the surface because it is meaningless to cover them up with senseless compromises. Moreover, such hidden controversies would eventually break into the surface anyway, often in a more intense and radical manner than otherwise. Therefore, political views should be out in the open since clear and obvious views create more favorable conditions for the evolution of political consensus.

4. Conclusion:
The Orbán Government's Philosophy of Democracy

In conclusion, beginning with the present and looking towards the future, let us try to answer the question how much and in what way the Orbán government's activity has influenced the evolution of the character of the new Hungarian democracy and how much the 1998 election will affect the 21st century political processes in Hungary.

As a preliminary opinion, I would say that the Orbán government played, in its first two years, and will continue to play, a significant role in forming the new Hungarian democracy. On one hand, it has brought to the surface the markedly divided and conflict-laden character of political relations in the country, something left latent during the first two election cycles, and institutionalized those differences into the characteristic features of the new democracy. On the other hand, the Orbán government simultaneously took steps to create the consensus needed for a long-term political compromise, although its significance and handiness to practical politics would only later be revealed.

Now these two statements need evidence to support them, which I will try to provide.

The most mature approach to analyzing the problem of Hungary's democracy can be found in Dutch political scientist Arendt Lijphart's famous models of democracy.[12] Lijphart makes the distinction between majority and consensual democracies. The essence of majoritarian democracy is the ability of a party that wins an election to be able to gain power and use it to implement and enforce its political ideas and program without negotiating or compromising with the opposition. Therefore, neither consensus nor compromise with the opposition is necessary and the government party or parties completely assume the political responsibilities for governing until the end of the election cycle. In this model, which is mostly characteristic of Anglo-Saxon countries with two-party systems—Britain, Canada, New Zealand, Australia, and the United States—political parties and political competition can be intense and the two major parties compete in order to gain control of political power.

Lijphart's alternative model is the consensual model in which the governing party or parties do not consider governing power as their exclusive privilege. On the contrary, they share the responsibility of governing with the other political parties through continuous negotiations and agreements. The consensual principle is implemented via different constitutional techniques such, general coalitions, great coalitions in government, veto right for parties including non-governing parties in deciding important political questions, a consensus-based legislative process in the parliament, and the prevalence of the confederative principle at the national level. The consensual model exists in a significant number of continental democracies—Belgium, the Netherlands, Switzerland, Austria until 1999—and is seen in governmental elements in several other countries as well. In this model there is always a multiparty system, although party and political competition is limited and moderated due to the existance of consensual principles.

One has to ask why it is that the majoritarian principle and strong competition prevail in Anglo-Saxon countries while the consensual principle as well as cooperation and self-constraint on political competition are so influential in continental countries. Lijphart gives a clear and unambiguous answer. He says that the majoritarian principle and strong competition function well in countries where the political culture is homogeneous and where there are a few basic values and norms which are accepted by every party and political actor and no longer up for debate. This is found in the Anglo-Saxon countries where due to a homogeneous political culture, forceful political competition between two large parties is "endurable" since the competition takes place under definite constitutional and normative constraints and the real challenge for a political party is to capture the political center.

The situation is the exact opposite in the consensual model. In these countries strong political oppositions and ideological divisions divide politics, public life, and society as well—ethnic differences in Belgium, religious differences in Holland, and linguistic differences in Switzerland—and under such conditions political culture is not homogeneous but fragmented. Therefore, in these divided and ossified societies, the Anglo-Saxon model of two-party political battle and competition would be life threatening since the differences in political/ideological goals and social groups are so deep that, if it were concentrated in two opposing parties with nobody or nothing to limit the contest, opposing parties and rivalry would reach such depths that they would endanger social and political peace.

In other words, competition can be allowed to be especially strong when there is consensus among parties concerning the basic values and norms of democracy, while limitation on party competition through consensual principle is needed when ideas concerning the functioning of democracy and the state are especially divided and fragmented among parties and political and social groups.

Let us see in which direction the new Hungarian democracy started out after the 1990 transition and how much and in what manner the Orbán government's post-July 1998 activities affected the profile of Hungarian democracy. Can Lijphart's typology be used unconditionally in Hungary or is a new model, different from both the majoritarian and the consensual models, unfolding in Hungary?

After the 1990 free elections and until May 1998, Hungarian democracy approached Lijphart's majoritarian model, although some consensual elements can be detected in it. Significant evidence for this conclusion comes from the Antall-Tölgyessy Pact, mentioned above, announced on May 2, 1990 which entailed an agreement between the leading government party, the MDF, and the biggest opposition party, the SZDSZ. This Pact introduced, on the German model, the constructive no-confidence motion which made the Prime Minister practically un-removable, giving the importance of a chancellor to the position. In addition, the Pact also decreased the number of laws requiring a 2/3 vote to just twenty. Therefore, a government led by a strong prime minister, in possession of a par-liamentarian majority, has great freedom to implement its political vision with constraints to negotiate with the opposition reduced to a few major issues. The Pact also contained an agreement about the office of President of the Republic: both parties considered the SZDSZ candidate, Árpád Göncz, suitable to fill the post of a weak or medium weak presidential office, a position that symbolizes the unity of the country but does not limit the government's power. One has to mention though that between 1990 and 1994 Árpád Göncz used certain constitutional opportunities granted to him to influence politics and, thus often went beyond the role of symbolic head of state, thereby becoming a "medium strong" president. Göncz did this when, in his view, the Antall government engaged in power-mongering or anti-democratic initiatives.

The Pact between the MDF and SZDSZ provided freedom to the next government to exercise power and left only a small area where consensus operated. Why did the political elite decide on this and why did they think that the majoritarian principle would be more practical in the new Hungarian democracy? The answer is that during those "heroic times" there existed a certain trust con-cerning common goals among the party elite of those groups which were changing the country's regime. In return for choosing the President of the Republic, the SZDSZ accepted a radical decrease in the limits on the government's power because the SZDSZ assumed that the MDF would use that power to implement only common regime-changing goals. That is, that the MDF would use political power, not misuse it. As a result, based on plans of the elite, a chancellery type government formed in 1990 which laid the foundation for the majoritarian model in Hungary by reducing the number of consensual elements in the political system. As a matter of fact, it happened in Hungary in a much stronger measure than in the German or Austrian democracies where strong legal, institutional, and normative consensual constraints counter-balance the chancellery system, especially in Austria.

The views of those who created this system were logical: the elite of the parties attempting to change the regime assumed that, in spite of all internal arguments, there was a kind of agreement between them and the other anti-communist parties, some common ground, that, since the country's political culture is rather homogeneous, strong competition could be built on it.

However, in half a year, by the end of 1990, this agreement quickly crumbled. The relationship between the MDP and the SZDSZ had deteriorated completely. The SZDSZ accused the government of an authoritarian and "Horthy era-esque" governing style, while the MDF accused the SZDSZ of anti-nationalism, an overly radical and excessive opposition, and incitement of public opinions. A final and spectacular disintegration of the trust between the governing parties happened in October of 1990, during the so-called taxi strike, when the SZDSZ suggested that the government had become illegitimate and could, and ought, to be replaced ahead of time. From then onwards, the government-opposition relationship deteriorated into hostility, and especially because of István Csurka, still a member of the MDF, the SZDSZ, hand in hand with its former staunch enemy, the MSZP, ventured out on extra-parliamentary politics through the organization Democratic Charta. That is, they took anti-governmental politics to the streets. It should be noted that the FIDESZ did not join this course.[13]

In retrospect, it is obvious that with this kind of engagement in politics, the presumed homogeneous political culture had disintegrated. In fact, the SZDSZ and the MSZP went so far as to declare the legally elected MDF government to be anti-democratic and, as such, to be rejected. On the other hand, however, the MDF broke its connections with the two opposition parties and, using the opportunities offered by the chancellery-type system, switched over to majoritarian type of government.

After the 1994 elections the situation was slightly altered during the four-year period of the Horn government when the MSZP-SZDSZ coalition, with 72% of the vote and a more than two-thirds parliamentary majority, adopted certain consensual elements of governing, e.g. an opposition-friendly distribution of committee memberships and enforcement of government-opposition parity in nominating the presidents of different advisory boards. All these, however, only mitigated but did not abolish the dominant majoritarian model. These gestures were made by an incredibly large "majority" government and, therefore, hardly encroached upon that government's almost unlimited scope of action and superiority in government decision making. (Let us consider our everyday relationships: when one gains power or dominates over another person in relationships—a wife, husband, colleague or lover—s(he) usually takes mitigating and special steps in order to make the situation bearable for the other party.)

It is even more important to note that, by then, the elites of the opposing party groups were motivated not by the consensual principle but by the majoritarian principle as well as by vigorous competition among them. This had been the case during the Antall government and it was further stabilized and deepened by the Horn government. The two dividing issues—being anti-socialist and anti-successor party versus being succesor party or sympathetic to the successor party, and being nationalistic (or popular) versus being cosmopolitan (or urban)—as viable ideological, attitudinal, and cultural orientations were consolidated as the defining issues for Hungarian political life during the 1994-1998 period and sharply defined the two camps. As a result, the Horn government, in spite of its technical and consensus oriented gestures, installed a majoritarian type governing style because it did not consider the opposition ideologically worthy of a compromise. In its view the opposition was anti-European, old-regime conservative, professionally incompetent, occasionally racist, and not a suitable partner for serious cooperation. Obviously, the opposition parties did not fail to express serious ideological criticism indicating that the government party was communist, anti-national, and socially insensitive. Both camps behaved in a majoritarian manner and more and more powerfully stressed the importance of political competition.

At this point, however, we have to think about what the logic of the Lijphart model dictates. If a nation's political culture, at least at the elite level, becomes strongly fragmented and if the elites are following the consensual model (such as Switzerland, Belgium, the Netherlands, and the Scandinavian states), then the parties ought to act to tone down the competition between them and extensively enforce consensual principles and institutionalization. The reason is that the lack of commonly accepted norms for a basic consensus combined with overly-vigorous competition could be "life threatening" to domestic politics.

In my view, the activities of the Orbán government since coming to power in July of 1998 are a response to this very issue. From their experiences during the two election cycles between 1990 and 1998, the FIDESZ concluded the following:

1) In Hungary there was a peaceful revolutionary change of regime which, however, did not end with the first free elections. Political and social competition with the successor party to the communist party (and its supporters) must continue until a base of political or social power equal to them are established.

2) The social, ideological, and cultural differences dividing the two big political camps are so deeply rooted in Hungarian history (the popular-urban antagonism) and are still so present in everyday life that their suppression by some kind of an illusionary consensus

would not solve anything. On the contrary, these latent differences would surface more vehemently anyway and then be impossible to control. Therefore, a clear recognition and forthright statement about those areas of conflict, along with political competition in those areas, is advisable in order to set the stage for some future consensus.

After the hesitancy of the Antall government and the overbearance of the Horn cabinet, the Orbán government unequivocally decided to pursue a majoritarian type of governance. This is visible in its concentration of governing institutions (such as establishing the chancellery office), in its avoidance of the two-thirds laws, in its calls for consensus, periodically, in a multitude of official changes, in its powerful and definite political style that muffles arguments, in a certain relentlessness that irritates the opposition, and in its strategy to dominate those political and other topics engrossing the attention of the general public. The fact that it allowed the virtual political consensus on foreign policy that existed in previous years to break down in certain areas is also an indication of the prevalence of majoritarian governance. This process began during the Kosovo War and continued during the talk about accession to the European Union talks, continued during talks about Hungary's relationships with neighboring countries, and continued even after the Austrian Freedom Party had come into Austria's governing coalition.

The recognition that conflicts between political parties in Hungary are vastly deeper than those among parties in western democracies underlies the activities of the Orbán government. While divisions between parties in Western Europe and in other developed democracies were treated and mitigated—that is "democratized" in Hungary it is democratization itself that makes it possible for basic antagonisms to come to the surface and for battles to be fought. While in the West major political poles have already established their social base of support, thus balancing and limiting one another, in Hungary these social forces are unbalanced, fragmented, and out of proportion to each other. Therefore, a major political struggle among them cannot be avoided.

However, the question needs to be asked whether the FIDESZ's belief in governing by a majoritarian model is well-founded when such governance contradicts the logic of the "classic" Lijphart theory. The problem is that, theoretically, the majority-based and strongly competitive model should be applied only if it is underpinned by a homogeneous political culture such as in Anglo-Saxon countries. If there is fragmentation, as in Hungary, and added on is party competition by two forceful "main" parties, the danger is that will prevail an intensive movement to the political extreme so that, eventually, a Weimar type situation might occur. If there is nothing to put a break on political or social competition, if that competition becomes self-reinforcing, and if more and more radicalization occurs, this could lead to the destruction of democracy. Is it then justified to apply a majoritarian model built on a situation of social fragmentation?

Well, based on the logic of Lijphart's theory and based on Hungarian circumstances, the application of the majoritarian principle is truly dangerous. However, at this point in time one has to step out of the confines of classical theorizing and to notice that in Hungary the majoritarian model functions under completely different historical and political conditions than exists in western democracies. While competition in the West takes place within a framework of democratic law and order, in Hungary, and probably in several other new Central European democracies, competition is closely connected to the process of democratization itself. In other words, in Belgium or Northern Ireland ethnic, religious, or linguistic conflicts do not relate directly to the existence or non-existence of democracy *per se* but are, *sui generis*, about ethnic conflicts and conclude or do not conclude in some kind of a constitutional solution or in territorial or political separation. In Hungary the conflicts between socialists and anti-socialists and between cosmopolitans and nationalists are about ideas pertaining to who and in what manner democracy will be defined and formed and how to make it stable. These conflicts and divisions are not only Hungarian identity, but are mostly about the type of democracy that Hungary will enjoy. While there is no consensus on the terms of how and in what way to establish democracy in Hungary and what characteristics it will have, the basic political goal for all the essential political parties is the same: to create democracy. Therefore, competition and democratization cannot be divided from one another—everybody wants democracy, but they each want a different democracy.

Thus, in spite of strong and radical differences, there is a deep congruency among the parties on the need to create democracy and this goal is the final measure and judgment on the activities of the political actors. In other words if, in a Western European country, ethnic, religious, and ideological differences become strained at the same time that government is run under majoritarian institutions and competitive political principles instead of consensual ones, then democracy might easily be damaged because these conflicts manifest as divisions independent of and self-determining of democracy. Thus, the 4th French Republic managed to diffuse a major system crisis only by introducing a semi-presidential system,[14] while in Italy centrifugal[15] political forces forced the system to implement a comprehensive constitutional reform. In Hungary deep conflicts among political parties manifest in a different way. They break out as part of the process of implementing democracy as well as due to the stake that actors have in the maintenance and stabilization of democracy. In other words, even during strong debates when political actors strongly clash, there is an inherent agreement among all political actors on the desirability of democracy. It just means that everybody means something different by it. In any case, the inherent agreement on democracy is the guarantee that alternating winners in the political and party contest would use their power to introduce some type of democratic system and not to destroy democracy in favor of authoritarianism. However, this fact is also accompanied by the fact that successive governments also keep announcing a *tabula rasa* in order to correct the "miserable" mistakes committed by previous governments and to "finally" establish the best possible democracy for the country. This attitude introduces a "jerking" motion into political and social processes. But the fact is that, in the meantime, democracy as a goal and an abstract norm has been established.

This is the point I mean when I say that the majoritarian model in Hungary—and probably in most of the new democracies as well—offers only a partial explanation for the character of these new democracies. Rather, it is part of a wider system of new political terms and conditions which suggests a new and original Central European model which could be called conflict democracy for the following reasons:

1) On one hand, the lines of conflict are well marked and after several decades of suppression they need to be aired. This need for competition keeps pushing consensus into the background.

2) On the other hand, as in every new democracy every political party fights its battles under the aegis of the goal of creating a "true" democracy. Therefore, radical competition does not endanger democratic institutions nor the norms of democracy. In other words, in conflict democracies both conflicts and democracy coexist.

Consequently, one significance of the Orbán government's activities lies in the fact that it systematically enforced a characteristic of the Hungarian political condition and Hungarian electoral politics already into the political race. This may not have been very pleasant from desire for a consensus, but is an inescapable phenomenon in the first phase of a new post-communist democracy. Therefore, the majoritarian model is the manifestation of a deeply unique and original conflict situation.

It is also clear that, parallel with forcing a definite competition among political actors, the Orbán government has striven to take symbolic steps necessary to develop a consensus acceptable to everybody in order to create a generally acceptable democratic tradition. Since the FIDESZ is a nationalistic party, in order to gradually develop a social consensus it considered it essential to commemorate the millennial anniversary of Hungarian statehood and the fact that the 2000 millennium was the one thousandth anniversary of St. Stephen's founding of Hungary. For this reason, the Holy Crown and coronation regalia, symbols of national unity, were transferred from the National Museum to the Parliament Building on January 1, 2000 where an extraordinary session was convoked in connection with the passage of the accompanying Act of the Holy Crown. However, this attempt to generate a sense of national unity was not shared by all political parties since two opposition parties, the SZDSZ and the MSZP, boycotted the event.

So it seems that competition was stronger that consensus in this instance and that is a stronger principle than the consensual one and debates about national identity, ethnicity, and history had not been laid to rest either.

However, history proves, time and again, that contemporary rivals who never accept or recognize even the simplest and prophetic initiatives succeed several years later by descendents or political generations not affected by their sentimental or honor-bound concerns and often appreciate initiatives taken to forge a national consensus in the old "heroic" days.

The question is whether the Orbán government's goal of intensifying certain political conflicts or its striving for national consensus becomes its legacy.

Notes

1. See Tamás Fricz, *Egy következmények nélküli ország* [A country without consequences] (Budapest: Századvég, 1998).

2. See Tamás Fricz, "Ungarn im Mai 1998. Die dritten freien Wahlen. Aufbruch in die politische 'Wechselwirtschaft'". *Berliner Osteuropa Info*, no. 11 (1998).

3. The following comprehensively analyzes the 1998 election campaign: *Parlamenti választások, 1998* [Parliamentary elections: 1998], eds., Antal Bőhm, Ferenc Gazsó, and István Stumpf, (Budapest: Századvég–MTA Politikai Tudományok Intézete, 2000).

4. With respect to the FIDESZ-FKGP relationship, the essay by László Kövér, key figure in the FIDESZ, is an important analysis of the coalition. "A FIDESZ-Magyar Polgári Párt és a Független Kisgazdapárt koalíciós megállapodása 1998-ban" [The coalition agreement of the FIDESZ-Hungarian Bourgeois Party, and the Independent Smallholders' Party in 1998]. *Magyarország Politikai Évkönyve* (*MPÉ*), (Budapest, 1999), pp. 336-346.

5. See Tamás Fricz, "Hungary" in *Democracy in the New Europe: the Politics of Post-Communism*, eds., I. Smith and E. Teage (The Greaycoat Press, 1999), pp. 77-96.

6. S. H. Barnes, P. McDanough, and P. A. Lopez, "The Growth of Democratic Legitimacy in Spain," *American Political Science Review*, no. 9 (1986).

7. See P. Bourdieu, *Outline of a Theory of Practice* (Cambridge: Cambridge University Press, 1979).

8. It was Ervin Csizmadia who initiated a debate about the role of the parties' background institutes in general and about the role of the FIDESZ background institutes in particular in the *Politikatudományi Szemle* (Political Science Review), See Ervin Csizmadia, "Pártok és agytrösztök. Think-tank szervezetek Nyugat-Európában és Magyarországon," [Parties and brain trusts: Think-tank organizations in Western Europe and in Hungary], *Politikatudományi Szemle*, no. 4 (1998) and comments in the following issues: 1999/1, 1999/2, 1999/3, and 1999/4.

9. In order to write this chapter the following comprehensive analyses provided essential help: Attila Ágh, "Fideszvilág Magyarországon: a

politikai voluntarizmus egy éve" [FIDESZ-world in Hungary: A year of political voluntarism], *Mozgó Világ*, no. 7 (1999); Endre Babus, "Agyakba döngölni" [Pounding it into heads], *Heti Világgazdaság*, (Budapest, June 26, 1999); Mihály Bihari, "Politikai libikóka, avagy kormányzati váltógazdálkodás, 1990-1998" [Political see-saw or governmental shift economy, 1990-1998], *MPÉ* (1999), pp. 265-271; *"Képzeljetek embert"* [Imagine a human being]— Political Science Essays for the 60th Birthday of István Schlett, eds., Mihály Bihari and András Cieger (Korona – ELTE ÁJK Political Science Department, 1999); András Bozóki, "A polgári radikális kormány" [The bourgeois radical government], *MPÉ* (1999), pp. 272-278; Ervin Csizmadia, "Démonok, frusztráltak, félelemkeltők, avagy mit kezdjünk az Orbán-kormánnyal?" [Demons, the frustrated, the frightening: What shall we do with the Orbán government?], *Magyar Hírlap*, (January 9, 1999); László Kéri, "Első polgár. Az Orbán-kormány első évének kérdőjelei" [The first bourgeois: The question marks in the Orbán government's first year], *Mozgó Világ*, no. 7 (1999); László Kéri, "A második polgári év" [The second bourgeois year], *Kritika*, (February 2000); László Kövér, "A FIDESZ-Magyar Polgári Párt és a Független Kisgazdapárt koalíciós megállapodása 1998-ban" [The coalition agreement of the FIDESZ-Hungarian Bourgeois Party, and the Independent Smallholders' Party in 1998], *MPÉ* (1999), pp. 287-346; László Lengyel, "Ezerkilencszáznegyvennyolc" [1948], *MPÉ* (1999), pp. 287-297; János Simon, "A harmadik szabadon választott ... (Parlamenti képviselők orientációi, attitűdjei, és értékei 1998-ban" [The Third Freely Elected ...The Orientation, Attitudes, and Values of the MPs in 1998], *MPÉ*, (1999), pp. 133-147; and Pál Tamás, "A generációs mumus" [The generational bogey-man], *Magyar Hírlap*, (February 27, 1999).

10. For this issue see the writing of Chancellery Minister István Stumpf, *Kormányváltás 1998-ban* [Change of governments in 1998], (Budapest, 1999), pp. 324-335.

11. See Tamás Sárközy, "Az Orbán-kormány szervezeti felépítése" [The structural build-up of the Orbán government], *MPÉ*, (Budapest, 1999), pp. 312-323.

12. A. Lijphart, *Democracies. Patterns of Majoritarian and Consensus Government in Twenty-One Countries* (New Haven – London: Yale University Press, 1984).

13. At this point it is necessary to clarify István Csurka's political significance. Csurka is the dare-devil of Hungarian domestic politics. He carries on the tradition of the Hungarian "vernacular" (not populist) movement from between the two world wars while providing it with right-wing radical or extreme political content. While he is similar to extreme right-wing politicians appearing throughout Europe (from Le Pen to Haider or Gilstrup, from Anders Lange to Fini), he is also a uniquely Hungarian phenomenon. He entered the political scene via the MDF in 1987/88, becoming its Vice-Chairman. However, in 1992 he turned against the moderate politics of the Antall government and aimed for an internal power takeover. The two larger opposition parties, the SZDSZ and MSZP, considered this to be a political shift to the extreme right. What is more, they perceived the danger of fascism. The movement called Democratic Charta, founded by the SZDSZ in 1991, acted to oppose these events. Pressed by circumstances Prime Minister József Antall was forced to move against Csurka and company. In June 1993 they were expelled from the MDF and soon Csurka founded an independent party, the *Magyar Igazság és Élet Pártja* [The Party of Hungarian Justice and Life] which carries on his right-wing radical and sometimes extreme politics. They managed to step over the electoral threshold and enter Parliament during the 1998 parliamentary elections. They have a narrow but very active elector base.

14. Political science distinguishes between presidential, semi-presidential, and parliamentarian government systems. The presidential system is characterized by the central role of the president of the state. He directs the government and has veto power vis-á-vis parliament: a classic example is the United States. In the parliamentarian system, parliament is at the center with the president (king or president of the republic) having a rather symbolic role. The semi-presidential role is in-between the two systems, with France as a typical example. Here, the president of the republic directs his ministers and the prime minister and has very strong "licenses" generally and towards the parliament in particular. Yet parliament retains its independence and its control over the government, and is not solely the executor of the president's will.

15. G. Sartori lists the Italian party system among extreme polarized party systems. One of its main characteristics is the prevalence of centrifugal forces in the electoral system and, as a result, parties are

polarized both in the direction of the extreme right and to the extreme left which threatens to cause the disintegration of the whole party system. See G. Sartori, *Parties and Party Systems. A Framework for Analysis*, (Cambridge University Press, 1976, Vol. I.).

BIOGRAPHIES OF KEY PERSONALITIES

Aczél, György (1917-1991)

Hungarian communist politician. Deputy Minister of Cultural Affairs (1957-67). Secretary of Central Committee of MSZMP (Hungarian Socialist Worker's Party) (1967-74 and 1982-85), Deputy Premier from 1974 to 1982; director general of the Institute of Social Science of the Central Committee between 1985 and 1989. From November of 1956 to 1988 the member of the Central Committee, and that of the Political Committee from 1970 to 1988.

Antall, József (1932-1993)

Hungarian historian and politician. Worked at the Semmelweis Museum of Medical History since 1964, director general of it between 1974 and 1990.Foundation member of the MDF (Hungarian Democratic Forum) (1988), president of the party since 1989. Prime Minister from May of 1990 to December of 1993.

Bauer, Tamás (1946-)

Hungarian economist. Member, later senior member of the Institute of Economy of the MTA (Hungarian Academy of Sciences) between 1968 and 1988. Professor at the University of Frankfurt since 1988. Member of the MSZMP (1966-74), was expelled. Foundation member of the SZDSZ and one of the signatories of the notice of the New March Front (1988). MP from 1994 to 1998.

Berecz, János (1930-)

Hungarian politician. Head of the Foreig Affairs Department of the MSZMP's Central Committee (1974-1982); editor-in-chief of the *Népszabadság* (1982-1985). Secretary of the ideology and propaganda affairs of the Central Committee (1985-89); member of the Central Commitee(1980-89), the Political Commitee(1987-89) and the reorganized MSZMP's Central Commitee (1989-91). Managing director of the Patriot Sport Ltd. since 1994, chairman of the Ezotrade Co. since 1995.

Bethlen, István count (1874-1946)

Hungarian big landowner and consevative politician. Prime Minister between 1921 and 1931.

Bihari, Mihály (1943-)

Hungarian lawyer and political scientist. University lecturer since 1973, university teacher since1993; teaches philosophy of state and law, sociology, later political studies. Responsible editor of the *Társadalmi Szemle* since 1990. Member of the MSZMP (1972-88), was expelled. Foundation member of the MDF and the New March Front, manager of the Publicity Club (1988-89); MP since 1994.

Bíró, Zoltán (1951-)

Hungarian literary historian.Teacher at the Teacher's Training College of Szeged since 1988. Had taken part in the foundation of the MDF since 1987 that's why he was expelled from the MSZMP in 1988. Member of the presidium of the MDF (1988-90), its chairman in 1989. He left the MDF in 1990. Between May and December of 1991, the chairman of the National Democratic Union, then its co-president until 1996. Editor-in-chief of the *Hitel* (1988-92).

Biszku, Béla (1921-)

Hungarian communist politician. Secretary of the MSZMP's Central Committee (1962-78).

Bocskai, István (1557-1606)

Hungarian big landowner and politician. Prince of Transylvania (1604-1606).

Bod Péter, Ákos (1951-)

Hungarian economist. Collaborator of the Institute of Controlled Economy of the National Central Planning Bureau.

Minister of Industry and Commerce (1990-91), President of the Hungarian National Bank (1991-94); managing director of the EBRD in London since 1995. Member of the MDF (1989-96), worked out its financial program. Member of the MDNP (Hungarian Democratic People's Party) since 1996. MP from 1990 to 1991.

Bokros, Lajos (1954-)

Hungarian economist. Worked at the Financial Reseach Institute from 1980 to 1987. Head of department at the Hungarian National Bank since 1989. President-director of the Budapest Bank (1991-96). Minister of Finance (1995-96), Senior Adviser to the World Bank (1996-97), section director since 1997. President of the Stock Exchange Council of Budapest (1990-95). Member of the MSZMP (1976-89), then the MSZP (Hungarian Socialist Party) since 1989.

Boldvai, László (1960-)

Hungarian economist and politician. Parlamentary expert of the MSZP (1992-94). From 1979 to 1989 member of the MSZMP, that of the MSZP since 1989. Treasurer of the party and MP since 1994. Vice-President of the Budgetary and Financial Board (1994-95), its member since 1996.

Boross, Péter (1928-)

Hungarian politician. Political State Secretary of the Prime Minister's Office (May-July of 1990), Minister without Portfolio controlling the Security Services (between July and December), then Minister of the Interior (from December of 1990 to 1993), Prime Minister (1993-94).

Bossányi, Katalin (1948-)

Hungarian journalist. Principal contributor of the *Népszabadság, Heti Világgazdaság, Magyar Hírlap* since 1978. Vice-president of the National Association of the Hungarian Journalists (1986-88). Chargé d' affairs of the Publicity Club (1988-89, then since 1993). Member of the management of the New March Front since 1988, spokeswoman of the Democratic Charta since 1991.

Bölcs, István (1935-)

Hungarian journalist and teacher. Editor of the *168 óra* (1982-94), was expelled, then rehabilitated in 1994.

Chrudinák, Alajos (1937-)

Hungarian journalist. Member of the Hungarians' World Union since 1996.

Csengey, Dénes (1953-1991)

Hungarian writer. Contributor of the *Hitel* since 1988. Member of the MDF's presidium (1989-91), its MP (1990-91).

Csoóri, Sándor(1930-)

Hungarian poet and writer. Contributor of different journals (*Szabad Ifjúság, Irodalmi Újság*, etc.) since 1953. Representative of the opposition since the 1980s: participated in the preparation of the negotiations at Monor (1985) and at Lakitelek (1987). Foundation member of the MDF since 1987. President of the editorial board of the *Hitel* (1988-92), its editor-in-chief since 1992. Chairman of the Hungarians' World Union from 1991 to 2000.

Csúcs, László (1942-) Hungarian lawyer and politician. Collaborator, later head of department of the Ministry of Finance from 1970 to 1992. Vice-president of the Hungarian Radio (1992-94). Member of the Assembly of the Capital since 1994. Head of the faction of the MIÉP (Hungarian Justice and Life Party).

Csurka, István (1934-)

Hungarian writer and politician. Member of the presidium of the Hungarian Writers' Association since 1981. One of the initiativers of the MDF in 1987, member of its national presidium (1988-93), its vice-president (1991-92). Was expelled from the MDF in 1993. President of the MIÉP since 1994. Editor-in-chief of *Magyar Fórum* (1989-90). MP from 1990 to 1994, and again since 1998.

Debreczeni, József (1955-)

Hungarian teacher, publicist and political scientist. Member of the Board of the National Radio and TV since 1996. Member of the MDF since 1987, was expelled in 1993. One of the foundation members of the Hungarian Civil Democrats' Association in 1995. Member of the Union of the Hungarian Civil Collaboration since 1996. MP between 1989-1994.

Demszky, Gábor (1952-)

Hungarian politician, lawyer and sociologist. Took part in democratic opponent movements since 1977, founded the AB Independent Publisher in 1981. Editor of the *Hírmondó*, the contributor of the *Beszélő* and the *Máshonnan Beszélő* since 1983. Was prohibited from publication in 1984. Foundation member of the Network of Free Initiatives, then that of the SZDSZ (Free Democrats' Alliance). Chief-Mayor of Budapest.

Eörsi, István (1931-)

Hungarian writer and dramaturgist. Member of the National Commitee of the SZDSZ since 1989.

Eörsi, Mátyás (1954-)

Hungarian lawyer and politician. Foundation member of the Network of Free Initiatives, then that of the SZDSZ. MP since 1990; chairman of the Committee of Foreign Affairs of the Parliament from 1994 to 1997.

Esterházy, Péter (1950-)

Hungarian writer. Member of the Széchényi Academy of Literature and Arts since 1993, that of the Academy of German Language and Poetry since 1994, awarded with Kossuth-prize in 1994.

Farkas, Mihály (1904-1965)

Hungarian communist politician. Minister of Defence (1948-53). One of the leaders of the violation procedures. Expelled from the party in July then sentenced in 1957. Released with amnesty in 1961, thereafter publisher lector.

Farkas, Zoltán (1952-)

Hungarian journalist, editor of the *Mozgó Világ* since 1990. The chargé d' affairs of the Publicity Club (1988-89).

Farkasházy, Tivadar (1945-)

Hungarian journalist, humorist. Editor-in-chief of the *Hócipő* since 1989. The spokesman of the Democratic Charta since 1991.

Fekete, János (1918)

Hungarian economist. The Hungarian governor of the IMF (1982-88), MP from 1985 to1990, the chairman of the ad hoc commitee of the reform affairs.

Fekete, Sándor (1927-)

Hungarian writer, journalist, literary historian. Foundation member of the New March Front.

Fenyő, János (1954-1998)

Hungarian photo-actor, businessman, journalist and publisher. Founded the Vico Ltd. in 1989, and was its managing director-president until his death. Publisher of many dailies and magazines. An own printing shop and a lot of real estate enterprises belonged to his business group. He was murdered.

Fényi, Tibor (1954-)

Hungarian historian and journalist. Foundation member of the Danube Circle and one of those who worked out the SZDSZ's program of the change of regime.

Fodor, Gábor (1962-)

Hungarian lawyer and politician. Minister of Culture and Education (1994-1995). Foundation member of the FIDESZ in 1988, its vice-president in 1993, then in the same year left the party. Member of the SZDSZ since 1994, its chargé d' affairs since 1996. MP since 1990. Chairman of the Committee of human rights, minority and religion affairs of the Parliament (1990-93).

Fodor, Tamás (1942-)

Hungarian actor and director. Member of the curatorium board of the Hungarian Radio Public Foundation since 1996. Member of the SZDSZ since 1989, that of the National Council and MP (1990-94).

Fónay, Jenő (1926-)

Hungarian engineer. The chairman of the Association of the Hungarian Political Prisoners (POFOSZ), since 1989.

Gerő, Ernő (1898-1980)

Hungarian communist politician. Minister of Transport since 1945, Minister of Finance since 1948, Minister of the State since 1949, Minister of the Interior since 1953, Vice-Premier between 1952-56. Member of the MKP (Hungarian Workers' Party) since 1948. One of the main responsible people for the violations of law after 1945.

Giczy, György (1953-)

Hungarian theologist , politician and journalist. Contributor of the *Új Ember*, a catholic weekly paper since 1980. Foundation member of the KDNP (Christian Democratic People's Party) since 1989, its president since 1995. MP since 1990.

Gombár, Csaba (1939-)

Hungarian sociologist and political scientist. Principal contributor of the Finance Researches Co. (1989-90); president of the Hungarian Radio (1990-93); chairman of the editorial board of the *Politikatudományi Szemle* since 1992; member of the Advisory Board of the Prime Minister in August-September of 1994.

Göncz, Árpád (1922-)

Hungarian writer, literary translator and politician. He was sentenced for life for his 1956-activities, released with amnesty in 1963. In 1988 foundation member of the Network of Free Initiatives, later that of the SZDSZ, member of the National Council in 1989-90; chairman of the Writers'

Association (1989-90). President of the Hungarian Republic from 1990 to 2000. Honorary President of the Hungarian Pen Club since 1994.

Grósz, Károly (1930-1996): Hungarian communist politician. First Secretary of the Party Committee of Budapest (1984-87), member of the Central Committee of the MSZMP since 1980, secretary-general of the the party (1988-89).

Győri, Béla (1942-)
Hungarian journalist. Responsible editor of a radio program, called *Vasárnapi Újság* (1979-94), was relieved in 1992, then worked at the general editorial office of the religious programs (1993-94). Spokesman of the MIÉP since 1993.

Gyurkó, László (1930-)
Hungarian writer, journalist, theatre director, foundation member of the New March Front in 1988.

Hack, Péter (1959-)
Hungarian lawyer and politician. Foundation member of the Network of Free Initiatives in 1988, later that of the SZDSZ, simultaneously member of the FIDESZ (1988-89). Member of the National Council of the SZDSZ since 1988, its chargé d' affaires since 1990. MP since 1990, chairman of the Constitutional and Judicial Committee since 1994, vice-chairman of the SZDSZ faction (1994-99).

Hankiss, Elemér (1928): Hungarian sociologist. Collaborator of the Institute of Literary Sciences of the Hungarian Academy of Sciences (1965-90), and its Institute of Sociological Researches since 1994. President of the Hungarian Television (1990-94), Chairman of the Curatorium of the Open Society Public Foundation since 1989.

Hann, Endre (1946-)
Hungarian social-psychologist. Managing director of the Medián Public Opinion and Market Research Ltd. since 1989. One of the founders of the Publicity Club in 1988. Foundation

member of the Network of Free Initiatives and the SZDSZ in 1988.

Harag, György (1925-1985)

Romanian stage director of Hungarian nationality. The chief director of the theatres of Marosvásárhely (since 1960), and Kolozsvár (since 1974).

Haraszti, Miklós (1945-)

Hungarian writer. One of the founders of the *samizdat* movement. The founder-editor of the periodical *Beszélő* (1977), foundation member of the Network of Free Initiatives in 1988. Member of the directory board of the curatorium of the Hungarian Radio Public Foundation since 1997. Member of the SZDSZ since 1989, member of its National Council since 1991. MP in 1990-1994.

Havas, Henrik (1949-)

Hungarian journalist, titular state secretary of the Prime Ministerial Office in 1995.

Hegedűs, István (1957-)

Hungarian sociologist, professor at the University of Economics of Budapest since 1996. Member of the advisory board of the Hungarian News Service Co. (SZDSZ) since 1997. Member of the FIDESZ (1988-94), foundation editor of the *Fidesz Pressz* in 1989. MP (1990-94), the vice-chairman of the Committee of Foreign Affairs (1990-93).

Hegyi, Gyula (1951-)

Hungarian journalist. Contributor of the *Magyar Hírlap* since 1976. Chargé d' affairs of the Publicity Club (1990-91), spokesman of the Democratic Charta. Member of the MSZMP (1979-89), that of the MSZP since 1995, chargé d' affairs since 1997, MP since 1994.

Hernádi, Gyula (1926-)

Hungarian writer. The scenario writer of Jancsó Miklós' films, chairman of the Association of the Independent Hungarian

Writers since 1991, member of the Academy of the Hungarian Arts since 1992.

Horn, Gyula (1932-)

Hungarian diplomat and politics. Diplomat between 1961-69, later collaborator of the Department of Foreign Affairs of the MSZMP's Central Committee, its leader (1983-85). State Secretary of Foreign Affairs (1985-89), Minister of Foreign Affairs (1989-90). President of the MSZP (1990-98), Prime Minister (1994-98).

Horthy, Miklós (1868-1957)

Hungarian naval officer and politician. Governor of Hungary from 1920 to 1944.

Horváth, János (1941-)

Hungarian journalist, worked for the Hungarian Television since 1969, the organiser and director of the Tv-2 (1988-89), the principal contributor of the Hungarian Television.

Ilkei, Csaba (1939-)

Hungarian journalist. Editor of the Hungarian Television since 1969. Member of the MDF (1988-91), MP (1990-94).

Jancsó, Miklós (1921-)

Hungarian director, president of the Association of the Hungarian Film and TV Artists since 1986, MP-candidate of the SZDSZ in 1994, vice-president of the Happiness Party till 1996, member of the Széchényi Academy of Literature and Arts since 1993, its president since 1994.

Jászi, Oszkár (1875-1957)

Hungarian sociologist and politician. The leader figure and theoretician of the Hungarian civil radicalism.

Kádár, János (1912-1989)

Hungarian communist politician. Minister of the Interior (1948-50), was arrested and sentenced for life on the basis of made-up charges (1951). Rehabilitated in 1954. Member of the Imre Nagy government in 1956. Member of the MSZMP's

Central Committee (1956-88), its first secretary (1957-85), then its secretary-general (1985-88), later its president (1988-89). Prime Minister (1956-58 and 1961-65).

Király, Zoltán (1948-)

Hungarian journalist and politician. Editor-reporter at the studio of the Hungarian Television in Szeged (1978-91), MP between 1985 and 1994. Member of the MSZMP (1974-88), foundation member of the New March Front in 1988, expelled from the MSZMP. Member of the presidency of the Movement for the Democratic Hungary in 1989, President of the Hungarian Social Democratic Party (1993-94), member of the MSZP since 1997. Spokesman of the Democratic Charta since 1993.

Kis, János (1943-)

Hungarian philosopher and politician. One of the founders of the democratic opposition, the editor of the *samizdat* periodical *Beszélő* since 1981. Chargé d' affairs of the Network of Free Initiatives and the SZDSZ (1988-91), its president (1990-91).

Konrád, György (1933-)

Hungarian writer. Publishing of his works was banned till 1988. Taught world literature at Colorado College (1987-88). President of the International PEN Club (1990-93), that of the Academy of Fine Arts of Berlin-Branderburg since 1997. Member of the National Council of the SZDSZ. Spokesman of the Democratic Charta since 1993.

Kósa, Ferenc (1937-)

Hungarian film director. Member of the MSZMP (1964-89), leader of the Reform Union in 1989, member of the MSZP's presidium since 1989. MP since 1990. Chairman of the Committee of Culture and Press since 1994.

Kőszeg, Ferenc (1939-)

Hungarian editor and politician. Contributor of the *Beszélő* since 1981, its editor-in-chief (1990-94). One of the founders of the Independent Legal Aid Service, one of the beginners of the Network of Free Initiatives (1988). MP since 1990.

Kun, Béla (1886-1938)

Hungarian communist politician. The founder and leader of the Party of Hungarian Communists. The real leader of the Soviet Republic as the member of the Revolutionary Governing Council (commissar of foreign-, later military affairs) since March of 1919.

Kuncze, Gábor (1950-)

Hungarian economist and politician. Minister of the Interior and coalition vice-premier in 1994-98. Member of the SZDSZ since 1992. Chargé d' affairs (1994-97 and since 1998), president of the SZDSZ (1997-98). MP since 1990, faction leader in 1993-94 and since 1998.

Lengyel, László (1950-)

Hungarian economist. Collaborator of the Financial Research Co. since 1987, its scientific director (1989-90), its president-managing director since 1990. Member of the government committee of privatisation since 1990. Worked out a lot of reform proposals for exceeding the Kádár-model since 1981. Participated in the meetings in Monor (1985) and Lakitelek (1987), was expelled from the MSZMP in 1988. One of the founders of the New March Front in 1988. The chargé d' affairs of the Publicity Club in 1988-89.

Lovas, István (1954-)

Hungarian journalist. Editor of the Free Europe Radio in Munich (1984-90), press-correspondence in New York.

Magyar, Bálint (1952-)

Hungarian sociologist and politician. Scientific collaborator (Research Institute of World Economy of the Hungarian Academy of Sciences, etc.) from 1977 to 1990. One of the editors of *Medvetánc* in 1981-89. Minister of Culture and Education in 1996-98. Member of the council of the Network of Free Initiatives in 1988, foundation member of the SZDSZ since 1988, its chargé d' affairs in 1988-91 and since 1992; its campaign-chief in 1990 and in 1994. President of the party since 1998. MP since 1990.

Mécs, Imre (1933-)

Hungarian electrical engineer and politician. He was sentenced for death—later for life—for his participation in the 1956 revolution in 1958, released with amnesty in 1963. One of the leaders and organisers of the *Százak levele* written to the parliament in 1987—the basis of the Network of Free Initiatives—and the SZDSZ (chargé d' affairs in 1988-96). MP since 1990, the chairman of the Committee of National Defence since 1994.

Mindszenty, József (1892-1975)

Hungarian catholic prelate. Archbishop of Esztergom since 1945, cardinal since 1946.

Nagy, Imre (1896-1958)

Hungarian agricultural economist, communist politician. Member of the MKP (Hungarian Communist Party from the end of 1944 to 1955. Minister of Agriculture, later Minister of the Interior (1944-46). Minister of Provisions, later that of ingathering and vice-prime minister. Prime Minister in 1953-55. Prime Minister again since October 24, 1956. Escaped from the Soviet invasion to the Jugoslavian Embassy, was dragged to Romania on November 24. Was sentenced for death in a conception action and executed on June 16 of 1958. His judgement was invalidated by the Supreme Court in 1989, and was reburied with his companion solemnly.

Nagy, Sándor (1946-)

Hungarian politician. The secretary of the Central Council of the Hungarian Trade Unions (1984-88), its general-secretary (1988-90), the president of the Hungarian Trade Unions' Coalition (1990-95). Member of the MSZMP (1966-89), that of the MSZP since 1994, its vice-president in 1998-99. MP in 1980-85, 1988-90 and since 1994, chairman of the Council of the Audit Office. Vice chief of the faction (1998-99).

Németh, Miklós (1948-)

Hungarian economist and politician. Worked at the economic political department of the MSZMP since 1987, president of the Cabinet in 1988-90. Vice-president of the European Reconstructional and Developmental Bank since 1991. Member of the MSZMP (1976-89), that of the MSZP since 1989. MP in 1988-91.

Nahlik, Gábor (1948-)

Hungarian mechanical engineer and economist. Vice-president of the MTV (Hungarian Television) in 1992-94, collaborator of the National Radio and TV Corporation (FKGP).

Nyers, Rezső (1923-)

Hungarian politician and economist. Member of the MSZMP's Central Committee (1957-89). Leader of the elaboration of the economic reforms of 1968. State Minister in 1988-89, president of the MSZMP (June-October of 1989), that of the MSZP (October, 1989-May, 1990). Foundation member of the New March Front in 1988. Member of the board of supervision of the Hungarian National Bank since 1993.

Oltványi, Ottó (1925-)

Hungarian journalist, general director of the MTI (Hungarian News Service) (1990-93). Chairman of the owners' advisory board of the MTI Co. since 1997 (MSZP).

Ómolnár, Miklós (1954-)

Hungarian journalist. Editor-in-chief of the *Ifjúsági Magazin* since 1996. Member of the FKGP (Independent Smallholders' Party) since 1989. MP in 1990-1994, was expelled from the party in 1991.

Orbán, Viktor (1963-)

Hungarian politician. One of the founders of the István Bibó Trade College since 1983, one of the editors of the *Századvég* since 1984. Member of the Central European Researchers' Group (1988-89). Foundation member of the FIDESZ since March of 1988, its president (1993-2000). MP since 1990, chairman of the European Integration Affairs' Committee of the Parliament, the leader of the FIDESZ faction (1990-93). Prime Minister since 1998.

Pető, Iván (1946-)

Hungarian historian and politician. Member of the committee of the Democratic Trade Union of Scientific Workers in 1988, one of the initators of the Network of Free Initiatives, one of the editors and authors of the program of the SZDSZ. Chargé d' affairs of the SZDSZ (1989-91), its president (1992-97). Vice-president of the Liberal Internationale since 1994. MP since 1990, the faction leader of SZDSZ (from October, 1990 to November, 1991 and 1994-97).

Pitti, Zoltán (1945-)

Hungarian economist, president of the APEH (Office of Taxation and Financial Affairs' Control) in 1994-96.

Pokol, Béla (1950-)

Hungarian political scientist. Collaborator of the Committee of Political Sciences of the MTA. Member of the Advisory Board of the Cabinet (1989-90). Personal advisor of József Torgyán, the FKGP's president (since 1995).

Pozsgai, Imre (1933-)

Hungarian politician. Worked in the country apparatus, later in the central one of the MSZMP since 1957. Minister of Culture (1976-80), Minister of Education (1980-82), general secretary of the Patriotic People's Front (1982-88), State Minister (1988-90). Member of the MSZMP's Central Committee (1980-89) Vice-president of the MSZP in May-November, then left the party.

Rákosi, Mátyás (1892-1971)

Hungarian communist politician. General secretary of the MKP, later that of the MDP (Hungarian Workers' Party) since 1945, its first secretary (1953-1956), State Minister (1945-52), Prime Minister (1952-53). Lived in the Soviet Union from August,1956 to his death.

Réger, Antal (1940-)

Hungarian journalist. MP (1975-90). Member of the National Committee of the MSZP (1989-90).

Révai, József (1989-1959)

Hungarian communist politician. Minister of Popular Culture (1949-53), leader ideologist of the cultural life. Member of the MDP's leadership.

Révész T., Mihály (1945-)

Hungarian lawyer. Scientific collaborator of the MTA (1970-80), university lecturer at the Eötvös Loránd University's Faculty of Law since 1980. One of the leaders of the reorganisation of the Hungarian Social Democratic Party in 1989. Personal advisor of Gyula Horn, Prime Minister in 1994-96. The chairman of the board (MSZP) of the National Radio and TV.

Schamschula, György (1944-)

Hungarian economist, lawyer and politician. Political state secretary of the Ministry of Labour (1991-93), Minister of Transport, Telecommunication, and Water Affairs (1993-94). Member of the MDF (1988-96). Economical advisor of József Antall, the president of the MDF in 1990. MP since 1990 (that of the MDF in 1990-96, after that independent, then in September-October of 1996, of FKGP).

Semmelweis, Ignác (1818-1865)

Hungarian obstetrician, the "rescuer of mothers". His epoch-making discovery that the so far usually fatal puerperal fever caused by an infection , which can be prevented by disinfection.

Seres, László (1963-)

Hungarian journalist. Foundation member of the Anarchist Group of Budapest in 1990.

Sólyom, László (1942-)

Hungarian lawyer. University teacher since 1983, the fields of his researches are civil legal history and comparative civil law. President of the Constitutional Court since 1990, the legal advisor of the unofficial environmental protection movements since the 1980s, participant of the Danube Circle. Foundation member of the MDF in 1987, member of its board since 1989. The chargé d' affairs of the Publicity Club in 1988-89.

Soros, György (George, 1930)

Hungarian born American businessman. Founded the Soros Foundation in 1983, which was also spread out to Hungary in 1984.

Speidl, Zoltán (1942-)

Hungarian journalist. Member of the MSZMP (1971-89), the MDF (1989-96), that of the MDNP (since 1996). MP in 1990-94.

Suchman, Tamás (1954-)

Hungarian lawyer and politician. Administrative officer in Marcali from 1975 to 1989, then director of the Marcali branch of Budapest Bank (1989-94). Responsible minister without portfolio for privatisation (1995-96), Minister of Industry, Commerce and Tourism (September-October of 1996). Member of the MSZMP (1983-89), that of the MSZP since 1989. MP since September, 1990. Vice-faction leader since 1999.

Surányi, György (1950-)

Hungarian economist. Scientific collaborator of the Institute of Financial Researches (1977-86). Secretary of the Bank Reform Committee (1983-86). Consultant of the World Bank in Washington (1986-87). Chief advisor of the committee of controlled economy of the Cabinet, later that of its economy political secretariat (1988-89), state secretary of the National Central Planning Bureau (1989-90), president of the Hungarian National Bank (1990-91 and since 1995).

Szabad, György (1924-)

Hungarian historian and politician. The field of his researches is the Hungarian civil transformation. Member of the FKGP (1945-46), the foundation member of the MDF since 1987, member of its presidency (1989-94). Member of the MDNP since 1996. MP in 1990-1998, President of the Parliament (1990-1994). Member of the board of the Union of the Hungarian Civil Co-operation since 1998.

Szabó, Miklós (1935)

Hungarian historian. The scientific collaborator of the Institute of the Historical Sciences of the MTA since 1967. Author of *samizdat* issues, held illegal lectures, the spokesman of the Network of Free Initiatives in 1988. Member of the National Council of the SZDSZ since 1988, its chargé d' affairs in 1988-90. Member of the managing board of the National Council in 1991. MP (1990-98).

Szabó, Zoltán (1955-)

Hungarian mathematician and politician. The political state secretary of the Ministry of Culture and Education since 1995, member of the MSZMP (1977-89), spokesman of the reform circles in Budapest, member of the MSZP since 1989, the vice-president of its national committee (1992-95). The spokesman of the Democratic Charta (1991-93). MP since 1994. Vice-faction leader since 1999.

Szálasi, Ferenc (1897-1946)

Hungarian politician. The fascist parties were joined together into the Arrow-Cross Party with his leadership. On 15 October, 1944 the Nazis put him onto power with putsch.

Szamuely, Tibor (1890-1919)

Hungarian journalist and communist politician. Commissar of Defence and Education during the Soviet Republic, the leader of the Red Terror as the president of the so called, "Behind the Front" Committees.

Szent-Iványi, István (1958-)

Hungarian social anthropologist and politician. Political state secretary of the Ministry of Foreign Affairs (1994-97). Member of the Council of the Network of Free Initiatives (1988), chargé d' affairs of the SZDSZ (1988-89 and since 1992). MP since 1990, secretary of the Committee of Foreign Affairs (1990-92), its vice-president (1992-94), its president since 1997. Faction leader of the SZDSZ (1997-98).

Tamás Gáspár, Miklós (1948-)

Hungarian philosopher and politician. The editor of the *Utunk*, a weekly in Kolozsvár (Romania) in 1972-78. Has been living in Hungary since 1978, scientific collaborator at the Institute of Philosophy of ELTE (1979-81), was expelled because of his opposition attitude. Contributor of the *samizdat* press. Had taught at American, English and French universities since 1986. Professor at the Institute of Philosophy of ELTE since 1989, the director of the Institute of Philosophy of the MTA (1991-94). Spokesman of the Network of Free Initiatives in 1988, the chargé d' affairs of the SZDSZ (1988-90), president of the National Council (1992-94). MP (1990-94).

Tellér, Gyula (1934-)

Hungarian sociologist and literary translator. Member of the board of the council of MTV Public Foundation (FIDESZ) in 1996-98. Head of the political analytic major department of the Premier's Office since 1998. Foundation member of the Network of Free Initiatives in 1988, later that of the SZDSZ (1988-94), member of the National Council (1991-94). MP (1990-94).

Torgyán, József (1932-)

Hungarian politician and lawyer. Member of the FKGP in 1956, he joined the reorganisation of the party in 1988. President of the FKGP since July of 1991. MP since 1990, member of different Parliament committees (e.g. that of the constitutional and judicial committee), faction leader (1990-91 and 1994-98). Minister of Agriculture and Religion Development since 1998.

Tóth Gy., László (1948-)

Hungarian political scientist and publicist. Leader of the cultural secretariat of the Cabinet since 1998. One of the founders of the Hungarian Civil Democrat Union in 1995.

Tölgyessy, Péter (1957-)

Hungarian lawyer and politician. Scientific collaborator of the Institute of Political and Juridical Sciences of the MTA since 1981, constitution-lawyer. Participated in the writing of the *Fordulat és reform* in 1987. Member of the SZDSZ (1989-96), took part in the Opponent Round Table negotiations. Chargé d' affaires of the SZDSZ (1989-90 and 1992-94), member of the National Council (1989-96), president of the SZDSZ (1991-92). He left the party in 1996. MP since 1990 (1990-96: SZDSZ, 1996-98: independent, since 1998: FIDESZ)

Vágvölgyi B., András (1959-)

Hungarian journalist. Worked at an international social research institute in Vienna, wrote articles for the *Beszélő* and the *Irodalmi Újság* in Paris. Member of the Democratic Trade Union of the Scientific Laborers, the FIDESZ and the SZDSZ in 1988. PR man of the reburial ceremony of Nagy Imre (1989), took part in the Round Table negotiations, the advisor foreign affairs of the FIDESZ, founder-editor of the *Magyar Narancs*, its editor-in-chief (1991-98). Chargé d' affaires of the Publicity Club (1993-94).

Varga, János (1927-)

Hungarian archivist. Chief director of the Hungarian National Archives (1978-90). President of the Revolutionary Committee of University Students in 1956. Member of the MDP (1949-56), that of the MDF since 1990, MP (1990-94).

Vásárhelyi, Miklós (1917-)
Hungarian journalist and historian. The press chief of the Imre Nagy government since November 1, 1956. Was sentenced for five years in the Imre Nagy legal proceedings, released with amnesty in 1960. The collaborator of the Institute of Literary Sciences of the MTA since 1972. Soros György's personal representative at the MTA-Soros Foundation (1984-89), president of the Curatorium of the Soros Foundation since 1989. Signed the declaration of solidarity with the Charta '77 in 1979. Foundation member of the New March Front and the Network of Free Initiatives (1988), hat of the SZDSZ since 1988, member of the National Council since 1989. MP (1990-94).

Vastagh, Pál (1946-)
Hungarian politician. University lecturer since 1973. Minister of Justice (1994-98). Member of the MSZMP in 1966-89, that of the MSZP since 1989, MP since 1990.

Vitányi, Iván (1925-)
Hungarian sociologist and essayist. Member of the Information Political Council of the Cabinet (1989-90). Founding member, managing secretary of the New March Front (1988), the spokesman of the Democratic Charta since 1993. Member of the MKP (1945-48), the MDP (1948-56), that of the MSZMP (1972-89), and the MSZP since 1989, member of the presidium (1989-94), chairman of the National Committee (1990-96). MP since 1990.

Völgyes, Iván (1936-)
Political scientist. Co-president of the Erasmus Foundation for Democracy and the Center of Safety Political and Defence Researches. Chief advisor of General Electric. His field of research is the 20th century Central European-Hungarian politics.

CONTRIBUTORS

BÁRÁNY, ANZELM (1958)

Graduated from the department of German at ELTE University, Budapest, and also studied international relations at the Budapest University of Economics. Won scholarships from the German *Bundestag* and the *Institut für die Wissenschaften vom Menschen* in Vienna.

DICZHÁZI, BERTALAN (1957)

Graduated in chemical engineering from the Budapest Polytechnic University in 1981. From 1990 has been serving in various institutions administering the privatization of the county's economic structure.

FRICZ, TAMÁS (1959)

Holds a BA in economics (School of Finance and Accountancy, Budapest, 1981) and an MA in philosophy (ELTE University, Budapest, 1989). He is research fellow at the Institute for Political Science of the Hungarian Academy of Sciences since 1990. He is the author of several books. His latest volume is: *Party Systems in Europe*, Budapest (2000).

GERGELY, ANDRÁS (1946)

Ph.D., graduated from the department of history at ELTE University, Budapest. Professor of history—specializing in the 19th century reform era and the 1848 revolution. He is the author of several books. For his research on Széchenyi was awarded the Knight Cross of Merit of the Hungarian Republic.

ILLÉS, ZOLTÁN (1961)

Obtained degrees in chemical engineering and biology form the Polytechnic University of Budapest, and has lectured at several universities in the United States. In 1998 was elected a member of Parliament, where he is chairman of the committee on Environmental Protection.

KAHLER, FRIGYES (1942)

Ph.D., obtained degrees from the universities of Szeged and Debrecen, judge in 1968, in 1987 vice-president of the Heves County Court and in 1991 became head of department in the Ministry of Justice. Since 1994 he has been a judge at the Veszprém County Court while continuing to teach at the departments of law at Miskolc University and also Péter Pázmány Catholic University. He has published numerous books on the revolution of 1956.

MARTONYI, JÁNOS (1944)

Ph.D., graduated from the university of Szeged in 1967. During 1989-90, he was government commissioner for privatization, and after the 1990 elections, he was appointed state secretary, first at the Ministry of International Economic Relations and then, from 1992, at the Ministry of Foreign Affairs. He is head of the department of international law at the University of Szeged and has taught at the College of Bruges. He became Minister of Foreign Affairs in 1998.

MATOLCSY, GYÖRGY (1955)

Ph.D., graduated from the Budapest University of Economics. From 1991 to 1995, he worked at the London-based European Bank for Reconstruction and Development. In 1991, he founded the Privatization Research Institute. He has published several books on the Hungarian economy during the transition. He became Minister of Economics in 2000.

MEDGYESY, BALÁZS (1972)

Graduated from the department of agricultural economics at the University of Budapest, teaches regional environmental policy and modeling at the University of Horticulture and Food Industry.

MELLÁR, TAMÁS (1954)

Ph.D., graduated from the faculty of economics at the University of Pécs and took up teaching positions at the same university. From 1988 to 1989 he was a visiting researcher at Princeton University in the United States. In 1998 was appointed president of the Central Statistical Office. He has written widely on economics.

MOLNÁR, ATTILA KÁROLY (1961)

Ph.D., graduated at ELTE University, Budapest, lecturer at the same university's department of the history of ideas. He also teaches at the University of Miskolc and the Péter Pázmány Catholic University. He is the author of "A protestáns etika Magyarországon" (*Protestant Ethics in Hungary*).

ŐRY, CSABA (1952)

Graduated from the law department of ELTE University, Budapest. From 1982 to 1988 he worked at the sociology research institute of the Hungarian Academy of Sciences. State secretary at the Ministry of Social and Family Affairs.

SCHMIDT, MÁRIA (1953)

Ph.D., graduated in history and German at ELTE University, Budapest. Her main areas of research have been 20th century Hungarian and world history, and she has held scholarships at the following universities: Vienna, Innsbruck, Oxford, Paris, Berlin Technische Universitat, Tel Aviv, Jad-Vashem

(Jerusalem), New York, Bloomington and the Hoover Institute in Stanford. Her major publications include: "Kooperáció vagy kollaboráció: A Budapesti Zsidó Tanács" (*Co-operation or Collaboration: The Jewish Council of Budapest*) 1990; "Ávós világ" (*The Communist Secret Police in Hungary*) 1991; "Diktatúrák ördögszekerén" (*On the Wings of Dictatorships*) 1998. Director Institute on the XXth Century, Budapest.

SEPSEY, TAMÁS (1956)

Graduated in 1974 from ELTE University, Budapest, worked as a lawyer. From 1994 to 1998 a member of the Parliament (MDF).

TELLÉR, GYULA (1934)

Ph.D., a sociologist and translator, from 1990 to 1994 member of the Parliament (SZDSZ). His analyses of contemporary social and political issues continue to appear frequently in the press.

TÓTH GY., LÁSZLÓ (1948)

Graduated from ELTE University, Budapest. He is author of several books analyzing the Kádárist inheritance for post-communist Hungary.

TŐKÉCZKI, LÁSZLÓ (1951)

Graduated in history and German from ELTE University, Budapest. In 1990 he became editor of *Hitel*, in 1992 of *Protestáns Szemle* and in 1994 *Valóság*, while writing also on contemporary political issues for the daily press. His latest book is a political biography of István Tisza.

Name Index

Aczél, Endre (1944-)
Hungarian journalist. 19
Aczél, György 19, 358, 369,
463, 499
Adenauer, Konrad 202
Áder, János (1959-)
Chairman of the Hungarian
Parliament since 1998. 523
Ady, Endre (1877-1919)
Hungarian poet and publi-
cist. 353-354
Alexa, Károly (1945-)
Hungarian literary historian
and critic. 23, 59
Antall, József 4, 29, 34, 43, 46-
49, 51-52, 54-55, 58-59, 71,
81-82, 84, 115, 118-120,
122, 133, 136-137, 140, 147-
156, 158-162, 207, 272, 284,
329-330, 335-336, 350, 357,
359, 364, 366, 368-371, 375,
400, 412, 463, 470, 534-537,
544-545, 548-549, 557-558,
560, 562
Applebaum, Anne 376, 474
Árkus, József 26
Aron, Raymond Claude Ferdi-
nand 355

Árpád (850?-907?)
Hungarian chieftain. 365
Árpási, Zoltán (1946-)
Hungarian journalist. 18
Babits, Mihály (1883-1941)
Hungarian poet, writer, liter-
ary translator and essayist.
351
Baker, James A. 250
Baló, György (1947-)
Hungarian journalist. 6, 44,
479
Bánó, András(1949-)
Hungarian journalist. 353
Bárd, Károly (1951-)
Hungarian lawyer and politi-
cian. 200
Barnes, S. H. 535
Bartók, Béla (1881-1945)
Hungarian composer, piano
artist, musical scientist. 354
Bauer, Tamás 115, 463, 466,
469
Beck, Tamás (1929-)
Hungarian politician and
economist. 31
Bedő, Iván (1952-)
Hungarian journalist. 61

Békés, Imre (1930-)
  Hungarian lawyer. 201
Belkin, F. 189
Bell, Martin 66
Benda, László (1951-)
  Hungarian journalist. 5
Berecz, János 9, 26, 65, 486
Berlusconi, Silvio 53-54
Bernrath, Hans Gottfried 57
Bernstein, Eduard 441-442
Bertelsmann, Carl 30-32, 35, 62
Bethlen, István 150
Bibó, István (1911-79)
  Hungarian lawyer and histo-
  rian. 221-222, 354
Bihari, Mihály 10, 201
Bíró, Zoltán 119
Bismarck, Otto von 17
Biszku, Béla 436, 474
Bocskai, István 375
Bod Péter, Ákos 43
Bokros, Lajos 99, 251, 272,
  282, 293, 526, 528, 545
Bölcs, István 353
Boldvai, László 485
Boross, Péter 84, 161, 330, 336,
  358, 366, 369, 470
Bossányi, Katalin 16, 18
Bourdieu, Pierre 136, 537
Brain 45
Brezhnev, Leonid Ilyich 31
Bruck, András 69

Bruhács, János (1939-)
  Hungarian lawyer. 204
Budai, György 485
Burke, Edmund 307
Camus, Albert 36
Carrell, Rudi 63
Ceausescu, Nicolae 31
Chrudinák, Alajos 5, 53, 55
Csengey, Dénes 9-11, 33, 36
Csikós, József 15, 23
Csillag, István (1951-)
  Hungarian lawyer and econ-
  omist. 76
Csintalan, Sándor 476
Csoóri, Sándor 115, 119, 149,
  353-355, 358, 361-362, 365
Csúcs, László 52-53
Csurka, István 7, 19-21, 24, 51-
  52, 59, 115, 119-120, 356-
  362, 364-365, 470, 559
Csutár 349
Czakó, Gábor (1942-)
  Hungarian writer and artist.
  9
Dahrandorf, Ralf 483
Deák, Ferenc (1803-76)
  Founder of the 1867 Comp-
  romise. 59, 208
Debreczeni, József 24, 221
Demszky, Gábor 31, 115, 466,
  481
Domány, András (1949-)
  Hungarian journalist. 6

Domokos, György 347-350, 355, 360
Donáth, László (1955-) Hungarian Lutheran priest, MSZP's MP since 1994. 470
Drake, Sir Francis 47
Durkheim, Émile 297
E. Fehér, Pál (1936-) Hungarian journalist and critic. 16
Eichmann, Karl Adolf 347
Eisenhower, Dwight David 359
Eörsi, István 9
Eörsi, János 10
Eörsi, Mátyás 28, 375
Eötvös, Pál (1939-) Hungarian journalist and publicist. 31
Erhard, Ludwig 48
Estaing, Giscard d' 119
Esterházy, Péter 37, 345, 479
Fabriczky, András 27
Faludy, György (1910-) Hungarian writer, poet and literary translator. 354
Farkas, Mihály 349
Farkas, Zoltán 35-36
Farkasházy, Tivadar 61
Fekete, Gyula (1922-) Hungarian writer. 26
Fekete, János 13
Fekete, Sándor 18
Fényi, Tibor 18

Fenyő, János 32
Fodor, Gábor 15, 467, 470, 522
Fodor, Tamás 36
Földvári, József (1926-) Hungarian lawyer. 207
Fónay, Jenő 364-365
Franco Bahamonde, Francisco 535
Frankfurter, Felix 25
Fricz, Tamás (1959-) Hungarian politician and publicist. 106, 474, 520
Friedman, Milton 449
Gádor, Iván 65, 353
Gerő, Ernő 349, 359
Giczy, György 18, 524
Gombár, Csaba 48, 51-52, 54, 360
Göncz, Árpád 360, 365-366, 370, 470, 558
Gonzalez Marquez, Felipe 535
Greco, Juliett 355
Grezsa, Ferenc (1957-) Hungarian physician, pshy-chiatrist and entrepreneur, MP (MDF). 50
Grósz, Károly 179
Győrffy, Miklós (1943-) Hungarian journalist. 5, 19
György, Péter (1954-) Hungarian aesthetician. 65
Györgyi, Kálmán (1939-) Hungarian lawyer; Supreme

Prosecutor (1990-2000). 200-201

Győri, Béla 20

Gyurkó, László 5

Hack, Péter 463

Halberstam 15

Hanák, Péter (1921-97) Hungarian historian. 362-363, 369-370

Hanák, Péter Mrs. 362

Hankiss, Elemér 48-49, 52-54, 63, 65, 360

Hann, Endre 23

Hanthy, Kinga 70

Harag, György 354

Haraszti, Miklós 8, 20, 23, 25, 34, 115

Hatvany, Lajos (1880-1961) Hungarian writer and literary organiser. 353

Havas, Henrik 6

Havel, Václav 159

Hayek, Friedrich August von 449, 465

Heckenast, Gusztáv (1811-78) Hungarian bookseller, publisher and printing office owner. 11

Hegedűs, István 23

Hegel, Georg Wilhelm Friedrich 295-296

Hegyi, Gyula 470

Hernádi, Gyula 7

Herpai, Attila 11

Hirschler, Richárd 9

Hitler, Adolf 340, 350

Hofi (Hoffmann), Géza (1936-) Hungarian actor, humorist. 6

Honecker, Erich 31

Horn, Gyula 4, 30-31, 48, 54-55, 67, 87, 122-123, 126, 135, 140, 272-273, 277, 291, 329, 335-337, 415, 480-481, 486, 491, 520, 526, 528-530, 536, 544-545, 547-551, 560, 562

Horthy, Miklós 118, 353-354, 368-370, 375, 459, 507, 559

Horvát, János 16, 66

Horváth, István (1944-) Hungarian journalist. 30, 33

Ignáczi 353

Ilkei, Csaba 18

Illyés, Gyula (1902-83) Hungarian poet, writer, dramatist and literary translator. 212, 354

Jancsó, Miklós 470

Jászi, Oszkár 353

Javorniczky, István (1952-) Hungarian journalist. 66

Jobbágyi, Gábor (1947-) Hungarian lawyer. 204

Juszt, László (1952-) Hungarian journalist. 70

Kádár, János 1, 3-6, 13, 16, 22,

31, 49, 54, 61, 65, 107-109, 122, 129, 133-134, 192, 196, 237, 240, 242-244, 283, 290, 326, 331, 337, 339, 342-344, 357, 359, 434, 438-439, 441, 447, 452, 459, 468, 471, 473, 478, 491, 496-497, 499, 501-507, 509, 524

Kahler, Frigyes 187, 207

Kecskés Székely, János 70

Kelemen, Iván 38

Kende, Péter (Pierre, 1927-) Hungarian political scientist and sociologist. 358, 370, 372-373

Kepenyes, János 29

Kepes, András (1948-) Hungarian journalist. 66

Kerényi, Imre (1943-) Hungarian director. 329

Kereszty, András (1942-) Hungarian journalist. 46

King Matthias (1443-90) (Hunyadi) King of Hungary (1458-90). 66, 289

Király B., Izabella (1944-) MP (1990-94), was expelled from the MDF (1993). 470

Király, Tibor (1920-) Hungarian journalist. 201

Király, Zoltán 18

Kis, János 8-9, 115, 375, 463, 469

Koestler, Arthur 346

Kohl, Helmut 119, 367

Kolianov, J. 189

Konrád, György 7, 354, 360-361, 470

Kornis, Mihály (1949-) Hungarian writer and theatrical expert. 467

Kósa, Ferenc 36

Kósáné Kovács, Magda (1940-) Hungarian politician, member of the MSZP. 476

Kőszeg, Ferenc 8, 329, 374

Kotz, László 76

Kovács, Zoltán (1952-) Hungarian journalist. 69

Kuhn, Thomas Samuel 317

Kun, Béla 19, 358

Kuncze, Gábor 66, 68, 375, 479

Lajos, György 166

Lakatos, Ernő 16, 486

Landerer, Lajos (1800-54) German-birth printer and publisher in Hungary. 11

Landeszmann, György 367

Langmár, Ferenc (1958-) Hungarian journalist. 70

László, József (1954-) Hungarian journalist and manager. 66

Lengyel, László 49, 130

Lenin, Vladimir Ilyich Ulyanov 12, 19, 45, 499

Lijphart, Arendt 555-557, 561, 563
Lipset, P. A. 111, 535
Locke, John 295
Lőcsei, Gabriella (1945-) Hungarian journalist. 70
Lomax, Bill 346, 488-489
Lopéz, Portillo y Pacheco 535
Lovas, István 70
Lusztig, Péter (1946-) Hungarian police officer, lawyer, later MP (MSZP). 374
Madách, Imre (1823-64) Hungarian poet and dramatist. 65
Magyar, Bálint 115
Makovecz, Imre (1935-) Hungarian architect. 343
Marjai, József (1923-) Hungarian diplomat and communist politician. 242
Marquard, Jürg 30-31
Marshall, George Catlett 3, 235, 250
Marton, Frigyes (1928-) Hungarian director and humorist. 18
Marx, Karl 441-442
Maxwell, Robert 31, 33-34
Mazowiecki, Tadeus 24
McDonough, P. 535
Mécs, Imre 67-68, 478-479
Megyeri, Károly 16

Mellár, Tamás 267, 492
Mélykuti, Attila (1947-) Hungarian journalist. 10
Menuhin, Yehudi 349
Mester, Ákos (1940-) Hungarian journalist. 65, 353
Michnik, Adam 24
Mill, John Stuart 295, 316
Milton, John 295, 316
Mindszenty, József 373
Moldova, György (1934-) Hungarian writer. 6
Molnár, Attila 464, 483
Montaigne, Michel Eyquem de 294
Montesquieu, Charles-Louis de 306
More, Thomas 294
Murdoch, Keith Rupert 30, 33-34
Nagy, Imre 12, 28, 68
Nagy, Sándor 32, 486
Nahlik, Gábor 52
Németh, László (1901-75) Hungarian novelist and playwright. 354
Németh, Miklós 46, 56, 77, 80, 88, 179, 207, 327
Németh, Zsolt (1963-) Hungarian political scientist, vice-president of the FIDESZ since 1993. 523

Nixon, Richard Milhous 47
Novák, Attila 363
Nyers, Rezső 31
Oltványi, Ottó 59
Ómolnár, Miklós 18
Orbán, Ottó (1936-)
    Hungarian poet, writer and
    literary translator. 354
Orbán, Viktor 65, 122, 126, 376,
    486, 520-521, 523, 530, 532,
    534, 536-537, 543-544, 546,
    548-552, 554-555, 557, 561-
    562, 565-566
Oistrakh, David Fyodorovich
    349
P. Szűcs, Julianna (1946-)
    Hungarian art historian and
    art critic. 18
Pálfy G., István (1945-)
    Hungarian journalist. 19, 48,
    53-55, 61
Pálfy, József (1922-)
    Hungarian journalist. 16
Palmer, Mark 33
Perlman, Itzhak 349
Pető, Iván 375, 463-464
Petőfi, Sándor (1823-49)
    Hungarian freedom-fighter
    poet. 10-11
Pitti, Zoltán 92
Plato 295-296
Pokol, Béla 57, 352

Polonyi, Péter (1935-)
    Hungarian journalist, China-
    expert. 361
Popper, Karl 294-299, 308-309,
    311-312, 316, 319-320, 483
Pozsgay, Imre 9-10, 19-20, 54
Rácz, Aladár (1886-1958)
    Hungarian cymbalo artist.
    349
Rádai, Eszter 53
Radnóti, Miklós (1909-44)
    Hungarian poet and literary
    translator. 354
Rákosi, Mátyás 54, 60, 108,
    190, 339, 342, 345, 349-350,
    359, 373, 432, 436, 452, 459,
    468, 478
Rau, Johannes 57
Rawls, John 316
Réger, Antal 18
Révai, József 190
Révész T., Mihály 481
Révész, Sándor (1956-)
    Hungarian journalist. 59,
    154, 349, 369, 463
Ritshkov, N. 189
Róbert, László (1926-)
    Hungarian journalist. 18
Rokkan, S. 111
Sándor, István (1947-)
    Hungarian journalist. 15
Sára, Sándor (1933-) Hungarian
    cameraman and director. 5

Sárközi, György (1899-1945)
Hungarian writer, poet and
literary translator. 354
Sartre, Aron 355
Schamschula, György 56
Schlett, István (1939-)
Hungarian historian and po-
litical scientist. 39, 201
Schmidt, Helmut 57-58, 250
Schmidt, Mária (1954-)
Hungarian historian. 339,
473-474
Semmelweis, Ignác 147
Seres, László 70
Simmel, Georg 297
Sneé, Péter (1953-)
Hungarian journalist. 8
Sólyom, László 10, 23, 176
Soros, György (George) 246-
247, 358, 483
Speidl, Zoltán 18
Spiró, György (1946-)
Hungarian writer, poet, liter-
ary historian and translator.
354-355
St. Stephen (975?-1038)
The first Hungarian king
since 1000. 554, 566
Stalin, Yosiph Vissarionovich
370
Stern, Isaac 349
Stumpf, István 548
Suchman, Tamás 47

Sugár, András (1933-)
Hungarian journalist. 61
Sükösd, Mihály (1933-)
Hungarian writer, essayist
and publicist. 62
Surányi, György 66
Szabad, György 22, 149, 327
Szabó, Albert 356
Szabó, László (1931-)
Hungarian journalist. 16
Szabó, Miklós 60, 349-350,
368-369, 466-467, 479
Szabó, Tamás (1953-)
Hungarian economist. 84
Szabó, Zoltán 470
Szájer, József Zoltán (1961-)
Hungarian lawyer member
of the FIDESZ' presidium.
523
Szálasi, Ferenc 349
Szamuely, Tibor 358
Szekfű, András (1943-)
(Karafiáth) Hungarian soci-
ologist and film historian. 9
Szentgyörgyi, Albert (1893-
1986)
Hungarian biochemist (No-
bel-prize). 349
Szent-Iványi, István 484
Szerb, Antal (1901-45)
Hungarian literary historian,
writer, literary translator and
essayist. 354

Szigethy, Gábor (1942-)
Hungarian literary man and director. 23
Szokai, Imre (1950-)
Hungarian economist. 485
Szűcs, Gábor (1950-)
Hungarian journalist. 70
Szűcs, Jenő 40
Szűk, László 201
Takács 199-202
Talleyrand, Charles Maurice de 220
Tamás Gáspár, Miklós 17
Tamás, Pál (1948-)
Hungarian sociologist. 37
Tellér, Gyula 432, 468
Tocsik, Márta 126, 485, 528, 540
Tőke, Péter (1945-)
Hungarian journalist. 26
Tölgyessy, Péter 362, 544, 557
Torgyán, József 115, 123, 548
Tóth Gy., László 351, 462
Tóth, Bálint (1929-)
Hungarian poet, writer and literary translator. 46
Tóth, Gyula 100
Uexküll, J. 168
Uncle Potyka 470
Ungvári, Tamás (1930-)
Hungarian writer, critic and literary translator. 62
Urban 24
Vágvölgyi B., András 23

Vajda, Mihály (1935-)
Hungarian philosopher. 44
Vajda, Péter (1950-)
Hungarian film editor. 68
Vajda, Tibor 375
Vándor, Ágnes 69
Varga, Csaba (1941-)
Hungarian lawyer. 201
Varga, János 167, 173, 176
Várkonyi, Tibor (1924-)
Hungarian journalist. 61
Vas, István (1910-)
Hungarian poet, writer, literary translator and essayist. 354
Vásárhelyi, Miklós 61, 465
Vastagh, Pál 11
Vékás, Lajos (1939)
Hungarian lawyer. 201
Vicsek, Ferenc (1950-)
Hungarian journalist. 6, 53
Vitányi, Iván 468, 470, 490
Völgyes, Iván 347
Waigel, Theo 470
Walesa, Lech 12, 159
Weber, Max 47
Wolffson, Michael 347
Zala, Tamás (1930-)
Hungarian historian, public writer and journalist. 354
Zétényi, Zsolt (1941-)
Hungarian lawyer and politician. 199-203

Zhdanov, Victor Mihailovich 190

Zhivkov, Todor 31

Zinner, Tibor (1948-) Hungarian legal historian. 207

Zsolt, Péter 65

Place Index

Auschwitz 363, 376
Baja 28
Balatonboglár 87
Battonya 11
Békéscsaba 29
Berlin 12, 358
Beszterce 191
Bonn 30
Bős 167, 169
Bratislava 168
Budapest 11, 27-28, 30, 33, 35, 147, 168, 170, 174, 179, 182, 191-192, 202, 233, 263-264, 271, 352, 359, 405, 462, 466
Debrecen 28, 168, 191
Eger 192
Esztergom 191
Gdansk 12
Gödöllő 168
Gütersloh 31
Gyömrő 191
Gyöngyös 28
Győr 28, 176, 191
Hollywood 36, 46, 342, 358
Kaposvár 28
Kecskemét 172, 191
Kosovo 551, 553, 562
Kunszentmárton 482

Lakitelek 9, 48, 148
Lakos 191
Miskolc 28, 176, 191
Mohács 353, 369, 372
Mosonmagyaróvár 176, 191, 201
Munich 8
Nagymajtény 353
Nagymaros 167, 169, 176, 178-179
New York 205-206, 356, 358
Nyíregyháza 168, 176
Ófalu 178
Oxford 263
Ózd 191
Paks 178
Paris 306, 409, 410, 411
Pécs 28
Pest 34
Recsk 11
Répcelak 87
Salgótarján 192, 205, 206
Sárbogárd 191
Sopron 168, 174
Szársomlyó 170
Szeged 168
Szekszárd 28
Szombathely 28, 168, 191

Tatabánya 192
Tel-Aviv 358
Tiszakécske 191
Tokyo 252
Trianon 233-235, 353, 370, 498
Vienna 147, 358

Világos 353
Visegrád 34, 159, 229
Yalta 1, 189, 237, 240, 244, 265, 370
Zsurk 482

Volumes Published in

"Atlantic Studies on Society in Change"

No. 1   *Tolerance and Movements of Religious Dissent in Eastern Europe.* Edited by Béla K. Király. 1977.

No. 2   *The Habsburg Empire in World War I.* Edited by R. A. Kann. 1978

No. 3   *The Mutual Effects of the Islamic and Judeo-Christian Worlds: The East European Pattern.* Edited by A. Ascher, T. Halasi-Kun, B. K. Király. 1979.

No. 4   *Before Watergate: Problems of Corruption in American Society.* Edited by A. S. Eisenstadt, A. Hoogenboom, H. L. Trefousse. 1979.

No. 5   *East Central European Perceptions of Early America.* Edited by B. K. Király and G. Barány. 1977.

No. 6   *The Hungarian Revolution of 1956 in Retrospect.* Edited by B. K. Király and Paul Jonas. 1978.

No. 7   *Brooklyn U.S.A.: Fourth Largest City in America.* Edited by Rita S. Miller. 1979.

No. 8   *Prime Minister Gyula Andrássy's Influence on Habsburg Foreign Policy.* János Decsy. 1979.

No. 9   *The Great Impeacher: A Political Biography of James M. Ashley.* Robert F. Horowitz. 1979.

No. 10   *Special Topics and Generalizations on the Eighteenth and*
Vol. I*   *Nineteenth Century.* Edited by Béla K. Király and Gunther E. Rothenberg. 1979.

No. 11   *East Central European Society and War in the Pre-*
Vol. II   *Revolutionary 18th Century.* Edited by Gunther E. Rothenberg, Béla K. Király, and Peter F. Sugar. 1982.

* Vols. no. I through XXXVI refer to the series *War and Society in East Central Europe*

609

No. 12
Vol. III
From Hunyadi to Rákóczi: War and Society in Late Medieval and Early Modern Hungary. Edited by János M. Bak and Béla K. Király. 1982.

No. 13
Vol. IV
East Central European Society and War in the Era of Revolutions: 1775-1856. Edited by B. K. Király. 1984.

No. 14
Vol. V
Essays on World War I: Origins and Prisoners of War. Edited by Samuel R. Williamson, Jr. and Peter Pastor. 1983.

No. 15
Vol. VI
Essays on World War I: Total War and Peacemaking, A Case Study on Trianon. Edited by B. K. Király, Peter Pastor, and Ivan Sanders. 1982.

No. 16
Vol. VII
Army, Aristocracy, Monarchy: War, Society and Government in Austria, 1618-1780. Edited by Thomas M. Barker. 1982.

No. 17
Vol. VIII
The First Serbian Uprising 1804-1813. Edited by Wayne S. Vucinich. 1982.

No. 18
Vol. IX
Czechoslovak Policy and the Hungarian Minority 1945-1948. Kálmán Janics. Edited by Stephen Borsody. 1982.

No. 19
Vol. X
At the Brink of War and Peace: The Tito-Stalin Split in a Historic Perspective. Edited by Wayne S. Vucinich. 1982.

No. 20
Inflation Through the Ages: Economic, Social, Psychological and Historical Aspects. Edited by Edward Marcus and Nathan Schmuckler. 1981.

No. 21
Germany and America: Essays on Problems of International Relations and Immigration. Edited by Hans L. Trefousse. 1980.

No. 22
Brooklyn College: The First Half Century. Murray M. Horowitz. 1981.

No. 23
A New Deal for the World: Eleanor Roosevelt and American Foreign Policy. Jason Berger. 1981.

No. 24
The Legacy of Jewish Migration: 1881 and Its Impact. Edited by David Berger. 1982.

No. 25
The Road to Bellapais: Cypriot Exodus to Northern Cyprus. Pierre Oberling. 1982.

No. 26
New Hungarian Peasants: An East Central European Experience with Collectivization. Edited by Marida Hollos and Béla C. Maday. 1983.

No. 27 *Germans in America: Aspects of German-American Relations in the Nineteenth Century.* Edited by Allen McCormick. 1983.

No. 28 *A Question of Empire: Leopold I and the War of Spanish Succession, 1701-1705.* Linda and Marsha Frey. 1983.

No. 29 *The Beginning of Cyrillic Printing — Cracow, 1491. From the Orthodox Past in Poland.* Szczepan K. Zimmer. Edited by Ludwik Krzyżanowski and Irene Nagurski. 1983.

No. 29a *A Grand Ecole for the Grand Corps: The Recruitment and Training of the French Administration.* Thomas R. Osborne. 1983.

No. 30 *The First War between Socialist States: The Hungarian*
Vol. XI *Revolution of 1956 and Its Impact.* Edited by Béla K. Király, Barbara Lotze, Nandor Dreisziger. 1984.

No. 31 *The Effects of World War I, The Uprooted: Hungarian*
Vol. XII *Refugees and Their Impact on Hungary's Domestic Politics.* István Mócsy. 1983.

No. 32 *The Effects of World War I: The Class War after the Great*
Vol. XIII *War: The Rise Of Communist Parties in East Central Europe, 1918-1921.* Edited by Ivo Banac. 1983.

No. 33 *The Crucial Decade: East Central European Society and*
Vol. XIV *National Defense, 1859-1870.* Edited by Béla K. Király. 1984.

No. 35 *Effects of World War I: War Communism in Hungary, 1919.*
Vol. XVI György Péteri. 1984.

No. 36 *Insurrections, Wars, and the Eastern Crisis in the 1870s.*
Vol. XVII Edited by B. K. Király and Gale Stokes. 1985.

No. 37 *East Central European Society and the Balkan Wars, 1912-*
Vol. XVIII *1913.* Edited by B. K. Király and Dimitrije Djordjevic. 1986.

No. 38 *East Central European Society in World War I.* Edited by B.
Vol. XIX K. Király and N. F. Dreisziger, Assistant Editor Albert A. Nofi. 1985.

No. 39 *Revolutions and Interventions in Hungary and Its Neighbor*
Vol. XX *States, 1918-1919.* Edited by Peter Pastor. 1988.

No. 41   *Essays on East Central European Society and War, 1740-*
Vol. XXII   *1920.* Edited by Stephen Fischer-Galati and Béla K. Király. 1988.

No. 42   *East Central European Maritime Commerce and Naval*
Vol. XXIII *Policies, 1789-1913.* Edited by Apostolos E. Vacalopoulos, Constantinos D. Svolopoulos, and Béla K. Király. 1988.

No. 43   *Selections, Social Origins, Education and Training of East*
Vol. XXIV *Central European Officers Corps.* Edited by Béla K. Király and Walter Scott Dillard. 1988.

No. 44   *East Central European War Leaders: Civilian and Military.*
Vol. XXV   Edited by Béla K. Király and Albert Nofi. 1988.

No. 46   *Germany's International Monetary Policy and the European Monetary System.* Hugo Kaufmann. 1985.

No. 47   *Iran Since the Revolution—Internal Dynamics, Regional Conflicts and the Superpowers.* Edited by Barry M. Rosen. 1985.

No. 48   *The Press During the Hungarian Revolution of 1848-1849.*
Vol. XXVII Domokos Kosáry. 1986.

No. 49   *The Spanish Inquisition and the Inquisitional Mind.* Edited by Angel Alcala. 1987.

No. 50   *Catholics, the State and the European Radical Right, 1919-1945.* Edited by Richard Wolff and Jorg K. Hoensch. 1987.

No. 51   *The Boer War and Military Reforms.* Jay Stone and Erwin A.
Vol.XXVIII Schmidl. 1987.

No. 52   *Baron Joseph Eötvös, A Literary Biography.* Steven B. Várdy. 1987.

No. 53   *Towards the Renaissance of Puerto Rican Studies: Ethnic and Area Studies in University Education.* Maria Sanchez and Antonio M. Stevens. 1987.

No. 54   *The Brazilian Diamonds in Contracts, Contraband and Capital.* Harry Bernstein. 1987.

No. 55   *Christians, Jews and Other Worlds: Patterns of Conflict and Accommodation.* Edited by Philip F. Gallagher. 1988.

No. 56   *The Fall of the Medieval Kingdom of Hungary: Mohács*
Vol. XXVI *1526, Buda 1541.* Géza Perjés. 1989.

No. 57   *The Lord Mayor of Lisbon: The Portuguese Tribune of the People and His 24 Guilds.* Harry Bernstein. 1989.

No. 58   *Hungarian Statesmen of Destiny: 1860-1960.* Edited by Paul Bödy. 1989.

No. 59   *For China: The Memoirs of T. G. Li, Former Major General in the Chinese Nationalist Army.* T. G. Li. Written in collaboration with Roman Rome. 1989.

No. 60   *Politics in Hungary: For A Democratic Alternative.* János Kis, with an Introduction by Timothy Garton Ash. 1989.

No. 61   *Hungarian Worker's Councils in 1956.* Edited by Bill Lomax. 1990.

No. 62   *Essays on the Structure and Reform of Centrally Planned Economic Systems.* Paul Jonas. A joint publication with Corvina Kiadó, Budapest. 1990.

No. 63   *Kossuth as a Journalist in England.* Éva H. Haraszti. A joint publication with Akadémiai Kiadó, Budapest. 1990.

No. 64   *From Padua to the Trianon, 1918-1920.* Mária Ormos. A joint publication with Akadémiai Kiadó, Budapest. 1990.

No. 65   *Towns in Medieval Hungary.* Edited by László Gerevich. A joint publication with Akadémiai Kiadó, Budapest. 1990.

No. 66   *The Nationalities Problem in Transylvania, 1867-1940.* Sándor Bíró. 1992.

No. 67   *Hungarian Exiles and the Romanian National Movement, 1849-1867.* Béla Borsi-Kálmán. 1991.

No. 68   *The Hungarian Minority's Situation in Ceausescu's Romania.* Edited by Rudolf Joó and Andrew Ludanyi. 1994.

No. 69   *Democracy, Revolution, Self-Determination. Selected Writings.* István Bibó. Edited by Károly Nagy. 1991.

No. 70   *Trianon and the Protection of Minorities.* József Galántai. A joint publication with Corvina Kiadó, Budapest. 1991.

No. 71   *King Saint Stephen of Hungary.* György Györffy. 1994.

No. 72   *Dynasty, Politics and Culture. Selected Essays.* Robert A. Kann. Edited by Stanley B. Winters. 1991.

No. 73   *Jadwiga of Anjou and the Rise of East Central Europe.* Oscar
           Halecki. Edited by Thaddeus V. Gromada. A joint publication
           with the Polish Institute of Arts and Sciences of America,
           New York. 1991.

No. 74   *Hungarian Economy and Society during World War Two.*
Vol. XXIX Edited by György Lengyel. 1993.

No. 75   *The Life of a Communist Revolutionary, Béla Kun.* György
           Borsányi. 1993.

No. 76   *Yugoslavia: The Process of Disintegration.* Laslo Sekelj.
           1993.

No. 77   *Wartime American Plans for a New Hungary. Documents*
Vol. XXX   *from the U.S. Department of State, 1942-1944.* Edited by
           Ignác Romsics. 1992.

No. 78   *Planning for War against Russia and Serbia. Austro-*
Vol. XXXI *Hungarian and German Military Strategies, 1871-1914.*
           Graydon A. Tunstall, Jr. 1993.

No. 79   *American Effects on Hungarian Imagination and Political
           Thought, 1559-1848.* Géza Závodszky. 1995.

No. 80   *Trianon and East Central Europe: Antecedents and*
Vol. XXXII *Repercussions.* Edited by Béla K. Király and László
           Veszprémy. 1995.

No. 81   *Hungarians and Their Neighbors in Modern Times, 1867-
           1950.* Edited by Ferenc Glatz. 1995.

No. 82   *István Bethlen: A Great Conservative Statesman of Hungary,
           1874-1946.* Ignác Romsics. 1995.

No. 83   *20th Century Hungary and the Great Powers.* Edited
Vol. XXXIII by Ignác Romsics. 1995.

No. 84   *Lawful Revolution in Hungary, 1989-1994.* Edited by Béla K.
           Király. András Bozóki Associate Editor. 1995.

No. 85   *The Demography of Contemporary Hungarian Society.*
           Edited by Pál Péter Tóth and Emil Valkovics. 1996.

No. 86   *Budapest, A History from Its Beginnings to 1996.* Edited By
           András Gerő and János Poór. 1996.

No. 87   *The Dominant Ideas of the Nineteenth Century and Their
           Impact on the State.* Volume 1. *Diagnosis.* József Eötvös.

Translated, edited, annotated and indexed with an introductory essay by D. Mervyn Jones. 1997.

No. 88 *The Dominant Ideas of the Nineteenth Century and Their Impact on the State.* Volume 2. *Remedy.* József Eötvös. Translated, edited, annotated and indexed with an introductory essay by D. Mervyn Jones. 1997.

No. 89 *The Social History of the Hungarian Intelligentsia in the "Long Nineteenth Century," 1825-1914.* János Mazsu. 1997.

No. 90 *Pax Britannica: Wartime Foreign Office Documents*
Vol.XXXIV *Regarding Plans for a Post Bellum East Central Europe.* Edited by András D. Bán. 1997.

No. 91 *National Identity in Contemporary Hungary.* György Csepeli. 1997.

No. 92 *The Hungarian Parliament, 1867-1918: A Mirage of Power.* András Gerő. 1997.

No. 93 *The Hungarian Revolution and War of Independence, 1848-*
Vol. XXXV *1849. A Military History.* Edited by Gábor Bona. 1999.

No. 94 *Academia and State Socialism: Essays on the Political History of Academic Life in Post-1945 Hungary and East Central Europe.* György Péteri. 1998.

No. 95 *Through the Prism of the Habsburg Monarchy: Hungary in*
Vol.XXXVI *American Diplomacy and Public Opinion during World War I.* Tibor Glant. 1998.

No. 96 *Appeal of Sovereignty in Hungary, Austria and Russia.* Edited by Csaba Gombár, Elemér Hankiss, László Lengyel and Györgyi Várnai. 1997.

No. 97 *Geopolitics in the Danube Region. Hungarian Reconciliation Efforts, 1848-1998.* Edited by Ignác Romsics and Béla K. Király. 1998.

No. 98 *Hungarian Agrarian Society from the Emancipation of Serfs (1848) to Re-privatization of Land (1998).* Edited by Péter Gunst. 1999.

No. 99 *"The Jewish Question" in Europe. The Case of Hungary.* Tamás Ungvári. 2000.

No. 100 *Soviet Military Intervention in Hungary, 1956.* Edited by Jenő Györkei and Miklós Horváth. 1999.

No. 101   *Jewish Budapest.* Edited by Géza Komoróczy. 1999.

No. 102   *Evolution of Hungarian Economy, 1848-1998.* Vol. I. *One and a Half Centuries of Semi-Successful Modernization, 1848-1989.* Edited by Iván T. Berend and Tamás Csató. 2001.

No. 103   *Evolution of Hungarian Economy, 1848-1998.* Vol. II. *Paying the Bill for Goulash-Communism.* János Kornai. 2000.

No. 104   *Evolution of Hungarian Economy, 1848-1998.* Vol. III. *Hungary: from Transition to Integration.* Edited by György Csáki and Gábor Krassai. 2000.

No. 105   *From Habsburg Agent to Victorian Scholar: G. G. Zerffi (1820-1892).* Tibor Frank. 2000.

No. 106   *A History of Transylvania from the Beginning to 1919.* Vol. I. Edited by Zoltán Szász and Béla Köpeczi. 2000.

No. 107   *A History of Transylvania from the Beginning to 1919.* Vol. II. Edited by Zoltán Szász and Béla Köpeczi. 2001.

No. 108   *A History of Transylvania from the Beginning to 1919.* Vol. III. Edited by Zoltán Szász and Béla Köpeczi. 2001.

No. 109   *Hungary: Governments and Politics, 1848–1999.* Edited by Mária Ormos and Béla K. Király. 2000.

No. 110   *Hungarian Minority in the Voivodina.* Edited by Enikő A. Sajti. 2001.

No. 111   *Hungarian Successes.* Edited by László Somlyódy. 2001.

No. 112   *Hungary and International Politics in 1848–1849.* Edited by Domokos Kosáry. 2000.

No. 113   *Social History of Hungary from the Reform Era to the End of the Twentieth Century.* Edited by Gábor Gyáni, György Kövér and Tibor Valuch. 2000.

No. 114   *Genuine Social Democracy: Struggles against Fascism and Communism in Hungary, 1944-1948.* Róbert Gábor and Vilmos Vass. 2000.

No. 115   *Hungarian Relics. A History of the Battle Banners of the 1848-49 Hungarian Revolution and War of Independence.* Jenő Györkei and Györgyi Cs. Kottra. 2000.